The Good Gardener's Guide

The Good Gardener's Guide

A critical guide from the publishers of Which?

Published by Consumers' Association
and Hodder & Stoughton

Acknowledgements

EDITOR
Jane Wafer

RESEARCHED BY
Clare Bassett
Pamela Castledine
Elizabeth Dobbs
Peter McHoy
Rosemary Ward

EDITORIAL ASSISTANT
Tricia Black

The editor wishes to acknowledge
the help given in the production of
this book by the staff
of *Gardening from Which?*.

First published in Great Britain by
Consumers' Association
14 Buckingham Street, London WC2N 6DS and
Hodder & Stoughton Ltd
47 Bedford Square, London WC1B 3DP

Cover illustration by Julie Tennent

Wafer, Jane
    The good gardener's guide.
    1. Nursery dealers — Great Britain —
    Directories   2. Garden Centres (Retail trade)
    — Great Britain — Directories
    I. title   II. Consumers' Association
    381'.415'02451   SB44

ISBN 0 340 37221 4

Typeset by Gee Graphics Ltd

Printed and bound in Great Britain
by Anchor-Brendon Ltd.,
Tiptree, Essex

Contents

Introduction

Gardening has never been more popular. More and more people are growing plants, feeding their lawns and building patios and ponds. Consequently, the gardening industry is booming: garden centres are springing up, long-established nurseries are being given a face-lift and big chains such as Sainsbury's Homebase are getting in on the act. This means that gardeners have more choice of plants, tools and chemicals. What's more, the choice is often on their own doorstep. Plants which a few years ago might be considered a rarity can now be found in local garden centres.

More choice must be good for the gardener but it can also make life confusing. What price should the gardener be prepared to pay for *Juniperus* 'Skyrocket' – £1? £3? or £5? We've seen it selling at all three prices. And what about quality? While putting together this *Guide* we've seen garden centres offering excellent plants that any gardener should be pleased to buy. We've also seen rubbish on sale – sometimes at ridiculously high prices. So where should gardeners go to get a good deal? This *Guide* aims to steer them towards some of the garden centres and nurseries from which they can get high-quality plants – the first priority of any good gardener – and a good choice of gardening tools and equipment. It also gives advice on what to look for when buying and tells gardeners where to go for further information or how to get in touch with fellow enthusiasts.

The first and longest chapter of the *Guide* has grown out of the Good Garden Centre Guide which first appeared as a report in the April 1983 issue of *Gardening from Which?*, published by Consumers' Association. Experience gained in compiling this report showed that garden centres were as many and varied as gardeners themselves. Some were little more than old-fashioned nurseries selling a few composts and fertilisers on the side; others were highly organised hypermarkets, open seven days a week, 52 weeks a year, with piped music, shopping trolleys and special offers. The original report included only 'true' garden centres where one could buy a reasonable range of gardening equipment as well as plants, but many gardeners evidently still preferred to buy their plants from small, family-run nurseries where they valued the personal service, home-grown plants and cosy atmosphere, even if they had to rummage among the flowerpots to find what they wanted. So to produce a fully fledged guide we've inspected more than 600 garden centres and nurseries throughout Great Britain and Northern Ireland, and selected more than 400 to put in the *Guide*. Many nurseries concentrate on a particular type of plant: conifers, roses or alpines, say; in this section of the *Guide* we've included only those that sell a wide enough range to interest most gardeners. Details of how to use the entries are given on page 10.

If you can't buy what you need at your local garden centre – perhaps you want something really unusual – the second section of the *Guide* should be able to help you. There you will find details of over 400 nurseries that have either built up a reputation for selling a particular type of plant – clematis, for example – or which concentrate their efforts on a particular area – water-gardening, say. Each entry in the section covers a different subject, and in addition to a list of specialist suppliers gives advice on how the plants are sold and what to look for when buying. We've also suggested some species or varieties to try – popular ones that should be easy to find, and more unusual ones for which you may have to hunt further afield.

The third section of the *Guide* covers societies and organisations, providing a starting-point for gardeners who want to pursue specialist interests further, or who wish to get advice, or who simply like belonging to societies. National and large regional organisations are included, though there are also many local groups that may interest you too – the larger organisations should be able to tell you about those in your area. Entries are arranged alphabetically under the name of the society or organisation.

In the fourth and final section we have given general advice on what to look for when buying gardening tools and equipment. We have covered the basic toolkit, and what it's likely to cost if you're starting from scratch, and also larger purchases like sheds and greenhouses which you may want to think about for the future. This is largely aimed at the new gardener, but more experienced gardeners with a little more money to spend may be interested in the pros and cons of newer labour-saving ideas such as spot weeders and nylon line trimmers, or may simply want to expand the scope of their gardening activities, say by investing in a greenhouse.

1 Good garden centres and general nurseries

How we chose the garden centres and nurseries

All the garden centres and nurseries included in this chapter of the *Guide* have been recommended to us and checked out by one of our team of inspectors. Our inspectors are all keen, experienced gardeners, but are not connected with the trade in any way. Inspections are unsolicited – no garden centre or nursery is inspected on request or pays to be in the *Guide*. Inspections are also carried out anonymously so that establishments are not able to spruce themselves up for the occasion or give our inspectors special attention – they are treated just like any other customers.

When considering a garden centre or nursery for inclusion in the *Guide*, we've looked first and foremost at the range of goods it stocks and the quality and price of plants – no amount of piped music and fancy displays can make up for a poor choice and high prices. We've tried to judge each place on what it sets out to do – we wouldn't downrate a traditional nursery for not providing a cafeteria or selling powered tools, for example. Entries cover many different types of establishment from small, family-run nurseries to large hypermarkets selling everything from shrubs to swimming pools. Some have been included because they provide a good, all-round service to gardeners; others because they cater well for particular aspects of gardening – they carry a comprehensive range of tools and equipment, say, or a good range of high quality plants. Some of the garden centres and nurseries our inspectors visited still had a lot of room for improvement, but we've included them either because they show a lot of promise, or simply because they provide a reasonable service for gardeners in areas for which we have no other entries.

Many garden centres and nurseries are omitted simply because we have not heard of them or do not know enough about them, and some of these may be just as good as those in the *Guide*. You can help us to expand and improve the *Guide* by recommending any good ones you know about, using the report forms at the end of the book. You can also help us to keep up to date with those that already appear in the *Guide* using the same forms. If you consider any entry to be incorrect, inadequate or misleading, you would be doing us and your fellow gardeners a service by letting us know.

In each entry we aim to highlight the important qualities and defects of the garden centre or nursery and to convey its essential character so that you will be able to tell if it is the sort of place you would enjoy visiting and whether it will satisfy your needs. Your impression of a garden centre or nursery may depend a lot on when you visit it. A popular centre can be very crowded at weekends and you may only be able to find untrained, part-time cashiers to help you out, whereas the same centre visited during the week can offer peaceful, off-peak shopping with personal service from fully-qualified staff. Stocks may vary considerably from season to season, or even from one week to the next. Plants may arrive at a garden centre looking fresh and lovely, but deteriorate rapidly if neglected or kept in unsuitable conditions. Given adequate feedback about the places which feature in the *Guide*, we hope to build up a more complete picture of what they are like all year round.

How to read the entries

Any town or village for which there is an entry is indicated on one of the following maps. Entries themselves are arranged in alphabetical order of place name. Each entry has two main parts – a description of the garden centre or nursery, followed by relevant information such as facilities and opening hours. The description is drawn mostly from our inspector's report and so generally reflects what the garden centre or nursery was like in the summer of 1984. However, many of these establishments are changing rapidly – practically all those we contacted were planning expansions or improvements for 1985 – so we also sent the proprietors or managers a detailed questionnaire for them to tell us more about their garden centre or nursery, the facilities provided and any plans for future developments. Where they have completed the questionnaire, we have been able to include these details in the entry to give you an idea of how a garden centre or nursery is developing. On the other hand, when the questionnaire has not been returned, we have sometimes been unable to obtain accurate information about opening hours, facilities and so on, and have had to leave this part of the entry blank. In any case, if you are travelling a long distance to a garden centre or nursery it is always advisable to telephone first to check the opening hours since they are inclined to vary a bit with the season and weather conditions, particularly if the centre or nursery is off the beaten track.

PRICES

To enable us to compare the cost of plants, we collected the prices of a range of plants that were in stock at the time of our inspections (summer). From this information, we calculated a basket price for each garden centre and nursery and compared it with the average basket price. We found a huge variation – at the cheapest nursery the price of plants in our basket was as little as £12.25, while at the other end of the range, the same plants cost more than £39. In the entries, we have given ratings of £ to ££££££ – very cheap to very expensive. Those rated £££ or ££££ were within a few pounds of our average basket price shown below.

Shopping basket

	average price £ [1]
Betula pendula 'Youngii'	1.64
Juniperus 'Skyrocket'	1.80
Cotoneaster x hybridus 'Pendulus'	1.64
Prunus cerasifera 'Atropurpureum'	1.41
Aucuba japonica 'Variegata'	2.28
Pyracantha	1.15
Blackcurrants	1.48
Gooseberries	1.87
Strawberries	0.39
Dianthus neglectus or *D. nitidus*	0.66
Helianthemum	0.65
Michaelmas daisies	0.90
Sedum	0.79
Phlox maculata	0.89
Rosemary	0.99
Thyme	0.65
Calluna vulgaris	0.67
Erica carnea	0.68
Hedera helix	2.70
Clematis 'The President'	3.08

total basket price £26.32

[1] Price of trees and shrubs varies with the size, so we've worked out prices per 30 cm (1ft) in order to make comparisons.

DISTINCTIONS

Garden centres and nurseries can earn three types of award. This year we have only made provisional awards, to be ratified in future years as we learn more about the garden centres and nurseries and how they are developing.

✿ **flower** This is given to establishments selling either a very good range of high quality plants, or a more limited but particularly interesting selection.

✎ **hand fork** This is given to garden centres stocking a particularly comprehensive range of gardening equipment, from hand tools and composts to greenhouses and paving.

★ **star** Awarded only to garden centres and nurseries which have met with the whole-hearted approval of our inspectors. They must have a good selection of high quality plants and a comprehensive range of gardening equipment, and must also excel in other ways, such as in the layout and facilities and services they provide.

International Garden Centre

Some of the garden centres in this *Guide* are members of International Garden Centre (British Group). These are marked with the IGC symbol. IGC arose in 1968 from an association which represented European garden centres. It now covers 14 different countries, each with its own national group representing its own special national interests. The British Group is one of the largest – there are well over 1,000 garden centres in the UK and about 140 of them are members of IGC.

IGC (British Group) has produced a code of practice which aims, among other things, to improve standards in garden centres. They carry out inspections to keep a check on standards at their members' centres, and in 1983 started a scheme for giving awards of merit for aspects in which a centre excelled, the range and presentation of sundries, for example. You may see certificates for these awards displayed in IGC centres. IGC also arranges for the training of garden centre staff through courses run by horticultural colleges. It does not run any central pricing or buying schemes, so you can't expect to find the same choice of stock or goods at the same prices at all IGC centres. However, you should find a reasonably comprehensive range of gardening equipment as well as plants because members of IGC have to be fully fledged garden centres – IGC does not encompass nurseries or really small, family-run centres (if you prefer these, steer clear of the IGC sign).

IGC members are well represented in this *Guide* – we have included 102.

Leisuregro

In 1981, some garden centres in Scotland broke away from IGC to form their own organisation called Leisuregro. They started primarily as a group for promotion and bulk buying, but they also inspect garden centres before allowing them to join, and visit members regularly to keep a check on standards. At the time of publication of our *Guide*, they had 15 members, and 10 of them appeared in the *Guide* – these are marked with Leisuregro's butterfly symbol.

Facilities for the disabled and elderly

Gardening is a hobby enjoyed by many elderly people and people with a wide range of disabilities, yet very few garden centres and nurseries have good facilities for them. In our inspections, we checked for features such as parking facilities, ease of access to all parts of the centre and clarity of labelling. No garden centre or nursery scored full marks for all of these features, but those which came out best are marked with the wheelchair symbol in the *Guide*. Some centres are limited in the changes they can make – they can't do much about a steeply sloping site, for example – but most have plenty of scope for improvement. We think it is time that garden centres and nurseries put more thought into catering for their less able customers. In the meantime, if you have any particular problems, we suggest you telephone garden centres and nurseries before visiting to check on the site and facilities.

LABELLING

Labels should be large and clear and easy to see by people who have difficulty bending or reaching. We found that one in five garden centres and nurseries had really poor plant labels – they were difficult to decipher even for agile people with good eye-sight! Weathering was the the most common problem – labels on older stock were often washed out or faded – though some handwritten ones were illegible even when new. The quality of labels varied a lot, even between plants at the same centre. Where present, large labels for groups of plants were generally much better than individual plant tags. They were often informative, well positioned and easy to read. One good idea adopted by some centres was to label the groups of plants clearly to help you make your choice, and to provide individual plant tags at the check out – this gets around many of the problems with weather-worn labels and makes sure you go home with the correct information about the plants you have bought. However, at most centres labelling is clearly an area in which there is plenty of room for improvement. If you have problems we suggest that you borrow a catalogue or price list from the centre to help you.

PARKING

There should be facilities for parking close to the nursery or garden centre, and easy access from the car park with no steps or obstacles. Nearly all the centres we inspected had parking nearby, though very few had spaces reserved for the disabled. This is a very cheap way of helping the disabled, particularly when parking space is limited. At about a third of the centres visited, the car park presented some sort of problem – steps, turnstiles, busy roads to cross, or a rough or gravelled surface.

ACCESSIBILITY

All parts of the garden centre or nursery indoors and out, including any cafeteria, should be accessible to wheelchair users. Ideally surfaces should be smooth and flat, and all paths and doorways wide and easy to negotiate. About a third of the centres inspected provided good access and a few even provided wheelchairs for customers' use, but a tenth were totally unsuitable for wheelchair users. Gravel paths, rough ground, narrow gangways and doors, steep slopes and steps can all present problems.

SEATS FOR RESTING

Shopping at garden centres, particularly some of the large ones spread over several acres, can prove to be very tiring, so even the fittest, able-bodied visitor may welcome a sit-down. Less than a third of the centres visited provided places to rest.

REFRESHMENTS

Fewer than a third of the garden centres and nurseries inspected had refreshment facilities suitable for wheelchair users. Many had no refreshment facilities at all, so if you're travelling a long way it's best to plan ahead so you don't go hungry or thirsty.

TOILETS

Most of the garden centres and nurseries we inspected had toilets, but very few of these were suitable for disabled users. A good browse round a centre can take several hours, so lack of toilet facilities can be a serious drawback.

STAFF

Helpful staff can make all the difference. Many centres provide trolleys or carts to help you transport your goods to the car, and staff are usually willing to carry your purchases and may even accompany you round the site. You might be well advised to telephone the centre first to find out what their attitude is, and be prepared to ask for help if you need it. It goes without saying that you are much more likely to get this sort of personal service if you are able to avoid the busiest period such as weekends.

England

ABINGDON Oxfordshire

map 4

Tesco Garden Centre

Marcham Road, Abingdon OX13 6QL   Tel Abingdon (0235) 33143

In the south-east corner of Abingdon bypass (A34) at the Marcham Road intersection, about 2 miles west of Abingdon

As one might expect from a 'superstore' complex, a lot of the marks go for a very clean and tidy layout, excellent facilities and wide array of equipment and bits-and-bobs. Trees are being grown to provide shelter but at the moment the wind across this site can be bitterly cold. Nevertheless, this is a good place for one-stop-shopping, with a cafeteria, petrol station, Tesco store and Sandfords DIY Centre all contributing to a well-serviced set-up. As one would imagine, all types of garden sundries are sold including Tesco own-brand products. Composts and chemicals deserve particular mention. The indoor plant arrangement is excellent, clearly labelled and obviously well cared for, and at the time of our visit there was a wonderful display of summer bedding plants. The selection of plants would satisfy most needs, the only notable shortage being fruit trees. Quality overall is quite good. The layout is compact and plants are arranged alphabetically with 'headboard' leaflets giving information on cultivation. Plants are also individually labelled. Even so, it may take you a while to work out the layout of the beds, and our inspector did find a few strawberries lurking amidst the alpines! The manager is happy to deal with queries and there are one or two casual labourers to help with carrying purchases.

Prices £££
Facilities Parking, 1,000 cars. Toilets. Restaurant. Play area. Garden advice. Delivery service. Free price list for garden buildings and machinery. Plant catalogue for reference only
Open Mon to Thurs 9am to 8pm (closes 6pm Mon to Wed in winter), Fri 9am to 9pm, Sat 8.30am to 6pm, Sun 9am to 6pm (Sun 10am to 5pm in winter)
Credit cards Access, Visa

ABRIDGE Essex

map 4

Crowther Nurseries

Ongar Road, Abridge RM4 1AA   *Tel* Stapleford (040 28) 581

On the south side of the A113, Chigwell to Ongar road, 1 mile east of Abridge

Strong and vigorous container-grown plants are the backbone of this nursery, situated near the River Roding. Plants are available only in the appropriate season, and this policy, along with good irrigation and care, ensures the high standard of health evident in the stock. Conifers and shrubs are a constant feature and they are displayed in independent sections and arranged alphabetically. Straightforward, rectangular beds make for easy examination of the plants (although shingle paths can make the going a bit tricky) and there are some unusual varieties to be discovered. Hand tools, chemicals, peat and fertilisers fill up the covered area and everything can be seen at a glance. Another small unit contains houseplants and a farm shop which specialises in goats' milk and its products, such as yoghurt. The goats themselves, from kids to adult milkers, are out in the fields in fine weather. Greenhouses, sheds, fencing and paving are stocked and if you are not much of a DIY person then the landscaping service might appeal. The owner is generally on hand to deal with queries, but other staff are reasonably knowledgeable and pleasant – loading is always done without any fuss. On Sunday afternoons pony rides are available for children (weather permitting).

Prices ££££
Facilities Parking, 22 cars (plus 30 overflow). Toilets. Vending machines and ice cream. Garden advice service. Delivery service. Free price list for paving, sheds etc. Free catalogue for roses, soft fruit and top fruit
Open Tues to Sun 9.30am to 6.30pm
Credit cards Access, Visa

ACLE Norfolk   map 4

Clippesby Garden Centre

Clippesby, near Great Yarmouth   *Tel* Fleggburgh (049 377) 367
NR29 3BJ
In Clippesby village 3 miles north-east of Acle. Turn off the A1064 at Billockby on to the B1152, take first turning left at Clippesby village

Houseplant fanciers will find this centre a boon. An exceptional range of mature indoor plants is beautifully arranged inside a glasshouse, and the display created is very interesting and informative without being ostentatious. The centre is a good place for a day out with the family. It is located in a sheltered, rural setting which is combined with a touring caravan site and holiday apartments, so visiting tourists might like to browse around to see how Clippesby compares with their local centres. The centre will cater for coach parties if warned in advance. On the whole this medium-sized centre is compact and well organised with trees, shrubs and other plants placed in display beds outside. Labelling is generally good and often provides cultural information, but it might be necessary to seek out the staff for some prices. The range and standard of plants is good though there were not many roses, alpines or heathers on sale when we inspected. On the other hand there was a wealth of fuchsias and ivies – in fact an exhaustive and exceptional array. There is also a good range of small cacti. Only a rudimentary supply of tools and sundries is stocked, but there are all sorts of fertilisers and pesticides. Local crafts products are sold, and if you want to find out more about local events and sights there is copious information displayed for your perusal. One warning is to watch your head among the multi-span glasshouses: the eaves are low and can be hazardous.

Prices ££££
Facilities Parking, 100 cars. Toilets. Play area. Cafeteria. Garden advice service. Delivery service. Free plant price list
Open Every day 9am to 5.30pm, 30 Mar to 30 Sept only. Closed in winter
Credit cards Access, Visa

ALBRIGHTON Shropshire   map 2

Roses and Shrubs   ★

Newport Road, Albrighton,   *Tel* Albrighton (090 722) 3233
near Wolverhampton WV7 3ER
*On the A41 Albrighton bypass, by Cosford Aerodrome, 1 mile from
the M54 junction 3*

This is a particularly good place to go in inclement weather, as a lot of the site is under cover, but in any weather condition it can offer a wide choice of plants and sundries. The centre is arranged into distinct sections each providing a different range of goods. Signposting and layout are excellent both outside and in. There is no problem with crowding yet they have managed to supply nearly everything the amateur gardener could want. A full range of composts and fertilisers and a wide variety of books and fish are just some of the accessories on offer. Lawnmowers, sheds and fencing are the only obvious items missing. The plants are set out around the site in attractive displays and they are in excellent health and conscientiously labelled. The climbers, conifers and alpines are very well represented, and one of our inspectors was impressed by the Acers which were numerous and very reasonably priced. The shrubs are of a high standard and the quality of plants is generally very good. Houseplants are superb and the wonderful selection of bulbs and corms sold also deserves a special mention. Most plants are grown on nearby sites. The staff are cheerful and willing and there are always trained staff on duty to cope with the more difficult problems. Some additional features are the range of packet seeds from all the main suppliers, and a pottery which visitors are encouraged to wander round.

Prices £££
Facilities Parking, 400 cars. Toilets. Cafeteria. Garden advice service. Delivery service. Free price list for plants
Open Every day 8am to 8pm (closes 5pm in winter). Closed Christmas and Boxing Day and New Year's Day
Credit cards Access, Visa

ALFOLD Surrey   map 5

Medland Garden Centre and Nursery

Horsham Road, Alfold GU6 8JE   *Tel* Loxwood (0403) 752359
On the A281 between Horsham and Guildford

A garden centre for plant-lovers, large sections are set aside for raising plants and the range offered is 'faultless'. The comprehensive selection is well set out and of first-class quality – our inspector thought the fruit trees were most impressive. Labelling is rather variable. Labels for groups of plants provide cultural and descriptive information in clearly readable print, but at the time of our inspection some individual labels were weather-worn and prices not always legible. New computerised labelling was being introduced in early 1985 which should hopefully have improved the situation. Smooth pathways, very good signposting and an excellent layout make browsing through the outdoor stocks a pleasure, but if you prefer houseplants these are displayed in a lovely, shaded greenhouse. Separate covered areas house the horticultural sundries, including an indoor fish pond with some quite large inhabitants. Most garden tools and sundries are available, including the larger items such as buildings and fencing, and there's a massive display of ornamental and clay pots. Staff members are alert to the needs of the customers and help out where they can. If you are still hungry for information, the bookstall has a range of interesting material to thumb through. The centre is spread out over a wide area and there is still room for considerable expansion.

Prices ££££
Facilities Parking, 80 cars. Toilets. Coffee machine. Play area. Garden advice service. Delivery service. Free price list for plants and sundries. Plant catalogue 40p
Open Mon to Sat 9am to 5.30pm, Sun 10am to 5pm (closed 1pm to 2.30pm)
Credit cards Access, American Express, Visa

ALLINGTON Kent   map 4

Kent Garden Centre   ★

London Road, Allington,   *Tel* Maidstone (0622) 677367
Maidstone ME16 9XX
1½ miles from Maidstone on the A20 to London. Take junction 5 off the M20

A fine range of tropical fish, live coral and marine accessories were the first things to catch our inspector's eye. The high standard and interesting displays continue throughout the centre, though the layout and atmosphere is functional rather than ornamental, and it gives the impression of being a massive DIY complex with a great array of gardening equipment and sundries. These range from tree-felling saws and spare parts for mowers to wrought ironwork, swimming pools and fancy pottery. The aquatic and pet section sells reptiles, tropical birds and cold-water fish, as well as live coral, and they all looked very healthy when we inspected. If you are looking for plants, there's a wide range on offer. For the house or greenhouse you can browse through the exotic tender plants, including a good selection of cacti. For the garden there is a wide range of hardy plants, displayed on waist-high benches and arranged in logical and helpful groupings. They are all extremely healthy, and some excellent labelling explains what is what. However, if you need any help, the staff are considerate and efficient, and the manager is readily available to answer queries. A plant information centre is planned for the future. A fast-food kiosk provides tea, coffee and snacks.

Prices ££££
Facilities Parking, 160 cars. Toilets. Play area. Garden advice service. Delivery service. Catalogue of sundries 50p
Open Every day 8.30am to 6.30pm (closes 5.30pm in winter). Closed Christmas Day
Credit cards Access, Visa

ALMONDSBURY Avon   map 3

Park Garden Nurseries   ✿

Over Lane, Almondsbury   *Tel* Almondsbury (0454) 612247
BS12 4BP

Near the Almondsbury flyover where the M4 and M5 cross. Over Lane is just off the A38 on Almondsbury Hill

This family-run nursery has been described as a 'quiet retreat' as it lies in a virtual sun trap with a background of rising wooded landscape. A nursery rather than garden centre, the concentration here is on the plants and not gardening equipment, though at present there's a wide range of stoneware and ornaments and first-class hanging baskets are made-to-order. The plants are of good quality throughout – poor plants are either removed or placed in their 'bargain offers' section. The layout is good with raised beds for display and there are plans to expand these. There are also large greenhouses where many of the young plants are kept and the public are invited to browse, but these immature plants are not yet for sale. Roses are not stocked because Sandays Nurseries, rose specialists, are ½ mile away. All plants are individually labelled with their variety and price, while their 'habit' is described either on the label or on a large group notice. Plenty of trolleys, trays and containers are available and all areas are staffed by helpful people who offer to carry your purchases before you even need ask.

Prices ££££
Facilities Parking, 100 cars. Toilets. Play area. Garden advice service. Delivery service. Free plant catalogue. Plants sold by mail order
Open Every day Mon to Sat 9am to 6pm (closes 5pm in winter). Closes Christmas week
Credit cards Access, Visa

AMBLESIDE Cumbria   map 2

T R Hayes & Sons   ★

Lake District Nurseries, Ambleside   *Tel* Ambleside (0966) 33434
LA22 0DW
Just south of Ambleside on the A591

This family firm is proud of its tradition of 'Serving the gardeners and visitors of the Lake District since the days of Napoleon'. It is a large garden centre near Lake Windermere with a tremendous range of stock. Our inspector felt one would need a week to see everything properly. It has been well planned with clear signposting. Plant labels give the size, colour, flowering time and soil requirements. Plants are rather expensive, but are excellent in all respects. There is a particularly good collection of dwarf conifers and a selection of shrubs for immediate planting. The choice of herbs was felt to be rather limited at the time of our inspector's visit. Almost all gardening sundries can be found here, but gardening machinery is kept at a separate centre 5 miles away in Windermere itself. Umbrellas, trolleys and a wheelchair are available for customers' use. The catalogue gives a history of all the plants available and also describes the garden design and construction service offered.

Prices £££££
Facilities Parking, 200–300 cars. Toilets. Coffee lounge. Garden advice. Delivery service. Plant catalogue 30p, price list free. Plants sold by mail order
Open Mon to Sat 9am to 6pm (or dusk), Sun 10am to 6pm (or dusk). Closed Christmas and Boxing Day and New Year's Day
Credit cards Access, Visa

AMERSHAM Buckinghamshire   map 4
Hyrons Nursery & Garden Centre

Orchard Lane, Amersham HP6 6AW   *Tel* Amersham (024 03) 5695
Entrance in Orchard Lane off Woodside Road (the A404 Amersham to Chesham road)

This garden centre is situated in the outskirts of Amersham within a secluded residential area. Although a small site, it has been well planned to full advantage and provides gardeners with a surprisingly large choice of stock. The variety of plants available is good, particularly in the rhododendron, rose, conifer, fruit tree and shrub sections. Many of them are grown in their own nurseries and the standard of all the stock is consistently very good. Labels are reasonable both for groups and individual plants. They have no illustrations or specific growing instructions, but there are free leaflets on specialist plants available, and a catalogue giving prices, descriptions and some growing advice. Plants are arranged alphabetically in accordance with the catalogue, so it is easy to find the ones you want. There are two small greenhouses for bulbs, seeds, houseplants and ornaments. Sheds, greenhouses and fencing are sold, and the cramped indoor areas stock tools and sundries. Because the centre is so small, usually only the knowledgeable cashier is available to answer questions, but there are experienced staff who can help if need be.

Prices ££££
Facilities Parking, 30 cars. Toilets. Garden advice service. Delivery service. Plant catalogue 40p or free
Open Mon to Sat 9am to 5 pm (closes 1pm to 2pm)

ANGMERING W. Sussex   map 5
Manor Nursery

High Street, Angmering BN16 4AW   *Tel* Rustington (090 62) 6977
In a cul-de-sac off Angmering High Street. Turn north off the A27 Worthing to Littlehampton road

A nursery recommended for the quality and value for money of its stock, and the first-rate advice given to customers. It stocks a very wide variety of trees, shrubs, fruit trees, dwarf conifers and houseplants, and a reasonable range of most other plants, all of top quality. Manor Nursery grows most of its stock at its own nearby nursery, and specialises, among other things, in cacti and carnations. The site is well laid out and labelling is generally very good, though let down by some unreadable, weathered labels. Few gardening sundries are stocked except for the basics such as composts and chemicals, though a range of stoneware and terracotta containers is available.

Prices Information not available
Facilities Parking, 60 cars. Toilets. Vending machines. Garden advice service. Delivery service. Free plant price lists in season
Open Every day 8am to 5pm. Closed Christmas Day

Roundstone Garden Centre

Roundstone Bypass,   *Tel* Rustington (090 62) 76481/2/3
Angmering, Littlehampton BN16 4BD
On the A259 Worthing to Littlehampton road, 3 miles east of Littlehampton

This centre has an excellent layout with wide gangways, plants alphabetically arranged and clear signposts. It is a large centre covering virtually every aspect of gardening. In terms of plants the range and quality is very good across the board, with houseplants reigning supreme. The only drawback is that the wide range can sometimes make finding a specific plant a little difficult. An automatic watering system keeps plants looking fresh even in the driest weather. When our inspector visited he found that labels on individual plants were poor, but group labels were quite good. The centre tells us a lot has recently been done to improve any substandard labels. The range of sundries is very comprehensive with some interesting extras. A franchise operation stocks an imaginative range of garden buildings from the standard conservatories, to gazebos and a Wendy House which children are encouraged to explore. Features include a gift shop, a 'bargain' corner in the sundries section, a wine cellar with free tasting of the 'wine of the week' and a fruit, vegetable and health food store. The final novelty which must not go unmentioned is the spectacular water feature, now augmented by an outdoor fish pool fed by a small, cascading waterfall. There are two long fish ladders running alongside containing Japanese Koi carp, Sarasa Comets, Blackmoors and Golden Orf. A real treat. Staff will put themselves out to help you and some of them are exceptionally knowledgeable.

Prices ££££
Facilities Parking, 600 cars. Toilets. Coffee shop. Garden advice service. Delivery service. Free descriptive pamphlets
Open Every day 8am to 5.30pm (closes 5pm in winter). Closed Christmas and Boxing Day
Credit cards Access, Visa

ARDLEIGH Essex   map 4

Notcutts Garden Centre

Station Ford, Ardleigh, Colchester   *Tel* Colchester (0206) 230271
CO7 7RT
*On the outskirts of Ardleigh, approximately 5 miles north-east of Colchester on the
B1029 road to Dedham*

The main London to Clacton railway line is the backdrop to this centre.
Wide, shingle paths lead to the different plant areas, each of which is
identified by a clear notice above head height. The site is well laid out with
plants logically arranged in alphabetical order. A large section of the plant
area is covered with a protective shading material, and a pleasant walk
through a rhododendron garden provides a nice break from the more
practical displays. There is a reasonable, all-round selection of plants and
they are maintained in good condition – however, prices are high.
All stock is grown at the company nurseries in Woodbridge and Bagshot
and details of all plants are given in Notcutts' catalogue – any plants not in
stock can be ordered. The labelling is easy to read and illustrations are often
provided. Most plants are priced individually. If your interests lie more
with tools and equipment, the range sold is comprehensive. Sheds and
greenhouses can be ordered, and the centre stocks fencing, paving, garden
furniture and ornaments. There is an advisory kiosk with leaflets and
reference books available and Notcutts also offers a full garden planning
service – they will even visit your garden.

Prices ££££££
Facilities Parking, 400 cars. Toilets. Vending machine. Play area. Garden advice
service. Delivery service. Catalogue and price list £1.50
Open Mon to Sat 8.30am to 5.30pm, Sun 10am to 5.30pm (closes 5pm Sat and Sun in
winter). Closed Christmas and Boxing Day
Credit cards Access, Visa

ASHBY DE LA ZOUCH Leicestershire   map 2

Staunton Harold Nurseries

Ashby de la Zouch LE6 5RU   *Tel* Melbourne (03316) 2769/3365
*3 miles north of Ashby de la Zouch, near the junction of the A453 with the B587
Melbourne road at Lount*

A good choice for a day's outing as well as a good place to buy very cheap
plants. This nursery is set in a landscaped park with an extensive lake – a
big attraction for both casual visitors and coachloads. These grounds
belong to the Cheshire Homes and are open to the public. There's a craft
centre next door to the nursery. The nursery itself covers 5 acres and the
stock is spread out so you can see plants in their natural surroundings
rather than the usual regimented rows. A walk round is relaxing and
satisfying, encompassing a wide range of plants. Plants are grown at the
nursery itself and at another site at Kings Mill. Cut flowers and houseplants
are sold in a large covered area. Family fruit trees are a speciality,

particularly apples. Emphasis is largely on selling plants, and sales of sundries are kept to the minimum – no tools, greenhouses or sheds, but you'll find fertilisers, garden furniture and ornaments. The tea rooms in the adjacent craft centre offer a variety of home-made produce and there's a caravan nearby for ices and drinks which is open in spring and summer. The nursery is fairly well laid out and signposted, but our inspector had trouble finding the pay desk!

Prices £
Facilities Parking, 100 cars. Toilets. Play area. Garden advice service. Delivery service. Price list
Open Every day 9am to 8pm (closes 5pm in winter). Closed Christmas Day
Credit card Access

ASHFORD Kent map 4

Bybrook Barn Garden Centre

Canterbury Road, Ashford TN24 9JZ *Tel* Ashford (0233) 31959
On the A28, Ashford to Canterbury road about ½ mile from Ashford town centre

Approached from the Ashford direction, this garden centre is well-signposted and easy to find. It provides a good selection of high quality garden plants which are well-displayed in the outdoor area, as well as a small selection of good quality houseplants inside. All plants are clearly and correctly labelled and labels are generally informative, particularly those on the trees and shrubs. Wide gravel paths lead through a well laid out, though fairly compact area, and most items are clearly visible. An interesting idea to stimulate the gardener's imagination is that of having a special monthly display. A theme is chosen and followed through, such as 'plants for leaf colour', and a printed leaflet is issued listing and describing the plants which are set out. A nice idea which must pay dividends both for the gardener and the centre. Indoors there is a shop selling smaller garden sundries as well as good quality fruit and vegetables, conserves and unusual biscuits. A sizeable greenhouse contains a reasonable selection of the larger garden equipment. Displays of paving are laid out in small patios and there is also a wide range of fencing, stoneware urns and pots, and an excellent collection of lawnmowers – a servicing and repairs department will also help you out if your mower is defunct. Children will be interested in the dwarf rabbits, displayed with their hutches and pens. Alternatively there is a '10p' kiddies mechanical ride. The young staff are courteous and helpful.

Prices ££££
Facilities Parking, 100 cars. Toilets. Delivery service. Free price lists for conifers, heathers, roses, paving and walling, and fencing
Open Every day, 9am to 5.30pm
Credit cards Access, Visa

Awards given this year are only provisional. We need plenty of feedback to let us know what the garden centres and nurseries are like all year round. Please use the report forms at the end of the book.

BAGSHOT Surrey
map 5

Notcutts Garden Centre

Waterers Nurseries, London Road,
Bagshot GU19 5DG
Tel Bagshot (0276) 72288

On the A30 just west of Bagshot, between Bagshot and Camberley

Pleasantly situated on the Surrey–Berkshire border, this is the home of the 'test tube' orchid. Since Notcutts took over this centre there have been great improvements and now only the very hard to please would come away disappointed. The total range of traditional gardening ware is stocked with a particularly good choice of moulded plastic ponds and other water-gardening equipment. Greenhouses, sheds, swimming pools, and fish and tropical fish equipment are all sold under franchise. Although there are no lawnmowers at present, a plan for the near future involves setting up a large display accompanied by a maintenance service. The selection of plants is comprehensive, though expensive: of excellent quality, pleasantly weed-free and looking fresh and upstanding. Azaleas and rhododendrons are a speciality and they are grown in the adjoining nursery along with perennials, shrub roses and fruit. Other plants are grown at Notcutts Nursery in Woodbridge. Labelling is first class as well – an unusual feature among garden centres! The whole centre is spacious and clean. The outside has been planned with easy access to all sections and the inside, with wide and uncluttered gangways, is also easy to negotiate. The staff are very helpful, though few in number, and they have a large collection of reference books and pamphlets to help get to the bottom of any query they can't answer themselves. Umbrellas are handed out on inclement days – and there are plenty of trolleys available for customers' use.

Prices ££££££
Facilities Parking, 150 cars. Toilets. Vending machines. Play area. Garden advice service. Delivery service. Free price lists for furniture, bulbs etc. Plant catalogue £1.50. Plants sold by mail order from Notcutts Garden Centre, Woodbridge (see WOODBRIDGE)
Open Mon to Sat 9am to 5.30pm, Sun 10 to 5.30pm. Closed 4 days over Christmas and New Year's Day
Credit cards Access, Visa

BAR HILL Cambridgeshire
map 4

Tesco Garden Centre

15 Viking Way, Bar Hill,
Cambridge CB3 8EL
Tel Crafts Hill (0954) 82123

5 miles north of Cambridge at Bar Hill on the A604

A purpose-built centre with raised beds for plant displays and slab paving paths. Everything is clearly signposted and labelling is excellent, with photographs, descriptions and details of cultivation provided. The atmosphere may be a little impersonal and antiseptic for some, but the quality of the plants is really most impressive. There is strict quality control and houseplants have sell-by dates, after which they are reduced in price. It is situated in the middle of a large modern housing estate and a lot of its custom comes from local people or those shopping at the Tesco foodstore. The plants stocked reflect this clientele as the range appears to be aimed at people with 'new gardens' and there is little out of the ordinary. Gardeners looking for the exciting or unexpected could be disappointed. Those who enjoy the building and hardware side of things will find a good all-round supply of items from hand and power tools to a good water-garden section which sells lighting, pumps and waterfalls. Cold-water fish are soon to be stocked. Most of the larger sundry items are also available, including greenhouses, sheds and fencing, but paving is not sold. The inside area is large and pleasant with wide aisles, so getting around is no problem. Staff are eager to help and the assistant manager is most knowledgeable – a catalogue is also available, although it is not always in stock. A cafeteria serving coffee, tea and meals is located in the main building. The complex includes a petrol station and superstore.

Prices £££
Facilities Parking, 170 cars. Toilets. Cafeteria. Garden advice service. Delivery service for greenhouses. Free price lists for greenhouses, sheds and garden machinery. Plant catalogue for reference
Open Mon to Fri 9am to 8pm, Sat and Sun 9am to 6pm (closes 5.30pm Mon, 6pm Tues and Wed in winter)
Credit cards Access, Visa

BARNSTAPLE Devon map 3
St John's Garden Centre

St John's Lane, Barnstaple EX32 9DD   *Tel* Barnstaple (0271) 43884
On the outskirts of Barnstaple, about 1 mile east of the town centre and ¼ mile off the A361 to South Molton

'One of the best-stocked and best-organised centres that I have been to' our inspector commented. This is a family-run business and the result is efficiency and full-hearted co-operation. The centre consists of five vast greenhouses which each devote themselves to magnificent floral displays with the changing seasons, from cyclamen, cacti and capsicum at Christmas to polyanthus and primroses come Easter – a glorious sight. But this is not all, for outside there is at least an acre of ground which is host to a wide range of trees, fruit and shrubs. Expansions are being planned all the time, and a play area and demonstration garden are in the pipeline. The state of health of plants is generally good, particularly that of the trees and shrubs. Group labels are very good and easily read from the paths, 'even wearing bifocals'! The labelling on heathers and alpines, however, could do with improvement. Most larger items of gardening equipment are sold here including fencing, sheds, greenhouses and construction materials, and a reasonable range of other sundries except for power tools. There is a separate well-stocked department devoted to water gardening and fish.

 Garden centres and nurseries awarded with a hand fork symbol stock a particularly comprehensive range of gardening equipment.

Prices £££
Facilities Parking, 120 cars. Toilets. Cafeteria. Garden advice service. Delivery
service. Free price list and catalogues for trees, shrubs, roses and conifers
Open Mon to Sat 9am to 6pm, Sun 10am to 5pm (closes Sun 12am to 2pm)

BARTON Lancashire   map 2

Barton Grange Garden Centre

Garstang Road, Barton,   *Tel* Preston (0772) 862551
Preston PR3 5AA

On the A6, 2 miles north of junction 32 on the M6, 5 miles north of Preston

Whether you've got a window box or an acre plot, there'll be something of
interest for you here. This is a large centre on a self-contained site which
includes a 3-star hotel conference centre. It sells a large range of
non-garden as well as garden materials, so there are things to interest both
the casual visitor and the serious gardener. The outdoor section is well
organised with raised beds for plants, well-stocked fish and water-garden
sections, and comprehensive signposting. Labelling is excellent. Indoor
areas contain many non-gardening items, while garden tools and sundries
are limited to a wide selection of chemicals, hand tools, furniture and
ornaments. A new leisure garden section shows a line of cascade
swimming pools and similar items. There is a very good all-round selection
of plants; conifers and shrubs are specialities – most are grown on site and
are of excellent quality. There's also an impressive indoor plant area where
an information desk has recently been opened. There are ample free leaflets
on all manner of garden topics. Staff are friendly and very knowledgeable.

Prices £££
Facilities Parking, 200 cars. Toilets. Restaurant and cafeteria. Garden advice service.
Delivery service. Weekly leaflets on plants
Open Every day 9am to 5pm
Credit Cards Access, Visa

BASINGSTOKE Hampshire   map 4

Homebase

Winchester Road, Basingstoke   *Tel* Basingstoke (0256) 55658
RG22 6HN

*On the A30, 2 miles south of Basingstoke towards Winchester, 200 yds from
Brighton Hill roundabout*

This is a pleasant centre to wander round and it takes a strong will to be
able to resist buying something. The stock of plants does not compare with
what a good nursery would be able to offer, but the range available is
nevertheless very good. The houseplant section is especially impressive
with all the common and some of the more unusual species on hand. All
the plants, whether indoor or out, are in excellent condition. Labelling is
thorough, but there is little in the way of planting instructions. The huge
indoor area caters above and beyond the needs of the gardener and if DIY is
close to your heart there will be something for you here – the line of goods

ranges from nails to complete bathrooms. The ordinary gardener is also well catered for. There's a comprehensive range of all the smaller gardening materials inside, and fences and greenhouses are kept outside. The entire establishment has been well organised and clearly signposted and there is plenty of room throughout to trundle your purchases around by trolley. The staff are very approachable, and notices dotted about state that they are trained and their presence is for the customer's benefit. Watching them work makes it obvious that they are plant people first, salesmen second. Our inspector would happily go back 'again and again' and has had no problems with any previous purchases.

Prices £££
Facilities Parking, 200 cars. Toilets. Vending machines. Garden advice service. Delivery service
Open Mon to Thurs 9am to 8pm, Fri 9am to 9pm, Sat 9am to 6pm. Closed Christmas Day
Credit cards Access, Visa

BATH Avon   map 3

Fred Daw Prior Park Garden Centre

Prior Park Road, Bath BA2 4NF   *Tel* Bath (0225) 27175
At the bottom of Ralph Allen Drive, 100 yds from the Lower Bristol road

A pleasure to visit, Fred Daw's garden centre is neat, clean and tidy, and sells a good range of plants and gardening sundries. It is set on a steeply sloping site on one of Bath's principal hills – this could be a problem for those who are short of breath or disabled. The frontage has been nicely landscaped with a stream and the centre is well set out with paths running in terraces across the slope. Plants are in alphabetical order and you'll find a wide selection of good-quality stock, though nothing really unusual. Plant labels were rather variable: some gave lots of information, others were less detailed or missing altogether. There's a large greenhouse containing houseplants and an extensive covered area housing a wide range of garden tools and equipment, and larger items such as sheds, fencing and furniture are also sold. The staff are very helpful and any questions you have can be referred to the manager or his assistant, both of whom are very knowledgeable.

Prices ££££
Facilities Parking, 40 cars. Toilets. Ice creams. Garden advice service. Delivery service. Free price list for fencing
Open Mon to Sat 8.30am to 5.30pm, Sun 10am to 5pm

Whiteway Garden Centre

Whiteway Road, Bath BA2 2RG   *Tel* Bath (0225) 21162
On the road between Newton St. Loe and Combe Down connecting the A4 and A367

One could happily spend an hour or two browsing round this pleasant centre with its extensive views of the surrounding countryside. The plants and gardening sundries stocked should satisfy most shoppers, and the layout is very good. It covers a large area, both indoors and out, and the exterior section is terraced with steps and ramps built between levels. The sundries section is excellent in all respects, while the range of plants covers all areas. Many of the plants are grown in the associated nursery and so the quality is good right across the board. Whiteway's are specialist bulb growers too, so if you want to build up your spring display, a visit here can be most worthwhile. Most labels are clearly written and informative, although on some prices have been omitted or lost. Information is readily provided by the staff, but at times they are very busy. Leaflets on many subjects are available which can help out on many of your gardening problems. If you are an avid gardener, the centre also keeps details of gardening courses run by Bristol University which might interest you.

Prices £££
Facilities Parking, 200 cars. Toilets. Vending machine. Play area. Garden advice service. Delivery service. Free price list. Catalogue, £1.25
Open Mon to Fri 9am to 6pm (closes 5pm in winter), Sat 9am to 5pm, Sun 10am to 5pm. Closed 3 days at Christmas
Credit card Access

BEACONSFIELD Buckinghamshire   map 4
Beaconsfield Garden Centre   ⊗ ★

London Road, Beaconsfield   *Tel* Beaconsfield (049 46) 2522
HP9 1SH
On the A40, ½ mile west of Beaconsfield Old Town centre

'A caring garden centre' says our inspector, and although plants are rather expensive you can expect value for money. It is spacious throughout and very nicely and effectively set out. The car park is quite small but an overflow area caters for late-comers. The large greenhouse holds a range of indoor plants which are most attractively displayed, and a series of extra buildings contains the tools and equipment. The range of garden furniture and ornaments is impressive – a marquee is used in summer to exhibit furniture. The exterior plant area excels in its offerings of bedding plants, superior dianthus, petunias and busy lizzies. The herbs and alpines looked strong and sturdy at the time of our visit and the standard of the trees was very high. On the whole the condition of all plants was good and their labelling informative and consistent. All the staff, from casual workers to full-time professionals, are out to please. There are plans to expand the plant area and to redevelop the shop area, providing a cafeteria and small lecture room.

Prices £££££
Facilities Parking, 200 cars. Toilets. Ice cream and soft drinks. Play area. Garden advice service. Delivery service. Free price lists for garden furniture etc. Plant catalogue 95p (free to customers making a large purchase)
Open Every day 9am to 6pm (7.30pm Fri), closes 5.30pm in winter. Closed Christmas Day
Credit cards Access, Visa

BEELEY Derbyshire

map 2

Chatsworth Garden Centre

Calton Lees, Beeley, Matlock
DE4 2NX

Tel Matlock (0629) 734004/5

On the main road through Chatsworth Estate, adjoining Calton Lees car park

This newly established centre is set in the Chatsworth Estate. Opened to the public in May 1983, it is still not entirely finished but shows a lot of promise. There are many gardening and recreational products already available in the spacious indoor area, including children's swings and cast metal signs made to order, power tools and lawnmowers. There's a display pool with specimen Koi carp in all sizes. Garden furniture is in good supply and a large outside area is under franchise to a firm specialising in walling and paving. There are plans to stock greenhouses and garden buildings, and these will be displayed alongside the walling and paving area. A show ground for swimming pools and chalets is also in the pipe-line. The centre is well laid out with plenty of room to browse even during busier times, and all paths are paved or concreted. The plant beds are not that large, but they have still managed to fit quite a variety into the space available by having just a few specimens of each. All plants are container grown and bought in. They are rather expensive but the standard is consistently good. The choice of conifers is greater than in the other plant sections, but when a further site for hardy nursery stock is completed the stocks of trees and shrubs should improve. Labelling is variable, some offering useful instructions, but most simply stating name and price. There is an information desk in the centre of the main area where you may get some extra help with enquiries. The outside staff keep themselves busy watering and tending the plants, but appear helpful when approached. There are trolleys supplied to carry goods to the car, and if you feel in need of refreshment there's a coffee shop with an adjoining patio.

Prices £££££
Facilities Parking, 70 cars (plus large overflow). Toilets. Restaurant, cafeteria and vending machines. Garden advice service. Delivery service
Open Every day 10am to 6pm (closes 1pm to 2pm). Closes 5pm in winter. Closed 25 Dec to 1 Jan
Credit cards Access, Visa

BELBROUGHTON Hereford and Worcester

map 3

Beechcroft Nurseries

Madeley Heath, Belbroughton,
Stourbridge DY9 9XA

Tel Belbroughton (0562) 710358

Between Halesowen and Bromsgrove. Leave the A491 at Fairfield roundabout, taking the turning to Romsley

This centre concentrates on its plants, and the quality and variety are excellent. For the enthusiastic gardener there is a marvellous choice of conifers, heathers and fruits and some unusual and choice trees and shrubs, most of which are grown on site. At the time of our visit all the plants in stock seemed to be in a very healthy condition, with the possible exception of the perennials. The narrow paths detract a bit from the overall layout but there is a pleasant demonstration garden of heathers and conifers to balance that out. At the time of our inspection many labels suffered from the common problem of fading, but the centre tells us this has been rectified. A small sundries area stocks a selection of furniture and ornaments in addition to the hand tools and chemicals needed by every gardener, but no larger items are available. Pond equipment can be ordered for you. A centre which is well worth exploring for those who like to stumble upon a new plant of interest with every visit.

Prices ££££
Facilities Parking, 150 cars. Toilets. Vending machines. Garden advice service. Free specialist plant lists
Open Every day 9am to 5.30pm (8pm Wed in Apr, May and June). Closes 5pm in winter. Closed Christmas and Boxing Day and New Year's Day
Credit cards Access, Visa

BELTON Lincolnshire
map 2

Belton Garden Centre

Belton, near Grantham NG32 2LN   *Tel* Grantham (0476) 63700
On the A607, 3 miles north of Grantham

This centre is situated in pleasant surroundings on the edge of the countryside and just across the way from the National Trust property of Belton House. Most popular varieties of plants are sold. They are grown on the associated family nursery from which stocks are constantly replenished. There are few rare plants on sale but the collection of alpines is quite extensive. Our inspector found the smaller range of herbaceous perennials to be of very good quality, as were the healthy-looking conifers, trees and shrubs. The centre was undergoing redevelopment and expansion, but at the time of inspection it consisted of a well-laid-out exterior site, an undercover area containing a good range of small tools and sundries, and a separate greenhouse for indoor plants. The signposting and labelling were being improved. The absence of any power tools, sheds or fencing is a noticeable omission for a centre of this size, and the choice of greenhouses could do with extending. However, fish and water-gardening equipment is very good. A member of staff wanders the premises to answer questions and to be generally available to assist customers. There is a very nice play area in which you can leave the children, and a coffee shop was due to open early 1985.

Prices £££
Facilities Parking, 150 cars. Toilets. Play area. Garden advice service. Delivery service
Open Mon to Sat 9am to 6pm, Sun 10am to 5pm. Closed Christmas week

---

BILLESDON Leicestershire
map 4

County Garden Centre

Tilton Lane, Billesdon LE7 9FG   *Tel* Billesdon (053 755) 248

On Tilton Lane, 500 yds off the A47 midway between Billesdon and Houghton-on-the-Hill

The owners of this family concern are also landscape gardeners so they can provide good advice on any gardening subject. This is a useful centre, particularly for those living in the local area or coming out from Leicester. It doesn't offer everything one might expect to find at a garden centre, but the selection is not bad, and the plants are of a very good quality. They pride themselves on their conifer collection and the high standard and reasonable prices of these make the centre well worth a visit. The heather section is also first class. On the other hand there were no roses, herbs or fruit in stock when our inspector visited, possibly due to the time of year. Inside there is a good choice of well-kept houseplants and you will also find a good range of hand tools, though no power tools. The aquatics and fish section also offers an interesting and varied choice if you are keen on water gardening. If you are planning to spend a little more time relaxing in the garden, there is a wide choice of garden furniture on show, which can be made to order – sheds can also be bought this way. The site is well organised, but labelling could definitely do with a facelift – it is often faded and carries little cultural information. The staff are unobtrusive and customers can wander freely without being pestered – but there is always someone close at hand if you do need help. A children's play area and pets corner are planned.

Prices £££
Facilities Parking, 30 cars. Toilets. New play area. Delivery service. Free plant price list
Open Every day 9am to 6pm (closes 5pm in winter). Closed Christmas

---

BIRDBROOK Essex   map 4
Boltons Garden Centre

Robert Bolton and Son, Birdbrook,   *Tel* Ridgewell (0440 85) 246
Halstead CO9 4BU
On the A604 between Haverhill and Halstead, near the village of Baythorn End

The Bolton family business is known nationally and internationally for its specialisation in sweet peas, which can be seen as a massive show of colour in their growing fields where next year's seed crop is raised. However, this has not prevented them from gathering together an excellent range of quality stock of a less specialist nature which has obviously been chosen with a good deal of care and thought. Ornamental trees, shrubs, roses, alpines and herbs are all available and the selection is very good for a medium-sized centre. You will also be able to refurbish your pond from a selection of aquatic plants and waterlilies. The plants all show signs of being closely tended. This can be seen not just from their condition, but in the sensible and tidy layout of the display areas where plants are protected and supported whenever necessary. Inside, in well demarcated sections, can be found a range of tools and sundries sufficient to keep most active gardeners happy. A comprehensive selection of larger items is also sold, including greenhouses, sheds, fencing and paving. Labelling is very good in all aspects, and the staff will always help out with extra information. The Boltons themselves are on hand much of the time and their enthusiasm is contagious; they have created a business with an important specialist side, but where this complements rather than dominates the rest of the enterprise. It is the charming family nature of the place and the quality of stock which should encourage more than one visit.

Prices ££££
Facilities Parking, 40 cars. Toilets. Vending machine. Garden advice service. Delivery service.
Open Every day 9am to 5.30pm (closes 4.30pm in winter)
Credit cards Access, Visa

BIRMINGHAM W. Midlands   map 4

Bourneville Garden Centre

Maple Road, Bourneville B30 2AE   *Tel* 021-472 0303
About 5 miles south-west of Birmingham between Selly Oak and Cotteridge, situated in Stocks Wood and reached via Linden Road (A4040)

The personal approach is very much a feature of this family-run firm. It is set in a lovely woodland area next to the village green. A wide, well-surfaced driveway leads into the car park. The site has been divided equally between outdoor and indoor sections and the layout is excellent, with easy access to all areas and large, clear signposts. The line of tools and accessories kept in stock is more than adequate and a recent development has been the extension of the display area for garden pools and fish tanks. Only those customers in search of power tools will be disappointed, although lawnmowers are available. Most common plants are stocked; prices are low and quality very high – particularly noticeable among the wide variety of conifers on show. Customers who are fascinated by the art of bonsai will appreciate the good specimens on display in the new 'speciality' area. New displays and improvements are in evidence all round the centre, and our inspector was pleased to note a general improvement in labelling since his last visit, though more emphasis on large labels covering cultivation and plant habit would be an added bonus. Staffing levels are ample, except at the checkout where short queues sometimes form, and all staff are helpful. Tree surgery, landscaping and replanting services are available.

Prices ££
Facilities Parking, 65 cars. Toilets. Vending machines. Garden advice service. Delivery service. Free price list for landscaping materials
Open Mon to Sat 9am to 6pm (open to 8pm Thurs to Fri)
Credit cards Access, Visa

BISHOPSTEIGNTON Devon   map 3

Jack's Patch Garden Centre

Newton Road, Bishopsteignton,   *Tel* Teignmouth (062 67) 6996
Teignmouth TQ14 9RG

On the A381 Newton Abbot to Teignmouth road, at Bishopsteignton

This 15-acre site has a wonderful position on high ground overlooking the Teign estuary, Shaldon and part of Teignmouth beach. Hidden by trees from the main road, the excellence of the centre first strikes the visitor in the form of a delightful display of seasonal decorative plants in the large entrance hall. This sets the tone for the rest of the visit, for somebody here really loves plants. Almost all the plants sold are grown on the centre's own nurseries. There is a small but unique range of alpines and rock plants and a good selection of heathers and fuchsias. Some 'surprise' shrubs make an appearance along with a very good stock of dwarf conifers and a small, but special range of container-grown trees. The overall representation of stock is not at all comprehensive, but it is great fun to browse over what there is, for everything has obviously been grown and tended with care. The lovely, well-planted rockery and display gardens deserve a perusal as well. The quality of plants is outstandingly good, and for fresh-looking, sturdy stock this place takes some beating. Our inspector thought that labelling could do with some improvement both in legibility and content, though the garden centre tells us they have greatly improved this since our inspector's visit. The centre is quite new but is already undergoing improvements and expansion. Hopefully it will retain its clear layout and the owners' attention will not be distracted from the actual plants. A small range of tools and a good selection of chemicals and composts is available, but as yet none of the larger ranges of tools and equipment (a big expansion is planned in this area). A franchise for fish and aquatic plants is planned for spring 1985.

Prices £££
Facilities Parking, 150 cars. Toilets. Vending machines (snack bar planned). Play area. Garden advice service. Delivery service. Free plant price list
Open Every day 9am to 5.30pm (closes 5pm in winter). Closed Christmas Day

BISLEY Gloucestershire map 3

Tythe Barn Gardens

Bisley, near Stroud GL6 7AD   *Tel* Gloucester (0452) 770626
150 yds east of Bisley High Street, at the crossroads, 4 miles from Stroud

A small nursery with unusual, well-grown and sensibly priced plants which will be of great interest to the keen gardener. The site can be a little difficult to find, but there are signposts from the main street of this hilltop Cotswold village. Practically all plants sold are propagated on the nursery and its position ensures that they are really hardy since it can be very cold and windy, and that they are all suited to the local Cotswold limestone soil. The range of plants is not huge but there are some unusual varieties to be discovered including a specialist collection of hydrangeas and daphnes. The selection of herbs is very good and these are sold off as mature plants. The owners are planning to increase propagation facilities and growing-on beds in the near future. Labelling is restricted to the name and price on each plant, but the friendly husband and wife team will answer all your questions for you. A sideline taken up by the centre is the supply of very good quality garden furniture which is made partly at the attached metal workshop. Compost is available on request, but otherwise there are no garden sundries sold.

Prices £££
Facilities Parking, 15 cars. Toilets. Garden advice service. Design service
Open Wed to Sun and bank holidays 10am to sunset. Closed Mon and Tues. Closed 1 Dec to 28 Feb except by prior arrangement

---

BLACKFORDBY Leicestershire   map 2

Bluebell Nursery   ✿

Blackfordby,   *Tel* Burton-on-Trent (0283) 222091
Burton-on-Trent DE11 8AJ
Off the A50 at Blackfordby, 2 miles west of Ashby-de-la-Zouch. The centre is situated at the rear of the Bluebell Inn

A medium-sized nursery devoted entirely to hardy plants. The site is well laid out and there are good paths and clear signposting. This sensible planning makes it easy for the visitor to explore the very good selection of cheap plants, which includes unusual varieties. The nursery is a specialist grower and can offer a choice of rare trees, shrubs, perennials and alpines. At the time of our inspection, it was only the fruit section which offered a rather limited range; however, the fruit the nursery does have is all certified virus-free and there are plans to extend the selection in the future. The vast majority of plants are grown at the nursery and they are all kept in very good condition. They are generally well labelled, although you may find the occasional label which has faded and is difficult to read. The staff are most friendly, and this coupled with the large stock of plants makes the nursery well worth a visit. A small range of houseplants and water-plants are soon to be introduced. For those with a thirst, there is an attractive pub and beer garden next door.

Prices ££
Facilities Parking, 20 cars. Toilets. Garden advice service. Delivery service
Open Every day 9am to 5pm. Closed Christmas and Boxing Day
Credit cards Access, Visa

BLACKPOOL Lancashire   map 2

Trebaron Garden Centre

350 Common Edge Road,   *Tel* Blackpool (0253) 691368
Blackpool FY4 5DY
On the B5261, at the back of the airport, 2 miles from the centre of Blackpool

The owners are obviously keen on keeping their premises neat, tidy and well ordered, and this is reflected in the appearance of the centre. The outdoor section is very attractively and clearly laid out: there are good notices designating the various plant areas, paved pathways are kept clean and all shrubs and trees are well supported and protected. The inside area is smaller, but is not excessively cluttered. There are plans to extend this, to include a leisure department and an enlarged houseplant section. The range of chemicals, hand tools, and composts is fairly comprehensive and there is an adequate choice of greenhouses, furniture, paving and fencing. No electrical tools are stocked though, nor any water-gardening equipment or fish. Among the plants you will find a wide variety of houseplants, heathers and perennials. The selection of trees, shrubs, roses and fruits is also reasonable, and all plants are generally of very good quality. Each plant group is excellently labelled and the typed labels for trees and shrubs are good. More seating and more accessible toilets would be handy. A new and very promising centre, it will be interesting to see how it develops over the next few years.

Prices £££
Facilities Parking, 100 cars. Toilets. Vending machines (restaurant and cafeteria planned for spring 1985). Play area. Garden advice service. Delivery service. Free price lists for sheds, fencing, ornaments etc.
Open Every day 9.30am to 5pm. Closed for Christmas
Credit cards Access, Visa

BOLD HEATH Cheshire   map 2

Pilkington Garden Centre

Bold Heath, Widnes WA4 0UU   *Tel* 051-424 6264
On the A57 Liverpool road 3 miles west of Warrington

This medium-sized centre offers the standard range of plants of a reasonable quality. The choice of alpines and water-garden plants is particularly good, and in season there is a comprehensive choice of bulbs and seeds. Most gardening sundries are stocked and there is a particularly good selection of greenhouses and a nice display of artificial flowers. A range of leisure equipment is sold including barbecues, camping equipment and garden furniture. Plants are labelled with growing instructions and plant groups have illustrated labels. The staff were not overly helpful when our inspector visited, though the manager proved to be keen to help with problems. There's an information desk, and free pamphlets are available. A new training programme for staff has been implemented since our inspection, and alterations planned for the site include a redesigned plant area and an extension to the sundries area.

Prices ££££
Facilities Parking, 200 cars. Toilets. Vending machines (cafeteria planned for 1985). Garden advice service. Delivery service
Open Mon to Sat 8.30am to 5.30pm (opens 9.30am Mon), Sun 10am to 5.30pm (closes 5pm every day in winter). Closed Christmas and Boxing Day
Credit cards Access, Visa

BOLTON Greater Manchester   map 2

Routledges

Ravenswood Nurseries,   *Tel* Bolton (0204) 41952
465 Chorley New Road,
Heaton, Bolton BL1 5OG

On the A673, mid-way between Bolton and Horwich

Set on a south-west slope in a pleasantly wooded area, this nursery is well worth a visit for local gardeners. It stocks a good, general range of cheap plants, with fruit trees, rhododendrons, conifers and evergreen shrubs being especially well represented. They are in good condition; the trees and shrubs are mainly grown by the centre and are noticeably the best. Groups of plants are well identified, but there are no cultural details or illustrations provided. Individual labelling is limited to the larger varieties and this again is fairly basic. However, a catalogue offers some more descriptive information as well as a current price list. The display area and layout are quite good, although the pathways are a little congested. This situation should be improved shortly. In terms of garden equipment and hardware, this is not a big supplier. Furniture is sold, tubs and ornaments are displayed around the site and there is a small shed stocked with insecticides. Apart from these and the ubiquitous composts there is little else in the way of sundries. As a small local enterprise this fulfils its function well, and the nursery and office staff are helpful.

Prices ££
Facilities Parking, 30 cars. Toilets. Plant price list/catalogue 10p
Open Mon to Fri 8am to 5.30pm, Sat 9am to 5.30pm (closes 5pm every day in winter). Closed Christmas and New Year's Day
Credit cards Access, Visa

BOOKER Buckinghamshire   map 4
Booker Garden Centre   &c ⫰

Clay Lane, Booker,   *Tel* High Wycombe (0494) 33945
near High Wycombe SL7 3DH
Situated 500 yds off the B482 Marlow to Stokenchurch road, adjacent to Wycombe Air Park

Our inspector liked the welcoming atmosphere of this large centre. It is set in pleasant open countryside, very close to the Booker Airfield. A large variety of garden and home needs are catered for, from 'pet accessories' to pine log chalets. The covered section is made of glass, which creates a bright cheerful atmosphere for the display of tools and sundries. The choice of barbecue-ware, garden furniture and water gardening equipment is wide, and the aquatic section was due to expand in early 1985 with the introduction of a tropical fish house. The centre also stocks a good range of lean-to greenhouses. There is now a separate sales, service and parts section for lawnmowers and electrical appliances (closed Wednesdays). Among the sundries you can find jams and honey, china flowerpots and floral displays. The houseplant section offers specimen plants and preplanted arrangements for the house and office. At the time of our inspection the centre had a good selection of soft fruits, but the range of trees and conifers was more limited. Plants were rather expensive and the condition variable – there were some very healthy, fresh-looking shrubs and heathers but sad-looking herbs and trees. Labels on the whole are informative, although some are weather-worn. If in doubt ask at the information shed in the middle of the centre – they are sure to be able to assist. At our last inspection we noticed a sparsity of signposting but this has improved recently. The layout of the exterior areas is still rather cramped with some fairly narrow paths. The indoor section is undergoing expansion and improvement.

Prices £££££
Facilities Parking, 60 cars. Toilets. Vending machine. Garden advice service. Delivery service. Free price list and catalogue for sundries
Open Mon to Sat 8.30am to 6pm (May to June closes 8pm), Sun and bank holidays 9.30am to 6pm (closes 5.30pm every day in winter)
Credit cards Access, Visa

BOURNEMOUTH Dorset map 4

Saxonbury Nurseries

56a Saxonbury Road, *Tel* Bournemouth (0202) 423824
Southbourne, Bournemouth BH6 5ND
Off the Bournemouth ring road. Take the Ilford Lane exit at the junction of the A3060 and A35, take the 7th turning on the right into Saxonbury Road

'There is an excellent range of plants and trees, the shrubs are good and the herbaceous perennials are particularly interesting ...I thought it was super!' enthused our inspector. This is rather a small centre and it is tucked away in a residential area, surrounded by back gardens on all sides – access is along alleys between the houses. There is room to park in the quiet neighbourhood roads. The site is extremely well laid out and is kept spotlessly tidy. A couple of pathways are a little on the narrow side, but this must be put down to the huge stock of plants in the grounds. Many of the plants are grown on site and all rate ten out of ten for their quality and health. Displays are tasteful and orderly, while plastic signs clearly designate each plant group. Individual pots are not generally labelled but each tree and shrub carries its own tag with prices and some growing advice. If you require additional help, it is easy to pick out the staff members and they readily offer useful advice and suggestions. Although this centre is a nursery and not a fully fledged garden centre, chemicals, composts and a good collection of terracotta and stone containers are made available. The wide range of interesting plants will be of great interest to keen gardeners.

Prices £££
Facilities Parking, 9 cars. Toilets. Garden advice service. Delivery service
Open Mon to Sat 9am to 5.30pm (closes 5pm in winter), Sun 9.30am to 1pm. Closed Christmas Eve to New Year's Day

---

BRADLEY Staffordshire map 2

Foster Nurseries

Oak Lane, Bradley, Stafford ST18 9EA *Tel* Stafford (0785) 780208
3 miles out of Stafford on the A518 Newport road, turn left to Bradley and the centre is on the southern side of the village

The approach to this nursery along several miles of narrow, winding lanes can be a bit of a trek, but on arrival the very attractive and inviting layout makes up for the effort. The centre itself has recently developed from an existing nursery business. Signposting is comprehensive so it's easy to find what you want, and pathways are adequate. Plants are cheap and the range extensive, with the nursery specialising in rare trees and shrubs and also producing a lot of bedding plants and hanging baskets. The choice of varieties for most plants is good and the quality is superb – all sub-standard specimens are removed to one side. Water-plants are limited to bog-plants. A large indoor area is devoted to the smaller tools and sundries such as ornaments, hand tools, chemicals and composts. Paving and fencing are also sold but no other larger accessories. Staff are exceptionally good, and all seem knowledgeable. Additional information is provided by printed, full-colour, group labels and clear, individual tags giving planting instructions. The centre provides a landscaping service and a floral service for offices and exhibitions, as well as participating in local flower shows. Work is still in progress to develop the site (a toilet block is planned) but our inspector was most impressed, commenting, 'This garden centre has an air of positive confidence. I feel it will be the major centre in Staffordshire.'

Prices ££
Facilities Parking, 200 cars (plus overflow). Toilets. Vending machines, ice cream and confectionery. Play area. Garden advice service. Delivery service. Free plant catalogue. Plants sold by mail order
Open Every day 9am to 7pm (closes 6pm in winter). Closed for Christmas
Credit cards Access, Visa

BRAMPTON Cambridgeshire map 4

Brampton Garden Centre

Buckden Road, Brampton, *Tel* Huntingdon (0480) 53048
Huntingdon PE18 8NF
On the A141, 2 miles south of Huntingdon, between Brampton and Buckden

A purpose-built garden centre which lies at the edge of an attractive village. A lot of thought seems to have gone into the design of this centre. There is a lovely show of plants in the front of the site which are well established and all clearly named. The design of the display blocks has been carefully tended to, with the plants and customers both benefiting. Trees are fixed securely to frames and climbing plants have special frameworks built round them to save them from careless knocks or blustery winds. Walkways are very well set out and kept clean. Both young and mature conifers are available, all very healthy-looking, and the climbers range from the common-or-garden varieties to rarer ones such as Actinidias. Group labels are clear and precise, containing lots of detail, although for more specific after-care information there are printed leaflets available or trained staff can be called on for advice. The excellent collection of houseplants, kept in a separate greenhouse, is worth perusing. A large covered area for pot plants and garden furniture is planned. A large selection of dried grasses, ornamental flowers and flower arranging accessories will be of interest to some. There is a very good range of composts, seeds and chemicals, and most other sundries are stocked in reasonable amounts.

Prices £££
Facilities Parking, 60 cars (plus 150 overflow). Toilets. Play area. Garden advice service. Delivery service. Free price lists for fencing, paving, sheds, greenhouses, walling and roses
Open Mon to Sat 9am to 5.30pm, Sun 10.30am to 5.30pm
Credit card Access

BRANKSOME Dorset   map 4

Homebase

Poole Road, Branksome, Poole BH2 5QJ   *Tel* Poole (0202) 762133
On the A35 between Bournemouth and Poole at the junction of Alder Road, Ashley Road and Poole Road

The centre is part of the Homebase DIY store and is situated in a built-up, commercial development area, along with other large chain stores. It is a useful place for gardeners planning to launch into major landscaping or building projects, since the selection of building materials and all general sundries is very good. There is a large display area for paving, building blocks, fencing and other materials, while smaller accessories and a good selection of houseplants are found in a nicely organised, covered section. The only omission from the range is water-gardening equipment. Plants are set out on trays at waist height so customers can take a close look at each purchase, and the pathways are all level and clear which is a great help to the less-able gardeners. There is nothing of specialist interest, although the selection of shrubs and alpines is quite good. On the whole most types of plants are available but only in limited numbers. Quality is usually fairly good; any poor plants are mainly end-of-season stock. Group labelling is clear and informative, but prices on individual plants are sometimes faded. Any questions must be referred to the main information desk in the shop where somebody will be called to help.

Prices £££
Facilities Parking, 205 cars. Toilets. Garden advice service. Delivery service
Open Mon to Fri 9am to 8pm, Sat 8.30am to 6pm. Closed at Christmas
Credit cards Access, Visa

BRANSGORE Dorset   map 4

MacPenny's of Bransgore

154 Burley Road, Bransgore,   *Tel* Bransgore (0425) 72348
near Christchurch BH23 8DB
4 miles north of Christchurch in Bransgore village, on the Burley to Christchurch road

A very pleasant, wooded situation is the location of this well-stocked nursery which grows most of its own plants. The adjacent gardens show off some mature and rare species which will be of particular interest to those with a semi-shaded, acid-soil garden. The gardens are also used to

39

test new varieties. The range of shrubs, herbaceous perennials and heathers is excellent, while dwarf conifers and alpines, water-plants and herbs are also extremely well represented. There are large stocks of field-grown trees and in 1985 more of these will be containerised for all-year sales. All are in very good condition and labels for groups of plants are informative, though not illustrated. There are not very many individual labels, but if you request at the checkout each plant will be labelled for you. Overall, the wide range of plants is reasonably laid out, though signposting is a little sparse. The emphasis at MacPenny's is definitely on plants; however, a limited selection of composts and a small number of chemicals and ornaments are stocked. The staff are easily located and very helpful people. An interesting craft shop is a useful diversion for the non-gardeners in your family. A friendly nursery, selling some unusual plants.

Prices £££
Facilities Parking, 75 cars. Toilets. Garden advice service. Delivery service
Open Mon to Fri 8am to 5pm, Sat 9am to 5pm, Sun 2pm to 5pm. Closed Christmas and Boxing Day

---

BREAGE Cornwall   map 3

Trevena Cross Nursery   ❀

Breage, Helston TR13 9PF   *Tel* Germoe (073 676) 3880
At Breage, 2 miles west of Helston off the A394 Helston to Penzance road

A father and son business which is of real interest to gardeners in the area. On this gently sloping site you'll find an excellent collection of hardy plants entirely suited to the local environment. The centre is exposed to the salty sea atmosphere and blustery winds (although there is a large windbreak) and so the plants, which are mostly raised on the premises, are acclimatised to local conditions. The nursery also sells sub-tropical plants such as palms and tree ferns. It is a comparatively small set up, but the area the public sees is only a part of the whole and behind the scenes there are many more plants ensuring that replacement stocks are always on hand. The extensive range of plants is of a uniformly high standard. Labelling is good. Group labels are large and placed up high, while individual plants have clear and informative illustrated labels. The centre is chiefly a nursery, but there is also a greenhouse containing many of the essential gardening sundries, with the principal exceptions of power tools and greenhouses. An additional house has been built since our inspection and further extensions and improvements are planned. Sheds, fencing, paving and garden ornaments are stocked. The site is pleasantly laid out and kept weed free. The owners are both very hard working and knowledgeable men, ready and keen to help with any problems. If they are not around ring the loud bell and they will make themselves known. This centre is well thought of locally and deserving of support and encouragement.

Prices £££
Facilities Parking, 70 cars. Play area planned. Garden advice service
Open Mon to Fri 9am to 5pm, Sat and Sun 10am to 5pm. Closed 25 Dec to 4 Jan

BRIDGEMERE Cheshire   map 2
Bridgemere Garden World

Bridgemere,   *Tel* Bridgemere (093 65) 239/381/182
near Nantwich CW5 7QB
On the A51, 8 miles south-east of Nantwich, 1 mile north of Woore

'A garden centre that is exciting and stimulating whatever time of year it is
visited.' It's a very large, efficient centre situated on the border between
Cheshire and Shropshire, and is very popular, attracting people from miles
around. The car park is huge, with easy access from the main road, and the
centre is on a regular bus route from the Potteries and Crewe. The layout is
excellent with wide paths and clear signposting. An extensive area under
glass houses a very wide selection of houseplants as well as garden tools
and accessories. The choice of tools is somewhat limited, but you can buy
most types of gardening equipment here. The range of plants, on the other
hand, is extensive, including some rare and unusual varieties as well as
run-of-the-mill stock. Most of the plants are grown on site and are of good
quality. Labelling is also of a high standard and many labels have colour
illustrations. Staff are very much in evidence in the covered sections of the
centre, and there's a large information desk. Outside, a new information
centre opened in spring 1985. Informative display gardens show
what the plants will look like in your garden and give ideas on plant
groupings. Facilities are good – there is an excellent cafe serving home-
made food all day (coachloads can be catered for by arrangement), and
a food hall selling a variety of goods such as jams, biscuits and sweets.
Displays inside and out are continually changing, introducing new
products and ideas. A very pleasant place to visit and highly recommended
for its extensive range of plants.

Prices £££
Facilities Parking, 1,000 cars. Toilets. Cafeteria. Play area (planned for spring 1985).
Delivery service. Free price list for plants. Plant catalogue and gardening guide £1.40
Open Mon to Sat 9am to dusk, Sun 10am to dusk (closes 5pm every day in winter).
Closed Christmas and Boxing Day
Credit cards Access, American Express, Visa

BRIGHOUSE W. Yorkshire   map 2
Charles Kershaw

The Nurseries and Garden Centre,   *Tel* Brighouse (0484) 713435/6
Halifax Road, Brighouse HD6 2QD
On the A644 Brighouse to Halifax road, about 1 mile from Brighouse

This large centre is roomy both outside and in, well arranged throughout,
and filled with plenty of plants and sundries. A complete range of
gardening accessories and equipment is available from the largest items to
the smallest. The selection of hand tools and chemicals is particularly good,
but the power tools are rather limited. Greenhouses, sheds, fencing and
paving are sold and there is a florist and floral art section. The sundries area
inside is all laid out on one level with good, wide aisles, so it's fairly easy to

get around and find what you want. A reasonable range of plants is stocked covering both common and more unusual varieties. They are cheap but the quality was very variable when our inspector visited, and it pays to have a close look at anything before you buy. However, the inspection took place in the middle of general rebuilding and re-organisation when quality control can become difficult. Our inspector found some very good rock plants and houseplants. Labelling was somewhat lacking – many plants were unlabelled and unpriced, while instructions and cultural information were very scarce. Part of this problem is solved by the very useful leaflets which are available, and the centre also plans to introduce a new labelling system. Fruit fields, where you can pick your own raspberries, blackcurrants, redcurrants, gooseberries and rhubarb, are open in season. A small cafe offers home-made cakes, snacks, teas and coffee.

Prices ££
Facilities Parking, 250 cars. Toilets. Tea room. Garden advice service. Delivery service. Free price lists for trees and shrubs and roses. Free information leaflets. Plant catalogue 30p. Plants sold by mail order
Open Mon to Sat 9am to 8pm, Sun 10am to 6pm (closes 6pm every day in winter)
Credit cards Access, Visa

BROCKWORTH Gloucestershire   map 3

Golden Vale Garden Centre

Shurdington Road, Brockworth   *Tel* Gloucester (0452) 862334
GL3 4PU
On the A46 Cheltenham to Stroud road, at Brockworth, 450 yds north of Crosshands/Birdlip roundabout

One of the Wyevale Group, this is an all-round centre supplying a good range of plants and a more limited range of gardening materials. The well-organised outside area is protected by mesh netting and this houses the general plant beds, as well as some special displays featuring seasonal plants. At the time of our inspection, there was a very good selection of sturdy trees and shrubs, although they were rather expensive. Our inspector found that group labels were a little variable and individual labels difficult to read but the centre tells us these problems have been rectified. Indoors the layout is good, and the wide range of furniture, ornaments and barbecue equipment stocked deserve a special mention. Houseplants are kept in tip-top condition. The centre doesn't sell larger items such as greenhouses, sheds and paving, but there's a very nice outdoor display of water garden accessories which appears to be one of the few in the area. Staff are a little elusive but they can be recognised by their red uniforms. They are cheerful and willingly offer to carry purchases. Trained horticulturalists are available to deal with gardening problems

Prices £££££
Facilities Parking, 200 cars. Toilets. Garden advice service. Limited delivery service. Plant catalogue £1.95, includes a £2 voucher
Open Mon to Wed 9am to 5.30 pm, Thurs and Fri 9am to 7pm, Sat 9am to 6.30pm,

Sun 10am to 6.30pm (closes 5.30pm every day in winter)
Credit cards Access, Visa

BROXBOURNE Hertfordshire   map 4

Chime Garden Centre

Old Nazeing Road, Broxbourne   *Tel* Hoddesdon (0992) 466646
EN10 6RJ

*Around 3 miles from Broxbourne in Keysers Estate. Old Nazeing Road is off the
B194 near Broxbourne station*

Quite difficult to find if you don't know the area for you must turn into the
Keysers Estate to reach the centre. Once there you will find a marvellous
range of gardening equipment which is all laid out in separate sections in a
covered area. All the products are up-to-date and it's not only the gardener
who will find something of interest; inflatable boats are an interesting type
of garden accessory! There was plenty of garden furniture on offer at good
reductions when our inspector visited. You can also buy turf, cement,
sand, stone and other landscaping materials, and most other types of
gardening equipment and sundries are sold, including larger items such as
sheds and fencing. Demonstrations are occasionally given, such as the use
of barbecue equipment. A 'for sale and hire' section might be useful for
some of your major landscaping plans. The centre can be crowded at
weekends, but it is well organised with signposts and notices for all the
different areas. They seem to stock most standard plants and the quality is
generally good – any poor specimens are sold off cheaply. The staff are
extremely helpful and often busy watering, but will readily stop and escort
you to the section you are looking for. Trolleys are available to take away
your acquisitions.

Prices £££
Facilities Parking, 200 cars. Toilets. Play area. Garden advice service. Delivery
service. Free paper gives prices, details of special offers etc.
Open Mon to Sat 8.30am to 6pm, Sun 9.30am to 5.30pm (closes 5pm every
day in winter)
Credit cards Access, Visa

Rochfords Garden Centre

High Road, Turnford, Broxbourne   *Tel* Hoddesdon (0992) 464526
EN10 6BH

*On the B176 at Turnford. Take the Broxbourne exit off the A10, go over the
Turnford roundabout and past Hertfordshire College.*

This centre is set just off the A10 in a landscape which is part rural and part
built up with pre-war houses. It has been around for donkeys years and
was once one of the biggest houseplant growers in the country. However,
it has recently stopped growing its own plants and now buys them in, so it
remains to be seen whether the same standards of excellence prevail. The
centre houses nearly all its plants in greenhouses, some of which look a
little old, but they are extremely well laid out and there is plenty of room
for wheelchairs and pushchairs. A small area outside has supplies of trees

and other plants. The general range of plants is first class, but perhaps slightly limited within each group. However, most gardeners would be satisfied with the choice. The quality of plants is good, they seem strong and sound, well cared for and watered. Each plant section has large illustrated and informative labels attached to a board at its rear. Individual labels are computer printed with name, colour, size and price, but they are often faded. At the time of our inspection, there was an adequate range of sundries, but no sheds, greenhouses, power tools or mowers. (A new section for greenhouses, sheds, fencing and paving was due to open in late 1984.) Rochfords has recently opened an aquatic centre called 'Water World' where there is a magnificent range of fish (costing up to £250!) as well as ponds and water plants. An attractive coffee shop provides refreshments, and the staff at the centre are cheerful and friendly and make themselves available to answer questions if needed, but are not pushy. The centre arranges lectures and talks on houseplants, plant care, propagation and so on.

Prices £££
Facilities Parking, 150 cars (plus overflow). Toilets. Coffee bar. Garden advice service. Delivery service
Open Every day 9am to 6pm (closes 5pm in winter)
Credit cards Access, Visa

BULVERHYTHE E. Sussex   map 4

Hastings Garden Centre   🐛♿

Bexhill Road, Bulverhythe,   *Tel* Hastings (0424) 443414
St. Leonards TN38 8AR
Just off the A259, behind the civic amenities at Bulverhythe

A large centre, well laid out, roomy and nicely organised. The under cover area contains a comprehensive range of tools and sundries for the practical gardener, including some very good books on gardening. There are few power tools other than lawnmowers available. Outside you will find an area devoted to larger items such as fencing, building materials and sheds and a reasonable choice of plants, particularly among the conifers and shrubs. The centre has several specialities, including specimen Cupressus and Cedrus, magnolias and Dracaena palms. All plants are kept in good condition. Good, clear labelling provides some in-depth guidance, especially for the trees and shrubs. Overall layout is good, both indoors and out, with wide paths and quite good signposting. However, the greenhouses and sheds are a bit of a walk from the car park and the centre, and the refreshment area, although nice, is too small for comfort. There are few staff available to answer queries on outdoor plants and only the cashier to direct you around the sundries, but staff are generally polite and quite helpful. A garden furniture showroom is planned. All in all a clean, tidy and bright establishment with everything for the gardener in one place.

Prices £££££
Facilities Parking, 100 cars. Toilets. Restaurant. Garden advice service. Delivery service. Price lists for some products, plant catalogue 95p or free to customers making large purchases

Open Every day, summer 9am to 6pm (closes 7.30pm Fri), winter 9am to 5.30pm.
Closed Christmas Day.
Credit cards Access, Visa

BURBAGE Wiltshire   map 4

Conifer Cottage Nurseries/Garden Centre

High Street, Burbage,   *Tel* Marlborough (0672) 810618
Marlborough SN8 3AA
South of Marlborough on the A345 Salisbury road

This is a small, family concern which has concentrated on a number of
aspects of gardening including conifers, clematis and water gardening.
Other plants are also stocked, including a fairly good range of heathers and
some unusual shrubs and trees from New Zealand. Plants are generally in
very good condition and there are many different sizes available. To help
those shoppers with less experience, there are flower and shrub beds
planted around the sales area so plants can be seen in situ. Mature trees
and shrubs are arranged to demonstrate height, spread and autumn colour.
An interesting new addition in the pipeline is a Japanese garden. Many
plants are propagated on site so there is a nursery section as well as the
show area. The small but well-stocked aquatics section includes
water-plants, fish tanks, pools, water ornaments and unusual fish. This is
one of the few sources of water-gardening equipment in the area, and the
centre is planning to expand this section. Other sundries available are hand
tools and furniture – customers requiring greenhouses, paving or sheds can
order them, but they are not kept in stock. Because the site is encircled by a
housing estate, room is limited and the layout is somewhat cramped with
very narrow pathways. However, the centre endeavours to convey a
cottage garden atmosphere. Labelling is poor and sometimes non-existent.
However, staff were at work touching things up while our inspector was
visiting. If you are having any problems the staff will help and there are
books available for customers to refer to for horticultural advice. It's worth
combining a visit to this centre with a walk in Savernake Forest. This is
about a mile from the village and has some good areas of beech forest,
several ancient oaks and many interesting flowers and fungi.

Prices £££
Facilities Parking, 20 cars. Toilets. Garden advice service. Delivery service
Open Every day 9am to 5pm (closes 12.30pm Tues). Closed Christmas and
Boxing Day

BURTON Cheshire   map 2

Gordale Nurseries

Chester High Road, Burton, S. Wirral L64 8TF   *Tel* 051-336 2116
*On the A540 Hoylake to Chester road, near the turnoff to Burton. About 7 miles
from Chester*

One of the many centres which has been working away at improving
facilities and expanding displays over the last few years. Further

improvements planned include an information centre and a play area. It now offers a quite outstanding selection of high-quality plants. There is a good collection of conifers and the choice of heathers and alpines is superb. Clematis are also numerous, taking pride of place in a large selection of climbers. All specimens are thriving, especially the smaller plants such as heathers and alpines. Nearly all labelling is easy to read, but more instructions would be welcome. The centre is large all round with the indoor section being particularly spacious. Chemicals, composts and hand tools are stocked in large quantities. A special feature is the really large variety of garden furniture ranging from rustic wooden and cast iron to more modern plastic and metal furniture. Both old and new garden ornaments and containers are also on offer. There is no water-gardening equipment, but this is probably due to the presence of a large, water-garden specialist next door. Power tools, construction materials and garden buildings are not available. Staff are expert and friendly.

Prices £££
Facilities Parking, 500 cars. Toilets. Vending machine. Garden advice service. Delivery service
Open Mon to Fri 9am to 5pm, Sat and Sun 9am to 6pm (closes 5pm every day in winter). Closed Christmas and Boxing Day
Credit cards Access, Visa

BURY ST. EDMUNDS Suffolk   map 4
Dogwood Nursery

Symonds Road, Moreton Hall   *Tel* Bury St. Edmunds (0284) 68243
Estate, Bury St. Edmunds IP32 7BW
By the A45 trunk road. Take the 'East Bury St Edmunds' exit from the A45 and follow the signs to Moreton Hall Estate Residential

This nursery is deceptively small considering the wide range of goods it stocks. The site is a little crowded, particularly in the shop (this area is to be extended), but it is well planned so this is not a great disadvantage. The nursery provides as wide a variety of plants as possible, rather than filling up space with a lot of the same thing, so most gardeners would be hard pressed to find any shortcomings in the selection on offer. Plant quality is generally good. Labelling is more patchy with some labels being very good, while others are severely weatherworn. The tools and sundries section is less comprehensive than the plants, but unless you are after the larger items like greenhouses or power tools you should have no trouble fulfilling your requirements. There are provisions for water-gardening enthusiasts and the selection of good-quality garden ornaments and statues offered is imaginatively displayed. The nursery offers a garden design service. The proprietor is most helpful.

Prices £££
Facilities Parking, 50 cars. Toilets. Garden advice service. Delivery service
Open Every day 9.30am to 5.30pm (9am to 5pm in winter). Closed 4 days at Christmas

BUTTERCRAMBE N. Yorkshire   map 2

Aldby Gardens

Buttercrambe, near Stamford Bridge, York YO4 1AU
On the A166 York to Bridlington road, 3 miles east of Stamford Bridge

A visit to this nursery could easily be incorporated into a lovely day out for the family. The nursery is in the walled garden of a large house about a quarter of a mile from the River Derwent. At Stamford Bridge, also on the Derwent, you will find some pleasant riverside walks, an old corn mill, a large waterfall and a restaurant. Most of the plants sold at Aldby Gardens are grown on the premises and there are some unusual ones to be found among the more ordinary stock. The standard of health of the plants is very good, probably because they are well tended by the excellent staff. Labelling, on the other hand, could do with some improvement. The collection of houseplants is refreshing – it manages to avoid the run-of-the-mill to some extent, but doesn't spill over to the very expensive, exotic species. Although this is primarily a plant centre, there is a small covered area which stocks some sundries such as hand tools, chemicals and ornaments. The staff take the time to explain the best way to care for any of your purchases. Often as not they will give you helpful instructions without being asked. A small shop sells vegetables grown on the premises and cold drinks.

Prices £££
Facilities Parking, 40 cars. Toilets. Play area. Garden advice service
Open Tues to Sun 9.30am to 5pm (closes 4pm in winter)

CALNE Wiltshire   map 4

Bowood Garden Centre

Bowood Estates, Calne SN11 OLZ   *Tel* Calne (0249) 816828
Off the A4 at Derry Hill village, adjoining the entrance to Bowood House and Gardens

The Earl of Shelburne opened this centre at the start of the 1983 season, making the specialist trees and other plants found on his estate available to the general public. The estate, known as the Bowood Pleasure Grounds and Arboretum, covers 82 acres and there are trees growing here which are reputed to have been raised from seeds planted between 1770 and 1785! The garden centre faces a mammoth task, but things have started to consolidate and there are signs that it will grow into a very pleasant centre. The speciality is obviously trees and shrubs and there is little sign of the mundane in the varieties on show. A general range of other plants is also kept in stock so there are things to look at even if you don't want to buy trees. An additional attraction are the rhododendron gardens, at their best in May and June. The quality of the plants is generally good. They are laid out in groups and quite reasonably arranged. Labelling is rather variable but there are some helpful details on the individual plants. A superb, specially designed conservatory houses an information centre and stocks some of the smaller garden accessories including a range of books, but there is no pretence of competing with the modern, well-stocked garden centre. Staff are unobtrusive but happy to assist if needed. An adventure playground, excellent restaurant and garden tea room are within the estate rather than at the centre so to use them you must pay the entrance fee to the grounds.

Prices ££££
Facilities Parking, 1,000 cars. Toilets. Restaurant within the estate. Play area. Garden advice service. Delivery service. Plant catalogue 30p
Open Every day 11am to 5pm, Mar to Oct only
Credit cards Access, American Express, Visa

CAMBERLEY Surrey   map 5

Copped Hall Cottage Gardens   ❀

Stonegate, Camberley,   *Tel* Camberley (0276) 22468
Surrey GU15 1PD

Turn off the A30, Camberley to Bagshot road at the Jolly Farmer into Maultway, over the M3 bridge, take the second right followed by the second left into Stonegate

It is quite easy to miss this centre on approach since it is very badly signposted; in fact our inspector drove past it the first time, but it is situated on a quiet road where it is easy to park the car. The site itself is very small and because of the large number of plants stocked, the paths are quite narrow, but clear signposting makes it easy to find one's way about. Conifers, shrubs, trees and fruit bushes are available in great variety. All plants are cheap and of very good quality and well labelled with instructions. For the space available, the stock of hand tools is most impressive. The indoor area is a little cluttered, but the layout makes the best use of the space available and there are plans for further reorganisation. Paving and sheds are not sold, but greenhouses can be ordered. Garden furniture and ornaments may also be purchased, including a large range of stone pots and troughs, and wooden tubs and barrels. Grass seed and traditional fertilisers are packed by the nursery in bags of various sizes. A second shop in Camberley town centre (2–4 Grace Reynolds Walk) stocks a supplementary range of garden sundries which includes chemicals, furniture and hand tools. Staff members will often approach customers with offers of assistance, and advice is happily given. A pleasant centre, especially if you enjoy the intimacy of a small establishment.

Prices ££
Facilities Garden advice service. Delivery service. Free leaflets and reference material available
Open Mon to Sat 9am to 6pm (closes 1pm Tues), Sun 10am to 6pm
Credit cards Access, Visa

   Garden centres and nurseries which provide the best facilities for disabled visitors are marked with the wheelchair symbol. Most centres show plenty of room for improvement in this area and we think it is time they gave more thought to their less able customers.

CAMBRIDGE Cambridgeshire   map 4
Beehive Garden Centre

Beehive Shopping Centre,   *Tel* Cambridge (0223) 358844
Coldhams Lane, Cambridge CB1 3ER
On Coldhams Lane, at the Newmarket Road end, 1 mile from the town centre

This centre is something of a paradox, for although it is part of a modern
shopping complex it does not just stock the run-of-the-mill items typical of
a modern garden centre. It's main strength lies in the more specialist plants
it sells which are often difficult to find elsewhere. Irises, fuchsias, heathers,
unusual bulbs, old-fashioned roses, a wide variety of water-plants and a
good choice of potato tubers are just some of the specialities. These are
usually of very good quality. The more common shrubs and plants offer
less choice and are generally in a poorer condition. The centre is at its best
in May and June when many stocks are new and healthy. Labelling also
suffers the test of time and labels are only legible on the new stock. In the
tools and sundries section, you might also find those bits and pieces you
haven't been able to obtain elsewhere, such as lawncare tools, soil warming
cables and lots of different hose attachments. The range of gardening
equipment stocked is comprehensive and includes all the larger items such
as sheds, greenhouses, fencing and paving. Overall the site gives a messy
and disorganised appearance. However, there are plans to improve this.
Staff are very helpful, but are few and far between, not really adequate to
look after this centre as it deserves. A supermarket, department store,
petrol station and coffee lounge are some of the other facilities offered by
the complex.

Prices £££
Facilities Parking, 60 cars. Garden advice service. Delivery service. Catalogues for
roses and fruit 5p
Open Tues, Wed, Thurs and Sat 9am to 5.30pm, Fri 9.30am to 7pm, Sun 10am to 5pm
(closed Sun Jan and Feb)
Credit cards Access, American Express, Co-op Handycard, Diners Club, Visa

CANTERBURY Kent   map 4
Canterbury Garden Centre

Littlebourne Road,   *Tel* Canterbury (0227) 68298
Canterbury CT3 4AF
On the A257 about 1½ miles from Canterbury centre

This is a roadside garden centre in rural surroundings which occupies a
3-acre site. Access is easy and there is ample car parking space. The centre
is set out on several levels (there are ramps to the shrub areas) and
incorporates a plant display area, a large shop for sundries and a
showroom for garden machinery and furniture. Greenhouses, sheds,
paving and fencing are also supplied and there are plans to display
swimming pools. The outside area has been sensibly laid out and all the
signposting is very clear; inside, however, the shop is rather crowded
though this is to be improved. The range of plants available is reasonably

49

wide and overall quality is generally good. Labelling could do with some improvement – this is promised in the near future. At the time of our inspection, each plant was labelled with its botanical and common name, but this had often faded beyond recognition. The staff are considerate and knowledgeable and they will usually take it upon themselves to carry goods and load your car. This centre provides a very useful service to those in the area.

Prices £££
Facilities Parking, 30 cars. Toilets. Vending machines. Play area. Garden advice service. Delivery service
Open Tues to Sun 8.30am to 5.30pm.
Credit cards Access, Visa

Kent Garden Centres

London Road, Upper Harbledown,   *Tel* Canterbury (0227) 454264
Canterbury CT2 8NA
2 miles north of Canterbury off the A2 Canterbury bypass

Perhaps a centre to explore more for its range of gardening accessories than anything special in the way of plants. It seems to stock everything a gardener could need. The area devoted to sheds and greenhouses is extensive, power tools and lawnmowers are very well represented and the array of books was one of the most impressive our inspector had seen for some time. The indoor space is arranged in an orderly fashion, but the exterior could be better. However, the outside was being reorganised when our inspector visited. The centre is new and still developing. The overall quality of plants was generally good, but only the more common varieties were stocked – the reorganisation should allow room for a wider range. Indoor plants were mostly in a healthy condition. Group labels were not too bad but those on individual plants were poor. They carried little in the way of information and many were missing altogether – possibly due to the alterations being made. The staff are courteous and helpful.

Prices ££££
Facilities Parking, 110 cars. Toilets. Vending machine. Play area. Garden advice service. Delivery service. Plant price list 20p, sundries catalogue 50p
Open Every day 8.30am to 6.30pm (closes 5.30pm in winter). Closed Christmas Day
Credit cards Access, Visa

CAPEL ST. MARY Suffolk   map 4
By Pass Nurseries

Capel St. Mary, near Ipswich   *Tel* Great Wenham (0473) 310604
IPN 2JR
At Capel St. Mary, 7 miles south of Ipswich on the A12

This centre was re-organised in 1984 and now presents a very fresh and clean appearance. The complex is set out on flat ground and there are seats dotted about, so it is particularly convenient for disabled and elderly gardeners. The plants are all arranged alphabetically with wide paths separating the clearly identified sections. This outside section takes up about one third of the total site. It has a very good range of healthy plants, although the specialist gardener might find it wanting. They are all carefully and clearly labelled, offering illustrations and details on plants. Garden buildings, including garages and conservatories, occupy another third of the available space, and the rest of the area has been well laid out for the display of indoor plants and garden accessories. The choice of these is above average with a particularly good range of barbecues and books. This nursery produces flower seed (customers are welcome to visit the seed production glasshouse) and specialises in flowering houseplants and bedding plants. The staff are very good and appear to enjoy their work. Improvements planned include the addition of a restaurant (opening spring 1985) and play area, and expansion of the car park and covered shopping area.

Prices £££££
Facilities Parking, 120 cars. Toilets. Garden advice service. Delivery service. Free information leaflets
Open Mon to Sat 9am to 5.30pm, Sun and holidays 10am to 5pm. Closed Christmas Day
Credit cards Access, Visa

CAR COLSTON Nottinghamshire   map 2

Frosts Gardening Centre

Foss Way, Car Colston,   *Tel* East Bridgeford (0949) 20767
near Bingham NG13 8JA
On the A46 Foss Way, about 1½ miles north of the Saxondale crossroad (about ¾ of a mile north of RAF Newton)

The open countryside and surrounding small villages make a pleasant rural setting for this centre. Frosts have a wholesale nursery across the road and there's a landscape gardening firm next door. These support and complement the services offered by the centre itself. The trees and shrubs are mostly grown at the nursery and are strong, healthy specimens. Bare-rooted stock can be obtained during the dormant season. Herbaceous perennials are bought in and on the day our inspector visited these showed signs of suffering. All labelling is legible, although there is little in the way of detail such as plant habit or description. The containerised plants occupy a plot of about half an acre which is easy to get around and well-organised. Tools and sundries are available including a good range of terracotta and reconstituted stone containers, while the landscaping firm adjacent stocks an impressive range of fine conservatories and summerhouses, as well as building materials, railway sleepers, gates and wattle fencing. Staff are friendly and although they don't have an outstanding knowledge of plants they are always ready to help. There are no refreshments or toilets on the premises, but there is a Little Chef restaurant next door.

Prices £££
Facilities Parking, 50 cars. Garden advice service. Delivery service. Free price list for soft fruit, trees, roses, etc.

Open Every day 8.15am to 6pm (closes 5pm in winter). Closed Christmas Day
Credit cards Access, Visa

CASTLE CARY Somerset map 3

Hadspen House Nursery

Hadspen House, Castle Cary *Tel* Castle Cary (0963) 50200/50427
BA7 7NG
2 miles east of Castle Cary on the A371

This nursery has an excellent stock of plants – mostly herbaceous
perennials and hardy shrubs but also water-plants and conifers. They are
all in very good condition and keen gardeners will be impressed by some of
the rare and unusual varieties available, particularly among the Hostas.
The adjacent garden occupies about 8 acres of sheltered, south-sloping land
and here the visitor can see the trees, shrubs, roses and rare Australasian
plants set out. An additional feature is the ornamental pool, covered with
waterlilies and surrounded by some beautiful species. The nursery is
situated beside Hadspen House and its grounds and is reached by a rough
track which is well signposted. The atmosphere is entirely peaceful and
particularly pleasant thanks to the kindly young owner. He and his two
staff offer all the advice one may need as to plant culture, which
complements the adequate but rather uninformative labelling. They are
also helpful in terms of carrying and loading even though the car park is
quite close. No sundries are stocked. If you happen to visit on a Sunday
you can take advantage of the teas served from 2pm to 5pm in the
'gardener's cottage'.

Prices Information not available
Facilities Parking, 30 cars (overflow unlimited). Toilets. Refreshments. Garden advice
service. Delivery service. Free plant price list
Open Tues to Sat 10am to 5pm, Sun and bank holidays 2pm to 5pm. Closed all Jan
and Sun Nov to Mar

CHAPMANSLADE Wiltshire map 3

Row Farm Garden Centre

Row Farm, Chapmanslade, *Tel* Chapmanslade (037 388) 260
Westbury BA13 4AB
*On the A3098 at its junction with the A36 Bath to Salisbury road, midway between
Westbury and Frome*

This is a pleasant centre set just off the main road with an expansive
nursery area behind, including beautiful rose fields and 20,000 rose trees.
Because it supplies its own centre, you can buy plants of different ages such
as trees and conifers ranging from small to very large. There is a good
general range of most sorts of plants (but no houseplants), with shrubs and
trees all of very good quality and adequately labelled. The plants for sale
are all arranged alphabetically and the logical system works towards a very
fine layout throughout. A medium-sized building holds most things a

gardener needs in the way of tools, fertilisers and sprays, while the centre also stocks sheds and greenhouses, fencing and paving, a few garden chairs and tables and water-gardening plants and equipment. The nursery also provides a contracting service for garden construction and alteration and will take on work anywhere within a 30-mile radius. Staff are friendly and helpful. The nursery holds a special rose open day the second weekend in July.

Prices £££
Facilities Parking, 20 cars. Toilets. Garden advice service. Delivery service. Free price list for roses, fruit trees and sheds. Plant catalogue 20p
Open Mon to Sat 9am to 6pm (closes 5pm in winter), Sun 10am to 5pm. Closed Christmas and Boxing Day

CHELMSFORD Essex   map 4
Cramphorn Garden Centre

Cuton Mill, Chelmsford CM2 26PD   *Tel* Chelmsford (0245) 466466
Just off the A12 at Cuton flyover on the east side of Chelmsford, about 1 mile from the town centre

Between two vast housing estates and a large industrial estate, this huge centre fits the local scale. It is easily reached off the main road and offers a big car park with overflow space. Exiting right on to the busy road can be a problem, so if frustration sets in, go left down to the roundabout about 100 yards away and swing back. All departments are well stocked and most gardening needs must surely be met here. In the well laid out, though slightly crowded interior you can find a wide range of tools, including Cramphorn's own Cuton brand. The chemicals and fertilisers section deserves to be singled out for praise, while there is also a very good pets section and a DIY department for the non-gardeners in your family. A tool hire department and refreshment facilities are planned. Paths can easily accommodate trolleys and wheelchairs, and signposting and labelling are both satisfactory. A very extensive range of plants is available, arranged in groups alphabetically. The garden plants were in very fine condition when our inspector visited, and the houseplants rated from fair to good. Staff are easy to find. However, checkouts are sometimes unmanned and this can result in long queues on a busy day. Our inspector tells us this centre is improving all the time. Different displays are put on throughout the year, such as a Dutch bulb display and summer craft show.

Prices ££££
Facilities Parking, 180 cars. Toilets. Play area. Garden advice service. Delivery service. Price lists, brochures and catalogues for numerous products
Open Every day 8.30am to 6pm (closes 5pm in winter). Closed Christmas and Boxing Day
Credit cards Access, Visa

Garden centres and nurseries are changing fast. Practically all those we've included in the Guide *were planning improvements for 1985, so we need as much feedback as possible about the ones you visit to keep us up to date. Please use the report forms at the end of the book.*

CHENIES Hertfordshire
map 4

Chenies Garden Centre

Chenies, near Rickmans-
worth WD3 6EN

Tel Little Chalfont (024 04) 4545/6/7/8

On the A404 midway between Amersham and Rickmansworth

Why not combine a visit to this centre, set in pleasant rural surroundings, with a call at the nearby Chenies Manor House and make an outing of it? This is a large centre with wide walkways, clear signs and an effectively organised interior area. The outdoor section is devoted to plants, landscaping materials and large garden buildings; one greenhouse contains garden furniture and another houses excellent indoor plants. Tools, seeds and small sundries are available under cover in a separate area – there is a particularly vast selection of china and plastic flower pots. There is a good range of prices and brands in the tool section – the only shortage appeared to be mowers and large power tools – and an excellent choice of greenhouses and wooden buildings such as lean-to's and sun rooms. A recent investment has been the stocking of swimming pools. A new cold- and warm-water fish section has been built. You need to pay more than one visit just to have a good look at all the equipment and accessories available. The quality of plants is generally very good, although when our inspector visited some showed signs of end-of-season blues. On the whole labelling is illustrated and descriptive and usually legible. The staff, when approached, are friendly and helpful and trolleys are made available for car loading. The centre provides an emergency service for problems such as tree and accident damage.

Prices £££
Facilities Parking, 90 cars. Toilets. Vending machines and confectionery. Garden advice service. Delivery service
Open Every day 9am to 5.30pm. Closed Christmas and Boxing Day and New Year's Day
Credit cards Access, Visa

CHESTER Cheshire
map 2

Grosvenor Garden Leisure

Wrexham Road, Belgrave, Chester
CH4 9EB

Tel Chester (0244) 672856

On the A483 Chester to Wrexham road, 3 miles south of Chester

You don't have to be green-fingered to enjoy a day here. This centre, close to the village of Pulford and adjacent to Eaton Hall, the Duke of Westminster's estate, is a delightful place to browse. There's a large and well displayed range of plants including some more unusual ones. They are quite expensive but of very good quality and there's a six-month guarantee on container-grown trees and shrubs. They are clearly and concisely labelled. Most garden machinery is sold and serviced here, and there is a comprehensive selection of larger items such as fencing, paving, garden furniture and ornaments as well as a demonstration swimming pool. The centre also offers a landscaping service. A new area has been opened to display greenhouses, sheds and other buildings. Special features include landscaped gardens, a new houseplant section, a camping display and a pets and aquatic centre. There is a restaurant housed in a converted nineteenth-century lodge which offers lunches, teas and 'chef's specials'. The staff are extremely courteous and helpful even on a weekend when busy and hard-pressed.

Prices £££££
Facilities Parking, 600 cars. Toilets. Restaurant and cafeteria. Play area. Garden advice service. Delivery service
Open Mon to Fri and bank holidays 9am to 5.45pm, Sat and Sun 10am to 5.45pm (closes 5pm every day Oct to Mar). Closed Christmas
Credit cards Access, Visa

CHESTER-LE-STREET Durham   map 2
Lambton Park Garden Centre

Lambton Park, Chester-le-Street   *Tel* Durham (0385) 855154
DH3 4PZ

In Lambton Park Estate, on the A183 between Chester-le-Street and Sunderland, about 2½ miles from the centre of Chester-le-Street

This centre borders on a large country estate which boasts its own castle and was at one time a wild animal park. Now its grounds offer a pleasantly secluded spot for this well-laid-out establishment. The centre provides a range and variety of items well able to satisfy most gardeners. There's a reasonable selection of plants, generally of high quality – conifers and trees seem to be in particularly good supply. The plants are well spaced, many of them raised on beds or platforms, and informatively labelled. One of the main attractions at the centre is the aquatics section with its numerous small ponds, a 10ft artificial waterfall, and a wide selection of water plants. Cold-water fish are sold and tropical fish are to be stocked in the near future. For the children there is a pet centre where they will see birds, mammals, reptiles and amphibians. The gardening accessories range from gum boots to goats and the only items missing are power tools. The collection of greenhouses and sheds is well worth looking at and there is a good selection of books on gardening and cookery, and a wide variety of artificial flowers and plants. A separate section is provided for houseplants. Staff vary from youngsters to more experienced people working in their specialised departments – all are friendly and helpful.

Prices £££
Facilities Parking, 400 cars. Toilets. Coffee shop. Vending machines. Play area. Garden advice service. Delivery service. Price list and catalogue for sundries 50p
Open Every day 9am to 6pm (closes 5pm in winter)
Credit cards Access, American Express, Diners Club, Visa

If you consider any entry to be incorrect, inadequate or misleading, you would be doing us and your fellow gardeners a service by letting us know. There are report forms at the end of the book.

CHESTERFIELD Derbyshire map 2
Van Dyke Bros.

Southgate House Nurseries,   *Tel* Chesterfield (0246) 810236
Clowne, Chesterfield S43 4TD
On the A619 Worksop to Chesterfield road, about 6 miles from Worksop

The strength of this centre lies in its outstanding collection of high-quality houseplants. These dominate a large greenhouse area and there are as many as 50 specimens of any one variety. Plant containers, pots and tubs are also a feature. If you are less keen on indoor greenery and want to add to your garden, there is also a reasonable range of outdoor plants for sale. Almost all the plants stocked are in excellent condition, although the fruit trees and roses were poorly when our inspector visited. The conifer section deserves a special mention both for the range and quality available. Gardening accessories are limited to a few hand tools and a useful choice of composts and fertilisers. There are no signposts, but large group labelling is very clear and easy to read. More detailed labelling with planting instructions is not provided. Staff consist of the owners and several working gardeners, all of whom are prepared to answer questions. Adjoining the centre is a tea room which serves teas and snacks, and a hotel where you will find a bar and a full meal service.

Prices Information not available
Facilities Parking, 200 cars. Toilets. Tea room (closed on Mon)
Open Every day 8am to 7pm (closes 5pm in winter)

CHICHESTER W. Sussex map 5
Chichester Garden Centre

Bognor Road, Merston,   *Tel* Chichester (0243) 789276
Chichester PO20 6EG
On the A259 Chichester to Bognor Regis road, about 1½ miles east of Chichester town centre

This is an excellent all-round garden centre and it is popular locally. The large outdoor section contains sheds, greenhouses and swimming pools, as well as hardy plants. Indoors are all the other sundries you might want, including barbecue equipment. A section is set aside for houseplants. The paths are not particularly wide, but the overall layout is very good. Both plants and trees are clearly labelled with some detailed information on most. The range of the plant stock is reasonable and the quality is very good. There are plenty of staff on the premises, including some fully qualified horticulturalists, and they are all happy to help.

Prices ££££
Facilities Parking, 100 cars. Toilets. Restaurant. Play area. Garden advice service. Delivery service. Plant catalogue 95p
Open Every day 9am to 6pm
Credit cards Access, Visa

CHIGWELL Essex   map 4

Garden Cottage Nurseries

Rolls Park, Chigwell IG7 6DJ   *Tel* 01-500 1636

On the A113, close to the junction of Chigwell High Road, Chigwell Lane and Abridge Road, about ½ mile outside Chigwell village

The helpfulness of the staff, the quality of plants and the uncommon varieties available give this centre a pleasant atmosphere and make it a place of interest for most gardening enthusiasts. It is not very easy to find your way about as there is little signposting, but our inspector felt things had improved since the last visit, with evidence of a general tidying up and a little more order in the presentation. The outside area comprises display and growing areas, as well as several propagation houses. This is worthy of exploration as there are lots of surprises among the shrubs and trees – the home-grown alpines and rhododendrons are notable specialities, and there is a fine display of summer- and winter-flowering heathers of excellent quality. The range on sale reflects the season, and overall the condition of plants is good – some are excellent; plants are carefully tended. Labelling is confined to individual plants and is adequate, particularly for the heathers; otherwise there is little to identify the plant groups. A large greenhouse is devoted to indoor plants and there are some interesting species to be found here. The sundries department is limited to composts and chemicals. A very helpful and knowledgeable staff will gladly answer questions, suggest what to plant or direct you around the site. Definitely a place to visit for those with an eye out for the unusual, although possibly not esoteric enough for the professional plantsman.

Prices £££
Facilities Parking, 12 cars. Toilets. Garden advice service. Delivery service
Open Tues to Sat 8.30am to 5pm, Sun 9.30am to 1pm
Credit card Access

CHIPPING NORTON Oxfordshire   map 4

The Hardy Plant Nursery

Banbury Road,   *Tel* Chipping Norton (0608) 41642
Chipping Norton OX7 5SY

Off the A361, about ½ mile east of Chipping Norton

This is a place which is perfectly adequate for most ordinary needs and fills the gap in gardening services locally. It stocks a good variety of trees, shrubs, conifers and soft fruit, the fruits including some of the more unusual types such as tayberries. The choice of climbers available is also interesting. Plants stocked tend to be lime loving or tolerant, due to the nursery's position. Houseplants and cut flowers in autumn are also available. Quality is generally good. A run-of-the-mill range of hand tools is stocked, but no larger equipment, though there are nearby stockists for paving and fencing and garden machinery. Ornaments and composts complete the picture. Everything is attractively laid out on a gravelled surface, with some plants set out on raised beds. Labelling could do with improvement, and the centre tells us that it will try to do this. There are few group labels and individual plant labels are often inaccessible. There was only a cashier on hand on the weekday afternoon when our inspector visited.

Prices £££
Facilities Parking, 30 cars. Toilets. Vending machines. Delivery service
Open Tues to Sun 10am to 6pm. Closed Mon except bank holidays. Closed all Jan

---

CHISLEHURST Kent   map 4

Coolings Nurseries and Garden Centre

Willow Grove, Chislehurst BR7 5RA   *Tel* 01-467 5064
A turning off Chislehurst High Street

A compact, well-organised centre which is large enough to be well-stocked but small enough to be friendly – there's a family atmosphere about the whole place and everything is well looked after. The centre is strictly for the gardener, all frills are dispensed with. It is well planned, all the space is taken up, but nothing looks too crowded. There is a heated area for houseplants and another covered area containing seeds and some tools, but as there is little room they don't stock the larger items. There is a good choice of plants available at a high standard. The bedding plants and container-grown shrubs and other plants are all grown by the nurseries and are of high quality – our inspector felt they were as good as any he had ever seen. Plants are displayed on raised benches. Labelling on the whole is satisfactory and the staff are very pleasant and if unable to deal with your problem they will find someone who can.

Prices ££££
Facilities Parking, 50 cars. Toilets. Garden advice service. Delivery service. Free price list for bedding plants in spring
Open Mon to Sat, Christmas to mid-Feb 8.30am to 5.30pm, mid-Feb to July 8am to 6pm, July to Christmas 8am to 5.30pm
Credit cards Access, Visa

CHISWELL GREEN Hertfordshire   map 4

Burston-Tyler Rose and Garden Centre

North Orbital Road, Chiswell Green,   *Tel* St Albans (0727) 32444
St Albans AL2 2DS
On the A405 at Chiswell Green, midway between the M10 roundabout and junction 6 of the M1

The grounds of this centre are well laid out. They are all level so it is easy to get around if you are in a wheelchair or pushing a pram and there are wide paths made of concrete slabs and good, eye-level signposting which is easily seen from the pathways. The exterior and interior areas are both sizeable. The former offers a reasonable selection of very good-quality plants, as well as peats, fertilisers and some of the bulkier garden materials;

the latter contains greenhouse heaters, barbecues and general sundries, including a selection of gardening books. Altogether the choice of tools and sundries is quite acceptable and includes the large items such as sheds, greenhouses, paving and fencing, but there are no power tools, lawnmowers or pond equipment. The staff are not abundant, but quite cheerful and happy to help. Some very useful written advice is provided on all plants, free of charge. General information is also given on the large, clear group labels, although the small plant tags are often faded and difficult to read. The centre provides a free garden planning service which includes a visit to the customer's garden.

Prices ££££
Facilities Parking, 200 cars. Toilets. Vending machines. Garden advice service. Delivery service. Roses sold by mail order
Open Every day 9am to 6pm (closes 5pm in winter). Closed Christmas and Boxing Day
Credit cards Access, Visa

CHORLEYWOOD Hertfordshire   map 4

Highlands Water Gardens Nurseries

Solesbridge Lane, Chorleywood   *Tel* Chorleywood (092 78) 4135
WD3 5SX
Solesbridge Lane is off the A404 at Chorleywood

These gardens have a very good reputation in the area and are well known. As the name suggests, they specialise in water gardening so their plants and sundries range is heavily biased in this direction. There are a few alpines and conifers kept in stock, but it is really for the pond, pool, stream or lake that you should be shopping. At the time of our visit extensive alterations were being carried out on the water system so it was not possible to see the centre at its best. However, the plants on display looked very healthy, and it is likely that this is true when the whole centre is working. The gardens are laid out in long rectangular concrete water beds and the extensive range of aquatic plants is neatly displayed. If you haven't yet built your garden pond there is an extremely wide range of plastic bases to choose from in all shapes and sizes. If possible it is worth trying to take your purchase away yourself since an additional delivery charge can jack up the price quite a lot. Indoors, all the bits and pieces needed to keep your display in good order are well arranged and carefully priced. For decorating the pond, there are statues and fountains of all types from which to select. A considerable and varied stock of ornamental fish is very well displayed, and the staff in this department are particularly knowledgeable and courteous. The manager of the centre is also most helpful and readily accessible to customers. Certainly deserving of some time if you are at all keen on this aspect of gardening.

Prices Information not available
Facilities Parking, 200 cars. Toilets. Garden advice service. Free price list and catalogue
Open Mon to Sat 9am to 5pm (opens 10am Sunday). Closed at weekends in winter
Credit cards Access, American Express, Diners Club, Visa

CHRISTCHURCH Dorset map 4

Stewarts Garden-Lands

Lyndhurst Road,   *Tel* Highcliffe (04252) 72244
Christchurch BH23 4SA

On the A35 Bournemouth to Southampton road, at the east end of the Christchurch bypass 2½ miles from Christchurch

This centre is situated on the edge of the New Forest and it covers a wide area both inside and out. The front part of the site has been attractively landscaped with Italian pools and the rest of the grounds are well laid out and clearly signposted. There is a very extensive choice of gardening equipment, including a particularly good selection of barbecues and garden furniture and a wide range of tools. Larger items such as sheds and greenhouses are also stocked and the only obvious omissions are fencing and paving. The centre's redevelopment programme even includes installation of a swimming pool. The plants themselves are well represented with the conifers deserving a special note. The trees, shrubs and herbaceous perennials are tended with care, but our inspector found some scrappy specimens about in other sections. Labelling was not very good – some trees and shrubs had no prices or identification at all (but the centre tells us that this has been rectified). Qualified and experienced staff are generally available to deal with horticultural problems. Trolleys are provided to carry goods around the site and to the car. The centre offers garden landscaping and interior landscaping services.

Prices ££££
Facilities Parking, 250 cars. Toilets. Restaurant and cafeteria. Garden advice service. Delivery service. Price lists for bulbs, roses, fruit and interior landscaping
Open Every day 9am to 6pm (late night opening Thurs and Fri). Closed Christmas and Boxing Day
Credit cards Access, Visa

CHURCH CROOKHAM Hampshire map 4

Redfields Garden Nursery Centre

Ewshott lane, Church Crookham,   *Tel* Fleet (025 14) 24444/5
Fleet GU13 0UB

Off the A287 Farnham to Odiham road, 1½ miles south of Fleet on the outskirts of Church Crookham

Built only a few years ago, this garden centre is now well established and already enjoys a good reputation locally for quality and service. There have been substantial improvements quite recently with an extension to the car park, now very large, and a dramatic increase in the stocks of sundries which now run to sheds and greenhouses as well as a wide collection of tools, ornaments and larger items including paving and garden furniture. The supply of peat and composts is enormous, and the new fish and aquatics area is first class and beautifully laid out. Plans are still in hand for development, the latest addition to be a small refreshment area. There's a good range of most plants, all in very good condition. Any poor specimens are put aside into the bargain corner. Two small greenhouses contain delicate plants, and there are 'netting houses' for an impressive display of azaleas and rhododendrons. The layout is sensible with wide concrete paths and large signs. An electrically operated entrance and exit makes getting around with your arms full significantly easier! There are plenty of staff members about, all wearing uniforms, and they are friendly and willing.

Prices £££
Facilities Parking, 160 cars. Toilets. Garden advice service. Delivery service. Plants sold by mail order
Open Every day 9am to 6pm. Closed Christmas and Boxing Day
Credit cards Access, Visa

CHURCHDOWN Gloucestershire   map 3
Hurrans Garden Centre

Cheltenham Road East,   *Tel* Churchdown (0452) 712232
Churchdown, near Gloucester GL3 1AB
On the B4063, 2 miles from Gloucester town centre and ½ mile from Staverton Airport; 3 miles from junction 11 of the M5

A very pleasant centre for the enthusiastic amateur gardener, offering talks from visiting horticultural specialists on Sundays, organised trips to the Chelsea Flower Show, and information packs and leaflets. The quality found at this centre is consistently very good whatever the time of year, and scrappy plants are quickly removed from sight. There is an excellent range of conifers and heathers, as well as a good basic selection of most other plants. A pleasing choice of alpines is attractively displayed in a rockery. The sections are clearly defined and well signposted with good wide paths leading from one area to another. Labelling is clear and descriptive and staff are willing to search for any additional information you need – they are easily recognisable in their blue gingham shirts. A basic range of equipment for most garden jobs is stocked, from fencing panels, sheds and furniture to decorative flower-arranging materials, although paving and lawnmowers are missing. The aquatics department is being improved and will feature landscaped pools, more ornaments and cold-water fish, and a wider selection of waterplants.

Prices ££££
Facilities Parking, 140 cars. Garden advice service. Delivery service. Some price lists available through the year covering both plants and sundries
Open Every day 9am to 6pm (closes 8pm Thurs and Fri, opens 9.30am Fri). Closes 5pm every day in winter. Closed 3 days over Christmas
Credit cards Access, Visa

CLAYGATE Surrey   map 5
Kennedys Garden Centre

Oaken Lane, Claygate, near Esher KT10 0RH   *Tel* 01-398 0047

Just off the A309 Kingston bypass near Hinchley Wood station

Our inspector felt it would be possible 'to build, furbish and stock a new garden from scratch without looking elsewhere': quite impressive for a centre of this size. There is a pervasive atmosphere of 'pride in presentation' and this is particularly evident in the immaculate layout. The exterior is set out as a garden with well-kept lawns, lovely flower beds and seating in the shade, and the whole site is tidy, clean and clearly signposted. It is a pleasant place for a restful walk whether you want to make any purchases or not. Every gardener's interest is catered for among the plants, with dwarf conifers and alpines of particular merit. The quality is good throughout with below-par plants being quickly removed. Labelling is clear and helpful and it is interesting to see some labels on individual plants showing their origins: for example, some are written in Spanish! Other pot labels offer names, growing advice and a description. The staff admit they are not experts but any question will quickly result in the production of a reference book for everyone to grapple with together. A comprehensive and varied stock of sundries is available with separate areas set aside for sheds, greenhouses, fencing and paving. There are plans to extend the shop and provide a cafeteria and children's play area.

Prices ££££
Facilities Parking, 120 cars. Toilets. Delivery service. Free price list for hardy plants
Open Every day, 9am to 6pm in summer, 8.30am to 5.30pm in winter. Closed 3 days over Christmas
Credit cards Access, Visa

CLAYTON-LE-WOODS Lancashire   map 2

Park View Garden Centre

600 Preston Road,   *Tel* Preston (0772) 35563/39266
Clayton-le-Woods, near Chorley PR6 7EH
1 mile from the M6 on the A6 between Preston and Chorley

This is a large centre, well laid out and clearly signposted. It has been divided into many different departments, each manned by different staff and with its own till. This can create problems as you have to pay for things separately as you go along rather than in one go at the end of your visit. The centre stocks a good range of tools and sundries, covering most sorts of goods from the small to the large, including a separate aquarium sales department. There are good displays of fencing, paving, sheds and other garden buildings. A reasonable selection of plants is stocked and they are of good quality, but old stock is not always up to scratch, so pick your plants carefully. Labels for groups of plants have been very well done, but at the time of our inspection some were weathered and difficult to read. All in all a pleasant place to wander around with no pressure to buy. When our inspector visited, the staff varied somewhat from department to department: those in the houseplant section were excellent, but they were difficult to find in the hardy, outdoor plants section. There is also a garden advice centre.

Prices Information not available
Facilities Parking, 100 cars. Toilets. Cafeteria. Play area. Garden advice service. Delivery service. Free price list for sundries
Open Mon to Sat 9am to 6pm, Sun 10am to 6pm
Credit cards Access, Visa

CLEOBURY MORTIMER Shropshire map 3

The Hollows Nursery

Prescott, near Cleobury Mortimer, *Tel* Stottesdon (074 632) 629
Kidderminster DY14 8RR
1½ miles from the village of Stottesdon, which is between Bridgnorth and Cleobury Mortimer

The strength of this nursery is that most plants are grown on the site and customers can be assured that they are hardy and accustomed to all local weather conditions. The couple who run the nursery know their plants and are aware of their differing requirements, and the results are for the most part excellent. Any plant which might have been sitting around for too long and is beginning to look pot bound will have its price knocked down without you needing to ask. The range is very good and the prices cheap, and although they don't have vast numbers of varieties of any one type of plant, they can offer some of the more unusual plants. The conifer collection is particularly good. This is perhaps not an ideal place to visit when the weather is bad because the indoor area is very small and the grass paths can get slippery but the nursery will lend you wellingtons! The selection of garden accoutrements is limited mainly to the smaller items although they do stock paving and a small amount of garden furniture and pond equipment. A good nursery offering friendly, personal service.

Prices ££
Facilities Parking, 12 cars. Toilets (on request). Garden advice service. Delivery service. Free plant price list
Open Every day except Tues 9am to 8pm (closes at dusk in winter)
Credit card Access

COAL ASTON S.Yorkshire map 2

Ward's Nurseries and Garden Centre

Eckington Road, Coal Aston, *Tel* Dronfield (0246) 412622
Sheffield S18 6BA
East of Coal Aston, on the B6056, Eckington to Dronfield road

An impressive and attractive centre which has been carefully and thoughtfully planned. It covers a large area, but the signposting and sensible landscaping make it easy to single out the section you want. The system is well organised, leaving no empty or forgotten spaces, and sections are continually restocked. There are plenty of large trolleys and baskets to transport your goods and they are easy to manage on the wide pathways. The range of plants should keep most shoppers happy, and the speciality of the house is heathers. Plants are individually potted, all given adequate elbow room and watered by an overhead spray system – the result is excellent, healthy specimens. Trees are spaced a little tightly so one can get wet walking throught this section. Excellent group labelling gives descriptive and cultural information. The range of garden equipment does not cover all areas, but most standard items are stocked and the displays of fencing, pots and ornamental troughs are extremely good – warnings are posted not to lift the heavy ornaments without help. Our inspector warmed to the staff who he felt were obviously keen to please. Smokers are discouraged at the entrance by polite notices suggesting that plants don't appreciate ash, and dogs, other than guide-dogs, are also discouraged.

Prices £££
Facilities Parking, 100 cars. Ice cream. Garden advice service. Delivery service
Open Every day 9am to 6pm (closes 5pm in winter). Closed Christmas and Boxing Day
Credit cards Access, Visa

COCKERMOUTH Cumbria   map 2
Oakhurst Garden Centre

Lamplugh Road, Cockermouth   *Tel* Cockermouth (0900) 822180
CA13 0DT
About ½ mile from the centre of Cockermouth on the A66

A surround of trees and attractive permanent show beds add to the pleasing aspect of this sloping site. It is a handy centre for those in the locality, but might be too limited at present to justify travelling great distances. However, the owners tell us that they are still developing the centre, so things may change. The large exterior section has been fairly well laid out with wide paths and reasonable signposting. The area is mainly occupied by a good selection of trees, shrubs and conifers, as well as a lot of Leylandii hedging. Most other standard plants are stocked, and it was only the choice of perennials, houseplants and soft fruits which was noticeably depleted at the time of our inspection. The overall quality of the plants is good. At the time of our inspection, the quality of the labelling was not of the same standard, though the centre tells us it has made improvements in this area. There is not much coverage of the larger garden accessories, but the range of the smaller bits and pieces is quite wide, resulting in a clutter in the small display area available (however, the new shop opening for spring 1985 and extended covered area should hopefully overcome this). Among the gardening sundries you will find chemicals and composts, furniture and ornaments, fencing and a few hand tools. A husband and wife team make up the staff of the centre and between them they manage to be wherever they are needed and are helpful and knowledgeable as well. The sloping site may make it difficult for some to push trolleys up to the car park and for those less-able visitors.

Prices £££
Facilities Parking, 50 cars. Toilets. Play area. Garden advice service. Delivery service
Open Mon to Sat 9am to 5.30pm, Sun 10am to 5.30pm

CODICOTE Hertfordshire   map 4
Jackman's Garden Centre

High Street, Codicote, near Welwyn   *Tel* Kimpton (0438) 820433
SG4 8XA

On the B656 Welwyn to Hitchin road at the north end of Codicote village

Set in a pleasant rural area in the Hertfordshire countryside, Jackman's
offers a good service to gardeners who are generally content with the more
common plants, and the variety and condition of shrubs for sale is
excellent. Brick-sided, raised beds and trough tables hold most plants, but
when our inspector visited, some of the paths were blocked by fallen
plants. Otherwise the layout is fine and the indoor facilities are particularly
uncluttered and attractive. The indoor area stocks a very good range of
tools and sundries with a special emphasis on gardening books and
handtools. An impressive array of glasshouses is on show and the centre
also sells sheds, swimming pools and garden furniture. The quality of
plants is generally good, although when inspected some were scorched,
pot-bound or in need of a drink – the perennials were particularly scraggy.
Illustrated plant signs are well detailed, but individual labels are rather
disappointing, often faded with prices that are difficult to read. A small
coffee lounge and snack bar caters for the hungry, and a nice touch is that
newspapers, magazines and childrens books are laid out for reading. For
those interested in water gardening there is a corner showing you 'how to
construct a pond with a fountain'. Wheelbarrows and trolleys are available
for collecting goods.

Prices ££££
Facilities Parking, 150 cars. Toilets. Cafeteria. Play area. Garden advice service.
Delivery service
Open Every day 9am to 6pm (closes 5pm in winter). Closed 25 to 29 Dec
Credit cards Access, Visa

CODSALL Staffordshire   map 2
Codsall and Wergs Garden Centre

Wergs Hall Road, Codsall,   *Tel* Codsall (090 74) 2461/2
near Wolverhampton WV8 2HJ
*4 miles west of Wolverhampton on the A41, turn right down Wergs Hall Road at
Crown public house*

This centre covers a 6-acre plot and it is surrounded on all sides by
farmland. A large car park can usually cope with the number of visitors, but
the small friendly staff can get absolutely swamped at peak times. The
principal feature of this centre is the wide range of goods it has in stock,
especially in the garden hardware section – the one problem is that it seems
to have expanded and spread itself a little wide before being able to fully
cope and it might need another season or two to completely settle in. The
centre has been undergoing extensive redevelopment since 1982 which
should be completed in 1985. There are no complaints about the layout
which has been well thought out, designating specific areas to each type of

product. A full range of sundries can be found here, including building materials. The centre specialises in aquatic equipment, including fish, and also has a greenhouse and shed display centre. At the time of inspection, the selection of plants was adequate for most gardeners. The plants' state of health was variable, with herbs, trees, conifers and alpines looking very good and roses and shrubs less so. The labelling needed major improvements, being very scrappy indeed. There is an attractive camping equipment display run by a separate firm next door which might be of interest to some members of the family, and it makes an interesting complement to the wide range of goods available at the garden centre. Improvements are promised in quality and maintenance of plants, labelling and number of staff following the redevelopment. When forthcoming, they should make a great difference.

Prices £££
Facilities Parking, 100 cars. Toilets. Vending machines. Garden advice service. Delivery service. Price lists and sundries catalogue
Open Mon to Sat 8am to 6pm, Sun 9.30am to 6pm (closes 5.30pm Mon to Sat, 5pm Sun in winter). Closed Christmas Day
Credit cards Access, Visa

COLCHESTER Essex   map 4

By Pass Nurseries   ☆ ★

Ipswich Road, Colchester CO1 2YF   *Tel* Colchester (0206) 865500
At the Ipswich Road, Cowdray Avenue roundabout on the northern section of Colchester's inner ring road

Although the name suggests that this centre is on the Colchester bypass, the access is actually off the smaller road leading into Colchester itself. Here the entrance is wide and safe and opens on to a well-planned and ample car park. This is a fine example of a large centre. It is very well maintained and organised, and the grounds are tidy and clearly marked. All the paths outside are in good repair, although some are just grassed ways, and they separate the area into distinct sections each containing a particular type of plant. Each plant is carefully labelled, while information panels by each section are clear and instructive. The range is extensive, especially among the alpines and herbs, and when our inspector visited it was impossible to find any signs of neglect. A good sprinkler system keeps everything well watered. The gardening equipment section is very comprehensive, offering a range which includes cultivators and a camping display as well as polyester flowers and a water-pet section. The indoor departments are all neatly assembled and clean. Staff throughout the premises are polite and helpful.

Prices ££££
Facilities Parking, 250 cars. Toilets. Restaurant adjacent to the centre, vending machines on site. Garden advice service. Delivery service. Free information leaflets
Open Mon to Sat 8.30am to 5.30pm, Sun and holidays 10am to 5pm. Closed Christmas Day
Credit cards Access, Visa

The Gardener at W & G

Williams & Griffin,   *Tel* Colchester (0206) 571212
Cowdray Avenue, Colchester CO1 1XY

On the eastern section of the A604, old Colchester bypass, 1 mile from the town centre

This centre sits between a railway line and the old bypass road, with access from the service road which runs parallel to the main road. The centre has been purpose-built and each product or plant has been allocated space according to the popularity and turnover expected. The selection of tools and sundries is very comprehensive and an especially large area has been assigned to the display of powered garden machinery and spare parts. Garden furniture is also a speciality. The more popular lines of plants have also been catered for, as well as alpines, herbs and houseplants. The plants are of good quality and the houseplants in particular are in excellent condition, benefiting from the care and attention of a dedicated staff: The outdoor plants are all containerised and are laid out in well-irrigated, clean beds. They are arranged in alphabetical order, each named and priced individually, with informative labelling accompanying each section. The layout of the centre, both inside and out, is excellent and our inspector had no complaints at all. The staff can be quite difficult to track down, but once found prove to be very helpful. In the houseplant section they are particularly good. Take special care when leaving the site: the old bypass is a very busy road.

Prices ££££
Facilities Parking, 150 cars. Toilets. Vending machines. Play area. Garden advice service. Delivery service. Free catalogue of gardening sundries
Open Every day 9am to 5.30pm. Closed Christmas and Boxing Day and New Year's Day
Credit cards Access, American Express, Diners Club, Visa

COLESHILL Warwickshire   map 3

Melbick Nurseries

Leisure, garden and aquatic centre,   *Tel* 021-779 2683
Chester Road, Coleshill, Birmingham B46 3HY

On the junction of A446 and A452, between Coleshill and Stonebridge

This nursery appealed to our inspector because of its informality and the choice and variety of stocks in all departments. The approach to the centre is quite difficult as it is situated between two dual carriageways and has four entrances, but once there the location is pleasant and the car parking ample. The inside area houses furniture, fish, books and a beautiful presentation of houseplants. It could be improved by defining the display areas more clearly. Outside there is a considerable area for the trees, shrubs, heathers and other plants. This has been well organised, but paths are a little too narrow for easy access by wheelchairs and pushchairs. A large area has been allocated to the display of greenhouses and sheds, which come in all shapes and sizes. In the plant section there are price reductions offered for any bulk purchases, such as large numbers of conifers. When our inspector visited, the quality of the plants was quite reasonable and only the roses looked a bit tired. Many plants are grown on site including herbaceous and alpine plants and some hardy nursery stock, and hanging baskets are made up in season. Grouping in alphabetical order makes it easy to find the plants you are after and each group is well identified. Individual labels are all typed, but some suffer from fading. Staff are mainly young and are not trained in horticulture but the cashier is quite knowledgeable and very helpful. The pets and aquatics sections are due to be modernised and enlarged.

Prices £££
Facilities Parking, 100 cars (plus 200 overflow). Toilets. Light refreshments. Garden advice service. Delivery service. Plant catalogue 25p
Open Every day 8.30am to 5pm. Closed Christmas and Boxing Day and New Year's Day
Credit cards Access, Visa

COMBE MARTIN Devon   map 3

Buzzacott Manor Garden Centre   ✿

Combe Martin EX34 0NL   *Tel* Combe Martin (027 188) 2359
2 miles east of Combe Martin, on an unclassified road off the A399

An enthusiastic young couple run this centre and they have made great strides since its beginning. It is rather off the beaten track, down a long, very rough track, but the surroundings are pleasant and there is a large area for walks or for children to play. A pleasant coffee lounge sells homemade cakes, Cornish pasties, delicious hot doughnuts and, in summer, cream teas, and these can all be eaten in the attractive courtyard. The site occupies around 2 acres, most of which is devoted to plants. The layout is still in need of some improvement, but things are getting better. A brand-new building now houses the sundries and a healthy collection of indoor plants, and there are stands for gardening books and seeds. Larger items of gardening equipment are sold such as sheds and paving but no greenhouses. A good range of cheap plants is usually stocked, allowing for seasonal shortages. Conifers, particularly the dwarf varieties, heathers and alpines were found in profusion the day our inspector visited. There were also some unusual shrubs. All were in excellent condition, well tended and cared for. Labels are generally poor and you have to stoop and contort yourself in order to read a lot of them – but this is not so true for the heathers and alpines which are displayed on raised beds. The husband-and-wife team are always in attendance and they are most helpful and knowledgeable, and will cheerfully advise on any horticultural problems.

Prices ££
Facilities Parking, 100 cars. Toilets. Restaurant and cafeteria. Play area. Garden advice service. Delivery service
Open Every day 10am to 6pm (closes at dusk in winter). Closed Christmas and Boxing Day and New Year's Day
Credit card Visa

CONGLETON Cheshire

map 2

Astbury Meadow Garden Centre

Newcastle Road, Congleton
CW12 4RL

Tel Congleton (026 02) 6466

2½ miles south of Congleton on the A34 Congleton to Newcastle road

This is a centre of above-average standard, stocking a comprehensive range of plants and sundries. The layout is based on a grid-iron pattern with excellent paved or gravel paths – it is easy to follow and well signposted. Labelling is variable – good for the plant groups, but unhelpful on individual plants except for climbers and fruit trees. The range of goods in stock is excellent for the size of the centre – almost too much choice! Within the plant section, most types of plants are available but, because of the restricted space, there is little of any one thing and the tendency is towards overcrowding. Plant quality was variable when our inspector visited – very good for ornamental and fruit trees and shrubs, but poor for the herbs, roses and houseplants, with the rest of the stock somewhere in the middle – a lot of this could have been due to end-of-season weariness though. The variety of garden accessories is also most impressive. Shelves are packed with books and tools, chemicals and electrical appliances. Furniture, artificial flowers, barbecue equipment and fish tanks fill up the floor space. Even the larger items such as garden buildings and paving are stocked. Again, the result is that it is rather too crowded for convenient inspection. Helpful and courteous staff are on hand, and the atmosphere is friendly and leisurely. Little Moreton Hall, a lovely Tudor house owned by the National Trust, is nearby and worth sparing time to visit after shopping at the centre.

Prices ££££
Facilities Parking, 250 cars. Toilets. Delivery service
Open Every day 9am to 6pm (closes 5pm in winter). Closed Christmas and Boxing Day and New Year's Day
Credit cards Access, American Express, Diners Club, Visa

COPTHORNE W. Sussex

map 5

Snowhill Plant Centre

Snowhill Lane, Copthorne, Crawley
RH10 3EY

Tel Copthorne (0342) 712545

Just off the B2037 (easily seen from the road) at its junction with the B2028

This centre has only been going a couple of years under the present ownership and facilities are still sparse. But on the whole it seems to be running very smoothly. The emphasis here is on plants, though a reasonable range of tools and sundries is stocked including chemicals and composts as well as larger items such as sheds, paving, garden furniture and ornaments and pond equipment. When our inspector visited, the range of plants was reasonable and of very good quality. The conifers were the most impressive and the rhododendrons, situated in their own shaded area, also rated very highly. There are some unusual houseplants kept in the greenhouse and some excellent-quality hanging basket plants. Several acres have just been planted with strawberries and summer 1985 will see the first 'pick-your-own' crop. When inspected, group labelling of plants was not comprehensive but the standard was generally acceptable and individual labels were good. If in doubt don't hesitate to ask the advice of the staff – they received high marks for friendliness and co-operation. The centre offers a landscaping service.

Prices £££
Facilities Parking, 45 cars. Toilets. Garden advice service. Delivery service. Free plant price lists
Open Mon to Sat 9am to 6pm (Fri opens 9.30am), Sun 10am to 6pm (closes 5pm every day in winter)
Credit cards Access, American Express, Diners Club, Visa

COSTESSEY Norfolk   map 4
Pettitts Garden Centre

Townhouse Road, Costessey,   *Tel* Norwich (0603) 742535/744900
Norwich NR8 5BU
In the village of Costessey, 1 mile north of the A47, 5 miles west of Norwich

Definitely a place to be visited by the houseplant enthusiast, for this is where the centre excels. All the plants are grown at the adjacent nursery and the selection and quality are superb. But the centre also stocks a reasonable choice of most popular outdoor plants, though roses and herbs were rather scanty when our inspector visited. The heathers and conifers are of good quality, and the rest of the stock is also reasonable. Most plants are clearly, correctly and informatively labelled, but not always priced. (The centre tells us labelling and pricing have both been improved since our inspector visited.) The grounds are quite small so the layout has had to be compact with no space available for demonstrations or displays. All the outdoor areas are fully paved and the general impression is of a neatly arranged, tidily kept site. The gardening accessories section is small; there are no greenhouses, sheds, fencing, or items such as water-gardening equipment; however, the range of composts and chemicals is very good and a handy feature is that you can buy fertiliser by the pound weight instead of pre-packaged. Future plans include the extension of the sales area and a cutting down on wholesale trade in favour of developing the garden centre. The friendly staff are eager to be of assistance.

Prices £££
Facilities Parking, 60 cars. Toilets. Vending machines. Garden advice service. Delivery service
Open Every day 9am to 5.30pm
Credit cards Access, Visa

Prices vary a lot at garden centres and nurseries. We've calculated a basket price for plants and given ratings from £ to £££££ – very cheap to very expensive.

CRAMLINGTON Northumberland map 2

Cramlington Garden Centre

Station Road, Beaconhill,   *Tel* Cramlington (0670) 733762
Cramlington NE23 8BJ
On the A1068 at the junction of the Bedlington and Ashington roads, on the fringe of the Bassington industrial estate

This centre is situated on the edge of an industrial estate, but has been nicely landscaped and there are views on to open land to the south and west. There are some lovely, formally planted beds which are attractive to the eye and stimulate the imagination. However it is the excellent range of tools and sundries and not the quality of the plants which is the strength of this centre. Shelves are stocked with an extensive range of items for both home and garden. A gift section offers jams, pickles and toiletries, while for the more garden-minded almost anything in the line of tools and sundries is available. Chemicals and composts are sold, along with sheds, greenhouses, mowers and paving. There is even a tropical fish room containing an interesting display which will attract the children. At the time of our inspection the range and quality of the outdoor plants was a disappointment, with the trees and shrubs the best bet out of a fairly mediocre choice, but this varies seasonally. There are plans to further extend the tree and shrub area and to modify the checkout in order to ease customer flow. The indoor plants, on the other hand, are very good and there is quite a variety to choose from, including lots of ferns. The layout is sensible throughout; the alleyways and paths are wide, allowing easy access to all sections, but signposting is variable. Labelling also suffers from inconsistency. It is a pleasant centre to walk around and there are helpful and knowledgeable staff on hand to advise.

Prices £££
Facilities Parking, 400 cars. Toilets. Cafeteria. Play area. Garden advice service. Delivery service. Free price lists for sheds, greenhouses, fencing, pools, composts, trees and shrubs
Open Every day from 9am to 8pm (closes 5.30pm in winter)
Credit cards Access, Visa

CRANBORNE Dorset map 3

Cranborne Garden Centre

Cranborne, near Wimborne   *Tel* Cranborne (072 54) 248
On the B3078 north of Wimborne St. Giles

This centre may not suit the serious gardener, but if you are happy in a cosy but chaotic atmosphere then you may well enjoy a visit. Garden ornaments and statuary are a special feature, and some specially made for the centre and imported from Italy – birdbaths at £275, for example – but cheaper ornaments are stocked as well. The garden centre is found in the grounds of an old manor house which was King John's Hunting Lodge. A beautiful avenue of beech trees, wild gardens and yew hedges create a setting which is quite idyllic and makes up for many of the centre's shortcomings. The range of plants sold is generally good, depending on the season. There are some interesting shrubs and clematis to browse around and the choice of herbaceous perennials has recently improved. Plants are mainly well looked after, though at the time of our inspection some were pot-bound. Plant labels were variable and some plants had no labels at all, while other plants were often not in the correct place anyway. There's a small shed for fertilisers, pots and compost, and a large but rather cramped shop selling 'garden extras' and gifts. There's also a covered area for garden furniture. The cashier is pleasant and there are two qualified staff who can help with your queries.

Prices ££££
Facilities Parking, 150 cars. Toilets. Garden advice service. Delivery service
Open Mon to Sat 9am to 5pm, Sun 2pm to 5pm

CREDITON Devon   map 3

Crediton Garden Centre

Barnstaple Cross, Crediton EX17 2EP   *Tel* Crediton (036 32) 3110
Off the A377 about 5 miles from Crediton on the Barnstaple side

This centre is not that easy to find, but visitors will be rewarded for their perseverance, not least by the superb setting. Views overlooking hills and woodlands attract many 'regulars' who bring lunches and picnic by the site. Our inspector recommends this as a 'very good small garden centre'. It is indeed a small enterprise run by a son and father-in-law team. These two are most pleasant and will happily talk about gardens and gardening at some length – they also load up your car without being asked. There is a good selection of cheap plants kept in stock and they are in excellent condition with some particularly outstanding heathers and young seedling plants. Labelling is better than at many of the major centres: it contains concise detail and is easy to read. Tools and sundries of the smaller varieties are available, and sheds and fencing can be ordered as the centre acts as agent for a local manufacturer. The general arrangement of the site is very good – it has been well organised and nicely laid out. All paths are paved, providing a good surface for the disabled and elderly. The car park is quite small but adequate. This small and comprehensive centre offers a more friendly and personal atmosphere than some of the larger places, and it is well suited to serve the nearby countryside and towns.

Prices ££
Facilities Parking, 60 cars. Garden advice service. Delivery service
Open Mon to Sat 8am to 5pm, Sun 10am to 12.30pm, 2pm to 5pm. Closed 1 week at Christmas

CREWKERNE Somerset   map 3

Clapton Court Gardens and Plant Centre

Crewkerne TA18 8PT   *Tel* Crewkerne (0460) 73220
3 miles south of Crewkerne on the B3165 to Lyme Regis

Clapton Court Gardens is a very interesting and beautiful garden of some 10 acres, with both formal and woodland settings and many rare and unusual plants, shrubs and trees, including the largest ash tree in mainland Britain. The plant centre stocks many uncommon container plants, shrubs and alpines. In the glasshouse (open March to July) there is a specialist collection of several hundred varieties of pelargoniums and fuchsias. All the excellent and unusual plants make a wonderful array. They are expensive but of good quality and the layout is attractive with displays clearly arranged and labelled. No gardening accessories are stocked apart from a few ornaments and terracotta and Chinese pots. Although staff are not always in attendance, a vigorous shake of the handbell will bring someone out to help. Admission to the garden centre and glasshouse is free, but there is a charge of £1.20 for adults, 30p for children and £1 for senior citizens for entrance to the gardens. Special rates are given to coach parties, and meals are served by arrangement. Home-made cream teas are served on Sundays and bank holidays and most weekdays from April to September.

Prices ££££££
Facilities Parking, unlimited. Toilets. Tea room. Garden advice service. Catalogue for plants and shrubs, fuchsias and pelargoniums 65p including p&p (one section only 36p)
Open Mon to Fri 10am to 5pm, Sun 2pm to 5pm. Closed Sat, except in May and Easter Sat (open 2pm to 5pm)

CROCKERTON Wiltshire   map 3

Lakeside Garden Centre   ✐ ♿ ★

Crockerton Shopping Centre,   *Tel* Warminster (0985) 217413
Crockerton, Warminster BA12 8AP
On the A350 Shaftesbury road, about 2 miles south of Warminster

Lakeside Garden Centre is part of the Crockerton Shopping Centre, a complex which comprises a cash and carry warehouse, furniture showroom and post office as well as the garden centre. Good signposting on the main road marks out the way to the site, and the setting is really rather beautiful. An old gravel pit has been converted into a lake, behind which is a sweep of tree-lined hills. Ducks, geese and other wildlife gather round the water and if any members of your party are not keen on gardening, a walk by the lake is most enjoyable. For the gardening enthusiasts, a large outside area is devoted to a good general range of plants and trees. This section is very nicely laid out with wide, tarmac paths. A useful feature is a small shelter half way round to offer protection in case of a cloudburst. Although the signposts are few, the landscaping of the site makes it easy to spot most areas. The stock of shrubs and conifers is particularly good, and under cover the large specimen houseplants and standard fuchsias are plentiful. Everything is of very good quality, but quite expensive. Many of the plants are grown by Scotts Nurseries of Merriott in Somerset, a closely associated nursery. Labelling varies, depending on the supplier, but it is generally quite satisfactory, with only those on the 'slow moving' plants suffering from fading. As far as the tools and sundries are concerned, the range here includes almost anything the standard garden might need. Sheds and greenhouses are available to order and for bargain hunters there are some second-hand items for sale, such as plastic containers adapted for use as water butts. Only the cashier and one gardener were visible at the time of our inspection. Trolleys are provided to assist in carrying goods.

Prices £££££
Facilities Parking, 400 cars. Toilets. Vending machines. Garden advice service. Delivery service. Free plant price list. Free loan of plant catalogue, 35p if retained
Open Mon to Sat 8.30am to 5pm (closes 8pm Thurs and Fri), Sun 10am to 5pm. Closed Christmas and Boxing Day
Credit cards Access, Visa

CROYDON Surrey   map 5
Thomas Butcher

60 Wickham Road, Shirley,   *Tel* 01-654 3720/4254
Croydon CR9 8AG
On the A232 from Croydon to West Wickham and Bromley, at Shirley, on the eastern outskirt of Croydon

This is not an outstanding find, but it provides a service to local Croydon residents by offering good-quality stock. Most standard plants are provided, although at the time of our visit the roses and fruit sections were awaiting an autumn restock. All container-grown stock is well watered and weed free, but when our inspector visited some plants were rather overgrown. The outdoor display area at the rear of the centre is attractive and the signposting is very good. Our inspector found that it can be a bit tricky to find what you are looking for, but the centre has now been reorganised so hopefully this problem has been solved. The labels for groups of plants are good and carry useful illustrations, but individual labels are sometimes patchy. A pleasant and well-laid-out indoor area contains a good range of houseplants and garden accessories – these include a wide variety of chemicals, composts, and hand tools. Fencing, furniture and ornaments are also on sale, but the larger power tools, garden buildings and paving are not available. Telephone enquiries are dealt with courteously and helpful information is forthcoming from both the staff and the supervisor. A comprehensive catalogue provides prices, descriptions and handy hints – worth picking up.

Prices ££££
Facilities Parking, 12 cars. Toilets. Garden advice service. Delivery service. Free price lists and catalogues for plants, seeds and corms
Open Mon to Sat 8am to 5.30pm
Credit cards Access, Visa

Garden centres and nurseries are changing fast. Practically all those we've included in the Guide *were planning improvements for 1985, so we need as much feedback as possible about the ones you visit to keep us up to date. Please use the report forms at the end of the book.*

DARLINGTON Durham

map 2

Elm Ridge Gardens

Coniscliffe Road,
Darlington DL3 8DH

Tel Darlington (0325) 462710

1 mile from Darlington town centre on the A67 to Barnard Castle

This is a centre which rates very highly in all respects. It is a moderate size and the site is divided between an excellent supply of sundries and a good choice of all sorts of plants. It has been very well laid out and clearly signposted with wide, well-built tarmac paths. The indoor area is spotless and stock is well displayed. Plants are expensive but quality is first class and the range is impressive, especially the choice of trees, shrubs and roses. Some are grown in the centre's own nursery. Every plant in the centre is labelled and group labels are large and informative. Indoors a large selection of houseplants includes some unusual specimens, such as airplants. A shop has recently opened on the site selling artificial flowers and other items for the flower arranger, and the centre is an Interflora agent so a good choice of cut flowers is also available. Staff are plentiful and are able to deal knowledgeably with your questions. They will also happily carry goods to the car if you need help. Once you have restocked the garden to your heart's content, it's worth taking a walk along the lovely River Tees, about ¼ mile away.

Prices £££££
Facilities Parking, 30 cars. Toilets. Ice creams and soft drinks. Garden advice service. Delivery service. Free plant price list
Open Mon to Sat 8am to 6.30pm (closes 5.30pm in winter)
Credit cards Access, Visa

DONCASTER S. Yorkshire

map 2

Pennells Garden Centre

Thorne Road, Doncaster DN2 5DX

Tel Doncaster (0302) 23460

Just north-east of Doncaster on the A18

'A pleasure to walk around', commented our inspector after visiting this most attractive centre. On arrival, one is struck immediately by the beautiful appearance of the site and the obvious care which has gone into setting it up. There is not one weed to be seen, nor any old boxes piled up in corners. Both inside and out the layout is straightforward and everything is tidy. Bold signposts direct you to appropriate areas and all the plants are arranged from A to Z making it easy to find what you want. Closer to hand, there are labels with illustrations and instructions on many of the plants. The range of plants is varied, offering a reasonable, all-round choice. Quality is high and the staff provide good plant care – they are very helpful altogether and will give advice with a smile, as well as being more than ready to assist with loading up the car. All aspects of garden care are catered for and the requisite equipment supplied. A separate area is turned over to sheds and greenhouses, while the smaller tools and sundries, along with houseplants, are nicely arranged under cover. Definitely worth a visit – a 'gardeners' garden centre', though plants are rather expensive.

Prices £££££
Facilities Parking, 100 cars. Toilets. Play area. Garden advice service
Open Mon to Sat 8.30am to 5.30pm. Sun and bank holidays 10am to 5.30pm. Closes 5pm in winter
Credit cards Access, Visa

DONNINGTON Berkshire   map 4
Sherrards

The Garden Centre, Wantage Road,   *Tel* Newbury (0635) 47845
Donnington, Newbury RG16 9BE
On the B4494 Newbury to Wantage Road, 2 miles north of Newbury, just north of Donnington

Recommended for its range of plants, particularly the very wide choice of herbaceous perennials. It is a medium-sized site and has been carefully laid out. Plants are arranged alphabetically, as well as being grouped according to soil requirements, for example, 'lime-hating deciduous shrubs'. There are no problems with over crowding and everything is generally in good order. The pathways are wide, but quite rough. The range of plants is good and apart from the comprehensive collection of herbaceous perennials it includes a good selection of conifers and unusual plants. The unusual plants are grown in the centre's own nursery and the centre offers a 'plant finding service' for anything which is not stocked. Unfortunately, plants are expensive and their condition varied at the time of inspection, possibly due to the drought: the conifers and deciduous shrubs were generally doing well but some other plants were suffering from lack of water. The labelling is a little patchy, some suffering from the usual problems of fading. Few gardening accessories are stocked, but there is a good range of seeds, chemicals and composts and a good choice of hand tools. (Sherrards are intending to decrease this side of the business in order to concentrate on plants.) There's also a small selection of houseplants. The staff are more than satisfactory at their jobs and most are skilled plantsmen.

Prices ££££££
Facilities Parking, 40 cars (plus 40 overflow). Toilets. Garden advice service. Delivery service. Plant catalogue £1.60 plus 60p p&p
Open Every day 9am to 5pm. Closed Christmas and Boxing Day
Credit cards Access, Visa

DORKING Surrey   map 5
Butchers Country Garden Centre

Reigate Road, Dorking RH4 1NT   *Tel* Dorking (0306) 884845
On the A25 between Reigate and Dorking, about 1 mile east of Dorking

The strength of this centre lies in its outstanding range of trees and shrubs, particularly the selection of grafted standards. There is also an excellent choice of water plants and a good selection of conifers. At the time of our visit the herbaceous perennials, alpines and soft fruits were rather limited, but this usually varies through the season. The trees and shrubs are well maintained, but again the alpines and perennials were felt to be suffering from end-of-season weariness. Illustrated and informative labels are generally provided, particularly on shrubs. Houseplants are all labelled with their names and these are on display in a large greenhouse area which they share with garden furniture. The overall range of tools and sundries is somewhat limited, excluding all power tools, water-gardening equipment and garden buildings. However, the choice of ornaments is quite good, and there is a small selection of fencing, hand tools and composts. The indoor show area is rather small and could do with some tidying up, but otherwise the centre is well laid out with attractive gardens and a large area devoted to the trees and shrubs. Staff can be elusive, but there are people available to help with car loading. A centre which caters well for the local neighbourhood, but which varies noticeably with the time of year.

Prices ££££
Facilities Parking, 30 cars. Toilets. Garden advice service. Free plant price list and catalogue
Open Every day 8am to 5.30pm (closes at 5pm and all day Sun in winter)
Credit cards Access, Visa

DURHAM Durham   map 2

Poplar Tree Nursery and Garden Centre

Hall Lane, Shincliffe, Durham DH1 2NP   *Tel* Durham (0385) 47553
In Shincliffe village just outside Durham City on the A177 Durham to Stockton-on-Tees road

Quite a small centre on the edge of an attractive country village, Poplar Tree offers a good range of plants and tools for its size. Most plants are bought in and almost all plant groups are represented in some form. There is a good selection of rockery plants and heathers as well as roses and conifers, and on the day of our inspection there were as many as six different varieties of blackcurrant bushes available. The small alpines, saxifrages and heathers are of good quality as are the trees and azaleas, and one of our inspectors was particularly impressed by the range of quality conifers. Houseplants and herbaceous perennials were looking rather lack-lustre when inspected, probably due to the prolonged hot weather. The overall labelling was variable – individual tags were generally faded with small lettering, but the group labelling was more legible and helpful and included illustrations. The general layout of the centre is quite good and paths are reasonably wide. The indoor area is kept tidy and has been neatly organised and can be pleasantly cool in summer. A good range of chemicals and hand tools is kept but there are no expensive tools or lawnmowers. A small selection of books and a choice of greenhouses, sheds, fencing and paving complete the picture. The centre is also an agent for Rolawn turf. Although there is some room for expansion and improvement, this centre still offers a wide range and friendly service.

77

Prices £££
Facilities Parking, 140 cars. Toilets. Vending machines and ice creams. Garden advice service. Delivery service. Free price lists for garden buildings
Open Mon to Sat 9.30am to 5.30pm (closes 5pm Sat), Sun 10am to 5pm

EARLS BARTON Northamptonshire
map 4

White Mills Garden Centre

Station Road, Earls Barton, *Tel* Northampton (0604) 810846
Northampton NN6 OPE
Off the main A45 ring road, on a side road to Grendon and Castle Ashby

The choice and quality of heavy duty garden machinery is a particular feature of this garden centre. A large separate area has a very good display of power tools, rotavators, trimmers and the like, which staff members will readily demonstrate. For those with slightly less ambitious plans there is a comprehensive line in hand tools as well. Most types of gardening equipment are sold. General sundries are found in the sizeable covered section, while greenhouses, sheds and similar items are kept outside. The layout shows an amount of foresight and most sections are easily visible from all areas. There are sometimes problems of overcrowding, but our inspector felt this was probably more a sign of satisfied customers returning than anything else. Plants are fresh and clean and, as well as an impressive collection of fruit trees, there is a good choice of roses and a fair selection of conifers and shrubs. Plants are sensibly organised and clearly identified by illustrated and informative labelling. The staff show enthusiasm and have a reasonable knowledge of their products.

Prices ££££
Facilities Parking, 250 cars. Toilets. Coffee shop. Play area. Garden advice service. Delivery service. Free price lists for various products. Plant catalogue 50p (refundable with purchases over £5)
Open Mon to Sat 9am to 5.30pm. Sun 10am to 5.30pm. Closed Christmas week
Credit cards Access, Visa

EASINGTON Durham
map 2

Easington Garden Centre

Thorpe Nurseries, Easington, *Tel* Easington (0783) 270430
Peterlee SR8 3UA
Off the A19 on the B1432 road into Easington, just north of Peterlee

This centre is situated on the outskirts of an urban area and caters very much for the DIY contingent of gardeners. In fact the range of sundries far exceeds garden needs and includes everything from clothes airers and fire grates to curtain track and roofing felt. Gardeners need not feel left out though because most of their requirements have been seen to as well. There are artificial flowers on sale and the range of hardwood garden furniture is worth investigating. Most larger items of gardening equipment are sold and a franchise for greenhouses and sheds is in the pipeline. The outdoor area is rather crowded and wider paths would be an advantage, but on the whole the plants have been well displayed and the weeds are kept at bay. The selection is somewhat limited by the space available; even so they have managed to supply quite a good range of quality plants – roses, dwarf conifers and flowering trees are the most numerous. The labelling is variable with individual tags often indistinct and group labels either well illustrated and clear or handprinted and difficult to decipher. The staff are readily available and well informed and happily put themselves out to help carry heavy items to the car. The area of the centre is to be increased shortly.

Prices ££££
Facilities Parking, 60 cars. Toilets. Vending machines. Play area. Garden advice service. Delivery service
Open Mon to Sat 8am to 5pm, Sun 9am to 12.30pm

EAST PECKHAM Kent
map 5

Brookside Nursery and Garden Centre

Seven Mile Lane, East Peckham, near Tonbridge TN12 5JG   *Tel* East Peckham (0622) 871250

Off the A20 at Wrotham, at the junction of Hale Street and Seven Mile Lane (B2016)

A well-stocked centre off a main road, but with a pleasant countryside atmosphere. The large car park allows quick, trouble-free access and the site itself is very well laid out and tidily kept. Smaller plants such as alpines and dwarf conifers are displayed on raised benches so that it is simple to find the variety you are looking for. The selection is wide with some lesser-known species adding a little spice to shopping. A good stock of shrub roses makes an added bonus for those customers with plans for a rose garden. All plants are well watered and weed-free and any specimens which don't make the standard are sent off to the bargain corner where you can chance your luck with a cheap purchase. It is nice to see a large range of traditional clay pots to choose from, and all the usual garden tools and sundries can be found apart from lawnmowers and power tools. The centre also stocks a very good range of greenhouses. The cashiers cannot provide much information but the manager is available to answer queries. The labelling on all plants is clearly printed and there are good, descriptive, handwritten labels to help out as well. A new sales area, extra car park and new toilets are planned for 1985.

Prices £££
Facilities Parking, 200 cars. Toilets. Vending machines. Play area. Garden advice service. Delivery service. Free price lists for roses, shrubs etc.
Open Mon to Fri 9am to 6pm (closes 5.30pm in winter), Sat and Sun 9am to 7pm (closes 6pm in winter). Closed Christmas and Boxing Day
Credit cards Access, Visa

Awards given this year are only provisional. We need plenty of feedback to let us know what the garden centres and nurseries are like all year round. Please use the report forms at the end of the book.

ECCLESHALL Staffordshire map 2

Fletchers Garden Centre

Bridge Farm, Stone Road, *Tel* Eccleshall (0257) 851057
Eccleshall ST21 6JY
On the A520 towards Stone, ¼ mile east of Eccleshall

The spacious layout, grassed avenues, well-equipped play area and picnic
site all make this centre a very good spot for an afternoon out. The excellent
and attractive site shows off an extensive range of stock in linear beds with
wide paths and lawns dividing them. There's a wide selection of plants,
especially among the small shrubs and conifers (eleven varieties of
cotoneaster, for example) though trees and larger shrubs are not so
numerous. All plants are of a very high quality and labelling is generally
very good. A large area is devoted to a display of greenhouses,
conservatories and sheds while a speciality of the house is the
water-gardening and fish exhibit. Ornaments, furniture and construction
materials are available, but there are no power tools in stock and only a
very small selection of hand tools. A garden furniture showroom is
planned. The sundries and houseplants are nicely organised in a small,
indoor area where there is no feeling of crowding. Children will enjoy the
aviaries and the pets corner with its wide range of animals. There is usually
a plantsman available to help customers, while a library of books and an
advice notice board are provided for self-service information.

Prices £££
Facilities Parking, 60 cars (plus overflow). Toilets. Vending machines. Garden advice
service. Delivery service
Open Every day 9am to 6pm (closes 5pm in winter)
Credit cards Access, Visa

EDWALTON Nottinghamshire map 2

Wheatcroft Garden Centre

Landmere Lane, Edwalton *Tel* Nottingham (0602) 216061
NG12 4DE
*At the junction of the A52 ring road and the A606 Nottingham to Loughborough
road, 3 miles south-east of Nottingham*

On high ground in open agricultural land lies Wheatcroft's, a centre well
known for its roses, which are grown in the surrounding fields. The centre
is a good place for a browse. The display areas are large, double
back-to-back beds with wide flagstone paths cutting between them. A 20ft
high roof of greenhouse shading keeps the plants cool on hot, sunny days.
Wide doors and level ground make it easy to push trolleys around, and
those in wheelchairs will also find access all round the centre easy. Sales
plots are set about 1ft above the ground and there are high notices at the
end of each section identifying the plants, some having colour illustrations
and details of plant habit. The labels on individual pots vary from those
carrying descriptions and pictures to others which are indecipherable tags

(the centre tells us these have since been replaced by computer-produced labels). Most types of plants are sold, but the choice of varieties is fairly limited (though improving), with the obvious exception of the roses. Overall quality is high. The indoor shop is large and extensively stocked. Sundries are well arranged and easy to find. There is a very good range of garden ornaments and furniture for sale but no paving and few power tools. A showcentre has been opened for greenhouses and sheds. The water gardening section has been discontinued. The information desk is worth a visit because there is a good chance of being offered a cup of tea while they track down the answer to your question. Staff are friendly and helpful, and the centre has a good reputation for being co-operative in replacing failed stock. There is a large play area and a pleasant picnic area. A new toilet block and cafeteria are to be opened in 1985.

Prices £££
Facilities Parking, 200 cars. Toilets. Play area. Garden advice service. Delivery service. Free catalogue and price list for roses
Open Every day 9am to 5.30pm (closes 4.30pm in winter)
Credit cards Access, Visa

ELMSTEAD MARKET Essex map 4
Unusual Plants

White Barn House, Elmstead Market, *Tel* Wivenhoe (020 622) 2007
Colchester CO7 7DB
Approximately 5 miles east of Colchester on the Clacton road

These large beautiful gardens are devoted to rare and unusual shrubs, trees and plants, and are bound to be a joy to any avid gardener. Not only can you wander through several acres of picturesque gardens, but you are invited to take a hamper with you and picnic with the family. This is a nursery, not a garden centre, so the concentration is on plants and there are no tools or sundries stocked. Unusual varieties are on offer and you will find things here which are not available at 'run-of-the-mill' centres; on the other hand you may have problems if you are only interested in popular plants. There is an excellent selection of Hostas. All plants and shrubs are of good appearance and they are nicely laid out with wide paths for access. Group and individual labelling is good and wooden labels are provided free for you to mark the name and variety of the plants you buy. The price list or catalogue is pretty essential, but gives you value for money. Advice is available on request from qualified members of staff. Car parking is adequate although it might get crowded at peak times.

Prices Information not available
Facilities Parking, 50 cars. Toilets. Vending machines. Plant catalogue £1, price list 20p
Open Mon to Sat 9am to 5pm (closes 4pm in winter). Closed for lunch 1pm to 1.30pm. Closed bank holidays and for 2 weeks over Christmas and New Year

---

 Establishments awarded with a flower symbol sell either a very good range of high-quality plants, or a more limited but particularly interesting selection.

EWELL Surrey

map 5

Seymours Garden and Leisure Centre/Seymours Garden Centre (Horticulture)

By-pass, Ewell KT17 1PS   *Tel* 01-393 0111 (Garden and Leisure)
or 01-394 1133 (Horticulture)

On the A240 Ewell bypass, 1 mile from Epsom

Our inspector described this as a 'gardening factory' which is very popular with people who want to buy everything in one fell swoop. The range of garden accessories supplied is faultless. Two businesses run by members of the same family co-exist on the same site and complement each other in the goods and services they offer. The Garden Centre (Horticulture) stocks gardening sundries such as hand tools, mowers and greenhouses, and also sells a wide range of quite expensive plants. The Garden and Leisure Centre, on the other hand, specialises in building materials including natural stone, turf and top soil, and also sells water-gardening equipment, garden furniture and barbecues. They run a garden construction service which includes the building and maintenance of swimming pools. During inclement weather you can browse round inside among the seasonal displays, for example of fuchsias, geraniums and petunias. Out of doors the range of common plants is absolutely huge and there are some more unusual specimens hidden away, for instance, a connoisseur's corner for alpines and a good range of evergreens. The condition of the plants is rather more variable. At the time of our inspector's visit the conifers and roses were particularly healthy, but the shrubs were only in fair shape and several deciduous trees showed signs of neglect and poor grafting. This might be the result of a slow turnover among the less popular varieties. Many of the plants are grown on site. The site has been reasonably well laid out with the plant sections arranged alphabetically, but the signposting could be a little more helpful and the information on individual plant labels is patchy. The indoor sections containing the houseplants and tools suffer from being overcrowded. The staff can be rather rushed on a weekend, but are generally quite helpful. This is a very large site with a huge range of goods, plants and services. Improvements are planned including the development of a new shop for the sale of mowers and garden machinery, and extension of the car park.

Prices £££££
Facilities Parking, 120 cars. Toilets. Restaurant. Garden advice service. Delivery service. Free newsheet and price lists covering paving, walling, fencing etc. Price lists and catalogues for plants and lawnmowers 10p and 20p
Open Garden and Leisure Centre, every day 8.30am to 5.30pm. Garden Centre (Horticulture), Mon to Sat 8am to 5.30pm, Sun 10am to 5pm, bank holidays 9am to 5.30pm. Closed Christmas and Boxing Day and New Year's Day
Credit cards Access, Visa

 Star awards are given to garden centres and nurseries which met with our inspector's whole-hearted approval.

EXETER Devon   map 3
Elmfield Nurseries

New North Road, Exeter EX4 4AH   *Tel* Exeter (0392) 74351
On the A3072, Tiverton to Crediton road, about ½ mile from Exeter city centre

This is a small nursery of interest to the keen gardener who is after plants of
outstanding quality. The layout consists of a series of glasshouses and
outdoor beds of chrysanthemums, one of the nurseries' specialities. Other
specialities include the production of spring and summer bedding plants,
geraniums, fuchsias and cyclamens. People come from all over to visit the
nurseries which are a great attraction particularly at weekends. The range
of plants available is limited but all are very healthy. The layout is neat and
tidy with most plants kept in the various greenhouses. Labelling is clear,
but it has been kept very simple so cultural or descriptive details are not
included – however, there are a small number of staff on the site and they
are friendly and helpful. The stock of sundries cannot compete with the
standard garden centres and there is little on offer apart from a small stock
of composts and chemicals. There is one aspect of the nursery which can be
a severe problem, particularly for the elderly and disabled, and that is its
position on a steeply sloping stretch of land. Facilities are limited, but cars
can be parked on the road fronting the nursery or across the way on a
side road.

Prices £££
Facilities Toilets. Free rose catalogue
Open Mon to Fri 8.30am to 5pm, Sat and Sun 9am to 4pm (closes 12 noon at
weekends in winter). Closed 1 week after Christmas

St. Bridget Nurseries

Old Rydon Lane, Exeter EX2 7JY   *Tel* Topsham (039 287) 3672/3/4
Main centre on the A38 between Middlemore and Countess Weir roundabouts;
second centre, Clyst-St-Mary, near Exeter, on the A3052 Exeter to Sidmouth road

The nurseries comprise two branches – the main centre on the rural
outskirts of Exeter and a smaller secondary centre 2 miles away in open
countryside. Both centres are well laid out and signposted and indoor areas
are clean, tidy and well stocked. Only plants, fish, building supplies and
greenhouses are supplied at the smaller centre, but there's a wide range of
other sundries at the main branch. At the main centre there is a very
extensive range of plants, especially roses, conifers and fruit trees, mostly
grown on their vast 200-acre nursery. The quantity of plants makes it
virtually impossible for every specimen to be kept in prime condition, but if
you make a careful selection you will not fail to find a very good-quality
plant. Large, clear signs designate each section, and group labels are
informative and well illustrated. Some individual labels are difficult to read
but you can get a useful catalogue on request which gives prices,
descriptions and general advice on planting, cultivation and pruning. Wide
level paths pass through rows of stone-edged bays and even in the
extensive outside area of growing fields it is not too difficult to find your
way around. Nicely organised in all respects with a helpful staff.

Prices £££
Facilities Parking, 150 cars (main site), 100 cars (second site). Toilets. Coffee shops and snacks (main centre), vending machines (second site). Play area. Free price list for plants, Handbook 75p
Open Mon to Sat 8am to 5pm, Sun 10am to 4.30pm. Closed for Christmas
Credit cards Access, Visa

FARNHAM Surrey map 5
Badshot Lea Garden Centre

Badshot Lea, near Farnham GU9 9JK   *Tel* Aldershot (0252) 333666
On the A324 mid way between Farnham and Aldershot, about 2 miles from Farnham

It is hard to fault the quantity of stock at this centre. Apart from non-gardening items such as jams and an exceptional range of dried and silk flowers, there is a wide range of hardware which includes ponds, greenhouses and machinery (with a workshop for repairs). The choice of plants is equally impressive and they are kept in a healthy condition. There is a separate area housing a mass of indoor plants – a very helpful assistant is on hand with hints on care. A nice touch is the sale of moss at 90p a carrier bag full. There are some landscaped areas for displays and the layout is generally good. Signposting has been improved since our last visit and now consists of well-marked sections, as well as a large 'You are here' board showing the overall plan of the site. Two attractively presented stalls at the entrance sell vegetables. The young staff are extremely helpful.

Prices £££
Facilities Parking, 250 cars. Toilets. Vending machines. Play area. Garden advice service. Delivery service. Free price lists for plants and sundries. Plant catalogue 95p
Open Mon to Sat 9am to 5.30pm, Sun and bank holidays 9.30am to 5.30pm
Credit cards Access, Visa

Forest Lodge Garden Centre

Holt Pound, Farnham GU10 4LD   *Tel* Bentley (0420) 23275
On the A325 Farnham to Petersfield road, about 2 miles south of Farnham

In a wooded rural setting with easy access from the main road, this is a pleasingly landscaped site of about 6 acres. The centre sells no particularly rare plants but stocks practically everything else the keen gardener could want. It is spacious and well laid out with the stock attractively presented, and the paths are wide with good signposting. In addition to a good range of tools and gardening materials, you will find flower arranging accessories, equipment for barbecues and a large houseplant section. The furniture and 'outdoor living' areas are particularly good and fencing, paving and water gardening equipment are also sold. As far as plants go there is a reasonable overall selection, possibly with the exception of fruit which was thin on the ground at the time of our inspection. Our inspector tells us that the quality is always very good, as is the labelling. Staff are sometimes hard to find and, although friendly and helpful, cannot always answer your gardening queries. A very clean and attractive restaurant

provides food for those in need, and a pleasant patio area is made available
if you prefer to eat outside.

Prices ££££
Facilities Parking, 350 cars. Toilets. Restaurant. Delivery service
Open Mon to Sat 8.30am to 5.30pm, Sun 9am to 5.30pm. Closed Christmas and
Boxing Day and New Year's Day
Credit cards Access, Visa

FELBRIDGE E. Sussex   map 5
Cramphorn Garden Centre

Copthorne Road, Felbridge,   *Tel* East Grinstead (0342) 28881
East Grinstead RH19 2PD
On the A264 2 miles north-west of East Grinstead

A large centre in a semi rural setting offering a good range of plants and
sundries at very reasonable prices. The outside area has a well laid out
plant section, with shrubs and trees arranged alphabetically and separate
sections for conifers and other plant groups. A formal, decorative pool
makes an eye-catching display and all sorts of garden ornaments are on
show leaving you spoilt for choice. A separate yard contains paving and
composts. A huge indoor shopping area houses all types of sundries
and a small selection of houseplants. Lots of different propagators of
all shapes and sizes are stocked and the unusual garden gadgets are fun to
look through, but there is a rather limited range of mowers and power
tools. The plants stocked range from an excellent choice of conifers and
wisterias to many more unusual species. They are generally well grown
and nicely cared for. Labels are informative, but when our inspector visited
some were suffering from the common problem of sun-stroke and were
hardly readable. Staff are ready with advice and assistance, but it would be
an improvement if they had some distinctive clothing to make them easier
to find. Information leaflets are available. Dogs are allowed into the centre
on a lead which is an advantage for dog owners because there is no shade
in the car park.

Prices ££££
Facilities Parking,100 cars. Toilets. Ice creams sold in spring and summer. Garden
advice service. Delivery service. Handbook on plants and general information, £1.95
(contains 4 x £1 vouchers)
Open Mon to Sat 8.30am to 5.30pm, Sun 9am to 6pm (closes 5pm Sun in winter).
Closed Christmas and Boxing Day
Credit cards Access, Visa

FERNDOWN Dorset   map 3
Haskins Garden Centre

Ringwood Road, Tricketts Cross,   *Tel* Ferndown (0202) 872282
Ferndown BH22 9AL
On the A31 between Ferndown and Ringwood, about 1 mile east of Ferndown

A very large centre indeed, well laid out with bold signposting and arches and seating dotted among the attractive display beds. Paths are level but could do with being a little wider to avoid trolley-jams at peak times. This centre is known locally as a good place to visit on a Sunday afternoon so it can get very crowded (the planned new entrance and checkout may alleviate this somewhat). The indoor site sells most of the gardening sundries the average enthusiast could want, including a good selection of pond liners and water-gardening materials and an impressive selection of artificial flowers. There is one whole area devoted to houseplants (soon to be enlarged) and another to cold-water fish (sold from April to September). If you are looking for the larger accessories there is a good selection of greenhouses, sheds and garages at one end of the site, but there are no lawnmowers or power tools stocked. A swimming pool department is to be introduced in the near future. You will find more than just the run-of-mill plants here, such as a good display of high-quality water plants and an interesting collection of airplants. The conifer section is very comprehensive. Plants are quite expensive, but are very good indeed. Plant labels are good and instructive, and in most cases plants are individually priced. Staff are very helpful, some specialising in the sundries area and others being knowledgeable plantsmen. They will readily order anything not found in stock. At Christmas this centre has its own Father Christmas and the best display of decorations in the area.

Prices £££££
Facilities Parking, 300 cars. Toilets. Cafeteria. Garden advice service. Delivery service.
Open Every day 9am to 5.30pm (Wed closes 8pm, Sun opens 10am). Closes at 5.30pm every day in winter
Credit cards Access, Visa

FERRING W. Sussex   map 5

Worthing Garden Centre (incorporating Langmead's Farm Shop)

Littlehampton Road, Ferring,   *Tel* Worthing (0903) 42003
near Worthing BN12 6PW
On the north side of the A259 Littlehampton road

Access from either side of the dual carriageway to this garden-centre-cum-farm-shop is quite easy with the help of a slip road. Langmead's has been expanding over the last few years and offers a good, efficient service. There are numerous friendly staff who will put themselves to any task. The popular shop sells a large range of fruit and vegetables as well as the plants, seeds and sundries typical of most centres. Plenty of good-sized trolleys are available, in addition to the boxes and bags provided so that customers can choose and weigh up their own fruit and vegetables. The shop is very spacious and everything is well displayed. The sundries stocked include a small number of hand tools and ornaments and a large variety of garden chemicals and composts. The greenhouses and bedding areas are at the back of the shop and the range of plants displayed here is quite comprehensive, including a good selection of trees, shrubs, fruits, climbers and the smaller alpines and heathers. They all look healthy and show signs of being well cared for. Labelling is clear and often contains helpful hints. The centre has recently been taken over by new management, and extensive changes are planned including a new cafe and play area.

Prices Information not available
Facilities Parking, 200 cars. Toilets. Garden advice service. Delivery service. Plant catalogue 99p
Open Every day 8.30am to 6pm (closes 5.30pm in winter). Closed Christmas and Boxing Day
Credit cards Access, Visa

FINDERN Derbyshire   map 2

Oakdale Nurseries

84 Burton Road, Findern, Derby DE6 6BE   *Tel* Derby (0332) 514268
Just off the A38 Derby to Burton road, 4½ miles from Derby

A centre which would keep the average gardener content, but would probably leave the specialist wanting. This is a medium-sized establishment with an extensive indoor area, the older part of which can sometimes get overcrowded. Outside, the layout is good with wide paths and an attractive display. Signposting both indoors and out was rather lacking when our inspector visited, though the nursery tells us this has been improved. The plant groups have informative labels, some illustrated, and plants themselves are labelled individually and arranged in alphabetical order. A good range of sundries is on offer including larger items such as sheds, greenhouses and fencing, but not paving. The variety of plants available is adequate, particularly the range of alpines, herbs, conifers and aquatics, and the quality is generally fine. Many plants are grown at the nursery. For the flower arranger there is a good supply of the requisite materials and at Christmas they put up an excellent display of accessories for floral art and decorations. Floral arrangements and sprays are made up to order, and tubs, troughs and hanging baskets are also made up in season. The staff give useful advice on request and the nursery gives talks to local organisations.

Prices £££
Facilities Parking, 150 cars. Toilets. Cafeteria. Garden planning and advice service. Delivery service. Free plant price list. Free sundries catalogue
Open Mon to Sat 9am to 6pm (5.30pm in winter), Thurs closes at 8pm, Sun 9.30am to 6pm. Closed Christmas and Boxing Day
Credit cards Access, Visa

FISHER'S POND Hampshire   map 4

Foulis Court Nursery

Fisher's Pond, Eastleigh SO5 7HG   *Tel* Eastleigh (0703) 695162
Just south of Colden Common opposite Fisher's Pond Inn, on the A333 between Winchester and Fair Oak

A well-laid-out nursery specialising in herbaceous perennials and alpines – most are grown on site and the selection offered is extremely comprehensive, including some unusual varieties. There is also a range of other plants all of a consistently high quality. The large outside area is laid out in beds devoted primarily to the perennials and alpines, and the beautiful gardens which circle this nursery give a marvellous idea of how the different species and varieties look in certain plantings and arrangements. There are also several displays which show plants in their suitable environments such as a 'shade' display house and a delightful water garden area which is presently being improved. There is a very definite 'family' atmosphere at this nursery, with staff quietly working away in corners, but always alert to customers' needs. It does not have the bustle of the big garden centres, offering nothing in the way of accessories apart fom a few pieces of garden furniture. The centre operates a landscaping business and garden consultancy service. A small covered area houses the pay desk and a seeds sale area. Altogether a pleasure to visit.

Prices £££
Facilities Parking, 70 cars. Toilets. Play area. Garden advice service. Delivery service. Free plant price list and catalogue. Plants are sold by mail order
Open Every day 10am to 5.30pm. Closed during the Chelsea Flower Show and one week in Nov for stocktaking

---

FLOWTON Suffolk   map 4
Little Park Nursery

Flowton, near Ipswich IP5 4LN   *Tel* Offton (047 333) 334
About 2½ miles west of the A1100 at Bramford; follow the Flowton sign via Tye Lane and turn right by Flowton church

This family enterprise is set deep in rural Suffolk and yet only 5 miles from Ipswich. It is a small centre and the personal supervision offered by the proprietor gives it that added friendly atmosphere. The owners are new and have plans for expansion and extensions, but they already have a good, wide selection of conifers and deciduous trees as well as most other plants (houseplants are only stocked occasionally), and the small shop sells a good supply of garden sundries. Most types of gardening equipment are stocked, even larger items such as greenhouses, car ports, sheds and conservatories, but no fencing or paving. A display of tubs is neatly set out in the car port. The site is well laid out on level ground, and gravel or shingle have been used to surface the paths. The plants are arranged aesthetically rather than alphabetically – you may have to hunt for what you want, but the proprietor explained that this was an attempt to give examples of colour arrangements and contrasting leaf textures.

Prices £££
Facilities Parking, 30 cars. Toilets. Garden advice service. Delivery service. Free plant catalogue and price list
Open Tues to Sun 9.30am to 5.30pm (closes 4.30pm in winter)

If you're travelling a long distance to visit a garden centre or nursery, telephone first to check the opening hours. They may vary with the season and weather conditions.

FOULRIDGE Lancashire — map 2
Lakeside Garden Centre

Skipton Road, Foulridge,   *Tel* Colne (0282) 865650
near Colne BB8 7NN
Just outside Colne on the A56 towards Skipton

Attractive shrubberies and mature trees surround this centre, which is set
on a sloping site overlooking Lake Burwain and the historic Pendle Hill.
The centre buys in most of its plants and the range is fairly standard with
no marvellous surprises. The plants are generally kept in a satisfactory
condition, though their quality varies with the length of time they have
been on site. The overall layout of the centre is quite reasonable and shows
definite signs of improvement in progress. Trees and shrubs are arranged
alphabetically, so it's easy to find what you want. Labelling is quite clear,
but rather basic and it offers little in terms of instructions. Expansion is
taking place at the moment, but the tools and sundries section is as yet
limited to chemicals, composts, hand tools, a bit of furniture, ornaments
and paving. Staff are very helpful and offer plenty of assistance. There are
reasonable facilities available and if the plans for expansion go well, this
centre could realise a good potential.

Prices £££
Facilities Parking, 60 cars. Toilets. Light refreshments. Play area. Garden advice
service. Delivery service. Free catalogues for roses, conifers, shrubs, fruit trees
Open Every day 9am to 6pm (closes 8pm Tues in May and June, closes 5pm every day
in winter). Closed 3 or 4 days at Christmas
Credit cards Access, Visa

FRENSHAM Surrey — map 5
Harpers Garden & Leisure Centre   ✿

Fernborder Ltd, The Reeds Road,   *Tel* Frensham (025 125) 3244
Frensham GU10 3BP
Off the A287 Farnham to Hindhead road, 3 miles south of Farnham

'This is more than just a selling place – it emphasises the pleasure of
gardening and garden ownership', commented our inspector after a visit to
this most attractive centre. One of the highlights is a woodland walk which
is like a beautifully laid-out arboretum and includes ponds and seating – an
enjoyable place to spend some of your time at Harpers. It is quite a large
centre and much of the stock is raised on site. The selection is good and
plants are maintained in excellent condition, particularly the trees, shrubs,
heathers and conifers. The centre specialises in large, specimen trees and
shrubs and it is developing a collection of unusual shrubs. An attractive
array of top-class houseplants might also be of interest. Plant labels are
reasonably good, although some show signs of weathering. The
ornamental pools, lovely lawns, good pathways and clear signposting
make it a joy to explore the centre, and you can leave the children in a
fenced-off play area with its Wendy and tree houses while you do your
shopping. When it comes to tools and sundries the range available is fairly

limited. There's lots of garden furniture, some lawnmowers and wheelbarrows, a bit of trellising and stakes, one brand of paving and stone walling and a limited collection of greenhouses. The centre has quite a small staff but they are pleasant and the new owners are obviously making a great effort to please their customers. The good choice of healthy and mature stock and the very attractive layout and surroundings go a long way to achieving that goal. Future plans include the introduction of aquatic plants and pond equipment in early 1985 and possibly an aviary, butterfly house and putting course. The tea, coffee and home-made cakes are an added bonus for peckish customers.

Prices ££££
Facilities Parking, 100 cars. Toilets. Restaurant. Play area. Garden advice service. Delivery service. Lists for roses, fruit trees, conifers and shrubs
Open Every day 9am to 6pm (closes 5pm in winter). Closed Christmas and Boxing Day and New Year's Day
Credit cards Access, Visa

FRESHFIELD Merseyside   map 2
Dixon Garden Centre

61 Gores Lane, Freshfield, Formby,   *Tel* Formby (07048) 75793
near Liverpool L37 3NU
In Freshfield about ¼ mile north of Formby and ½ mile off the A565 Liverpool to Southport road

Located in a suburban setting where 'every house has a garden', this centre provides a valuable service to the casual gardening shopper. It is a small place but has a surprisingly large range of tools and garden accessories. The limited space available has been put to good use and the layout is very good, allowing easy access to all the different areas. For those in the locality it is convenient to have somewhere within easy reach where you can find greenhouses, composts, sheds, fencing, and tools for sale or hire. The range of plants is also admirable – all the popular varieties are stocked, but there are obviously limitations on the selection. Many herbaceous perennials and bedding plants are available in the spring, as well as the centre's own-grown vegetable plants. The overall quality is generally quite acceptable. The labelling consists of good, clearly written labels for groups of plants and adequate individual tags. Staff always make themselves available and are very helpful. This is not a place for a family outing, nor can it really compete with the large commercial centres, but as a useful source of plants and garden bits and pieces for locals it rates very well.

Prices £££
Facilities Toilets (on request). Vending machines and ice cream. Garden advice service. Delivery service
Open Mon to Sat 9am to 5.30pm, Sun 10am to 5pm, in summer. Mon to Sat 9.30am to 5pm, Sun 10am to 4pm (closes Wed afternoon), in winter
Credit cards Access, Visa

Prices vary a lot at garden centres and nurseries. We've calculated a basket price for plants and given ratings from £ to ££££££ – very cheap to very expensive.

GARFORTH W. Yorkshire   map 2

Saville Brothers Garden Centre

Selby Road, Garforth, Leeds LS25 2AQ   *Tel* Leeds (0532) 862183
On the A63 Leeds to Selby road, 7 miles from Leeds

When the weather is not ideal for gardening, you could do worse than to plan a day's visit to this area and include a stop off at this centre. Temple Newsam House and Lotherton Hall, both of historic interest, are within 5 miles of Saville Brothers, and the centre itself offers a choice of gardening and allotment equipment to keep most gardeners content for hours. Water plants and fish are sold. The selection of greenhouses is reputedly the best in the north, and for flower arrangers there is a delightful collection of artificial flowers and grasses. There is plenty of room for browsing, and the area is well signposted. If you manage to arrive on a sunny day, picnic tables are set out and there is a counter service for refreshments. A miniature railway runs all around the centre both inside and out. The quality and selection of cheap plants for sale is generally very good. Bedding plants are grown on site. At the time of our inspector's visit the conifer section was excellent. Although most labelling was good, providing useful and legible information, the alpines let the side down but the centre tells us it is making large changes in this section. It is not a bright new modern centre but has a lot to interest keen gardeners. The staff are generally friendly, though not all are knowledgeable.

Prices ££
Facilities Parking, 400 cars. Toilets. Restaurant and cafeteria. Play area. Garden advice service. Delivery service
Open Every day 9am to 6pm (closes 5pm in winter)
Credit cards Access, Visa

GLAZEBURY Lancashire   map 2

Bents Nurseries and Garden Centre ★

Warrington Road, Glazebury, Leigh   *Tel* Leigh (0942) 671028
WA3 5NT
On the A574 about ¼ mile from the junction with the A580 Manchester to Liverpool road

In a pleasant rural area with 'plenty of good pubs around' this centre is easily found and well worth a visit. Established as a nursery since 1939, it specialises in roses and shrubs. It is attractively laid out with plants arranged in blocks, and all sections are quickly spotted thanks to tall and distinctive signs. If you know just what you want and don't feel like browsing you can quickly find your area of interest without having to search through the stocks. The roses are a joy – there are massive stocks of good-quality bushes and standards – and alpines and trees are also represented. In fact most gardeners will find what they want here. Most plants are grown on site and are of very good quality. A superb display of fuchsias in hanging baskets made an eye-catching sight when our inspector visited. Labels are very good for the groups of taller plants, being

91

informative and prominent, but the smaller and individual plants are not so well labelled. There is a small lake with water birds on site which is a pleasant diversion from the task of shopping, and also a narrow-gauge railway for you to ride on. There are plans for extensive alterations to produce landscaped and demonstration areas, and to extend the play area and car park. Hand tools are sold and also most types of leisureware for the garden, from barbecues and gardening books to a fine choice of furniture. Fish and water gardening materials are housed in a separate building. There is a franchise offering greenhouses and home extensions, and others planned, for example, for landscaping, building materials and swimming pools. Staff are not pushy but they make sure customers are cared for. A modern coffee lounge offers light refreshments.

Prices ££££
Facilities Parking, 150 (plus overflow). Toilets. Coffee lounge. Play area. Garden advice service. Free plant price lists and catalogues
Open Mon to Fri, 8.30am to 6pm summer, 9am to 5.30pm winter. Sat and Sun 9.30am to 5pm. Closed Christmas and Boxing Day and New Year's Day
Credit cards Access, Visa

GODSTONE Surrey   map 5

Knights Garden Centre

Nags Hall Nursery, Oxted Road,   *Tel* Godstone (0883) 842275
Godstone RH8 8DB
On the A25 between Oxted and Godstone, 1 mile from Godstone

The words 'outstanding' and 'excellent' appeared throughout our inspector's report on this centre and it is easy to see why. Plants are expensive but the selection of trees and shrubs is most impressive with a wide variety of sizes and prices. The only obvious omission from the range of excellent-quality stock is water-plants and these can be bought at the associated centre at Woldingham. Any variety of plant not in stock will be ordered if requested. If you are more interested in plants for the house, there are some excellent and unusual ones on display and the centre runs a floristry business. The stock of sundries is not totally comprehensive, but there's a good range of most small accessories and a wide choice of barbecue equipment, greenhouse heaters, garden ornaments and netting. If you require fencing or aquatic equipment and fish, a visit to Woldingham is again called for. The centre has undergone some reconstruction in recent years and most of the original buildings have been replaced – the interconnecting covered areas, each devoted to a separate aspect of gardening, are now all very well laid out and clearly marked. Paths have been widened and relaid with various kinds of slab paving – even the car park sports a new, smooth tarmac surface. This thoughtful organisation extends to the labelling as well, which excels in quality and consistency. Clear notices distinguish the various plant groups which are arranged both alphabetically and in groups reflecting individual requirements, for example, clay soil, shade, chalk-lovers. Fruit trees are helpfully marked with explanations about pollination and necessary planting distances. If you are still puzzled, pick out anyone in green overalls and your queries will be honestly and competently dealt with. The atmosphere is business-like, but this doesn't undermine the relaxed and friendly attitude which prevails. Displays are constantly changing so there are always new and interesting things to see as well as the reliable backbone of stock.

Prices ££££££
Facilities Parking, 60 cars. Toilets. Garden advice service. Hardy plant and houseplant catalogue 95p
Open Mon to Sat 8am to 5.30pm (closes 5pm Sat in winter), Sun 9am to 12.30pm
Credit cards Access, Visa

GOSFORTH Cumbria   map 2
Walkmill Garden Centre   ✿

Gosforth
About ½ mile west of Gosforth on the road to Wasdale

Gosforth village boasts a lovely church and most common amenities – and now it has the additional attraction of this pleasant garden centre. Half an acre is taken up by a series of glasshouses in which the 'delicate' gloxinias, geraniums and begonias are kept while, outside, twice that area is given over to displays of the hardier plants and fields growing soft fruits. The fields yield sought after supplies of fresh gooseberries, raspberries, blackcurrants and strawberries. The range of plants sold by the nursery is comprehensive and the condition of the rhododendrons, azaleas and conifers can only be described as excellent. Herbs and ornamental trees and shrubs also deserve a special mention. The stock is well set out amidst wide pathways and a most attractive rockery has been built featuring a series of small waterfalls and pools. Our inspector found the labelling to be generally satisfactory – often informative and illustrated. A good selection of the smaller garden sundries is available, ranging from window boxes to thermometers, as well as a very good choice of packet seeds. The hand tool section is small. Staff are often kept busy picking fruit; nevertheless they are easy to find and will readily set aside their tasks to assist customers.

Prices ££££
Facilities Parking. Refreshments. Garden advice service
Open No details available

GREAT AMWELL Hertfordshire   map 4
Van Hage's Nurseries and Garden Centre

Anwell Hill, Great Amwell,   *Tel* Ware (0920) 870811
near Ware SG12 9RP
On the A1170 just south of Ware

A good, all-round centre offering wide selections and good quality. It can't come up to the standard of a full-scale nursery in its range of plants, but for most domestic gardeners the choice is ample. The centre specialises in bulbs and seeds and also stocks specimen ornamental and flowering trees. The trees and herbaceous perennials were in particularly large supply when our inspector visited and the condition of plants was generally good. Labelling is reasonably good and prices are cheap. Apart from the extensive outside area there is a spacious interior section which stocks a good choice of tools and sundries with an especially nice range of garden furniture. Paving, fencing, greenhouses and the like are set up outside. A new building is to be built to house tropical fish, tanks, pumps and other pond equipment, and there are plans to introduce water plants. The staff comprises numerous unskilled assistants who are kept busy watering and working at the tills, and a few knowledgeable staff who man the several information booths. In 1984 the centre began a series of gardening lectures and homecraft demonstrations. These last the whole day and are given by their own experts. Children have a choice of amusements. There is a mini-farm where they will see llamas, deer, goats and peacocks or they can try a journey on the mini-railway. Toilets are pretty basic.

Prices ££
Facilities Parking, 1,000 cars. Toilets. Cafeteria. Mini-farm and railway. Garden advice service. Delivery service. Free seed catalogue. Plant catalogue 95p
Open Every day 9am to 6pm (Fri closes 8pm). Closes 5.30pm in winter. Closed 25 to 30 Dec
Credit cards Access, Visa

GREAT GADDESDEN Hertfordshire   map 4
Broadwater Garden Centre

Broadwater Nurseries,   *Tel* Hemel Hempstead (0442) 64684
Gaddesden Lane, Great Gaddesden,
near Hemel Hempstead HP1 3BW
About 3½ miles north-east of Hemel Hempstead on the A4146

This is a neat and tidy place where you will find a good, general range of stock. It is situated in an area of natural beauty and is bordered on two sides by the River Gade. Of medium size, it has been well laid out, although there are no signposts at present to help you round. The indoor section for tools and sundries is small, but overcrowding is not a problem. The accessories sold don't include power tools and water-gardening equipment, but otherwise you will find most things. There's a small selection of hand tools, but a good choice of sheds (made by the centre), conservatories and greenhouses. There are no obvious omissions from the range of plants sold, and the selection of trees and shrubs is especially good. They are all of good quality. Labelling is satisfactory when it is there, but there are some parts where it is lacking. Our inspector found the staff friendly and willing to answer queries; however, they did not seem to be sure about some of the prices. The shop and houseplants areas are to be extended and will include a coffee bar. Worth dropping by if you are in the area and need a good, basic garden centre.

Prices ££££
Facilities Parking, 160 cars. Toilets. Garden advice service. Delivery service. Free price lists
Open Every day 9am to 6pm (closes 5pm in winter). Closed Christmas Day
Credit cards Access, Visa

GREAT TORRINGTON Devon   map 3
School Lane Nurseries

School Lane, Great Torrington   *Tel* Torrington (0805) 26270
EX38 7AJ
In Torrington, about 100 yds from the A386, 200 yds north-east of the town centre

This is a nursery which, in season, can provide a good service to the local
community. It concentrates more on plants than sundries, but there is a
shop in the town centre which deals with this side of the gardening market.
You will, however, find some paving, fencing, ornaments and furniture on
display, as well as the hand tools and composts one would expect. As a
small nursery, it is predominantly devoted to trees, shrubs, smaller plants
and houseplants. There is nothing of remarkable interest, but the range is
fairly wide and the choice of bedding plants and geraniums in season is
very good. Most plants are bought in, so stocks are sometimes sold out and
prices do have a tendency to fluctuate – because of this there are not many
prices marked, and in fact labelling generally could be improved. There are
very few staff, so it might be necessary to hunt someone out in order to get
assistance. Parking is available 25 yards down the road from the nursery in
a public car park. A useful, local nursery, but not worth travelling great
distances to visit.

Prices £££
Facilities Delivery service
Open Every day 8am to 5.30pm (closes 5pm in winter)
Credit card Visa

GREAT WARLEY Essex   map 4
Warley Rose Gardens

Warley Street, Great Warley,   *Tel* Brentwood (0277) 221966
Brentwood CM13 3JH
On the B186, 300 yds north of the intersection with the A127

For those gardeners with a liking for roses this centre is worth a visit – they
are specialist growers of roses, as well as other hardy nursery stock, and
they offer a good selection of all varieties. There is also a wide variety of
trees, shrubs and fruit bushes and a good range of water plants. The quality
of plants is high, though they are also quite expensive. The plants have
clearly written labels with helpful instructions and there is a labelled
demonstration bed at one end of the centre. Most tools and sundries are
available with the exception of power tools; sheds, fencing and
greenhouses are not on show but may be ordered. The range of water
gardening equipment and wooden garden furniture is particularly choice.
Overall the outside area is well marked and set out and although the indoor
section can be quite crowded, it is well organised. Rebuilding was
underway in late 1984. Raised beds were planned and sections containing
tools for the disabled and plants for the blind. The staff are friendly and
helpful and willingly transport goods to your car.

Prices £££££
Facilities Parking, 60 cars (plus 150 overflow). Soft drinks and confectionery. Garden advice and planning service. Delivery service. Price list and catalogue for hardy woody plants 20p, lists for some other plants free. Plants sold by mail order
Open Winter, Mon to Thurs 9am to 5pm, Fri and Sat 9am to 6pm. Summer, Mon, Wed and Thurs 9am to 5pm, Tues, Fri and Sat 9am to 7pm. Closed Sun
Credit cards Access, Visa

GREETLAND W. Yorkshire   map 2
Riverside Garden Centre

North Dean, Stainland Road,   *Tel* Elland (0422) 71011
Greetland, Halifax HX4 8AN
On the B6113, ½ mile from Elland centre

This is a fairly new centre, but it already boasts a good stock of plants (both outdoor and indoor) and sundries. Outside, the plants are all neatly laid out in sections on gravel beds. They are well looked after and the eye-level pictures carry instructions on how and when to plant. The selection of alpines was particularly impressive when our inspector visited, and they were easy to examine, being set out on raised beds. Generally the range of plants stocked is comprehensive, though the choice of trees is a little limited. In terms of tools and sundries, greenhouses and lawnmowers are the only major items not sold. The choice of ornamental tubs and pots, fish-ponds and tools is good. The interior section is nicely laid out, clean and shaded. A wide variety of houseplants is a bonus for enthusiasts and these are maintained in very good condition. Customers are invited to use a houseplant reference book if they want specific details, but the staff are very helpful themselves and obviously know what they sell. There is a play area nearby and the installation of a vending machine is planned.

Prices £££
Facilities Parking, 50 cars. Toilets. Garden advice service. Delivery service
Open Every day 8.30am to 8pm (closes 5.30pm in winter)
Credit cards Access, Visa

GRIMSBY Humberside   map 2
Pennell & Sons

Garden Centre, Humberston Road,   *Tel* Cleethorpes (0472) 694272
Grimsby DN36 4RW
On the A1031 on the fringe of the suburbs to the south of Grimsby

Tidy, well cared for and efficiently organised are the words which first come to mind on seeing this centre. The layout comprises paved pathways with plants arranged in clearly signposted, rectangular areas. The outside plot is not that large, however, so it can get congested when there are a lot of people with trolleys about. The covered area is sizeable and allows ease of access and ample room for a wide range of goods. All the paraphernalia for the DIY gardener is stocked, including a good range of tools with 'king-size' versions for the taller enthusiasts, and gardening clothes in the form of jerkins, anoraks and boots. The main emphasis out of doors is on the shrubs. All specimens are well watered and healthy looking. Plants are quite expensive, and their number can be quite low since fresh stock is brought in regularly from their nurseries. Group labelling is clear and generally carries illustrations and information. You need the catalogue to check on prices. Staff are also available to deal with problems.

Prices £££££
Facilities Parking, 75 cars. Toilets. Ice cream and confectionery. Play area. Garden advice service. Delivery service. Free price list for nursery stock, catalogue 20p
Open Mon to Sat 8.30am to 5.30pm, Sun and bank holidays 10am to 5.30pm. Closed 25 and 26 Dec and 1 Jan
Credit cards Access, Visa

GWENNAP Cornwall   map 3

Burncoose and South Down Nurseries

Burncoose, Gwennap,   *Tel* Stithians (0209) 861112
Redruth TR16 6BJ
On the A393 between Redruth and Falmouth, 3 miles from Redruth

This centre is the result of a merger between Caerhays Castle Gardens and South Down Nurseries and any keen gardener should have an enjoyable time browsing among the interesting varieties of plants on sale and visiting the famous gardens. The large site of 30 acres provides plenty of opportunity for exploration and a spring visit can be particularly rewarding as the shrubs and trees are at their best at this time of year. The nursery is giving the gardens a major facelift and doing some replanting so they are likely to get even better. Admission to the grounds is 50p, but you can just visit the nursery site, situated in the walled garden, if you prefer. Building works were in progress when our inspector visited and plans include a new car park, bigger sales area and an office, shop and refreshment facility. At the present there is a good layout comprising display beds around the walls and several polythene tunnels providing covered show areas. The paths are wide, but somewhat rough in places. The nursery specialises in 'new and rare' plants, and the range of camellias, azaleas, hebes and magnolias is excellent – all are cheap and in fine condition. Labels are not of such a high standard though, since they usually give only the name of a plant. However, there are a few display beds where plants are grouped according to their preferred habitat – windy, alpine, for example – and here the large labels supply some useful information. The proprietor is very knowledgeable and will undoubtedly give any additional help needed. This is not really a garden centre, the only sundries available being chemicals and composts – it is a place for plant-lovers, run by gardeners not salesmen, and if you are keen on great variety and interesting species, there is plenty on offer.

Prices ££
Facilities Parking, 40 cars. Toilets. Garden advice service. Delivery service. Free plant price list, plant catalogue 40p. Plants sold by mail order
Open Every day 9.30am to 5pm (closed 1pm to 2pm). Closed at Christmas

HANDCROSS W. Sussex map 5

Handcross Garden Centre

London Road, Handcross RH17 6BA *Tel* Handcross (0444) 400725
*On the A23 London to Brighton road, about one mile south of the village of
Handcross*

A large centre located on a busy dual carriageway, well signposted and
easy to find. The setting itself is rural and the centre is well laid out on
various levels (this could present a problem for the elderly or disabled).
You'll find virtually everything you need amongst the comprehensive
stocks of plants, tools and sundries. At the time of inspection there was a
particularly good selection of trees, including dwarf conifers, as well as lots
of good-quality indoor plants. Plants are rather expensive but good, with
few pot-bound specimens in evidence. Some very nice mature plants are
available, such as specimen Cupressus and Cedrus and 12ft Dracaena
palms. Labelling is quite good with most plants having a small price tag
and label, while each plant group is fronted by a picture and description of
the plant and its requirements. Signposting could be better. The centre
offers a good range of tools and sundries with a particularly large display of
sheds and greenhouses. A garden furniture showroom is planned. A large
selection of cold- and warm-water fish for the pond or tank is available and
should be of interest to most people if only to look at – certainly a good way
to keep the children amused. The aquatic area is expanding to include
plants, ponds, equipment and small mammals as well as fish. If you need
any advice with a difficult problem there is always one member of the staff
who should be able to help.

Prices £££££
Facilities Parking, 80 cars. Toilets. Ice cream and soft drinks (cafeteria planned). Play
area. Garden advice service. Delivery service. Price lists for some products, free plant
catalogue for customers making a large purchase
Open Every day, summer 9am to 6pm (closes 7.30pm Fri), winter 9am to 5.30pm.
Closed Christmas Day
Credit cards Access, Visa

HARDEN W. Yorkshire map 2

Sandy Banks Garden Centre

Wilsden Road, Harden, Bingley *Tel* Cullingworth (0535) 274653
BD16 1BL
At Harden ½ mile from the B6429 on the road to Wilsden, 2 miles south of Bingley

Amateur gardeners will find everything they need in an average season at
this centre. It is set in a quiet rural district with good access from the road
and a large parking area. There are three separate indoor areas which are
very clean, spacious and superbly laid out. Tools and sundries are to be
found in abundance, particularly barbecues. A few greenhouses and
numerous garden ornaments are kept outside. Sheds, fencing, paving,
garden furniture and ornaments are also sold. One section concentrates
entirely on water life, showing a wide range of pool liners and providing

advice specifically about water gardening. The fish are an impressive sight and cost from as little as 50p to as much as £80. Well-organised outside plots allow plenty of space to move round, and for relaxation there's a woodland walk. Groups of plants are labelled with pictures and cultural instructions. Individual labelling is also quite good, but some handwritten tags are unreadable. The trees are strong and healthy and the wide selection of conifers is in very good condition. On the whole a reasonable range of plants of good quality is stocked. It is pleasant to amble around the centre, and the staff are obliging but no pressure is put on you to buy. There is sometimes a queue at peak times. The centre is convenient to visit for those without transport as there is a bus stop directly outside.

Prices ££££
Facilities Parking, 120 cars. Toilets. Confectionery and cold drinks. Play area. Garden advice service. Delivery service
Open Every day 9am to 6pm (closes 5pm in winter)
Credit cards Access, Visa

HARESFIELD Gloucestershire
map 3

Haresfield Garden Centre

Bath Road, Haresfield, Stonehouse   *Tel* Gloucester (0452) 721081
GL10 3DP
Four miles south of Gloucester, adjacent to the M5 exit 12

The centre sells an especially good range of garden construction materials, conservatories, sheds and greenhouses, and also offers a garden building erection service. These items take up a lot of space but there is still room for a good selection of most common plants. Conifers take the pride of place and are of particularly good quality. Most of the trees and shrubs were also in satisfactory condition when our inspector visited, and were reasonably well labelled – group labels were informative, and plants were also individually labelled. One interesting feature was the selection of water-lilies on show. The layout of the outdoor section was very good and clearly signposted. Small pot plants are set out on raised beds so they may be easily examined and are less likely to be damaged. The centre does suffer from one common fault – a cramped interior where too much has been packed into too small a space, but the centre has been re-organising this area in order to reduce the problems. The stocks of tools is rather limited. The staff are friendly and helpful. A pleasant, fenced-in play area with swings and slides is provided for children.

Prices ££££
Facilities Parking, 80 cars (plus 100 overflow). Play area. Garden advice service. Delivery service. Price list for sundries 50p. Plant catalogue 50p. Leaflets for all buildings
Open Every day 9am to 6pm (closes 5pm in winter)
Credit cards Access, Visa

If you consider any entry to be incorrect, inadequate or misleading, you would be doing us and your fellow gardeners a service by letting us know. There are report forms at the end of the book.

HARKER Cumbria map 2

Border Garden Centre

Osborne Garden Centres, Harker,   *Tel* Rockliffe (022 874) 676
Carlisle CA6 4DS
Three miles north of Carlisle on the A7; ½ mile from Junction 44 on the M6

The tiny village of Harker lies in lovely rural surroundings and plays host to this sizeable centre. A large tarmac car park lies off the main road and there is direct access from here to the centre. Indoor plants are kept in greenhouses and a large covered area contains a section for chemicals and tools on one side, fencing, netting and the larger sundries on the other. For those who have major landscaping projects in mind, a small part of the centre is let to a company which sells, hires and repairs cultivators, large mowers, chainsaws and other machinery. A wide range of good-quality plants is on sale and all are well labelled with growing instructions included for plant groups. The staff are friendly but unobtrusive and readily answer queries or help with carrying purchases. A camping exhibition run by a separate business concern is adjacent to the centre, accessible directly from the car park.

Prices ££££
Facilities Parking, 50 cars. Toilets. Drinks and confectionery. Play area. Garden advice service. Delivery service. Free price lists for fencing, paving, fruit trees etc.
Open Mon to Sat 9am to 5.30pm. Sun 10am to 5pm (late night opening Thurs and Fri in summer). Closed Christmas and Boxing Day and New Year's Day
Credit cards Access, Visa

HARROGATE N. Yorkshire map 2

Harrogate Garden Centre

53 Grove Road, Harrogate HG1 5EP   *Tel* Harrogate (0423) 503386
Grove Road joins King's Road and the A59 Harrogate to Skipton road. The centre is near the fire station, opposite Grove Road station

A very useful centre for locals, particularly as it can be reached without a car. It is sited in an inner-suburban area of Harrogate and has rather restricted quarters as a result. However, the centre is being re-designed to make the best use of the limited space, and for a small, urban garden centre there are a lot of goods on offer. The shop contains a wide range of sundries with a particularly extensive stock of chemicals and composts. Larger items such as greenhouses and fencing, tubs, troughs and urns are also available and the staff will order power tools, pond equipment and sheds on request. The variety of plants stocked is also surprising for the size of the site. Bedding plants, alpines, herbaceous plants and shrubs are grown nearby on the centre's own nursery; the selection of alpines and herbaceous plants is particularly good. Planted troughs and hanging baskets are sold in season. Our inspector found the condition of the plants rather mixed. There were some good ones but also some tired old stock. However, the stocks of trees, shrubs and roses were renewed in October, after our inspector's visit. Qualified and helpful staff are available to answer your questions. Overall this is a good, local garden centre offering a personal service and carrying a wide range of stock in all seasons.

Prices £££
Facilities Garden advice service. Delivery service. Rose catalogue for reference
Open Mon, Tues, Thurs and Fri 9am to 5pm, Wed 1pm to 5pm, Sat 9am to 5.30pm, Sun 10am to 5pm Easter to August bank holiday only

Moorland Nurseries and Garden Centre

Maurice Wilson and Sons,   *Tel* Harrogate (0423) 866054
Forest Moor Road, Knaresborough,
near Harrogate HG5 8JY
Forest Moor Road joins the A661 and B6163. It is parallel to and 1 mile south of the A59 Harrogate to Knaresborough road

The policy of this centre is to stock plants only at the appropriate planting time and ruthlessly reduce prices at the end of each season to clear the way for new arrivals. Thus alpines and perennials appear in the spring, but are gone by high summer and heathers come in for the autumn season through to the spring. Many of the plants are grown on site and by disposing of plants through the use of the bargain basement and the bonfire, a very high quality of stock is maintained. The tall plants are given sheltered positions and the smaller plants are set out on raised beds. This ensures a healthy stock and good presentation. The layout is excellent – spacious and always neat and tidy. Shrubs and trees (including top fruit) are always in stock and although the range is limited it has been imaginatively chosen to offer some interest in all areas, plus the occasional delightful surprise. So if you are prepared to be a little versatile with your shopping list you will undoubtedly be rewarded. A good range of houseplants is also stocked and many of these are grown on the site. Hand tools, chemicals, composts, flower arranging accessories, and ornaments are the extent of sundries kept in store. A recent venture has been a water garden and fish section but this was very limited at the time of our inspection. Plans for the future involve extending this section as well as introducing a toilet block, additional parking space, a furniture section and an improved information desk. The staff are usually at work on the site but they can be summoned by the counter-bell and you will find them well informed. All-in-all an impressive plant centre with some very good bargains to be had during the frequent clearances of seasonal and damaged stock.

Prices Information not available
Facilities Parking, 35 cars. Garden advice service. Delivery service. Some price lists for selected lines
Open Every day 9am to 5pm. Opens 10am Sat and Sun from Nov to Feb. Closed 25 to 30 Dec

HARTFIELD E. Sussex   map 5
Perryhill Nurseries

Hartfield TN7 4JP   *Tel* Hartfield (089 277) 377
One mile north of Hartfield on the B2026

Perryhill Nurseries justifiably calls itself 'the plant centre for the discerning gardener'. This is a nursery in the true sense of the word, as almost all the plants are propagated on site and the emphasis is on the growth and sale of plants to the exclusion of all sundries. The selection is far wider than the average garden centre, though prices are rather expensive. A catalogue is available, but the centre warns customers that only small quantities of the rarer plants are available. The quality of plants is excellent, and the staff, being trained nurserymen, are most helpful and knowledgeable. The labelling is above average and the problem of faded labels at the end of the season was being dealt with when our inspector called. The layout is carefully planned with clear signposting, well-spaced plants at waist level and artistic arrangements of hothouse plants. Their specialisation in the growth of quality plants has led to very high standards and a remarkably wide range. To use the words of our inspector this is 'an exciting place to visit and a pleasure to any appreciative gardener'.

Prices £££££
Facilities Parking, 50 cars. Garden advice service. Delivery service. Plant price lists 5p to 10p. Plant catalogue 60p
Open Every day 9am to 5.15pm (closes 4.30pm in winter). Closed Christmas and Boxing Day and New Year's Day (depending on the weather)

HARTLEY WINTNEY Hampshire — map 4

Coach House Garden Centre

Hartley Wintney RG27 8HY   *Tel* Hartley Wintney (025 126) 2400
On the A30 between Hook and Hartley Wintney, 8 miles from Basingstoke

This is a large garden centre selling a reasonable range of plants including a good collection of heathers and alpines. The quality of plants is generally good and the majority are well labelled. Building materials, a large range of sheds and greenhouses, and even swimming pools (sold by a separate company on site) are stocked, and there's a heated area for houseplants. Access to the centre is quite difficult – it is off a dual carriageway and up a small track, but the owners are hoping to open up the entrance and extend the car park, which will greatly improve things. The centre itself is quite well set out, though all outside displays are on a slope which could prove problematic for those in wheelchairs. Extensive alterations to the layout are underway and additional features planned include a play area for children, a fishery section and a pet food and sundries department. A new covered area for peat and fencing is being built, and concrete paths laid. The indoor area is roomy and well set out, stocking houseplants, seeds and a reasonable range of tools and sundries, particularly garden chemicals. Staff are unobtrusive, but helpful if approached.

Prices ££££
Facilities Parking, 35 cars. Toilets. Vending machine. Garden advice service. Delivery service
Open Mon to Fri 8.30am to 5.30pm, Sat and Sun 9am to 5.30pm. Closed 3 days at Christmas
Credit cards Access, Visa

HASSOCKS W. Sussex   map 5
Straffords Garden Centre

Brighton Road, Hassocks BN6 9LX   *Tel* Hassocks (079 18) 5232
On the A273 Brighton road on the south side of Hassocks, 3 miles south of
Burgess Hill

A small garden centre set in pleasant countryside with lovely views of the
South Downs. It stocks an impressive line in seeds and a comprehensive
choice of composts and fertilisers. All small garden accessories are readily
available, the main omissions from the range of sundries being heavy
garden machinery, building materials and furniture. The ornaments,
greenhouses and sheds should be well able to meet demand. The centre
does not get congested but on our first inspection the displays were not
particularly well signposted or organised – a second visit showed great
improvements. Paths are wide, allowing wheelchairs and pushchairs
access to all plant areas as long as you keep one eye out for the kerbs.
Houseplants have patchy labelling, but all plants outside are fairly well
marked. The quality of plants is generally good, with the houseplants
looking in prime condition. Carnations, roses, fruit trees and other plants
are grown on the adjoining nursery, Allwoods. Honey from the local bee
farm is sold along with lemon cheese and marmalade. The staff are cheerful
and able to help out. This centre was in the process of being revamped
when inspected, and further improvements are planned.

Prices £££
Facilities Parking, 35 cars (plus 150 on nursery at weekends). Toilets. Garden advice
service. Delivery service. Price list for Allwoods carnations 10p. Free catalogue for
sheds and greenhouses
Open Every day 8.30am to 5.30pm in summer, 9am to 5pm in winter
Credit cards Access, Visa

HATHERSAGE Derbyshire   map 2
Riverside Garden Centre

Castleton Road, Hathersage   *Tel* Hope Valley (0433) 51435
S30 1AH
2 miles from Hathersage, on the A625 Hathersage to Castleton road

A very nice little garden centre, clean and well kept. It provides a good
service to the local neighbourhood and is still developing, but at the
moment is not perhaps worth a long journey unless you are planning an
outing in the beautiful Derbyshire countryside. The centre has been very
well organised and because of its size it is easy to see across the whole site
from any part of it. Nevertheless, there is also signposting to help you find
what you want and wide pathways to facilitate access. Plants are cheap;
individual specimens are very well labelled. All plants are kept free
from weeds and any litter is kept in abeyance. The stock of tools and
sundries is neatly assembled in a covered area, and although the range is
adequate for the centre there is nothing special. You will find the usual
stocks of chemicals, composts and hand tools, as well as a selection of

fencing, paving, furniture and some garden ornaments. Greenhouses, sheds, pond equipment and lawnmowers are all available to order. The plant stocks were rather low at the time of our inspector's visit, but there were some more unusual shrubs available and a reasonable range of dwarf and slow-growing conifers. The centre is undergoing refurbishment. Developments planned include a picnic area on the riverside, new display beds and a covered walkway from the car park. If you require any assistance there is a bell in the shop to summon staff, who you'll find friendly and helpful. The centre offers a landscaping and design service and also carries out garden maintenance and tree surgery.

Prices ££
Facilities Parking, 40 cars. Play area. Garden advice service. Delivery service. Plant catalogue 20p
Open Every day 8.45am to 6.30pm (closes 4.30pm in winter). Closed Christmas and Boxing Day
Credit cards Access, Visa

HEDDON-ON-THE-WALL Northumberland   map 2
Hall's of Heddon Nursery Centre   ✿

West Heddon Nurseries,   *Tel* Wylam (066 14) 2445
Heddon-on-the-Wall, Newcastle-upon-Tyne NE15 0JS
Off the B6318, about 8 miles west of Newcastle city centre. About 1 mile north-west of Heddon-on-the-Wall

Our inspector 'could have stayed all day' at this marvellous plantsman's nursery. It is run by Mr Hall and his family and retains a natural, true nursery atmosphere. It is not a fashionable garden centre and stocks no sundries other than chemicals and composts, but the plants are all in excellent condition and are beautifully kept. Most are pot-grown but certain items are available bare-rooted or rootballed in the dormant season. The trees and conifers are set out in frames, while shrubs, clematis and heathers are on raised brick stands with surfaces of moist, gritty cinders. The labelling is generally large and informative, and all pots have at least a name and price tag. The selection should satisfy both beginners and dedicated gardeners. At the time of our inspection the choice of dahlias, chrysanthemums, heathers and conifers was terrific. Some useful facilities are the phone-in order service which saves waiting, and the convenient collection point at their Newcastle shop if you are without transport. If the plant you want is out of stock the nursery will do their best to obtain it – either from their other nursery at Ovington (collection can be made from the more convenient of the two), or from elsewhere. The Ovington nursery specialises in alpines and herbaceous plants, with a selection of these being carried at Heddon. The owners are extremely kind and knowledgeable and staff are expected to help where they can. Chairs are willingly brought out for anyone who needs to sit down.

Prices £££
Facilities Parking, 25 cars. Toilets. Garden advice service. Delivery service. Free price lists, catalogue 15p

Open Mon to Fri 8am to 4.30pm, Sat and Sun 10am to 5pm (closes 4pm Sat and Sun in winter). Closed Christmas and Boxing Day and New Year's Day

HENLEY-ON-THAMES Oxfordshire   map 4
Toad Hall Garden Centre

Marlow Road,   *Tel* Henley-on-Thames (0491) 574615
Henley-on-Thames RG9 3AG
1 mile north-east of Henley-on-Thames, on the A4155 Marlow road

This is a centre offering a wide selection of plants of very good quality and size. It is located in a converted, walled garden in a pleasant rural setting. The centre also stocks a comprehensive range of garden accessories which includes the larger items such as sheds, greenhouses, fencing, paving, and even wood-burning stoves. New and second-hand machinery is a useful feature among the sundries, and a service section is also provided. Several large, indoor areas contain the houseplants and sundries. These sections are well signposted and the pathways are generally negotiable, except for the occasional blockage caused by overflowing stock. Outside, the displays are well laid out, and wide concrete paths and good signposting make it easy to find what you want. The outside section is given over mainly to plants, and they are all marked out with prominent group labels. Those for fruit trees and vines carry some particularly useful information. Polyanthus, impatiens and winter-flowering pansies are all grown on site and are a special feature along with a vast choice of hanging baskets. The staff are 'very willing to give advice – and the advice is good', reported our inspector. A centre which rated well and deserves a visit.

Prices £££
Facilities Parking, 235 cars. Toilets. Vending machines and ice cream. Play area. Garden advice service. Delivery service
Open Every day 9am to 5.30pm (closes 5pm in winter). Closed Christmas and Boxing Day
Credit cards Access, Visa

HERMITAGE Berkshire   map 4
Fairfield Nurseries and Garden Centre   ★

Hermitage, Newbury RG16 9TG   *Tel* Hermitage (0635) 200442
On the B4009, 4 miles north of Newbury. Take exit 13 off the M4 and follow signs northwards to Hermitage

A very large site with something of interest for everyone. Fairfield is known locally as a nursery – bedding plants and many geraniums and fuchsias are grown on site – but a considerable area is also devoted to paving, fencing, and garden buildings as well as non-gardening items such as camping equipment. There's a good range of chemicals, tools, ornaments and all the other gardening bits and bobs which just might come in handy, and an excellent fish section containing both tropical and cold-water species. The layout, indoors and out, has been well planned with wide paths dividing neat rectangular beds of container-grown plants. The range of plants is very good, particularly for dwarf conifers, and any plants not available can be ordered. In addition there is an intriguing collection of exotic greenhouse plants, including orchids in flower, attractively displayed and at a reasonable price. The quality of plants, tender and hardy, is generally very good. In addition they occasionally have some very good bargain offers. If you need any advice on plant cultivation, the staff are consistently polite and helpful and there's also a plant information centre. Fully recommended for its range of goods and services and the quality of its plants.

Prices ££££
Facilities Parking, 250 cars. Toilets. Vending machine. Play area. Garden advice service. Delivery service. Free information leaflets
Open Mon to Fri 9am to 5.30pm, Sat 9am to 5pm, Sun 10am to 5pm
Credit cards Access, Visa

HERSTMONCEUX E. Sussex   map 5

Lime Cross Nursery

Herstmonceux, Hailsham   *Tel* Herstmonceux (0323) 833229
BN27 4RS
Just east of Herstmonceux village, on the A271 Hailsham to Battle road

This 1½-acre site is devoted almost entirely to a select range of extremely healthy and well-maintained, container-grown plants. The nursery concentrates on a small range of plants, mainly heathers and conifers, particularly the slow-growing varieties. Trees and shrubs are also available and there are a few greenhouses filled with indoor plants, primarily cyclamen. Though the range is limited, what they do provide is done very well and the selection within each category is very impressive. Great care has been taken with the labelling which is large and clear and contains all the background information a customer would need to have success with any purchase. The site is very well organised, with wide gravel paths and large clear signposts, so it's very easy to get around and find what you want. Lime Cross sells few sundries other than peat, fertilisers and compost. Staff keep themselves busy working among the plants, but a ring on the bell will bring someone out to help. Not a comprehensive nursery, but well worth exploring if you are interested in the range they cover.

Prices ££££
Facilities Parking, 30 cars. Toilets. Garden advice service. Delivery service. Free plant catalogue
Open Every day 8.30am to 5pm

HEXHAM Northumberland   map 2

Tynedale Nursery Garden Centre   ✿

Alemouth Road, Hexham   *Tel* Hexham (0434) 602282/605137
NE46 3PJ
On the southern side of Hexham close to the A69 bypass, about 100yds from the town centre

This is a very popular centre which is often full, leading to some problems of congestion. However it is worth making the effort to see the great array of goods which they have managed to assemble in quite a small area. (If the car park is full try the main town one opposite.) A large glasshouse is devoted to a wide selection of good-quality houseplants – Easter, Christmas and other seasonal plants are particularly good. There is also a large tools and sundries section containing a full range of items. As a consequence the space left for plants is rather limited and cramped. Even so the site is well organised and clearly signposted. Most common plants are kept in stock and the overall quality is very good. The emphasis is on a very good range of conifers, both slow-growing and dwarf forms, imported from Holland. Individual labels will tell you the name and price, and plant areas are designated by large hanging signs. The staff are full of good advice both for plants or tools and sundries but one has to wait at busy times. Additional attractions are the pet shop and a small tea room.

Prices £££
Facilities Parking, 35 cars. Cafeteria
Open Every day 9am to 5pm
Credit card Visa

HITCHIN Hertfordshire   map 4
Grove Road Garden Centre

Grove Road, Hitchin SG5 1SE   *Tel* Hitchin (0462) 51519
On the north-east edge of town, ¾ mile from the centre, Grove Road leads off
Bancroft (the main street)

This small, open-air centre is found near the Catholic church in the town centre of Hitchin. It is obviously geared to the town dweller and offers limited but good-quality stock as well as facilities for ordering many things not kept on the premises. A small indoor area houses the checkout as well as some chemicals and hand tools. A new shop is planned. Other gardening equipment available includes furniture and ornaments, sheds, greenhouses, fencing and paving. The choice of plants is quite small and you certainly couldn't call it comprehensive, although the quality is very good and prices low, and the centre is very convenient for locals who have small, undemanding projects in mind. The site is easy to get around and all the plants are labelled and priced, but labels don't give you any instructions. The owner is knowledgeable and helpful and there are assistants to take heavy goods to the car. The centre also provides a landscaping and garden construction service.

Prices ££
Facilities Parking, 10 cars. Toilets. Garden advice service. Delivery service
Open Tues to Sat 9am to 5.30pm, Sun 9am to 1pm

Harkness Rose & Plant Centre

Cambridge Road, Hitchin SG4 0JT   *Tel* Hitchin (0462) 34027/34171
On the A505 midway between Hitchin and Letchworth town centres

This centre, set on a hill in rural surroundings, offers a treasure trove for the rose enthusiast. Harkness are rose specialists and there is one section of the centre entirely devoted to a rose display. The rose fields are open to visitors from July to September. However, for those interested in other plants a good selection of ornamental shrubs is also available as well as a choice of other plants. All plants are arranged on gravel beds and are well watered and of good quality. The owners have plans to double the plant area in the near future. Labelling and pricing is consistent, particularly for the roses, where details of features such as colour, height and fragrance are provided. The centre is of medium size and pathways are surfaced with concrete, making it easy to walk about. A warehouse is stocked with a variety of tools and accessories, but it is large enough not to suffer from over-crowding. Apart from a particularly good range of chemicals and seeds to look through, the selection of sheds and summerhouses is worth inspecting, but there are no greenhouses. This is a long-established, family business and at least one member of the family is on duty most of the time. Otherwise there are only a few staff but they are helpful. There is a camping centre adjacent which sells tents, trailers and caravans.

Prices £££
Facilities Parking, 300 cars. Toilets. Ice cream. Garden advice service. Delivery service. Free price list for roses. Plant catalogue 20p. Plants sold by mail order
Open Mon to Sat 9am to 5pm, Sun and bank holidays 10.30am to 5pm. Closed Christmas Day to New Year's Day
Credit cards Access, Visa

HOCKLEY HEATH W. Midlands   map 4
Pasture Croft Nurseries

Tithe Barn Lane, Hockley Heath,   *Tel* Earlswood (056 46) 2214
Solihull B94 5DJ
Between Tanworth-in-Arden and Earlswood, ¼ mile off the B4023

'Every single plant was in first-class condition – well watered, growing profusely and green, green, green' wrote our inspector after visiting these nurseries. This praise is partly offset by the limited range of plant stock available, though there's a good selection of conifers and a reasonable range of shrubs, as well as alpines, heathers and perennials. Bedding plants and hanging baskets are a speciality of the nursery and are produced in large quantities in season. The growing area comprises at least 5 acres and is set in open country. There are no chemicals or sundries offered for sale and attention is fully concentrated upon growing the stock. The outside display is excellent, with easy access to the entire site, but it is necessary to wander around to find where the different plants are. Those plants which are up for sale are well labelled. Several of the huge greenhouses and polythene tunnels which occupy part of the site are open to inspection by the public as is the private garden which shows clearly labelled mature specimens of most of the shrubs offered for sale. The nurseries tend to emphasise the growing rather than the selling side of the business, partly because of its out-of-the-way location, but the staff are cooperative and most helpful if customers do have any requests. Worth a trip if you are stocking up your garden and want good-quality plants but nothing out of the ordinary.

Prices £££
Facilities Parking, 10 cars. Toilets. Garden advice service. Delivery service. Free plant price list
Open Every day 9am to 7pm (closes at dusk in winter). Closed 12am to 2pm Sun

---

HOLKHAM Norfolk map 4

Holkham Gardens

Holkham Park, Wells-Next-The-Sea NR23 1AB   *Tel* Fakenham (0328) 710374

On the A149 near Wells-Next-The-Sea

The walled kitchen garden of the Earl of Leicester's Estate is the splendid setting for this beautiful nursery. The gardens were designed by Samuel Wyatt and built in the 1780s. They are a fine example of walled gardens of this period, and the ornamental borders are deserving of a visit even if you have no intention of buying anything. If you do want to make a purchase, the mature plants growing in the borders give a marvellous feel of what the plants could look like in your garden. There is a very wide range for sale and the quality is really excellent. Most are grown in the grounds from cuttings or seeds, and those which are bought in are grown on before being sold. It gives a delightful atmosphere to see all the old buildings of the 6-acre site being put to use today in propagating and distributing this collection of trees, shrubs and garden plants. There is no detailed labelling and plants carry a name tag only. The staff are very helpful and it is not unusual to overhear them advising customers not to buy yet, or that certain plants are not up to sale quality. They also give detailed advice on how to care for and treat all purchases. There is no gardening equipment sold here and no indoor area – even the pleasantly informal sales area is outside.

Prices £££
Facilities Parking, 100 cars. Toilets. Garden advice service
Open Mon to Sat 10am to 5pm (closes 1pm to 2pm), Sun 2pm to 5pm
Credit cards Access, Visa

HORNCASTLE Lincolnshire map 2

Crowder's Nurseries and Garden Centre

Lincoln Road, Horncastle LN9 5LZ   *Tel* Horncastle (06582) 7686
On the A158 Lincoln road 1 mile north of Horncastle town centre

This garden centre has been around for over 100 years and prospective customers used to be collected from Horncastle railway station in a horse and trap. Not quite the same story today, but the modernisation and expansion have been well thought out and the centre still provides a friendly service. It is situated in open countryside on the edge of the Lincolnshire Wolds and offers plenty of facilities and scope for a day out for all the family. The excellent, well-signposted layout comprises an outside area for plants, an adjacent area for items such as garden walling and pools, and several buildings housing a mass of tools and sundries. The show gardens are a popular attraction and there is also a pleasant courtyard used to display garden seating, tubs and pots and other patio items. Trees and shrubs are still the speciality here, and there is an excellent choice, most raised in their own nurseries. They are alphabetically arranged and carry distinctive yellow labels with photographs and explicit growing instructions. Other plants are also well represented, although sometimes a popular variety is missing. Quality appears to be very good. The easily identifiable staff are courteous and helpful and there is an information desk specifically for garden problems. The attractive coffee shop and adjoining health food store offer light meals and home-made cakes.

Prices ££££
Facilities Parking, 400 cars. Toilets. Restaurant and cafeteria. Play area. Garden advice service. Delivery service. Gardening Guide catalogue £1.50
Open Every day 8.30am to 5.30pm (opens 9am Sun). Closed Christmas, Boxing and New Year's Day
Credit cards Access, Visa

HORNINGSEA Cambridgeshire   map 4

Ansells Garden Centre

High Street, Horningsea,   *Tel* Cambridge (0223) 860320
Cambridge CB5 9JG
North-east of Cambridge on the B1705, 1 mile north of the A45

Ansells Garden Centre is pleasingly situated on the edge of the village of Horningsea. The outdoor area is large and the signposts and gravel paths make it easy to negotiate the displays of trees and shrubs. Large descriptions above the plants are also useful, and the centre is neat and well organised. All the standard plants are stocked here and are in good condition. They also have some of the lesser-known varieties – there were seven different varieties of grapevine on offer the day we inspected. Tropical fish, turtles and snakes enhance the water-gardening section which is separated off from the rest of the comprehensive equipment area. A wide selection of greenhouses are erected for you to browse around, and a good selection of garden ornaments offers a variety of statues, vases, tubs and the like. Overall the supply of tools and sundries is good with the one omission of power tools and lawnmowers. The staff are friendly and willing.

Prices ££££
Facilities Parking, 100 cars. Toilets. Vending machines. Garden advice service. Delivery service. Free plant price lists
Open Mon to Sat 8am to 5.30pm, Sun 9.30am to 5.30pm (closes at dusk every day in winter). Closed Christmas and Boxing Day
Credit cards Access, Visa

If we've missed out on a good garden centre or nursery, tell us. There are report forms at the end of the book.

HORSHAM W.Sussex   map 5
Howards Nursery Centre

Plummers Plain, Horsham   *Tel* Lower Beeding (040 376) 255
RH13 6HX

On the A279 south-east of Horsham about 3 miles west of Handcross

A wide main entrance and large car park make for easy access into this
centre from the main road. Our inspector thought the very good range of
fuchsias and large display of greenhouses were two features particularly
worthy of mention at Howards. A special service for greenhouse erection is
also provided by the firm. A reasonably large stock of containerised plants
should prove useful to many local shoppers – don't expect anything
remarkable though. Some plants such as geraniums, fuchsias, cyclamen
and shrubs are grown on site. The labelling is adequate and quality is
generally very good. The stocks of sundries include peat, fertilisers and
compost as well as paving, water-gardening equipment and some
furniture. The site is large and has some good, wide paths, but generally it
is inadequately signposted. (There are plans afoot to try to improve this.)
The indoor area, on the other hand, is first class. The proprietors are
usually available to help customers with problems and they will order items
not in stock if requested.

Prices ££££
Facilities Parking, 70 cars. Toilets. Play area. Garden advice service. Delivery service.
Free price lists for plants, paving, bulbs etc
Open Every day 8am to 6pm (closes 5.30pm except Fri in winter). Closed Christmas
and Boxing Day
Credit cards Access, Visa

Nightingale Garden Centre

Nightingale Road, Horsham   *Tel* Horsham (0403) 50441
RH12 2NW

*Just off Hurst Road (A281) in Nightingale Road, via Gladstone Road, about five
minutes' walk from Horsham station*

'This is a place for plant lovers, not for those who want a day out with the
kids and like to return home with a second-rate plant as evidence of a
happy day.' It is a small, urban nursery, very pleasantly located within an
old, walled garden. The site is secluded and sensibly adapted, and the
plants found here will give joy to all gardeners. The limited space places
certain restrictions on the stock: for instance, only a limited range of trees is
available. However, conifers, heathers and perennials are comprehensively
represented, and without exception the quality of all the plants is good.
The vigour of the plants is due, at least in part, to the vigilance of the staff
who keep a sharp look-out for pests and disease and spray regularly. An
irrigation system ensures a steady supply of water to the neatly arranged
rows of plants. Labelling is neat and informative and it is backed up by the
sound advice offered by the small number of staff. The site is kept clean
and ship-shape. There is a covered area at one end which displays

111

ornamental fish pond fittings and barbecues, furniture and other sundries. A modified corn store provides a three-level display area where tools, insecticides, pots and the like are assembled. The selection of power tools and greenhouses is limited, but in all other respects the stock is perfectly adequate for most gardeners' needs. All round a creditable, efficient and well-ordered business.

Prices ££££
Facilities Parking, 15 cars. Toilets. Garden advice service. Delivery service
Open Every day 8.30am to 5.30pm. Closed Christmas and Boxing Day
Credit cards Access, Visa

Tates Garden World

Brighton Road, Horsham RH13 6QA   *Tel* Horsham (0403) 55456
On the A281 Brighton road just south of Horsham

Attractively arranged on a large 10-acre site, this centre greets the visitor with some fine displays. Raised beds, stone-flagged pathways and clearly signposted sections all work together to create well-laid-out grounds. The very impressive range of plants is set out alphabetically. Most are grown on site and the quality is first rate with no signs of neglect or bad stock – this is no doubt helped out by automatic spray watering of the plant beds. Our inspector remarked that the 'dwarf conifers were a picture!' Although the smaller, typed labels are sometimes difficult to read due to fading, the group labels are professional and clear. In the hardware department the coverage is pretty comprehensive. Lawnmowers, garden machinery, furniture and sheds are all stocked. The greenhouses are particularly well set up in a separate and well-spaced-out display area and there is a swimming pool centre and 'Petworld'. Plans for the near future include an adventure playground, camping centre and new garden furniture showrooms. The staff are helpful and give directions when requested. They are always available to carry goods and there are numerous trolleys on hand as well. There is a tea room with some tables and chairs out on the lawn.

Prices ££££
Facilities Parking, 350 cars. Toilets. Cafeteria. Play area (opens 1985). Garden advice service. Delivery service
Open Every day 9am to 6pm. Closed Christmas and Boxing Day
Credit cards Access, Visa

HUDDERSFIELD W. Yorkshire   map 2
Hampsons Garden Centre

Long Lane, Dalton,   *Tel* Huddersfield (0484) 23519/29159
Huddersfield HD5 9SD
In Dalton, 1½ miles north-east of Huddersfield town centre. Take the A629 for 1 mile, turn left at Junction Inn traffic lights into Broad Lane which becomes Long Lane; centre is ½ mile along on the right (but not visible from the road)

This centre offers superb-quality, cheap plants in beautiful display beds. A plan of the layout greets you at the entrance and there is clear signposting to direct you around the rest of the site. The flagged paths, leading through a range of common and less common plants, are kept clean and dry. A smart aluminium-framed greenhouse contains an outstanding collection of indoor plants. The labelling of both outdoor and indoor plants is consistently informative and legible. Inside is a limited range of tools in the middle price bracket, a good range of quality garden furniture, and a selection of artificial flowers which cannot go un-noticed. The larger gardening materials, such as sheds and greenhouses, are stored in a separate area, but you will find no power tools or lawnmowers for sale. Our inspector was struck by the friendliness of the staff – 'from the lady in the cafe to the driver of the delivery van.' There is an exceptionally good refreshments area – clean, carpeted and providing a good selection of snacks.

Prices ££
Facilities Parking, 200 cars. Toilets. Restaurant. Garden advice service. Delivery service. Free price lists for greenhouses, conservatories and sheds
Open Every day 9am to 8pm. Closes 5.30pm in winter. Closed Christmas week
Credit cards Access, Visa

HULL Humberside   map 2

Homebase   ♿

Priory Way, off Hessle Road,   *Tel* Hull (0482) 506055
Hull JU13 9NT
In the western outskirts of the city, just off the A1105 Hull to Hessle road

The surroundings of this centre are rather uninspiring, but it is convenient for west Hull and the suburbs. This particular Homebase has only recently opened and the stocks all look to be in very good condition. You won't be able to find anything very unusual here, but it has provisions for the needs of most gardeners all under one roof, plus a DIY section. Our inspector thought that the plants were well looked after and the shop well maintained. The staff also appear to be concerned and helpful. Labelling is generally good, both for individual pots and for groups of plants, with clear print and planting information on display boards. The range of accessories is comprehensive, excelling in the selection of garden building materials such as paving and fencing. There is also a good collection of gardening books. Among the plants, most common ones are stocked. The selection of houseplants is well above average. A very large car park is designed to deal with the numerous customers who come to take advantage of the garden centre and the supermarket, DIY store, Laura Ashley shop and petrol station, also on the same site.

Prices £££
Facilities Parking, 752 cars. Toilets. Garden advice service. Delivery service
Open Mon 9am to 6pm, Tues to Thurs 8.30am to 8pm, Fri 8.30am to 9pm, Sat 8.30am to 5.30pm. Closed Christmas
Credit cards Access, Visa

IRON ACTON Avon

map 3

Parkers Garden and Aquatic Centre

Wotton Road,
Iron Acton BS17 1UG

Tel Rangeworthy (045 422) 761

On the B4058 Wotton-Under-Edge road at Iron Acton

As the name suggests, the aquatics department is an important feature of this centre and makes it worth a visit in itself. Paving and walling are also specialities, and as this section expands there are plans afoot to move it to an adjacent plot, thus opening up more space to plants. Garden ornaments are also stocked and wrought-iron work is made to order. The centre opened just two years ago and has been steadily expanding and establishing its reputation. Improvements in facilities are planned. All tools and sundries are stocked, and the shop area is laid out with careful thought. There are no particular specialities in the plant line but the overall range is quite reasonable and stocks appear to be increasing with the growing demand. They are all healthy and well tended but the labelling could do with improvement. The outside layout is open and there are wide paths surfaced with stone chippings. The staff of this family concern are helpful and always make time to discuss things with customers. The centre offers a landscaping service. A hard-working establishment which deserves to succeed.

Prices £££
Facilities Parking, 50 cars. Ice cream and cold drinks. Play area. Garden advice service. Delivery service. Free price list for all sundries, catalogue for sundries and aquatic plants 50p
Open Every day 10am to 6pm
Credit cards Access, Visa

IVYBRIDGE Devon

map 3

Endsleigh Garden Centre

Ivybridge, near Plymouth PL21 9JL

Tel Plymouth (0752) 892254

Beside the A38, 8 miles from Plymouth, about ½ mile west of Ivybridge

This garden centre received warm praise from our inspector for its 'emporium' of sundries and its wide stock of plants (most of which are grown at their nursery in Milton Abbot which is also open for plant sales). It is arranged in a clear and logical manner, with each group of plants assembled sensibly, and good, wide pathways crossing between them. Signposting is easy to follow and once you have located a particular section of plants, the general labelling is informative although individual labels could be improved with some more details. Price lists are handed out for customers' reference. All plant stock is well cared for and looked healthy when our inspector visited, even though weather conditions were adverse. The staff were at work tending the plants and maintaining their quality. The selection is wider than average and includes all the usual types of plants, subject to seasonal variations. Apart from the extensive outdoor plant area, there is a covered plant-growing area and a large, enclosed section which contains a comprehensive collection of garden sundries of all shapes, sizes and types. A concessionnaire runs a water-garden department located in a separate building. The centre is well organised and well run by its professional staff. They are friendly, helpful, knowledgeable and always somewhere on hand to deal with customers' questions. An attractive cafeteria provides on-site refreshments with an outside seating area for the sunnier days of the year.

Prices £££
Facilities Parking, 300 cars. Toilets. Restaurant. Garden advice service. Delivery service. Free plant price list and catalogue
Open Mon to Fri 9am to 6pm, Sat 9am to 5pm, Sun 2pm to 5pm (closes 5pm every day also in winter)
Credit cards Access, Visa

KELSALL Cheshire
map 2

F. Morrey and Son

Forest Nursery, Kelsall, near Tarporley   *Tel* Kelsall (0829) 51342
CW6 0SW
On the A54 on the Nantwich side of Kelsall village

This nursery has an attractive setting, in rolling countryside on the edge of Delamere Forest. There is plenty on offer for the serious gardener, who will find not only the more common varieties of shrubs, heathers, alpines and conifers, all beautifully displayed, but also a number of more unusual ones. The fruit was very impressive – the list reads like an Italian ice cream selection: 'Vines, currants, cherries, apricots, peaches, cobnuts, quince, boysenberry and youngberry'. The emphasis is very much on high-quality plants – most are grown in their own nursery and are not container-grown so are only available in the correct season. There is little signposting in the nursery, but the area isn't large enough to present real problems. More difficulty results from lack of clarity on the group labels and the fact that code letters on labels have to be matched to price code lists on displays around the centre. Otherwise individual labels are good, with clear and concise growing instructions. The indoor shop is very small and crowded and only chemicals, composts, and hand tools are stocked. Outside there's a good collection of garden ornaments, urns, vases and tubs. This is a place to go if you are looking for high-quality plants at a reasonable price and if you know what you are looking for – not for impulse buyers. The owners and staff are always on hand to advise customers and are very helpful.

Prices £££
Facilities Parking, 20 cars. Toilets. Garden advice service. Price list and plant catalogue 15p. Rose price list
Open Mon to Sat 8.30am to 5.30pm

KENDAL Cumbria
map 2

Webbs Garden Centre

Burneside Road, Kendal LA9 4RT   *Tel* Kendal (0539) 20068

On the A591 Windermere road, ½ mile north of Kendal town centre. Bear right by St. Thomas' Church into Burneside road; the centre is 300 yds along on the right

Easily accessible from town, this is a useful spot to drop into while shopping if you want to pick up a few gardening odds and ends. The range of sundries and hand tools is extensive and there is also a comprehensive selection of seeds, though no larger items such as greenhouses and sheds. There are no obvious gaps in the plant section though, and the stock is kept in good condition – plants are healthy and growing well. Many are grown on site or at a nursery outside Kendal, in particular, dwarf conifers, shrubs and bedding plants. Labels for groups of plants bear clearly printed information including a description, soil requirements and other helpful details. Most plants are arranged on raised beds so it is quite easy to inspect them. The overall layout is reasonably well done with paths which are wide enough to prevent any problems with congestion – however, the signposting could be improved. The knowledgeable staff are easy to find and are full of helpful advice – if you want help with loading the car they are happy to lend a hand. The 'gardeners' cafe' is an attractive place offering home-made cakes and sandwiches, jacket potatoes and other snack meals. Improvements for spring 1985 include new display beds in the houseplant shop and refitting of the furniture showroom and cafeteria.

Prices ££££
Facilities Parking, 60 cars. Toilets. Restaurant. Garden advice service. Delivery service. Free price list for plants in season
Open Mon to Sat 8.30am to 5.15pm (closes 5pm in winter), Sun 10.30am to 5pm (opens 2pm in winter)
Credit cards Access, Visa

KESTON Kent

map 5

Cramphorn Garden Centre

Oakley Road, Keston
BR2 6AG

Tel Farnborough (0689) 59419/54040

At the junction of the A233 and A232, 2 miles south of Bromley

Highly recommended by our inspector as a place offering something for everyone. This is not an enormous centre but the selection both inside and out is most comprehensive. The layout is straightforward with nice, wide paths and clear signposting. There is a very wide choice of tools and small sundries as well as an area turned over entirely to greenhouses and sheds. The children will find the pets section entertaining with its parrots, budgies, rabbits and hamsters, and for the garden pond there is a collection of cold-water fish. Any DIY fanatic will be satisfied by the stocks available, and for garden care in dry weather the excellent selection of hoses and fittings could prove most useful. As far as the plants go there is an 'enormous' choice of heathers, so many that it is difficult to know where to start. Our inspector also noted a 'super selection of conifers' and an impressive range of trees and shrubs. You can buy fruit trees either trained or untrained, and the houseplants are well represented with the best collection of air plants our inspector had ever come across. The only plants which weren't in tip-top condition were the cacti. All plants are labelled with price and name, and there are also informative group labels. Apart from the features already mentioned you might enjoy the pottery, vases and flower arranging sections or the 'mind-boggling' selection of jams, honey, spices and Eastern condiments. For your information, there are imaginative display boards showing methods of pruning fruit trees and pollination charts. To round it off the staff are easy to spot and nothing seems to be too much bother for them to deal with.

Prices ££££
Facilities Parking, 130 cars (to be extended). Toilets. Garden advice service. Delivery service and free use of pick-up. Free price lists for garden buildings and building materials
Open Every day 8.30am to 6pm (closes 5pm in winter). Closed Christmas and Boxing Day
Credit cards Access, Visa

KEYNSHAM Avon   map 3
Hurrans Garden Centre   ★ ⊛ ♿

Hicks Gate, Keynsham,   *Tel* Bristol (0272) 778945
near Bristol BS18 2AD
South-east of Bristol on the A4 Bath road

This centre is very nicely laid out and a few hours spent browsing and examining some of the displays is a 'joy', according to our inspector. Pathways are broad, and clear signposts show which direction to take. The centre is large and offers a wide range of goods. The supplies among the garden accessories include swimming pools, camping equipment and building materials, and there's a greenhouse area where staff are always on hand to advise on sizes, prices and construction. The range of tools has been well thought out and there's a wide variety and large quantity to choose from. At the time of our inspection, the stocks of plants were not so comprehensive and many varieties were unavailable – however, this was due to seasonal variation and most plants are available at the appropriate time of year. They are kept in very good condition and look healthy and pest free, and it is a pleasure to note the good standard of labelling which carries descriptions, pictures and details on how and when to plant. Help is freely given by the staff who cheerfully hunt round for wayward plants. Overall, an extremely good centre, quite expensive for plants, but providing ample stimulation to customers stuck for ideas in their own gardens.

Prices £££££
Facilities Parking, 1,000 cars. Toilets. Restaurant. Garden advice service. Delivery service
Open Mon to Wed and Sat 9am to 6pm, Thurs and Fri 9am to 8pm, Sun 10am to 6pm (closes 5pm every day in winter). Closed 3 days at Christmas
Credit cards Access, Visa

If you're travelling a long distance to visit a garden centre or nursery, telephone first to check the opening hours. They may vary with the season and weather conditions.

KILLINGHALL N. Yorkshire   map 2

Daleside Nurseries

Killinghall, Harrogate HG3 2AY   *Tel* Harrogate (0423) 56450
On the A61 between Harrogate and Ripon, 2 miles north of Harrogate on the north side of Killinghall

This friendly family nursery is just 2 miles from Harrogate which is called by some 'the floral town of Europe'. It is set in a pleasant rural area in an attractive village. The car park and smallish shop lie in the middle of this 40-acre site and from here one gets a good view of the rest of the grounds. There is no signposting, but the principal areas are fairly obvious. The site is sensibly organised and has good wide paths. Individual plants are adequately labelled and there is helpful, descriptive information for the group sections. The excellence of the plants is the most noticeable feature of this nursery – most of them are grown on site. Heathers are a speciality and an excellent range can be seen on display. Slow-growing dwarf conifers also deserve a special mention for the number and variety offered. There are demonstration gardens for viewing shrubs, heathers and conifers (no dogs allowed). The emphasis may be on the plants, but a reasonable supply of sundries is also stocked. Due to the competitive prices from nearby superstores, they no longer keep power tools but furniture, greenhouses and an extensive range of ornaments are still available. The staff are experienced and give advice freely. An attractive place offering quality, expertise and patience.

Prices ££££
Facilities Parking, 60 cars. Toilets. Garden advice service. Delivery service. Free catalogue on trees and shrubs
Open Mon to Sat 8.30am to 5.30pm, Sun 10am to 12am and 1.30pm to 5pm (closes half an hour earlier every day in winter)
Credit cards Access, Visa

KINGS ACRE Hereford and Worcester   map 3

Wyevale Garden Centre

Kings Acre, Hereford HR4 0SE   *Tel* Hereford (0432) 265474
About 2 miles north-west of Hereford on the A438 Brecon road

This is a large and well-stocked garden centre on the outskirts of Hereford. The indoor area houses most garden equipment with the notable exception of mowers and power tools which can be bought 'over the road' from another firm. There is a very good range of paving, walling and rock garden materials, as well as garden and pool statues.The plant section is comprehensive with a particularly wide choice of dwarf conifers, heathers and alpines. The plants are of good quality and well watered, but they are rather expensive. The centre is well laid out with good signposting, and labelling for plant groups is informative. A new system of individual labelling was being introduced in spring 1985. The information kiosk in the plant sales area is not continually manned but the rest of the centre is adequately staffed – look out for the conspicuous red jerseys. The staff are reasonably knowledgeable and helpful and include a number of trained horticulturalists. An attractive restaurant area is found at one end of a conservatory, and snack lunches are available with special portions for children. If the children are getting fractious, show them the enclosed pool area where at the push of a button or a flick of a switch fountains will spring to life. An excellent centre with an eye to the needs of urban and suburban gardeners.

Prices £££££
Facilities Parking, 150 cars. Toilets. Restaurant. Garden advice service. Delivery service. Plant catalogue £1.95, but includes vouchers worth £4
Open Mon to Sat 9am to 6pm, Sun 10am to 6pm (closes 5.30pm every day in winter)
Credit cards Access, Visa

KINGSTON NEAR LEWES E. Sussex map 5

Sussex Country Gardens

Newhaven Road, Kingston near Lewes   *Tel* Lewes (0273) 473510
BN7 3NE
On the Lewes to Newhaven road (C9, formerly the A275) at the junction with the road to Kingston

On the edge of the South Downs, this fairly new centre is run by two qualified horticulturalists who have a special interest in chalk-loving plants. It is therefore well worth a visit from people in the area or anyone who finds it difficult to deal with gardening on a chalky soil. The centre also specialises in other types of plants such as coastal plants and old-fashioned roses. The knowledgeable staff are happy to give advice on what and how to plant, and because of their interest and the location there is a good selection of plants suitable for the local soil. There are also special sections for rare and unusual alpines and shrubs. An interesting collection of trees is stocked, for example Liriodendron, but many of the more common ones had sold out when our inspector visited. The quality of plants is good, particularly the trees and shrubs and houseplants which are set out in a nice display. The centre is well organised inside and out, with gravel paths off the main pathway, good signposting and alphabetical arrangements for the shrubs. The labelling is comprehensive, clear and informative. A general plan at the entrance of the centre would be very helpful. A covered area houses a range of tools and sundries. No paving is stocked, but there are some sheds, small greenhouses and summerhouses on show, and a separate building deals with lawnmower sales, servicing and repairs. Staff are more than willing to obtain items not in stock and phone you when they arrive. There are plenty of trolleys to carry off your purchases. When we inspected, car parking had recently been expanded to cope with demand and other extensive alterations were planned.

Prices ££££
Facilities Parking, 100 cars. Toilets. Garden advice service. Delivery service. Rose catalogue £1.50
Open Mon to Sat 9am to 5.30pm, Sun 10am to 5pm. Closed Christmas and Boxing Day and New Year's Day
Credit cards Access, Visa

KINGSWINFORD W. Midlands map 3

Ashwood Nurseries and Aquatics

Greensforge, Kingswinford,
near Stourbridge DY6 0AE
Tel Kingswinford (0384) 273436

About ½ mile off the A449 6 miles south of Wolverhampton

There was nothing but praise in our inspector's report on this centre. It has been thoughtfully and imaginatively laid out around rock gardens, water spectacles, shrubbery, and heather and conifer gardens. The owner has recently started a native plant reserve at the back of the site which is being extended and developed all the time. It is a centre where there is obvious enthusiasm among the staff and they are actively involved in trying to promote good gardening in the locality. In the winter courses are offered on different aspects of gardening, from greenhouse management to alpine care. The nurseries raise their own Lewisias and have won several awards for their specimens. Unusual houseplants, including insectivorous plants, are kept in a separate hot-house. The centre also specialises in rhododendrons, alpines, dwarf conifers and heathers, and the range of these plants is tremendous. Herbaceous perennials and bedding plants are stocked, but only the more unusual varieties are kept out of season. Much of the plant material is grown on the site, with the result that it is always of a high standard. Staff will actually replace a poor specimen at the cash till if they feel the customer has made a bad choice. All labelling is clear and long lasting and you can find additional cultivation hints in specialist leaflets. Only small items are stocked in the sundries section. You will find fertilisers, garden ornaments, furniture, hand tools and pond equipment, and the bookshop is one of the best in the district. There is also a florist section which sells fresh cut flowers, silk and dried flowers and grasses, and offers an Interflora service. Specialist staff are on hand to deal with customer queries.

Prices £££
Facilities Parking, 100 cars (plus 100 overflow). Toilets. Garden advice service. Delivery service. Free price lists for shrubs, trees, roses, fruit, alpines, heathers and Lewisias
Open Mon to Sat 9am to 6pm (Sun opens 9.30am). Closed Christmas and Boxing Day
Credit cards Access, Visa

KIRBY CROSS Essex map 4

Frinton Road Nurseries

Kirby Cross CO13 0PD
Tel Frinton (025 56) 4838

On the B1033 between Kirby Cross and Frinton-on-Sea

A small but well-laid-out centre offering good-quality plants at reasonable prices. The range of named varieties and species of trees, shrubs and other plants is very good and all are clearly labelled with photographs and prices. A small but adequately stocked glasshouse contains a selection of healthy houseplants. There is a wide choice of top-of-the-range greenhouses and conservatories and a good collection of garden furniture. In the main building an average stock of the better-known brands of tools and sundries is kept. Outside you will find walling, paving and natural rock garden stone at a range of prices. A small but adequately stocked glasshouse contains a range of good-quality houseplants. The extension under way at the rear of the main building will hopefully relieve the cramped conditions which are the centre's principal drawback. There are few staff but they are happy to help you out.

Prices £££
Facilities Parking, 50–60 cars. Play area. Toilets. Garden advice service. Delivery service. Free price lists for paving, fencing, greenhouses etc. Free catalogue for plants
Open Mon to Sat 8.30am to 5.30pm. Closed Sun
Credit cards Access, Visa

KIRKHAM ABBEY N. Yorkshire map 2
Kirkham Abbey Garden Centre

Kirkham Abbey, York YO6 7JS   *Tel* Whitwell-on-Hill (065 381) 658
About ½ mile off the A64 York to Scarborough road at Whitewell Hill, about 10 miles east of York

This is a small nursery situated by the side of the River Derwent, across the bridge from Kirkham Abbey ruins. When inspected it had only been open for about 18 months so was still developing. At present it is nicely kept and has a reasonable selection of conifers, shrubs, perennials, hard fruit, alpines and herbs. Everything is in good health, but the labelling, apart from on the trees, is very scrappy – the nursery tells us that it will try to correct this. A small covered area stocks a selection of accessories which is adequate for the size of the nursery – primarily small tools, composts, pool liners and ornaments, though fencing, paving and furniture are also available. The site is sensibly laid out so that there is plenty of room in the interior area, and easy access via wide flagstone paths outside. Helpful staff are ready to deal with customers' troubles, while a licensed coffee lounge caters for the hungry.

Prices £££
Facilities Parking, 50 cars. Toilets. Garden advice service. Delivery service
Open Every day, 9am to 7.30pm in summer, 9.30am to dusk in winter
Credit cards Access, Visa

KIRTON IN LINDSEY Lincolnshire map 2
Fairgardens Plant Centre

Station Road, Kirton in Lindsey   *Tel* Kirton Lindsey (0652) 648631
DN21 4JR
At Kirton in Lindsey, about 7 miles south of Scunthorpe. Take the B1400 or B1205 turning off the A159 Scunthorpe to Gainsborough road

A very wide range of garden accessories and an excellent choice of trees and shrubs are the features which make this centre special. Most of the large outside area is turned over to these plants, which are all arranged alphabetically and are of a very good quality. Most other plants are stocked, all of which are cheap, but at the time of our inspection their quality did not match that of the trees and shrubs. The houseplants, on the other hand, were of excellent standard and well cared for. Labels for groups of plants were good and often provided descriptions and growing tips; however, individual tags needed some improvement (these are now computerised). If your interests lie more with the building and maintenance side of gardening then there is plenty on offer as well. The whole gamut of tools and sundries is available from fish and fertilisers to paving and power tools. The all-round layout of the centre is reasonable, though our inspector thought the inside area was rather jumbled. He also felt that some of the staff had rather an unfortunate 'take it or leave it attitude'. The car park and toilets could do with improvement, but in spite of these criticisms the centre is worth a visit particularly if you are looking for gardening equipment or want to stock your garden with trees and shrubs.

Prices ££
Facilities Parking, 70 cars. Toilets. Vending machines. Garden advice service. Delivery service. Free price list for greenhouses, sheds etc
Open Mon to Sat 9am to 7.30pm, Sun 10am to 7.30pm (closes 5pm every day in winter). Closed Christmas and Boxing Day and New Year's Day
Credit cards Access, Visa

KNAPHILL Surrey — map 5

Knap Hill Garden Centre

Slocock & Knap Hill Nurseries, *Tel* Brookwood (048 67) 81212/5
Barrs Lane, Knaphill,
Woking GU21 2JW
In Lower Knaphill, 1 mile from the A322 Bracknell to Guildford road. Bear left at the bottom of Anchor Hill into Barrs Lane; the centre is 200 yds along on the right

Our inspector's comment was 'for general interest and as Chelsea gold medalists, it's a must'. These nurseries have been established for 190 years in the pleasant quiet of rural Surrey. There is a large well-organised outside display area. Plants are quite expensive but of good quality. There's a comprehensive range – the conifers and azaleas are particularly impressive and the rhododendrons also excel. 'Waterers Walk' takes visitors through an avenue of trees and is a special feature at Knaphill. It is part of the unique collection of unusual trees, some of historic importance, which have been grown on the site. If you are interested in the culinary side of the garden then there is quite a wide selection of healthy-looking herbs. Labelling on all plants is pretty good – easy to read and informative. There is a spacious indoor shop which houses a very good range of tools and sundries with the exception of lawnmowers, and most garden buildings and construction materials can be purchased. A separate area is devoted to an impressive display of camping equipment, including tents and all the related paraphernalia, and there are plans to introduce a swimming pool display area. The 'Loft Shop' stocks a selection of horticultural gifts. The staff are well able to deal with customer queries, but a few more smiles wouldn't go amiss. Umbrellas are on hand for rainy days and there is a selection of free handouts if you want to ponder over particular problems. For the hungry, there is a restaurant on site, and the centre also sells fresh fruit and vegetables.

Prices £££££
Facilities Parking, 100 cars. Toilets. Restaurant. Play area. Garden advice service. Delivery service. Free price list for greenhouses and sheds. Plant and sundries catalogue 50p. Plants sold by mail order
Open Mon to Sat 9am to 5pm, Sun 10am to 5pm (closes 4pm every day Jan and Feb). Closed 2 days at Christmas and New Year's Day
Credit cards Access, Visa

KNOCKHOLT Kent map 5

Whiteleggs Nurseries and Garden Centre

Knockholt, near Sevenoaks TN14 7LJ   *Tel* Knockholt (0959) 32187
Off the A21 about ⅓ mile from Knockholt Pound, travelling towards the church on the Cudham to Biggin Hill road

A medium-sized nursery selling good, healthy plants at reasonable prices but you need to take wellington boots because of the state of the paths! A small paved area contains a selection of trees, shrubs, perennials and heathers, but the rest of the nursery's pathways can get totally waterlogged due to daily watering. There are numerous varieties of conifers and shrubs on offer for those with more than a passing fancy. The selection includes some large trees up to 15ft. Overall, plants are of very good quality. Labels for shrubs give informative, helpful instructions while perennials and trees could do with more details about the plants and their cultivation. There are no frills among the stocks of sundries – no mowers or greenhouses – but a small selection of most practical gardening accessories. A small indoor area under glass houses this equipment as well as a display of houseplants – overcrowding can be a frustration. The overall layout of the centre could be improved if areas were more clearly signposted, however if you can't find what you are looking for staff are friendly and helpful. From Monday to Friday customers can get detailed advice on planting and garden layout.

Prices ££££
Facilities Parking, 50 cars. Toilets. Ice creams. Garden advice service. Delivery service
Open Mon to Fri 8am to 5.30pm, Sat 9am to 5.30pm, Sun 10am to 5pm (closes at dusk every day in winter)
Credit cards Access, Visa

KNUTSFORD Cheshire map 2

Caldwell & Sons

The Nurseries and Garden Centre,   *Tel* Knutsford (0565) 4281/2
Chelford Road, Knutsford WA16 8LX
On the A537 to Chelford and Macclesfield, ½ mile from Knutsford

Caldwell's is a small family business which was started by the present owner's ancestors in 1780. It is known for its good service and high standard, and for plant-lovers is definitely worth a visit. The site is divided physically by the A537, one side dealing exclusively with houseplants which are exceptionally good but pricey, and the other with hardy plants and garden sundries. The site is well signposted and the paths are wide though some are unmade. The nursery offers a good range of quality stock, specialising in small trees and shrubs; heathers and climbers are well represented too. All plants are grown on Caldwell's own nurseries; there are allied rose, tree and shrub nurseries nearby at Ollerton and tree and fruit nurseries 5 miles away at Goostrey. An indoor area deals with tools, seeds and books and a limited line of larger materials and machinery, such as fencing, paving and pond equipment. The flower-arranging sundries are a speciality which meets a local demand. The staff are knowledgeable, courteous and always available to give advice when needed. They will make advisory visits to customers' gardens and also offer a planting service.

Prices ££££
Facilities Parking, 90 cars. Toilets. Vending machines. Garden advice service. Delivery service. Free price lists for plants and brochures on stoneware, pool equipment etc. Plants sold by mail order
Open Mon to Sat 8.30am to 5.30pm (closes 5pm Sat), Sun 10am to 5pm. Closes at dusk in winter. Closed Christmas and Boxing Day
Credit cards Access, Visa

Fryer's Nurseries

Manchester Road, Knutsford   *Tel* Knutsford (0565) 2642
WA16 0SX
On the A50, 1½ miles north of Knutsford

This is primarily a rose nursery but also stocks a reasonable range of other plants and a good choice of smaller gardening sundries. So after a pleasant wander through the rose fields (open July to October) there is plenty to look at among the terracotta tubs and lawn spreaders. The roses are guaranteed and there are masses to choose from, including bush, climbing, shrub, standard and miniature roses. Trees, conifers and shrubs are also on display in large quantities with a fair collection of alpines and heathers. The general health of plants is good. The centre is quite nicely laid out with wide paths and plenty of room in the garden shop to browse around. The range of tools and seeds is extensive and you will also find fertilisers, books and barbecues. There is even a display of swimming pools and related equipment, but other larger items such as building materials, power tools and garden buildings are missing. Signposting is inadequate outside, but the staff are very helpful and more than happy to direct visitors around. The proprietor, Mr Fryer, is often on the premises and is happy to answer your queries. There are big, informative labels for the plant groupings and smaller plants also have very helpful hints on them. Some individual labels are washed out. It is a pleasant drive through some beautiful Cheshire countryside to get here and a very enjoyable walk round on arrival.

Prices ££££
Facilities Parking, 100 cars (plus overflow). Toilets. Garden advice service. Delivery service. Price list and catalogue for roses 10p
Open Mon to Sat 9am to 5.30pm, Sun 10am to 5.30pm. Rose field open to 9.30pm. Closed Christmas and New Year
Credit cards Access, Visa

KNYPERSLEY Staffordshire — map 2

Jackson's Garden Centre and Nurseries

Tunstall Road, Knypersley,   *Tel* Stoke-on-Trent (0782) 513405
Stoke-on-Trent ST8 7AB
On the A527 just south of Biddulph

The old stone buildings and cobbled yard of what was once a smallholding can still be seen within the grounds of this small plant centre. Raised beds set out around the car park are filled with displays of all the plants for sale in the nursery. Plants are cheap, carefully labelled and nicely tended, and the arrangements show the relative sizes, shapes and colours of mature specimens – very useful before making any purchases. The range of plant stock includes most run-of-the-mill types and there is a good selection of conifers. They are all laid out alphabetically in rows between fairly wide, flat paths. Each group of plants has a large, clear informative sign, and basic descriptions and prices are attached to individual pots. Everything is well kept and of very good quality. Apart from the small outside plant area there are plants for the house and hanging baskets displayed in a medium-sized greenhouse. For tools and sundries the choice is rather small. The shop is obviously just a sideline and the hand tools, water-gardening equipment and composts seem to have been on the shelf for some time. The owner, when around, is very pleasant and helpful. The other staff member, the cashier, hasn't the horticultural knowledge but is very cheerful. You can drive your car right up to the cash desk so loading is no problem. This cannot really be classed as a fully fledged garden centre, but as a general nursery it is very good.

Prices ££
Facilities Parking, 20 cars. Garden advice service. Free price list
Open Every day except Tues 10am to dusk. Closed in snowy weather

LACOCK Wiltshire — map 3

Whitehall Garden Centre

Lacock, Chippenham SN15 2LZ   *Tel* Lacock (024 973) 204
On the A35 Lacock bypass, 4 miles from Chippenham and 3 miles from Melksham

A centre highly recommended for its plants – rated ten out of ten by both inspectors who visited it. In addition to the regular lines, it stocks some unusual varieties and some very good specimen plants. The 5-acre site has an excellent layout with plenty of space to walk about. The outside is devoted to shrubs and trees while aquatic plants, perennials and bedding are kept under cover. Labelling is very good with each item marked individually and big notices set out alphabetically to mark the groups of plants. Plants are arranged partly alphabetically and partly by size so that it is not always possible to see all the varieties from one group assembled together. There is a very good range of sundries with the exception of power tools. Greenhouses, sheds, fencing and paving are sold under franchise, and garden furniture and ornaments are also stocked. The water gardening section is particularly noteworthy. Camping equipment is shown annually at a major exhibition. The staff do not all profess to be experts but they are very enthusiastic and there are two qualified plantsmen who answer any queries. The coffee lounge is pleasant and children will enjoy the play area. The centre is well located overlooking the Wiltshire Downs and adjoining the National Trust property of Lacock.

Prices ££££
Facilities Parking, 75 cars (plus overflow). Toilets. Restaurant. Play area. Garden advice service. Free promotional leaflets
Open Mon to Sat 9am to 5pm, Sun 10am to 5pm
Credit card Access

LAMBLEY Nottinghamshire   map 2
Floralands Garden Centre

Catfoot Lane, Lambley,   *Tel* Nottingham (0602) 268137
Nottingham NG4 4QL
5 miles east of Nottingham. Catfoot Lane is off the B628 near the Travellers'
Rest pub

In a pleasant rural setting outside the city of Nottingham, this centre is situated on a hillside overlooking farmland. The sloping site has been extensively terraced over the years so that there are flat areas for the shrubs and plants, sheds and greenhouses and the indoor accessories areas. The indoor areas are all connected by ramps which helps out visitors with wheelchairs or pushchairs, but the elderly might find the slope a little tiring. It is a medium-sized centre catering principally for town and city gardeners and this is reflected in the division between outdoor and indoor display areas. There is an above-average selection of garden furniture and barbecue equipment and a good display of water gardening sundries and fish in season. Some tools and garden buildings are available, but no paving is stocked. There's a camping exhibition in season. The layout and signposting in some parts could be better. Stocks of plants are extensive and the centre is known locally for its impressive selection of clematis. There is also a good range of heathers, trees and houseplants which are well displayed in an old greenhouse containing some delightfully mature specimens. However, the varieties available within some groups of plants are limited, particularly among both hard and soft fruits. The quality throughout is very good, conifers being especially noteworthy. Labelling, however, is rather variable. Staff can be difficult to locate – it would be helpful to the customers if they wore some sort of identifying clothing or badges. This garden centre is continually improving and is well worth a visit.

Prices £££
Facilities Parking, 500 cars. Toilets. Cafeteria. Play area. Delivery service. Free catalogue for aquatics
Open Every day 9am to 6pm (closes 7pm Easter to June). Closed 3 or 4 days over Christmas
Credit cards Access, Visa

LANCASTER Lancashire   map 2
Ashton Hall Garden Centre

Ashton-with-Stodday,   *Tel* Galgate (0524) 751767
near Lancaster LA2 0AJ
On the A588 Lancaster to Glasgow road, 3 miles south of Lancaster

This centre, within the old, walled garden of Ashton Hall, has seen continual improvement since our last inspection. A newly installed watering system means that all the plants are kept in prime condition and care is obviously taken to see that nothing sub-standard is left on display. Many of the plants are grown at the centre's nearby nursery. The water-gardening section and pool area have been extended recently and are very nicely laid out. Even the labelling is being renewed and labels are clear and easy to read. The overall layout is already very good and paths are wide. The stock is very comprehensive – all common plants are available, with particular mention earned by the wide selections of perennials and strong, sturdy trees. The range of shrubs is most interesting and there are some excellent specimen plants. There is also a large house containing pot-plants. Greenhouses and power tools are not stocked by this centre, but the smaller garden accessories are well provided for and the high-quality barbecue equipment is worth a look. Fencing, paving and furniture are sold and sheds are to be stocked in the future. There is an aviary and a small reptile and fish house for the children to explore when they are tired of shopping. The staff are consistently helpful and cheerful – the centre prides itself on its 'staff qualifications'.

Prices ££££
Facilities Parking, 50 cars. Toilets. Coffee shop. Play area. Garden advice service. Delivery service
Open Mon to Sat 8.30am to 5.30pm (closes 8pm Thurs and Fri). (These times may change from April 1985)
Credit cards Access, Visa

LECHLADE Gloucestershire   map 3
Lechlade Garden and Fuchsia Centre

Fairford Road, Lechlade GL7 3DP   *Tel* Faringdon (0367) 52372
On the A417 Cirencester road, ½ mile west of the village of Lechlade

A specialist centre offering an extensive indoor display of fuchsias as well as a large number of geraniums and silver foliage plants – including some marvellous dianthus. They are all attractively and imaginatively laid out –

the fuchsias are displayed in a jungle setting. They are available as rooted cuttings and plants from April onwards. The plants are well looked after and are labelled individually with group headings, but if you want any more information there are excellent descriptive booklets on the cultivation of these select plants. There are also stocks of shrubs and other plants, but the centre has sensibly decided not to spread itself too wide and has concentrated upon its chosen area. There is however a good selection of other garden centre items, including a nice range of gardening boots and shoes in all sizes. Garden ornaments and furniture are plentiful and all the larger sundries are available, even power tools. It is a rewarding and interesting place to visit.

Prices ££££
Facilities Parking, 100 cars (plus overflow). Toilets. Play area. Garden advice service. Delivery service. Free fuchsia catalogue
Open Mon to Sat 9am to 5.30pm, Sun and bank holidays 10am to 5pm
Credit cards Access, Visa

LEEDS W. Yorkshire   map 2
Homebase

Moor Allerton Centre, King Lane,   *Tel* Leeds (0532) 693166
Ring Road, Leeds LS17 5NY
3 miles north of Leeds, on the A6120 outer ring road between the A61 Harrogate and the A660 Otley roads

This centre is part of a major shopping complex which comprises a Sainsbury's, Homebase DIY and Laura Ashley, not to mention the library, Wimpy and pub. These are all newly built in this suburban setting and are very attractive to those who want to buy all their weekend shopping at once, including bits and pieces for the garden. The car park is extensive, catering as it does for vast numbers of shoppers. Inside the garden centre itself, the layout is very good with easy access along wide paths and good signposting. Tools and sundries are competitively priced and well displayed, providing a range which covers all normal gardening requirements. All the larger items such as greenhouses, sheds and mowers are also sold, and there's a good selection of fencing and paving. The houseplant display is attractively designed with sloping glass sides and all plants on waist-high gravel beds. There are some interesting varieties available and the plants are very healthy. The selection of outdoor plants is quite adequate, although you are unlikely to find anything very much out of the ordinary. They are generally of a very good quality – our inspector was especially impressed with the condition of the bedding plants – and since all smaller varieties are on raised beds, they are easy to inspect and the small, individual labels are easy to read. Most trees and shrubs carry large glossy labels which provide a photograph and a description. The staff are mainly young. They are easy to find and eager to help with information or carrying. An information desk for the whole Homebase store is always manned.

Prices £££
Facilities Parking, 742 cars. Toilets. Garden advice service. Delivery service

Open Mon 9am to 6pm, Tues to Fri 8.30am to 8pm, Sat 8.30am to 5.30pm, Sun 9am to 6pm. Closed 3 days at Christmas
Credit cards Access, Visa

Plantland

York Road, Whinmoor, Leeds LS15 4NF   *Tel* Leeds (0532) 731949
On the A64 Leeds/Tadcaster/York road, 5 miles from the city centre

It is difficult to see the turning to this centre until you are almost on top of it, so keep your eyes peeled. Once inside, things are relatively straightforward. The centre is of medium size, the inside being divided between a section for all the 'necessary' garden equipment, and an area housing an attractive display of pot plants. The larger outside area is devoted entirely to plants, a third of which are under a glass roof which can be handy for wet-weather shopping. Things are well spaced outside, so that there are no problems with getting around. The interior displays are also tidily arranged. The tools and sundries available are limited, but cover most simple needs, except for power tools, greenhouses and sheds. The selection of hardy plants is very good and specimens are usually healthy and of good quality. The landscaping business run by the centre means some unusual conifers and semi-mature trees are stocked: this also encourages a quick turnover, keeping stock fresh and weed-free through the season. The centre also runs an indoor landscaping service, for example, for offices and shops, and so specialises in indoor and artificial plants. Our inspector thought the labelling was the best he'd seen for some time – all plants were marked and both group and individual labels provided planting instructions and other information. The staff are available to answer questions or to carry goods to the car.

Prices ££££
Facilities Parking, 100 cars. Toilets. Garden advice service. Delivery service. Free plant price list
Open Every day 9am to 7pm (closes 6pm in winter). Closed Christmas and Boxing Day
Credit cards Access, Visa

LEICESTER Leicestershire   map 4

James Coles and Sons

Thurnby Nurseries, 66 The Parade,   *Tel* Leicester (0533) 412115
Oadby, Leicester LE7 9QB
Just outside the eastern boundary of Leicester on the north side of the A47, Leicester to Uppingham and Peterborough road

It is the quality of plants, both indoor and outdoor, which makes these nurseries worthy of attention. They make no pretence of being a garden centre and there are no gardening tools or equipment sold, but you will find composts and peats. Most of the plants sold are grown in the nurseries and their speciality is trees, including a good selection of conifers. Every-thing is easy to find and the shrubs are helpfully arranged in alpha-betical order. Plants are well labelled – the houseplant labels are especially useful as they provide descriptive and cultural hints. The friendly and very knowledgeable staff are on site to help customers in any way possible.

Prices ££££
Facilities Parking, 30 cars. Toilets. Garden advice service. Delivery service. Plant price list free, catalogue 60p
Open Every day, 9am to 5.30pm in summer, 9.30am to 4.15pm in winter. Closed Christmas Day

---

Leicester Garden Centre

Melton Road, East Goscote LE7 8QY   *Tel* Leicester (0533) 605515
On the A607, Melton Mowbray to Leicester road between Syston and Rearsby

This large centre is one of the Wyevale group. The surroundings – close to the main road and near the overspill village of East Goscote – have little aesthetic appeal, but it has a good choice of stock to offer those in the area, and there are plans to re-landscape the garden centre surroundings. The logical layout, clear signposting, and wide, level paths make it an easy place to get round. There are large boards, often illustrated, which designate plant groups. Individual labels are less satisfactory. Greenhouses and sheds are sold under franchise. About half the centre is under cover and is devoted to such items as furniture, chemicals, barbecue equipment and gnomes. There is a good selection of books. The overall range of plants is quite good, including most popular varieties, but they are rather expensive. New houseplant and water-plant sections have recently been set up. Quality of the plants was rather variable at the time of our inspection, so it is worth having a close look at anything you are planning to buy. However, standards are usually good. Professionals among the staff will willingly answer specialist queries when available. Umbrellas are on loan in wet weather, and there are plenty of barrows and baskets available.

Prices £££££
Facilities Parking, 200 cars. Toilets. Ice cream and confectionery. Garden advice service. Delivery service. Plant catalogue £1.95 (includes vouchers worth £4)
Open Every day 9am to 6pm (closes 5.30pm in winter). Closed Christmas and Boxing Day
Credit cards Access, Visa

Palmers

St Johns, Narborough Hill,   *Tel* Leicester (0533) 863323
Leicester LE9 5BS
On the A46, 1 mile south of the M1 junction 21

The average gardener should be satisfied with the stock on offer at this centre. The selection of plants is reasonably good although most species are only represented by one or two varieties. On the day of our inspector's visit the heathers, shrubs and conifers in particular were in good condition. The individual plants are all priced and have good colour labelling; however signposts and labels for groups of plants could do with improvements. It is not too difficult to find your way around though as all the sales areas are connected and the site is spacious with good paths. A large covered area holds a very good range of most tools and sundries, with an interesting assortment of earthenware pots. The greenhouses and sheds are housed separately. Our inspector saw no sign of power tools or water-garden accessories. There are some fine-quality indoor plants in their own glasshouse. There is always an experienced horticulturalist on the staff as well as several younger members – all are very willing and attentive. The centre is undergoing some general reconstruction and the owners hope to continually improve all areas.

Prices Information not available
Facilities Parking, 200 cars. Garden advice service. Delivery service
Open Mon to Sat 9am to 5.30pm, Sun 10am to 5pm
Credit cards Access, Visa

LELANT Cornwall   map 3

Lelant Garden Centre

Nut Lane, Hayle TR27 6LG   *Tel* Hayle (0736) 753731
Just off the A30 between Hayle and St. Ives on the edge of the village of Lelant

A branch of the Wyevale Group set in pleasant rural surroundings near the Hayle estuary, a favourite haunt of bird-watchers. Within the grounds there is a pond with wild water plants and tame ducks. The centre is well designed with two buildings for seeds, garden furniture, chemicals and tools, and an open area protected by netting for plants. There appears to be a big turnover of plants, with frequent deliveries. Generally there is a good selection for the everyday gardener. When our inspector visited for a second time, the centre was offering an impressive selection of hydrangeas, hebes, fuchsias and pelargoniums, and a blaze of colour was created in the entrance hall by a display of some beautiful plants. A good variety of houseplants is contained in a glasshouse and there is a separate area for alpines and herbs. The stock is grouped alphabetically with informative, printed labels, particularly useful to those with limited horticultural knowledge. Plants are of excellent quality but quite expensive. The sundries meet the needs of the average gardener. The stock of chemicals, fertilisers, peats and composts was singled out by our inspector for special praise. Next door to the garden centre is a workshop for lawnmower servicing and a hire service for power tools. There are few staff but they are cheerful and efficient.

Prices £££££
Facilities Parking, 150 cars. Toilets. Restaurant. Play area. Garden advice. Delivery service. Free price list for sheds, greenhouses, fencing and pond equipment. Plant catalogue 75p
Open Mon to Wed 9am to 5.30pm, Thurs and Fri 9am to 7pm, Sat 9am to 6.30pm, Sun 10am to 6.30pm (closes 5.30pm every day in winter). Closed Christmas and Boxing Day
Credit cards Access, Visa

 Establishments awarded with a flower symbol sell either a very good range of high-quality plants, or a more limited but particularly interesting selection.

LEVEN Humberside
map 2

The Cedars Nurseries

South Street, Leven, near Beverley   *Tel* Leven (0401) 42313
HU17 5NY
*About 6 miles from Beverley, in the village of Leven on the A165 Hull to
Bridlington road*

This nursery started from modest beginnings and has developed and
improved its range of stocks carefully and professionally. The family
business is run by the owners who have a keen interest in plants and
gardening. The site is small but well laid out and not too crowded. Few
garden accessories are stocked (only fencing and garden ornaments) but
the overall choice and quality of plants is good. Most are grown on site. The
trees on offer are nothing out of the ordinary, but the choice of shrubs is
better. They seem to keep an eye out for new varieties suitable for the local
area, so it is worth looking out for these. There are some very good-quality
indoor plants which are displayed in a new purpose-built glasshouse.
There are not always enough staff on hand at busy times, but they are
always terribly helpful. This is a nursery with consistently high standards
and our inspector felt more than happy at recommending it. There are
plans to extend both the indoor and outdoor areas, to display all plants on
benches and to build display beds. Keep a sharp eye out when approaching
the nursery because it is situated on a bend and is easily missed.

Prices £££
Facilities Parking, 50 cars. Toilets. Play area. Garden advice service. Delivery service.
Free plant catalogue and price lists in season
Open Tues to Sun 9.30am to 6.30pm (closes 5.30pm in winter). Closed Mon except
bank holidays

LEYLAND Lancashire
map 2

Auldene Nurseries

Southport Road, Ulnes Walton,   *Tel* Croston (0772) 600271
Leyland PR5 3LQ
On the A581 between Chorley and Croston, 1 mile east of Croston

This garden centre is situated on the west side of the small village of
Eccleston along a popular holiday route from Chorley to the seaside town
of Southport. It is a small compact centre and cannot really compete with
the well-equipped, larger garden centres as far as facilities and range of
stock go, but the quality of plants largely compensates for this. It offers a
reasonable range of most popular plants without any special emphasis on a
particular type, although the conifer section is particularly good. The plants
are of good quality, cheap and well identified with group labels. Labelling on
individual plants could be more detailed and does not provide any growing
instructions, but there are plans to install a computer printer in order to
rectify this. Most of the run-of-the-mill sundries are available including
hand tools and a good supply of peat and composts as well as some larger

items such as greenhouses, sheds and garden furniture. The centre is very well laid out with nice wide paths and attractive displays of plants. About half the area is under cover and this includes an impressive houseplants section. Staff are all dressed in 'Auldene Garden Centre' T-shirts and it is their welcoming and cheerful spirit which makes the centre special.

Prices ££
Facilities Parking, 55 cars. Toilets. Vending machines, sweets and ice creams. Garden advice service. Free price lists for greenhouses, sheds and roses
Open Mon to Sat 9am to 5.30pm, Sun 10am to 5pm
Credit cards Access, American Express, Visa

LICKEY Hereford and Worcester map 3

Little Heath Lane Nurseries ✿

Little Heath Lane, Lickey, *Tel* Bromsgrove (0527) 78174
Bromsgrove B60 1HY
1 mile north-east of Bromsgrove, down a turning off the B4096 at Lickey End.
2 miles from exit 4 of the M5

This is a good, all-round centre, although the emphasis is on the plants. The selection is particularly wide among the conifers, shrubs and bulbs, but alpines and heathers are also well represented. A special attraction at the nursery is its range of wild garden plants, native trees and shrubs. A wild-life garden is being extended to provide walkways through the native plants. The quality of plants is generally good, being particularly impressive in the large houseplant section. If you are an enthusiastic, indoor-plant lover, the art of bonsai is an interesting challenge and there is an area devoted entirely to this feature. The centre arranges special events which include bonsai weekends and bulb festivals. Group visits can be organised and talks are given. Within the covered section of the centre you will also find a fair range of small tools and sundries, plus water-gardening equipment and a range of floristry products. Emphasis is placed on organic gardening products. No greenhouses or large tools are available but most of the other larger accessories are stocked, including a good selection of paving with a demonstration patio and a range of barbecue equipment. Everything has been nicely laid out. The pathways are wide and all the doorways offer plenty of elbow room. Inside there is a pleasant spaciousness so that it is not difficult to get to any section. Plant labels are also well done, although some alpine labels were unclear when our inspector visited. Unfortunately there has been little attempt at including any cultural instructions, either on individual plants or on labels for different plant sections. The nursery tells us it is in the process of relabelling the sections. Advice is readily given by the helpful staff and they will also do any loading or carrying required. Overall a reliable, all-round place offering no gimmicks, just good stock.

Prices ££££
Facilities Parking, 120 cars. Toilets. Vending machines. Play area. Garden advice service. Delivery service
Open Mon to Sat 9am to 5.30pm, Sun 10am to 5pm (closes ½ hour earlier in winter). Closed Christmas Day and New Year's Day
Credit cards Access, Visa

LINCOLN Lincolnshire

map 2

Pennells Garden Centre

Newark Road, South Hykeham, Lincoln   *Tel* Lincoln (0522) 682088
LN6 9NH
On the A46 Lincoln to Newark road, about 3 miles south of Lincoln city centre

'Popular but pricey', says our inspector, but for the less experienced
gardener this centre is probably easier to deal with than the many outlying
specialist nurseries in the area. It is large and stocks almost anything you
might need in the garden, including a comprehensive selection of tools and
sundries and larger items such as greenhouses, sheds and paving. The
centre specialises in clematis, and also stocks a very good range of trees and
shrubs which are supplied directly from Pennells wholesale nursery in
Lincoln. The choice of perennials is more limited. Group labels are
descriptive and legible, but when our inspector visited, labels on some
individual trees and shrubs were indistinct (we are told that these have
since been improved). It can be difficult to locate people in the grounds and
the one or two staff at the cash desk have to deal with queries and the cash
tills which can cause hold-ups at busier times. The centre tells us they are
planning to enlarge the shop area and improve the till area to ease
congestion.

Prices £££££
Facilities Parking, 100 cars. Toilets. Play area. Garden advice service. Delivery
service. Free plant price list, plant catalogue
Open Mon to Sat 8.30am to 5.30pm, Sun 10am to 5.30pm (closes 5pm every day
in winter)
Credit cards Access, Visa

LISS Hampshire

map 4

Tates Garden World

Farnham Road, Liss,   *Tel* Liss (0730) 892196
near Petersfield GU33 6LJ
On the A325 Farnham to Petersfield road, about 1 mile south of Liss

The approach to Tates is not well signposted and the entrance can easily be
missed, so keep a good lookout. (There are plans to improve the signs.) The
layout of the centre is excellent – the wide concrete paths, broad aisles and
large, clearly arranged shop are of particular help to the disabled – and clear
signposts help you locate the different sections. The variety of stock is very
good, with a comprehensive range of accessories and an emphasis on
building products such as stone, slabs and pillars. The less ambitious
shoppers can purchase ready-made sheds and glasshouses or any other
standard garden sundries including water-garden equipment. A pet

---

*Garden centres and nurseries awarded with a hand fork symbol stock a
particularly comprehensive range of gardening equipment.*

section offers a collection of fish, and there are numerous books to choose from. The centre is planning to introduce new departments such as a camping sales centre and a swimming pool section. At the time of our inspection, there was a wide choice of trees and shrubs while the herbaceous perennials were awaiting a restock. There is no apparent specialisation and the overall range is adequate. Quality was a little variable the day our inspector visited, but only end-of-season perennials and roses were under the weather and otherwise quality was good. Labels for groups of plants are excellent, but individual plant tags are less impressive. However, improvements are being made in this direction. If you have any queries, the staff are easy to spot. There are a couple of specialists on site who will deal with any horticultural problems.

Prices ££££
Facilities Parking, 150 cars. Toilets. Play area (opens 1985). Garden advice service. Delivery service. Free price list for greenhouses, conservatories and building materials. Free plant catalogue
Open Every day 9am to 6pm. Closed Christmas and Boxing Day
Credit cards Access, Visa

LITTLE BYTHAM Lincolnshire
map 4

Rasell's Nurseries
✿

Little Bytham,   *Tel* Castle Bytham (078 081) 345
Grantham NG33 4QY

On the B1176 Grantham to Stamford road, between Little Bytham and Castle Bytham

Many unusual plants can be found at this nursery and it deserves a visit from any keen gardener, although it is probably not a suitable venue for a family outing. The interest in plants can be seen from the 9 acres of excellent-quality specimens, mainly grown by the nursery, and the enthusiasm of the nurseryman who is happy to spend time discussing and exchanging points of view on various plants. The nursery excels in its selection of fruit trees and seasonal pot-plants as well as ornamental trees, shrubs, soft fruit, roses and conifers. In fact there is generally very good coverage and quality across the board. Labelling is not quite of the same standard; group labelling is good, but individual plants have to make do with a name tag or even no tag at all. The whole site is devoted to outdoor plants and they are fairly well organised. There are no signposts to point you in the right directions but there are wide, mainly mud, tracks to get you there. Only composts are available in the gardening accessories line. Staff are extremely helpful and generally available to help with loading goods.

Prices £££
Facilities Parking, 14 cars. Toilets. Garden advice service. Delivery service. Free price list and catalogue for plants. Plants sold by mail order in small quantities
Open Mon to Sat 9am to 5pm, Sun 10am to 1pm

★ *Star awards are given to garden centres and nurseries which met with our inspector's whole-hearted approval.*

LITTLE MARLOW Buckinghamshire   map 4

Thames Valley Garden Centre ★

Pump Lane, Little Marlow SL7 3RB   *Tel* Marlow (062 84) 72922
At the junction of the A404 and A4155, midway between Marlow and Bourne End

Expert planning lies behind this large centre. The spacious, attractive
layout and excellent selection of house and garden stocks have earned our
inspector's praise. A covered way lined with conifers and tubs runs
through the centre and offshoot paths are wide and clearly signposted. All
sections are well marked and informative, and small plants are displayed
on raised beds. At the time of our inspector's visit shrubs, herbs, conifers
and water plants were in plentiful supply – and there were five varieties of
strawberry plants. Group labels had helpful instructions. The overall
quality of trees and plants was good. Stocks of tools and sundries are
extensive, especially in the lawnmower and shed lines, and there's a good
selection of stone containers. However, the range of garden chemicals and
furniture is limited. Staff are readily available to answer queries – a 'plant
consultant' will help with more specialised information. There is some car
parking outside the building, but the large car park was being resurfaced in
early 1985.

Prices ££££
Facilities Parking, 400 cars. Toilets. Vending machines. Garden advice service.
Delivery service.
Open Every day 9am to 5pm. Closed Christmas period
Credit cards Access, Diners Club, Visa

LIVERPOOL Merseyside   map 2

Buckels Nursery and Garden Centre

Copplehouse Lane/Field Lane, Fazakerley,   *Tel* 051-525 2712
Liverpool L10 0AG
Behind the GEC factory on the East Lanes Road (A580) down Stonebridge Lane,
6 miles north-east of Liverpool town centre

This nursery, in the middle of a Liverpool housing estate, comprises a
greenhouse, shop, two acres of ground for the retail section and numerous
heated greenhouses for raising pot plants to sell to local gardening shops.
All plants are container grown, and the selection of trees, dwarf conifers,
heathers, roses and shrubs is very good. Soft fruit and fruit trees were
notably thin on the ground and in rather poor condition at the time of our
inspection, but this was most likely due to the time of year. The other
plants all seemed to be well cared for and houseplants are worth exploring,
with prices ranging from 40p to £165. Generally the plants are cheap.
Houseplants, bedding plants and vegetables are all grown on site. If lucky,
you might be able to take advantage of one of the discounts on offer which
are advertised on a billboard at the entrance to the centre. The labelling is
generally good, with helpful hints for the different plant species, and name
and price on most individual pots. If you are having any difficulties the
staff will willingly help out. They don't have uniforms, but are not hard to

identify and are happy to pop next door to pick up any plant temporarily out of stock – the advantage of being next door to the wholesale outlet. As well as plants, the centre stocks a good range of hand tools and composts and also an excellent selection of pots, containers and baskets. Sheds, garden furniture and ornaments and pond equipment are also sold.

Prices ££
Facilities Parking, 28 cars. Toilets. Garden advice service. Delivery service. Free plant price lists
Open Mon to Fri 9am to 5.30pm (closes 7pm Thurs), Sat 9am to 5pm, Sun 10am to 5pm (Apr to June closes 7pm Tues and Wed)
Credit cards Access, Visa

LONDON, GREATER   map 6

Armstrong Waterford Garden Centre

108–116 Waterford Road,   *Tel* 01-731 4717 or 01-732 2262
Fulham SW6 2EU
At the junction of King's Road, Chelsea, and the New King's Road

Rather inauspiciously set behind a high wire fence, this centre in residential London is certainly worth a visit. It is a small centre aimed primarily at the town gardener and will not come up to the expectations of those used to large 'supermarket' style sites. However, it offers a cheerful, low-key atmosphere and is very convenient for Londoners. It is not a place to take the family as it gets rather crowded and offers few of the facilities of the big centres. It is easy to get to either by bus (11, 14, 22, 28) or underground (Fulham Broadway) but if you arrive by car you will have to find space in the neighbouring side streets. There is a wide variety of stock packed into a small space, including chemicals, composts, and a very good range of attractive terracotta pots and containers of all shapes and sizes. Teak garden furniture is also a speciality. Many larger items such as fencing, paving, heavy garden machinery and greenhouses are not available. The plant stock changes with the seasons but the range is good overall and it is possible to come across a few rarities which makes up for the occasional shortage of common varieties. Plants in poor condition are sold off cheaply so that the quick turnover assures a good standard. There are some exotic indoor plants including orchids, but also many easy-to-care-for houseplants. Some improvement could be made in the labelling, particularly for the perennials. The staff, although small in number, are very rarely in a hurry and quite content to pass the time dealing with customers' queries. A pleasant place with a good atmosphere.

Prices ££££
Facilities Garden advice service. Delivery service
Open Mon to Sat 8.30am to 6pm, Sun and bank holidays 10am to 6pm (5pm in winter). Closed Christmas Day
Credit cards Access, Visa

Awards given this year are only provisional. We need plenty of feedback to let us know what the garden centres and nurseries are like all year round. Please use the report forms at the end of the book.

Clifton Nurseries

5a Clifton Villas, W9 2PH   *Tel* 01-289 6851
Two minutes from Warwick Avenue Tube station

This centre is hidden away down a narrow alley at the back of a Victorian
terrace – look for the signs in Clifton Villas. Its location can cause one major
difficulty – parking. There is nowhere on site to leave a car, nor is it very
easy to find a space on the nearby streets (although parking restrictions are
lifted at the weekend). However, the centre has taken this into account and
staff are kept quite busy taking trolleys backwards and forwards to
customers' cars. There is a range of goods on offer suitable to the small
town garden. The plants cover an adequate range for town gardening,
varying with each season and including specimen plants and topiary. Trees
and shrubs generally are in good condition, and there were also some good
bedding plants available when we inspected, but they were expensive.
Many individual plants have labels containing helpful details,
and most group labelling is quite good. The site is very small and this puts
limitations on the number of garden accessories they can keep in stock.
One wouldn't really expect to see rotavators and greenhouses in the middle
of a London centre, and the range here caters nicely for the main type of
gardening in the local neighbourhood – patio and window-box gardening.
There are ornaments and furniture, tubs, window boxes, fencing, hand
tools and chemicals. The size of the site also has had an effect on the layout,
and paths are extremely narrow making passage in a wheelchair
impossible. A lot of work is going on at the moment building a new
entrance, shop and conservatory. Staff are most helpful, but are often busy
with the many customers.

Prices ££££££
Facilities Toilets. Garden advice service. Delivery service
Open Mon to Sat 8.30am to 6pm (closes 5.30pm in winter), Sun 9.30am to 1.30pm
Credit cards Access, Visa

Clock House Nursery

Forty Hill, Enfield EN2 9EU   *Tel* 01-363 1016
*Just off the A10 Cambridge road about 2 miles north of Enfield, nearly opposite the
gates of Forty Hall*

The plants at this nursery are of marvellous quality and very good value.
Many are grown on site. Unusual plants are often to be found while
browsing and even in mid-winter there is plenty on display. Several large
greenhouses contain plants such as fuchsias and geraniums in season.
Azaleas and rhododendrons are wisely set aside in their own shaded
corner and trees and shrubs are very well laid out outside. A lot could be
done to tidy up this nursery – it is generally disorganised with empty
flowerpots lying around and weeds proliferating along the paths – but it is
a working nursery, not a show-piece garden centre. The sparsity of signs
and directions means that, in order to find something specific, you must
look through all the plants or constantly ask the staff. Labels are helpful
and informative, though many plants in the stock area and occasionally

new batches put out for sale are unlabelled. There is a small range of sundries, mainly peat and composts, although there are plans to expand stocks in the future. Overall it is a friendly place where you can always be sure to find some exciting surprises and often at a very good price. The quality of the plants cannot be understated. One warning – queues at the cash desk are a weekend hazard. There are no refreshment facilities on the premises, but you could always pay a visit to Forty Hall across the way which has very pleasant gardens and a cafeteria.

Prices ££
Facilities Parking, 100 cars
Open Every day 8am to 5pm (closes at dusk in winter). Closed Christmas and Boxing Day

---

Cramphorn Garden Centre

Cattlegate Road, Crews Hill, Enfield EN2 9EA   *Tel 01-367 0422*
On the northern boundary of Enfield. Turn off the A10 or A1005 to Crews Hill

On the northern boundary of Enfield, this centre is surrounded on all sides by wholesale and retail, general and specialist nurseries, so there is easily enough in the area to keep you occupied for an afternoon's shopping. Since this centre gets especially busy at weekends this is the time they bring in their professional staff, who are helpful with both advice and assistance. Refreshments are also limited to the weekends in the form of a small, indoor coffee bar. The centre is nicely organised, clearly signposted and well maintained. The large indoor area houses a very wide range of sundries from tools to greenhouses, while outside you'll find plants, stoneware and fertilisers. The flower arranging accessories are particularly good. There is a good choice of brands for most of the gardening materials and equipment. There is a reasonable choice of plants with an exceedingly wide selection of variety and colour in conifers, but a sharp eye may be needed when choosing plants as quality was rather variable when our inspector visited – the heathers and fruit trees were good, but standards overall were let down by very poor clematis, weak and leggy fruit bushes, and perennials and alpines which were below par. Group labels were informative in most areas, but individual paper labels and supplementary handwritten ones were blurred and hard to read. Gerbils, hamsters and cage-birds in the pets corner provide distractions for the children.

Prices ££££
Facilities Parking, 140 cars. Toilets. Coffee bar. Garden advice service. Delivery service. Price lists, brochures and catalogues for numerous products.
Open Every day 8.30am to 6pm (closes 5pm in winter). Closed Christmas and Boxing Day
Credit cards Access, Visa

Greenford Road Garden Centre

Greenford Road, Sudbury Hill, Harrow HA1 3QF   *Tel 01-422 5730*
Off the A40 at Greenford flyover, towards Harrow

A smallish, family-run nursery with a good range of plants, but which doesn't profess to have everything for everyone. Their stock would satisfy most average, non-specialist gardeners. The display of miniature roses is very fine and there are some unusual varieties of shrubs as well as those you would normally expect to find. Quality is generally good, any older and poorer specimens being put to one side. Most plants are labelled and group labelling is conveniently placed at eye level with some good specialist information – on lime-hating plants, for instance. There is a very small, well-stocked section for seeds, tools and sundries; the wider selection of fencing and paving shares space with the cars in the gravel car park. Overall, sensibly laid out on simple rectangular lines, it's easy to find your way around this small centre. It has a family business atmosphere and the husband and wife team are very helpful

Prices Information not available
Facilities Parking, 50 cars. Garden advice service. Delivery service
Open Every day 8.30am to 6pm (closes at dusk in winter). Closed Christmas week

---

Hanworth Garden Centre

Adrian Hall Ltd, Feltham Hill Road,   *Tel* 01-890 1778/5057
Feltham TW13 7NA
From the A316 (Chertsey Road) take the turning to Hanworth and Lower Feltham

This centre has a lot to offer, particularly if you are after gardening equipment and sundries. There is a spacious indoor area stocking a wide selection of items for the home and garden, and outside an extensive range of rockery and paving. Mowers are the only type of power tool stocked. There's a good choice of pool liners and a plentiful array of water plants available to stock a pond, but no fish. The centre is well arranged with good wide paths for easy access to different sections. There are some more unusual trees and shrubs stocked along with houseplants, conifers and heathers, but at the time of our inspector's visit the variety of herbs, alpines and herbaceous perennials was small. The plants are of good quality and seem well cared for. Plant names are displayed on group labels, while individual tags sometimes offer a little more information. Our inspector found that many labels had dropped off and lay scattered around on the ground. There are specialist staff on duty in various parts of the centre and they are also willing to help load the heavier building materials.

Prices £££
Facilities Parking, 120 cars. Toilets. Ice cream and confectionery. Play area. Garden advice service. Delivery service. Free price list for building materials
Open Mon to Fri 9am to 5.30pm, Sat 8am to 5pm, Sun 9am to 5pm. Closed 4 or 5 days over Christmas
Credit cards Access, Visa

Hurrans Garden Centre

Temple Gardens, Holloway Lane,   *Tel* 01-897 6075/6
West Drayton UB7 0AE
Close to Junction 4 of the M4, on the A3044 2 miles from West Drayton

Set rather inauspiciously between the M4, gravel pits and wasteland, this centre is nevertheless a very good all-round centre and a first choice if one wants to be sure of a wide range of 'in season' garden requirements. Its comprehensive nature is complemented by a good layout both inside and out with attractive permanent displays and occasional special arrangements, for example, a model vegetable garden and a rockery. There are wide paved paths and separate screened areas for different types of plants. A large indoor display houses most sundries including furniture, tools and books, but there are no power tools and little aquatic material. Midland Buildings operates its own area for sheds and garages, but there is no fencing or paving. Most popular plants are well-represented but are rather expensive. High sales result in plants of generally good quality with older plants offered at half price. The fruit trees were the only plants not up to standard when our inspector visited, but these were old stock. Plant groups were identified by eye-level, illustrated labels but the information provided was limited. (The centre tells us this was due to re-organisations.) All individual pots have labels. The staff are generally helpful and there are special information desks inside and out.

Prices £££££
Facilities Parking, 300 cars. Toilets. Vending machines and confectionery. Garden advice service. Delivery service. Free price lists for bulbs, roses, furniture etc.
Open Mon to Wed 9am to 6pm, Thurs and Fri 9am to 8pm, Sat 9am to 6pm, Sun 10am to 6pm (closes 5pm every day in winter). Closed 25, 26 and 27 Dec
Credit cards Access, Visa

Neal's Nurseries

Heathfield Road, Wandsworth SW18 2PH   *Tel* 01-874 2037
Off Trinity Road, by Wandsworth Common

The stocks at this centre are surprisingly good for an urban area. It has a new covered indoor area for tools and sundries, stocking most items except greenhouses and fencing, but plants are the main feature and there's a comprehensive selection of unusual species. Many of the plants are kept under a covered way. At the time of our inspection, all the plants were robust-looking and seemed well cared for, but they were expensive. Group labels were good, but many of the individual plant labels were faded. Staff were friendly and helpful.

Prices ££££££
Facilities Parking, 100 cars. Toilets. Vending machine. Garden advice service. Delivery service
Open Mon to Sat 8.30am to 5.30pm (closes 4.30pm in winter), Sun 9am to 4.30pm (closes 4pm in winter). Closed 4 days at Christmas
Credit cards Access, Visa

Phoebe's Garden Centre

2 Penerley Road, Catford SE6 2LQ   *Tel* 01-698 4365 or 01-697 6101
In the centre of Catford, on the A21 ¼ mile from the south circular junction

141

This centre is easy to pass by without noticing. It is hidden away at the bottom of a narrow alley and surrounded on all sides by the gardens of Victorian houses. This suburban setting calls for a centre of just this type, offering an adequate selection of goods for the local town gardener. The restricted area means that organisation is important and this has been quite nicely handled with logical layout patterns, good signposting and an all round neat and tidy appearance. A two-bay glasshouse contains a reasonable supply of garden accessories, excepting lawnmowers and power tools, though the centre stocks spares and carries out servicing and repairs. There's a selection of sheds and greenhouses and an attractive aquatic section which is set out in its own small glasshouse displaying plenty of fish and water plants. The centre also sells fencing and paving and runs a landscaping service. On the plant side, it stocks a wide range, but with the limited space available, the choice of plants in each section can be rather poor. Exceptions to this are the collections of conifers and heathers which are very good. The heathers were in superb health on the day our inspector visited, but at the other extreme some trees seemed thin and drawn. Overall, though, the condition of the plants is very good. Labelling, however, is patchy and improvement wouldn't go amiss. Hopefully this will happen when computer labelling is introduced. At present it varies from large illustrated labels with plentiful instructions to faded, handwritten tags which are indecipherable. The staff are very friendly, and although they don't pressurise customers in any way, they are always there to help.

Prices £££
Facilities Parking, 15 cars. Vending machines. Garden advice service. Delivery service. Free catalogue and price lists for paving, walling, fencing etc.
Open Mon to Sat 9am to 5.30pm, Sun 9am to 12.30pm. Closed 4 days over Christmas
Credit cards Access, Visa

Syon Park Garden Centre

Syon Park, Brentford TW8 8JG   *Tel* 01-568 0134
In Park Road, Isleworth, off the A315 about 8 miles from central London

Set in the landscaped parkland estate of the Duke of Northumberland, this is very much a garden centre for an outing. In the summer months Syon Park has facilities and attractions for everyone, including the London Butterfly House, a motor museum, extensive parkland and Syon House and gardens. However, the centre's reputation does not rest solely on its setting; it boasts extensive ranges of most plants and there is an intriguing display of unusual specimens and a 'plant of the week'. Although the layout is generally good it can sometimes be difficult to find a specific plant quickly, but the very size of the stock makes for interesting browsing. Most plants are in good condition, and it was pleasant to see that their bonsai trees had improved considerably since our inspector's last visit. Any second-rate stock is put up for sale at a reduced price. The outdoor area has wide paths which are clearly signposted. The indoor area has a wide selection of tools and sundries, including books, pottery, flower-arranging materials and wholefoods. Larger items of garden equipment are also

stocked including greenhouses, sheds, fencing, paving and
water-gardening equipment. Labelling is informative and staff are friendly.

Prices ££££
Facilities Parking, 2,000 cars. Toilets. Restaurant, cafeteria and vending machines.
Garden advice service. Delivery service
Open Every day 9.30am to 6pm (closes 5pm in winter). Closed Christmas week
Credit cards Access, Diners Club, Visa

Wolden Nurseries and Garden Centre

Cattlegate Road, Crews Hill, Enfield EN2 9DW   *Tel* 01-363 7003
*Opposite Crews Hill Station. From A10 Cambridge road, or the A111, follow signs
to Whitewebbs and Enfield town centre*

This centre is to be found on the northern boundary of Enfield, an area
which is the home of many general and specialist nurseries. Wolden is
quite a small place, but it tries to stock as wide a range as possible which
results in rather cramped quarters. However, the different sections are well
laid out although the numerous extensions from the main building cut
across plant beds and create lots of different and unrelated areas. Once you
orientate yourself there are good-quality, well-maintained plants to browse
among. The range is fairly comprehensive with a particularly good choice
of alpines and shrubs. Some plants are grown on site including the alpines,
bedding plants and houseplants. The tools and sundries section offers the
customer a limited range of lawnmowers and greenhouses in addition to a
reasonable selection of the standard composts and hand tools, and some
paving, fencing, furniture and ornaments. There's also a range of artificial
flowers plus all the materials needed for flower arranging. The staff are
friendly and well informed and they will help with any information not to
be found on plant labels. Although this is a small and rather cluttered site
with few extra facilities, it offers good-quality and modestly priced seasonal
plants – and the building work in evidence suggests that improvements are
on the way.

Prices ££
Facilities Parking, 100 cars. Toilets. Garden advice service. Delivery service.
Free catalogue
Open Mon to Fri 8am to 5.30pm, Sat and Sun 8am to 5pm. Closed Christmas
for 4 days
Credit cards Access, Visa

LONDON COLNEY Hertfordshire   map 4

Ayletts Nurseries

North Orbital Road, London   *Tel* Bowmansgreen (0727) 22255
Colney, St. Albans AL2 1DH
*2 miles south-east of St. Albans on the A405, near the A6 roundabout at
London Colney*

A large nursery in a semi-rural setting just off the very busy North Orbital
Road. It stocks a good range of popular and specialist plants and is famous

for its dahlia collection. Each autumn a dahlia festival is held which includes floral display competitions and a honey show. Generally, plants tend to be a bit expensive. Fuchsias are another speciality and there is also a wide variety of fruit and houseplants. The quality is very good and there is a particularly wide selection of healthy-looking conifers and flowering trees. The centre is spaciously laid out, both indoors and out, and well signposted. Labels for groups of plants are informative, but individual labels are variable. The nursery does, however, offer a host of helpful leaflets on herbaceous perennials, fruit, conifers, climbing and wall plants and roses. These contain information on the plants themselves and their after care. The lists of plants for specialist purposes, such as winter colour or acid soil, can prove very useful. Indoors there is a flower shop and a good display of hand tools and garden furniture, but no power tools or mowers are available. Greenhouses, sheds, paving and fencing are also sold. Staff are helpful and friendly and the centre offers a full garden design service.

Prices £££££
Facilities Parking, 150 cars. Toilets. Vending machines. Garden advice service. Delivery service. Free price list and catalogue for dahlias. Free catalogue for all plants. Plants sold by mail order
Open Mon to Fri 9am to 5.30pm, Sat 9am to 5pm, Sun 9.30am to 5pm
Credit cards Access, Visa

Bygrave Garden and Leisure Centre ✿ ✄

North Orbital Road, London *Tel* Bowmansgreen (0727) 26100
Colney, St. Albans AL2 1DL
2 miles south-east of St. Albans on the North Orbital Road (A405). On the right-hand side of the dual carriageway travelling west from London Colney roundabout

A large centre just off a very busy road. It must be approached from the west for direct access off the dual carriageway, and if travelling from the east you'll have to use the flyover. The large car park is able to cope with demand and a nice restaurant selling hot meals as well as coffee, tea and cakes is reached directly from the parking area. In addition to a wide range of good-quality plants, this centre has an excellent variety of garden sundries. More unusual non-gardening items include playground equipment for your own home, equipment for the angler, swimming pools and even a pet shop and aviary. Mowers and hedgetrimmers are kept in a separate building with a very helpful attendant who is full of advice and suggestions.The layout of the centre is fairly good and there is not too much problem in finding one's way about. Plant labels are adequate but sometimes difficult to read where they have faded in the sun. Improvements are in progress, including changes in the layout, installation of an automatic watering and feeding system and better labelling. Staff are efficient and you should have no difficulty in obtaining information.

Prices ££££
Facilities Parking, 250 cars. Toilets. Restaurant with wine cellar. Play area. Garden advice service. Delivery service. Free price lists for plants and sundries

Open Every day 8.30am to 5.30pm. Closed 25, 26 and 27 Dec
Credit cards Access, American Express, Diners Club, Leicester Card, Visa

LOSTWITHIEL Cornwall

map 3

Penlyne Nursery

Duchy of Cornwall Woodlands, *Tel* Bodmin (0208) 872668
Cott Road, Lostwithiel, Bodmin PL22 0ET

Cott Road is a turning off the A390 St. Austell to Liskeard road, about 1 mile north of Lostwithiel

This nursery got an enthusiastic report from our inspector: 'An excellent nursery and probably the best in Cornwall for shrubs and trees'. It is set in a forestry estate on the edge of Lostwithiel and is a wonderful haven for wildflowers, butterflies and birds. The site is rather exposed and set on a steep slope overlooking the river Fowey. It is an attractive spot with a picnic area and forest trails cut through the unspoilt woodland – there are plenty of benches spaced along the paths for the less energetic members of your party to take a breather. The nursery is pleasantly unmodernised. It specialises in conifers, and also ornamental trees such as Prunus and Sorbus. Apart from a tiny office it's all open – a large acreage with an extensive spread of roses and varied trees, open-ended greenhouses and polythene shelters for more tender plants. Well-made cinder paths divide the rows of shrubs but signposts are non-existent and you have to rely on the large labels at the end of the rows and the fact that the layout is rational. Plants are not individually labelled and it can be difficult to find what you want without some advice, but the staff are knowledgeable and helpful. The nursery concentrates on the sale of plants to the virtual exclusion of tools and sundries. The only accessories stocked are chemicals and fertilisers, though sheds and fencing can be ordered. The variety of plants is excellent – vast numbers and selections of flowering and foliage shrubs, hedging and climbing plants, ornamental hardwood and coniferous trees. You can also find specialised tender shrubs for growing only in sheltered, coastal areas. The quality is first class and the plants are cheap. This is clearly a place where pride has been taken in nurturing local and unusual species. You would be well advised to look through a catalogue in advance of a visit; some initial homework on these extensive stocks would prove very useful.

Prices ££
Facilities Parking, 25 cars. Toilets. Garden advice service. Plant catalogue 20p
Open Mon to Sat 9am to 5pm. Closed for public holidays

LOWESTOFT Suffolk

map 4

Ashley Nurseries and Garden Centre

London Road, Kessingland, *Tel* Lowestoft (0502) 740264
Lowestoft NR33 7PL

3 miles south of Lowestoft on the A12

A nice centre offering a good variety of plants and a comprehensive range of tools. A friendly and well-informed staff are on hand who will try to order any plant you ask for, if it is not in stock. The range they do carry is quite adequate and there are some more unusual items to be found. Quality is generally very good, and end-of-season plants are sold off cheaply. Labelling is excellent, easily read both on the individual plants and for plant groups. A fully-stocked tools and sundries section can provide everything from fish and flower-arranging equipment to greenhouses. Paving is displayed in various patterns, giving some ideas on how their stock may be used. Interwoven fencing is available, while other sorts may be ordered. The centre is reasonably large and the layout outside is particularly good. Most of the interior area is devoted to garden accessories but there is also a range of houseplants displayed. Overall there is plenty under cover to keep you happily busy during rainy spells. Staff will help out if there is any heavy loading to do.

Prices ££££
Facilities Parking, 150 cars. Toilets. Cafeteria. Garden advice service. Delivery service. Free price list for some plants
Open Every day 9am to 5.30pm (closes 5pm in winter). Closed Christmas and Boxing Day and New Year's Day
Credit cards Access, Visa

LYMINGTON Hampshire   map 4

Spinners   ✿

School Lane, Boldre, Lymington   *Tel* Lymington (0590) 73347
SO4 8QE
On the outskirts of Boldre village which is off the A337 Lymington to Brockenhurst road. About 1½ miles north of Lymington

Our inspector liked the informal atmosphere of this nursery where the owner cannot even boast a pocket calculator to add up the bills! It may not be to everyone's taste but is a real find for an enthusiastic gardener who dislikes the modern 'family outing' centre. It is set in the midst of some quiet and beautiful countryside and has a show garden (open April to September) with mature examples of the plants available from the nursery. There are many connoisseur plants scattered around the nursery in a rather haphazard, higgledy-piggledy fashion. Plants for sale and nursery stock are all mixed together and some of the paths are narrow, but within this collection you'll find many plants which are not available in other places. Some are not even listed in the usual reference books. The plant arrangement is apparently a deliberate policy by the nursery to show plants as they should be grown. Speciality plants suitable for different levels of shade or for acid soils are particularly plentiful, and a keen gardener could do with hours to browse. The quality is always very good and prices are cheap; labelling is rather poor except for some of the groups of plants. Many labels have been removed so that rare or difficult plants are only purchased by enthusiasts who know what they're buying. The owner is an expert; very welcoming and terribly enthusiastic. Not a good place for those who like supermarket shopping or who are looking for an afternoon out with lots of active children, but for the keen gardener, a real find. As our inspector said, 'I bought plants here for which I've been searching for years'.

Prices ££
Facilities Parking, 12 cars. Toilets. Garden advice service. Catalogue and price list 30p
Open Every day 9am to 6pm (closes at dusk in winter)

MAIDENHEAD Berkshire   map 4
K.R. Hunt Nursery and Garden Centre

Holyport Road, Maidenhead   *Tel* Maidenhead (0628) 21927
SL6 2EY
Junction of the Holyport road with the A308 Windsor to Maidenhead road

A small, suburban garden centre lacking the range of facilities and products usually available at the larger centres, but nevertheless having a substantial nursery with good-quality plants. A good proportion of the plants are grown on the site and consequently are beautifully fresh and strong-looking. The plant range is adequate and the choice is perfectly reasonable for the average gardener who does not want to be wildly adventurous. The choice of conifers, herbaceous perennials and soft fruits is particularly comprehensive and the herbaceous perennials are large and sturdy. The centre has a well-designed layout and wide gravel paths. There is no signposting or labels showing types of plants, but individual labels are descriptive and reasonable. A small selection of tools and ornaments and a wider choice of chemicals and composts are also sold. Houseplants are stocked and there's a floristry department. Staff are cheerful and will readily carry goods to your car.

Prices £££
Facilities Parking, 50 cars. Toilets. Garden advice service. Delivery service
Open Every day 9am to 5pm. Closed over Christmas
Credit cards Access, Visa

MAIDSTONE Kent   map 4
Notcutts Garden Centre

Bearsted Road, Maidstone ME14 3JH   *Tel* Maidstone (0622) 39944
Just off the A249 near Maidstone

The setting for this new centre is the pleasant country surroundings of the Weald of Kent. It is a large centre which had only been open for a year when we inspected in 1984 and had managed to avoid the overcrowding of equipment and stores commonly found at garden centres. Plants are carefully laid out, some on waist-high benches surfaced with gravel. They are all labelled with prices and other relevant information. The centre specialises in hardy nursery stock and supplies many good-quality but expensive plants including mature specimens (particularly among the trees). They are generally well tended. All sorts of equipment and sundries are stocked, in particular a good range of greenhouses. A very large area of

147

camping equipment and tents might be of interest to visitors who are not so keen on gardening. The children can be kept busy at the pick-your-own fruit farm or with the strawberries and cream offered in the coffee lounge. Staff are found in each section and offer helpful guidance.

Prices £££££
Facilities Parking, 320 cars. Toilets. Cafeteria. Play area. Garden advice service. Delivery service. Plant catalogue and price list £1.50
Open Every day 9am to 5.45pm. Closed 4 days over Christmas, and New Year's Day
Credit Cards Access, Visa

MAPPERLEY Nottinghamshire
map 2

Brookfields Home and Garden Centre

Brookfields Nurseries,   *Tel* Nottingham (0602) 268200
431 Mapperley Plains, Mapperley,
Nottingham NG3 5RW
On the B684 1½ miles beyond Mapperley

This garden centre has been under new management for four years and if the improvements in layout and plants continue then it has a bright future. It already offers a good range of plants, including an impressive choice of heathers and some of the more unusual perennials. Dwarf conifers and unusual trees and shrubs are also a speciality. Finding the right plant can be rather confusing though, as trees and perennials may be sitting under a large sign saying 'bedding plants', and plants of the same variety may be kept in more than one place. Nevertheless labelling is clear and almost all the plants are individually marked. Many of the plant groups have labels with descriptions and illustrations which are perfectly adequate. When our inspector visited, the overall quality of the stock was good. The centre stocks most tools and sundries but within each category the choice is small. There are plans to begin stocking fish next season. At present only ice creams and cold drinks are available in the way of refreshments, though a tea room is also planned. Attractive flower beds surround a large play area where children can amuse themselves on the swing and climbing frame.

Prices £££
Facilities Parking, 100 cars. Toilets. Ice creams and cold drinks. Play area. Garden advice service. Delivery service. New catalogue available from spring 1985
Open Every day 9am to 6pm (closed 5.30pm weekdays Nov to Mar). Closed Christmas and Boxing Day and New Year's Day

---

MAPPLEBOROUGH GREEN Warwickshire
map 4

Mike Davis Nurseries

Mappleborough Green, near Studley   *Tel* Studley (052 785) 3288
B80 7BH
On the A435 Birmingham to Alcester road, in the village of Mappleborough Green opposite the Boot Inn

Our inspector was very impressed with many aspects of this nursery – the range of smaller sundries, the friendliness of the staff and the condition of the plant stocks. It is a fairly large site and is very well laid out indeed. The sundries section includes flower arranging accessories, stone ornaments, rockery stone and ponds, as well as the standard tools and composts. There are no garden buildings or power tools though. A very wide selection of rock plants, shrubs, trees, and other plants is displayed outside, many of which are grown on site. Ornamental trees can be reserved by customers and collected in the autumn and winter as bare-root stock. A small glasshouse contains the indoor plants. Quality is particularly good and anything past its best is sold off very cheaply indeed. Group labelling is good but some individual tags are weathered. However, there are some helpful hints on positioning and other cultural details. Nothing is too much trouble for the staff and you will find them most anxious to please and obviously getting great job satisfaction out of doing so.

Prices £££
Facilities Parking, 140 cars. Toilets. Ice cream and soft drinks (vending machines to be introduced). Garden advice service. Delivery service. Free price lists for building materials and roses
Open Mon to Fri 9am to 6pm, Sat and Sun 10am to 6pm (closes 5pm every day in winter). Closed Christmas and Boxing Day
Credit cards Access, Visa

MARLDON Devon   map 3

Style Park Gardens   ⊛ ★

Moles Lane, Marldon, Paignton   *Tel* Kingskerswell (080 47) 3056
TQ3 1SY

Just off A3022 (Torbay Ring Road) at the roundabout at the top of Hamelin Way;
take the road signposted for Abbotskerswell

A centre which is beautifully located (though on a very windy site) in open countryside near the coast and moors. It draws large crowds during the holiday season and the car park within the centre is rather small to deal with these numbers, but there is an overflow space about three minutes walk down the lane. The general layout is excellent, with ramps and wide, smooth paths which gently slope up to the indoor section where you'll find an outstanding array of houseplants. Other shops in the spacious indoor area carry a comprehensive range of all chemicals and fertilisers, tools, garden buildings, pond equipment and other sundries. There is little signposting in the shops (although there are plans to improve this), while outdoors it is adequate. Labels for plant groups are clear and useful though individual labels are not always clearly priced. Plants are cheap and quality is good even during long dry spells. Most trees, shrubs and climbers are grown by their own nurseries, but alpines, perennials, houseplants and roses are bought in. When selecting a tree or shrub, make sure the one you choose is healthy – sometimes groups of pots are pushed closely together and laterals may get broken or puny plants left unnoticed. Staff are helpful, friendly and knowledgeable. Altogether a very impressive centre but lacking 'surprise' plants.

Prices ££
Facilities Parking, 50 cars (plus overflow). Toilets. Garden advice. Delivery service.

Free price lists for most plants. Gardening guide 95p. Water gardening list 50p
Open Mon to Sat 9am to 5pm, Sun 10am to 5pm (closes 4.30pm in winter). Closed 4 days over Christmas
Credit cards Access, Visa

MAYFORD Surrey map 5

Jackmans Garden Centre

Egley Road, Mayford, Woking *Tel* Woking (048 62) 4861
GU22 0NH

On the A320 Woking to Guildford road, about 3 miles north of Guildford

'Comprehensive selection and space were the impressive features', was our inspector's verdict of this semi-urban centre. It is quite a large centre, covering about 4½ acres and the greenhouses, ornaments, fish and plants have all been given plenty of room to spread out. The layout is reasonable and signposting is very good; but labelling is not perfect, either due to weathering or absence of information such as prices. The quality of many of the plants is very good, and when one of our inspectors visited the trees, shrubs and climbers were in particularly good shape. The herbaceous perennials are displayed in a shaded section. There is a wide selection of gardening equipment and hardware, including mowers and power tools which are sold on concession, and a good selection of tubs and pots, garden furniture, sheds and greenhouses. Plans for the future include a self-contained houseplant shop, a children's play area and a coffee shop. The staff in the different departments are generally helpful, although there are not always very many about. Easily accessible from Guildford and Woking, this centre offers good general coverage for the non-specialist gardener.

Prices £££
Facilities Parking, 250 cars. Toilets. Garden advice service. Delivery service. Plants sold by mail order
Open Mon to Sat 9am to 5pm, Sun 10am to 5pm. Closed 25 to 28 Dec, 31 Dec, 1 Jan
Credit cards Access, Visa

MERRIOTT Somerset map 3

Scotts Nurseries (Merriott)

Merriott TA16 5PL *Tel* Crewkerne (0460) 72306
2 miles north of Crewkerne, 500 yds east of Merriott church

This is a well-established nursery for the serious gardener, situated in the centre of an unspoilt village. It's devoted mainly to hardy plants but also sells a good selection of tools and sundries including furniture and ornaments, though no power tools or very large items. The centre is well organised both inside and out with wide, paved paths and clear signposting. The smallest plants are displayed on raised benching and climbers are well supported. There is a good selection of high-quality plants, most of which are grown by the nursery. Staff are easy to find in the shop (but not outside) and the atmosphere is friendly.

Prices ££££
Facilities Parking, 50 cars. Toilets. Vending machines. Garden advice service.
Delivery service. Free plant price list, plant catalogue £1
Open Mon to Fri 7.45am to 5pm, Sat 9am to 5pm, Sun 2pm to 5pm

---

MIDDLETON Greater Manchester map 2
All-In-One Garden Centre ❦ ★

Rochdale Road, Middleton,   *Tel* Rochdale (0706) 32793
Manchester M24 2RB

On the A664 about 6 miles from Manchester city centre, between Junctions 19 and 20 of the M62

This centre offers good-quality plants at cheap prices. Both outdoor
and indoor sections have been well organised with shrubs arranged
alphabetically and wide paved paths providing easy access throughout the
site. Tools and sundries are available to suit most tastes and needs, with a
particularly large selection of garden sheds and glasshouses and a
comprehensive range of water-gardening equipment and aquatic plants.
Paving, sand, stone and similar construction materials are stacked in a large
yard outside. All trees and other plants are of good quality and are
maintained in excellent condition. The range of shrubs, alpines and trees is
particularly good. Alpines and heathers are all individually labelled with
informative tags while the rest of the plants have prices marked and large,
helpful group labels. The numerous staff make themselves available to
assist with car loading and they are all cheerful and happy to answer
questions. They are easily recognised by their red and brown uniforms.

Prices ££
Facilities Parking, 150 cars. Toilets. Garden advice service. Delivery service. Free
price list for building materials. Plant catalogue 95p
Open Summer, Mon to Fri 9am to 8pm, Sat and Sun 9am to 6pm. Winter, Mon to Sat
9am to 5.30pm, Sun 10am to 6pm
Credit cards Access, Visa

MIDDLETON CHENEY Oxfordshire map 4
Middleton Home & Garden Centre

Chacombe Road, Middleton Cheney,   *Tel* Banbury (0295) 710804
Banbury OX17 2OA

At Chacombe crossroads on the B4525 Banbury to Northampton road, 3 miles east of Banbury

This is an attractive and well-stocked centre which provides a service in an
area which suffers from a dearth of gardening suppliers. The garden
accessories include a good selection of all basic hand tools, chemicals and
composts. There's also a sizeable area devoted to larger items such as
fencing and a choice of garden buildings, rustic furniture and pool
equipment. Most of the larger plants are sensibly arranged in alphabetical
order, while the smaller alpines, heathers and herbs have been set out at
waist height. This, coupled with the good and durable labelling, creates an

attractive and clear layout. The overall selection of plant stock is good, and our inspector was especially impressed by the number of roses available. Everything is maintained in a healthy condition, the only complaint being that some trees were suffering from minor wind damage when inspected. There are plenty of helpful staff who will happily order items for you which are not in stock. Baskets and trolleys are provided.

Prices £££
Facilities Parking, 120 cars. Toilets. Ice cream and confectionery. Play area. Garden advice service. Delivery service. Free price list for fencing, paving, sheds and greenhouses
Open Every day 9am to 5.30pm
Credit cards Access, Visa

MILBURY HEATH Gloucestershire map 3
Severnvale Garden Centre 🌺 ✀

Milbury Heath, Falfield,   *Tel* Falfield (0454) 412247
Wotton-under-Edge GL12 8QH
On the A38 at Milbury Heath, 3 miles north of the M4/M5 Almondsbury interchange

You will find this large garden centre in the pleasantly isolated rural area overlooking the Severn Vale. It is set in well-laid-out grounds. A main car park is located amidst lawns and flowerbeds and there are ample overflow facilities if needed, all providing easy access to the site. The centre is attractively arranged, partly in the open and partly under a pergola-type roof, and asphalt paths give a sound footing. A very large indoor shop area is located under shaded glass and an extensive range of tools and sundries is available, including a wide choice of garden furniture and barbecue equipment. If there is something they haven't got in stock they're happy to try to acquire it for you. The centre stocks greenhouses, and other items such as sheds, fencing and paving are sold under franchise. Most common plants are sold and they are in good condition, though expensive.
Not all small plants are individually labelled, so it can be difficult to find the prices and details of those you want to buy. Staff are always available and offer sensible advice. If you are tired and hungry after shopping, a very good restaurant offers a varied menu of hot meals and specialises in the sale of local cider.

Prices £££££
Facilities Parking, 500 cars. Toilets. Restaurant. Garden advice service. Delivery service. Plant and garden advice catalogue £1.95, includes £2 voucher
Open Mon to Wed 9am to 5.30pm, Thurs and Fri 9am to 7pm, Sat 9am to 6.30pm, Sun 10am to 6.30pm (closes 5.30pm every day in winter)
Credit cards Access, Visa

MILFORD Derbyshire map 2
Riverside Garden Centre

Makeney Road, Milford, Derby DE5 0RU   *Tel* Derby (0332) 841191

On A6 at Milford, 5 miles north of Derby adjacent to Strutt Arms Hotel

This small centre is set in delightful surroundings, bordering on both sides of the River Derwent. From the car park, you cross the river by a footbridge and from here you can enjoy the views of the riverbanks and small island with its ducks and rabbits. The centre is compact with a well-organised interior. The stock of sundries is particularly good and includes – for entertainment only – a cage of parrots and an aviary of pheasants. The range of plants is, on the whole, limited, but they are cheap. Conifers are a speciality and are best in terms of quantity and quality. At the time of inspection, labelling didn't give any planting or growing advice and staff were slow to assist, but once aroused proved helpful. The cafe and craft shop were far from completion, but good food was available in the pub next to the car park; alternatively, you can use the picnic area among the wild fowl. You may not find everything you need here but this centre makes the most of its surroundings and provides a very pretty setting for a day out.

Prices ££
Facilities Parking, 300 cars. Toilets. Play area. Garden advice service. Delivery service
Open Every day 8.30am to 5.30pm
Credit card Access

MILFORD Surrey   map 5

The Secrett Garden Centre

Portsmouth Road, Milford,   *Tel* Godalming (048 68) 4553
near Godalming GU8 5HL
On the A3100, 1½ miles south-west of Godalming towards Milford

A map at the entrance is a helpful start to a visit around this attractive centre, and there are also useful sign boards singling out different plant sections. The centre is fairly large and its wide range of stock is nicely displayed within a landscaped garden which has a pond and garden seats. Tender plants are kept under cover. The many hardy species sold, including some unusual varieties of shrubs and a comprehensive conifer section, are arranged between the good, wide paths. There are some beautiful bedding displays, changing with the season. Staff remove inferior plants quite regularly so the quality of those left on display is generally very good. Surplus stock is sometimes sold off at half price at the end of the season. Labelling provides hints about suitable growing conditions and, apart from some signs of weathering, is basically quite good. There is a very large furniture section which includes barbecue equipment, and the choice of plant pots and containers is substantial. Chemicals, composts and books also contribute to an interesting range of sundries. Fencing and paving are also stocked, but no sheds or greenhouses. The staff are keen on their work and will always find someone who can answer a query if they are unable to help you themselves.

Prices ££££
Facilities Parking, 300 cars. Toilets. Ice creams and confectionery. Play area. Garden advice service. Delivery service
Open Mon to Sat 9am to 5.30pm, Sun (Mar to June) 10am to 5pm
Credit cards Access, Visa

MILTON KEYNES Buckinghamshire   map 4
Cramphorn Garden Centre   ✕

Avebury Boulevard,   *Tel* Milton Keynes (0908) 604011
Secklow Gate, Central Milton
Keynes MK9 3BY
Central Milton Keynes, near the main shopping centre and adjacent to the Beefeater
Restaurant

Marmosets and chinchillas are possibly not every gardener's dream, but
this centre's pet section certainly deserves a mention for its rarity value.
Children will be fascinated by the parrots and monkeys and snakes and
you'll be lucky to get away with just a hamster! Meanwhile for the more
conventional shoppers there is a very good range of all tools and sundries
kept both indoors and out. This includes many larger items such as
conservatories, greenhouses, sheds and building materials. The wide paths
lead all around the grounds and the inside sections are clearly signposted
and roomy enough to avoid problems with congestion. The selection of
roses, shrubs and conifers is very good and the conifers were in fine shape
when inspected. The roses were also looking especially lovely. But our
inspector would like to have seen a slightly better collection of houseplants
and cut flowers. A range of seasonal plants is grown under glass and is
open to public view. Labelling offers some helpful instructions but many
are worn and difficult to read. The staff are fairly helpful and are willing to
load cars if requested. A small coffee shop serves Rombouts coffee.

Prices ££££
Facilities Public car park nearby. Cafeteria. Garden advice service. Delivery service
(use of Borrovan). Brochures and catalogues for various ranges stocked
Open Every day 8.30am to 6pm (closes 5pm in winter). Closed Christmas and
Boxing Day
Credit cards Access, Visa

MOLESCROFT Humberside   map 2
Molescroft Garden Centre

114 Woodhall Way, Molescroft,   *Tel* Hull (0482) 881172
near Beverley HU17 7JP
Off the B1248, 1 mile north-west of Beverley

This is a good, small nursery which fulfils the needs of the local market
town and its environs. The overall selection of plants is quite reasonable for
a place of this size and they are very well maintained – the range of shrubs,
trees, bedding plants and vegetables is particularly good. A glassed-in area,
kept beautifully cool in hot weather, contains an attractive display of
bright, healthy houseplants; or if you are intrigued by the Japanese art of
bonsai, there is also an interesting collection for you to examine. For those
who head straight for the hardware department, the good range of hand
tools from various manufacturers is worth a look. In addition to these, the
centre stocks sheds, fencing and paving, as well as furniture and

ornaments, but large power tools and greenhouses are absent. Both inside and outside sections are adequately laid out. Plants are not arranged alphabetically, but rather to please the eye. Some of the labels suffer from fading but staff will happily help out if there are problems.

Prices £££
Facilities Parking, 15 cars. Garden advice service. Delivery service. Free plant price list and catalogue
Open Every day 9am to 5.30pm (closes 5pm in winter). Closed Christmas week
Credit cards Access, Visa

MORPETH Northumberland map 1
Heighley Gate Nursery Garden Centre

Wooler Road, Morpeth NE61 3DA *Tel* Morpeth (0670) 513416
On the A697 to Coldstream Wooler, 3 miles north of Morpeth

This centre is still being developed, but our inspector feels it is heading in the right direction. There is a good, wide choice of both plants and gardening equipment and the layout is effective, with everything clean and tidy and clearly signposted. The shrubs and plants are well organised, but the labelling is variable. In most cases there are large general notices for each group with an accompanying picture, but sometimes the writing is not too clear. Many plants are grown on site and they are generally in good condition. The range is very good in all areas, and one of the impressive features is the choice of sizes available, particularly noticeable among the shrubs where you can either purchase an 'instant garden' for a price or, if you are willing to wait, there are good-quality smaller versions for a more reasonable outlay. The plants are all set out on gravel and are roofed over. The tools and sundries area includes all accessories except for sheds and lawnmowers. A new area for garden furniture is planned. The aquarium has some interesting features and the stock of fish is very good, as is the aquatic plant area. There are also aviaries which may interest the children, and picnic and play areas for them to let off steam. The staff are cheerful and helpful, and although they are not all knowledgeable, expert advice is available if asked for. Baskets, trolleys and umbrellas are provided.

Prices £££
Facilities Parking, 300 cars. Toilets. Vending machines. Play area. Garden advice service. Delivery service. Plant catalogue 95p
Open Mon to Fri 9am to 6pm (closes at 5pm in winter), weekends and bank holidays 9.30am to 5pm. Closed Christmas and Boxing Day and 1 and 2 Jan

---

NANTWICH Cheshire map 2
Stapeley Water Gardens

London Road, Stapeley, Nantwich *Tel* Crewe (0270) 623868
CW5 7LH
On the A51 Nantwich to Stone road 1 mile south of Nantwich

Stapeley Water Gardens is a centre of particular interest to those keen on water gardening. Displays of fountains, pools and fish are featured, and their 'dancing waters' are synchronised to music, much to the delight of the children, while in their water equipment shop can be found a large selection of all types of water garden supplies. There is also an area devoted entirely to swimming pools. The centre offers a large collection of furniture and garden ornaments incorporating water features, as well as a good supply of sheds and greenhouses. On the other hand they do not have any power tools or mowers. The range of plants available and their quality is variable and on the day of our inspector's visit the stocks of shrubs, trees (ornamental and fruit) and soft fruit (only strawberries) were low. The herbs, shrubs and herbaceous plants were not in very good condition, though the rhododendrons, houseplants, specialist conifers and many smaller plants were of good quality. All plants were labelled, although not all with illustrations. Some of the labels had faded, but the staff are pleasant and willing to help out if you have problems. For snacks, teas and coffee a small cafeteria is provided on-site with a picnic area adjacent if you prefer to sit outside (cafeteria food only).

Prices ££££
Facilities Parking, 3,000 cars. Toilets. Cafeteria and 'burger bar'. Play area. Garden advice service. Delivery service. A to Z of water gardening 25p or 2 first-class stamps. Free price lists and leaflets. Aquatic plants sold by mail order
Open Mon to Fri 9am to 6pm, Sat and Sun 10am to 7pm (closes 5pm every day in winter). Closed 2 weeks over Christmas
Credit cards Access, Visa

NATLAND Cumbria
map 2

R Holmes & Sons
❀

The Nurseries, Natland, near Kendal   *Tel* Sedgwick (0448) 60224
LA9 7QL
On the edge of the village of Natland, 2 miles south of Kendal on the Natland to Sedgwick road

Surrounded by fields, just off a quiet country road, this is a good 'local' nursery especially for bedding plants and shrubs. A smallish indoor area sells chemicals, composts and tools, while flowering potplants are housed in a glasshouse; but the real area of interest is outdoors. Recent expansion has allowed plenty of room for an impressive selection of their own-grown bedding plants and biennials in season, and the wide, hard-surfaced paths facilitate access to a good range of healthy shrubs, heathers, conifers and rockery and herbaceous plants. Plants are very cheap and quality is good, though our inspector spotted mildew on the gooseberries! Individual plants are only labelled with name and price and there is no general information or cultural instructions for plants groups. A little more signposting would also be a helpful addition. Staff are always around to give advice and will help with carrying heavy goods to the car park. Overall, this nursery is a good source of plants at reasonable prices.

Prices £
Facilities Parking, 25 cars. Toilets. Vending machines. Free price lists for roses, heathers, conifers etc.

Open Mon to Fri 8.30am to 6pm, Sat 9.30am to 5.30pm, Sun 9.30 to 1pm
Credit cards Access, Visa

NETHER ALDERLEY Cheshire map 2
S.E. Matthews

Alderley Park Nurseries,   *Tel* Alderley Edge (0625) 582087
Nether Alderley, Macclesfield SK10 4TH
On the A34 Wilmslow to Congleton road, 100 yds from Monk's Heath traffic lights

This is a family-run, moderate-sized nursery which retains an emphasis on plants, particularly shrubs and dwarf conifers, rather than gardening sundries. The plants are not displayed in any systematic way, but are arranged to illustrate contrasts in habit and foliage, or to show plants requiring similar soil and climatic conditions. Almost all are labelled clearly with information on suitable position, description and price. Group labels are also good – they are distinct and permanent. Our inspector found the plants generally strong and of good quality. Changes in progress when we inspected should hopefully improve the indoor section which was rather crowded and ill-lit. The site is continually developing, with paths being paved and facilities for the disabled being improved. There is a modest display of hand tools as well as a few lawnmowers. Chemicals, composts and artificial flowers complete the list of smaller sundries, but you will also find greenhouses, ornaments and furniture available. This centre gives a pleasant atmosphere and an impression of honest trading. It offers the Interflora service and evening demonstrations are held in summer and winter. The staff are helpful with enquiries, and if they can't answer a question, customers are referred to senior personnel.

Prices £££
Facilities Parking, 200 cars. Toilets. Play area. Restaurant. Garden advice service. Delivery service. Free plant price list, catalogue 20p
Open Every day 8am to 6pm (closes 5pm in winter). Closed Christmas and Boxing Day and New Year's Day
Credit cards Access, Visa

NEWCASTLE-UPON-TYNE Tyne and Wear map 2
B&Q Retail

Sands Industrial Estate, Haxham Road,   *Tel* 091-488 8144
Swalwell, Newcastle-upon-Tyne NE16 3DJ
Adjacent to the slip road from the A69 at Swalwell going west

This is a DIY superstore as well as a garden centre so there is plenty to attract both the home-improvers and the gardeners in your family. Our inspector was pleasantly surprised by the consistently high quality of the plants available. The range is quite reasonable, but it concentrates on the more popular, run-of-the-mill varieties, so you are unlikely to find anything unusual. There is a wide range of items which the gardener should find of interest. Building materials, barbecues, a fair variety of paving, and a good display of sheds and greenhouses are just some features of the comprehensive sundries section. Non-gardening items include self-assembly furniture. Both the outside and indoor areas are closely packed with goods, but all displays are well set out so the layout works well. Staff are not always easy to find though, and their horticultural knowledge is somewhat limited. Labelling is only fair so this cannot help very much in providing instructions or information. Supermarket trolleys can be used for transporting your goods and there is a clean and pleasant refreshment area.

Prices ££££
Facilities Parking, 150 cars. Toilets. Cafeteria and vending machine. Delivery service. Free shed and greenhouse catalogue
Open Mon to Sat 9am to 8pm
Credit cards Access, Visa

Peter Barratt's Garden Centre

Gosforth Park,   *Tel* Newcastle-upon-Tyne (0632) 365597
Newcastle-upon-Tyne NE3 5EN
On the A189, 4 miles from the city centre adjacent to Gosforth Park race course

A fairly new centre set in open countryside adjacent to the race course. Outdoor plants are well set out and generally in alphabetical order and the excellent selection of houseplants is nicely displayed in the large covered area. Most popular plants are stocked as well as some more unusual varieties and the range of conifers is quite extensive. The quality is generally good and there are a reasonable number of plants from which to choose. There's a wide range of tools and spare parts, and a good selection of sundries including ornamental pots, tubs, and artificial flowers. A new section of 'farmhouse products' sells jams, biscuits and sweets, and the range of books on gardening and homecraft makes for an enjoyable browse. The centre also has a large display area for paving and walling materials and there are plans to extend the greenhouse and shed department. Our inspector noticed that improvements had been taking place, particularly in the layout and among the display beds. There is also a new stock of fish for outdoor pools to add to the already excellent range of tropical fish. Staff at the centre are friendly and helpful.

Prices £££
Facilities Parking, 170 cars. Toilets. Vending machines. Play area. Garden advice service. Delivery service. Free price lists for greenhouses, sheds and building products
Open Every day 9am to 5.30pm. Closed 25 and 26 Dec and 1 Jan
Credit cards Access, Visa

Willow Dene Garden Centre

Great Lime Road, Forest Hall,   *Tel* Tyneside (091) 2681003
Newcastle-upon-Tyne NE12 0A8
On the Great Lime Road, about 5 miles north of the town centre, towards Killingworth

The country-like setting, surrounded as it is by woodlands and trees, belies the suburban location of this centre. It is an attractive site and is undergoing expansion and improvement in many quarters. A wooded area with a stream marks one of the boundaries of the grounds and there are some pleasant features dotted round the site such as conifer displays and a water garden with a running well. The firm offers a landscape gardening service and there are landscaping plans for the centre itself which will be interesting to follow. At the moment there are wide flagstone pathways and some plants are on low terraces, reached by the occasional single step. The range of plants, particularly conifers and heathers, is very good, and they are in mainly good condition. Unusual varieties and many different sizes can be picked out from among the run-of-the-mill stock. Labelling is variable, some illustrated and offering useful instructions, others faded and lacking prices. The centre tells us it intends to improve this where it can. There is a reasonable range of hardware, including a selection of hand tools and furniture. Greenhouses should be stocked by spring 1985. The choice of containers, pots and tubs is very good, and the centre will supply you with fencing or paving stones to order. The owners are very helpful, but there are not many staff around and it is often necessary to return to the office for information. There is a patio with seating if you want to relax and a play area is planned for the near future.

Prices £££
Facilities Parking, 25 cars. Vending machines and ice cream. Garden advice service. Delivery service
Open Mon to Fri 9am to 5.30pm, Sat 9am to 5pm, Sun 9.30am to 4.30pm
Credit cards Access, Visa

NEW MALDEN Surrey   map 5

Homebase   ⁄ ♿

229–253 Kingston Road, New Malden KT3 3RU   *Tel* 01-949 7141
On the A2043 Kingston Road about 1 mile south-east of Kingston town centre

The setting is suburban and the centre is typical of the Homebase stores. This branch is relatively new and tends still to suffer from limited stocks. The plants kept are generally the seasonal ones, of which there is a wide choice, but the excellent range of dwarf rhododendrons and some of the choice shrubs tend to be snapped up by the public very quickly and do not get replaced for some time. The outside area has clear signposting and wide paths. Larger gardening accessories are displayed, including a good selection of patio and building materials, sheds and greenhouses and all manner of terracotta pots and stone troughs. Smaller garden sundries are just as well represented, including some decorated earthenware. The only noticeable omission is water-gardening equipment and fish. There's a DIY section which may interest the non-gardeners in the family. The staff keep the weeds down and conscientiously water, but although they are always happy to try to answer questions, they don't really have the experience or knowledge to compete with a professional nurseryman.

Prices £££
Facilities Parking, 195 cars (plus 51 overflow). Toilets. Garden advice service. Delivery service

Open Mon to Thurs 9am to 8pm, Fri 9am to 9pm, Sat and Sun 9am to 6pm. Closed 24 and 25 Dec
Credit cards Access, Visa

NEW MILL W. Yorkshire   map 2

Totties Nurseries   ❀

J A Bentley, New Mill,   *Tel* Holmfirth (0484) 683363
near Holmfirth HD7 1UN
From the A635/A616 crossroads in New Mill take the road to Holmfirth and
Manchester for 50 yds, turn left up hill to Scholes/Totties, turn right at the top
of the hill

Set high up in the Pennines, this nursery has lovely views overlooking the valley. Its situation ensures that the plants raised in its large propagation and growing-on area are sturdy and hardy and are likely to survive almost any conditions. The nursery specialises in conifers and other trees but also grows many other plants such as heathers, alpines, herbaceous perennials and bedding plants. Plants are cheap and nicely arranged in beds about 5ft wide divided by wide gravel paths. The grounds are devoted to outdoor plants of every description, and only the roses are not propagated on the site. The selection of heathers, alpines and apple trees is particularly impressive and the quality of plants all round reflects the knowledge of the nurserymen who run the centre. Plants are identified by a label placed at the front of the display bed and some have clearly printed tags – only the occasional hand-written label has faded. This is primarily a plant centre and does not offer many extra facilities, but there is a small shop which sells a few chemicals, pots and trellises. The staff are all experienced horticulturalists and they are kept busy caring for the plants when not serving customers, but nevertheless are always quite happy to deal with any questions about cultivation. Customers are welcome to browse through the fields and look at the nursery stock.

Prices ££
Facilities Parking, 60 cars. Garden advice service. Free descriptive lists of plants
Open Mon to Fri 9am to 7pm, Sat and Sun 9am to 6pm (closes 5pm or at dusk every day in winter). Closed Christmas and New Year

---

NEWQUAY Cornwall   map 3

Algarnick Nurseries, Cornwall

Quintrell Downs Greenhouse   *Tel* Newquay (063 73) 77402
Centre, Quintrell Downs, Newquay TR8 4LH
On the A3058 at Quintrell Downs, 3 miles from Newquay

It's well worth dropping in to this centre if you live in the area and need plants suitable for a windy coastal garden. It specialises in container-grown shrubs and trees which will do well under these adverse conditions. At the time of our inspection, the speciality plants had fared best when it came to labelling; the remaining species had washed-out tags or nothing at all (the centre tells us that labelling has since been improved). Quality overall was variable when inspected. The centre covers quite a small site with a layout which could well be improved with better signposting. (We are told that both layout and signposting are being updated.) The paths are adequate and plant sections are well spaced out. A large glasshouse run under separate management stocks a very pleasing range of good, healthy indoor plants. A satisfactory range of all common tools and sundries is available, including larger items such as sheds, fencing and paving, and the centre also specialises in custom-made cedarwood greenhouses and porches. Staff are very courteous and helpful and always on hand with advice and muscle.

Prices £££
Facilities Parking, 30 cars. Toilets. Garden advice service. Delivery service. Free price lists for greenhouses, sheds and plants
Open Mon to Sat 9am to 5.30pm
Credit card Visa

NORMANTON W. Yorkshire   map 2

Birkwood Nurseries

Birkwood Farm, Altofts,   *Tel* Wakefield (0924) 892573
Normanton WF6 2JE
3 miles north of Wakefield, off the A642, 1 mile down the road marked Stanley Ferry

This nursery supplies some good-value, peat-based composts, basic fertilisers, and growing bags – both branded and non-branded. Early each season these are sold at a discount which provides a cheap way of buying in your year's supply. Excellent quality home-grown bedding and vegetable plants are available in spring and the centre also sells a fairly wide range of other plants at low prices. The shrubs and conifers are of particularly good quality. The garden equipment section is a bit limited in range, but you will find fencing, paving and ornaments, as well as the composts and hand tools. A few sheds and greenhouses on display in the car park are sold by franchise. The centre has grown up from small beginnings and its development has been rather haphazard. The layout, therefore, isn't very good and reflects the lack of overall planning. There are few signposts and paths are either gravel, paving or matting over soil, and on a wet and windy day a visit can be a little trying. At the time of our inspection the labels for plant groups offered little in the way of information – simply price and name, while individual labels were often missing. However, the nursery tell us that signposting and labelling have now been improved. Birkwood Nurseries are attached to a farm shop which sells fresh vegetables and meat for freezing, and there's a pick-your-own fruit section. Planned expansion includes a larger houseplant section, a water-gardening section and a play area.

Prices ££
Facilities Parking, 50 cars. Toilets. Vending machines. Garden advice service
Open Every day 9am to 5.30pm (closes 9pm in fruit picking season)
Credit cards Access, Visa

NORTH SHIELDS Tyne and Wear

map 2

Cleveland Road Nurseries

Cleveland Road,
North Shields NE29 0PF

Tel North Shields (0632) 582536

Near the coast, off the B1304, Hawkes Lane. Turn into Cleveland Road opposite North Shields football ground

This nursery was taken over 10 years ago when it was suffering from neglect. Now it is efficiently run and is geared to the customer's needs in every way. It is a 'plant-care' centre rather than a garden 'supermarket', so it concentrates on offering healthy, interesting plants rather than fancy presentations or huge numbers of plants. All plants are container-grown and the best choice is in the spring and early summer. However, the selection is generally wide all year, particularly in the shrub section. The shrubs are kept in very good condition and the heathers also deserve to be singled out for being in tip-top shape. All labelling is very good with prices marked throughout and some illustrations. The owners are skilled people and they run this family business in a thoughtful and caring manner. They have provided a nice layout indoors, and although there are no special features outside, the general appearance is very pleasant. A large wooden shop holds general sundries such as hand tools, chemicals and composts. Paving and ornaments are also available, but the nursery largely devotes itself to plants. There is no car park, but you can park in the street. (Note that the telephone number is due to be altered in 1985.)

Prices ££££
Facilities Garden advice service. Delivery service
Open Every day 9.30am to 5pm (closes 4.30pm in winter)

NORTH WALSHAM Norfolk

map 4

LeGrice – The Plant People

Norwich Road, North Walsham
NR28 0DR

Tel North Walsham (0692) 402591

On the B1150 Norwich road, ¼ mile within the southern boundary of North Walsham

A wonderful place for rose lovers and the whole nursery can easily provide any gardener with several hours of happy browsing. A lot of the 45-acre site is open to the public, and the 5 acres of fragrant rose fields which can be visited from July to September deserve a special mention. There are some attractive and mature show gardens which give an idea of what your young container purchases might look like in a few years' time. The plants here are all clearly labelled. The wide range of roses is complemented by a good choice of quality trees, conifers, perennials and rhododendrons. The amount of stock actually put out for sale at any one time is kept small so that turnover is rapid and plants are kept in the nurseries until needed to replenish supplies. Most of the exterior selling area is paved and the lawns around the show gardens are all mown and well kept. Signposting is good and labelling is remarkably clear and instructive. There are information points dotted around the centre or you can pick up the free, informative rose catalogue. This centre concentrates on its propagation and doesn't try to be everything to everybody; however, it stocks many of the larger items such as sheds, fencing and paving. The centre also offers a landscaping service. Of particular interest are the special events where the nursery's own experts demonstrate various skills and techniques through the day or over a weekend, such as fruit pruning or herb growing. On an ordinary day the staff are all found working around the beds and gardens, but they are trained and experienced and always happy to help.

Prices ££££
Facilities Parking, 60 cars (plus 100 overflow). Toilets. Cafeteria. Play area. Garden advice service. Delivery service. Free price list for roses and other plants, free catalogue for roses. Roses sold by mail order
Open Mon to Sat 9am to 5pm, Sun and bank holidays 10am to 5pm. Closed 25 Dec to 1 Jan
Credit cards Access, Visa

NORTHAM Devon   map 3

Northam Garden Centre

Northam, Bideford EX39 3QE   *Tel* Bideford (023 72) 4403
On the edge of Northam, 2 miles from Bideford

This is a good garden centre for a suburban area and it offers a very useful facility to the local neighbourhood. It is nicely located on the edge of open countryside, but still integral with its more immediate residential surroundings. A small car park is easily reached from the road, and it provides adequate space for a centre of this fairly small size. The site is well planned in theory, although in practice the alphabetical order is not always followed and individual sections are not very clearly designated. The indoor shop, however, is more consistently arranged and it stocks pretty much all that the average gardener would need, including heavy machinery and greenhouses. The centre runs a repair service for machinery and stocks a good selection of spares. They also run a landscaping and contracting service. On the plant side, the range stocked is quite reasonable and so is the quality, though the condition varies somewhat according to how long they have been sitting about. New stock always appears bright and healthy, while some of the older plants were a bit weary looking when our inspector visited. Labelling on individual plants needs some attention where it has faded or has no price marked. Improvements planned at the centre include an irrigation system and a play area for children. Staff are helpful and cheerful, although not all experts, and you should be able to find someone to answer your general queries.

Prices £££
Facilities Parking, 15 cars. Toilets. Ice cream. Garden advice service. Delivery service. Free price lists for paving, sheds, roses, trees etc.
Open Every day 8am to 6pm (closes 5pm in winter). Closed Thur pm all year, Sun pm Jan and Feb
Credit cards Access, Visa

NORTHAMPTON Northamptonshire map 4

Northampton Vale Garden Centre

Newport Pagnell Road,
Northampton NN4 0BU

Tel Northampton (0604) 65725

On the B526 Northampton to Newport Pagnell road, adjacent to the Queen Eleanor pub, 2½ miles from the town centre

You will receive a friendly welcome at this garden centre. A commissionaire is posted at the entrance to greet and direct customers, and many other helpful staff are available, even at busy times. The centre is well organised with clear signposting. Plants are quite expensive but the range is very good with a superb selection of shrubs, conifers and other trees, and overall quality is excellent. A large undercover area is devoted to indoor plants. General descriptions of each plant are clearly displayed and all-in-all labelling is very good. The indoor section is well laid out and there is plenty of space for manoeuvring between the main displays. Gardening sundries from pets to greenhouses are plentifully supplied. Fencing, paving and landscaping services are available from a company adjacent to the centre, and there's also a display of camping equipment and swimming pools. For children there are a few electrically-operated 'rides' and in the entertainment centre next door there is a large, old-fashioned working merry-go-round and a display of ancient working organs – the pride of place going to a Grand Wurlitzer which gives regular recitals. Definitely an impressive centre stocking almost anything you might need for the garden.

Prices £££££
Facilities Parking, 150 cars. Toilets. Restaurant. Garden advice service. Delivery service. Plant handbook £1.95
Open Mon to Sat 9am to 6pm (June and July open to 8pm Thurs and Fri), Sun 10am to 6pm. Closes 5.30pm every day in winter. Closed Christmas and Boxing Day
Credit cards Access, Visa

NORTON ST. PHILIP Somerset map 3

Oldfield Nurseries

Trowbridge Road,
Norton St. Philip, near Bath BA3 6NG

Tel Limpley Stoke (022 122) 2104

Near Norton St. Philip, on the A366 close to its junction with the A36. About 8 miles south of Bath

This nursery is sited in an established garden around an old house. It is a place for plant-lovers and has never diversified into supplying gardening equipment. The range of plants is very wide with the only omissions being houseplants and waterplants. Plants are available in all sizes and are obviously well grown. The nursery propagates most of them itself and specialises in those which like lime and clay soils. There are often unusual varieties to be found. The nursery will also take orders for plants it doesn't have in stock. Our inspector loved the serious atmosphere where customers can pick and choose plants without being distracted by extraneous 'offerings'. The staff are knowledgeable as well as cheerful and willing to help. A great attraction of this centre – particularly in the summer – are the spectacular exhibition beds and rock gardens (which are to be extended). Professional horticulturalists run courses from April to September on a variety of topics such as garden planning, flower arranging, shrubs and hedges, soil and composts or garden history. The nursery also offers a garden design service.

Prices £££
Facilities Parking, 60 cars. Toilets. Garden advice service. Free price list and catalogue
Open Mon to Sat 8.30am to 5pm, Sun 11am to 5pm

NORWICH Norfolk   map 4

Mousehold (Cash and Carry) Garden Centre

63 Mousehold Lane, Norwich   *Tel* Norwich (0603) 413272
NR7 8HP

On Norwich ring road, between Wroxham and Salhouse roads. On the north-east side of Norwich, above Mousehold Heath

This is a small centre, located in a built-up area just off the busy ring road, but the shelter offered by walls and fencing gives one a sense of seclusion. The size of the centre must obviously limit its range and general appeal, but it is a very friendly place and seems to cater for a regular, local clientele. Many plants have been cleverly fitted into the space available with a care and attention which contributes to the attractive appearance. There are good paths, neat plant beds and a general well-thought-out display. The plants are very cheap and are all of good quality – the heathers and dwarf conifers were exceptionally fine and the selection quite impressive. There is a reasonable range of plants, but few specimens on show of any one type. However, large stocks are held at a nearby site. The sundries section is well arranged in a tiny shop – but it is very crowded and there is little room to move around. Hand tools, furniture and paving are stocked and there are even two sheds and three greenhouses on display. The staff are usually at work among the plants but they are willing to help and advise whenever needed. The centre hopes to expand shortly to include water-gardening and a play area.

Prices £
Facilities Parking, 20 cars. Toilets. Garden advice service. Delivery service. Free price list for garden buildings
Open Every day 9am to 5pm

Notcutts Garden Centre

Daniels Road, Norwich NR4 6QP   *Tel* Norwich (0603) 53155
On the Norwich ring road, on the south side of the junction with the A11

Notcutts in Norwich supplies an excellent range of hardy, home-grown plants, but at a price. There are many types of shrubs available, the fruit tree section offers a good choice, and vegetables and bedding were in plentiful supply when our inspector visited. There is really little that the average gardener needs which can't be found at this establishment, and plants are all well grown and maintained, resulting in stock of first-class quality. Labelling carries informative hints, and labels for groups of plants are all illustrated. The range of tools and sundries is not exceptional but is quite comprehensive and includes both the smaller bits and pieces and the items at the larger end of the market (greenhouses, sheds and pond equipment are sold under franchise). The layout is good and signposting is clear throughout. Easily-wheeled trolleys are on hand to transport purchases to the car park. Some extra features include the pet centre with its fish, birds and beasts, a small craft shop and a coffee shop selling rolls, salads, pies and drinks. Help is available from the staff if required.

Prices ££££££
Facilities Parking, 380 cars. Toilets. Cafeteria. Play area. Garden advice service. Plant catalogue £1.50
Open Every day 8.30am to 5.30pm. Closed for 4 days over Christmas and New Year's Day
Credit cards Access, Visa

NOTTINGHAM Nottinghamshire   map 2

Homebase   ⚡ ♿

Castle Marina Park, Castle   *Tel* Nottingham (0602) 413800
Boulevard, Nottingham NG7 1GY
About ½ mile from Nottingham centre, just off the A6005, between the Nottingham to Derby railway line and the Nottingham to Beeston canal

This is essentially just one part of a large DIY complex. The range of gardening equipment sold is very comprehensive – you'll find everything from trowels to lawnmowers in the tools section, and there are some good building materials, composts and terracotta pots. There's also an interesting range of books on all aspects of gardening. The selection of plants is also satisfactory, but you are unlikely to find anything very out of the ordinary. The display of ericas impressed our inspector and the strongest lines at the time he visited seemed to be the shrubs and alpines. All plants are carefully weeded and watered and as a result are in fine condition. Good, permanent plastic labels offer coloured illustrations. The layout caters well for those less able to get around since there are no steps to negotiate and the paths are nice and wide. The doors are also a good width and they open and close automatically, which is a help for anyone in a wheelchair or with a trolley. It can be difficult to find any staff members, but if you ask at the Information Desk in the main store someone will be called to assist – there are horticultural experts available to deal with gardening questions. A coffee lounge provides light refreshments and there is a public house adjacent.

Prices £££
Facilities Parking, 322 cars (plus 34 overflow). Toilets. Coffee house. Garden advice service. Delivery service
Open Mon to Thurs 9am to 8pm, Fri 9am to 9pm, Sat 8.30am to 6pm. Closed Christmas
Credit cards Access, Visa

Nottingham Garden Centre

Clifton Lane, Wilford, *Tel* Nottingham (0602) 815656
Nottingham NG11 7AT
About 3 miles south of Nottingham, on the edge of Wilford

The entrance to this centre immediately creates a favourable impression
with large bowls of seasonal plants throwing out a lovely splash of colour.
Further exploration of the centre will not disappoint you. The layout is
good, with wide paths and many raised beds. Plants are quite expensive.
The range and quality of stock in the trees and shrubs section
deserve a special mention – it includes plenty of conifers and some
good fruit trees. If you have a liking for houseplants, there's a selection of
popular ones in fine condition which are worth looking at. They are set out
in a tasteful display, with a fountain playing in the middle. The garden
accessories department has been depleted since the centre stopped selling
greenhouses, lawnmowers and power tools – competition from large stores
was too great. Nevertheless there are still plenty of ornaments, plastic
pools, furniture and hand tools available, and fencing and paving are also
supplied. There are also many non-gardening items for sale. Our inspector
found the staff were helpful and quite willing to search out particular
plants. In our inspector's opinion 'this is a well-planned, well-stocked, and
attractive garden centre', and for those without cars it is easily accessible by
public transport. A small coffee lounge provides tea and coffee.

Prices £££££
Facilities Parking, 110 cars. Toilets. Cafeteria. Garden advice service. Delivery service
Open Every day 9am to 6pm (closes 5.30pm in winter). Open Sun, Mar to Oct for
plants only
Credit cards Access, Visa

OAKHANGER Hampshire map 4
Springfields Nursery

Oakhanger, near Bordon GU35 9JD *Tel* Bordon (042 03) 2528
On the road from Blackmoor to Oakhanger, 2 miles off the A325

The atmosphere at this nursery is one of a pleasant and helpful gardeners'
centre, and it seems unlikely that the owners intend to, or even want to,
turn it into an all-purpose, modern garden centre. It is found on a quiet,
country lane and first-time visitors might have problems finding it, but it is
well known locally. Some plants are displayed outside while other, more
tender plants are found in greenhouses and polythene-covered areas –
these include indoor plants and any 'specials' as well as a wide range of
excellent, home-raised fuchsias, begonias, geraniums, dahlias and the like.
These are beautifully arranged and most attractive. The outside sections are
rather more tatty, with weeds and broken brickwork detracting from the
displays, although when our inspector visited there were signs that this
was being 'smartened up'. Stocks were very low when inspected,
consisting mainly of trees, containerised roses and shrubs, but the spring
and autumn periods usually offer a better choice. All plants were in

167

reasonable condition, but the labelling could have done with some attention. The emphasis here is very much on growing, and the nursery doesn't stock the full range of garden sundries found at many large centres. However, most average gardeners would find their simpler needs satisfied – there's a reasonable selection of hand tools, garden furniture and ornaments, as well as a limited amount of fencing and paving. The staff are very pleasant and they will offer to order any special plants not in stock or replace unsatisfactory ones (within reason!) and deliver locally free of charge.

Prices ££££
Facilities Parking, 100 cars. Toilets. Vending machines. Garden advice service. Delivery service
Open Every day 9am to 5.30pm (closes 5pm in winter). Closed for a few days over Christmas
Credit cards Access, Visa

ORMSKIRK Lancashire   map 2
Warbreck Garden Centre

Lyelake Lane, Lathom,   *Tel* Ormskirk (0695) 22960
Ormskirk L40 6JW
On the B5240, 1 mile from junction 3 of the M58 and 2 miles from Ormskirk

This centre is set on a sloping site, sheltered on all sides by trees. It offers a fairly good range of plants, at very acceptable prices. When our inspector visited, dwarf conifers were available at a very reasonable cost, and a wide variety of roses – floribunda, hybrid tea, climbers and standards – were selling from 99p. All plants are container-grown and they are well maintained. The labelling varies from adequate, on the trees and conifers, to good – illustrated and informative – on shrubs and climbers. Some permanent display beds are being planted out to show off the shrubs and conifers in a garden setting. Other plants are grouped by variety, and the trees and shrubs are particularly well set out with plenty of room for inspection and identification. Indoors, the walkways are rather narrow and could become congested on a busy day. The garden accessories department boasts a range of tents and camping equipment and barbecues as well as a selection of sheds and greenhouses. There is a good range of composts and fertilisers, but the selection of tools and ornaments is rather limited. Fencing and paving are available from 1985. Other changes planned include a new shop, cafe and play area. If you need any information about what is in stock, or advice about planting and growing, the staff are able and willing to help.

Prices £££
Facilities Parking, 150 cars. Toilets. Ice cream. Garden advice service. Delivery service. Plant catalogue for reference
Open Every day 8.45am to 6pm (closes 5.30pm in winter). Closed 4 days from Christmas Day, 3 days from New Year's Day
Credit cards Access, Visa

ORTON WATERVILLE Cambridgeshire   map 4

Notcutts Garden Centre   ♀ ⫻ ⊛ ♿

Oundle Road, Orton Waterville,   *Tel* Peterborough (0733) 234600
Peterborough PE2 0UU

*Just off the A605 west of Peterborough by the entrance to Nene Park, close to the
East of England Show Ground*

A pleasant place to spend an afternoon particularly as the centre is close to
various leisure facilities, five minutes' walk from Nene country park and
adjacent to Ferry Meadows. An attractive, airy coffee lounge supplies light
meals or there is a public house next door which serves morning coffees.
The centre is generously laid out and well signposted so that it doesn't
suffer from crowding on a busy day. Most garden accessories are stocked,
with a particularly good supply of greenhouses, sheds, pots and
ornaments. A swimming pool franchise was installed in 1984, and the
centre was also developing a franchise for garden machinery. The centre
sells a very good range of healthy-looking trees, shrubs and other plants,
but they are expensive. Most of the hardy plants are produced at
Notcutts own nurseries. This centre has apparently improved considerably
over the past three years. Labelling is generally good, usually giving some
indication about culture and habit. Staff are helpful and pleasant.

Prices £££££

Facilities Parking, 360 cars. Toilets. Coffee shop. Play area. Garden advice service.
Delivery service. Plant catalogue £1.50. Free price lists for roses, furniture, fencing etc.
Plants sold by mail order from Notcutts Garden Centre, Woodbridge (see
Woodbridge)

Open Mon to Sat 8.30am to 6pm, Sun 10.30am to 6pm. Closed for New Year's Day
and a few days over Christmas

Credit cards Access, Visa

OSGODBY N. Yorkshire   map 2

Fruit Farm Garden Centre

Osgodby, near Selby YO8 7HG   *Tel* Selby (0757) 703171

On the A63, 2½ miles east of Selby

This centre suffered severe damage in gales in 1984 and at the time of our
inspection work to restore greenhouses and other essential equipment had
led to other areas, such as the car park, being neglected. Hopefully things
should all soon be back in order and then there will be nothing to detract
from your enjoyment of this centre. It covers about two and a half acres,
and stocks should satisfy the ordinary gardener. A good selection of trees is
well presented, each one securely supported along the perimeter fence.
The display beds for plants are also neatly laid out. Houseplants, bedding
plants and other seasonal or tender species are kept under cover in a large
glassed-in area. The selection of smaller tools and sundries is reasonably

*If we've missed out on a good garden centre or nursery, tell us. There are report
forms at the end of the book.*

comprehensive, but there is only a small stock of sheds, greenhouses and garden machinery. A farm shop on the premises sells bread, cakes and fruit and vegetables, and they will make up sandwiches for you on request. Planned developments include toilets and a cafeteria.

Prices Information not available
Facilities Parking, 70 cars. Refreshments. Garden advice service. Delivery service
Open Every day 9am to 7pm (closes 5pm in winter). Closed Christmas, Boxing and New Year's Day

---

OTLEY W. Yorkshire   map 2

Stephen H. Smith Garden Centre & Nurseries

Pool Road, Otley LS21 1DY   *Tel* Otley (0943) 462195
On the A659 1 mile east of Otley

This centre is situated in pleasant rural surroundings just off the main road. It has been undergoing re-organisation which is due to be completed soon and promises to offer some new and attractive display beds. The signposting of the various sections could still be improved though. The selection of plants is not aimed at the specialist, but the average gardener will find what he is looking for (at a price), with an exciting choice among the excellent range of quality heathers. The overall quality is a little variable with old and new stock in very different condition – this was particularly apparent with the clematis and some rather overgrown and leggy trees. The labelling suffers from the same problem, but the centre tell us a new labelling system is being introduced in 1985. There is an extensive area stocked with tools, fertilisers, machinery and a large garden produce section. Garden furniture and florist supplies are also stocked, along with all the larger items such as sheds, greenhouses, fencing and paving. Staff are courteous and helpful and will come to help you out if you ask at the cash desk.

Prices £££££
Facilities Parking, 140 cars (plus overflow 100 cars). Toilets. Ice cream and confectionery. Play area. Garden advice service. Delivery service
Open Mon to Fri 8.30am to 8pm (closes 5.30pm in winter), Sat 9am to 8pm, Sun 9.30am to 6pm (closes 5pm Sat and Sun in winter). Closed 4 days over Christmas
Credit cards Access, Visa

OTTERY ST. MARY Devon   map 3

Otter Nurseries Garden Centre

Gosford Road, Ottery St. Mary   *Tel* Ottery St. Mary (040 481) 3341
EX11 1LZ
1 mile south of A30 on the Ottery St. Mary road. Turn off the A30 at Pattersons Cross (monument)

This centre caters for a large area of east and mid Devon and generally gives good value. Definitely worth a visit if you are a dabbler in dwarf conifers, the nurseries' speciality, or if you would enjoy browsing around their choice selection of trees and shrubs, most of which are grown on site. These are generally of good quality. Each plant has a simple plastic tag, while eye-level labels give details of the characteristics of the plants and any environmental conditions required. Any further facts can be obtained from one of the senior staff members who are always happy to answer questions. All staff are courteous and they will point you in the right direction whenever signposting proves inadequate. A large undercover area houses a good supply of garden sundries and the centre also stocks a very wide selection of conservatories, greenhouses and furniture. Brick and concrete base work and greenhouse erection will be undertaken by builders from the centre (within about a 40-mile radius) and three landscaping teams keep busy in the more immediate vicinity. Facilities are generally quite good and further improvements are already underway. When our inspector visited, they had also obtained planning permission to construct a new office, restaurant and toilet block – work is expected to begin in July 1985.

Prices £££
Facilities Parking, 100 cars. Toilets. Vending machine (cafeteria opening Feb 1985). Garden advice service. Delivery service. Price list and plant catalogue 40p, free with purchases over £1. Specialist plant lists free
Open Mon to Sat 8am to 5pm, Sun 9am to 5pm. Closed 25, 26 and 27 Dec

---

OWERMOIGNE Dorset　　　　　　　　　　　　　　　　map 3

Galton Garden Centre　　　　　　　　　　　　　　

Wareham Road, Owermoigne,　　　　　　*Tel* Warmwell (0305) 852324
near Dorchester DT2 8BY
On the A352 Wareham to Weymouth road 8 miles east of Dorchester

Without doubt a centre for a day out with the family, not just because of the proximity to some attractive coastal beauty spots, but also because of the extensive range of things to do and see at the centre itself. Children can be kept busy in the excellent adventure playground, leaving the keen gardeners free to browse. You will find everything from collectors' plants to flower arranging demonstrations. Displays are all organised logically and imaginatively, and the wide pathways and clear signs make it easy to get around the centre – there are no 'pokey' corners. The large covered area offers excellent shopping in wet weather and there is enough on display here to keep a gardener occupied for some time. There are good bargains among the composts and chemicals, an extensive book section and a very colourful array of silk and dried flowers (with evening classes held in flower arranging). There's a large houseplant section and an impressive enclosed water garden area, both of which are to be extended further, while in other areas round the centre there are power tools, garden buildings and construction materials. Plants are of a high standard throughout. Climbing plants, heathers, and dwarf conifers all deserve special mention, and the range of shrubs includes everything from the most mundane to some unusual items. At the time of our inspection there was a bright display of lilies in stock. Any unusual plants not on hand will be ordered at the customer's request. Large signs above plant groups provide interesting information – even to the extent of a recipe for quince jelly. Individual labels are printed or clearly hand written. Each department has a specialist staff member on hand to deal with queries and all other staff are easily identified by their uniforms. This is a friendly welcoming centre where it is enjoyable to pass the time and pleasant to look at the frequently changing displays which always offer new ideas. There are events held through the year, from visits by famous horticulturalists to local radio 'question times' and films on ways and means of cultivation and propagation. An inviting cafe offers home-made snacks, and barbecues are held each weekend during the summer months. A new restaurant is planned.

Prices *££££*
Facilities Parking, 300 cars. Toilets. Restaurant. Play area. Garden advice service. Delivery service
Open Every day 9am to 6pm (closes 5pm in winter)
Credit cards Access, Visa

OXFORD Oxfordshire   map 4

Johnsons Garden Centre   ✿

Southern Bypass, South Hinksey,   *Tel* Oxford (0865) 730368
Oxford OX1 5AR
In a service road parallel to the A34 Southampton road, 2 miles from Oxford city centre. Leave the A34 at signs to South Hinksey

From the main road this looks like little more than a side stall, but it soon opens out to a medium-sized centre, backing on to a very attractive rural landscape. The centre consists of a small indoor area and an outside space of about two acres (both areas are to be increased). The building which houses garden commodities is cramped but shelves are neatly organised and unless there is a real crowd inside it is not too difficult to get around. The size obviously limits the amount of equipment that can be stocked, and this is particularly reflected in the line of power tools and garden furniture available, but outside there is a good display of paving, walling and rockery stone, and an impressive collection of stoneware. Greenhouses are also well represented. The gently sloping site contains a wide variety of most plants and their condition is particularly good, all stock being sturdy and well watered. Any sub-standard specimens are quickly whisked away. Labelling is quite good with different coloured labels for different varieties. Although the paths are not overwide, the plants are arranged in neat rows. There are some pleasing touches in the design of the centre, from a patio area delightfully decorated with troughs, which contained a very colourful show of begonias, fuchsias and geraniums when our inspector visited, to a more permanent feature of a series of large fish tanks placed along the sloping plot and filled with many varieties of fish. The water circulates through to an attractive rock and water garden with a fish pond holding some very large inhabitants indeed. A water gardening specialist is available five days a week to give advice. Staff are friendly and helpful.

Prices £££
Facilities Parking, 50 cars. Toilets. Garden advice service. Delivery service
Open Every day 8.30am to 6pm (closes 5pm in winter). Closed Christmas and
Boxing Day
Credit cards Access, Visa

PAMBER END Hampshire   map 4

Elm Park Garden Centre and Nursery

Aldermaston Road,   *Tel* Basingstoke (0256) 850587
Pamber End, Basingstoke RG26 5QW
*On the A340, Basingstoke to Aldermaston road, 5 miles from Basingstoke just south
of Pamber End*

A must for the rose-lover, this centre stocks 150 varieties, but the list of
plants doesn't stop here and the overall range is also good. It includes a
special section on lime-hating plants and a lovely display of various,
healthy water-plants. All plants exhibit signs of quality, although the
labelling was less satisfactory when our inspector visited. Some of it was
badly weathered and group labelling was sparse, but the centre tells us it
has introduced outdoor, plastic labels since our inspection. Advice is
always available from the staff, though they are not that easy to find;
notices refer prospective purchasers to the shop. This consists of a
good-sized area and it is well laid out and pleasantly cool on a hot day.
Sundries range from troughs and containers to composts and chemicals,
and you will find plenty of paving and building materials as well as
barbecue and patio equipment. However, garden buildings and power
tools are not stocked nor are hand tools. There is good access to an area
where you can collect heavy or bulky goods and in fact access is easy
throughout the centre, which is well set out all on one level and has good,
wide gravel paths.

Prices £££
Facilities Parking, 50 cars. Toilets. Vending machine. Garden advice service. Delivery
service. Free price lists for peat, paving, roses, fruit etc.
Open Every day 8.30am to 7.30pm (closes 5.30pm in winter). Closed Christmas Day
to New Year's Day
Credit cards Access, Visa

PAR Cornwall   map 3

The Plant Centre

Par Moor, Par PL24 2TY   *Tel* Par (072 681) 4854
1 mile to the west of Par on the A3082

The friendly, interested staff and wide range of stock make this centre
worthy of praise. It is a small place, developed on the site of a derelict tin
mine, and it specialises in plants. However, there is a small area devoted to
garden accessories such as tools, fencing and paving, furniture, ornaments,
lawnmowers and chemicals and composts. The plant section is well laid out

with plants protected under tunnels. Paths are wide, but do tend to get a little waterlogged after a watering session – this problem should have been overcome by the installation of a new irrigation system. There is a comprehensive plant range and the standard is generally very high. In season the displays of fuchsias are very beautiful. Labels for groups of plants have descriptions and illustrations, while individual labels bear a name and price only. The staff are easy to find and most helpful if you have any problems. Occasional altercations occur in the ill-designed car park – cars tend to get 'boxed in' and the peaceful nature of the plant centre does not always permeate through to a gardener behind the wheel! The centre is fairly new and still developing – eventually the parking problem should be solved. There are beaches, golf courses and other holiday facilities in the area so perhaps you could combine a visit to the centre with a family day out.

Prices £££
Facilities Parking, 40 cars (plus 100 overflow). Toilets. Garden advice service. Delivery service. Plant price list and catalogue 20p
Open Every day 8am to 6pm (closes 5pm in winter)

PEMBURY Kent   map 5
Whiteleggs Garden Centre

Tonbridge Road, Pembury TN2 4QN   *Tel* Pembury (089 282) 2636
On the A21 opposite Pembury Hospital

A good, ordinary garden centre serving local needs. It is set on sloping ground in woodland and there's a pleasant landscaped garden walk between the car park and nursery area. The outside area is well laid out. When our inspector visited, the range of plants was rather patchy though there was a good selection of shrubs and he thought the fuchsias worthy of special mention. The plants were obviously of good quality when first brought in, but were not all kept up to scratch. Plants are reasonably well labelled, though the system of codes for pricing can be confusing. The range of aquatic plants is good and the 'expert' who runs the aquaria really knows and loves his fish and will give sensible advice. The shop area looks cramped and overcrowded, but is nevertheless well organised to make full use of the available space and there are plans to extend it. Most garden sundries are stocked including larger items such as greenhouses, fencing and paving. Staff are identified by their overalls and are very helpful.

Prices ££££
Facilities Parking, 200 cars. Toilets. Vending machines and ice creams. Garden advice service. Delivery service
Open Mon to Fri 8am to 5.30pm, Sat 9am to 5.30pm, Sun 10am to 5pm (closes at dusk every day in winter)
Credit cards Access, Visa

If you consider any entry to be incorrect, inadequate or misleading, you would be doing us and your fellow gardeners a service by letting us know. There are report forms at the end of the book.

PENKRIDGE Staffordshire   map 2

Stanelli's Garden Centre

Bungham Lane, Penkridge,   *Tel* Penkridge (078 571) 2387
Stafford ST19 5NP

On the western outskirts of Penkridge, 8 miles south of Stafford. Bungham Lane is a turning off the A449

This centre started out as a landscaping business and so the long experience of Mr Wright, the proprietor, enables him to deal with any queries about garden design. The centre is of average size and occupies a long narrow strip of land. The site has been generally well organised, and the large indoor area, although crowded, is nicely laid out. A large percentage of the centre is given over to garden ornaments, furniture and paving. Equipment for flower arranging is also sold, as well as a good range of indoor plants. A flower arranger is often on hand to give advice and help to customers. The larger garden sundries such as power tools and garden sheds are not stocked. A wide selection of plants, shrubs and trees is available, but there is nothing of a more specialist nature. The quality is generally good, although it is important to be careful when choosing. Prices are quite high. Labelling is reasonable.

Prices £££££
Facilities Parking, 50 cars. Toilets. Delivery service. Price lists
Open Every day 8am to 6pm (closes 5pm in winter). Closed a few days at Christmas
Credit card Visa

PETERSFIELD Hampshire   map 4

Baileys Garden Centre

College Street, Petersfield   *Tel* Petersfield (0730) 62001/2
GU31 4AY

In Petersfield on the A3 one-way system (Portsmouth to Guildford section)

Large trees on its northern boundary give this centre a pleasant air, protecting it from the bustle of the main road and the surrounding built-up area. Access is reasonably easy, but make sure you get into the correct lane of the one way system! Known locally for backing up their claim of 'satisfaction or replacement' without too much trouble, they offer a good service to the gardener. Plants are arranged in an orderly fashion but narrow aisles indoors and ungenerous paths outside, sometimes obstructed by overgrown plants, can make manoeuvering rather difficult (wider paths are planned). Some gardeners might find the range of plants limited, but alpines and heathers are well represented and conifers, shrubs and trees offer a reasonable choice. Prices are fairly high, but quality of plants is generally good, while labelling varies from excellent 'trade printed' signs to very patchy individual tags. The free catalogue is helpful if you are in doubt. This branch of Baileys doesn't stock many of the larger gardening sundries but they make a feature of pots, ornaments and furniture.

Prices £££££
Facilities Parking, 30 cars. Advice service. Delivery service. Free plant catalogue. Free price lists for plants, bulbs, fencing, walling etc.
Open Mon to Sat 8.30am to 5.30pm (closes 7.30pm Fri), Sun 9am to 5.30pm (closes 5pm every day in winter). Closed 5 days over Christmas
Credit cards Access, Visa

PETERSTOW Hereford and Worcester map 3

Pengetherly Nurseries

Peterstow, Ross-on-Wye
HR9 6LL

Tel Harewood End (098 987) 284

Just north of Ross-on-Wye, on the A49 Hereford to Ross road

A smallish centre with a reasonable range of shrubs, trees and other plants for its size, but those gardeners keen on conifers are in for a marvellous surprise because the scope and quality of the conifer selection is outstanding. There is also an excellent choice of standard roses as well as the normal Hybrid Teas and Floribundas, and a good choice of perennials. All their plants are healthy and, even in very dry weather, are always well-watered. Houseplants are displayed in a separate, spacious section. The layout of the centre is easy to follow. Paths are good and wide and labelling is clear both for plant groups and for individual pots. There is a small shop containing quite a reasonable variety of sundries, but don't expect a great choice of hand tools and there are no power tools or water gardening equipment. The earthenware pots on sale are particularly reasonably priced as well as being attractive. Ice cream and apple juice are the only refreshments on offer, although the centre sells its own tomatoes, honey and apples in season. (A tea room is planned.) Staff are always on hand to offer advice and answer queries.

Prices ££££
Facilities Parking, 50 cars. Toilets. Ice creams. Garden advice service. Delivery service. Free price lists for some plants
Open Every day 9am to 5pm. Closed for Christmas week

PEWSEY Wiltshire map 4

Peter Jones

Manningford Nurseries,
Manningford Abbots,
near Pewsey SN9 6HY

Tel Marlborough (0672) 62232

2 miles west-south-west of Pewsey. Take the Pewsey exit from the A345, go through Manningford Abbots and the nursery is 1½ miles along by the railway

This is an attractive little country nursery which only opened fairly recently. It is run by Peter Jones who is well known locally for garden design and for his lectures, both at local societies and at the nursery. His enthusiasm and knowledge are translated into the interesting plants he stocks and the useful recommendations given about what to plant where. The plant stocks are still being built up, but there is already a good range including some less usual ones such as plants of the 18th and 19th centuries. The layout covers about 2 acres of land, a third of which is devoted to plant beds, the rest to potted plants, four greenhouses, and an attractive garden. The paths are either gravel or grass and any awkward corners are being improved as the working area expands. There are plans to build an Elizabethan garden and a water-garden. No tools are available, but the nursery sells composts and peat in addition to some very nice terracotta pots and Italian urns. When the owner is not on hand the rest of the staff are guaranteed to be helpful and pleasant. Day-long horticultural courses are held in winter and spring.

Prices ££££
Facilities Parking, 18 cars. Toilets. Garden advice service. Delivery service
Open Every day except Wed, 8.30am to 5pm. Closed Sun 1pm to 2pm

---

PICKERING N.Yorkshire   map 2

The Roger Plant Centre   ✿

Malton Road, Pickering   *Tel* Pickering (0751) 72226
On the A169 towards Malton. The nurseries are a mile north of Pickering on the same road (towards Whitby)

The nursery and plant centre are both situated on the rich farmland of the Vale of Pickering with views south to the Yorkshire wolds and north to the moors. The nursery was established in 1913 and customers can look round the entire 300-acre site (take your wellingtons, it can be muddy), but all sales take place at the plant centre. The home-grown plants are first class – the roses are particularly good. Houseplants are also sold and some exotic indoor plants, including orchids, are kept under thermostatically controlled conditions. You can buy bulbs, potatoes, parsnips and swede turnips from the farm at the appropriate times of year. The centre also sells composts, tools and a limited range of teak and cast iron furniture. The centre has been well laid out with concrete paths and raised beds for alpines and houseplants. More raised beds are planned for dwarf conifers and herbaceous perennials. Plants are arranged alphabetically so it is easy to find what you want even among the hundreds of different varieties. The range of plants is very impressive – 250,000 plants raised each year for containers alone. All stock is suitable for growing in the north. Container-grown plants can be bought at any time of year, and bare-rooted stock in season. Plant labels give only the name and price, but further information is given in the catalogue. Staff are long-serving and knowledgeable and there is even a telephone advice service.

Prices £££
Facilities Parking, 80 cars. Toilets. Vending machines. Garden advice service. Delivery service. Plant price list and catalogue 50p. Plants sold by mail order. Postal address: R V Roger Ltd, The Nurseries, Pickering, North Yorkshire YO18 7HG
Open Mon to Sat 9am to 5pm, Sun 1pm to 5pm, bank holidays 10.30am to 5pm. Closed 25 Dec to 1 Jan
Credit cards Access, Visa

PINCHBECK Lincolnshire — map 2
Birch Grove, the Spalding Garden Centre

Pinchbeck, Spalding PE11 3XY   *Tel* Spalding (0775) 85490
On the A16 Spalding to Boston road, 3 miles from Spalding, about 1 mile north of Pinchbeck

Our inspector was pleasantly surprised by this centre which has much improved since our last visit. It is a moderately large site with compact neat beds and a good indoor sales area. The centre is arranged thoughtfully with wide paths making access easy and clear signposting pointing you the right way. 'Special offer' displays have large signs announcing their presence. Labelling is generally good and prices are cheap and clearly marked. The plants have a well-cared-for feel to them and there is an interesting selection of conifers, alpines and climbers to tempt the visitor. There is also a small selection of houseplants. The range of tools and sundries is fairly comprehensive and includes plenty of chemicals and seeds. A particularly charming aspect of the centre is the presence of some lovely bird houses and cooing doves for sale – if you want something special for your garden, you may be tempted by romantic thoughts of a dovecot. Pet and horse supplies are currently stocked separately in two mobile cabins on the site. The centre offers numerous sheds and sunhouses of all shapes and sizes, and fencing, paving and garden ornaments are also stocked. Staff are all able to deal with gardening enquiries and are willing to order items not available in the sundries section. There is a small cafe for refreshments. A new covered area is planned to include a pet shop, indoor plants and a cafeteria.

Prices ££
Facilities Parking, 300 cars. Toilets. Cafeteria. Play area. Garden advice service. Delivery service. Plant catalogue available in spring 1985
Open Every day 9am to 6pm (closes 5pm in winter)
Credit card Access

PLYMOUTH Devon — map 3
Plymouth Garden Centre

Fort Austin Avenue, Crownhill,   *Tel* Plymouth (0752) 771820
Plymouth PL6 5NU
On the A38 at Crownhill, 3 miles from Plymouth city centre

This centre is located on the suburban outskirts of Plymouth and provides a good service to the populace of the city. The setting is unusual – in an 1850s fort. The original walls of the fort, with a guardhouse inset, form the frontage to the garden centre, and at the rear you'll find natural woodland surrounded by a moat. The growing area is largely screened off by lime trees planted when the fort was built. The outside area of the centre is partly given over to the larger and more messy garden accessories – peats and manures (sample sacks open for inspection), paving and pots. Greenhouses, sheds and heavy building materials are sold by franchise. A good selection of sundries, including both hand and power tools, is found in a medium-sized shop. This area is kept tidy, but even so, things are cramped and not very attractively displayed. There is a good-sized shop for houseplants and the selection here is very good – part of this shop is to be turned into a shade house. Among the hardy outdoor plants the range of plants, trees and shrubs is fairly good and it includes some of the less common perennials and an interesting array of herbs. Trees and shrubs were in excellent health when our inspector visited, and the conifers and roses were also good. Generally plants are well cared for and of good quality. Labels for groups of plants give some brief details and illustrations. Tags on individual plants are reasonable, though they tend to suffer from fading (a new computer labelling system is being introduced). The garden centre is well signposted, but some improvements in the layout are needed as the arrangement can be confusing, with soft fruit popping up in the middle of the shrubs, and a 'Connoisseur's Corner' in the middle of nowhere in particular. Staff are easy to find and they can be very helpful.

Prices £££
Facilities Parking, 200 cars. Toilets. Vending machine. Play area. Garden advice service. Delivery service. Free catalogue and price list for plants
Open Mon to Sat 9am to 5.30pm (closes 5pm in winter), Sun 10.30am to 5.30pm
Credit cards Access, Visa

PODINGTON Northamptonshire   map 4
Podington Nurseries and Garden Centre

31 High Street, Podington,   *Tel* Rushden (093 34) 53656
Wellingborough NN9 7HS
In the centre of Podington, 2½ miles from Rushden. Take the turning off the A6 just outside Rushden

Podington Nurseries is found in the centre of the village and it is easily located if you keep an eye out for the signs. Our inspector felt this centre was run by people who 'are garden-minded, and not just in the business for money'. The plants are of a good overall quality, the one detracting feature being their somewhat cramped conditions. In fact, organisation and tidiness are the areas in which this centre falls down, but once you are accustomed to the general muddle there are some good items to be bought. The range of tools and sundries is reasonable and most larger items are now stocked, including sheds, paving and fencing. There are also plans to sell greenhouses and to develop a water garden display area. Plants, however, are the main concentration and the range is generally good. The labelling and identification are well done but there is no apparent order in their layout. The staff are eager to please and cheerful. A small refreshment area offers coffee and snacks.

Prices £££
Facilities Parking, 100 cars. Toilets. Light refreshments. Garden advice service. Delivery service. Free price list for paving, fencing and ponds
Open Every day 9am to 6pm. Closed Christmas and Boxing Day
Credit cards Access, Visa

PORT SUNLIGHT Merseyside
map 2
Green Hand Garden Centre

The Causeway, Port Sunlight Village,   *Tel* 051-645 6244
Bebington, Wirral L62 5DY
About 3 miles from Birkenhead

This centre is found at one end of extensive public gardens running
through the middle of the Leverhulme model estate. At the other end you
will find the Leverhulme Art Gallery. The site occupies about 3 acres in
which there are three separate courtyards; one contains stone and cement
slabs, peat and fertiliser; another has sheds and garden furniture; and the
third holds wooden fencing. At the rear of the grounds are display beds of
shrubs and trees, with rough walkways in between and very good
signposting. A roomy garden shop is well stocked with a choice of hand
tools and most other sundries, including artificial flowers. The selection of
plants is excellent throughout and our inspector spotted over 50 varieties of
heather. Quality is very good as well and any plants which are
sub-standard, either damaged or wind burnt, are removed and disposed
of. All labelling is informative and legible and every pot has a tag with
name and price. The staff are mainly helpful with recommendations and
advice, especially about what shrubs are suitable for different areas of the
country.

Prices £££
Facilities Parking, 200 cars. Garden advice service. Delivery service. Free price lists
for sheds and paving
Open Every day, 8.30am to 5.30pm in summer, 8am to 4.45pm in winter. Closed from
25 Dec for 10 days
Credit cards Access, Visa

POYNTON Cheshire
map 2
Brookside Garden Centre

Macclesfield Road, Poynton   *Tel* Poynton (0625) 872919/875088
SK12 1BY
On the A523 midway betwen Poynton and Hazel Grove

This is a fairly large garden centre where most of the stock is kept outdoors.
Many of the plants are grown at the associated nursery, 3 miles from the
centre. There is a wide range of plants of good quality, especially trees,
shrubs, conifers and heathers. The centre is fairly well signposted, but
some paths are narrow and difficult to negotiate. There is a balanced range
of garden accessories from the small hand tools and bottles of chemicals to
sheds and greenhouses and a small but reasonably well-stocked DIY
section. There's also a floristry department. Labels are adequate but
inconsistent – some easy to read and illustrated, others both difficult to find
and very faint. Staff are plentiful and helpful. In addition to the play area
there is a picnic area and a small railway, proceeds from which go to
various appointed charities. A new restaurant complex and garden
furniture showroom were due to open in spring 1985.

Prices ££££
Facilities Parking, 400 cars. Toilets. Restaurant. Play area. Garden advice service.
Delivery service
Open Mon to Fri 8am to 6pm, Sat 9am to 5.30pm, Sun 10am to 5.30pm (closes 5pm
every day in winter)
Credit cards Access, Visa

PRESCOT Merseyside   map 2
Prescot Garden Centre

Liverpool Road, Prescot L34 3LX   *Tel* 051-426 6455
On the A57 west of Prescot, close to the junction of A57 and A58

A series of visits suggests that this centre is getting better bit by bit and
might soon realise its full potential. A large nursery and numerous
greenhouses make up the site. The layout could still do with some
improvement. It is unkempt, has no signposting and is in need of either
flagging or tarmacking in parts to improve the state of the paths. Things are
better in the inside area where tools, ornaments, sundries and houseplants
are kept. The centre stocks a selection of most garden sundries including a
large collection of garden ornaments, as well as lots of paving, sand, peat
and the like. A selection of healthy, good-quality plants includes quite a
few dwarf conifers and a fair range of indoor plants. Overall the choice is
fairly standard. Labelling is poor – most name tags are washed out, prices
are hard to find and there are no group labels at all. The staff seem helpful
and will assist with carrying heavy goods to the car. This could be a very
good place with a little more care and attention to the layout and labelling.

Prices £££
Facilities Parking, 200 cars. Toilets. Vending machines. Garden advice service.
Delivery service
Open Mon to Fri 8.30am to 5.30pm, Sat 9am to 5.30pm, Sun 10am to 5.30pm

PRESTON Lancashire   map 2
Rosebank Nurseries and Garden Centre

Chainhouse Lane, Whitesake,   *Tel* Preston (0772) 36664
Preston PR4 4LB
3 miles east of New Longton between the A59 and A559

This centre is recommended for its specialist range of paving and fencing.
Any gardener planning a building or landscaping project could do worse
than a visit to Rosebank, where the construction materials stocked include
shingle, sand, paving and some beautiful rocks. These take up a large part
of this site and are obviously a feature. The other main strength of the
centre, its water-gardening section, is located across the road in a separate
area. The selection of aquatic plants is good and there are also many species
of fish on show. On the whole, the range of plants sold is rather limited and
the quality could really do with improvement, though prices are reasonable.
When our inspector visited, the shrubs rated best for selection and the trees
and conifers for healthy condition. The garden sundries stocked, apart

from fencing and paving, consist mainly of the smaller items like hand tools, ornaments, furniture and composts. Most of these are housed in an indoor section which, though overcrowded, is reasonably well organised. Improved signposting and labelling would be a help.

Prices £££
Facilities Parking, 30 cars. Toilets. Ice cream and confectionery. Garden advice service. Delivery service. Free price lists for walling, paving etc.
Open Every day 8am to 6pm (closes later at busy times). Closed Christmas and Boxing Day and New Year's Day

---

PRESTON Humberside

map 2

Sandhill Nurseries Garden Centre

Wyton Road, Preston, near Hull
HU12 8TY
On the B1239 about 6 miles east of Hull

Tel Hull (0482) 898370

Located in pleasant countryside, this centre is a family business comprising a garden centre and adjoining nursery. The range of conifers is particularly good, and the owners are hoping ultimately that it will fulfil the needs of even the specialist gardener. There is also a very good selection of popular trees and shrubs and a reasonable choice of most common plants. Many of the plants are home-grown and the quality is generally excellent. Some re-organisation was going on at the time of our inspector's visit, so it was a little difficult to judge the layout and labelling, though she felt the walkways were rather narrow. The nursery tells us that new raised display beds are now completed and they are improving their labelling. Inside, the centre is well arranged and there is a good, general stock of sundries to satisfy the average gardener's needs. One section is devoted entirely to artificial flowers while for those closer to nature there is a wide selection of pot plants in the main glasshouse. Fencing and paving are also sold, and greenhouses and sheds may be ordered. A very pleasant cafeteria offers hot and cold snacks and light meals. There is a nearby field for children to run around in and a proper play area is planned. Staff are very helpful and willing to answer customers' queries.

Prices £££
Facilities Parking, 200 cars. Toilets. Cafeteria. Garden advice service. Delivery service
Open Every day 8.30am to 8pm (closes 5.30pm in winter). Closed Christmas for 2 or 3 days

---

PULBOROUGH W. Sussex

map 5

Cheals Garden and Leisure Centre

Stopham Road, Pulborough
RH20 1DS
1 mile west of the double roundabout in Pulborough village centre, on the A283 to Petworth

Tel Pulborough (079 82) 2981

There is a wide selection of garden hardware stocked at Cheals, including everything from swimming pools to lawnmowers. The water-garden section contains an excellent collection of fish and a choice of pools and fountains. There's a wide range of garden furniture, a barbecue section and a machinery department which provides a hire service. The centre also offers a landscape design service. Plants are rather expensive. When our inspector visited, they were offering a good choice of dwarf conifers and water-plants, as well as lots of plump, healthy bulbs and some more unusual herbaceous perennials. There are also special displays of air plants, bromeliads and orchids for those interested in house and greenhouse plants. The centre has been undergoing major refurbishment and we look forward to seeing the results. The staff are very helpful and should be able to assist with any problems. If the children are getting fidgety, you can take a model train ride right round the centre for 20p.

Prices ££££
Facilities Parking, 70 cars. Toilets. Cafeteria. Play area. Garden advice service. Delivery service. Free price list
Open Mon to Fri 8.30am to 5.30pm, Sat 9am to 5.30pm, Sun 10am to 5.30pm. Closed Christmas and Boxing Day
Credit cards Access, Visa

Murrells Garden Centre

Broomers Hill Lane,
Pulborough RH20 2DU
Just east of Pulborough off the A283

Tel Pulborough (079 82) 2771

A smallish but well-stocked centre found on a country lane just off the A283. It is a small family business which has expanded over the last few years and is well worth supporting. There is a good selection of common plants and the owner specialises in some of the more unusual shrubs and other plants. They are all well looked after. A glasshouse is devoted to houseplants of wonderful variety – probably the best selection in the area. The centre is computerised and catalogues are provided which indicate what is available and have a code for price, height and other features. Plants are well labelled. It would be helpful if the various display areas were signposted but otherwise things are well laid out with carefully maintained walkways. (The centre tells us that the labelling and layout are being improved.) The indoor area is rather small and congested and there is no indication as to what is there or where to find it. They have an exceptional array of terracotta pots and quite a good selection of the smaller garden accessories such as hand tools, but no power tools or greenhouses. Peat and composts are in ample supply and paving is also sold. The proprietor and his small staff, although often harassed, obviously want to be helpful. If you need any help carrying your purchases away there are several 'lusty' lads to help out. Toilets are available in the owner's house nearby and refreshment at the nearby pub.

Prices ££££
Facilities Parking, 50 cars. Toilets. Garden advice service. Delivery service. Free price lists and catalogues for many products
Open Every day 9am to 5.30pm (closes 1pm to 2pm Sat and Sun)
Credit cards Access, Visa

RAYLEIGH Essex map 4

Cramphorn Garden Centre

Eastwood Road, Rayleigh   *Tel* Southend-on-Sea (0702) 527331
SS6 7LU

*On the north side of the A1015 Rayleigh to Southend-on-Sea road, approximately
2 miles east of Rayleigh town centre*

This is smaller than the Chelmsford branch of Cramphorn and the range of
goods is correspondingly narrower. Nevertheless it is a well-laid-out centre
with attractive display beds and well-ordered plant groupings. Our
inspector liked the imaginative displays of conifers and spring bulbs and
the good, informal display of houseplants. These are frequently changing
so that interest and impact are constantly being renewed. There is a large,
covered area for tools and sundries and the range of these is
comprehensive. Most goods from swimming pools and pet accessories to a
large variety of artificial flowers are available, but the choice of some items
is rather limited. The range of plants is reasonable and quality, on the
whole, is quite good. At the time of our inspection there was an abundance
of healthy shrubs and trees for autumn planting. Labels are usually very
informative with details of season, colour, dimensions, soil and site
requirements. The staff are generally helpful and knowledgeable.

Prices ££££
Facilities Parking, 60 cars. Garden advice service. Delivery service (use of Borrovan).
Free price lists and catalogues available for many products
Open Every day 8.30am to 6pm (closes 5pm in winter). Closed Christmas and
Boxing Day
Credit cards Access, Visa

RINGWOOD Hampshire map 4

B.S. Guy & Son

Belle Vue Nurseries, Ringwood   *Tel* Ringwood (042 54) 3113
BH24 3HW
2 miles east of Ringwood on the A31 road to Southampton

This is the only nursery our inspector knows of where it is almost cheaper
to buy plants than to propagate them oneself – and the range is enormous.
The selection includes both the common varieties and some interesting
surprises as well. The quality is very good across the board and although
the labelling is less than adequate, providing neither illustration nor
information, each plant is individually marked on purchase. The nursery
concentrates on plants and sundries are limited, although there are stocks
of smaller sundries and some larger items such as furniture, ornaments,
pond equipment, fencing and paving. One feature detracting from the
impression of the centre is the layout. Plants are scattered about the site at
random – small shrubs are to be found mixed with trees, and deciduous
with evergreen. The staff are easy to locate and are reasonably well
informed – quite able to give details of plant habit and descriptions when
asked.

Prices ££
Facilities Parking, 80 cars. Toilets. Garden advice service. Delivery service.
Free plant catalogue
Open Mon to Sat 8am to 5pm (closed 1pm to 2pm), Sun 9am to 12.30pm

---

ROMFORD Essex map 4

Sungate Nursery

Collier Row Road, Romford RM5 2BH   *Tel* Romford (0708) 40724

10 minutes' walk from Collier Row Shopping Centre and 2 miles from Romford town centre

Our inspector thought this centre rated 12 out of 10 for its range of garden accessories – praise indeed! The selection of garden furniture, ornaments, tubs, paving, and the like is excellent, and there is a good supply of hand and power tools and garden chemicals. The centre also sells larger items such as sheds and greenhouses and makes rustic furniture and fencing to any size and shape. There is a lawnmower repairs and sales workshop. The indoor area also has a small section set aside for houseplants. Outside there's a well-laid-out area crossed by good gravel pathways. Most common plants are sold and the choice of roses and conifers is particularly worth noting, as is the wide variety of shrubs. When our inspector visited, the fruit trees, roses, conifers and heathers were in good condition overall, though some other plants were rather straggly. The large, clear group labelling and reasonable individual labels provide satisfactory information. The staff are very helpful and seem to know what they are talking about. This, coupled with pleasant surroundings, large covered areas and a nice layout make for a worthwhile visit. Climbing frames, swings and slides, as well as a duck pond might amuse the children and for refreshment there is a pleasant, grassed-over area with tables and chairs where visitors can have coffee, biscuits and ice creams. A new area for water-gardening and tropical birds opened in spring 1985.

Prices ££££
Facilities Parking, 75 cars. Toilets. Cafeteria. Play area. Garden advice service.
Delivery service
Open Every day 9am to 6pm (closes 5pm in winter). Closed Christmas Day
Credit cards Access, Visa

ROMSEY Hampshire map 4

Hillier Plant Centre

Jermyns Lane, Braishfield,   *Tel* Braishfield (0794) 68407
near Romsey SO5 0QA
Off the A31, 2 miles north of Romsey, signposted Arboretum

This plant centre is attached to a large nursery which produces about 6,000 different plants, although some of these are not available directly from the centre and may have to be ordered. It lies in open countryside and more than 100 acres of the adjacent land is devoted to a marvellous arboretum displaying many unusual and interesting trees and shrubs. The retail nursery itself is of moderate size and it is nicely laid out. There are good-sized gravel paths and all areas are very well signposted. Shrubs are arranged alphabetically and according to their eventual height, and group labelling is excellent, instructive and consistent. Individual pots are all marked, but not in any detail. Overall, the selection is very good, particularly for trees and shrubs, although most other plants are also represented. They are quite expensive but all of very good quality and carefully attended by the skilled staff. The staff are very helpful and easy to locate if you have any queries. This is primarily a nursery, so the stocks of accessories are limited, but a small covered area offers a selection of chemicals, composts, fencing and hand tools. Well worth a visit, particularly for tree-lovers.

Prices £££££
Facilities Parking, 100 cars. Toilets. Garden advice service. Delivery service. Plants sold by mail order
Open Mon to Sat 9am to 5.30pm, Sun 10am to 5.30pm. Closed 25 to 29 Dec
Credit cards Access, Visa

Hilliers Garden Centre (Romsey)

Botley Road, Romsey SO5 8ZL   *Tel* Romsey (0794) 513459
Just off the A31 Bournemouth to Winchester road, in Botley Road on the eastern outskirts of Romsey

Our inspector was pleased to see the 'bargain' old stock perennials being watered with as much love and care as the more expensive plants – a very promising sign. This centre has recently been taken over by Hilliers, and the standard and range of stock have been continually improving. Recent changes include redesigning and landscaping of the outside area, and a children's play area and a greenhouse for house plant displays are in the pipeline. There are pleasant 'group planting' displays in addition to the ordinary beds, and these are specially set out to provide the customer with ideas and information. Small labels are being replaced by larger ones, and each group of plants is fronted by a large instructional notice. The range of stock is wide and increasing – at the time of our visit a new supply of grape vines had just arrived. Prices are quite high. The layout is becoming better with re-organisation, but at the time of our inspection the interior still needed some work done on it. The garden accessories department stocks hand tools, chemicals and furniture. Outside there is a separate area for paving, fencing, some very attractive terracotta ware and a good range of gravel and rocks for building rockeries. Friendly and helpful staff are readily available to give you a hand, and there is a garden advice service to assist with more complicated problems.

Prices £££££
Facilities Parking, 100 cars. Toilets. Garden advice service. Delivery service. Plant price list and catalogue 35p
Open Every day 9am to 5.30pm. Closed Christmas Day
Credit cards Access, Visa

ROSS-ON-WYE Hereford and Worcester   map 3
Hill Court

Walford, Ross-on-Wye HR9 5QN   *Tel* Ross-on-Wye (0989) 63123
Leave Ross-on-Wye on the B4288, fork right at the Prince of Wales sign and
continue for nearly 2 miles

Our inspector was charmed by this centre, which is set in the grounds of
Hill Court, a house dating from the 17th century. The avenues of trees, old
orchards and yew walk provide a lovely backdrop to the well-ordered
layout. About 2 acres are taken up by the centre and this comprises two
greenhouses (one for exotic plants and one for tomatoes), two walled
gardens, a sundries shop and a tea shop. Espalier fruit trees are displayed
in the larger, walled gardens and the shrub beds in front of these are
arranged by month, so the visitor can see when each plant is at its best.
There are good-sized gravel paths and all beds are marked in alphabetical
order. Group labels are extremely helpful, and individual labelling is legible
and comprehensive. There is no particular speciality on offer, but the range
covers most types of plants. Plants are all of good quality. The tools and
sundries are kept in the shop and include everything from wellington boots
to pot-pourri. The larger items such as sheds and greenhouses are being
introduced and new developments include a play area and herb garden.
Shortbread, cakes and a good cup of coffee are on offer if you are in need of
refreshment. The staff are most helpful and seem well able to deal with
queries.

Prices ££££
Facilities Parking, 80 cars. Toilets. Tearoom. Garden advice service. Delivery service
Open Every day 9.30am to 5.30pm
Credit cards Access, Visa

ROYTON Greater Manchester   map 2
Newbank Garden Centre

Turf Lane, Royton, Oldham OL2 6JH   *Tel* Shaw (0706) 844150
Turf Lane runs between the A663 and the B6194, 1 mile south-west of Shaw and
1 mile from exit 20 of the M62

This centre has an enormous covered area which houses a comprehensive
range of general gardening equipment, and a smaller, outside section
where you will come across some unusual finds among the plants. Given
the limitations of the site, the layout has been well planned. Paths are wide
and stone-paved while the signposting is easy to read. Labelling could be a
lot better; our inspector noticed quite a number of plants with faded labels,
incorrect information or no labels at all. The plants themselves are cheap,
healthy and well cared for. At the time of our inspection, conifers, heathers
and alpines were strongly represented while the herbaceous perennials
and shrubs were less plentiful. The centre specialises in conifers and
hedging and imports vast numbers of plants in the winter which it sells as
rootballed stock. There are a surprising number of plants sold here which

are not available at other local centres – *Waldsteinia ternata, Tellima grandiflora, Pachysandra terminalis,* to name but a few – and these might entice you to pay a visit. The range of tools and sundries is very comprehensive, only falling short in the garden buildings section where there is little choice on display. A new section called 'The Pot Shop' was being set up in early 1985 and should offer a good choice of plant containers. The staff are courteous and ready to help carry goods to the car. The main car park is across the road, but there is sufficient space by the centre for loading purposes. There is a farm shop on the site.

Prices ££
Facilities Parking, 200 cars. Toilets. Coffee shop. Garden advice service. Delivery service
Open Every day 9.30am to dusk (closes 6pm in winter and at dusk in Dec)
Credit cards Access, American Express, Diners Club, Visa

RUGBY Warwickshire map 4

Bernhard's Rugby Garden and Leisure Centre

Bilton Road, Rugby CV22 7DT   *Tel* Rugby (0788) 811500
On the A4071 1 mile south of Rugby town centre, between Rugby and Bilton village

This centre on the outskirts of Rugby stocks most of the better-known trees, shrubs and other plants, many of which are raised at its associated nursery. The conifers and heathers are particularly good. Prices are quite high but quality is good. There is a first-class selection of artificial flowers which will be of particular interest to those who enjoy flower arranging. If you don't want to do the work yourself, flower arrangements can be made to order or hired from about £10. Labels for plants are a bit variable with some having instructions and illustrations, others not. The centre is fairly compact and could become congested at the busier times of the week, but the parking facilities are adequate for most days. There is a separate building housing the mowers, trimmers, cultivators and other powered tools. A repair, servicing and hire service is also available. Most sundries are sold except for sheds and paving. Staff are courteous and happy to help out.

Prices £££££
Facilities Parking, 300 cars (plus overflow). Toilets. Tea and confectionery. Play area. Garden advice service. Delivery service. Free price lists of popular plants. Plants and sundries catalogues available for reference
Open Mon to Sat 9am to 6.30pm (closes 6pm in winter). Closed Christmas and New Year's Day
Credit cards Access, Visa

RUNCTON W. Sussex map 5

Manor Nursery

Pagham Road, Runcton,   *Tel* Chichester (0243) 781734
Chichester PO20 6LJ
On the B2166 Chichester to Pagham road, ¾ mile south-east of Chichester

This is a market nursery and specialises in a wide variety of high-quality, reasonably priced plants. The site consists of a large outside area for hardy outdoor plants and trees, and two greenhouses for the tender indoor plants – the range of these is very impressive. The vast majority of plants sold are grown at their nurseries and include cacti, poinsettias, carnations, primroses, cyclamen and many others. Wide concreted paths and walkways lead you around the whole site and each plant seen has its own waterproof label with a price and description. Sundry items are mainly limited to those essential for the care and maintenance of plants, but also include a selection of terracotta, ceramic and stone pots. This retail outlet has only recently been set up and it is still expanding and adding to its existing stock – it will be interesting to see how it develops.

Prices £££
Facilities Parking, 60 cars. Toilets. Vending machines. Garden advice service. Free price list for roses, bedding plants and trees
Open Every day 8am to 5pm. Closed Christmas Day

ST. ALBANS Hertfordshire   map 4

Notcutts Garden Centre

605 Hatfield Road, Smallford,   *Tel* St. Albans (0727) 53224/64922
St. Albans AL4 0HN
On the A414 Hatfield road, 3 miles from St. Albans

This large garden centre rates highly in most respects. The layout is well ordered with good-sized gravel paths joining all the clearly signposted sections. The outside area contains the plants and a good range of sheds, greenhouses and fencing materials. The spaciously arranged interior has a limited range of hand tools, but there are no power tools or lawnmowers stocked. Other sundries available include ornaments, furniture, water-gardening materials and fish. The array of plants is excellent, though expensive, and you would be unlucky to come away unrewarded. They are all kept in very fine condition, conscientiously watered and shaded when necessary. Group labels are easily spotted, as are those on each plant – sadly, there is little in the way of instructions or pictures. However, on the whole it is not difficult to locate what you want and for additional information you have the choice of consulting the staff or purchasing the excellent and informative catalogue. There is an interesting collection of gardening books if you want to explore any questions in depth.

Prices ££££££
Facilities Parking, 200 cars (plus 400 overflow). Toilets. Play area. Garden advice service. Delivery service. Plants price list and catalogue £1.50, plus 50p p&p
Open Mon to Sat 8.30am to 5.30pm, Sun 10am to 5.30pm (closes 5pm Sun in winter). Closed 4 days at Christmas and New Year's Day
Credit cards Access, Visa

Prices vary a lot at garden centres and nurseries. We've calculated a basket price for plants and given ratings from £ to ££££££ – very cheap to very expensive.

ST. AUSTELL Cornwall map 3
Prices Garden Centre

St. Austell Garden Centre, Boscundle, St. Austell   *Tel* Par (072 681) 2197

On the A390 just before its junction with the A3082, 1½ miles from St. Austell

A pleasant wooded area is the home of this well-arranged centre. There is ample room to get around, and the outside area is divided into sections containing plants, furniture, building materials, and sheds and greenhouses. Tools and other small gardening sundries and houseplants are kept in a covered area. There is a good, general range of gardening equipment and a reasonable range of plants. Plants are of good quality and include a particularly good selection of bulbs, shrubs and fruit trees. Eye-level signs for the shrubs, trees and fruits carry useful information and illustrations: the smaller alpines, heather and herbs are identified by individual labels. Willing and helpful staff are on hand to give advice or to lend a hand with any heavy loading. There are no refreshment facilities and no toilets.

Prices £££
Facilities Parking, 100 cars. Garden advice service. Delivery service. Free price lists
Open Mon to Sat 8.30am to 5.30pm, Sun and bank holidays 10am to 5pm. Closed Christmas and Boxing Day and New Year's Day
Credit cards Access, Visa

SANDY Bedfordshire map 4
Bickerdike's Garden Centre

London Road, Sandy SG19 1DZ   *Tel* Sandy (0767) 80559

On the A1, 3 miles north of Biggleswade, ½ mile north of the Sandy roundabout

A small but beautifully presented centre with a good supply of the more popular shrubs, trees and other plants. The layout is especially good, comprising a main paved path off which are raised beds for plants and timber frames supporting container-grown shrubs and trees. Firm gravel surrounds all the plant areas. The excellent selection of conifers is nicely set out in a peat bank, and customers are invited to remove those they want or to ask an assistant. The only criticism of the layout would be that there is a bit too much path at the expense of stock, and that the alphabet system is a bit obscure – our inspector never did find 'M to S'! Plants are generally healthy and clean, all watered by 9.30am. However, fruit bushes showed signs of mildew and aphids when our inspector visited. Group labels are suspended at eye level and are very informative. Each plant has a name and price tag. The stock of tools and sundries is well balanced, though there are no power tools or lawnmowers. The decorated containers in terracotta and simulated stone particularly took our inspector's fancy. Larger items including sheds, greenhouses, fencing and paving are also sold. A large, contoured car park provides adequate space, although there is more room round the side. There are slides for the children if they get bored and the landscaping and loggia, with its hanging baskets, flower troughs and trees, make it a pleasant place for shopping.

Prices £££
Facilities Parking, 150 cars. Toilets. Play area. Garden advice service. Delivery service. Free price lists for plants, paving, walling, fencing, and garden buildings
Open Every day, 9am to 5.30pm
Credit card Access

SAWBRIDGEWORTH Hertfordshire map 4

Greenscape Garden Centre

High Wych Road, Sawbridgeworth *Tel* Harlow (0279) 722338
CM21 0HJ
Near Sawbridgeworth, 2 miles from Harlow

This centre used to be called Rivers. It has changed hands, but the old manager is still there and the centre has not altered much, though improvements are planned. It has proved to be a reliable centre for buying plants. Our inspector bought soft fruits here ten years ago and they are still very productive. It specialises in figs and vines which are grown on site. The range of plants on sale is reasonable and they are kept well watered and in a healthy condition. However, stocks can get rather depleted out of season and it would be wise not to expect a good choice at off-peak times. Labelling of plants is good, especially the group labelling. Inside, a range of tools and fertilisers is set out to advantage in a small space. Greenhouses, fencing and paving materials are not available but most ordinary garden sundries can be bought, including barbecues. This is a medium-sized centre with a small but helpful staff.

Prices £££
Facilities Parking, 300 cars. Toilets. Garden advice service. Delivery service. Plant price list and catalogue
Open Mon to Sat 9am to 6.30pm (closes 5pm in winter). Closed Christmas Day
Credit cards Access, Visa

SCAYNES HILL W. Sussex map 5

Scaynes Hill Nursery

Anchor Hill, Scaynes Hill, *Tel* Haywards Heath (0444) 86673
near Haywards Heath
On the A272 Lewes road, just south of Scaynes Hill

Four years ago the site of this centre was a wilderness, but it is slowly taking shape as more and more of the area comes under cultivation. It is well laid out, attractive and tidy, and shows a lot of promise. At the moment much of the stock is bought in from outside, but increasingly plants will be grown on site. At the time of our inspection the range of stock clearly reflected seasonal variations. The land which has already been reclaimed from the wild has been well organised and labelling is good, with some plants having details of cultivation. The condition of most plants is good with only the occasional sad specimen. Since this centre is slowly being built up from scratch there are not as yet many sundries available, but you will find chemicals, composts and garden ornaments. When our inspector visited, only one person was on duty selling the plants and answering queries, but she was helpful and friendly and it was at an off-peak hour. Fresh vegetables grown in the grounds and free-range eggs can also be purchased here.

Prices Information not available
Facilities Parking, 20 cars. Garden advice service
Open Every day (further information not available)

SHEFFIELD S. Yorkshire

map 2

Abbey Lane Nurseries

Abbey Lane, Sheffield S7 2QZ   *Tel* Sheffield (0742) 360408

3 miles south of the city centre where the A621 crosses the ring road at Beauchief corner. The centre is 100 yds along Abbey Lane

This small nursery is located on the edge of woodland, but the surroundings are steadily becoming built up. It is a family-run business and offers a select stock centring around an excellent choice of home-grown conifers. There is no attempt to attract gardeners of every ilk: they concentrate on their limited range, and what they do they do well. All the plants are in excellent condition, obviously well cared for and informatively labelled. The whole site is very small, but it has been nicely laid out. In addition to the conifers the choice of plants consists of a good range of alpines and heathers, and some trees, shrubs and interesting ferns. Garden pools and pool liners of all shapes and sizes are available and a limited supply of fencing. They also stock sheds and paving but no greenhouses or mowers. An attractive feature is the tubs and troughs which are planted out and placed around the centre. A landscape gardening service is provided which takes on large estates as well as gardens of ½ acre and less. A lecture service is also offered. The staff are few in number but very considerate.

Prices ££££
Facilities Parking, 8 cars. Toilet. Garden advice service. Delivery service when linked with landscape work. Free price list for bedding plants, dwarf conifers, hardy plants. Free catalogue for dwarf conifers
Open Mon, Wed, Thur, Fri and Sat 9am to 6pm (opens 10am, closes at dusk in winter). Closed Tues and Sun. Closed Christmas Day

---

Abbeydale Garden Centre

Abbeydale Road South, Dore,   *Tel* Sheffield (0742) 369091
Sheffield S17 3LB

On the south-west side of Sheffield, 4 miles from the centre on the A621

In an attractive, suburban setting close to Millhouses Park and Abbeydale Industrial Hamlet, this centre is rather like the proverbial 'curate's egg' – good in parts. It is well laid out and plus points noted by our inspector last year included a well-designed car park, making the best use of a long, narrow area, a large stock of stone and terracotta pots and tubs and a selection of interesting varieties of houseplants. Our inspector's main criticism of this centre was the mixing of some old, tired plants with new, healthy arrivals. At the time of inspection shrubs, trees and conifers were in reasonable condition and the centre was awaiting new deliveries. Labelling was patchy, varying from non-existent to quite helpful. The centre stocks greenhouses, sheds, fencing and garden ornaments. A separate building houses a furniture and glassware shop and there is an attractive coffee shop adjacent to the car park. Alterations are in progress in the indoor area. The average city gardener would find the sundries and plants satisfactory. The keen gardener might be harder to please but careful plant selection would have its rewards.

Prices £££
Facilities Parking, 200 cars. Toilets. Restaurant and cafeteria. Garden advice service. Delivery service
Open Every day 9am to 6pm (closes 5.30pm Jan to April). Closed Christmas and Boxing Day and New Year's Day
Credit cards Access, Visa

Ferndale Nursery & Garden Centre

Dyche Lane, Coal Aston,   *Tel* Dronfield (0246) 412763
Sheffield S18 6AB

About 5 miles south of Sheffield city centre, 1 mile south of the Norton roundabout

This is a fairly small, well-arranged centre where wide paths give very comfortable access to all parts of the site; flooring is good and surfaces outside are hard – gravel or paved. Ramps connect the different indoor levels ensuring easy access for customers with wheelchairs and pushchairs, and although there are some steps outdoors the main path is also ramped. The plants are logically set out and clearly labelled in groups – the centre is not really large enough to warrant signposting. There is a good selection of most common gardening equipment, though the centre lacks furniture, lawnmowers and other power tools. There are only a few water-gardening accessories and aquatic plants, and no fish. The range of plants would satisfy most gardeners – shrubs, dwarf conifers, herbs and houseplants probably being the best represented. These plants were in very good health when our inspector visited, as were the ornamental trees, but it was disappointing to see containerised fruit trees and bushes, which were really too old to grow on into good croppers, still for sale. The general appearance of the site is very attractive. Staff are clearly identifiable in their bright red overalls; they can offer a little knowledgeable help and are certainly welcoming. Extensive changes are to be made to the outdoor area and toilets are under construction (including one for the disabled and baby changing facilities).

Prices £££
Facilities Parking, 70 cars (plus 100 overflow). Garden advice service. Delivery service.
Open Every day 9am to 6pm (closes 8pm Fri and 5.30pm every day in winter, except

Sun 5pm). Closed Christmas and Boxing Day and New Year's Day
Credit cards Access, Visa

Huttons Nurseries

Long Lane, Loxley, Sheffield 6   *Tel* Sheffield (0742) 337134
On the B6077, Bradfield road, about 5 miles from Sheffield city centre

Huttons is located in a rather isolated setting amidst hilly countryside just
outside Sheffield. It is a nursery rather than a garden centre, so if your
plans are for a family outing, this is not the place to choose. Some fencing,
ornaments, hand tools and composts are available, but stocks of sundries
are small as the nursery concentrates on plants. The small, well-organised
covered area is turned over almost completely to a collection of houseplants
(plans for a new glasshouse are in the pipeline). The emphasis among the
outdoor plants is on conifers and heathers – there is a very good selection
and the standard is high. There is also a fair selection of other popular
species, particularly trees and shrubs. Bedding plants, alpines, fruit and
conifers are all grown on site. Labelling is acceptable overall, but best for
the trees and shrubs. Prices are low.

Prices ££
Facilities Parking, 30 cars. Ice cream. Delivery service
Open Every day 9am to 7.30pm (closes 7pm in winter)

Valleyside Garden Centre

Bell Hagg, Manchester Road,   *Tel* Sheffield (0742) 301925
Sheffield S10 5PX
On the A57 Manchester road 3½ miles west of Sheffield city centre

Quite a small but attractive site in the suburbs of Sheffield, this centre
comprises a fairly large outside display area but a rather crowded interior
(there are plans to extend this). In spite of limited space, the centre is well
organised both inside and out and clearly signposted so that it is not too
difficult to track down what you are after. Most garden accessories are
stocked and if you have a soft spot for water gardening the department
here is well worth exploring. Fish, snails, mussels and an excellent
selection of plants make up an interesting display. Fencing, paving, garden
furniture and ornaments are sold and a lawnmower sharpening service is
also offered, but there are no new machines on sale. Outside there is a
reasonable range of plants. They are well tended and so of good quality.
Bedding plants, geraniums, fuchsias, conifers and shrubs are grown on
site. Sections are divided by railway sleepers and have large illustrated
labels which are placed up high. Individual plants are well marked and you
can ask for information leaflets or the catalogue for additional details. The
staff are courteous and willingly deal with questions.

Prices ££££
Facilities Parking, 60 cars. Toilets. Vending machines. Garden advice service.
Delivery service. Plant catalogue 40p
Open Every day 8.30am to 6pm (closes 5pm in winter)
Credit cards Access, Visa

SHELDWICH Kent map 4

Sheldwich Garden Centre

Sheldwich Lees, Sheldwich,   *Tel* Faversham (0795) 532274
near Faversham ME13 0NG

*At Sheldwich Lees, 2 miles south of Faversham off the A251 Faversham to
Ashford road*

This centre is more a place for the real plant fancier rather than the DIY
gardener. It is situated opposite a delightful village green, and the layout is
most attractive with plants arranged alphabetically in what used to be a
kitchen garden. In some corners, plants have been placed to form small
patio gardens which are very pleasant and have seats dotted around so that
you can rest your feet and think about what you want to buy. The overall
layout is very good and the arrangement of indoor plants makes good use
of limited space. There is a very good stock of cheap plants, and you will
be able to find some of the less popular varieties. At the time of our visit the
choice of clematis was particularly comprehensive. The concentration is
obviously on plants, and the general quality readily reflects this, with fine
healthy specimens of all indoor and outdoor varieties. The labelling of plant
groups is first class although individual labelling could be called only fair.
Tools and sundries are available in a very limited range with the exception
of a good choice of ornaments, peat and composts. Fencing, garden
furniture and pond equipment are also sold. Fruit and vegetables can be
bought on the premises. Although there is no play area for children, they
will undoubtedly find the aviary an exciting diversion. Staff are pleasant
and helpful.

Prices ££
Facilities Parking, 100 cars. Toilets. Vending machines. Garden advice service. Free
plant price list and catalogue
Open Every day 8am to 4.30pm. Closed Christmas Day

SHEPPERTON Surrey map 5

Uncommon Garden Centre

Walton Bridge, Shepperton   *Tel* Walton-on-Thames (0932) 222711
TW17 8LS

*On the A244 on the Shepperton side of Walton Bridge, about 500yds from Walton
Town Centre*

A picnic by the Thames at the nearby popular Cowey Sale could follow a
visit to this centre, which lies in pretty rural surroundings near to Walton
Bridge. The 2½ acre site contains first-class plants and because of the clean
and careful layout, weeds have little chance of a foothold – when they do
appear they are very small and very healthy! The range is good, most
standard plants are available and there's a particularly extensive choice of
alpines, herbs and heathers. Large notices identify the species to be found
in each bed, while each individual plant has a stick-in label with its name,
picture and environmental preferences. Shrubs bear labels giving the name

and price. However, the outside area is only half given over to plants; the other half is devoted to an impressive selection of garden buildings from conservatories and summer houses to saunas, chalet pools and spa baths.The covered section of the centre stocks a good range of the smaller sundries, including barbecue equipment and indoor plants as well as tools, composts and chemicals. The centre is planning to diversify further into the DIY market. There is a large coloured plan of the layout placed conveniently near the entrance. The staff are very friendly and their bright red T-shirts can be easily seen dotted about the centre. One or two plain-clothed gentlemen sporting lapel labels introduce themselves if you look like you need help – and they can be very helpful indeed.

Prices ££££
Facilities Parking, 220 cars. Toilets. Vending machines and ice creams (coffee bar planned). Garden advice service. Delivery service
Open Every day 8.45am to 5.45pm. Cloed Christmas and Boxing Day
Credit cards Access, American Express, Diners Club, Visa

SHERFIELD-ON-LODDON Hampshire   map 4

Baileys Garden Centre

Wildmoor Lane,   *Tel* Basingstoke (0256) 882776
Sherfield-on-Loddon, Basingstoke RG27 0HA
Just off the A33, Basingstoke to Reading road, opposite Sherfield-on-Loddon village

A very well-stocked centre which has been newly landscaped and now looks very attractive indeed. The layout is very good inside and the large outside area is filled with trees, shrubs and other plants, carefully grouped in alphabetical order which makes it easy to find what you want. The clear labelling also aids identification. Plants are quite expensive but the range is excellent and their high standard is due to conscientious watering and care lavished by the staff. The shrubs and trees were in pristine condition on the day of our inspection, in spite of the drought. There is a thriving area which deals with sheds, greenhouses, building materials, paving slabs and the like, while a covered area houses the other gardening tools and sundries. These were displayed in a manner which delighted our inspector – goods were neatly arranged with clearly marked prices, and sections were very well stocked. An extensive range of garden furniture is also sold for those who are not adverse to an occasional break from gardening. Unusual features include swimming pools and accessories, and antique furniture. A cold-water, tropical and marine fish centre and a greenhouse extension were both well underway by the end of 1984. Our inspector's conclusion was that 'there was everything one could need, or wish for, under one roof'. The staff are helpful and seem to be continually busy dealing with enquiries.

Prices £££££
Facilities Parking, 100 cars. Toilets. Ice cream and soft drinks. Garden advice service. Delivery service. Free price lists for bedding plants, bulbs, paving, fencing etc. Free plant catalogue

Open Summer, every day 9am to 5.30pm. Winter, Mon to Sat 9am to 5pm, Sun 10am
to 5pm. Closed 5 days at Christmas
Credit cards Access, Visa

SHIPLEY Shropshire map 3

Lealans Nursery

Shipley, Pattingham,   *Tel* Pattingham (0902) 700209
Wolverhampton WV6 7EZ
About 7 miles from Wolverhampton town centre, on the A454 Bridgnorth road

Quite a good, old-fashioned nursery with none of the frills offered by a
modern garden centre. The site is reasonably spacious and there are
extensive glasshouses, some used for growing cut flowers and others for
displaying indoor plants as well as the seeds and few composts and
chemicals which are sold. When our inspector visited, it was not very
systematically organised and labelling didn't help much – it was often
faded or non-existent, although the nursery tells us this has been
improved. The strongest feature of the nursery is the conifers – these offer
the widest selection and were very healthy when inspected. Otherwise our
inspector felt the range of other plants offered for sale was a bit patchy.
Quality was generally good, though there were a few neglected plants.
There was a wide range of houseplants in good condition, and a special
feature is made of hanging baskets and decorative bowls. The staff are
helpful and will volunteer to assist with any loading or carrying. There are
plans to provide a shop and toilet facilities, as well as increasing the range
of sundries.

Prices £££
Facilities Parking, 90 cars. Play area. Garden advice service. Delivery service.
Plants sold by mail order
Open Every day 8am to 6pm (closes 5pm in winter)
Credit cards Access, American Express, Visa

SHIRLEY W. Midlands map 4

Notcutts Garden Centre

Stratford Road, Shirley,   *Tel* 021 744 4501
Solihull B90 4EN
On the junction of the M42 and A34 between Shirley and Hockley Heath

This vast garden centre, mainly under glass, is one of the Notcutts group. It
scored highly for its alphabetical layout – 'impossible to fault' – and
beautiful presentation. Access from a busy road is well landscaped and
parking is easy. It is set in a pleasant, urban area which is soon to be
remodelled to accommodate a Tesco Superstore at the rear of the centre.
(The centre is to be rebuilt but will continue trading throughout the
building programme.) This will be handy for those Saturday shoppers who
want to 'kill two birds with one stone' and shop for the garden as well as
the house. Notcutts itself seems to stock everything from fish to phlox,
resulting in only one problem – finding them! A few more signposts would

be very helpful. All the larger items of gardening equipment are sold, including sheds, greenhouses, fencing, paving, barbecues and water-gardening equipment. Plants are expensive but in tip-top condition. There is a particularly good selection of common trees and shrubs. The centre offers a garden design and landscaping service. Staff are pleasant and helpful and there is an advice centre which is usually staffed, as well as a range of free leaflets. Described by our inspector as 'The very best garden centre I have ever visited!'

Prices ££££
Facilities Parking, 500 cars. Toilets. Vending machines. Play area. Garden advice service. Delivery service. Free price lists for roses, furniture, sheds etc. Plant catalogue £1.50. Plants sold by mail order from Notcutts, Woodbridge (see entry for WOODBRIDGE)
Open Mon to Sat 9am to 6pm, Sun 10.30am to 6pm (closes 5.30pm every day in winter). Closed 25 to 28 Dec and 1 Jan
Credit cards Access, Visa

SHREWSBURY Shropshire   map 2
Bayley's Garden Centre

Bayston Hill, Shrewsbury   *Tel* Bayston Hill (074 372) 4261
SY3 0DA
One mile south of Shrewsbury, on the A49 Hereford road

Bayley's is a nursery with a garden centre adjoining it. It is a medium-sized site situated in the rural outskirts of Shrewsbury. You can buy from Bayley's by mail order, selecting plants from their excellent, fully descriptive catalogue. Many customers purchase their garden stock this way, but a visit to the centre can also be rewarding. Many of the plants are grown on site – there is a good range of trees, shrubs and conifers and a satisfactory selection of most other standard plants. They are generally sturdy and healthy specimens and are identified by clear, informative group labelling – although pricing and labelling on individual plants needs some improving. Another advantage of the centre is the excellent professional staff on hand to give expert advice, even to the extent of advising customers against making certain purchases. Greenhouses, sheds and building materials are displayed outside, and indoors, amid a slightly crowded layout, there are many smaller sundries, including an extensive selection of hand tools. No power tools are available though, and at the time of our inspection there were no water-gardening supplies stocked, but a water-garden department is planned. A new greenhouse designed specially for indoor plants has recently opened and this might be of interest if you are short of a little greenery in the home. Tea, coffee, cakes and ice cream are provided by a small, on-site cafe.

Prices £££
Facilities Parking, 80 cars. Toilets. Cafe. Garden advice service. Delivery service. Catalogues for plants free and sundries 50p
Open Every day 8.30am to 5.30pm (opens 10am Sun)
Credit card Access

Percy Thrower's Gardening Centre

Portland Nurseries,   *Tel* Shrewsbury (0743) 51497
Oteley Road, Shrewsbury SY2 6QW
On the A5, 2 miles south-east of Shrewsbury town centre

The biggest centre in the area and one where you should go to purchase
tools and sundries or houseplants, but which lets the side down when it
comes to outdoor plants. The selection of gardening equipment is wide
with a good choice of brands and sizes. The tool section is very good and a
comprehensive range of seeds is kept in stock. You should find anything
you need in the way of garden hardware, as well as some non-gardening
extras such as toys, and everything is well organised and clearly divided
into sections. The houseplant department offers a collection of high-quality
plants which unfortunately outshines what is available among the hardy
range outside (though the centre told us they were improving the hardy
plant section for 1985). The exterior displays are well laid out and plants are
placed in alphabetical order, although a few signposts wouldn't go amiss.
The range is generally adequate and the fuchsias were particularly
impressive when we inspected. Labels for groups of plants are very good
and give information such as hardiness, eventual size, and flowers, all in
clear print. Each plant is marked with an identification tag only and this is
frequently illegible. For prices it is necessary to refer back to the group
label. There are plenty of staff about to help out and they are generally very
good, but the centre can get very busy, especially at weekends, so be
prepared to wait. A farm shop and craft section are planned.

Prices £££
Facilities Parking, 300 cars. Toilets. Coffee bar. Garden advice service. Delivery
service. Free price list and catalogue for hardy plants 15p
Open Every day 9am to 6pm (Wed, Thurs, Fri open to 8pm). Closes 5pm every day in
winter. Closed Christmas and Boxing Day
Credit cards Access, Visa

SIDCUP Kent   map 5

Ruxley Manor Nursery and Garden Centre

Maidstone Road, Sidcup DA14 5BG   *Tel* 01-300 0084/0900
On the A20, London to Dover Road about 1 mile south of Sidcup

A showpiece garden centre just on the edge of town overlooking farm land.
The approach road from the large car park leads past gardens which are
nicely planted out with bedding plants. The range of tools and sundries is
impressive with an excellent barbecue section and a good range of show
glasshouses and sheds. There is a good range of garden furniture, sheds,
garages and greenhouses as well as luxury extras such as swimming pools
and tropical and cold-water fish. The centre comprises a massive area laid
out with all your gardening needs, and clear signposting helps you to find
what you are after. Flower beds are well organised with wide paths
providing plenty of room to manoeuvre trolleys and prams. A good
selection of high-quality but fairly expensive plants is available.

When inspected, strawberries and herbs were not up to standard. There's an especially big choice of conifers and climbers and an area is set aside for unusual trees and shrubs. Our inspector found the staff helpful and well trained. The advice desk is particularly good and there is an excellent selection of free gardening leaflets. The system of labelling was good but, as is often the case, the weather had caused some deterioration. In addition to the attractive restaurant there is a shop selling fruit and vegetables.

Prices £££££
Facilities Parking, 700 cars. Toilets. Restaurant. Play area. Garden advice service. Delivery service
Open Mon to Sat 9am to 5.30pm (closes 5pm in winter), Sun 9am to 12am
Credit cards Access, Visa (Diners Club and American Express in restaurant)

SOBERTON Hampshire map 4
Kingfisher Plants

Selworth Lane, Soberton, *Tel* Droxford (0489) 877683
near Droxford SO3 1PX
About 600 yds off the A32, 2 miles south of Droxford

A centre with a lovely atmosphere where, according to our inspector, locals 'just come to visit and sit'. It is in a rural setting, tucked away in heavily wooded countryside and, as the name would suggest, it is mainly a nursery although the gardening sundries side is being developed. The growing areas provide interesting browsing for curious gardeners and the haphazard arrangement on a sloping site is pleasant and relaxing. Paths are on the narrow side and plant displays sometimes overgrown, but all is not chaos – signposting is clear, group labelling is very good and, at the time of our inspector's visit, all individual tags were in the process of being revamped. A comprehensive range of plants is available either from Kingfisher's or from the associated Fairoak Nursery. The conifer range is excellent, roses are good and there is a very good choice of bulbs, especially tulips. The quality varies from good to splendid. The full range of gardening tools and sundries found at large garden centres will never be carried by Kingfisher's, but there is a basic selection of hand tools and garden furniture. Paving, water-gardening equipment and sheds can be ordered through Fairoak. Work is taking place to install toilets, and further developments are planned to improve paths, facilities and the car park. This is a very pleasant informative nursery, well regarded locally.

Prices £££
Facilities Parking, 40 cars. Vending machine. Garden advice service. Delivery service. Free plant price list and catalogue
Open Every day 9am to 6pm. Closed Christmas and Boxing Day
Credit cards Access, Visa

Garden centres and nurseries which provide the best facilities for disabled visitors are marked with the wheelchair symbol. Most centres show plenty of room for improvement in this area and we think it is time they gave more thought to their less able customers.

SOUTHAMPTON Hampshire   map 4

Homebase

Lordshill District Centre, Lordshill, *Tel* Southampton (0703) 739782
Southampton SO1 8HY
On the A3057 between Southampton and Romsey, 3 miles from Southampton centre

This sizeable complex is in the middle of a large, new housing area. The site includes other shops and a pleasant pub, as well as the Sainsbury's Foodstore and Homebase DIY, and provides public facilities such as parking, toilets and a cafe. The garden centre is reached by walking through the DIY section to the tools and sundries and then on outside to the plants, fencing, ornaments and such like. On busy days, there is direct access to the gardening area. The whole centre is well laid out and clearly signposted. The wide aisles and paths make it particularly suitable for those with pushchairs, wheelchairs or trolleys. All types of gardening equipment are supplied. Building materials such as bricks and walling are plentiful and there is a useful information service linked to the DIY department. The centre provides a good, standard choice of plant varieties rather than anything particularly unusual. Nevertheless, when our inspector visited, there was an interesting collection of grapevines and some lovely clematis. Generally the quality was very good and labelling rated well for clarity and content. The centre and its helpful, knowledgeable staff provide a good service to the surrounding area and offer an excellent extension to a more mundane shopping trip. There is a machinery hire shop on the site and roof racks are loaned free for delivery.

Prices £££
Facilities Parking, 542 cars. Garden advice service. Delivery service
Open Mon 9am to 6pm, Tues and Wed 8.30am to 8pm, Thurs and Fri 8.30am to 9pm, Sat 8.30am to 5pm
Credit cards Access, Visa

Swan Garden Centre

Gaters Hill, Mansbridge Road,   *Tel* Southampton (0703) 472324
West End, Southampton SO3 3HW
On the A27 between Swaythling and West End village, close to Southampton airport

A comprehensive garden centre with some lovely riverside walks nearby, so why not pack a picnic and make an afternoon of it? Whatever you are after there is bound to be something here which should fit the bill. The centre is well laid out, arranged into several distinct areas each with its own speciality. One section deals with greenhouses and sheds and a second has a selection of swimming pools on show. If you are interested in fish there is an aquatic centre with a very good advice desk, and if you are more interested in eating them, the vegetable shop has fresh trout for sale. Hand tools are sold, but at the time of inspection the centre was waiting for a new franchisee to take over the lawnmower and power tool department – at the moment there is an electric tool hire shop offering its services. There's a good indoor display of garden furniture and decorative plant containers. Plants are set out on raised, waist-high benches with wide paved paths cutting between rows. Nothing is actually propagated on the site, but the range of plants bought in is very good and the quality high. Our inspector was agreeably surprised by the improvement in the health of the plants since his last visit. The staff are all pleasant and willing to help and there is a catalogue available which tells you what is in stock and gives some general hints on plant care.

Prices Information not available
Facilities Parking, 150 cars. Toilets. Ice creams. Garden advice service. Delivery service. Free plant catalogue
Open Every day 9am to 5.30pm. Closed a few days over Christmas
Credit cards Access, Visa

SOUTHWELL Nottinghamshire map 2

Hill Farm Nurseries and Garden Centre

Reg Taylor, Normanton, Southwell NG25 0PR *Tel* Southwell (0636) 813184
On the Hockerton road, 1 mile east of Southwell

A large garden centre and nursery, sensibly laid out with all sections clearly signposted. At the time of our inspection there were three separate greenhouses, one containing some very good quality houseplants including fine begonia specimens, a second housing a selection of shrubs, and the third set aside for composts and fertilisers, seeds, tools and various other sundries. Outside there are raised beds for alpines, heathers and the smaller shrubs, and an open area at the far end of the centre holds a large collection of fruit trees. Plants are mostly grown on the centre's three nurseries and are cheap. The overall range and quality of trees and shrubs is good, although our inspector noticed a few overgrown ornamentals. Illustrated labels offering brief plant descriptions are used for different types of shrubs. The sundries section includes a very large choice of garden furniture and an enormous selection of tubs, containers and stone ornaments. Fencing and paving are sold and also a selection of aquatic equipment, water plants and lots of fish. In fact the range of stock at this centre would easily meet most gardening requirements. Staff in all the sections are very helpful and they are forthcoming with their time and recommendations. The refreshment facilities are well above average and in warm weather the pleasant tea room extends into an open courtyard with tables and chairs – umbrellas open up to give shade on hot days. There is also a small country park and nature conservation area for you to explore.

Prices ££
Facilities Parking, 175 cars (plus 100 overflow). Toilets. Restaurant. Garden advice service. Delivery service. Free price lists for plants and sundries
Open Every day 10am to 5.30pm
Credit cards Access, Visa

H. Merryweather and Sons

The Nurseries, Halam Road,   *Tel* Southwell (0636) 813204
Southwell NG25 0AH
On a back road ¼ mile out of Southwell

Merryweather has been a fruit specialist for years, and it supplies an
excellent range of culinary fruit trees which is not limited to the standard
apples, plums and pears. More unusual still is a delightful aviary set aside
in one corner of an open-fronted building – these birds are not for sale but
are an attractive spectacle. The overall range of goods may not be as
comprehensive as in some garden centres, but it is quite adequate for most
needs. All the popular shrubs and conifers are there and some ornamental
trees. Alpines, heathers and herbs are also stocked and other plants such as
biennials, bulbs and perennials appear during the appropriate planting
season. There are some houseplants available, but the selection is not
extensive. The quality of all the stock is very good, and there are ranks of
small, healthy plants being grown in the reserve beds ready to replenish
supplies quickly. Illustrated labels are used whenever possible, and the
overall standard of labelling is quite satisfactory. Many improvements in
the layout have taken place over the last few years. The different sections
are uncrowded and all paths are paved. An indoor area contains seeds,
hand tools, fertilisers and similar sundries, including a substantial
collection of gardening books. A separate, open-fronted building stocks
numerous containers for the patio or house and these come in all shapes
and sizes, plain and fancy. There are not very many staff but they are
pleasant and will try to find the answers to any of your questions if they
don't know them themselves. A tea and coffee bar provides refreshments.

Prices £££
Facilities Parking, 100 cars. Toilets. Tea and coffee bar. Play area. Garden advice
service. Delivery service. Price lists
Open Every day 9.30am to 5.30pm (closes 5pm in winter). Closed Christmas and
Boxing Day

New Minster Water Gardens and Garden Centre

Fiskerton Road, Southwell   *Tel* Southwell (0636) 813186/813427
NG23 5RB
*On the eastern outskirts of Southwell, which is on the A612, 12 miles north of
Nottingham*

An enjoyable day can be had by gardeners and non-gardeners alike in this
centre set in delightful countryside. The layout is very orderly and
attractive with plants placed on raised beds which are separated by wide,
criss-crossing pathways. This area is laid out with the smaller plants at one
end graduating up to trees at the other, all clearly signposted. All around
the periphery are displays of plastic fish ponds, ornaments, furniture,
fencing and the like. The collection of plants includes a very varied stock of
roses which are all in excellent condition, as well as a good selection of
conifers. The selection of other plants is reasonable, though the choice is
somewhat limited. There is a large covered area, the principal features of

which are an extensive stock of fish (both tropical and cold-water), water-gardening equipment and a special 'fish advice' service. You will also find most tools, machinery and sundries, and a particularly well-stocked book counter. No sheds, greenhouses, fencing or paving are kept in stock, although there are plans for this in the future, and at the moment they may be ordered from a brochure. Staff are very helpful and courteous and readily give advice and information. A comfortable 'waitress service' dining room sells light lunches or there is a pleasant picnic area next to the coffee bar. Children can be left to play safely in an enclosed area with a 'fun castle'.

Prices £££
Facilities Parking, 80 cars. Toilets. Restaurant. Play area. Garden advice service. Delivery service
Open Every day 9.30am to 6pm (closed Tues from mid Sept to Mar)
Credit cards Access, Visa

SPROWSTON Norfolk   map 4

Sprowston Garden Centre   ❀ ✎

Blue Boar Lane, Sprowston,   *Tel* Norwich (0603) 412239
Norwich NR7 8RJ
Take the A1151 Wroxham road off the A47 Norwich ring road, proceed for 1 mile and turn right into Blue Boar Lane

This garden centre is set in pleasant wooded surroundings. There is a well-organised, clean and tidy indoor area stocking all kinds of gardening equipment and a miscellany of gifts. A separate section is devoted to the art of the flower-arranger and a special display shows some interesting examples of bonsai. There is also an excellent range of high-quality houseplants which deserves a special mention. All the larger items of gardening equipment are also available; there is a 'greenhouse centre' where expert advice is on hand, a special aquarium centre with display ponds and large fish containers, and a wide choice of speciality fencing. Outside, the displays are well laid out and signposted. A good selection of shrubs and some unusual plants add interest to a range which is generally satisfactory. At the time of our inspection, plant quality varied from fair to very good – plants of moderate quality were usually end-of-season stock and some were being sold off cheaply. Group labels are large and legible, providing helpful cultural instructions and often with full-colour illustrations. Plants are all labelled with name and price, but these have sometimes faded. Our inspector spent an enjoyable time among the attractive displays and the positive impression gained of this centre was consolidated by the friendliness and good advice offered by a mature and experienced staff. A coffee shop is planned for the near future.

Prices £££
Facilities Parking, 400 cars. Toilets. Vending machines. Play area. Garden advice service. Delivery service. Free plant price list and catalogue
Open Mon to Sat 8.30am to 5.30pm, Sun 10.30am to 5pm
Credit cards Access, Visa

STALBRIDGE Dorset

map 3

Station Road Nursery

L. A. Williams and Son, Stalbridge
DT10 2RQ

Tel Stalbridge (0963) 62355

Just off the main street in Stalbridge

This is a relatively small nursery and it does not aspire to being a fully fledged garden centre. The proprietor, Mr Williams, raises most of his own plants but buys in fruit bushes and trees. His propagated specimens are of very good quality, as are the houseplants. The range of plants is average with nothing of extraordinary interest, but there's enough to content most gardeners and prices are low. The nursery will order anything not in stock. Trees are sold bare-rooted in the winter months. All labelling is very clear and helpful, mainly printed and with coloured illustrations – but not every plant is marked. Besides the well-laid-out and clearly signposted exterior area, there is a greenhouse for indoor plants and a very small, but well set out, shop (about to be extended) for tools and sundries. A variety of peats, composts and chemicals are kept in stock and a small selection of hand tools as well as garden ornaments are also available. A new project centred around the aquatic side of gardening has been embarked upon, but is still in its infancy. The owners are pleasant and very knowledgeable. There is no car park attached to the nursery but you'll find a public car park just across the road.

Prices ££
Facilities Garden advice service. Delivery service. Free plant lists in season
Open Mon to Sat 8.30am to 5pm (closed Wed pm), Sun (Apr to Jul) 8.30am to 5pm

STANTON-ON-THE-WOLDS Nottinghamshire

map 2

Moores Nurseries

156 Melton Road,
Stanton-on-the-Wolds,
Nottingham NG12 5BQ

Tel Plumtree (060 77) 3717

On the A606 Melton road about 6 miles south-east of Nottingham

A nursery of medium size which stocks a few hand tools and chemicals but otherwise devotes itself entirely to inexpensive plants. The tendency is to stock heavily with seasonal plants rather than keeping a wide range on sale throughout the year. This means that the quality of the current plant range is excellent, but the out-of-season items are variable and can be a bit indifferent. A helpful feature is the presence of notices which inform customers when to expect the arrival of new stock. Labelling of shrubs and trees is good and descriptive, while on seasonal plants it can be poor. The staff offer sound advice and notices are displayed reminding the visitor about good plant care and warning against planting out fragile plants too early. The sales shop (a greenhouse) is well organised but congested.

Prices ££
Facilities Parking, 70 cars. Garden advice service
Open Every day except Tues, 10am to 5.30pm (closes 4.30pm in winter)

STAPLEFORD Nottinghamshire

map 2

Bardill's Roses Garden Centre ✿

Toton Lane, Stapleford,   *Tel* Sandiacre (0602) 392478
Nottingham NG9 7JB

On the A52 Stapleford bypass, 1 mile from the M1 junction 25, 6 miles from Nottingham

This centre is situated in a pleasant green-belt area surrounded by farmland. A series of large interconnecting greenhouses provides a light, airy and well-arranged display area for pot plants, furniture and most smaller tools and sundries. There is even an aquatic section with some cold-water fish if you have plans for restocking your pond. The only omissions are sheds and greenhouses. The overall range and quality of plants are good, but the centre's speciality is the roses which are grown and packed at the centre's own nursery. The layout of the outside section could do with some improvement (the centre tells us that this is now underway), but the labelling is very good with large, instructive signs perched in front of most different species, and smaller but equally adequate tags to be found on individual plants. The staff are friendly and knowledgeable. An attractive cafe is open all year round selling baked potatoes, salads and teas at quite reasonable prices. The play area is rather small but has swings for the children to play on, and the rabbits in the pets corner are also bound to attract their attention.

Prices £££
Facilities Parking, 350 cars. Toilets. Cafeteria. Play area. Garden advice service. Delivery service. Free price list and catalogue for plants. Free price lists for fencing, paving etc
Open Every day 8am to 6pm (closes 5pm in winter). Closed Christmas and Boxing Day
Credit cards Access, Visa

STARTLEY Wiltshire

map 4

Startley Hill Nurseries

Startley, Chippenham SN15 5HQ   *Tel* Seagry (0249) 720674
About 3 miles south of Malmesbury on the Upper Seagry to Sutton Benger road

A small nursery run by a keen orchid grower and his sister. The owner is welcoming, knowledgeable and enthusiastic without being pushy. The trees and shrubs offer the widest selection, and supplies change through the seasons. At our last inspection there was a very good cross-section of perennials and cottage-garden plants and obviously a lot of orchids. There are several greenhouses and open displays and the layout is good despite the lack of signposts (these are to be introduced). The range of sundries is limited to different types of peat, composts and chemicals. A good, old-fashioned nursery.

Prices £££
Facilities Parking, 23 cars. Garden advice service
Open Mon to Sat 8.30am to 6pm (closes 5pm in winter)

STEVENAGE Hertfordshire   map 4
Roger Harvey Garden Centre

Bragbury Lane, Stevenage SG2 8TJ   *Tel* Stevenage (0438) 811777
On the A602 Hertford road, 2 miles east of the A1(M) and 1 mile from Stevenage

This centre is located in some old farm buildings in an attractive setting. It is a lovely place to browse. Plants are not arranged alphabetically but grouped according to characteristics or common requirements, such as 'shade loving' or 'low growing' – possibly a problem if you want a specific plant, but a good idea if you are looking for plants for a purpose. The layout is pleasing to the eye and the paths are wide, allowing easy access. The large indoor section offers a good range of equipment and sundries with an excellent array of florist's supplies and a good number of superb houseplants. There are no greenhouses or sheds stocked but plans for 1985 include the introduction of garden buildings and conservatories. The outside section is rather small but provides display space for a good range of healthy specimens. Labelling was patchy when our inspector visited, though group labels were very good – informative and illustrated. The staff on hand are mostly involved in maintenance, but there is always one trained horticulturalist on site to help with customer's queries. A children's adventure playground was due for completion in early 1985.

Prices ££££
Facilities Parking, 250 cars. Toilets. Coffee bar. Play area (spring 1985). Garden advice service. Delivery service
Open Every day 9am to 6pm (April, May and June closes 8pm Thurs and Fri). Closes 5.30pm in winter. Closed for a few days at Christmas
Credit cards Access, Visa

STOCKSFIELD Northumberland   map 2
Tyne Valley Garden Centre

Mickley Square, Stocksfield   *Tel* Stocksfield (0661) 843263
8 miles east of Hexham, on the A695 in the village of Mickley Square

This is a medium-sized centre which has been under new management for the past couple of years during which time there have been significant improvements. The centre has an excellent layout with paved main paths, and firm gravel secondary paths so that access to all parts of the site and all display beds is very easy. The pathways are raked and clean, while the beds are all kept weed free beneath immaculate displays of very high-quality plants. The choice of plants should satisfy all but the most demanding gardener. The shrubs are worthy of particular mention, as are the conifers, amongst which you might find some interesting and rare varieties. All specimens are well labelled with both name and price. There is an area under glass with a good range of houseplants on show: other items include hand tools and composts. There is no space at this centre for the larger sundries such as sheds, greenhouses and power tools, but it does stock some fencing and paving, as well as furniture and ornaments. There are plans to include a water-gardening section with a display pond, and improvement to the sales area and expansion of the nursery stock are also underway. Staff are always available and are cheerful and ready to give advice when requested. The site and car park are on a slight slope which might become a litle tiring for the elderly or handicapped.

Prices £££
Facilities Parking, 25 cars. Toilets. Ice cream. Garden advice service. Delivery service. Free plant catalogue
Open Every day 9am to 6m (open to 8pm Thurs and Fri). Closes 5pm in winter
Credit cards Access, Visa

STOCKTON ON THE FOREST N. Yorkshire   map 2

Deans Garden Centre

Stockton Lane, Stockton on the Forest,   *Tel* York (0904) 400141
York YO3 9UE
Off the A64 York to Malton road. On a minor road to Stockton on the Forest, about 4 miles north-east of York city centre

This excellent centre is easily located amidst pleasant countryside just south of the York to Scarborough road. It covers a large site and presents a light and airy atmosphere. Paths and alleys have been arranged to create well-defined sections and plants are placed on raised staging where necessary. The different varieties are illustrated and prices are marked on each pot. The range of plants available is extremely good and they all show the healthy glow of good care. The indoor section houses a wide range of tools, fertilisers and other sundries, while the larger construction materials and garden buildings are displayed in a separate outside area. Beekeeping equipment is sold and you can also buy home-made preserves and honey in the shop. You may also find the 'gift' and floral departments of interest. Staff are distinguished by their green overalls. Their level of expertise is variable, though specialist questions can be answered by the more knowledgeable ones. You should be able to find nearly everything you need to stock and manage a garden or greenhouse at this centre.

Prices ££££
Facilities Parking, 200 cars. Toilets. Vending machine, confectionery and soft drinks. Garden advice service. Delivery service. Free lists for plants and sundries. Free catalogues for plants and beekeeping equipment
Open Every day 9am to 7pm (closes 5.30pm in winter). Closed Christmas Day, and sometimes between Christmas and New Year, depending on the weather
Credit cards Access, Visa

STONE CROSS E. Sussex   map 5

Stone Cross Nurseries and Garden Centre

Battle Road, Stone Cross,   *Tel* Eastbourne (0323) 763250
Pevensey BN24 5EB

On the A27 Polegate to Pevensey Road, 300yds east of Stone Cross

A centre with a rather weatherbeaten appearance, but which seems to have undergone some recent improvements, especially the large car park. It is in the middle of the village of Stone Cross and appears to be popular with the locals for it is often very busy. There is plenty to look at and it is enjoyable just to potter around the wide paths and browse through the good selection of shrubs, biennials and houseplants. Space at the centre itself is limited, but much of the stock is grown on nearby sites and includes shrubs, trees and conifers for coastal planting, and bedding plants, chrysanthemums, salads, vegetables and fruit. Generally the range of plants on offer is quite reasonable. The shrubs and trees are arranged in alphabetical order, but the small outdoor area could still do with more signposting. Labels are generally very good, although some suffer from the usual problems of fading and more helpful instructions in the herbaceous section would be welcome. The overall quality of plants is very good and our inspector spotted few weeds. Inside things are more clearly marked out and this well-organised section avoids the frustrations of overcrowding. The range of tools and sundries is reasonable. The water garden equipment is extensive with pools, fish and snails taking up a lot of the under-cover area. Fencing may be ordered, but no wooden fencing, only plastic-coated steel and wire mesh are available. The selection of garden furniture is quite small. The staff are easy to find and very friendly and helpful.

Prices £££
Facilities Parking, 60 cars. Toilets. Vending machines and light refreshments. Plant price list and catalogue 20p
Open Mon to Sat 8.30am to 5.30pm, Sun 9.30am to 5.30pm. Closed Christmas Day
Credit card Access

STONEHOUSE Gloucestershire   map 3
Kennedys Garden Centre

Ebley Road, Stonehouse,   *Tel* Stonehouse (045 382) 3846
near Stroud GL10 2LW
On the A419 about 1 mile west of Stroud and 2 miles east of Junction 13 on the M5

This is a centre with a very good range of most plants without any particular specialisation. The balanced but quite expensive range should satisfy any aspiring beginners as well as most die-hard gardeners. Conifers are available in large quantity with a fine selection to choose from. All are container-grown, and the general quality is above average. When our inspector visited, houseplants were of a particulary high standard, but a few trees were threatened by bad aphid attacks. The occasional weed or piece of moss was spotted as well as a few dead container plants left in display beds. In season there is an interesting range of made-up hanging baskets of superior quality. Layout is excellent both inside and out with most areas having wide, flat paths and good gangways – easy for negotiation by trolley, pram or wheelchair. Neat, raised beds make close inspection possible without a lot of bending and stooping. Group labels are large and easy to read, many including photographs and reasonable cultural details. Individual plant tags range from poor, faded and handwritten to very good, machine-printed labels. There's a well-balanced selection of garden machinery and accessories including summerhouses, sheds, stonework and water garden equipment. One building, which contains largely furniture, is closed on Sundays. Staff are reasonably knowledgeable and price guides and a general planting guide are available for the asking. The centre sits in pretty countryside with a view of the Cotswolds in the distance.

Prices £££££
Facilities Parking, 110 cars. Toilets. Delivery service. Free price list for hardy plants
Open Every day 9am to 6pm in summer, 8.30am to 5.30pm in winter. Closed Christmas Day
Credit cards Access, Visa

STONHAM ASPAL Suffolk map 4
Stonham Barns Plant Centre

Pettaugh Road, Stonham Aspal,   *Tel* Stowmarket (0449) 711755
Stowmarket IP14 6AS
On the A1120 Stowmarket to Yoxford road, just outside Stonham Aspal village 1 mile from the A140

A collection of farmbuildings has been tastefully renovated to house this centre which started as extensive pick-your-own fields. It has been consistently improving since opening and now offers excellent facilities for such a small site. As yet the range of gardening equipment and tools is not comprehensive but there is a selection of furniture, greenhouses, paving and sheds already available. Plans are afoot for further development and expansion. A reasonable choice of shrubs and a particularly good selection of conifers and alpines are in stock, as well as a general collection of other plants. The quality is good throughout. Individual labelling is accurate and much of it is nicely illustrated, but a definite improvement would be the addition of some larger signs to help locate and provide details about the various plant groups. The layout is otherwise very good with wide, paved paths helping those in wheelchairs or with prams or pushchairs. The staff give an excellent service and are all very friendly and informative, particularly the manager. There are some excellent additional services on the site, including a licensed restaurant which serves good lunches, a tea shop with an outside patio, and a farm shop selling local apples and pears, fruit juices and gifts.

Prices ££££
Facilities Parking, 100 cars. Toilets. Restaurant and cafeteria. Toilets. Play area. Garden advice service. Delivery service. Free plant price list
Open Tues to Sun 10am to 5.30pm

Garden centres and nurseries are changing fast. Practically all those we've included in the Guide were planning improvements for 1985, so we need as much feedback as possible about the ones you visit to keep us up to date. Please use the report forms at the end of the book.

STOURBRIDGE W.Midlands   map 3

Hurrans Roseacre Garden Centre

Kidderminster Road South,   *Tel* Kidderminster (0562) 700511
West Hagley, near Stourbridge DY9 0JB
On the A456 Kidderminster to Birmingham road, 4 miles south-east of Stourbridge,
just south of Hagley

A delightful place run by people who 'love gardens, gardeners and
gardening', says our inspector. Wide slabbed paths interspersed with fine
chippings and clear signposting provide an excellent layout for the
attractive displays of all sorts of plants. They are very well cared for and in
first-class condition, but they are quite expensive. Labels are distinctly
written and the large plaques for plants groups include information on
height, flowering period etc. A large covered area houses an ample range of
all kinds of tools and sundries with the exception of power tools and two
special features are worth noting: there is a permanent swimming pool
display with personnel on hand to talk to customers about installation and
maintenance, and the West Hagley Falcon Centre is on the site with a large
number of hunting birds such as hawks and falcons which are flown
regularly – a beautiful sight. Many of the sundries operate under franchise.
The staff are numerous and are easily spotted by their smart uniforms.
They are a knowledgeable group and are more than happy to assist. A
cafeteria is in the process of being built, and there are vending machines
and an excellent range of home-made cakes and biscuits.

Prices £££££
Facilities Parking, 300 cars. Toilets. Vending machines and confectionery. Garden
advice service. Delivery service. Free price lists for furniture, bulbs, roses etc
Open Mon, Tues, Wed, Sat and Sun 9am to 6pm, Thurs 9am to 8pm, Fri 9.30am to
8pm (closes 5pm every day in winter). Closed 25, 26 and 27 Dec
Credit cards Access, Visa

STOWMARKET Suffolk   map 4

Narey's Garden Centre

Spikes Lane, Stowmarket IP14 3QD   *Tel* Stowmarket (0449) 612559
1 mile north-west of Stowmarket on the A45 – look for the Spikes Lane sign

In an area with a shortage of established centres, Narey's gives a good
service and has become well known locally. It is quite small, but there is
room for several large greenhouses and an extensive garden shop, and
much of the site is under cover. Sections are very clearly indicated, and the
wide concrete paths make it easy for those with wheelchairs, pushchairs or
trolleys. A covered area boasts a good display of mowers and garden
furniture, but the stocks do not end there. The selection of tools, books and
gifts is very good and all other common gardening requirements can be
found, with the exception of water-gardening materials and fish. There is
even a display of above-ground swimming pools. The plant section is not
quite so complete and plants are rather expensive. Even so, there was a
reasonable choice on offer when we carried out our inspection, including a

211

good selection of houseplants and a nice collection of trees, and the quality was above average. Labelling is clearly readable and most labels are illustrated. One or other of the two partners should always be available to give advice. The play area with its climbing frames will help to keep the children out of mischief if the rest of the centre begins to pall.

Prices £££££
Facilities Parking, 100 cars. Toilets. Play area. Garden advice service. Delivery service. Free price list. Catalogues, sundries 50p, plants 95p
Open Every day 8.30am to 5.30pm (closes 5pm in winter)

STRATTON ST. MARGARET Wiltshire map 4
Kennedys Garden Centre ✿ ✎

Hyde Road, Stratton *Tel* Swindon (0793) 822224/825126
St. Margaret, Swindon SN2 6SB
North-east of Swindon on the A419

Kennedys can fulfil most of the needs of the enthusiastic amateur gardener. Whether your interest is houseplants, greenhouses, or just general garden plants, there is likely to be something here for you. The range of outdoor plants is very good, although somewhat seasonal, while for indoors the choice is very good indeed and the quality excellent. The tools and sundries section encompasses all smaller accessories as well as the main construction materials needed round the garden. The selection of posts, stakes and greenhouses is particularly good. Power tools and lawnmowers are sold by a separate company housed in its own building on site. The layout of the centre is orderly with plants set out alphabetically in blocks. There is plenty of room to walk around and the plant groups are easily recognised by the large, illustrated colour labels. Individual plants also have labels but these have sometimes faded from the sun and rain. Inside, the displays are attractively arranged in a light, airy building. There is an adequate number of staff working in the grounds and the shop, but be warned that things can get a little hectic on weekends. The shop is to be extended shortly and a cafeteria constructed.

Prices ££££
Facilities Parking, 150 cars. Play area. Delivery service. Free price list for hardy plants
Open Mon to Fri 8.30am to 6pm, Sat 9am to 6pm, Sun 10am to 6pm (closes ½ hour earlier every day in winter). Closed 25 to 27 Dec
Credit cards Access, Visa

STUDLEY Wiltshire map 3
Blounts Court Garden Centre

Studley, near Calne SN11 9NH *Tel* Calne (0249) 812103
Just off the A4, about 2½ miles west of Calne

If garden ornaments or furniture are on your shopping list, then this is a centre to visit since it probably has the best displays in the area. In addition there are greenhouses, building materials, barbecues and a select range of power and hand tools – in fact almost anything the day-to-day garden jobs might call for. Most of the outside area is devoted to a display of plants which, although not terribly well laid out, is nevertheless interesting. There is quite a reasonable selection of good-quality but quite expensive plants and there are plans to extend the growing areas and to begin raising perennials, annuals, flowers and conifers. Houseplants are available and are exhibited in walk-in greenhouses. Paths are narrow and are surfaced with grass or shale, but there are no proper walkways between trees and this area is liable to get muddy if it's been raining or they have been watering, so you may need your wellingtons. Printed labels on individual plants are clearly priced, while labels marking groups of plants are often illustrated and contain useful advice. Most labels are easily read. The staff are very helpful – willing to give advice but not at all pushy. A garden contract service is offered by the centre.

Prices £££££
Facilities Parking, 35 cars. Toilets. Ice cream and confectionery. Play area. Garden advice service. Delivery service. Plant catalogues 20p to 25p or free. Free sundries catalogue
Open Every day 9am to 5.30pm. Closed several days at Christmas and New Year's Day
Credit cards Access, Visa

STUDLEY Warwickshire   map 4
Peets Garden Centre

Alcester Road, Mappleborough   *Tel* Studley (052 785) 2631
Green, near Studley B80 7DL
On the A435, 3 miles from Redditch and ½ mile in the Birmingham direction from the Redditch–Henley crossroads (Dog Inn)

This medium-sized centre can't perhaps offer very much to the specialist gardener, but if your requirements are modest it is worth a visit. Stocks reflect the season. However, there is usually a reasonable collection of trees, roses and conifers, though they are rather expensive, and these are well maintained and in good condition. Many of the trees and shrubs are grown by the centre. Plant labels are quite good, but the outdoor layout could be a little better, although the trees and shrubs are clearly arranged. Indoors the layout is much better and the stocks consist mainly of the less bulky garden accessories – this includes hand tools, chemicals and composts for garden care, while for decoration and leisure there is fencing (large amounts can be ordered), furniture and assorted ornaments. Greenhouses are also stocked. The staff is small but nothing is too much trouble for them. The centre also undertakes landscaping projects and offers a garden design service.

Prices £££££
Facilities Parking, 70 cars. Toilets. Vending machine. Play area. Garden advice service
Open Mon to Sat 9am to 6pm, Sun 10am to 6pm (closes 5pm every day in winter). Closed Christmas and Boxing Day
Credit cards Access, Visa

SUDBURY Suffolk   map 4

Cramphorns Garden Centre

Newton Road, Chilton, Sudbury   *Tel* Sudbury (0787) 73628
CO10 0PZ

2 miles east of Sudbury on the A134 Sudbury to Colchester road

Part of the Cramphorn's chain, this centre is surrounded by lawns and
large nursery areas. The layout is very good. Plant groups are clearly
identified and all sections are signposted. Pathways are wide enough to
take trolleys, wheelchairs or prams. Labelling is good and is kept in
reasonable order. Some interesting set pieces liven up the display areas –
when our inspector visited there were collections of conifers and shrubs
showing autumn colouring and giving helpful ideas for the use of these in
garden design. Plants are of good quality and many are grown nearby: on
the whole you should have little problem finding something suitable. The
staff obviously keep an eye out for sub-standard plants since these are sent
down to the 'bargain' area. There are a lot of staff and the senior members
are very knowledgeable and deal pleasantly with all customers. The
sundries are displayed in the large indoor shop where the selection is very
wide indeed. There are no basics omitted from the range offered, and of
particular note are the seeds and bulbs. There is also a pets section where
the snakes and lizards, birds and fish should intrigue the younger members
of your party.

Prices ££££
Facilities Parking, 40 cars. Toilets. Garden advice service. Delivery service. Free
catalogues and price lists
Open Every day 8.30am to 6pm (closes 5pm in winter). Closed Christmas and
Boxing Day
Credit cards Access, Diners Club, Visa

SUNDERLAND Tyne and Wear   map 2

Clay's Garden Centre

Silksworth Lane, Sunderland   *Tel* Sunderland (0783) 220911
SR3 1PD

About 1 mile from the town centre. Take the A690 and follow signs to Silksworth

This garden centre stocks a good range of shrubs, as well as most common
trees and other hardy plants. Quality is generally good, both for outdoor
plants and houseplants. The layout is excellent, with plenty of room for
wheelchairs and pushchairs. Sections are clearly divided and signposted
and plants are organised alphabetically. More group labelling with some
details on habit and requirements of plants would be helpful, and the
printing is often unclear on the tie-on labels. However, the nursery tell us
they are preparing clearly printed, waterproof labels which should improve
the situation. They are also increasing their information facilities. There's
an average selection of tools and sundries with a good choice among the
chemicals and composts. The larger items, such as sheds, greenhouses,
fencing and paving are also available. This centre has recently been

extended and improved and the standards have been rising. A fish department completed in summer 1984 offers an interesting collection of accessories and tropical fish and a new cafe has been opened. Further plans include expanding the covered sales area and improving the car parking. The centre holds promotional events and there's an area selling fresh fruit and vegetables.

Prices £££
Facilities Parking, 100 cars (plus 100 overflow). Toilets. Cafeteria. Vending machines. Play area. Garden advice service. Delivery service. Free price lists for paving, walling and water gardening equipment
Open Every day 9am to 6pm (closes 5.30pm in winter). Closed Christmas, Boxing and New Year's Day
Credit cards Access, Visa

SWALLOWNEST S. Yorkshire — map 2

Swallownest Nurseries

P.W. and H.E. Bradley, *Tel* Sheffield (0742) 872240
Swallownest, Sheffield S31 0TT
On the main A57 Sheffield to Worksop road, at the junction with the A618, 1 mile from junction 31 of the M1 towards Sheffield

This nursery has grown up bit by bit as an extension of a wholesale nursery. This shows in its 'excessively informal' layout, and it has reached the size where some concerted re-organisation is needed, as well as some form of signposting and rather wider paths. It is a place for gardeners who know what they want rather than the browser. However, the indoor area has recently been improved and is now well arranged and some of the older sales beds are to be redesigned. There are several large greenhouses comprising the sales area of this nursery, and most of them are devoted to outdoor plants. The range is wide and includes a good selection of varieties suitable for growing locally. Many of the plants stocked are grown by the nursery. Trees and shrubs are container grown. All plants appear to be extemely well cared for, and the few older or neglected pots are put up for sale at bargain prices. The labelling is variable, that on older stock looking faded and weatherbeaten while newer plants carry typewritten tags with useful details about planting. This is essentially a nursery, and the garden sundries sold are restricted to composts, chemicals and hand tools. It has received many awards at local shows and the owners are very well versed about what plants will do well in the area.

Prices £££
Facilities Parking, 40 cars. Toilets. Garden advice service. Delivery service. Free plant list and catalogue
Open Every day 8am to 6pm (closes 5pm in winter). Closed Christmas Day
Credit cards Access, Visa

 Establishments awarded with a flower symbol sell either a very good range of high-quality plants, or a more limited but particularly interesting selection.

SWINDON Wiltshire map 4

Carrefour Garden Centre

Tewkesbury Way, Westlea Down,   *Tel* Swindon (0793) 872781
Swindon SN5 7DL
3 miles west of Swindon, 1 mile from junction 16 of the M4

This centre caters for quick, effective shopping rather than browsing. The layout is very good, and though the centre is small it stocks an extensive range of most gardening equipment. There's also a good DIY section. The centre is adjacent to a shopping precinct, so you can stock up for the garden at the same time as doing your ordinary shopping. At the time of our inspection, the condition of the plants was reasonable, though the alpine and herb beds were rather crowded. The selection of container-grown roses is good. Plant groups are adequately labelled but a lot of the labelling had faded at the time of inspection. There is no refreshment facility in the centre but there is a restaurant in the Carrefour supermarket next door. Staff are always cheerful and happy to help customers. Trolleys are provided for you to take goods to the car.

Prices £££
Facilities Parking, 1,000 cars. Toilets. Play area. Garden advice service. Delivery service
Open Mon to Thurs 9am to 8pm, Fri 9am to 9pm, Sat 9am to 7pm, Sun 10am to 5pm
Credit cards Access, Visa

SYSTON Leicestershire map 4

Fowkes Garden Centre

Foss Way, Syston, Leicester LE7 8NJ   *Tel* Leicester (0533) 693500
At Syston on the B6670, a turning off the A607, 4 miles north of Leicester city centre

The sheer extent of this centre and enormous range of goods stocked would appeal to any gardener. You can spend many happy hours browsing among the spaciously laid out indoor and outdoor areas – or just sitting in the gardens watching the fountains. An extensive range of tools and sundries is sold – virtually everything for the gardener including larger items such as greenhouses and sheds. There is a good range of landscaping materials, and water-gardening equipment is sold from March to August. There are plenty of popular plants to choose from but less in the way of specialist interest. Our inspector thought the tree section was the best in terms of choice and quality. The labelling is generally good with coloured photographs of plants, and extensive group descriptions with hints on plant care. Some labels were old and difficult to read when our inspector visited, but the centre tells us these are being replaced. Staff were not easy to recognise or find but more are being taken on to cover busy periods and in most other respects this is a well-organised centre.

Prices ££££
Facilities Parking, 300 cars. Toilets. Vending machines. Garden advice service.

Delivery service. Free price list and catalogue for plants, landscape materials and water gardening equipment
Open Every day 8am to 6.30pm (closes 5pm in winter)
Credit cards Access, Visa

TANSLEY Derbyshire map 2

Matlock Garden, Waterlife and Pet Centre

Nottingham Road, Tansley,   *Tel* Matlock (0629) 4699/4221
Matlock DE4 5FR
On the A615, 2–3 miles east of Matlock and 8 miles from the M1 exit 28

The main attractions at this garden centre are the indoor aquarium and all the water-gardening paraphernalia – fish breeding tanks, fountains, ponds and water lilies. A fair range of tools and sundries is sold. The centre concentrates on smaller items like books, seeds, hand tools, bulbs and houseplants, but fencing and garden furniture are also available. The houseplants are excellent and the centre prides itself on its collection of bonsai trees and accessories. There is also a wide range of trees, shrubs and other plants, and quality is very good across the board. Orientation is easy here with wide paths, clear signposting and adequate labelling (at the time of our inspection some individual labels were faded, but the centre tells us this has been rectified). Staff are easy to find and very willing and knowledgeable. Our inspector gives them high marks and told us that through all seasons this 'is the best centre that I have visited'. A coffee shop combined with a plant house is planned for 1985.

Prices £££
Facilities Parking, 120 cars. Toilets. Vending machines. Play area. Garden advice service. Delivery service
Open Every day 10am to 1pm, 2pm to 6pm (closes 5pm in winter). Closed 25 Dec to 1 Jan
Credit cards Access, Visa

James Smith (Scotland Nurseries)

Tansley, Matlock DE4 5EF   *Tel* Matlock (0629) 3036/7
On the B6014 Clay Cross road, 2 miles east of Matlock

A very large acreage is turned over to this nursery, and our inspector found it difficult to cover a quarter of the stock available. The number of specimens of each plant variety stocked is quite extensive, but do not expect to come here for water plants and houseplants or a wide choice of herbaceous perennials. The nursery grows its own plants, concentrating on trees, shrubs and conifers, as well as a collection of heathers and rhododendrons. The range and quality of these are excellent and they are cheap. Locating a particular plant can be difficult because of the size of the site and because a lot of the labelling is rather faint. However, the staff are excellent and very friendly. There is a catalogue available and if you require some very detailed advice then you are welcome to make an appointment. The nursery will supply planting plans free of charge with suggestions as to what might be suitable for a particular customer and they will also carry out planting within a reasonable distance. Certainly a nursery worth investigating if you are a real purist and can do without the trimmings of the garden centre – the only sundries available are tree guards, stakes and ties and peat.

Prices ££
Facilities Parking, 85 cars. Toilets. Garden advice service. Price list and catalogue. Plants sold by mail order
Open Mon to Fri 8am to 5pm, Sat 8am to 12pm (container department open to 5pm Sat), Sun 10am to 5pm. Closed a few days over Christmas

---

TARLETON Lancashire map 2
Dunscar Nurseries & Garden Centre

Southport New Road, *Tel* Hesketh Bank (077 473) 2684
Tarleton, near Preston PR4 6HY
Approximately midway between Preston and Southport on the A565

Attractive display beds throughout the exterior area demonstrate some excellent-quality plants to good effect. This centre has moved from being a small nursery to a modern garden centre without losing any of the traditional values and virtues of a nursery. The few staff are very hard-working and full of advice and they maintain the centre beautifully giving the public excellent-quality, home-grown plants at very reasonable prices. There's a wide selection of plants, with a marvellous number of common shrubs to choose from. A somewhat cluttered indoor area deals with a large range of supplies in a relatively restricted space – it succeeds in providing most small tools and sundries including a good range of furniture and tubs, and composts and chemicals in many shapes and forms. The centre misses out on lawnmowers, power tools, hard landscaping materials and greenhouses. The outside section of the site is well signposted and the paths are of a good size; meanwhile the centre is still expanding and improving and a play area should soon be available. The staff appear dedicated to the business and to enjoy their work thoroughly.

Prices ££
Facilities Parking, 75 cars. Toilets. Garden advice service. Delivery service
Open Every day 9am to 5.30pm (closed 12 noon to 1pm Mon to Fri). Closes at dusk in winter
Credit card Access

TAVERHAM Norfolk map 4
Taverham Nursery Centre

Fir Covert Road, Taverham, *Tel* Norwich (0603) 860522
Norwich NR8 6NN
Take the A1067 through Taverham past the Silver Fox pub. Fir Covert Road is the next turning on the right and the nursery is about ¼ mile along on the left

This is a nursery which is gradually expanding into a garden centre. A reasonable range of gardening equipment is already available, including paving, fencing, books, composts, garden ornaments and furniture, as well as ponds and waterfalls. There are plans to double the size of the shop area to accommodate the expanding stocks. Fertilisers are handily weighed out in any amount you require. Greenhouses, sheds and other large items are also sold. Most of the plants are stored inside, and each plant house is well labelled. Trees and hardy shrubs are kept in outdoor beds, but the wide selection of heathers and conifers, numerous houseplants and fuchsias, excellent-quality spring bedding and healthy clematis are all found under cover. Many of the plants are grown on site and at the time of our visit the nursery beds were full of a healthy young stock of heathers. Good, informative labelling is carried by most plants, but group labels are few and far between. Essentially a place to buy quality plants at very low prices and run by a staff always willing to advise and answer questions, or carry goods. A cafeteria and lecture room are in the pipeline.

Prices £
Facilities Parking, 600 cars. Cafeteria (open from spring 1985). Garden advice service. Delivery service. Free price list for some products
Open Every day, 8.30am to 5.30pm in summer, 9am to 5pm in winter

---

TENBURY WELLS Hereford and Worcester map 3

Treasures of Tenbury ✿

Burford House Gardens, *Tel* Tenbury Wells (0584) 810777
Tenbury Wells WR15 8HQ
Just off the A456 Kidderminster to Ludlow road, ½ mile west of Tenbury Wells by Burford Church

This large nursery, famous for its clematis, borders on Burford House gardens which are open to the public from 1 April to 28 October (you can visit at other times but by appointment only). It's a pleasure to wander around this beautiful estate near the banks of the River Teme, and see flowers and plants growing which you can then buy at the nursery. This really is a place for an outing as there is also a museum to browse around and a coffee house set out in a large glasshouse. The general air of Treasures is one of quiet elegance and warm welcome. Most of the plants sold are grown on site and the clematis are their pride and joy. They sell a large number of varieties and also house the National Clematis Collection. There is also a good range of trees, shrubs and other plants for the average taste, as well as a more select group such as some of the more unusual bedding plants and an extensive range of herbaceous plants. The layout is good throughout and tidily organised. Plants are in alphabetical order and there are large labels, clearly marked for each group. The selection of sundries is not comprehensive and doesn't include large items such as sheds and greenhouses, but there is a small, separately owned area under cover stocking hand and power tools; this also has a workshop and tool repairs department. The people in charge are knowledgeable, but not intimidating, and for keen gardeners this really is a treasure house.

Prices ££££
Facilities Parking, 75 cars (plus overflow). Cafeteria (open Apr to Oct). Garden advice

service. Clematis sold by mail order. Plant price list 65p. Clematis booklet £1.25 including p&p
Open Mon to Sat 9am to 5pm, Sun 2pm to 5pm (closes at dusk in winter)
Credit cards Access, Visa

TEWKESBURY Gloucestershire   map 3

Mythe Nurseries

Tewkesbury GL20 6EB   *Tel* Tewkesbury (0684) 293103
On the A38 road to Worcester, about ½ mile from Tewkesbury

This medium-sized site is well laid out and offers a reasonable service to those in the area. There is a large display area set aside for greenhouses and conservatories and some very attractive stone ornaments. There are two adjoining greenhouses which stock seeds, composts and a small range of hand tools, as well as a separate houseplant display. The goods are all well marked with prices and if the size you want is not on show, labels indicate the various options available. Outside there are tanks containing fish and plants for stocking a water-garden. If your interest lies with garden plants and not the hardware, the selection stocked offers a standard range of common varieties, but with nothing to interest the specialist. The choice is fairly small but the condition of plants on the whole is quite good. A particularly good range of well-tended heathers and herbs was noted by our inspector, and the choice of healthy herbaceous perennials was also reasonable. In terms of plant labelling this centre rated well. Each group label has detailed descriptions and plants themselves are all well identified. At the rear of the display area some faded tags were noticed in addition to a few scrappy shrubs – an area which looked a little forgotten. The staff are very pleasant, the site clean and tidy and there is a general sense of goodwill about the place. However, an increase in the range and variety of stock would be welcome and the centre tells us that plans are underway to bring this about. Ice creams and soft drinks are available.

Prices ££££
Facilities Parking, 60 cars. Toilets. Confectionery and cold drinks. Garden advice service. Delivery service
Open Mon to Sat 9am to 6pm, Sun 10am to 5.30pm (closes ½ hour earlier every day in winter). Closed Christmas and Boxing Day
Credit cards Access, Visa

THETFORD Norfolk   map 4

Thetford Garden and Leisure Centre

Lime Kiln Lane, Thetford IP24 2BU   *Tel* Thetford (0842) 63267
On the south side of the A11 in Thetford, just past the police station if heading towards Norwich

This centre is strategically placed to serve a large area of rural Norfolk. The layout is exceptional with plants tidily arranged within well-signposted areas and the spacious shops pleasantly set out with their plentiful stock. There is about an acre devoted to containerised plants, garden buildings and the like. Displays are carefully and attractively laid out including an array of flowers which provides seasonal colour. The quality of plants is uniformly excellent and the staff obviously take great care in tending them and maintaining their healthy condition. You should find most common varieties available – although there is a marked bias towards heathers, alpines and conifers, due to the centre's proximity to Blooms of Bressingham. Plant labelling is well above average, providing customers with plenty of information about the plants on display. They are easy to read and prices are clearly marked. The two shops stock a full range of the smaller sundries, and for those keen on water-gardening the extensive area for pool equipment and aquatic plants is worth investigating. The larger garden items such as greenhouses, sheds, fencing and paving are also sold. Recommended for its attractive layout, helpful staff and high-quality plants.

Prices £££
Facilities Ample parking. Toilets. Vending machines. Garden advice service. Delivery service
Open Every day 9am to 7pm (closes 5.30pm in winter)
Credit cards Access, Visa

THREE LEGGED CROSS Dorset   map 4

Three Legged Cross Garden Centre

Ringwood Road, Three Legged Cross,   *Tel* Verwood (0202) 822203
near Wimborne BH21 6RD
North of West Moors on the Horton road, 4 miles from Ringwood

A well-equipped centre in open countryside among a scattering of bungalows and farms. Large areas are devoted to sheds, greenhouses and summerhouses, garden furniture, water-gardening equipment and tools; and a covered area is well stocked with indoor and outdoor sundries, including plenty of fancy pots. There's a large display of tents and camping accessories in season. The centre is well laid out with fairly wide paths. There is little emphasis on specialised plants, but a wide choice for the average gardener. All the trees and plants our inspector saw looked in good shape. Labelling was reasonable though lacking plant-care instructions; staff were co-operative.

Prices £££
Facilities Parking, 100 cars. Toilets. Vending machines. Play area. Garden advice service. Delivery service
Open Mon to Sat 9am to 5pm, Sun 10am to 5pm
Credit cards Access, Visa

TOPSHAM Devon   map 3

Yeomen Gardeners

Highfield, Newcourt Road,   *Tel* Topsham (039 287) 3339
Topsham, Exeter EX3 0BU

Just north of the A377 Exeter to Exmouth road, turn left on entering Topsham from Exeter

This pleasant, rather small centre propagates much of its own stock in an adjoining nursery area and these plants are all carefully tended up to the point of sale. The proprietors are skilled horticulturalists with years of practical experience as well as being cheerful and willing to put themselves out to help customers. Besides providing a good, all-round stock of healthy plants, they offer a considerable landscaping business which will cater for all gardens within about a 25-mile radius. In terms of tools and sundries, this centre stocks a lot of the main types of gardening equipment but some of the larger items are not available, such as greenhouses, lawnmowers and other power tools. The well-laid-out and sensibly organised site displays everthing to advantage, while the wide paths and clear signposting aid access. Our inspector felt that the labelling would have benefitted by having additional cultural information – we are told this is to be improved – and a more boldly marked name and price.

Prices £££
Facilities Parking, 30 cars. Toilets. Vending machine. Play area. Garden advice service. Delivery service. Free plant price list and catalogue
Open Mon to Sat 8.30am to 5pm, Sun 10am to 4pm. Closed Christmas week

---

TROWBRIDGE Wiltshire   map 3
Fred Daw Garden Centre

288 Frome Road, Upper Studley,   *Tel* Trowbridge (022 14) 63927
Trowbridge BA14 0DT
On the A361 Frome road, ½ mile from Trowbridge town centre, opposite the Black Horse pub

Set in a pleasant area on the outskirts of town, this centre provides good-quality plants and a good range of gardening sundries. Conifers, shrubs and herbs offer the best choice to the customer and there is a small selection of ornamental trees. A water garden nursery is located within the site although its opening hours are slightly different from the main area. Plants are kept in very good condition. Smaller plants and herbs are placed in protective tunnels, and the alpine and heathers section is being developed. The labelling for plant groups is informative with useful illustrations: individual plants are marked with their name and price. The centre is laid out to give a great feeling of space, and care has been taken in signposting the different areas and in setting up displays. The only area our inspector felt was not up to scratch was the houseplant and book section which was rather cramped. Lots of different brands of seeds are stocked, and most items of gardening equipment are sold. The company next door stocks items such as paving, ornaments and sheds. Staff are helpful and show interest in customers' problems, but they are not always easy to find.

Prices ££££
Facilities Parking, 100 cars. Toilets. Vending machines. Play area. Garden advice service. Delivery service
Open Mon to Sat 9am to 5.30pm, Sun 10am to 5pm
Credit cards Access, Visa

TROWELL Nottinghamshire   map 2
Trowell Garden Centre

Stapleford Road, Trowell NG9 3QE   *Tel* Nottingham (0602) 326920
*On the Stapleford to Ilkeston road, about ½ a mile off the A52 Nottingham to
Derby road*

This is a sizeable and well-run centre which is divided into a large, covered
area containing sundries, seeds, composts and the like, and a hardy plants
section where shrubs are arranged alphabetically and each item is easy to
locate. The hardware department offers a good range of hand tools, and
fencing and paving are also stocked as well as a selection of plastic pools.
However, due to the competition from the large stores the centre has
decided not to stock greenhouses, sheds or lawnmowers any more. There
is a wide range of inexpensive plants, including houseplants, and an
impressive collection of dwarf conifers and shrubs plus a good selection of
heathers which are found with the alpines in a little plot of their own. Our
inspector thought the heathers and hebes were in admirable condition – in
fact with few exceptions quality was good all round. Labelling is above
average, with large, descriptive group labels posted above the plants, and
plainly marked individual tags with easy-to-read prices. If you need a break
in the middle of your shopping, there is an attractive coffee lounge serving
lunches from 12 noon to 2pm. It is cheerful and brightly lit and the staff are
most pleasant. Staff throughout the centre are friendly and helpful.

Prices ££
Facilities Parking, 150 cars. Toilets. Restaurant. Garden advice service.
Delivery service
Open Every day 9am to 5pm (opens 9.30am in winter). Closed Christmas and
Boxing Day

TRURO Cornwall   map 3
Chacewater Garden Centre   ⚞

Chacewater, Truro TR4 8QD   *Tel* Truro (0872) 560533
4 miles from Truro on the old Truro to Redruth road

Our inspector wrote, 'The indoor area is excellent and so well stocked that a
visit is a must'. Indeed, this does seem to be the case – all the major types of
gardening equipment and sundries are to be found, and the centre even
sells swimming pools! About three-quarters of the site is under cover and
all the goods housed within this spacious area are well arranged. There are
some large vines growing inside which present an unusual and interesting
foil to the tools and hardware. In contrast, the small outside area and the
range of plants stocked are disappointing: the grounds are poorly
maintained and disorganised and detract from an otherwise favourable
impression, while the choice of plants is limited and bitty in all sections.
However, what's there is of a good standard. Houseplants offer the widest
selection. There are plans to extend the shrub area. Plants are identified by
illustrated group labels – most individual labels and prices are either faded
or entirely absent. The staff are easily spotted and will willingly answer

your questions. The facilities could do with improvement; in fact the centre tells us that a cafe and new play area are planned.

Prices ££££
Facilities Parking, 100 cars. Toilets. Play area
Open Every day 9am to 7pm (closes 5pm in winter)
Credit cards Access, Visa

Carnon Downs Pet and Garden Centre

Quenchwell Road,   *Tel* Truro (0872) 863058
Carnon Downs, Truro TR3 4LN
Just off the A39, between Truro and Falmouth, 2½ miles from Truro

As its name implies, this centre has a special pets and aquatics section, but perhaps its most impressive feature is the range of hardware stocked. You will find all the gardening sundries and accessories you could dream of amidst the excellent selection of merchandise on offer and everything is well displayed and sensibly arranged in a brand-new glasshouse. At the time of our inspection, the rest of the centre, sadly, did not maintain this standard. Though cheap, the choice and quality of plants was only average and the exterior layout was somewhat haphazard. The site seemed to have developed in a disjointed way. Signposting was also in need of some improvement, while the labelling was 'higgledy-piggledy', so it could be quite difficult to find a particular plant. The exception to this was the small area devoted to annuals and bedding – the illustrated and detailed tags used here gave much more help to the uncertain or beginner gardeners. There was also room for improvement in the service offered by staff, but in spite of the criticisms, this centre is worth a visit, particularly if you are looking for gardening equipment. The centre tells us that our inspection was carried out at a time when extensive changes were under way and that many of the problems we found are now being dealt with along with further development of the site.

Prices ££
Facilities Parking, 600 cars. Toilets. Vending machines. Play area. Garden advice service. Delivery service. Free price list
Open Mon to Sat 9am to 5pm, Sun 10am to 5pm. Closed Christmas and Boxing Day
Credit cards Access, Visa

TWYFORD Berkshire   map 4
Kennedy's Garden Centre

Floral Mile, Twyford, near Reading   *Tel* Wargrave (073 522) 3933
RG10 9SW
On the A4 between Maidenhead and Reading, opposite the A3032 turning to Twyford

A large centre in a spacious rural setting, well back from the busy A4. The layout is well organised with a very extensive plant area, a building containing garden sundries and another large area devoted to items such as sheds, paving, garden furniture and greenhouses. There is a wide range of rock-garden pools in many sizes and finishes, with a watering can on hand to do your own testing! The range and quality of plants is usually good. Labels could do with some improvement, though the main plant areas are well signposted, and within each section there are often useful guides to growing requirements. Staff vary from being courteous and helpful to being rather offhand, so look out for a cheery face when seeking assistance. The younger children will certainly enjoy a visit to Kennedy's as there is a very good play area with shallow ponds and decoy ducks to play with. The centre also has displays of swimming pools and camping equipment and there is a farm shop.

Prices ££££
Facilities Parking, 650 cars. Toilets. Play area. Delivery service. Free price list for hardy plants
Open Mon to Fri 8.30am to 6.30pm, Sat and Sun 8.30am to 6pm (closes 5.30pm every day in winter). Closed 25 to 27 Dec
Credit cards Access, Visa

UPMINSTER Essex   map 4

Roots & Shoots Nursery and Garden Centre

Nags Head Lane, Upminster   *Tel* Ingrebourne (04023) 42469
Common, Upminster RM14 1TS
Next to Upminster Common, 2 miles south-west of Brentwood

This centre should be able to supply everything the suburban gardener needs, though it has some interesting extras such as large specimen plants for display. It can be something of a challenge to track down what you are looking for, but it is likely to turn up after some detective work. The rather 'bitty', badly signposted layout is probably attributable to a lack of planning as this centre has developed from some existing glasshouses and gardens. However, the pathways are quite wide, some made of gravel and others of rough concrete. The selection of tools and sundries is adequate and reasonably well organised, and although you will not find any garden machinery or buildings there is a good selection of ornaments and a choice of furniture. Hand tools, water garden equipment and composts are also stocked. The plant area contains a good selection of healthy, well-watered specimens – the conifers were particularly fresh and stout when we inspected the centre. Individual labelling usually consists of handwritten tags and there are some quite satisfactory group notice boards. However, more signposting would save a lot of time and frustration. The staff make up for many of the deficiencies of layout by keeping an eye out and asking customers if they need help when they spot a confused face. Four-wheeled wagons are provided to transport purchases to the car, and staff will also help out if needed. There are plans to improve the facilities at this centre to include a new garden shop, play area, toilets and vending machine.

Prices £££
Facilities Parking, 100 cars. Toilets. Garden advice service. Delivery service. Free price list for shrubs and fruit trees. Sundries catalogue 45p
Open Every day 9am to 6pm (closes 5pm in winter)

225

WALSDEN W.Yorkshire map 2
Gordon Rigg Nurseries ❀ ✄

Calder Bank Nurseries and *Tel* Todmorden (070 681) 3374
Garden Centre, Walsden,
Todmorden OL14 7TJ
About 2 miles from Todmorden on the A6033 to Rochdale, in Walsden

'We enjoyed the exploration – rather like Aladdin's cave', wrote one of our inspectors. Paths tend to be on the narrow side and indoor areas are apt to be crowded and disorganised; however, new racking was to be installed in 1985 which should help relieve the problem. The houseplant area, on the other hand, is kept neat and tidy. Despite its shortcomings the centre gives value for money, with a good range of plants at cheap prices, including exceptional houseplants and heathers. Generally plants are of good quality. Group labels are quite clear with illustrations and cultural information, but individual labels are more erratic. The selection of hand tools covers a wide price bracket and there is a very good range of garden and patio furniture, ornaments and mowers (ranging from hand mowers to ride-ons). The centre also sells a wide range of composts and fertilisers, some of their own manufacture, and most larger garden sundries such as greenhouses, sheds, fencing and paving. On the day one of our inspectors visited, a demonstration of the barbecue equipment was taking place. The check-out is reasonably efficient and you shouldn't have to wait long even when the centre is quite busy. It is well attended and particularly convenient for local people without cars.

Prices ££
Facilities Parking, 250 cars. Toilets. Vending machines. Children's rides. Garden advice service. Delivery service or loan of van
Open Mon to Fri 9am to 9pm, Sat 9am to 6pm, Sun 10am to 6pm (closes 5.30pm Sat and Sun in winter). Closed Christmas and Boxing Day

---

WARESLEY Cambridgeshire map 4
Waresley Park Garden Centre and Nursery

Waresley, near Sandy SG19 3BS *Tel* Gamlingay (0767) 50249
Just outside Waresley village on B1040 St Ives to Biggleswade road, 2 miles from Gamlingay

Our inspector was impressed by this centre because not only is it clean, tidy and well arranged, but 'every nook and cranny is of interest'. It has a character of its own and an ambiance which makes it a pleasure to wander around and browse at one's leisure. The unhurried atmosphere seems to be conducive to providing very healthy plants, many of which are grown on site. These include pelargoniums and fuchsias which present a superb array of colour and foliage in the spring. The range of plants is quite comprehensive and any omissions are usually due to end-of-season shortages. Dwarf conifers are the speciality of the centre, but the choice of clematis is also outstanding and the houseplant section has a lot of bright and interesting varieties for sale. The staff obviously care about gardening and their concern is reflected in the general condition of the centre. Everywhere is kept clean and weeded, sections are distinctly signposted, walkways are orderly and well surfaced, trees and shrubs are laid out alphabetically and labelling is very good. There are screened areas outside which provide cover for alpines and other plants which do better with some protection. The sundries section stocks most common items and has a good selection of furniture for its size, as well as an attractive display of greenhouses. Advice comes informally from some of the older staff members, and any plants not stocked will be ordered on request. A nice new coffee lounge serving home-made cakes and teas is a pleasing addition to an already satisfactory centre. A garden design and planning advice service were planned for 1985.

Prices £££
Facilities: Parking, 100 cars (plus 200 overflow). Toilets. Coffee shop. Play area. Garden advice service. Delivery service. General price guides. Catalogues due for publication 1985
Open Every day 9am to 6pm. Closed 25, 26 and 27 Dec
Credit cards Access, Visa

WARLINGHAM Surrey   map 5

Telkamps Garden Centre   🖉

Limpsfield Road,   *Tel* Upper Warlingham (088 32) 2404/5
Chelsham, Warlingham CR3 9YT
On the B269 south-east of Warlingham

This centre has grown up over the last 15 years from very modest beginnings to a thriving and busy place. It offers a wide range of good-quality stock, well laid out in alphabetical order. The outside section is quite spacious and includes three small gardens landscaped to demonstrate possible plant arrangements, and a protective tunnel for tender species. Bays are well marked with useful information such as the ultimate height of the plants and the best site for successful growth. Individual plant tags are rather patchy but the good outnumber the bad. Shrubs are mostly grown on site and offer the best selection, but there's also a reasonable range of other plants including roses, trees, fruits and conifers. Plants are generally in good health and shrubs and trees are particularly good. Garden sundries are in plentiful supply and you will find all types of hardware except for lawnmowers and power tools. There's also a good range of gardening books. Separate, outside plots contain greenhouses, fencing, garden ponds and swimming pools. Staff are very good. They cope well on busy weekends, deal courteously with telephone enquiries and help to carry goods if requested. Information is also provided by topical notices which explain such things as types of sprays to use for particular pests and diseases. A large, gravelled car park provides plenty of parking space.

Prices ££££
Facilities Parking, 100 cars. Toilets. Play area. Garden advice service. Delivery service. Free plant catalogue

Open Every day 9am to 5pm (opens 10am Sun). Closed Christmas
Credit cards Access, Visa

WARRINGTON Cheshire map 2
Cantilever Garden Centre

Station Road, Latchford,   *Tel* Warrington (0925) 35799
Warrington WA4 2AB
On the south side of Warrington, off the A50 and above the Manchester ship canal

Customers can have a pleasant time at this centre browsing around the
excellent displays of garden furniture, barbecue equipment and
houseplants, and partaking of a pleasant cup of coffee and some cake at the
Gingham Cafe. It is also a good source of non-specialist plants, offering a
comprehensive range and occasionally stocking some more sizeable shrubs
and conifers. The plants are generally of good quality, but it is worth
steering clear of the older stock which is frequently pot-bound and in poor
condition. The prices tend to be high. If your interests lie with
gardening hardware, then the range on offer in Cantilever's sundries'
department is very reasonable. Most aspects of garden care and
maintenence are catered for. The centre is located on the site of an old
railway station, so although in an urban area, there is satisfactory space.
However, improved signposting and labelling would make tracking down
particular items a lot easier (although the centre tells us that the lack of
signs is a deliberate policy – people didn't read them!). The senior staff are
cheerful and knowledgeable.

Prices ££££££
Facilities Parking, 120 cars. Toilets. Coffee shop. Delivery service
Open Every day 9am to 6pm (closes 5pm in winter). Closed 25 Dec to 2 Jan
Credit cards Access, Visa

WARWICK Warwickshire map 4
Warwick Nurseries ❁

Hinton Brothers, Warwick Nurseries,   *Tel* Warwick (0926) 492273
Guys Cliffe, Warwick CV34 5YL
On the A46 Kenilworth to Warwick road, on the outskirts of Warwick

It is an interesting ride from Kenilworth to this centre and it is easily
spotted right opposite Guy's Cliffe. It started life as a nursery but appears to
have graduated to a garden centre and now sells a reasonable range of tools
and sundries as well as plants. However, there are no power tools. When
our inspector visited no prices were marked (the centre tells us they were
being overhauled), and the sundries section of the centre looked as though
it has been set up as a concession to the customer while the real love was
still with the plants themselves. You can find trees and shrubs in very fine
condition, a wonderful range of conifers, and fruit trees of all sorts in
well-labelled, neat rows. The condition of all the plants reflects constant
attention and trees are securely staked. The walkways are wide and well
maintained and all the plant labels are clearly written, but the layout and

signposting is such that it is impossible to find your way about – you may have to wander around for some considerable time before finding the plant of your choice. It would be a great help to have a plan or map of some sort, and better signposting to tell the customer just where the different groups of plants are located. The members of staff are cheerful and chatty. The nurseries offer a garden construction and alteration service.

Prices Information not available
Facilities Parking, 20 cars (plus extra at back). Delivery service
Open Mon to Sat 8am to 5.30pm (closed 1pm to 2pm), Sun 9am to 12.30pm (closes 5pm weekdays in winter). Closed Christmas and Boxing Day
Credit cards Access, Visa

WASHINGTON W. Sussex   map 5

A. Goatcher & Son   ❀

The Nurseries, Rock Road,   *Tel* Ashington (0903) 892626
Washington, near Pulborough RH20 3BJ
Rock Road is a turning off the A24 about 200 yds north of Washington roundabout. The turning is signposted Thakenham and West Chiltington

This is an area of remarkable natural beauty and the nursery, situated on rising ground overlooking National Trust land, is a real 'plantsman's paradise'. It is a family firm which has been in business in the area for 130 years and its reputation for 'good, honest plant culture' survives today. There are no gardening gimmicks for sale and other than plants, there's only a small range of fertilisers available. The nursery specialises in ornamental trees, shrubs and perennials. Most of the 30-acre site is devoted to plant propagation and cultivation and the layout is conventional and pleasantly old-fashioned. Well-maintained, but bumpy, turf paths lead down to the three main nurseries: 'fruit' – devoted to fruit trees and flowering trees; 'conifer' – a wide range of conifers, rhododendrons, large shrubs and trees; and 'home' – containing mainly herbaceous plants and deciduous trees. The labelling is rather vague, but the staff will happily show you to where you want to go and there's also a comprehensive catalogue to help you. This is definitely a place for the serious-minded gardener who will take an interest in the wide range of unusual specimens grown. There are things here which you would never find in the average centre. Rose lovers will be disappointed though, since the propagation of these has been abandoned in favour of trees and shrubs. Although this is essentially a 'traditional nursery' there is a wide range of container-grown stock available. Visitors are always welcome to wander around, even when the staff are not there. All staff are competent and their enthusiasm shows in the pains they take to answer queries to your satisfaction.

Prices ££££
Facilities Parking, 20 cars. Toilets. Garden advice service. Delivery service. Free plant price list. Plant catalogue 30p, 55p including p&p. Plants sold by mail order
Open Mon to Fri 9am to 5pm (closed 12.30pm to 1.30pm), Sat 9am to 12am

✎ *Garden centres and nurseries awarded with a hand fork symbol stock a particularly comprehensive range of gardening equipment.*

WATERPERRY Oxfordshire map 4
Waterperry Gardens

Waterperry, near Wheatley OX9 1JZ *Tel* Ickford (084 47) 226
3 miles east of the A40, and 2½ miles from the junction of the A40 (M) and A418 at Wheatley

Waterperry Gardens are open to the public (admission 80p) and, with their excellent herbaceous and shrub borders, offer fascinating viewing for everyone. The keen gardener should also take the opportunity to see the stock and nursery beds. The nursery holds the National Collection of Kabschia Saxifrages. The sales nursery is set in the grounds of the Georgian house and has a good selection of houseplants and fruit bushes and trees, including some nice cordons. The trees, shrubs and indoor plants are of good quality. The small inside area is 'uninteresting' but stocks a few garden chemicals and seeds. Fresh fruit and vegetables are sold as well. Sadly, the centre seemed to have become a little run down since our last visit. This was reflected in the poor state of the hardy perennials which were looking unloved, dry and generally scrappy. Lack of care was also evident in the labelling, which was sparse and often faded and hard to read. However, the centre tells us these criticisms have been dealt with. The general layout remains good with well-organised and clearly laid-out sundries and good, broad pathways outside, and there are plans for a formal garden with areas for herbs and a knot garden. A large and airy tea room serves very nice refreshments which include salads and home-made cakes. Staff are a bit thin on the ground, but are friendly and will assist with any carrying or loading.

Prices £££
Facilities Parking, 60 cars (plus 100 overflow). Toilets. Tea room. Garden advice service. Free price list for soft fruit, catalogues for alpines and herbaceous plants 15p
Open Mon to Fri 10am to 5.30pm, Sat and Sun 10am to 6pm (closes 4pm every day in winter). Closed Christmas and Boxing Day, New Year's Day and 18 to 21 July
Credit cards Access, Visa

WELLESBOURNE Warwickshire map 4
Duncans Pet & Garden Centre

10 Warwick Road, Wellesbourne, *Tel* Stratford-Upon-Avon
near Warwick CV35 9NB (0789) 841847
On the A429 at Wellesbourne, 5½ miles east of Stratford-Upon-Avon

Our inspector's comment was 'one could easily stock a new garden, including a pool with fish and fountain, as well as patio furniture and tubs from the stocks at this centre'. Quite a feat for a small site tucked away behind a busy shopping street. The shop contains chemicals, hand tools and all the smaller garden sundries, as well as a Mynah bird which greets customers on entrance – a delight for children and adults alike. Other birds from parrots to zebra finches are sold as pets or for garden aviaries. There is no room for power tools and mowers, but the owner will gladly order them for you. At the back of the premises there is an 'oasis' of colourful plants. The range is obviously limited by the size of the site, but even so there is an abundance of conifers and a good choice of most common plants – anything not in stock can be ordered. (The site is due to be extended in 1985, allowing more room for plants.) The quality of all the plants is exceptionally good. Labelling varies from being very clear for the plant groups to less reliable on individual pots. However, when you buy the plants, you can obtain additional details from the garden centre staff either in writing or verbally. The centre has been very well laid out in order to make the best use of the space available and this enables it to stock garden furniture and ornaments, though not greenhouses, sheds, fencing or paving. Tropical fish and fish tanks are sold as well as cold-water fish, water-gardening equipment and water plants. The centre is very handy for those who are unable or unwilling to go to any of the larger places further afield and the staff are all extremely helpful and friendly, making the centre a pleasure to visit. Parking can be difficult on the main road, but there are some quieter streets round the back of the shop.

Prices £££
Facilities Parking, 11 cars. Toilets. Ice creams and cold drinks. Garden advice and design service. Delivery service. Free price list for fish tanks and accessories. Sundries catalogues 50p, refundable on return
Open Every day except Thurs, 9am to 6pm (closes 5.30pm in winter). Closed Thurs except during peak periods
Credit cards Access, Visa

WELLING Kent   map 5

Woodside Garden Centre   ✿

353 Shooters Hill, Welling DA16 3RP   *Tel* 01-319 2598
On the A207 Shooters Hill road, between Blackheath and Welling

A compact, orderly centre offering a wide range of all types of plants at average prices. It does not appear to get excessively busy so the staff are readily available and it's easy to move around the site. The paths are paved, and perennials and alpines are placed conveniently on raised beds. An alphabetical arrangement helps customers to find the plant of their choice. The only criticism of the layout is that the entrance is rather small, but there are plans to enlarge it. There is a comprehensive selection of plants, all of good quality. When our inspector visited, the range of shrubs and clematis was particularly good, and the conifers, herbs and rockery plants were in prime condition. Labels are generally machine printed and are often illustrated and supply details of habit and flowering periods. Houseplant enthusiasts will enjoy the good selection of houseplants and may be interested in the range of mature bonsai trees and suitable containers on show. A bonsai expert visits the centre every Friday to advise and instruct customers. Stone pots, terracotta-ware, and china plant holders are available in great variety so this might be a good opportunity to brighten up a patio or balcony. The first Sunday of each month sees a visit by a craftsman who makes hand-painted pottery for all occasions. For the more down to earth, there is an accessible display of hand tools, a large paving and stoneware section, a good range of fencing and pergolas and most of the smaller but handy bits and pieces for the garden. The larger sundries, including power tools, are few in number. The centre offers variety and value, and the introduction of new ranges helps to keep interest alive.

Prices ££££
Facilities Parking, 80 cars. Toilets. Vending machines. Garden advice service. Delivery service
Open Every day 9am to 5pm. Closed 3 days at Christmas
Credit cards Access, Visa

WELLINGTON Hereford and Worcester

map 3

Hermitage Fruits Nurseries and Garden Centre

Wellington, Hereford HR4 8BB   *Tel* Canon Pyon (043 271) 277
On the A49 4 miles north of Hereford, at the bottom of the south side of Dinmore Hill

An offshoot of the nearby Hermitage Fruit Farms, this centre lies on the plain of the Lugg with a backdrop of Dinmore Hill. Produce from the farms is sold, including apples, potatoes, lettuce and tomatoes, and honey and eggs from other local farms. You might also enjoy a spell in the pick-your-own tomatoes greenhouse (in season). The atmosphere here is not in the least commercial; it is a place which cares for its customers and looks after its plants. The stock of plants is good for a ¼-acre site, particularly the conifers and shrubs which are home grown, but there are obviously limitations in the varieties available. The centre is, however, large enough for comfort, very flat, and the hardcore paths are well kept. There might be an overall impression of confusion and muddle about the place, but in fact it is sensibly set out with plants arranged in alphabetical order and most plants carrying some sort of identification, though little in the way of other information. Staff are very knowledgeable and helpful. A large wooden hut contains a shop and reception area selling composts, chemicals and smaller tools and equipment. Paving and ornaments are also sold and the centre does claim that if you want something in particular they are happy to order larger items. There is no cafe and only one toilet which is located in a garden shed, basic but very clean (new toilets are planned).

Prices £££
Facilities Parking, 10 cars. Toilets
Open Mon to Sat 8.30am to 5pm, Sun 10am to 5pm. Closed Christmas and Boxing Day

---

WELLS Somerset

map 3

Browne's Garden Centre

Woodford Lane, Keward, Wells BA5 1QQ   *Tel* Wells (0749) 73050
On the edge of Wells, just off the A39 to Glastonbury

This small family business does not compete with the larger centres catering for substantial urban demand, but for local towns and a scattered rural population it provides an excellent service. The centre is enclosed by high hedging and so is well sheltered. The outdoor layout is random and chaotic, and as a first-time visitor you might well have a few problems locating the right plant, but the helpful staff on hand make up for the lack of organisation. The emphasis is on plants, particularly trees and shrubs, and once you have got the hang of the layout, there is a lot here worth seeing. The range is good and the quality generally high. At the time of our inspection the conifers were in excellent shape, shrubs and climbers looked very good, but the soft fruit were very much the worse for wear because of the drought. Labelling could be said to be patchy, varying from good to abysmal. Garden accessories of the smaller kind are available, including a good range of garden ornaments and some garden pools and furniture, but there are no power tools or sheds. Seeds and chemicals are well presented.

Prices ££££
Facilities Parking, 60 cars. Toilets. Garden advice service. Delivery service. Price lists for tools, sundries etc. free or 45p. Price list for trees and shrubs, free or 6p
Open Every day 9am to 5.30pm. Closed Christmas and Boxing Day

---

WEST MONKTON Somerset   map 3

Monkton Elm Nurseries and Garden Centre

West Monkton, Taunton   *Tel* West Monkton (0823) 412381
TA2 8QN
By the junction of the A38 and the A361, 2¼ miles north of Taunton

This garden centre is well set back from the A361 in semi-rural surroundings close to Taunton suburbs. It is a small centre, well laid out both indoors and out. It presents a generally tidy aspect and the plants are well presented. There are plans for a landscaped area with display beds. A shaded glasshouse creates a spacious indoor sales area where you will find an excellent display of houseplants (this area is being extended). The general emphasis is on plants because the centre is part of a commercial nursery whose produce is often on sale here. The range of shrubs deserves to be singled out for special mention, but all plants are generally in excellent condition and well cared for through all seasons. Group and individual labelling is consistent and legible. Power tools and lawnmowers are not stocked, but there are a good number of hand tools and a variety of chemicals. Sheds, fencing, paving and garden ornaments are also sold. The staff are cheerful and reasonably helpful. It is a good local garden centre for the Taunton area.

Prices £££
Facilities Parking, 60 cars (plus 150 overflow). Toilets. Vending machines. Delivery service
Open Every day 9.30am to 5.30pm (closes 5pm in winter). Closed between Christmas and New Year's Day
Credit cards Access, Visa

Garden centres and nurseries are changing fast. Practically all those we've included in the Guide were planning improvements for 1985, so we need as much feedback as possible about the ones you visit to keep us up to date. Please use the report forms at the end of the book.

WESTERHAM Kent   map 5
Westerham Heights Nurseries   ⚘

Hawley Corner, Main Road,   *Tel* Biggin Hill (0959) 71545
Westerham Hill,
Westerham TN16 2ED
South of Biggin Hill on the A233 Westerham to Bromley road

This is a small, family-run nursery set in the countryside near Biggin Hill. It
might be of particular interest to gardeners who are planning to make a
new garden pond or to restock an old one since there is a very good range
of aquatic plants and water-gardening equipment. The centre also runs a
landscaping service which specialises in rock and water gardens. If you are
not interested in ponds, but simply want to collect a few healthy plants for
the garden, then the selection of trees, shrubs, heathers and alpines offers a
good choice. Soft and top fruit are also well represented, and when our
inspector visited only the herbaceous perennial section was rather limited.
All plants are very healthy looking, particularly the trees. Excellent group
labels provide helpful information, though individual tags are sometimes
faded. The outside area is well laid out with paved paths. The inside,
however, is very small and feels cluttered. The number of sundries stocked
is small – only hand tools, chemicals and composts, together with some
furniture and ornaments. Only two or three staff are on hand, but they are
helpful and pleasant. For a nursery of this size there is a good range of
good-quality trees and shrubs at average prices.

Prices £££££
Facilities Parking, 20 cars. Play area. Garden advice service. Delivery service.
Plant catalogue 20p
Open Every day 9am to 6.30pm (closes 5pm in winter). Closed for Christmas
Credit cards Access, Visa

WESTON Lincolnshire   map 5
Baytrees Garden Centre

High Road, Weston, near Spalding   *Tel* Holbeach (0406) 370242
PE12 6JU
On the A151 at Weston, 2 miles east of Spalding

This centre is located just to the east of the famous tulip-growing area of
Spalding and creates special floral displays on site during the Spalding
Tulip Festival. It is a large 25-acre site, with beautiful display gardens and a
bright spacious indoor section devoted to gardening equipment and
sundries. A separate business supplies a good line in greenhouses and
sheds. Most other items are available although lawnmowers are only
stocked in the spring and summer. The site is well laid out with wide paths,
benches and clear signs pointing to the main display beds. The centre
specialises in roses, and there's also a very good selection of herbaceous
perennials, shrubs and water plants as well as conifers and fruit trees.
Plants are very cheap and were in excellent condition when inspected. They

carried helpful, informative labels, although some had faded in the sun.
Plenty of water gardening equipment is sold and there is an attractive pond
display. Children will be kept busy exploring the playhouse and the pet
section with its rabbits, guinea pigs and terrapins or simply watching the
birds in the aviary while you browse through the surrounding pot plants.
Special offers are regularly advertised in the local papers and due to its
popularity the centre can often be quite crowded. Guided tours are
arranged for organised parties. There are basic meals and snacks on sale if
you get hungry. The staff are courteous and helpful and although most of
them are employed for maintenance and up-keep there are professionals
on hand who will willingly share their experience.

Prices £
Facilities Parking, 500 cars, 50 coaches. Toilets. Restaurant, cafeteria and vending
machines. Play area. Garden advice service. Delivery service
Open Every day 9am to 6pm (closes 7pm in summer). Closed for Christmas and
Boxing Day

WESTONING Bedfordshire
map 4

Flitt Vale Garden Centre

Flitt Vale Nurseries, Flitwick
Road, Westoning MK45 5AA
Tel Flitwick (0525) 713213/712484
Between Westoning and Flitwick on the A5120

Our inspector felt this was an above-average garden centre, offering good
plants at fair prices. The range of plants is large considering the space
available, and our inspector was particularly impressed by an extensive
display of fuchsias all grown on site. Other plants grown include
geraniums, alpines and bedding plants. The overall quality of plants is
above average. The layout is good and everything is very tidy and well
labelled, but the arrangement of the shrubs is not entirely logical so you
might need help here. Most run-of-the-mill garden accessories are kept
except fencing and garden sheds. The selection of hand tools and furniture
is quite small, but there is an extensive line in lawnmowers and
the centre will maintain and repair all types of horticultural machinery. Fish
are sold on Saturday and Sunday only – the only time when knowledgeable
staff are available. This is a good place to buy cut flowers, as the choice is
wide. If you time your visit carefully, a stroll next door to the local cricket
pitch might offer a little afternoon's spectating.

Prices ££
Facilities Parking, 55 cars. Toilets. Vending machines. Play area. Garden advice
service. Delivery service. Free price lists
Open Mon to Sat 8.30am to 5pm, Sun 10am to 4.30pm
Credit cards Access, Visa

---

*Prices vary a lot at garden centres and nurseries. We've calculated a basket price for
plants and given ratings from £ to ££££££ – very cheap to very expensive.*

---

*Establishments awarded with a flower symbol sell either a very good range of
high-quality plants, or a more limited but particularly interesting selection.*

WHEATLEY Oxfordshire   map 4

Cramphorn Garden Centre

London Road, Wheatley, Oxford   *Tel* Wheatley (086 77) 3057/8
OX9 1XJ
On the A40 Oxford to High Wycombe road ½ mile outside Wheatley

This centre is situated in rural agricultural land with its back boundary
marked by a small stream. The outside display area is restricted to a long
narrow plot along the side of the road and the plants tend to be rather on
top of each other. However, despite its drawbacks, it is fairly well laid out
and stocks a reasonable range of plants and gardening equipment.There
are paved walkways and the plots are distinctly signposted, but it can be
very wet underfoot. The interior is a very pleasant building, spacious,
bright and clean but rather packed to the gills. The shop contains a wide
range of all the usual gardening equipment as well as a few out of the
ordinary items, such as budgie cages, dog baskets and animal pictures.
There is also an aquatic section, stocked up in the spring. The restricted
space outside has resulted in some shortages among the plant stocks –
though most types of plant are sold the choice of varieties is sometimes
limited. However, a good range of fruit trees has been fitted in and the fruit
area has a chart giving pollination requirements. A twelve-month
guarantee is offered on all container plants. The quality of plants is
generally good and a cut-price, no-guarantee section provides a home for
damaged plants. At the time of our inspection, individual plant labelling
was very poor – difficult to find and difficult to read – but the centre tells us
it is working to improve this. Large illustrated boards mark out the group
beds. A trained horticulturalist is usually available to answer your
questions, but the casual workers are not particularly helpful.

Prices ££££
Facilities Parking, 20 cars. Toilets. Cold drinks and confectionery. Garden advice
service. Delivery service (loan of van). Plant handbook £1.95
Open Mon to Sat 8.30am to 5.30pm, Sun 9.30 to 6pm (closes 5.30pm Sun in winter).
Closed Christmas and Boxing Day
Credit cards Access, Diners Club, Visa

WHITMINSTER Gloucestershire   map 3

Highfield Nurseries

School Lane, Whitminster,   *Tel* Gloucester (0452) 740266
Gloucester GL2 7PL
*On the edge of Whitminster. School Lane is a turning off the A38 Gloucester to
Bristol road, 1 mile from Junction 13 on the M5*

Highfield Nurseries grow their own plants and deliver them throughout
the country,so direct sales only constitute a small part of the turnover. This
is very much a place for the serious plantsman, and its traditional, natural
atmosphere can be a pleasant contrast to some of the large, modern centres
which stock everything. The sprawling exterior plays host to a vast choice
of trees, fruit and shrubs, particularly conifers and heathers. Pot-grown

miniature roses are available as well as a good choice of bush and standards growing in the ground. The staff appear to be nurserymen first and salesmen second, and it is very interesting to wander about the polythene houses to see the propagation and potting-on taking place. Although very busy with maintenance and watering, the staff will appear with the ring of a bell and give you knowledgeable help. As far as quality of plants is concerned this more than rivals the average centre with a consistent lush greenness in evidence. There was no sign of pests, disease damage or dead plants when our inspector visited. The layout of the nursery is a bit haphazard although signs are clear. Both the car park and all pathways are gravelled. Because the emphasis here is on the plants, the range of supplementary gardening items is kept to a minimum – just enough to tackle most basic gardening jobs. The one exception is a reasonable range of composts. Some fencing, ornaments and furniture can also be bought. Our inspector's one complaint was that it is a pity they don't raise and sell houseplants!

Prices ££££
Facilities Parking, 20 cars. Toilets. Play area. Garden advice service. Delivery service. Plant price list and catalogue 20p. Plants sold by mail order
Open Mon to Sat 8am to 5pm
Credit cards Access, Visa

WHITTLESEY Cambridgeshire   map 4

Burdetts Garden Centre   ❁

Eastrea Road, Whittlesey,   *Tel* Peterborough (0733) 202207
Peterborough PE7 2AH
On the A605 Peterborough to March/Wisbech road, about ½ mile east of Whittlesey town centre

This centre is a mixture of old and new buildings set on the edge of a small market town. It has grown up from a long-established nursery, first started in 1927. The surrounding countryside is very flat so there is a good level car park and access is very easy. The site is uncluttered and roomy, consisting of well-organised indoor and outdoor areas. The covered area encompasses a very good selection of sundries for all tastes, including storm porches, sun loungers and a large pets section as well as gardening equipment. The range and layout of barbecues, sheds and greenhouses is very good. Plants are inexpensive but well maintained. You will find a large choice among the conifers and some very lush specimens among the fruit trees. The centre specialises in geraniums, available in spring. Each plant group has a large price plate which is easily visible. Individual plants have name tags and all labelling is generally legible and useful. Trolleys are available for car loading and the staff will help out with carrying goods or answering any queries you might have. Some refreshment facilities would be an improvement, and toilets could do with being sited a little closer to the main buildings.

Prices ££
Facilities Parking, 100 cars (plus overflow). Toilets. Play area. Garden advice service. Delivery service

Open Every day 9am to 6pm (closes 5.30pm in winter). Closed Christmas and Boxing Day
Credit cards Access, Visa

WICKERSLEY S. Yorkshire   map 2
Springfield Garden Centre   ✿

Bawtry Road, Wickersley,   *Tel* Wickersley (0709) 547007
Rotherham S66 0BL
On the A631 by a Texaco garage site, 3 miles east of Rotherham

A friendly centre where the staff are always out to please the customer, to
the extent of ordering unusual plants at special request. It is a clean, tidy
site where plants are arranged in neatly defined blocks and the labelling is
concise and informative, although sometimes weathered. The centre is
attempting to concentrate its space and resources on stocking a wide range
of alpines, shrubs, trees, heathers, perennials and bedding plants. Recent
improvements include a redesigned alpine, herbaceous and bedding plant
area. The range of inexpensive plants already available should please most
buyers and they all show obvious signs of care and attention. A double
glasshouse area contains tools, sundries and indoor plants which would
satisfy all but the most demanding professional. Larger items such as
sheds, fencing and paving are also sold, but no greenhouses. Staff are on
hand all the time and are all helpful, right through to the cashier. Cold
drinks and crisps can be bought at the garage kiosk integral to the centre,
and there are plans to set up a proper tea room.

Prices ££
Facilities Parking, 40 cars. Toilets. Garden advice service. Delivery service. Reference
books loaned
Open Every day 9am to 6pm (closes 5pm in winter). Closed Christmas and
Boxing Day
Credit cards Access, Leicester Card, Visa

WICKFORD Essex   map 4
Alpha Garden Centre

208 London Road, Wickford   *Tel* Wickford (03744) 66093
SS12 0AR
On the western outskirts of Wickford on the A129 Billericay road

A centre which sells most gardening equipment, but a disappointing range
of plants. It covers a large, well-laid-out area with wide pathways. A
modern building containing tools and many gardening sundries is also
nicely organised. The stock of garden accessories is quite comprehensive
and includes a good range of tools (both hand and power), an entire
greenhouse devoted to water-gardening, and even a swimming pool
display area. A new garden furniture and tropical fish building is planned
for the near future. The range of plants stocked is small, though on the
whole they are of very good quality. When our inspector visited there were
few trees, and no soft fruit or herbs. The choice within any one category is

limited to one or two plants. The notable exception to this is the very large stock of heathers. Individual plants have either pre-printed or handwritten labels – many of the latter are difficult to read – but there is no sectional labelling of any sort. The selection of houseplants is poor, and at the time of inspection they were in very poor condition. However, a new houseplant conservatory is to be built which should give scope for a wider range. Other improvements planned include an enclosed planteria and a new restaurant and toilet block. A useful centre for locals in need of gardening hardware.

Prices ££
Facilities Parking, 120 cars. Toilets. Vending machines. Play area. Garden advice service. Delivery service. Free price list for paving, fencing, fish ponds and swimming pools
Open Every day 9am to 6pm (closes 5pm in winter)
Credit cards Access, Visa

Alton Garden Centre

Arterial Road, Wickford SS12 9JG   *Tel* Basildon (0268) 726421
Situated on the London-bound carriageway of the A127 about 2 miles from Rayleigh

A busy dual carriageway runs along beside this centre, but access is helped by a slip road leading directly to the centre. A good car park should cater for all comers and the site itself is nicely laid out. It is a large centre with an extensive plant display area where there are wide paths connected by ramps, and bold area signs indicating the whereabouts of various goods. The indoor section is also quite sizeable and the disabled and elderly should be warned that there are some steps in this area. Stocks are plentiful at Alton's. One of its specialities is the lawnmower department which offers not only a large choice for sale, but also servicing, spare parts and advice facilities. If you are planning to expand the leisure side of the garden, the range of paving slabs is very good, and there is a large covered area which sports a display of garden furniture and swimming pools. Other features are the good range of conservatories and, for the flower-arranging enthusiast, artificial flowers and decorative materials. A further development planned for 1985 was the introduction of a large water-garden section including a range of fish and fountains. As far as the plants go, the range is quite comprehensive, although you won't find anything very unusual tucked away. The selection of seasonal plants is quite impressive, so for those interested in bulbs or spring bedding a visit could be rewarding. All the plants are of good quality and any scruffy ones left on display are marked down in price. Labels are weatherproof and unfaded, but unfortunately there is little but the common name of the plant to read. The plentiful but unobtrusive staff are helpful.

Prices ££££
Facilities Parking, 150 cars. Play area. Delivery service. Free price lists for fencing, stonework, walling etc. Plant catalogue 95p
Open Every day, 9am to 6pm in summer, 10am to 5pm in winter
Credit cards Access, Visa

WICKWAR Gloucestershire map 3

George Osmond

Archfield Nursery, Wickwar, *Tel* Wickwar (045 424) 216
near Wotton-under-Edge GL12 8NA
On the B4060 midway between Wickwar and Chipping Sodbury

The first impression of this nursery is one of general muddle and
untidiness, but this can easily be forgiven after a glance round. This is very
much a 'working' nursery rather than a 'showpiece' garden centre, and the
seed boxes and packing cases lying around reflect a greater concern for the
plants than for the image created. However, a bit of a tidy-up wouldn't go
amiss. The site is a large one and the layout good. There are numerous
polythene greenhouses devoted to a vast collection of conifers at all stages
of growth. The rest of the centre is filled with an interesting and unusual
selection of container-grown herbaceous perennials, alpines and shrubs –
not to mention the immense variety of ericas (over 90 listed). All these
inexpensive plants are of top quality and are well maintained; on the day
of our inspection only a few trees looked a little weary. George Osmond,
the owner, is extremely helpful and has 30 years of experience to call on.
The rest of his staff are also excellent, although there are not enough of
them! If you are a keen collector or just an all-round plant-lover you are
bound to find a visit here fascinating. No tools or sundries are sold.

Prices ££
Facilities Parking in lane and field. Garden advice service. Free price lists and
catalogue for plants
Open Mon to Sat 8am to 7pm (closes at dusk in winter)

WIDECOMBE IN THE MOOR Devon map 3

Southcombe Gardens

Widecombe in the Moor,
Newton Abbot TQ13 7TU
*On a hill to the south-west of Widecombe village, 12 miles from Newton Abbot.
From Widecombe take the Ponsworthy road for ¼ mile, turn right at signs to
Southcombe*

This nursery is a treasure house of unusual plants set against a dramatic
Dartmoor backdrop. The gardens are on terraces which are cut deeply into
a steep hill, and a collection of old granite farm buildings completes the
picture. There will be nothing of interest here for the DIY gardener, but any
plant-lover will happily throw themselves into this absorbing place.
Gardeners looking for the range of common plants may be disappointed,
but if 26 varieties of helianthemum or 20 species and hybrids of dianthus
appeal to you, then a visit here is called for. The impressive arrays of
healthy, good-quality rockery plants, heather, trees, perennials and other
plants are pleasantly organised in groups on the terraced site, and plants
within each section are arranged alphabetically. Great care has been taken
to paint clear wooden labels giving brief, but relevant information

including area of origin. Our inspector said, 'This is a genuine plantsman's nursery, compared with many of the new supermarket centres'. The staff are all experienced and the proprietor is a bit of a 'character'. A comprehensive catalogue contains 28 pages of closely typed information and prices are included. There's a large garden in which you are welcome to picnic, and two cafes about ½ mile away.

Prices Information not available
Facilities Parking, 30 cars. Toilets. Garden advice service. Delivery service. Plant catalogue 40p
Open Every day 10am to dusk

WILLIAN Hertfordshire   map 4
Pioneer Nurseries

Willian, Letchworth SG6 2A   *Tel* Letchworth (046 26) 4100
Off the A6141 at Willian behind the Three Horseshoes pub

Not necessarily a place for an afternoon walkabout, but certainly a good place to go to purchase good-value plants and vegetables directly from the growers. This is a nursery first and foremost, so there are no garden sundries available. There is a large growing area and you will find many varieties to choose from, particularly among the wide collection of alpines. The plants are generally well tended, but at the time our inspector visited some seemed excessively dry. The grounds are well planned and gravel paths keep the mud and dust at bay. Labelling is adequate, although not all trees are priced. The farm shop offers some good garden produce to the public including home-grown tomatoes. Staff are cheerful and happy to help out with customers' problems.

Prices ££
Facilities Parking, 50 cars.
Open Mon to Sat 8am to 5pm, Sun 10am to 1pm
Credit cards Access, Visa

WILLINGTON Bedfordshire   map 4
Willington Garden Centre

Sandy Road, Willington   *Tel* Cardington (023 03) 777/8/9
MK44 3QP
On the A603 between Bedford and Sandy, 3 miles from the turn-off to Sandy

This is a professionally run garden centre which has developed from a nursery originally founded at the end of the last century. Now amidst a pleasant atmosphere there are signs of the modern world in the displays of barbecues, outdoor lighting and camping equipment. It is a fairly large centre and the planthouses and planteria are well maintained. A good layout allows ample space for trolleys and wheelchairs, and clear signposting shows you where to go, but the indoor shop with its bulbs, composts and small tools is rather badly lit and dismal (this area is to be improved). There is a good general range of healthy plants, though they are a little expensive. The emphasis is on trees and shrubs, some of which are bought in from other countries. However, this is not to the detriment of other types of plants such as the excellent spring bedding available in season. Perhaps the most striking aspect of Willington's is the enormous planthouse. There you will find specimen plants, exotic banana and grapefruit trees, bonsai trees and air plants, to name just a few. A 'beautiful haven' said our inspector. At the more mundane level, you will find most tools and sundries are stocked and there's an impressive selection of furniture and ornaments. There is also a good display of greenhouses and sheds, as well as plenty of fencing and netting. Paving and power tools, on the other hand, are much more limited. Staff are extremely keen and there are experts available in the different areas to advise you. The plant labels also provide easy-to-read and useful instructions. A treat for the gardener and the family.

Prices £££££
Facilities Parking, 285 cars (plus 500 overflow). Toilets. Coffee shop. Play area. Garden advice service. Delivery service. Plant price list and catalogue 75p
Open Mon to Sat 9am to 5.30pm, Sun and bank holidays 10am to 5.30pm. Closed Christmas
Credit cards Access, Visa

WILMSLOW Cheshire   map 2

Wilmslow Garden Centre

Manchester Road, Wilmslow   *Tel* Wilmslow (0625) 525700
SK9 2XX

One mile north of Wilmslow on the A34 Wilmslow to Manchester road

This is a pleasant place for a gardener to visit since its welcoming and pleasant atmosphere dominates any sense of a commercial enterprise. It is sited on slightly sloping ground and there is a lot of unused grassland where special attractions, sales and fairs are held. There is a large, shaded greenhouse and a sizeable exterior which is well laid out with broad paths. Although it presents an attractive appearance and is easy to get round, the big problem is finding things. Customers armed with a shopping list are likely to become infuriated with the absence of any map or logical arrangement of plants, and the small, uninformative labels. However, there is a considerable range of plants if you can find them, and they are of very good quality indeed, so perseverance is worthwhile. This is a fairly new centre, continually changing, and the current development programme includes improvement to signposting and information for customers. The tools and sundries section incorporates both the large and small items of gardening equipment and the selection is generally good. The centre has a particular interest in greenhouses, sheds and building bricks. A home-brewing agency and double-glazing exhibition are also set up in the large indoor area. Other features planned include a furniture and barbecue showroom, swimming pool centre and pets centre. Although the arrangement of plants is poor, this is compensated for by the helpfulness of the staff, the quantity and standard of the stock and the reasonable prices. A good licensed restaurant provides refreshment facilities.

Prices ££££
Facilities Parking, 100 cars (plus 50 overflow). Toilets. Restaurant. Play area. Garden advice service. Delivery service. Free price lists for walling, paving and fencing
Open Every day 9am to 6pm (closes 5pm in winter)
Credit cards Access, American Express, Diners Club, Visa

WINCHESTER Hampshire   map 4

Hillier Garden Centre

Winchester SO22 5DN   *Tel* Winchester (0962) 6741

About ½ mile from the city centre on the A3090 Romsey road, opposite the county hospital

Hilliers stocks many unusual varieties of plants to choose from, and also has a good overall range, but they are quite expensive. A special water garden section is of interest to those keen on this aspect of gardening. A comprehensive selection of chemicals and fertilisers is available as well as most hand tools, sheds and paving. Power tools are sold under franchise. Flower pots and gardening books are also well represented, along with a stock of jams and preserves to take home for your afternoon tea. The plants are well arranged and easily accessible along wide paths, but the indoor area was found to be a little cramped. If your interests lie more in the home than the garden there is an attractive display of houseplants with which to occupy your time.

Prices ££££
Facilities Parking, 80 cars. Toilets. Garden advice service. Delivery service. Catalogue for trees and shrubs £5.95. Plants sold by mail order
Open Mon to Sat 9am to 5.30pm, Sun 10am to 5.30pm. Closed for several days over Christmas
Credit cards Access, Visa

WINDERMERE Cumbria   map 2

Windermere Garden Centre

New Road, Windermere LA23 2LA   *Tel* Windermere (096 62) 2719
On the main road between Windermere and Bowness

Local gardeners will find that the selection of heathers and dwarf conifers sold here makes a visit well worthwhile. A small, family nursery, it specialises in these particular plants and although slightly less ambitious with the rest of the range, better-known varieties of shrubs and perennials are stocked in limited numbers, and you will find trees, fruits, roses and herbs. Plants sold are in good health. They are arranged in groups and the displays of heathers, alpines and dwarf conifers are most attractive. The site is not exceedingly large and most things are easily spotted – good signposting also helps out. Each plant is labelled with its name only and prices are not always marked. The owner and his family are very kind and will assist whenever customers are at a loss. General access is good, the pathways wide and surfaced with gravel to keep down the mud. Tools, houseplants, chemicals and other sundries are stored in a large glasshouse

area, but the selection is very basic. Some furniture and garden decorations
are available as well. This is not a place which supplies everything and
anything, but what it does it does well.

Prices £££
Facilities Parking, 30 cars. Garden advice service. Delivery service
Open Mon to Sat 9am to 5pm, Sun 10am to 4pm
Credit cards Access, American Express, Visa

WINDLESHAM Surrey   map 5

L R Russell Nursery Garden Centre

London Road, Windlesham GU20 6LL   *Tel* Ascot (0990) 21411/2
North side of A30, 1½ miles west of Sunningdale

A long-established, thoroughly well-organised garden centre and nursery
with a good perception of what the public needs. There is a general feeling
that they are a bit 'up market' in their aims and prices, but you certainly get
what you pay for. The layout is impressive and there's a map showing a
numbered location for each plant type. The entrance and exit hallways are
spacious with plenty of elbow room at the cash desks. The plant sales area
covers about 2 acres and is being expanded further. A covered area houses
sheds and greenhouses, while a comprehensive selection of the smaller
sundries, such as tools, ponds, chemicals and barbecues, is found
indoors. There's a showroom for mowers, tractors and other machinery,
and a service workshop on site. A speciality of Russell's is its garden
ornaments – they have several hundred pots and statues in stone, concrete
and earthenware. General garden tools and accessories are also very good.
On the plant side, there's a wide choice of variety and colour. The centre
specialises in flowering and ornamental shrubs and trees, including
camellias, azaleas, rhododendrons, hydrangeas and fuchsias. The range of
alpines, rock plants and exotic indoor plants is also excellent. Quality is
high; many of the plants are grown on site and are well cared for. Trees are
supported, shrubs staked, camellias shaded and even the alpines are clean
and tidy. A bargain section deals with those plants which have 'passed
their best'. The labelling is excellent and very informative and in addition
there is an 'advice chalet' where you can discuss your gardening problems.
There are staff in each section who are also able to advise you. Overall a
centre offering an immense breadth of variety, with surprises round every
corner.

Prices ££££££
Facilities Parking, 185 cars (extra for 50 cars planned). Toilets. Vending machines.
Garden advice service. Delivery service. Free price lists for some plants, garden
furniture, paving and walling. Free catalogue for hardy plants. Plants sold by mail
order
Open Mon to Sat 8.30am to 5.30pm, Sun 10am to 5pm. Closed Christmas and Boxing
Day and New Year's Day
Credit cards Access, Visa

WISLEY Surrey   map 5

RHS Enterprises   ❀

Royal Horticultural Society   *Tel* Guildford (0483) 224163/224124
Wisley Garden, Wisley,
Woking GU23 6QB
Off the A3, between Cobham and Ripley, 8 miles north of Guildford

The beautiful Wisley Garden stretches out behind this centre offering some fascinating sights for gardeners and non-gardeners alike. The arboretum, riverside walk, rhododendron garden and trial grounds are just some of the treats which contribute to an enjoyable family outing. Entry to the garden is free for RHS members, otherwise there is a charge (£1.60). The centre itself provides good-quality plants, plenty of choice and expert advice when needed. The alpines deserve to be singled out for offering an exceptional range of quality plants which would rival all but the specialist nursery. Many of the less common varieties of shrubs and plants are available, but this seems to be at the expense of some of the more common ones. All plants are well grown and there are some very mature specimens kept in stock. Our praise cannot extend itself to the labelling – when our inspector visited, many labels had been obliterated by the weather and plants were often not priced. Group labelling was slightly better. However, the centre tells us this has since been rectified. The layout of the centre was undergoing changes, and since the outside section was obviously in transition when our inspector visited, it is difficult to make any comment. However, in sections where the re-organisation and enlargement had been completed there were good, accessible pathways. The indoor section rates well for its layout, but since this is essentially a plant centre, the extent of sundries is limited to a handful of tools, containers and chemicals. Seeds, bulbs and some very fine houseplants are also on show. A large inform- ation centre and shop next door sells a wide selection of books as well as jams, honeys and gardening-related products. Other facilities include a picnic area, an enormous car park and country ice creams for sale. Inside the grounds of Wisley Garden itself there is a restaurant and cafeteria.

Prices ££££
Facilities Parking, 600 cars. Toilets. Restaurant and cafeteria (closed mid Nov to early Feb). Garden advice service. Booklets on rhododendrons, perennials, bulbs etc
Open Plants centre: every day 10am to 7pm (closes 6pm in winter). Closed Christmas week. Gardens: Mon to Sat 10am to 7pm (closes 4.30pm in Nov, Dec and Jan), Sun 2pm to 7pm (10am to 2pm reserved for members only). Closed Christmas Day
Credit cards Access, Visa

WOBURN SANDS Buckinghamshire   map 4

Frosts Garden Centre

Woburn Sands, Milton Keynes   *Tel* Milton Keynes (0908) 583511
MK17 8UE
South-east of Milton Keynes at Woburn Sands, on the Newport Pagnell road

The centre is located in the sleepy rural setting of Woburn Sands, a small town divided by the Bedfordshire/Buckinghamshire border. A large indoor area supplies everything even remotely connected with gardening, even ride-on mowers. Outdoors, plants are well displayed, but the layout is not entirely satisfactory. The car park entrance runs through the centre and pathways are not sufficiently wide for customers and their trolleys on a busy day. However, developments planned for 1985 include wider paths as well as demonstration gardens. There is a comprehensive labelling system and avenues are marked with large, clear labels, each section within an avenue having a sign which carries a short description. The plants themselves are arranged alphabetically and are labelled with name and price. Advice on growing is available from the extremely nice staff who, although always kept busy, are willing to stop what they are doing to help out and frequently offer their help voluntarily if you look lost. There is also an excellent information centre. The centre stocks a good range of inexpensive plants all of which are generally maintained in healthy condition. Containers are usually clean and free from weeds or mosses. Our inspector felt it was a place she would happily return to again.

Prices ££
Facilities Parking, 350 cars. Toilets. Coffee shop. Garden advice service. Delivery service. Free price list for some plants. Catalogue for trees and shrubs 75p
Open Mon to Fri 9am to 5.30pm (opens 10am Tues), Sat 9am to 5pm, Sun 10am to 5pm. Late closing Fri, Apr to June. Closed 3 days at Christmas
Credit cards Access, Visa

Kennedys Garden Centre

53 Newport Road, Woburn   *Tel* Milton Keynes (0908) 582511
Sands, Milton Keynes MK17 8US
On the A5130 north-east of Woburn Sands

A large centre stocking most items you might need for the garden. The indoor area exceeds the outside in size and contains a good range and display of most gardening accessories, as well as a small play area with swings and slides for children. It also includes a pet shop and florist's. It is well set out and there is a particularly nice arrangement of books and literature and a good display of garden furniture. The water garden section is large and comprehensive. Most large items of gardening equipment are stocked, including greenhouses, sheds, fencing and paving, but no heavy electrical garden tools. The exterior is organised with plenty of space between the neat rows of plants, but it is poorly signposted. However, plants are arranged alphabetically and once you have understood the system, this helps. Labelling could do with some improvement – the print is small and often washed out. The range and quality of plants, particularly conifers, is generally good, but they are quite expensive. There are only a few staff, but they are helpful.

Prices £££££
Facilities Parking, 300 cars. Toilets. Cafeteria. Play area. Garden advice service. Delivery service. Free price lists for trees, shrubs, paving and fencing. Free leaflets
Open Mon to Fri 8.30am to 5.30pm, Sat and Sun 9am to 6pm (closes half an hour

earlier in winter). Closed 3 days over Christmas
Credit cards Access, Visa

WOKINGHAM Berkshire

map 4

Heathlands Country Market

Heathlands Road, Wokingham
RG11 3BG

Tel Reading (0734) 782777

Take the Easthampstead road out of Wokingham, over the level crossing, turn right at the White Horse pub and the centre is ½ mile down this road

A useful combination of garden centre, farm shop and pick-your-own fields. The garden centre sells plants alone and has no supplies of gardening equipment. It occupies a small site in this pleasant country setting. Almost all the plants are arranged outside in well-sheltered, shaded grounds. There is a reasonable selection of stock including a good range of azaleas and fruit trees. All plants are very well looked after and this shows in their healthy appearance. Care has also been taken with the labelling: though some plants have only a handwritten label bearing the name and price, others carry small descriptive labels and plant groups are identified by large pictures. The manager is a plantsman with some 30 years' experience, and a professional gardener is on hand at weekends to give horticultural advice. There are plans to extend the display area and to build a house for indoor plants. The addition of some kind of play area for the children would also be welcome.

Prices £££
Facilities Parking, 200 cars. Toilets. Garden advice service. Delivery service
Open Tues to Sat 9am to 5.30pm (closes 5pm in winter), Sun 10am to 1pm
Credit cards Access, Visa

WOLDINGHAM Surrey

map 5

Knights Garden Centre

Rosedene Nursery, Woldingham
Road, Woldingham CR3 7LD

Tel Woldingham (905) 3142

Off the A22, 1 mile towards Woldingham

This is very much a centre for the keen gardener rather than the day-tripper. It is set in a pleasantly rural area and faces on to rolling fields. Popular plants are plentiful and there's a particularly good choice of shrubs, trees, conifers and heathers. They are all very well cared for, notably the excellent conifers and heathers. Plants are well laid out, in alphabetical order, with easy access along wide paths, and small plants are displayed on raised beds for easy viewing. Signposting is very good and the overall impression is of space and organisation. The larger plants are well marked, but labelling of the smaller ones is patchy. There is a wide selection of the smaller garden accessories as well as some fencing and furniture. The selection of pots and ornaments is very good, while there are some interesting items on offer for the flower arranger and bonsai enthusiast. The centre has recently been enlarged and now encompasses a large covered area for indoor plants. They plan to introduce a new outdoor fish unit as well as extending the shop area. This is a friendly and reliable centre and you'll find the staff (spotted by their green coats) knowledgeable and helpful.

Prices ££££
Facilities Parking, 75 to 85 cars. Toilets. Garden advice service. Delivery service. Free price list and catalogue for plants
Open Mon to Sat 8am to 5.30pm, Sun 9am to 12.30pm. Closed public holidays
Credit cards Access, Visa

WOODBRIDGE Suffolk   map 4
Notcutts Garden Centre

Ipswich Road,   *Tel* Woodbridge (039 43) 3344
Woodbridge IP12 4AF
Just off the A12 outside Woodbridge

Lovely mature trees and a landscaped garden provide a pleasant setting for this centre. The layout is very good, with excellent signposting, and there is a wide range of plants of top quality, all well labelled, but expensive. Basic sundries and water-gardening equipment are sold, and the range of garden furniture and ornaments is good. The quality and range of houseplants is excellent. The friendly uniformed staff are very knowledgeable. The centre has recently been enlarged to give more space for trees, slabs and fencing.

Prices ££££££
Facilities Parking, 200 cars. Toilets. Vending machines. Play area. Garden advice service. Delivery service. Free plant price lists, catalogue £1.50
Open Mon to Sat 8.30am to 5.45pm, Sun 10am to 5pm
Credit cards Access, Visa

WOODFORD Cheshire   map 2
Woodford Park Home and Garden Improvement Centre

Chester Road, Woodford, Bramhall   *Tel* 061-439 4955/4995
SK7 1QS
On the A5149 between Wilmslow and Bramhall

This is a large centre offering excellent facilities and yet still undergoing extensive development. A generous car park is located within the site and a large chart showing the plan of the grounds tells you immediately which way to go. In addition to this there are large signposts – so overall the layout makes it easy to get around. There is a sizeable covered area for equipment including dried flowers, lots of books and an extensive selection of tools (except for the larger powered machines). An excellent display of greenhouses, sheds and conservatories is also set up on site, and altogether there's little missing from the comprehensive stocks of sundries. A swimming pool and sauna display area is planned, and also a machinery sales, repair and hire service. On the plant side, the range sold is reasonable – except for the shrubs which were rather limited when we inspected. Some very attractive seasonal displays show off the stock well.

Other plants are arranged on raised staging and are generally of good quality. Both sectional and individual labelling is legible and prices are marked. Labels for the shrubs provide plenty of detail, but this unfortunately isn't true for the other plant types. The large number of customers can make it difficult to find a staff member free to answer technical questions, but once cornered they are most helpful. A full restaurant service is available seven days a week.

Prices £££
Facilities Parking, 250 cars. Toilets. Restaurant. Play area. Garden advice service. Delivery service. Free price lists for paving, fencing etc.
Open Every day 8am to 6pm
Credit cards Access, American Express, Diners Club, Visa

WOOLSINGTON Tyne and Wear   map 2
Cowell Nurseries

Main Road, Woolsington,   *Tel* Tyneside (091) 286 3403
Newcastle-upon-Tyne NE13 8DG
On the A696 Newcastle to Jedburgh road, about 1 mile south of Newcastle airport

This is a very good, small nursery which is improving and expanding with each year. The nursery concentrates on plants but also sells a complete but small range of hand tools, a good line in composts and peat and a limited choice of paving and fencing. The fine-quality plants are difficult to fault. Many are grown on site – fuchsias, cyclamen and primroses to name but a few. In the late summer and early autumn you can buy home-grown dahlias and chrysanthemums at the lovely cut-flower stall. Herbaceous perennials and heathers were in beautiful condition on the day our inspector visited and there were some very good alpines and conifers, though the choice of other trees was sadly limited. Wide paved areas and distinct display beds make up the sensible exterior layout. Signposting could be better, though once you have found your plants they are clearly labelled with prices and instructions. Staff are pleasant and ready to give advice at any time or to help with loading.

Prices £££
Facilities Parking, 90 cars. Garden advice service. Delivery service
Open Every day 8.30am to 7pm (closes 5pm in winter)
Credit cards Access, Visa

WORCESTER Hereford and Worcester   map 3
Palmers Nurseries

Worcester Garden Centre,   *Tel* Worcester (0905) 51231
Droitwich Road, Worcester WR3 7SW
On the A38 2 miles north of Worcester city centre, just outside the city boundary

This garden centre is supported by nearly 20 acres of growing land and it endeavours to supply a specialist range of shrubs, trees, climbers, and conifers. The nurseries behind the centre are not closed to the public, but the sales take place at the centre itself. It is a friendly, family-run place and the layout has been carefully thought out; wide paths lead around the flat site and each group of plants is placed in alphabetical order. Signposting is clear and labelling includes information on soil and light requirements as well as plant descriptions. The plants themselves are neatly displayed, well watered and looked after. The indoor area is small but well organised and offers a limited selection of the smaller garden tools and materials. There is also a choice of greenhouses and sheds, but no mowers or mechanical tools. The staff are plentiful and all of them are willing to help out with advice or loading the car. It has a good name locally for quality at a reasonable price.

Prices £££
Facilities Parking, 70 cars. Toilets. Ice cream and soft drinks. Garden advice service. Delivery service. Free price list. Plant catalogue 30p
Open Mon to Sat 8.30am to 5.30pm
Credit cards Access, Visa

WORKSOP Nottinghamshire   map 2

Dukeries Garden Centre

Welbeck, Worksop S80 3LT   *Tel* Worksop (0909) 476506
On the A60 Mansfield Road, 4 miles from Worksop

This is a new centre which has been built on the edge of the Duke of Portland's Welbeck Estate. It has been undergoing extensive reorganisation since a change in management in 1983, and developments planned include an adventure playground, a caged bird shop and a department selling garden construction materials. The car park is one thing which could certainly do with improvement – on the day our inspector visited there were enormous puddles of water, some up to 4in deep! The setting really is splendid and the site itself is well laid out with trees and shrubs displayed alphabetically in the large exterior space. The walkways have been made a little too narrow for comfort though. Signposting is very good, inside as well as out. There are several sizeable greenhouses stocking small selection of tools and sundries and a wide choice of chemicals and composts. The centre specialises in aquatics, not only cold-water fish, garden ponds and equipment, but also tropical and marine fish and reptiles. Greenhouses, sheds and garden furniture and ornaments are also stocked. The choice and condition of the houseplants is excellent and the large selection of air plants is very well presented. Conifers and shrubs are also kept in good health and there is a substantial choice on offer. Although labelling is clear and the layout simple to follow, a little more information could usefully be provided. This centre shows a lot of promise and is worth a visit.

Prices £££
Facilities Parking, 1,000 cars. Toilets. Restaurant
Open Every day 10am to 6pm
Credit cards Access, Visa

WORTHING W. Sussex   map 5

Tesco Garden Centre

Ranany Road, West Durrington,   *Tel* Worthing (0903) 64439
Worthing BN13 3ED

*Signposted off the A259 Worthing to Littlehampton road, 2 miles from Worthing
town centre*

Tesco Garden Centre concentrates on selling a lot of seasonal plants at the
appropriate times of year, thus ensuring a quick and large turnover of
stock. So, for those who know what they want, there is a good variety of
quality plants and shrubs on sale during planting time, at reasonable
prices. The fast-selling lines of bedding in the spring and bulbs in the
autumn are typical of plants to be found, but there is also a backbone of
trees and shrubs which includes a good range of fast-growing conifers for
hedging. All plants are well cared for. Labels for groups of plants are good;
they are clearly displayed and carry illustrations and descriptions of the
plants. Individual labels are more variable and while some are excellent,
others are very washed out. The outside area has been well laid out and
there is an excellent car park with spaces near all the basic amenities
reserved for the disabled. The tools and sundries section is
comprehensively stocked at all times of the year and will satisfy the needs
of the average gardener at reasonable prices. Sheds are delivered pre-built
and ready for immediate use. Staff are not always on hand, but can be
summoned by the cashier to give you help and guidance. A report on
Tesco's cannot be completed without some mention of the supermarket
adjacent to the centre which allows the more mundane shopping to be
dealt with on the same trip.

Prices £££
Facilities Parking, 400 cars. Toilets. Garden advice service. Reference catalogue for
shrubs. Free leaflets for greenhouses and sheds
Open Mon to Wed 9am to 8pm (closes 5.30pm in winter), Thur and Sat 8.30am to
8pm, Fri 8.30am to 9pm
Credit cards Access, Visa

WOTTON-UNDER-EDGE Gloucestershire   map 3

Midland Nurseries

Tytherington, Wotton-under-Edge   *Tel* Thornbury (0454) 413003
GL12 8QE

*Adjacent to the school in the centre of Tytherington village, 1 mile off the A38,
2 miles from Thornbury*

This nursery specialises in fuchsias, geraniums and bedding plants but also
sells a reasonable range of other plants. It is in a rural setting and, being
small, the layout is compact and clearly defined. The owner's son is keen to
specialise in clematis. When our inspector visited there were already many
of these crowding out one greenhouse, and the list of varieties available
will be of great interest to anyone anxious to branch out from the

251

Jackmaniis and Nelly Mosers. An excellent range of honeysuckle and other climbing plants is also worth exploring – the rest of the small area is turned over to shrubs, alpines, conifers and perennials. Quality of the specialist plants is excellent and the rest of the stock is also good. Labelling, however, is very patchy. All the staff are very helpful, and knowledgeable advice is provided by the owner and son. This is a traditional nursery, not a garden centre – no tools and sundries are stocked (though you can order greenhouses) and there are no extra amenities apart from a small car park. However, the nursery also owns a garden shop in the High Street, Thornbury, and this is fairly well stocked with container-grown shrubs, perennials and alpines, as well as seeds, bulbs and hand tools. The nursery runs open evenings for gardening clubs and horticultural societies.

Prices £££
Facilities Parking, 12 cars. Garden advice service
Open Mon to Fri 10am to 5pm, Sat and Sun 10am to 1pm. Closed Christmas and Boxing Day
Credit cards Access, Visa

WYCHBOLD Hereford and Worcester   map 3

Webbs Garden Centre   🐾 ★

Wychbold, Droitwich WR9 0DG   *Tel* Wychbold (052 786) 245
On the A38 between Bromsgrove and Droitwich, ½ mile from junction 5 of the M5

Although adjacent to a busy trunk road the centre lies well back and is screened by a mature cupressus hedge. To add to the country atmosphere there is a stream running by the centre where customers are encouraged to take picnics. It would be worth while bringing a hamper because the range of things to see could keep the family busy for some time. The centre covers 30 acres and there are franchisees with their own sizeable displays of greenhouses and summer houses, walling, paving and rockery stones and a camping exhibit. There is a wide selection of good-quality hand tools (although no power tools) and the display of dried grasses and flowers is both attractive and impressive. A wide range of garden ornaments and furniture is also sold. The centre is very well laid out with wide slabbed paths, clear signposts and consistently legible and informative labelling. This provides an ordered and healthy environment for the myriad of plants stocked which are all in prime condition. Webbs now houses the National Collection of forsythia – 24 varieties are on show including one from the Ming Tombs in China. Houseplants are a speciality and a further addition in this department is planned. The selection of bulbs sold in the autumn is superb and a vast selection of seed is stocked. The staff are easy to spot by their uniforms and are all helpful. A new and prominently sited information area is due to be built in 1985.

Prices ££££
Facilities Parking, 400 cars. Toilets. Vending machines. Picnic area. Play area. Garden advice service. Delivery service. Free seasonal price lists for many plants. Plant catalogue 50p
Open Mon to Sat 9am to 5.45pm (opens 9.30am Wed), Sun and bank holidays 10am to

5pm (closes 5pm every day Dec to Feb). Closed Christmas and Boxing Day
Credit cards Access, Visa

YELLAND Devon map 3
Yelland Manor Garden Centre

Pottery Lane, Yelland, *Tel* Barnstaple (0271) 860534
near Barnstaple EX31 3EL
Very near the centre of the village about 100 yds off the A39. Midway between
Bideford and Barnstaple

This is a small, family-run centre which serves the surrounding counties.
The quality of the trees and shrubs is reasonably good and the overall
stocks are quite comprehensive, including some old plum and apple
varieties. The tools and sundries department carries a small range of most
standard gardening equipment and materials, although our inspector
spotted no garden furniture or houseplants. The layout of the outside
section is not particularly commendable, being somewhat jumbled and not
clearly signposted. However, we are told that the centre was rearranging
many display beds and installing an automatic watering system at the time
of our inspection. The centre's policy is to have an 'informal' layout. The
indoor area is also disappointing – it is crowded and disorganised.
Nevertheless, the framework is there and provides a good foundation for
further improvements which we gather are to be made. The labelling is
variable. Some labels are typed, easy to read and informative, while other
plants bear no details at all, not even variety or price. When our inspector
called, there was only one member of staff on duty but normally there is
someone available to give expert help and advice. Generally the impression
of this centre is that it requires a little more care and effort in order to fully
realise its potential. Although there are no special toilet facilities, those in
the owner's home can be used on request.

Prices £££
Facilities Garden advice service. Delivery service
Open Mon to Sat 9am to 5pm (closed 1pm to 2pm), Sun 10am to 5pm (closed 1pm to
2.30pm). Closed Christmas

YORK N. Yorkshire map 2
Challis Garden Centre

Challis of York, Boroughbridge Road, *Tel* York (0904) 976161
York YO2 6QE
On the A59 to Harrogate, just outside York city boundary

A comprehensive centre on the suburban outskirts of York. The business is
based on the nearby wholesale nursery which grows houseplants, trees
and shrubs, and these are the centre's strongest areas. The condition of the
trees and shrubs at the time of inspection was good, but amidst their wide
range of other plants some poor herbaceous perennials, alpines and strawberries were evident (suffering from the drought). Plants are rather pricey.
A good site plan is set up at the entrance and signposting is clear. Outdoor

ENGLAND

sections are sensibly laid out by type of plant and season of interest (for example, dwarf conifers, summer-flowering shrubs, peat-loving plants). Labels for groups of plants were good, though when we inspected individual labels were erratic and there was room for improvement. Most larger items of gardening equipment and a wide range of tools and sundries are stocked, as well as non-gardening items such as preserves, flower-arranging materials and pet accessories. Sheds and greenhouses are sold under franchise and there's a wide range of garden furniture to choose from. Staff at the centre are generally helpful and the garden advice centre is open at peak times.

Prices £££££
Facilities Parking, 323 cars. Toilets. Vending machines and confectionery. Play area. Garden advice service. Delivery service. Plant price list and catalogue 15p
Open Every day 9am to 8pm (closes 6pm in winter). Closed Christmas and Boxing Day
Credit cards Access, Visa

Fairways Garden Centre

Heslington Lane, York YO1 5DY   *Tel* York (0904) 642864
Near the golf course on Heslington Lane

This centre has only just opened and although it may not make its name as a nursery, it is worth visiting for its vast stock of garden accessories. All the equipment and bits and pieces for the garden are stocked. The choice of plant containers is one of the best our inspector had ever seen – pots and tubs and troughs of every description, from small, fancy bowls to large clay patio containers. The larger items such as sheds, greenhouses, paving and power tools are stocked as well. The inside area takes up most of the site and the layout is excellent. The exterior area is much smaller and reasonably well arranged. Plant stocks were limited when our inspector visited and the labelling was not particularly good. The staff are few in number, but very courteous and helpful.

Prices Information not available
Facilities Parking, 140 cars. Vending machines. Delivery service
Open Every day 9am to 8pm. Closes 5.30pm in winter. Closed 3 days at Christmas and New Year's Day
Credit cards Access, Visa

Wales

Woodlands Services and Supplies

Brooklands, Mardy, Abergavenny   *Tel* Abergavenny (0873) 5431
NP7 6NU
On the A465 Abergavenny to Hereford road, just north of the village of Mardy,
about ½ mile from Abergavenny

This centre is worth a visit for local gardeners, though the selection of
plants probably doesn't warrant a long journey. Plants are mainly grown
on site and are well cared for and in good condition. The choice of plants is
reasonable and if your requirements are fairly standard then you shouldn't
be disappointed. The site is well laid out with wide gravel paths, and plants
are easily located. Large signposts mark the different sections which are
arranged alphabetically. Individual labelling could do with improvement –
our inspector came away with a few aches after all the bending and
stretching required to read them. Seeds and fertilisers are stocked in a
well-laid-out shop, while a larger shed area houses a very good selection of
garden ornaments, tubs and stone furniture. Houseplants should be
available from 1985. Hand tools, greenhouses, sheds, fencing and paving
can also be bought. There is no water-gardening equipment – a shame,
since there is a lovely stream running down the hill through the middle of
the site and it could be used to advantage. The stream is only covered at the
bottom of the hill, so do keep an eye on small toddlers.

Prices £££
Facilities Parking, 50 cars. Toilets. Ice cream. Garden advice service. Delivery service.
Price list and catalogue 50p
Open Mon to Fri 8am to 5pm, Sat 9.30am to 5pm, Sun 2pm to 5pm. Closed 7 to 14
days at Christmas and New Year
Credit cards Access, Visa

East-Lynne Gardens

Usk Road, Caerleon NP6 1LP   *Tel* Caerleon (0633) 422743
100 yds north of Caerleon on the main road to Usk, about 3 miles from Newport

East-Lynne Gardens is a nursery as well as a garden centre. All plants are
grown on the premises and they are of good quality and are well tended.
The range of dwarf conifers and heathers is particularly good, while
geraniums and fuchsias are also a speciality. Plants are arranged logically
and signposted so that most categories are simple to find, particularly as
the centre is quite small. Gravel paths provide a firm footing and the plots
are generally neat and well organised. Plant labelling, however, leaves a lot
to be desired. There are no group labels and only abbreviated tags on some

plants. There are hardly any prices marked at all. The indoor area is well lit and well arranged. It contains a basic range of tools and sundries. The water gardening section is fairly small, concentrating more on fish than on aquatic plants. Most larger accessories are stocked including greenhouses, sheds, fencing and paving. This centre has been developing over the years and has been slowly improving its presentation and range of goods. Even though it doesn't provide many of the facilities of the bigger centres, it's worth a visit for the inexpensive plants. Our main criticism is the inadequate labelling and pricing.

Prices ££
Facilities Parking, 70 cars. Ice cream. Garden advice service. Delivery service
Open Every day 9am to 6pm (closes 5.30pm in winter)

CARDIFF Glamorgan
map 3

The Dutch Nursery in Wales
✿

J. Deen & Son, Maes-y-Bryn Nurseries,   *Tel* Cardiff (0222) 777050
Bridge Road, St. Mellons, Cardiff CF3 9YJ
Just north of the M4, off the A48 Cardiff to Newport road east of Lisvane

This is a nursery with no frills attached. For quality plants at very reasonable prices it probably surpasses most other nurseries and garden centres in the area. The owner is a genuine horticulturalist and top-class grower, and the friendliness and cheerfulness of all the staff is a real pleasure. A comprehensive range of plants is stocked with the quality and selection of conifers being most impressive. The shrubs are also of good quality and those available tend to be the less-common varieties, so if you are after the run-of-the-mill you could be out of luck. One area where the nursery falls down is with its plant labelling – it could certainly do with improvement. The layout is also less than perfect and the access ways are narrow, but for all its faults with presentation, the standard and friendly atmosphere of this nursery more than compensate. Few sundries are stocked apart from fertilisers and composts, hand tools, sheds and an unusual collection of stone sinks and pots. A new houseplant centre opened in late 1984 and other changes to layout and presentation are planned.

Prices ££
Facilities Parking, 70 cars. Toilets. Vending machine. Garden advice service. Delivery service
Open Every day 8am to 8pm (closes at dusk in winter)

CASTLETON Gwent
map 3

Vale Garden Centre

Newport Road, Castleton,   *Tel* Castleton (0633) 680002
Cardiff CF3 8UQ
Just east of Castleton on the A48 between Cardiff and Newport

A well-landscaped site reputed to be one of the largest centres in the country. Its massive size obviously allows a vast range of goods to be stocked, including many not directly related to gardening such as camping equipment, swimming pools and pets, sold under franchise. There is a particularly good selection of tools of different brands as well as the larger gardening items such as greenhouses, sheds and mowers also sold under franchise. (Paving, stoneware and fencing are to be stocked from spring 1985.) All the separate areas in the centre are nicely laid out with wide paths. Plants are placed on raised staging about 2 ft off the ground, so that you don't have to bend much to examine them. Some more signposting would be useful considering the size of the site. Group labelling of plants, however, is informative and illustrated, and each plant is marked with a name and price. The overall quality is good with a wide range, but prices are a bit high. Not a place to visit if you want the intimacy of a small grower, but the choice here is enormous. There are qualified horticulturalists on the staff and their red uniforms make them easy to spot. All staff are very helpful and friendly.

Prices £££££
Facilities Parking, 500 cars. Toilets. Restaurant. Garden advice service. Delivery service. Plant and gardening catalogue £1.95, with £2 voucher included
Open Mon to Wed 9am to 6pm, Thurs and Fri 9am to 7pm, Sat 9am to 6.30pm, Sun 10am to 6.30pm (closes 5.30pm every day in winter)
Credit cards Access, Visa

DENBIGH Clywd   map 2

Green Fingers Garden Centre   ✿

Rhyl Road, Denbigh LL16 5TQ   *Tel* Denbigh (0745 71) 5279
On the north-east side of Denbigh, in Ryle Road (A525) adjoining the Kwick Save car park

This centre is situated in pleasant surroundings on the outskirts of the historic old town of Denbigh. It is a pleasant centre to visit, above all because of its straightforward layout and approach. It is of moderate size and purpose-designed so that display areas are well laid out. One shortcoming is that the paths are surfaced with gravel chippings which makes them awkward for pushchairs or wheelchairs. The range of equipment is limited and they stock no power tools, lawnmowers or water gardening equipment, but there is a comprehensive collection of fertilisers and garden chemicals. The selection of plants stocked is good, with an especially wide choice of ericaceous plants, particularly heathers. There is also an interesting range of rare ornamental trees and shrubs. Overall quality is very good. There is an orderly arrangement of labels and nearly all are illustrated. Where handwritten labels are used these are clearly written. It is particularly easy to inspect the alpines as they are placed on raised beds for the customer's convenience. The staff are knowledgeable and helpful and the owner is always available for expert advice.

Prices £££
Facilities Parking, 200 cars. Play area. Garden advice service. Delivery service. Free price lists for fencing, sheds and greenhouses

Open Nov to Feb, Tues to Sat 9.30am to 5pm, Sun 10am to 4pm. Mar to Oct, opens 9.30am, closes 5.30 Tues and Wed, 6pm Thurs, 7pm Fri, 5pm Sat and Sun. Closed Mondays except bank holidays

---

HAVERFORDWEST Dyfed map 3

Rhos Garden and Plant Centre ✿

The Rhos, Haverfordwest SA62 4AU *Tel* Rhos (043 786) 232
3 miles east of Haverfordwest, 1 mile south of the A40, follow the signs to Rhos and Picton Castle Gardens

A mile along a quiet country lane you'll find the hamlet of Rhos where this garden centre sits amid some lovely wooded countryside. The Cleddan estuary is only a couple of miles away. It is a small centre with a family atmosphere which grows and propagates a lot of its own plants. The range of plants stocked is comprehensive and they're all kept in good condition, including one or two 'treasures' dotted about such as rare varieties of decorative shrubs. The selection of dwarf conifers is very impressive. The group labelling is well done with a fair amount of illustration, although no instructions are given. There are plans to introduce a computer system for labelling and pricing in the near future. The layout of the outside section can be somewhat confusing, but once you get to grips with the system it works quite well. A pleasantly arranged covered section (soon to be extended) contains most tools and sundries and manages to keep up to date with new products. There are only one or two garden buildings and not much in the way of fencing, but there is a nice range of hand tools and spare parts and an outstanding range of high-quality troughs, tubs, urns and pots. The centre offers a landscaping service. The staff are very helpful and keen. They are a mixture of young, less experienced members and fully qualified people who have been at the centre for nearly 20 years.

Prices £££
Facilities Parking, 30 cars. Toilets. Vending machines. Garden advice service. Delivery service. Free price list for plants
Open Mon to Fri 8am to dusk, Sat 9am to dusk, Sun 10am to dusk (closes 6pm Aug to Mar)

Vincent Davies Garden Centre

Fishguard Road, Haverfordwest *Tel* Haverfordwest (0437) 3849
SA62 4BT
On the A40 Haverfordwest to Fishguard road, north of Haverfordwest

This centre has been expanding its accessories section for some time and consequently the space given over to the plants has diminished. However, it has always been possible to find something out of the ordinary amidst the bread-and-butter plants. The covered area housing gardening hardware and other bits and pieces is now quite large. It stocks a wide range of both power and hand tools, composts and chemicals. All of the larger items of garden equipment such as paving and greenhouses are also sold. The site also includes a fitted kitchen and bedroom centre. The selection of plants is somewhat smaller, although plant beds are being raised and re-organised to cope with a wider range of stock. Geraniums, fuchsias and pelargoniums are grown on the premises. Everything else is bought in and the stocks are very seasonal, with the main deliveries being in September and March. There were plans to introduce aquatic plants into the range in spring 1985. Plant quality is good and all potbound specimens are sold off at half price. Labelling is also very good: a lot of illustrations and good, big labels are used; there are few cultural instructions but wall charts are posted showing suitable sites for different plants. The staff are reasonably knowledgeable and will try to help if they can. This set-up is part of the Vincent Davies supermarket, so if you want to save yourself two journeys you can combine your weekly shopping trip with an exploration of the plants and sundries on offer at this centre. A very attractive cafe provides home-made food and friendly service.

Prices £££
Facilities Parking, 80 cars. Toilets. Cafeteria. Garden advice service. Delivery service. Sundries catalogue 50p
Open Mon to Sat 9am to 5.30pm (closes 7pm Fri), Sun 10am to 4pm

---

HAWARDEN Clwyd   map 2

Daleside Nurseries

Gladstone Way, Hawarden   *Tel* Chester (0244) 532041
CH5 3HF
On the A550 Queensferry to Hawarden road, just north of Hawarden

Set in a quiet residential area near the Dee estuary, this is a centre that offers a good service in a locality which is not well endowed with garden centres. Of medium size, it is basically well laid out and each section is clearly designated, so finding the right plant is not difficult. It used to be a wholesale nursery supplying local garden centres, and still specialises in bedding and plants such as tomatoes, cucumbers, melons, vegetables, fuchsias, and cyclamen. Hanging baskets are also sold in season. The bedding plant section is being expanded further in 1985. It carries a more than adequate range of plants and 'for its size' has a particularly large choice among the conifers and shrubs. Staff keep themselves busy watering and tending the plants and this has paid off in the good shape of their stock. When our inspector visited, labelling was somewhat patchy with problems of fading apparent on a number of outdoor plants (a new labelling system is being installed). The trees, shrubs and herbaceous plants are on display outside, while a covered area houses a good array of the smaller gardening bits and pieces. Peat and composts are extensively stocked and you can also obtain barbecue equipment here. If you are having troubles with your lawn the 'lawn-care equipment for hire' may interest you. However, this is not a place to head for if in search of garden buildings, big power tools or construction materials. There is only a vending machine to provide refreshment, but fruit, cut flowers and vegetables can be bought on the premises.

Prices ££££
Facilities Parking, 60 cars. Toilets. Vending machines. Garden advice service. Delivery service
Open Mon to Sat 9am to 5.30pm, Sun 10am to 5.30pm (closes 5pm every day in winter). Closed 10 days over Christmas and New Year

---

LLANBEDR Gwynedd   map 2
Aber Artro Garden Centre and Nursery

Llanbedr LL45 2PA   *Tel* Llanbedr (034 123) 301
Just out of Llanbedr on the Gwynfryn road

Down a lane, over a bridge and through a stables entrance might make access to this nursery a little awkward, but the site itself is very well organised and the space has been fully utilised with greenhouses, plant beds, orchard and office. The location is the converted kitchen garden of an old country house, set within some beautiful woodland by the Artro River. The paths around the grounds are flat and wide, with smooth surfaces making them suitable for the elderly or those in wheelchairs. An old-world atmosphere pervades the centre, and the staff show no sign of the hard-sell but are keen, informal and will attend to customers at the first signs of difficulty. The majority of plants are home grown. Stocks of hardy plants suitable for coastal regions are the best buy. Because the site is in a 'frost pocket' all the plants are particularly cold resistant and stock is generally strong and healthy. Although the selection is not that large, most common varieties are available and two interesting finds were evergreen honeysuckle and climbing hydrangea. There is also a good selection of hebe, azaleas, rhododendrons and pieris. Plants are usually very well labelled and provide a considerable amount of hand-written, descriptive information; lettering is rather small, though, and some writing has become weathered. If you are interested in gardening accessories, there is an affiliated shop about a mile down the road towards Llanbedr. It consists of a large building containing an excellent variety of tools and sundries, including a very good choice of seeds, as well as a yard full of sheds, fencing, furniture and greenhouses.

Prices £££
Facilities Parking, nursery 20 cars, garden centre 10 cars. Garden advice service. Delivery service. Plant price list
Open Mon to Fri 9am to 5pm. Closed Sat pm and Sun
Credit cards Access, Visa

LLANELLI Dyfed   map 3
Cefn Vale Garden Centre

Bynea, Llanelli SA14 9ST   *Tel* Llanelli (0554) 772189
4 miles from Llanelli on the A4070 to Swansea

Located on the main road in a light industrial area, this is a centre which doesn't offer a remarkable range of goods, but fills a need for the local gardening community. It has recently been taken over by the Wyevale group and since then some improvement and new building has taken place. This should have been completed early in 1985, extending the range of goods available. The layout is quite good – ample spacing allows easy viewing and plants are arranged alphabetically, some on raised beds. There is a reasonable range of most popular plants with a selection of shrubs and indoor plants of special interest. The overall impression of plant quality is good, but generally prices tend to be rather high. At the time of our inspection, most plants were labelled but some labels had suffered badly from fading. Descriptive labelling could be improved. Tools and sundries similarly offer a basic range of stock all attractively displayed – paving will be available from spring 1985. There are plenty of staff on hand and they can be quickly spotted by their uniforms. They are helpful when approached.

Prices £££££
Facilities Parking, 200 cars. Toilets. Cafeteria. Garden advice service. Delivery service. Plant catalogue £1.95 (includes vouchers worth £4)
Open Every day 9am to 6pm (closes 5.30pm in winter). Closed Christmas and Boxing Day
Credit cards Access, Visa

Swiss Valley Garden Centre

Felinfoel, Llanelli   *Tel* Llanelli (0554) 759712
On the A476 Llanelli to Llandeilo road, 2½ miles north of Llanelli

A good, all-round centre which should meet the requirements of most gardeners. Re-organisation and extensions were being carried out when our inspector visited, to provide a play area and display areas for furniture and bedding plants, so things are likely to get even better. The layout is reasonable with shrubs and trees arranged in alphabetical order, making it easy to find what you want. There is no signposting at present, though this is to be rectified. There is a comprehensive range of most garden accessories, but no lawnmowers or paving. Composts, chemicals, plant pots and seeds offer a particularly wide choice. The centre also sells a good range of plants and you should have no problem finding something to please you, particularly if you are after shrubs and conifers. The quality overall is good. Labelling was also commended by our inspector, consisting of clear, readable and informative notices at the back of each display and printed tags on all individual plants. There is also a selection of fact sheets available. The staff keep themselves busy tending displays which often requires extra work since the site can be windy and plants tend to get blown about.

Prices ££££
Facilities Parking, 60 cars. Toilets. Vending machine. Garden advice service. Delivery service
Open Mon to Fri 8.30am to 5.30pm, weekends and bank holidays 10am to 6pm. Closed 25 Dec to 1 Jan
Credit cards Access, Visa

★ *Star awards are given to garden centres and nurseries which met with our inspector's whole-hearted approval.*

Wellfield Nurseries

Tom Jones & Sons, Gorslas,   *Tel* Cross Hands (0269) 842257
Llanelli SA14 7HP

1 mile north of Cross Hands, 200 yds off the A476 (follow signs to the nursery)

This nursery has a very good selection of plants, all of outstanding quality.
There's a reasonable range of most plants, and an excellent selection of
conifers, deciduous trees and shrubs. Sundries are not really a feature here.
Stocks include the indispensable chemicals and composts, plus a few small
ornaments which are stored in a small, rather disorganised indoor area,
hand tools, furniture, greenhouses and sheds. The plants are well laid out
but some paths are rather narrow and there is no signposting, nor any
logical arrangement of plant species. Some sections have some very good
general labelling as well as individual tags, but this is slightly spoiled by
areas where there's no labelling at all. A working staff keep busy with plant
maintenance, advising the public and carrying goods to cars. A traditional
nursery not trying to be everything to everybody.

Prices £££
Facilities Parking, 12 cars. Toilets. Garden advice service. Delivery service. Plant
price list and catalogue 20p
Open Mon to Sat 8am to 5pm, Sun 10am to 5pm

LLANGAN S. Glamorgan   map 3

Timbersgreen Nursery and Garden Centre

St. Mary's Hill Road, Llangan,   *Tel* Pencoed (0656) 860168
near Bridgend CF35 5DR

*About 1 mile north of the A48. Turn off at the B4268 junction between Cowbridge
and Bridgend*

Not an easy place to find since the pleasant, hill-top site is not signposted.
The centre appears to meet the needs of the local community and our
inspector found evidence of this in the brisk business and the familiar,
friendly atmosphere. This is a family-run business and there is a nursery
adjacent to the centre which produces a large proportion of the stock. The
range of plants available is reasonable, with shrubs, heathers, trees and
dwarf conifers offering the greatest choice. The quality was variable at the
time of our inspection, but this could have been due to the time of year and
drought conditions. Sundries are to be found in a modern shop and include
garden furniture, chemicals and composts, pond equipment, lots of garden
ornaments and pots, and hand tools. Sheds and fencing are also available.
The presentation of this modest centre and nursery is somewhat patchy.
The car park and shop are well arranged while outside among the plant
displays things are much less orderly. There are few labels for groups of
plants and individual labels are difficult to find and read, but there are
plans to improve this area. In spite of the criticisms, this is a useful, local
garden centre with friendly, approachable staff.

Prices £££
Facilities Parking, 70 cars. Vending machine. Garden advice service. Delivery service

Open Every day 9.30am to 5.30pm (closed 1pm to 2pm Aug and Sept). Closed 25 Dec to 2 Jan
Credit cards Access, Visa

MARSHFIELD Gwent   map 3

Fletcher Garden Services   ✄

Marshfield, Newport CF3 8UB   *Tel* Castleton (0633) 680419
In Marshfield village, south of the A48 mid-way between Newport and Cardiff

A rather small but well laid out centre specialising in garden buildings. There is no signposting to help you find what you want, but the size makes that less important than in most centres. The range of sheds and greenhouses is good and most other sundries are available including water gardening equipment. Prices of gardening equipment and plants are very competitive and the shelves are packed with goods. Good-quality shrubs and conifers are stocked and there is the standard range of popular plants as well as a small selection of houseplants. The only plants not up to standard when our inspector visited were the herbaceous perennials which were suffering from lack of water. Group and individual labels were typed out, but some were a little faded. There are usually two staff available at the cash desk, but they were not noted for their friendliness.

Prices £
Facilities Parking, 50 cars. Toilets. Garden advice service. Delivery service. Free price lists for garden buildings, fencing, paving and gates. Sundries catalogue 25p
Open Mon to Sat 9am to 6pm, Sun 10am to 6pm (closes 5pm every day in winter). Closed for 2 weeks over Christmas

---

NANTGARW Mid Glamorgan   map 3

Caerphilly Garden Centre

Penrhos, Nantgarw,   *Tel* Caerphilly (0222) 861511
near Cardiff CF4 7UN
Turn off on the A470 Cardiff to Methyr Tydfil road ¼ mile up Nantgarw Hill

A windy site on high, open ground between two valleys. The centre has an attractively arranged interior which stocks a very wide range of chemicals, gadgets and furniture. All the larger items are also sold, including greenhouses, sheds, fencing, paving and pond equipment. The display areas outside are still being improved and developed. On the day our inspector visited there were some nice, newly laid out raised beds for alpines and shrubs with attractive walkways under arches. The rest of the layout, however, was fairly basic with no apparent rhyme or reason in its design. The condition of the plants was fairly average, although houseplants were very well cared for. If you are a rose fancier there is an impressive range of varieties to browse through. Labelling could be considerably improved both in content and legibility. Prices are always clear! All staff, indoor and out, are friendly and helpful. If other members of your party are showing signs of boredom there is a 'Noah's Ark Mall' with animals for the children to visit (40p) or three small shops selling local

wooden and metal crafts and pottery. Extensive improvements are
planned, designed to make the centre a good place for a day's outing for
the gardener and family.

Prices £££
Facilities Parking, 300 cars. Toilets. Tea room. Play area. Garden advice service.
Delivery service. Catalogues and price lists for some stocks
Open Every day 9am to 8.30pm (closes 5.30pm in winter)
Credit cards Access, Visa

PENHOW Gwent   map 3
Duckpool Farm Nurseries

Parc Seymour, Penhow,   *Tel* Penhow (0633) 400287
Newport NP6 3AE
Between Newport and Chepstow, ½ mile off the A48

This one-man enterprise does not supply the range of goods on offer at
large centres, nor can it deal with a vast influx of customers, but for the
keen and knowledgeable gardener, who is looking for quality in plants and
concern from staff, a recommendation is due. Peaceful, rural surroundings
enclose the small site. Facilities are few, access is tricky and the car park can
only manage about half a dozen cars. However, the site has been well
arranged, there is ample space between plant groupings, and paths are all
grassed over. The range of plants is not great, but it covers most areas of
interest and offers an excellent choice of ericas and a good number of
conifers. The real joy about these plants is that, although they are not well
presented and labels are non-existent, the quality is very good indeed.
There are none of the up-to-date methods familiar in so many centres and
most dealings have to go through the owner in the relaxed way common to
old-fashioned nurseries. As there is only the one man there it might be
necessary to wait a while before he is free to talk, but he is very helpful and
friendly when available. Nothing in the way of tools or sundries is
supplied.

Prices Information not available
Facilities Parking, 8 cars. Toilets
Open Tues to Sun 9am to 7pm (closes 4.30pm in winter)

PONTARDULAIS W. Glamorgan   map 3
Pontardulais Garden Centre

Alltygraban Road, Pontardulais   *Tel* Pontardulais (0792) 882561
SA4 1DX
On the A48 Swansea to Carmarthen road, 8 miles west of Swansea

This family-run centre is surrounded by hawthorn hedges and is set in
pleasant countryside. It is popular and many visitors come with their
children and take advantage of the play area and duck pond as well as the
plush, waitress-service tea rooms. Home-made cakes, fruit pies and an
outside seating area make this a great favourite. The selection of pots,

ornaments, fencing and paving steals the show, and these are all laid out around the car park. The rest of the sundries available consist of hand tools, greenhouses, sheds and an extensive range of fertilisers. A lot of the large, outside area is devoted to garden hardware, leaving the plant sections relatively small. The range of plants is rather sparse with just a few of each type on display. The main stocks are shrubs, conifers and trees. Overall quality is very good. The layout could do with some improvement. It is organised more like a garden than a garden centre and some plants are tucked away in corners. Paths are either very wide or extremely narrow and there is little which is clearly signposted. Labelling also needs attention. A place with plenty of potential, but in need of a wider range of plants and some re-arranging.

Prices £££
Facilities Parking, 100 cars. Toilets. Tea room. Play area. Garden advice service. Delivery service. Free price list for paving, sheds etc., catalogue £1.25
Open Every day, 8am to 6.30pm in summer, 9am to 5pm in winter
Credit card Visa

PONTYPOOL Gwent   map 3

Coed-y-Paen Garden and Leisure Centre

near Pontypool NP4 5SY   *Tel* Usk (029 13) 2348
Off the A449 Caerleon to Usk road at Llangibby or Llanbadach – follow Coed-y-Paen signs

This nursery is very small and its range may not be extensive, but it is very well laid out in an attractive position and is worthy of support while it becomes more established and broadens its range. Sitting on a hilltop, the site has lovely views overlooking Llandegffydd Reservoir. There are plenty of places to sit down and survey the setting and the display area. The outside area is being expanded and the selection of plants will no doubt increase to fill the space. At the moment there is a small range of most common varieties and they are generally in good condition, notably the trees, soft fruits and heathers. The only labelling provided is on individual plants and these do not contain any growing instructions, so it is necessary to ask the helpful couple who run the centre if you have any questions. It is also necessary to refer to them about prices, for these are seldom marked – rather a tedious process if you are doing a lot of shopping. The sundries department stocks a small selection of most things with the noticeable exception of any tools, hand or electric, and no paving. An additional feature for the casual visitor is a pottery and crafts section which shows good potential. If the new owners continue to 'find their feet' in the manner they have been, then this will develop into a very pleasant place to spend a few hours.

Prices Information not available
Facilities Parking, 100 cars. Ice cream. Play area. Garden advice service. Delivery service
Open Every day 8am to dusk. Closed a few days over Christmas

PYLE Mid Glamorgan

map 3

Glamorgan Vale Garden and Leisure Centre ✿ ⚑

Village Farm Industrial Estate, *Tel* Kenfig Hill (0656)
Pyle, Bridgend CF33 6NU 741443/743761
On the A48 mid-way between Bridgend and Port Talbot, a mile from junction 37 of the M4

The landscaping and planting around the centre has created a very attractive site at the entrance to a small industrial estate. The display areas have been well organised. The inside and outside areas are well balanced with the former devoted to a good selection of tools and indoor plants and the latter to plants and building materials. Lots of non-gardening items are sold and ceramics and silk flowers are a speciality. A new display area for greenhouses and garden buildings is planned. Plant quality is generally good – conifers, heathers, cacti and soft fruits are excellent. The range of plants is also good, particularly the conifers and heathers. Small plants are kept on raised beds. There is a good alphabetical labelling system, but labels tend to be descriptive and not particularly instructive. Advice is available at the information point, and staff are friendly and helpful. On a hot day it is nice to take a rest and sit down in the circular glasshouse cafe for a cup of tea and a snack. We recommend this centre for its comprehensive ranges of both plants and gardening equipment.

Prices ££££
Facilities Parking, 60 cars (plus overflow). Toilets. Restaurant. Garden advice service. Delivery service. Free plant catalogue
Open Summer Mon to Wed 9am to 6.30pm, Thurs to Sat 9am to 8pm, Sun 10am to 8pm. Winter Mon to Sat 9am to 5.30pm, Sun 10am to 5.30pm
Credit cards Access, Visa

RADYR S. Glamorgan

map 3

Ty-Nant Nursery and Garden Centre ✿

Pugh and Son, Morganstown, Radyr, *Tel* Radyr (0222) 842017
Cardiff CF4 8LJ
Just out of Cardiff. Take the A470 Cardiff to Merthyr Tydfil road, turn off at Castell Coch onto the B4262 towards Radyr. The centre is about 500yds along this road

Just off the main road in view of the imposing Castell Coch, this large centre is run as a friendly family business. It offers a good selection of all trees, shrubs and other plants and their quality is also satisfactory, although at the time of our inspection the perennials were suffering a little. About half the bedding plants and many houseplants are grown on site, and the centre also makes up and sells a considerable number of hanging baskets. Labelling for groups of plants is informative, but some individual labels suffer from fading. Both the indoor and outdoor areas are sizeable with the larger garden products such as sheds, paving and greenhouses having their own display section. The range of sundries is quite extensive, particularly the garden ornaments, but there are very few tools on display. The sections are nicely laid out with good paths and everything is kept tidy.

The number of staff is small but they are friendly and helpful and a display of their photographs adds to the family atmosphere of the place. A homely cafe supplies a good cup of coffee. Some problems occur on the access lane to the centre – there is a bend in the road which can cause considerable chaos at busy times.

Prices ££££
Facilities Parking, 100 cars (extra for 50 cars planned). Toilets. Restaurant. Garden advice service. Delivery service. Price list for sundries, sheds and greenhouses 50p, for paving, free
Open Mon to Sat 9am to 6pm, Sun 10am to 6pm. Closed 3 days over Christmas
Credit cards Access, Visa

RAGLAN Gwent   map 3
Welsh Tree Services

Abergavenny Road, Raglan NP5 2BH   *Tel* Raglan (0291) 690751
Two miles west of Raglan on the old A40 Abergavenny road, signposted Clytha at the Raglan and Abergavenny roundabouts

The centre is in a magnificent rural setting with outstanding views across to the Black Mountains. The countryside all around is beautiful, and with Raglan, Skenfrith, Grosmont and White Castle all near at hand, what better idea than to combine a visit to the centre with a day out touring the area. Welsh Tree Services caters for the local demand of country houses as well as for small gardens. The centre concentrates on trees, conifers, shrubs and fruit all grown in the adjoining nursery. They are well displayed and in fine condition. A reasonable range of other plants is kept but they were in rather a patchy state when our inspector visited. Signposting and labelling could be better (the centre tells us that these are being improved). Greenhouses, wood-burning stoves and double glazing are sold by concessionaires and there is a caravan and camping centre next door which is open from March to October. The indoor area is packed with sundries, but larger items such as power tools and lawnmowers are very limited in range. (The centre is planning to let more concession sites to include mowers and repairs.) A comprehensive choice of composts and garden pots is kept in stock. Staff are plentiful and friendly and the garden advice centre is prominently located. There is a clean and bright cafe on the premises where snacks or more substantial meals are available.

Prices ££££
Facilities Parking, 750 cars. Toilets. Cafeteria. Play area. Garden advice service. Delivery service. Free price lists for fencing, sheds, walling and rustic furniture
Open Summer, Tues to Sun 9am to 6pm. Winter, Tues to Fri 8am to 5pm, Sat and Sun 9am to 5pm. Closed Mon except bank holidays. Closed Christmas Eve to 2 Jan
Credit cards Access, Visa

SWANSEA W.Glamorgan   map 3
Swansea Garden Centre

Mill Lane, Blackpill, Swansea SA3 5BD   *Tel* Swansea (0792) 401509

Just west of the A4069 Mumbles road, at Blackpill in Swansea

This garden centre is set in very pleasant woodland with some lovely, mature trees. It is quite close to the beach at Swansea Bay and adjacent to Clyne Castle and Clyne Country Park. The centre is recommended for its wide stock of goods including tools, sundries and plants. There are no obvious omissions from the comprehensive range of plants, which includes a sizeable tree section and some good displays of shrubs and conifers. The outside areas next to the car park are the home for the larger, more cumbersome garden accessories including the standard sheds and paving not to mention a special swimming pool section. Greenhouses and power tools are not available. Smaller sundries and houseplants are kept in a large glasshouse complex. One of our inspector's criticisms of this centre was the layout and organisation. The indoor area is quite reasonable and surfacing outside is acceptable, but it can be very tricky to find what you are looking for. The signposting is poor and there appears to be no logic behind the way plants are arranged. There are no labels on display stands, and prices can be hard to locate. Plants were also rather neglected and weedy when inspected, with dead plants left out in the display beds. With a concerted effort to tidy up in some areas and a few more staff to help, this attractive centre could come into its own. A refreshment area offers home-made cakes.

Prices ££££
Facilities Parking. Toilets. Cafeteria. Garden advice service. Delivery service
Open Information not available

TAL-Y-CAFN Gwynedd   map 2
Bodnant Garden Nursery   ❀ ♿

Tal-y-Cafn, Colwyn Bay LL28 5RE   *Tel* Tyn-y-Groes (0492 67) 460
Just off the A470 Llanrwst to Glanconwy road at Tal-y-Cafn

A nursery concentrating on the production and sale of high-quality, rare ornamental trees and shrubs. It is found in the famous Bodnant Gardens in the Vale of Conwy. The surroundings are beautiful and one would find it difficult to resist spending some time in the Gardens themselves (set apart from the sales area). There is a charge of £1.50 made by the National Trust but entry is free for Fellows of the Royal Horticultural Society. The nursery may not be ideal for the beginner as the range of common-or-garden plants is limited and there are no tools or sundries, but they do stock herbaceous perennials, heathers, bulbs and conifers as well as shrubs and trees. There is an excellent selection of camellias, rhododendrons, magnolias, evergreen azaleas and rare and unusual plants such as Embothrium. Most are grown on the premises, quality is extremely high and prices reasonable. All plants and displays are labelled and the staff are most helpful. The nursery itself is comparatively small, but well laid out so that there is ample room to move around and inspect the merchandise. Well worth a visit, particularly if you love trees and shrubs.

Prices Information not available
Facilities Parking, 1,500 cars. Toilets. Kiosk serving light refreshments from April to

Sept. Garden advice service. Plant catalogue, 25p from shop or send an s.a.e. Plants sold by mail order
Open Mar to Oct, every day 9.30am to 5pm. Nov to early Mar, 9.30am to 4.30pm, (closed weekends in Jan and Feb). Closed for lunch 1pm to 2pm

TRELAWNYD Clwyd   map 2
Jackson's Nursery and Garden Centre

Trelawnyd, Dyserth, Rhyl LL18 6EB   *Tel* Dyserth (0745) 570680
On the A5151 close to Trelawnyd village, 2 miles off the A55 N. Wales trunk road

A comprehensive centre in a rural area near the North Wales coast. The layout is pleasant and orderly but inadequately signposted. A large and well-organised indoor area stocks garden accessories and nicely displayed houseplants. The centre specialises in the supply and erection of greenhouses and sheds, and a new water-gardening section was complete in 1984. Paving, garden furniture and ornaments are also sold. The quality of plants is generally very satisfactory, particularly the ericas and conifers, and the collections of these plants and the roses deserve a special mention. A rose propagation area is open to the public during the appropriate season and this can provide an interesting browse for the avid rose grower. Labelling was generally reasonable when our inspector visited, but some plants had been missed out and prices were often hard to find. There is a garden advice service and the staff are attentive and ready to answer questions. There are no refreshment facilities on site but there is a picnic area you can use. A toilet block was due to open in spring 1985.

Prices £££
Facilities Parking, 50 cars. Toilets. Play area. Garden advice service. Delivery service. Free price lists for roses, sheds and greenhouses. Price list for all nursery stock available from spring 1985
Open Every day 8.30am to 5pm
Credit cards Access, Visa

Scotland

ABERDEEN Grampian

map 1

Springhill Nurseries

Garden Centre, Lang Stracht,
Aberdeen AB2 6HY

Tel Aberdeen (0224) 693788

On the western edge of Aberdeen in the suburb of Mastrick. Lang Stracht runs from the ring road (Anderson Drive) to the A944

The setting amidst industrial units on the built-up edge of Aberdeen is uninspiring, but it's worth a visit to this nursery for the good-quality plants sold. There are about 1½ acres given over to container-grown plants , most of which are grown in a separate nursery area 10 miles from the city. The range of plants is good and the wide selection of alpines is conveniently displayed on waist-high shelving so they are easily inspected. Shrubs, trees, alpines, herbaceous and bedding plants are considered to be specialities. Labelling is variable, but it usually provides some descriptive information and each variety of shrub carries details of the plant and its aftercare. The external area is a little tight for space and the indoor area is rather crowded. The rock gardens display area is to be expanded, and a water-gardening section developed. The emphasis here is definitely on plants, but a range of tools and sundries is stocked which should satisfy the general needs of most gardeners. The number of staff is quite small, but barrows are provided for transporting goods to the car park.

Prices ££££
Facilities Parking, 60 cars. Toilets. Garden advice service. Delivery service. Free price lists for plants and sundries. Plant catalogue 30p
Open Every day 8am to 5pm (8.30am to 4.15pm in winter). Closed 25 and 26 Dec, 1, 2, 3 Jan and last Mon in Sept

W. Smith and Son

Hazlehead Garden Centre,
Aberdeen AB9 2QU

Tel Aberdeen (0224) 38658

3 miles west of Aberdeen centre in the suburb of Hazlehead, off Hazledene Road

There are several appealing features at this garden centre, not least of which is the attractive little show garden. Here you will find displays of many of the plants sold at the centre, all carefully labelled as in a botanic garden, and some of the greenhouses and sheds available for purchase are also shown being put to practical use. The entire site has been thoughtfully set out, the inside arranged on a simple linear plan and the outside with wide paths between plant beds and good signposting. A fairly large display room houses the pot-plants, while the range of tools and sundries is comprehensive. The shrubs, trees and other plants sold are typical of the area, and since they are propagated and cultivated at the centre they are hardy and suited to local conditions. The plants do tend to be quite expensive, though. Four grass seed mixtures are sold which the centre blends and mixes specifically for local soil conditions – very handy. The overall plant quality is good, with the shrubs better on average than the trees – roses are very healthy and provide a colourful splash throughout the summer. Most group labels are handwritten and are large enough to be easily read from a distance – some contain useful descriptive and cultural information. The helpful staff are easy to locate and even on the rainy day of our inspection they were out and about at work. Hazlehead Park is just across the road, so the children can let off steam while you enjoy browsing around the centre.

Prices £££££
Facilities Parking, 100 cars. Toilets. Vending machines. Garden advice service. Delivery service. Free price lists
Open Mon to Sat 9am to 5pm (closed Sat pm in winter)
Credit cards Access, American Express, Diners Club, Visa

ASHGILL Strathclyde   map 1

Fairview Nurseries and Garden Centre   ★

Ashgill, Larkhall ML9 3AE   *Tel* Larkhall (0698) 882951
At the Larkhall turning off the A74 midway between Garrion Bridge and Canderside Toll

The ex-mining village of Ashgill offers a treat to the gardener in the shape of this family-run nursery. The site is large and is carefully and thoughtfully laid out with no steps in any section. You will find all makes of tools here and somewhere among the acre of ornaments you're bound to find the pot of your choice. Greenhouses, sheds, frames and paving are all stocked as well as the smaller bits and pieces close to the gardener's heart. The comprehensive range of plants includes a marvellous collection of strong sturdy conifers, trees, bedding dahlias and chrysanthemums, and in the spring the choice of bedding annuals is impressive. Our inspector has special praise for the consistently good quality of the tomato plants and dahlias stocked at this centre. Some of the plants, including the bedding and vegetables, are grown in the adjoining nursery. All plants, indoors and out, are clearly labelled. A very good advice desk provides useful help year-round from professional gardeners, and the staff generally can't do enough for you. There are pleasant tea rooms which do 'high tea' and home-baking and if you still have the time and energy there is a rewarding time to be had at the picture gallery.

Prices £££
Facilities Parking, 50 cars. Toilets. Cafeteria. Play area. Garden advice service. Delivery service. Price lists for some plants
Open Every day 9am to 8.30pm in summer, 9.30am to 4.30pm in winter. Closed Christmas Day and New Year's week
Credit cards Access, Visa

Prices vary a lot at garden centres and nurseries. We've calculated a basket price for plants and given ratings from £ to ££££££ – very cheap to very expensive.

BERRIEDALE Highland map 1

Langwell Nurseries

Berriedale KW7 6HE   *Tel* Berriedale (059 35) 237
A mile off the A9 on a private road

These nurseries are found along a narrow and winding road next to
Langwell Gardens (open to the public June to October). The wooded valley
makes a lovely backdrop to the nurseries, and a visit can be combined with
a day out in lovely countryside. However, the serious gardener should
need no added incentive – this centre is worth a visit just for the plants. It
sells a wide range of good-quality plants suitable for growing in the area.
The choice of heathers is excellent and the selection of trees and shrubs and
fruit comes a close second. Wide gravel paths lead to the various display
areas. The houseplants and more tender outdoor varieties are kept in
several glasshouses, while the small shop stocks some chemicals and a few
tubs. The narrow door into the building can cause congestion, but once
inside it is orderly and well arranged. The staff are rather scarce but they
will readily show you around the site and can give some useful growing
tips. There are attractive refreshment areas both inside and out and a safe
area for children to play.

Prices Information not available
Facilities Parking, 100 cars. Toilets. Vending machines. Ice cream. Play area. Garden
advice service. Free plant price list
Open Mon to Fri 10am to 5pm, Sat and Sun 10am to 7pm (closed weekends in winter)

BLAIRGOWRIE Tayside map 1

James McIntyre & Sons

Moyness Nurseries and   *Tel* Blairgowrie (0250) 3135
Garden Centre, Coupar Angus Road,
Blairgowrie PH10 6UT
On the A923 Coupar Angus to Dundee road, ½ mile from Blairgowrie

This centre is sited in an attractive, tree-lined setting in the grounds of a
large country house. It offers a good service to customers and will replace
any failed plants immediately and order any items for you if they are not
kept in stock. The centre is of medium size and nicely laid out. It comprises
an exterior section, a display area and an indoor shop. There is a very good
range of tools and chemicals and the only items you won't be able to obtain
are sheds, water-gardening equipment and water plants. There is a
landscaping and garden design facility which offers free estimates. The
centre stocks a very good general range of plants. Quality is very
satisfactory and plants are neatly labelled and well packed and presented.
The nursery's speciality, soft fruit, deserves be singled out for mention –
you can buy it by mail order and all plants were of a high standard when
our inspector visited. The staff are happy to leave customers to browse
without pestering them, but always show an interest if approached for
help. A catalogue is also available.

Prices £££
Facilities Parking, 20 cars. Garden advice service. Delivery service. Free plant price list and free catalogue for fruit bushes. Plants sold by mail order
Open Mon to Sat 8am to 6pm (closes at dusk in winter)
Credit cards Access, Visa

CAIRNEYHILL Fife map 1

James Fairley & Co

The Rose Garden and Garden Centre, *Tel* Newmills (0383) 880223
Cairneyhill, Dunfermline KY12 8QT
On the A994 Dunfermline to Kilcardine road, 3 miles west of Dunfermline in the village of Cairneyhill

Overlooking farmland, on the edge of a small village, you'll find this surprisingly well-stocked centre. 'The best range of sundries I have seen', said our inspector and this is confirmed in the comprehensive list of goods stocked. Garden furniture and water-gardening equipment is sold, as well as the larger items such as fencing, sheds, and greenhouses. A wide range of plants is also available, all of very good quality, but a bit expensive. However, the centre's specialities are roses, trees and shrubs and many of these are grown on site. Labelling is excellent and the overall layout could be described as pleasant and well organised with good signposting. Even so there are plans to introduce more raised beds and pictorial labelling displays. A shop sells green groceries, cut flowers and chocolates, and also houses an Interflora agent who will make wedding displays and wreaths to order. A very impressive, family-run firm.

Prices £££££
Facilities Parking, 50 cars. Toilets. Vending machines. Play area. Garden advice service. Delivery service. Free price lists for plants in season
Open Every day 8am to 6pm (closes 5pm in winter). Closed Christmas and Boxing Day and 1 to 3 Jan
Credit card Access

CONON BRIDGE Highland map 1

Riverbank Nursery

Riverbank Road, Conon Bridge, *Tel* Dingwall (0349) 61720
near Dingwall IV7 8BT
In the centre of Conon Bridge, 2½ miles from Dingwall

This nursery is still partly under construction but it should prove to be a benefit to the local gardening community. It is found on the banks of the River Conon, well known for its salmon fishing, and the surrounding countryside is very pleasant. The nursery has been well laid out, and wide concreted paths have slopes rather than steps to help those in wheelchairs. A good-sized shop area faces an expansion programme, but at the moment there are hand tools and chemicals and some garden ornaments already available. The range of plants is quite good – many are grown on site – but we felt the quality was a little patchy. Development of the growing area for shrubs and trees is underway. Group labelling is illustrated and offers some helpful points on plant care and habit, but individual labels could do with some improvement. Toilets are being built and there is a nearby play area with a specially constructed BMX course for the older children. Further improvements in the display areas are planned, and altogether this nursery looks very promising.

Prices £££
Facilities Parking, 20 cars. Garden advice service. Delivery service
Open Mon to Sat 9am to 5.30pm (closes 5pm in winter), Sun 2pm to 5.30pm summer only. Closed 2nd week Aug

---

CROSSFORD Strathclyde
map 1

Sandyholm Garden Centre

Crossford *Tel* Crossford (055 586) 205
At Crossford on the A72 a few miles west of Lanark

A friendly centre in lovely countryside on the banks of the river Clyde. The quality and range of plants sold is generally good – the roses and shrubs offering the most choice. Most tools and sundries are stocked, with the exception of sheds and water gardening materials. Greenhouses, garden furniture and paving are set out on display and in the attractive covered area there is a good choice of other basic tools and accessories. A separate area contains a display of houseplants. The site has been generally well thought out. Labelling provides some very good instructions for shrubs, perennials and alpines, but there is a bit of touching up required for some of the more weathered tags. The staff are cheerful and will readily put themselves out to try to help customers. Some additional attractions are a pick-your-own-fruit area open during the appropriate season, an attractive coffee bar which supplies tasty home baking, and a pets' corner with donkeys to amuse the children.

Prices £££
Facilities Parking, 400 cars. Toilets. Restaurant and cafeteria. Play area. Garden advice service. Delivery service
Open Every day 9am to dusk (closes 5pm in winter). Closed in January

---

CUPAR Fife
map 1

Cupar Garden Centre

Cupar Trading Estate, Cupar KY15 4SX *Tel* Cupar (0334) 55766
Half a mile east of Cupar, just off the A91

The good quality of the plants and the comprehensive labelling single this centre out for recognition. Plants are kept in very good condition and at the time of our inspection there was an outstanding selection of fruit and ornamental trees. The choice of heathers, conifers, shrubs and trees was also good. The labels on individual plants are very good – no plants are left unlabelled and our inspector found as many as four types on one plant! The centre is found in a rather inauspicious setting – it is one of a set of units within the Cupar Trading Estate. However, the layout is attractive: a small outside area has displays of trees and shrubs arranged on a large lawn with gravel paths, while smaller species are placed on raised tables. Signposting is minimal, but because of the size of the place there is little chance of confusion. Our inspector found the interior suffered from being rather cramped, but it does offer quite a comprehensive line of tools and sundries. The smaller accessories are readily available, and larger items such as greenhouses, sheds and water-gardening equipment are also sold. Staff leave people to browse undisturbed but are there to give assistance and advice when required, and when approached the husband and wife team do their best to deal with queries.

Prices ££££
Facilities Parking, 50 cars. Toilets. Ice cream. Garden advice service. Delivery service
Open Mon to Fri 9am to 6pm, Sat and Sun 9am to 5pm in summer. Every day 9.30am to 5pm in winter. Closed from Christmas Eve to mid Jan
Credit cards Access, Visa

DALKEITH Lothian   map 1

Dobbie's Nurseries and Garden Centre

Melville Nursery, Lasswade,   *Tel* 031-663 1941
near Dalkeith EH18 1AZ
On the A7 (Gilmerton Road), 6 miles south-east of Edinburgh, ½ mile west of Dalkeith

Our inspector found this centre 'a pleasure to visit'. It is a spacious and well-planned site in pleasant (if rather dull) surroundings. There are large showbeds and gardens to demonstrate plant arrangements and two new ones have recently been planted, one for betula and the other for sorbus. There are also water-gardening displays and tropical and cold-water fish are sold. All garden equipment is stocked and there is a good selection of fruit trees, shrubs, roses, rhododendrons and clematis. The plants are mostly Scottish grown so are quite hardy. Plant stocks are largely in good condition but prices tend to be quite high. On the whole the labelling is very good, easy to read and helpful. Additional information can be found in the special hut devoted to colour photographs of shrubs in flower, or from the many helpful leaflets and catalogue. The centre also sells a comprehensive collection of books. All the larger items of garden equipment are stocked including a range of garden buildings and conservatories. Heavy materials are located next to the car park and there's a separate machinery centre. Landscaping materials are sold and there is a complete landscaping and garden construction service offered. The excellent centre for hardware and houseplants received the following accolade from our inspector: 'the houseplant section was one of the finest I have seen anywhere – all healthy plants'. The staff are all easy to find and there are experts on hand to deal with problems concerning both the plants and sundries. They are beginning to landscape the grounds, and a butterfly house, with shop, educational and insect sections, was due to open in April 1985, making this a pleasant place for an outing even for the non-gardeners in the family.

275

Prices £££££
Facilities Parking, 400 cars. Toilets. Vending machines. Play area. Garden advice service. Delivery service. Free plant price list. Plant catalogue 30p. Roses sold by mail order
Open Every day 8.30am to 6pm (closes 5pm in winter). Closed Christmas and New Year's Day
Credit cards Access, Visa

DOONFOOT Strathclyde map 1
Doonbank Garden Centre

Dunure Road, Doonfoot, Ayr KA7 4HR *Tel* Ayr (0292) 42334
On the A719 Ayr to Dunure road, 2 miles south of Ayr town centre

'The outside layout is the best I have ever seen', said our inspector, who was most impressed by its clear signposting, logical arrangement and wide paths. This large area is covered with a windbreak material and devoted to a good selection of outdoor plants, which are all in excellent condition. The labels for groups of plants are top rate, giving descriptions of the plants, while individual plants all have tags which show the common and botanical names. Tools and garden accessories offer an adequate range. Garden furniture is in good supply and there is some water-gardening equipment, though no fish. The other large, sundry items such as greenhouses, conservatories, fencing and paving are also sold. Soft toys are on display and may interest the children when they get fed up with the gardening paraphernalia. The pleasant, helpful staff will gladly load your car for you and they contributed greatly to the very favourable impression received by our inspector. A coffee shop sells home-baked foods, and although it is not very elaborate it is clean and functional. Plans for the future include enlarging the showroom, resiting the coffee shop and modernising the pot-plant house. The centre has pick-your-own strawberry fields, and if you still have energy when your visit is over, then Robert Burns' Cottage is not far away.

Prices ££££
Facilities Parking, 120 cars. Toilets. Cafeteria. Garden advice service. Delivery service
Open Mon to Sat 9am to 5pm, Sun 10am to 5pm. Closed Christmas and Boxing Day
Credit cards Access, Visa

DUNDEE Tayside map 1
Blackness Nursery

James Laurie & Son, Ninewells, *Tel* Dundee (0382) 68360
Dundee DD2 1PX
On the A85 Dundee to Perth road, about 2 miles west of Dundee town centre

It's the country garden atmosphere that strikes you first on arriving at this centre. Just by the River Tay, the site is down quite a narrow, steep road and the landscape and layout are quite lovely – rather like a park. The centre is well established. The plants are mostly grown on site or at a second nursery 10 miles away. The main display area is outside, where plants are well presented in neat sections. There are some more unusual varieties to choose from; the quality is always high and the plants are a good size. Some plants do not have prices marked, but labelling is usually readable and neat. The scope of sundries available is limited mainly to chemicals and composts. A very pleasant place to visit, with staff offering good advice and with time to help you out. The nursery is perfectly happy to replace failed plants.

Prices ££££
Facilities Parking, 15 cars. Toilets. Garden advice service. Plant price list and catalogue 50p. Plants sold by mail order
Open Mon to Fri 9am to 5pm, Sat closes 12am. Closed for public holidays

---

EDINBURGH Lothian   map 1

Morton Hall Garden Centre

30 Frogston Road East, Edinburgh EH16 6TJ   *Tel* 031-664 8698
On the south side of Edinburgh on the Ring Road section between Fairmilehead and Liberton

A medium-sized garden centre stocking a reasonable choice of plants throughout the year. The outside area is well set out, but the interior is small and rather cluttered. However, the centre was undergoing changes in layout at the time of inspection, and the indoor area was being extended which seemed to be relieving space problems. The centre stocks a good range of sundries and a more limited array of tools and machinery. Peat and compost are kept in a separate terraced section, and there is an extensive range of greenhouses to look at. One unusual feature of the centre is the Bee Keepers shop which stocks hive equipment and accessories. Plants are on display in the large outside area and also in several greenhouses around the site. The occasional poor specimen can be found, but quality is generally good. Plant stocks include some unusual and well-cared-for shrubs, but a poorer selection of trees. Labelling is fairly standard, consisting of name and price tag on individual pots and group labels which offer facts on how and where to grow the plant. Staff are extremely helpful, and are also happy to do some carrying for you.

Prices £££
Facilities Parking, 170 cars. Toilets. Vending machine. Play area. Garden advice service. Delivery service. Free plant catalogue
Open Mon to Sat 9am to 6pm, Sun 10am to 6pm (closes 5pm in winter). Wed late night opening 6pm winter, 8pm summer. Closed Christmas and New Year's Day
Credit cards Access, Diners Club, Visa

Pinegrove Garden Centre

Maybury Road, Edinburgh EH4 8DX   *Tel* 031-339 4702/6702
5 miles from the city centre. Take the Queensferry Road (Forth Bridge road) and at the Barton Hotel roundabout, turn left into Maybury Road

A popular garden centre in the semi-rural suburbs of Edinburgh and crowded at weekends. It sells an excellent range of conifers and shrubs and a good selection of most other plants. The majority of conifers and shrubs are home grown, and the heathers and most of the trees are raised in the Highlands, so are hardy. The quality of plants is generally good – the conifers are excellent – and the alpines were much improved from the previous inspection, though prices are high. The centre is well planned, though the shop tends to get crowded. There is a good range of healthy houseplants and the centre specialises in floristry. The collection of artificial flowers is 'splendid'. A good collection of tools, garden furniture, sheds, greenhouses, barbecues and garden ornaments is sold, and the centre also stocks garden machinery. Staff are reasonably friendly and helpful.

Prices ££££££
Facilities Parking, 60 cars. Toilets. Vending machine and ice cream. Garden advice service. Delivery service. Free plant price list
Open Mon to Sat 8.30am to 5.30pm, Sun 10am to 5pm (closes ½ hour earlier every day in winter). Closed 2 days at Christmas and 2 days at New Year
Credit cards Access, American Express, Visa

FOCHABERS Grampian
map 1

Christies Garden Centre

The Nurseries, Fochabers IV32 7PF   *Tel* Fochabers (0343) 820362
On the eastern fringe of the Speyside town of Fochabers, at the junction of the A96 and A98

Set adjacent to woodland in a rich farming area, this centre extends over some 15 acres of land. Most of this is devoted to the cultivation of plants and to providing cut flowers for the many Christies florists, but a good 2 acres holds the displays of container-grown plants for sale and a greenhouse filled with houseplants. The stock list includes a wide selection of most non-specialist plants and the trees, shrubs, conifers, fruits perennials and roses which are all grown at the nursery are of a very high standard. The range of tools and sundries concentrates on the smaller items and gardening gadgets. You will find every type of herbicide, insecticide, weed-killer and pet deterrent in stock, as well as pots of every size, shape and description. Furniture, popular gardening books, building materials and greenhouses are also supplied. The layout of the centre is excellent, especially inside where there are well-lit and uncluttered displays and sections are distinct and easily located. Outside, the paths are broad and firm and areas are signposted. Labelling varies from excellent, clear and informative to non-existent. If you can't locate sales staff, the people at the cash desks will summon assistance for you, either for loading goods or giving horticultural advice – most helpful and useful. When arriving at the centre, take extra care crossing the busy A98 (the car park is over the road from Christies) – it can be quite hazardous for youngsters and the elderly or infirm. Other features include a picnic area, an aviary, freely wandering white peacocks and a beautiful floral clock.

Prices £££
Facilities Parking, 200 cars. Toilets. Vending machine. Play area. Delivery service. Free plant catalogue

Open Every day 9am to 5pm
Credit cards Access, Visa

FORFAR Tayside   map 1
Lochlands Garden Centre

Dundee Road, Forfar DD8 1XE   *Tel* Forfar (0307) 63621/2
On the A929 Dundee road about 1½ miles south of Forfar

The farming countryside north of Dundee is the home of this good, general garden centre which stocks a little of everything. The layout is rectangular and rather uninteresting, but it is very functional. Large signs indicate the different plant groups and there are wide, grassed pathways leading down between individual beds. The range of plants is generally good and for visitors keen on trees, roses and shrubs the collection of these is more than satisfactory. Most plants are grown on the nursery attached to the centre. On the day our inspector visited some of the soft fruit was in poor shape and some trees were suffering from the drought, although the overall quality was good. Labelling was somewhat variable; group labels were very good for the trees, shrubs and roses, but individual plants were poorly marked. A large shed is devoted to a range of sundries which includes tools, greenhouses, pond equipment, lawnmowers and garden furniture, although the selection is not very great. There's also a fairly small range of houseplants. The staff are very pleasant and happy to help out. Events such as dog shows and car rallies are often held at weekends. The building of a new bypass in winter 1984 will increase the area of the centre to include a mini country park and picnic area.

Prices £££
Facilities Parking, 25 cars (plus 200 overflow). Toilets. Vending machine, ice cream and soft drinks. Delivery service. Free plant price list and catalogue (donation). Play area. Garden advice service
Open Every day 8am to 5.30pm (closes 5pm in winter). Closed Christmas and New Year's Day

FORRES Grampian   map 1
T. & W. Christie (Forres)

The Nurseries Garden Centre,   *Tel* Forres (0309) 72633/73477
Forres IV36 0EA
Towards the western end of Forres, to the north of the roundabout on the A96 Inverness road

Nurseries covering 140 acres in various sites in the area supply the vast majority of Christie's stock. Everything is replanted on arrival at the sales centre and allowed to grow naturally until ready for sale, and this seems to ensure a very high quality indeed. The plant beds are also kept very tidy by the young apprentice gardeners. There is a very wide range of plants in stock with the exception of house and water plants, and in the case of trees, there's a choice of several sizes for any one variety. It is quite a good idea to get hold of a copy of the comprehensive, descriptive catalogue before doing your shopping. This way one can browse at home and do a lot of planning beforehand. Plants can also be bought by mail order. The layout of the main sales area is very functional and immaculate. It is enclosed by high hedges, which also separate the different areas. The pathways are of hard-packed grit and quite wide enough for easy access – signposting is absent in the display area, but nevertheless it is no problem, even in this 4-acre site, to spot any particular area. Trees create an impressive background to the colours of the roses, perennials and varied shrubs. The indoor area is described by our inspector as 'minute, quaint, full of character and charm, redolent of yesteryear'. It stocks only proprietary garden chemicals and contains the office area. Labelling is, with rare exceptions, excellent and the staff, although unobtrusive, are always somewhere to be found and give friendly and courteous assistance. A place for the keen gardener – few frills.

Prices ££££
Facilities Parking, 15 cars. Toilet. Garden advice service. Free catalogue and price list for plants. Plants sold by mail order
Open Mon to Fri 8am to 5pm (closed 12 noon to 1pm), Sat 8am to 12 noon. Closed local Mon holidays

---

FORTROSE Highland   map 1
Canonbury Market Garden   ✿

Precincts Road, Fortrose IV10 8TS   *Tel* Fortrose (0381) 20194
On the edge on Fortrose, on the A832

This centre nestles on the edge of the small town of Fortrose on the coast of the Black Isle. It is in the middle of a region which abounds in beaches, museums, historic buildings, hill-walking, hunting, shooting and fishing, not to mention bird-watching, bowling and golf! For those of you enjoying a day out in this beautiful area, it's well worth sparing time to visit the garden centre. The quality of the plants is excellent and the range is comprehensive. Some are grown on site, others bought in. Some varieties are only stocked in small quantities but staff will willingly order anything you want. The high quality of the stock is partly the result of a tidy and clean environment, where plants have been arranged sensibly, and clear signposting and labelling make it unnecessary for the public to pick through them looking for what they want. At the moment there is a single greenhouse serving as a shop and only a very limited range of sundries is sold – chemicals and composts, and some furniture and ornaments. However, there are plans to improve the shop area. The growing area for soft fruit and vegetables is also to be extended and rhododendrons, azaleas and camellias introduced. The staff are very knowledgeable and go out of their way to be of service. Salad vegetables and soft fruit are sold in season. This nursery is recommended for its excellent quality at a reasonable price.

Prices ££££
Facilities Parking, 10 cars. Garden advice service
Open Mon to Sat 9am to 6pm (closes at dusk in winter). Closed in January

GLENCARSE Tayside   map 1

Glendoick Garden Centre

Glencarse, Perth PH2 7NS   *Tel* Glencarse (073 886) 260

Just east of the village of Glencarse off the A85, 8 miles east of Perth

The rhododendron enthusiast will find this centre a real treat, though other gardeners will also find that the quality of all the plants and the service makes a visit here worthwhile. There are plenty of staff who work at keeping the plants in tip-top condition, giving top-quality but quite pricey specimens. The normal range of popular plants is readily available, and as well as the excellent rhododendrons and azaleas there is a good selection of fruits, both soft and hard. The centre also specialises in peat garden plants and other plants suitable for Scottish conditions. Many of the plants are grown on site or at an associated nursery. Tools and sundries are generally well represented, including larger items such as sheds, fencing and paving, though the stocks of greenhouses are limited. The indoor section is pleasantly arranged. The exterior areas have been well organised and clearly signposted, and there are some well-landscaped beds. Group labels are large and easily visible, and individual labelling is also generally good. The staff are knowledgeable and willing to help and the manager is always in attendance to deal with any problems. There are no refreshment facilities on site but a small restaurant is located about 50 yds away.

Prices £££££
Facilities Parking, 35 cars. Restaurant. Play area. Garden advice service. Delivery service. Plant catalogue for own stock 50p, plant guide 70p
Open Every day 9am to 6pm in summer, 9.30am to 5pm in winter. Closed first 2 weeks of Jan
Credit cards Access, Visa

Linden Nursery and Garden Centre

Main Street, Glencarse PH2 7LX   *Tel* Glencarse (073 886) 222

On the A85 at Glencarse, 6 miles from Perth and 12 miles from Dundee

The access to this centre is off the main street in Glencarse. The car park is small, but if it's full you can park along the road outside. It is a small centre with rather narrow paths but the layout has been fairly well organised – the main problem occurs among the trees and fruit trees which are difficult to look at because of the lack of space between rows. Plants are arranged in groups but not signposted, though it's easy to cast an eye round to see what you are after. Group labels are descriptive, often carrying a colour photograph, though individual plants are generally marked with the price only (the centre tells us they are reorganising the labelling system). There is a good overall standard and any plants which are 'past it' are sold cheaply. The selection is generally acceptable although houseplant enthusiasts will be disappointed. The range of cultivars of fruit trees is excellent, particularly the apples and pears. The water-gardening section is also worth a look at: it has a good range of aquatic plants and a well-stocked fish section which is being expanded by the addition of a tropical fish house. If you want to make a pond or water feature in your garden, you will also find pumps, pool equipment and fibreglass pools. A limited range of hand tools and power tools is sold and you will also find paving, fencing, greenhouses and sheds. The two staff members are easy to find and very knowledgeable, but you might have to wait when the centre is busy.

Prices ££££
Facilities Parking, 15 cars. Toilets. Garden advice service. Delivery service. Water gardening catalogue 30p
Open Every day 9am to 6pm (closes 5pm in winter). Closed Christmas and Boxing Day and 1, 2 and 3 Jan

---

GLENROTHES Fife map 1
Roots Garden Centre

Caskieberran Road,   *Tel* Glenrothes (0592) 756407
Glenrothes KY7 6DR
On the south-west corner of Glenrothes, a short distance from the A911 Kinross to Leven road

This centre offers a solid and adequate range of goods for the undemanding gardener. A comprehensive selection of tools and sundries should provide most shoppers with what they need in terms of garden buildings, DIY and landscaping materials, ornaments and all the other gardening bits and pieces. There is a wide range of decorative walling and paving, as well as a good selection of garden furniture. The choice of plants is quite ordinary, but the quality is good and you shouldn't have too much trouble filling your trolley. Useful labels are clearly written and carry growing instructions as well as pictures of mature or flowering plants, but keep a lookout for careless labelling since there are a few mistakes. The overall layout is good, so it is easy to get around the large site, although it can be difficult to find staff as they are a bit thin on the ground. They are always helpful, though not all are well informed. The entrance road is to be surfaced and a new building erected to house a wider range of furniture and conservatories.

Prices ££££
Facilities Parking, 300 cars. Toilets. Vending machines. Garden advice service. Delivery service. Price list for water-garden sundries 50p. Plant catalogue 70p
Open Mon to Fri 8.30am to 6pm, Sat 9am to 6pm, Sun 10am to 6pm
Credit cards Access, Visa

HAZELBANK Strathclyde map 1
Silverbirch Garden Centre and Buttery

Hazelbank, near Lanark ML8 5QQ   *Tel* Crossford (055 586) 623
On the A72, 5 miles from Lanark, on the Lanark side of Crossford village

The woods and parkland along the Clydeside create the setting of this beautiful garden centre. It is one of the larger centres of the west of Scotland and the plant section is most strongly geared towards conifers and bedding plants as well as a good selection of lovely fresh-looking houseplants. However, most gardeners should find something to suit their needs among the well-maintained, good-quality but rather pricey stock. Excellent mature trees are available which might be of interest if you want to fill a space in your garden quickly. The labels on the smaller plants are clear with useful growing instructions, but on the trees it is sometimes difficult to read the weathered print. The tools and sundries again cater for most basic needs – there are no power tools, sheds or greenhouses – but the garden furniture is a special feature and there are some attractive, wrought-iron ornaments available. Our inspector commented that the staff 'could not be any nicer' and he enjoyed the visit very much. There is a tasteful 'old-fashioned buttery' serving lunches and afternoon teas. Pick-your-own fruit fields are attached to the garden centre and in season provide a pleasant diversion.

Prices £££££
Facilities Parking, 120 cars. Toilets. Buttery. Garden advice service. Delivery service
Open Every day 9am to dusk. Closed Christmas and New Year
Credit cards Access, Visa

INVERNESS Highland — map 1

Howdens Garden Centre

Telford Street, Inverness IV3 5LF   *Tel* Inverness (0463) 233647
On the old A9 Inverness to Beauly road, on the outskirts of Inverness

This is an attractively landscaped centre with pleasant grassy areas, rockeries and a pond all giving a natural garden atmosphere to the site which is located in a built-up area near the Caledonian Canal. A car park has recently been extended, but the new area is gravelled (the centre tells us that this will be tarmacked) and has a curb making it unsuitable for wheelchairs. The centre is generally well laid out with wide paths and is clearly signposted inside and out. The large area devoted to sundries is very comprehensive with stock ranging from floral art materials to a large selection of pesticides and seeds. Tools, landscaping materials, ornaments and greenhouses are all available. The only omission we noticed was garden sheds. A small area is turned over to a display of water-garden plants, and a slightly more generous amount of space houses a large collection of healthy pot plants. Otherwise there is a reasonable all-round selection of outside plants of which the roses reign supreme, their quality outstanding. Both ornamental and fruit trees are also well represented and in good condition. Some plants are grown on site including dahlias, chrysanthemums, fuchsias and begonias. At the time of our visit some stocks were low, notably shrubs, although those there were looked healthy. The range and quality of perennials, herbs and soft fruits was less good, but a lot of this is due to seasonal shortages. Group labels are illustrated and contain useful, easily read details. Each plant is priced and labelled as well. The staff can be difficult to find, but they will answer queries and carry goods if requested.

Prices £££
Facilities Parking, 80 cars. Toilets. Vending machine. Play area. Garden advice service. Delivery service
Open Mon to Sat 9am to 5.30pm, Sun 1pm to 5pm (Sun Mar to Oct only)
Credit cards Access, Visa

INVERURIE Grampian
map 1

Forbes Garden and Machinery Centre

Souterford Road, Inverurie AB5 9TP   *Tel* Inverurie (0467) 21402
On the B9222 to Old Meldrum, off the A96 Aberdeen to Inverness road, about 400 yards from Inverurie town centre

The mountain of Bennachie looks down over the geographical area known as the Garioch, and it is here you will find Forbes Garden Centre, in a pleasant rural setting on the edge of a busy town. It is largely geared to locals and meets the needs of the gardeners of northern Scotland. Parts of the site were successfully re-organised in 1984 and plant quality and maintenance were also on the up-and-up following the arrival of a new, experienced horticulturalist on the staff. The main lines of plant stocks (trees, conifers and shrubs) are generally in plentiful supply with others being more seasonal. The centre is quite small; but very compact. Only the shop suffers from congestion and even this is well laid out and manages to carry a wide range of goods. The centre stocks a good supply of equipment and sundries, but its main strength lies in garden machinery – the choice of mowers, trimmers, power saws and other tools is excellent, and a very good spares and repair service is provided. There is a small, water-garden demonstration area – this is to be enlarged as is the shrub area. The staff all wear uniforms so that finding someone to help you is not difficult, and they are always ready to advise customers. A tea room is planned for the near future.

Prices ££££
Facilities Parking, 55 cars (plus 25 overflow). Toilets. Vending machine. Play area. Garden advice service. Delivery service. Plant catalogue 70p
Open Every day 8.30am to 6pm (10am to 5pm in winter). Closed 1 to 7 Jan
Credit cards Access, American Express, Diners Club, Visa

KELSO Borders
map 1

Floors Castle Garden Centre

Floors Castle, Kelso   *Tel* Kelso (0573) 24530
TD5 7SF
2 miles north-west of Kelso off the B6397 Kelso to St. Boswells road, followed by a ¾-mile drive through the castle grounds

If you are keen on castles and need a few stocks for the garden then you could do worse than a combined visit to Floors Castle (open April to Sept.) and its garden centre. If you aren't put off by the long, bumpy drive through the grounds then you will come upon this well-laid-out centre positioned in an old walled garden of the castle. Part of this garden still supplies vegetables and fruit – including hot-house peaches – to the castle itself, and people are welcome to explore the 'private' area as well as the centre itself. The signposting is very good and many plants are set out in alphabetical order so that it is not too difficult to locate things. For those with no garden, or just keen on greenery indoors, there is a large selection of houseplants to explore. However, if outdoor plants are what's needed the range of shrubs, alpines, heathers is reasonable and for the kitchen garden there is a wide range of herbs. Most other common varieties are available. The selection of tools and sundries is rather limited, but furniture and ornaments, as well as fencing, are available in the larger range, and chemicals, composts and some hand tools are also stocked. The main detrimental feature of this centre is the condition of some plants – certainly at the time of our visit some specimens were pot-bound, others surrounded by weeds, although there was no sign of pests or disease. A little more plant care would not go amiss. Labelling on shrubs and conifers is good, while individual labelling is variable. If you require further information there are really only the cashier and young assistant available as the gardener can be difficult to find. They are very friendly though and will help within their knowledge and ability. A coffee shop offers a good choice of snacks, many of them home baked.

Prices £££
Facilities Parking, 200 cars. Toilets. Coffee house and cafeteria. Play area. Delivery service
Open Every day 9.30am to 5pm (closes 4.30pm in winter)
Credit cards Access, Visa

Mayfield Garden Centre

Mayfield, Kelso TD5 7AU   *Tel* Kelso (0573) 24124
The centre is 5 minutes' walk from the town centre, adjacent to the main car park and by the side of the River Tweed

This is a centre which many people seem to visit for an afternoon out and it is well suited to this. Situated near a riverside walk and picnic area, the centre itself offers a full range of plants and gardening materials. The layout is immaculate and there are separate areas devoted to houseplants, outdoor plants and garden sundries, as well as a purpose-built machinery building for the sale and repair of power tools and machines. The range of garden accessories is extensive and it is only the water gardening section which is limited, although even here there is a choice of pools and waterfalls. At the time of our inspection there was a very wide selection of shrubs and conifers, heathers and alpines, while most other plants are also available. The quality is excellent and labelling is good and easy to read. To supplement the information given here there are lots of free leaflets and trained personnel to provide expert advice. There are often special offers advertised at the entrance, so it's worth keeping your eyes open. The centre specialises in the production of onion and leek seed and is the home of the 'Kelsae Onion'.

Prices ££££
Facilities Parking, 50 cars. Toilets. Picnic area. Play area. Garden advice service.

Delivery service. Free price lists for seeds and plants. Catalogue for hardy plants 70p.
Seeds available by mail order
Open Every day 8.30am to 5pm (opens 9am in winter)
Credit cards Access, Visa

KILTARLITY Highland   map 1
Highland Liliums   ✿

Kiltarlity, By Beauly IV4 7JQ   *Tel* Kiltarlity (046 374) 365
*On the A832 Beauly/Kiltarlity road, 12 miles north-west of Inverness, following
signposts from Kiltarlity post office*

This excellent centre lies fifteen minutes' drive from Loch Ness and is set in
lovely countryside near the village of Kiltarlity. It is not a modern garden
centre, but is the place to go if you care about plants. Tools and sundries are
sold, but they definitely take second place. There's a marvellous and
healthy range of most popular outdoor plants including primulas, alpines,
heathers, shrubs and trees and a good choice of bedding plants in season,
and also a small number of very good-quality houseplants. A large area is
devoted to the plants and it is well laid out with mainly wide paths. The
signposting is easily readable and all labelling is informative, illustrated
and consistent. Many plants (including Liliums) are grown on site, and if
you want something unusual or which is not in stock they will do their best
to acquire it or propagate it for you. A small but well-organised space holds
a limited selection of hand tools and sundries including some ornaments
and pond equipment and the centre will order any larger construction
materials or garden buildings for you. The staff are very efficient and
courteous and will ask if you need help but won't pressurise at all. A
service for both indoor and outdoor landscaping is available. Some
refreshment facilities would be a welcome addition.

Prices £££
Facilities Parking, 30 cars. Toilets. Garden advice service. Delivery service. Free plant
price list
Open Mon to Sat 9am to 5pm. Closed 1st Thurs in Aug, Christmas and Boxing Day,
1 to 3 Jan

KIRKFIELDBANK Strathclyde   map 1
Gilchrist's Garden Centre   ✿ ♿

The Pleasance, Riverside Road,   *Tel* Lanark (0555) 3234
Kirkfieldbank, Lanark ML11 9TG
700 yards off the A72 at Kirkfieldbank Bridge

This is an excellent centre where the family can spend a pleasant day out.
Reasonably priced meals (children's portions half price) are available at the
versatile restaurant and a very attractive, pool-side cafe sells home-made
cakes and scones. Children can be amused in the play area or with the pet
rabbits, while the garden-lovers in the family explore the spacious and
extremely well-arranged centre. Under glass there is an excellent display of
houseplants in first-class condition, ranging from plants priced at 20p to

specimens selling for as much as £4,000. You'll also find a wide selection of chemicals, composts and hand tools, some interesting floral art equipment and a frozen food centre! Garden buildings, fencing, paving and patio accessories are all available. Water-gardening equipment is stocked, but for plants and fish you must visit the specialist centre about 200 yds away. The overall range of outdoor plants is good and anything not in stock will be ordered for you. Plants are maintained at a high standard and any end-of-season specimens which are not at their best are sold off at a fraction of the standard price to make room for new stock. Identification and labelling are very good and the staff have reference books for customers' use which contain detailed information about all the plants. Staff are very helpful in all respects – they do not pressurise customers and the trained personnel certainly know about their specific areas.

Prices Information not available
Facilities Parking, 600 cars. Toilets. Restaurant and cafeteria. Play area. Garden advice service. Delivery service
Open Every day 9am to 8pm (closes 5pm in winter). Closed Christmas Day and 2 days at New Year

---

LESLIE Fife   map 1

Maryfield Nurseries   ✿

Leslie, Fife KY6 3JU   *Tel* Glenrothes (0592) 741322
On the northern outskirts of Leslie on the Glenrothes road, about 3 minutes' walk from the centre

An established, family-run business set in the high-walled garden of a large, private house. It is something of a specialists' paradise with a remarkable range of alpine and rock-garden plants (25 varieties of gentian, over 80 heathers, for example). Trees and conifers are also outstanding and many of the trees are well established. No water-plants or bulbs are sold, but there is a good range of other plants and everything is in first-class condition. Identification and labelling have much improved since our last inspection and there is an entirely new range of glasshouses nearing completion. The staff are very knowledgeable and helpful – 'delightful, expert, caring and tolerant' were just some of the words of praise our inspector came up with. The layout is informal, with many different 'surprise' corners amidst the large area of frames, beds and walkways. Tools and sundries, other than basic fertilisers, are not stocked, but this is more than compensated for by the range of plants that you simply would not find in the average, modern garden centre.

Prices £££
Facilities Parking, 10 cars. Toilets. Garden advice service. Delivery service. Free plant price list. Plant catalogue 25p. Plants sold by mail order
Open Tues to Fri 8am to 5pm, Sat 8am to 4pm, Sun 10am to 4pm (closed 12am to 1pm daily). Closed Christmas Day and 1 and 2 Jan

---

If we've missed out on a good garden centre or nursery, tell us. There are report forms at the end of the book.

LUNDERSTON BAY Strathclyde

map 1

Cardwell Nursery Garden Centre

Lunderston Bay, Gourock PA15 1BB   *Tel* Gourock (0475) 521536
On the A78 coast road 3 miles south of Gourock

With lovely views overlooking the bay this is a centre which is a pleasure to
visit. It has been carefully laid out and a lot of paths have been created or
improved in the last couple of years – now both pathways and ramps are
wide, paved and easy to negotiate. A covered walkway is being
constructed through the shrub area. The plants are set out on raised beds
which are numbered and labelled, though a map would be useful to help
customers find the beds they want. However, the labelling itself is excellent
with many beds fronted by large cards offering details of plant
requirements and habit. Individual labels provide name and price only. An
extensive range of plants is available, the conifer, shrub, tree and
houseplant sections being the most complete, and there is no doubt that all
but the most demanding gardener would find something of interest here.
Plants are all container grown, many at Cardwell's own nursery. They are
well cared for and kept weed-free. One or two of the full-time staff are quite
knowledgeable. The part-timers are not experienced but are generally
pleasant. The 'sundries' side of the centre will also keep most gardeners
happy, whether interested in floral art or heavy construction. A separate
area provides room for a display of greenhouses and sheds, and a hire
service offers a range of equipment from small hand tools to cement mixers.
There are plans to expand the water-gardening section. There is a pleasant
tearoom which sells home-baking, and the balcony looks out over the bay.

Prices £££
Facilities Parking, 120 cars. Toilets. Cafeteria. Play area. Garden advice service.
Delivery service. Free price lists and leaflets for various products, plant catalogue 75p
Open Every day 9am to 8pm (closes 6pm in winter). Closed 2 days at Christmas and
2 days at New Year
Credit cards Access, Visa

METHVEN Tayside

map 1

Seven Acres Nursery

Methven, PH1 3SU   *Tel* Methven (073 884) 318
On the A85 5 miles west of Perth

In the midst of undergoing repairs and expansions, this nursery is in a
rather untidy phase, although the new management is working hard to
upgrade it and its potential is very good. It is located in a large walled
garden with some very pretty countryside around. There is a selection of
plants of very good quality which is more than likely to include something
suitable for most gardening requests. Much of the stock is grown on site
including bedding plants, perennials, fuchsias and geraniums. Labelling is
good and clearly typed, although some more group labels would be
helpful. The plants are the principal feature of the centre at the moment
and the layout of these is basically good. A new greenhouse and large

288

storage sheds are at present under construction, and as a result of a general improvement to facilities the tools and sundries section is likely to expand. Even so, there is already a small range of accessories stocked, including greenhouses, fencing and garden furniture. Sheds, paving, pond equipment and tools are not sold. The new staff are experienced and very friendly and will advise on appropriate building materials or recommend local landscape gardeners. They are also happy to carry goods and load the car. Worth a visit for the range of plants and worth keeping an eye on for future developments.

Prices ££££
Facilities Parking, 50 cars. Garden advice service.
Open Mon to Fri 8am to 5pm (closes 4.30pm in winter). Sat and Sun 8am to 5pm (July and August only)

MILNGAVIE Strathclyde   map 1

Findlay Clark Garden Centre   ⚙★

Boclair Road, Milngavie, Glasgow   *Tel* Balmore (0360) 20721
G62 6EP

Just east of Bearsden on the B8049 Boclair road

This is a garden centre that by all accounts has something for everyone, and at a very high standard. It is a large centre with a spacious, uncluttered indoor section and a well laid out and extensive exterior with 'all plants in their proper environment'. The sizeable car park is centrally located and from it one can easily spot where to go – each area is clearly signposted and has easy-to-read boards with helpful planting and aftercare instructions. The plants themselves have illustrated labels at eye level. The staff wear distinctive aprons so they are quickly spotted, and experts are available to help out on specific problems. The indoor section houses pottery, candles, and gardening books, as well as flower arranging equipment. The houseplants sold are superb and include a wide range of specimen foliage plants. Outside one can choose from a wide range of excellent, healthy and vigorous but quite expensive trees, climbers, dwarf conifers, roses, and heathers (heathers and seeds were being offered at a discount at the time of our visit). There are trolleys to transport one's purchases to the cash desk, but the organisation of the pay-out system is rather ill-conceived. The centre also boasts a good water-garden section, power tools for sale and hire (daily or weekly) and an attractive tearoom offering soups, sandwiches and home-made cakes. Wheelchairs are available for customers' use, and the whole site is designed with ramps.

Prices £££££
Facilities Parking, 200 cars. Toilets. Tearoom. Garden advice service. Delivery service. Free price lists for nursery stock, bulbs, fencing etc.
Open Every day, 9am to 6pm winter, 9am to 9pm summer
Credit cards Access, Visa

If you're travelling a long distance to visit a garden centre or nursery, telephone first to check the opening hours. They may vary with the season and weather conditions.

Duncans of Milngavie

Flower and Garden Centre, 101 Main Street, *Tel* 041-956 2377
Milngavie, Glasgow G62 6JJ
Just north of Bearsden on the A81, 7 miles north of Glasgow city centre

The first impression given by this centre is one of 'everything in its place'. It has obviously been carefully laid out and it is a pleasure to walk around. The paths and gangways are kept clear of obstructions and the whole site is immaculately clean and tidy. Plants are arranged alphabetically. They are clearly marked with name and price, and placed under signs which provide helpful instructions on cultivation and which are easily read from the walkways. There is a good range of well-known plants which are all of very high quality. The nursery itself concentrates on producing spring bedding plants and hanging baskets and also on forcing bulbs and azaleas for Christmas. The inside area reflects the same 'pristine' appearance as the outside. It is set on split levels and kept spotlessly clean, the one drawback being that it is so packed with stock that it can be difficult to negotiate and so may present a problem for the disabled. The range of tools and sundries has been arranged in an excellent display and includes most everyday items. A floristry offers an Interflora service, and the centre also stocks an extensive range of flowering and foliage houseplants. Pond equipment and garden ornaments are stocked and greenhouses can be ordered, but sheds, fencing and paving are not available. There's a good range of garden furniture. There are staff on hand and they are all friendly and helpful.

Prices ££££
Facilities Parking, 35 cars. Toilets. Play area. Garden advice service. Delivery service. Free price lists for roses, alpines, furniture etc. Scottish Gardening Guide 70p
Open Mon to Sat 8.30am to 5.30pm, Sun 10am to 5pm. Closed Christmas and Boxing Day and 1 and 2 Jan
Credit cards Access, American Express, Visa

NEWMACHAR Grampian map 1
Swailend Nurseries

Newmachar AB5 ONU *Tel* Newmachar (065 17) 2289
Between Dyce and Newmachar, ¼ mile off the A947

A good, old-fashioned nursery, well worth a visit, particularly if you are after heathers or conifers. It also specialises in bedding plants, and summer-flowering pot plants such as fuchsias and pelargoniums. Most are grown on site. The overall range of plants varies with the seasons, but quality is generally excellent even at the end of the season. Layout is functional rather than exciting. Although the labelling was very patchy and sometimes misplaced when our inspector visited, a good catalogue is available which provides detailed descriptions of plants coupled with useful notes on selection, planting and care under local conditions. A roomy, covered area houses the tools and sundries section, as well as providing space for indoor plants and propagation. The scope of the gardening hardware is not wide, but there are a few tools, a limited selection of chemicals, and a slightly bigger range of fertilisers and composts. Many of the handy bits and pieces such as ties, labels, canes and twine are also sold. The larger items are not stocked at present, but there are plans to expand into heavier goods. Our inspection took place the same day as a local show which probably accounted for the lack of staff – the cashier was knowledgeable though and provided help with a smile. Be careful when approaching the nursery – the last 100 yards is along an unpaved farm-track and visibility is restricted.

Prices ££££
Facilities Parking, 22 cars. Garden advice service. Delivery service. Free plant catalogue
Open Mon to Sat 9am to 5pm, Sun 10am to 4pm (closed Sun July to Feb)

PAISLEY Strathclyde   map 1
Dykebar Garden Centre

Barrhead Road, Paisley PA2 7AD   *Tel* 041-887 5422
1 mile from Paisley, near Hawkhead hospital on the A726

A small but imaginative centre set up among the outbuildings in the attractive grounds of Dykebar House. The quality of stock more than compensates for the small range, and at the time of our inspection there was a very passable selection of conifers. All plants, trees and shrubs are in excellent condition, and the houseplants are beautifully maintained. The layout is well organised with wide paths and attractively arranged plants. Labelling is generally good but there are no group labels: this is not too much of a problem if you have some basic knowledge, however, since you can see around the centre at a glance. The indoor area is particularly attractive with its array of houseplants and splendid floral arrangements and also a pets corner with a budgie aviary. The centre sells mostly the smaller gardening sundries, although there is some paving and fencing and a large stock of wooden garden seats. The good quality extends to the tea room where you can find home-made cakes and more substantial fare – even special dinners. Fresh fruit and vegetables and cut flowers are sold. Staff are easy to find and will take the time to discuss pros and cons of a particular plant or product with you.

Prices Information not available
Facilities Parking, 60 cars. Toilets. Tea room. Play area (planned for early 1985). Garden advice service. Delivery service
Open Every day 9am to 5pm. Closed 2 days at Christmas and 2 days at New Year

PEEBLES Borders   map 1
Kailzie Gardens

Kailzie, Peebles EH45 9HT   *Tel* Peebles (0721) 22054
About 2½ miles from Peebles on the B702

A beautifully scenic road following the route of the River Tweed leads the visitor to this small centre. It is part of the much larger Kailzie Gardens

Complex. Take a stroll through the Gardens themselves (admission 70p) and you can see the trees, shrubs and plants growing, giving you an idea of what they might look like in your garden. The rose gardens and wild fowl add to the peace and elegance of the atmosphere. Entrance to the garden centre, gallery and a restaurant in the stables is free. The restaurant serves simple home-made lunches, coffees and teas, or there is a picnic area for those who have planned ahead. Once in the centre, there are few signposts, but the walkways make getting around easy. The very small selection of sundries would probably only tempt the impulse buyer. The range of plants is not great, but they are all propagated on site, and the result is that they are all strong and healthy and should prove hardy in the local area, where conditions can get quite severe. The head gardener is available at most times to give help and advice and you can pick up plenty of ideas from a pleasant walk through the Gardens.

Prices £££
Facilities Parking, 150 cars. Toilets. Restaurant and cafeteria
Open Every day 11am to 5.30pm

PERTH Tayside   map 1
Tesco Garden Centre   ❀ ✍

Edinburgh Road, Perth PH2 8DX   *Tel* Perth (0738) 34540
On the south side of Perth on the main A912

A very good range of quality plants and gardening accessories is provided by this large, modern centre. It is located beside a Tesco supermarket, within a residential/industrial area which is quite pleasant despite the description. It would be helpful if there was a road sign directing customers to the centre's own car park, because many don't realise it is there and walk from the supermarket car park. You will find an excellent range of all gardening equipment and machinery in the large covered area. The whole site is well ordered and signposted. There is a complete range of popular plants all kept in good order. Labelling is neatly done although no detailed information is provided. Our inspector's one major complaint about the centre is the lack of interest or knowledge shown by the staff.

Prices £££
Facilities Parking, 6 cars (250 cars in main car park). Toilets. Garden advice service. Delivery service.
Open Mon to Fri 9am to 5pm, Sat 8.30am to 6pm, Sun 11am to 5pm (open to 8pm Wed to Fri in summer)
Credit cards Access, Visa

PITMEDDEN Grampian   map 1
Pitmedden Garden Centre

Old Meldrum Road, Pitmedden AB4 0PA   *Tel* Udny (065 13) 2317
On the west side of Pitmedden village, on the B9000

This centre's specialisation in house and garden pine furniture (made in the adjoining workshop) and the good range of conifers, ornamental shrubs and trees are just two aspects which single it out from the run-of-the-mill centre. Effort has also been made to display all the plants to advantage. Rather than siting them in ordered ranks, they are set out in interesting groups and the 'plant of the month' feature is both attractive and interesting. The outdoor area is clearly arranged and the informative, illustrated group labels are very helpful. The centre does have a few limitations though – washed-out individual plant labels and a crowded indoor section were criticised by our inspector. However, the overall range of plants and sundries is quite reasonable and in addition to the pine furniture there is an excellent choice of fencing and paving to be had. Staff are very helpful and well able to give advice. Additional features planned for the near future include a coffee shop, plant catalogue and credit card facilities. If you have time to spare after shopping at the centre, the National Trust for Scotland's Pitmedden Gardens are close at hand.

Prices £££
Facilities Parking, 20 cars. Toilets. Ice creams. Play area. Garden advice service. Delivery service. Plants sold by mail order
Open Every day, 9am to 5.30pm in summer, 10am to dusk in winter. Closed for 1 week at New Year

PRESTWICK Strathclyde   map 1
Airport Garden Centre

James Milroy and Sons,   *Tel* Prestwick (0292) 76221
Monkton Road, Prestwick
On the A74 Prestwick to Ayr road near the airport

A fairly small centre, but stocking a good range of gardening equipment and plants for its size. Alterations were underway at the time of inspection, but the centre was already well laid out and showed a lot of promise. There was a good range of plants, all in reasonable condition. The herbaceous and alpine plants were excellent and offered a particularly wide choice. Labelling was good, although the description of plants could do with improvement. The garden hardware and accessories section is also quite comprehensive with a good range of greenhouses. Our inspector found the staff helpful, even though they were busy changing stock. It's worth keeping an eye on this well-stocked centre to see what added attractions the alterations bring.

Prices ££££
Facilities Parking, 100 cars. Toilets. Garden advice service. Delivery service
Open Every day 9am to 8pm (closes 5pm in winter). Closed Christmas and Boxing Day and New Year's Day
Credit card Visa

Awards given this year are only provisional. We need plenty of feedback to let us know what the garden centres and nurseries are like all year round. Please use the report forms at the end of the book.

RUTHERGLEN Strathclyde map 1
Robert Bell & Sons

Westfield Nursery, Cathcart Road, *Tel* 041-641 6921
Rutherglen, Glasgow G73 2DT
On the road to Cathcart, ¼ mile from Rutherglen main street

This is a one-man business offering 'good, old-fashioned service' with no
extra frills or facilities. It is a nursery which will please the amateur
gardener and if you are interested in first-class plants, and personal service,
then you will enjoy spending time here. A comprehensive range of plants
takes up most of the site, but fertilisers and the like are also sold – these are
measured out to the required weight straight from large bins or bags, so
you can buy exactly what you need. On arriving at this centre you would be
forgiven for believing that chaos reigns – but somehow everything seems to
have its place and the owner knows exactly where that is. Most things are
labelled, but if you are in any difficulties he is constantly available to give
advice. Stocks tend to sell very quickly because of their excellent state of
health, and this quick turnover in itself helps to keep standards high. The
nursery is quite small, but even though space is restricted the width of
paths is adequate. There is no car park on site so you must find space in the
street; however, if you need to load goods into the car you can reverse up to
the entrance.

Prices Information not available
Facilities Information not available
Open Information not available

TAIN Highland map 1
Sandy's Garden Centre

Morangie Road, Tain IV19 1LY *Tel* Tain (0862) 3164
Just off the A9, take the northern exit from the town of Tain

Sandy's Garden Centre opened in 1984, just on the edge of the historic
town of Tain, and should be fully operational by spring 1985. It will be
interesting to see how it develops. It offers a popular range of plants and
sundries and is of average size, about a third under cover, a third devoted
to the hardy outdoor plants and the remaining area turned over to a shop
and service section. It has a good layout with wide pathways. Most
standard items of gardening equipment are stocked, and greenhouses,
water-gardening equipment and fish can be ordered. Most common plants
are also readily available – nothing of great rarity, but plenty to please most
gardeners, and good quality is the general rule. The labelling and staff
came in for our inspector's criticism – both tending to be either absent or
unable to provide useful information, but the centre tells us someone
should always be available to help customers. The centre provides a
landscape service.

Prices £££
Facilities Parking, 12 cars. Toilets. Garden advice service. Delivery service
Open Every day, 7.30am to 8.30pm in summer, 8am to 6pm in winter
Credit card Access

TILLICOULTRY Central   map 1

Sterlings Garden Centre

Moss Road, Tillicoultry FK13 6NS   *Tel* Tillicoultry (0259) 50655
Off the A908 Alloa road, near Tillicoultry town centre, 10 miles from Stirling

An attractive centre in a pleasant, country town and not a bad choice for an
afternoon out if you would also enjoy a visit to the adjoining pub/restaurant
or 'Britain's largest furniture centre' which are both part of the same
complex. The centre has been very nicely laid out. Much of the outdoor
section is roofed over and there are wide paths and good signposting. A
good range of first-class plants is on display – only the roses and soft fruits
were few in number when we visited. Each plant group is marked out with
a large sign and most plants have clear, individual labels. The shrubs are
especially easy to identify since they are arranged alphabetically and are
particularly well labelled. A large indoor area is devoted to garden sundries
and tools, a huge selection of gardening books and a beautiful display of
dried and artificial flowers. A separate greenhouse is also pleasantly set out
with a display of houseplants. The overall selection of garden accessories is
very good, but the selection of sheds is somewhat limited and greenhouses
and power tools are not stocked. Several staff members are found on the
site and they are willing to give assistance and advice where needed. The
centre offers an excellent display and comprehensive selection of quality
goods.

Prices £££
Facilities Parking, 200 cars. Toilets. Restaurant and cafeteria. Garden advice service.
Delivery service
Open Every day 9am to 8pm (closes 5.30pm in winter). Closed Christmas and New
Year's Day
Credit cards Access, Visa

Northern Ireland

BELFAST Co. Antrim map 7
Woodlawn Garden Centre

360 Saintfield Road, Belfast BT8 4SJ   *Tel* Belfast (0232) 704777
On the outskirts of Belfast, on Saintfield Road, the main Belfast to Carryduff road

Conveniently situated for Belfast's gardeners, this centre stocks a wide range of plants and gardening sundries. It occupies about two acres of land and is sensibly laid out with clear signposting, so it's easy to find your way around. The outside area at the front of the centre has a good selection of sheds, fencing, greenhouses, furniture, paving and ornaments on show, while the area at the rear of the site is devoted entirely to plants. The selection and quality of the trees and shrubs is particularly noteworthy – though the perennials were not quite up to scratch on the day of our inspection, probably suffering from the prolonged dry spell. The centre also stocks large trees, up to 15m high. The labelling is generally good throughout. The indoor section houses a mix of gardening tools and sundries which should cater for the average shopper, but the area is somewhat restricted so it can be diificult to get about at busier times. The houseplant sections will be a pleasure to any enthusiast as the range is very good and the quality high. Staff are approachable and try their best to handle customers' queries. A new landscaped garden provides a picnic and play area for children.

Prices £££
Facilities Parking, 120 cars. Toilets. Vending machines. Play area. Garden advice service. Delivery service. Free price lists and catalogues for fencing, sheds and greenhouses
Open Mon to Fri 9am to 5.30pm, Sat 10am to 5pm, Sun 2pm to 5pm
Credit cards Access, Visa

LARNE Co. Antrim map 7
Inver Nurseries and Garden Centre

Casements Brae, Inver, Larne BT40 3DD   *Tel* Larne (0574) 76351
Near the town centre beside Inver Park football ground

This is a centre sited on the side of a hill in pleasant surroundings. It is run by a family team who are extremely helpful. The variety and extent of stock surpasses most other local garden centres and nurseries. A very good plant selection includes excellent-quality trees which may be bargained for. Quality is high all round, but labelling could do with improvement – labels can be anything from poor to very good. A large and varied arrangement of garden ornaments and a lawnmower repair service are two features of the sundries department. This section also stocks hand and power tools, fencing, paving and garden furniture. A very comprehensive library and extensive free leaflets and papers are a useful contribution for the less knowledgeable shoppers. Sadly, the layout is in a sorry state – it suffers from lack of organisation and is overgrown in some areas, and the fact that the centre is on a slope does not help matters. (The centre say that their aim is to provide a wide range of plants in a small area, and this means the plants have to be close together which leads to lack of organisation.) With a few more staff to keep things in order, this could be one of the best centres in Northern Ireland.

Prices £££
Facilities Parking, 5 cars. Toilets. Garden advice service. Delivery service
Open Every day 10am to 5.30pm (closes 5pm in winter)
Credit card Access

LISBURN Co. Antrim   map 7

Texas Homecare Garden Centre   🦋

Antrim Street, Lisburn BT28 1AU   *Tel* Lisburn (08462) 76888
On the outskirts of Lisburn close to a pedestrian-only area

For those interested in gardening hardware, this centre offers a full and comprehensive range at competitive prices. There is an excellent selection of patio paving and furniture, and in the main store there is an extensive collection of unusual ceramic tiles suitable for porches and patios. Most other gardening sundries are kept in large quantities except for water-gardening equipment; in fact the quantity of sundries causes some problems as stock rather overflows (this area is undergoing re-organisation). The layout of the outer area is reasonably good and doesn't suffer from overcrowding, but things are arranged in a somewhat haphazard manner. Labelling of plants is very good – all items are individually priced and group labels are excellent. The quality of the plants is also of a very high standard, partly due to the high turnover allowing a constant influx of new, fresh specimens. All damaged or wilted plants are discarded as soon as they are noticed. The range of plant stock, however, was rather limited on the day our inspector visited (though expansion is planned for 1985) – there were no trees, shrubs, fruits or perennials available, but other plants such as conifers, alpines, roses, heathers and houseplants were reasonably numerous. The staff will gladly carry goods for the elderly or infirm, and disabled drivers may drive into the store area. Supervisors and managers are very helpful and anxious to please.

Prices Information not available
Facilities Parking, 1,000 cars. Toilets. Vending machines. Garden advice service. Delivery service
Open Mon, Tues and Sat 9am to 5.30pm, Wed to Fri 9am to 9pm, Sun 12am to 6pm. Closed Christmas Day and 12 July
Credit cards Access, Visa

MAGHERA Co. Londonderry   map 7

Mid-Ulster Garden Centre   🦋 ✿

35 Station Road, Maghera BT46 5BU   *Tel* Maghera (0648) 42324
On the east side of Maghera near the intersection of the A29 and A6

This is very much a plantsman's garden centre with an excellent range of stock including good-value unusual specimens, all in fine condition. A lot of the shrubs and conifers are grown on site and there is a written guarantee that none of the plants have been forced under glass, so you can be assured that 'what you see is what you get'. Heathers and conifers are a particularly strong point, while there are some interesting finds such as seaside plants and grasses hidden away in corners. Labels for groups of plants are excellent, giving clues to the best planting conditions and siting as well as aftercare, and a new computer labelling system has been introduced for individual labels. The centre is well laid out and signposted, and there's a heated indoor section stocking a large and varied collection of houseplants as well as fertilisers, chemicals and hand tools. Garden furniture and ornaments are also sold, and a new furniture showroom was due to open in February 1985. Patio planters, hanging baskets and other containers cater for the town gardener. New sections for paving and fencing were under construction in 1984, as was a new aquatic centre. A garden design service is offered and customers are invited into the design offices to watch the work in progress. The staff are keen to assist and the centre offers a service for finding rare and unusual plants.

Prices ££
Facilities Parking, 140 cars. Toilets. Coffee shop. Play area. Garden advice service. Free plant price list. Plant catalogue £2.25 (refundable on purchases over £20)
Open Mon to Sat 8.30am to 5.30pm, Sun 2pm to 5pm (closes 5pm every day in winter). Closed Christmas and Boxing Day

---

NEWTOWNSTEWART Co. Tyrone map 7
Baronscourt Nurseries and Garden Centre

Abercorn Estates, *Tel* Newtownstewart (06626) 61683/4
Baronscourt, Newtownstewart,
Omagh BT78 4EZ
3½ miles from Newtownstewart on the Drumquin road

This centre has an exceptional setting in the parkland of the Duke of Abercorn's estate. A large area is devoted to trees, while shrubs are kept in a walled garden of about four acres. There is a wide selection of other plants – extensive ranges of alpines and heathers – and a great deal of space is given over to the nursery area and propagation houses. Almost all plants sold are grown in the nursery: unusual trees and shrubs are a speciality, and several new varieties have been raised at Baronscourt. Quality of the plants is good and the prices cheap, but at the time of inspection labelling was poor and often washed out (the nurseries tell us this has been improved). The site is well laid out with paths laid using different types of paving to show what is available. Manoeuvring trolleys was difficult. The range of tools and sundries includes garden chemicals, composts, hand tools, sheds, hard landscaping materials, furniture and ornaments. Our inspector tells us that the nursery boasts 'one of the most up-and-coming plantsmen in the province – if not in the UK'. Improvements planned for 1985 included a tea room, improved checkout and a video advice service.

The nurseries have an agreement with two associated firms to provide a design and planting service.

Prices ££
Facilities Parking, 150 cars. Toilets. Garden advice service. Free plant price list
Open Mon to Sat 10am to 4.30pm, Sun 2pm to 4.30pm. Closed Christmas and Boxing Day

---

TEMPLEPATRICK Co. Antrim — map 7

Coleman's Nursery and Garden Centre

6 Old Ballyclare Road,   *Tel* Templepatrick (084 94) 32513
Templepatrick, Ballyclare BT39 0BJ

About 1 mile from the Templepatrick interchange with the M2, towards Templepatrick and 100 yds from the Pig 'n' Chicken roundabout

The range and number of plants stocked at this centre would surely satisfy both the beginner and the keenest gardener. There are simply vast stocks of every species and variety and on top of this the quality is exceptionally good in all cases and prices cheap. Almost all plants are marked with their botanical name, but some labels are hard to read due to weathering. The plants are arranged in a rectangular pattern which is straightforward, but paths in this area are somewhat narrow. This is not such a good place for buying gardening equipment. The inside shop area is very badly lit and our inspector felt it was rather sparsely stocked. However, the empty spaces on shelves suggested that this was an end-of-season shortage rather than a permanent feature and the centre tells us that it will be completely restocked in the spring. Anyone who loves plants will enjoy the opportunity to wander around the site freely without being pressurised to buy. The one staff member in attendance on the day of our inspection was most friendly and anxious to help. The centre offers a landscaping service which includes the installation of pools, patios and fencing. The centre has only recently entered the retail side of the trade and alterations are still planned, including a redesigned shrub area and display ground.

Prices ££
Facilities Parking, 50 cars. Garden advice service. Delivery service. Free price list and catalogue for plants
Open Mon to Fri 9am to 8pm (closes 5pm in winter), Sat 9am to 5pm, Sun 2pm to 5pm. Closed all day Sun in winter

2 Specialist nurseries

AFRICAN VIOLETS see SAINTPAULIAS

ALPINES AND ROCK PLANTS

It is no wonder that many gardeners become obsessed with alpines when they realise the potential and beauty of this tiny world, and just how many you can fit into a small area.

Most people immediately think of alpines as suitable for the rockery and nowhere else, but in fact they are at home in many places. The ground cover plants, such as acaena and thyme, are ideal in cracks and crevices in paths or the patio. Sinks or troughs can become miniature landscapes with a few well-positioned plants and stones. Alpines look lovely in a flat, raised bed or along the edge of the border, and, when you are really hooked, an alpine house can expand your scope considerably by allowing you to grow those that dislike our damp winters.

Wherever they are planted the conditions of their natural habitat – clean, sunny mountain regions – should be duplicated as closely as possible. The majority prefer a bright position and a quick-draining soil is imperative. It must have some organic matter, eg peat, in it but rock fragments, grit or very coarse sand are also necessary to ensure that it is sufficiently open and free draining. The ideal balance is a soil which retains moisture during the summer months, but never becomes saturated causing the alpines to sit with soggy roots during the winter.

Alpines are widely available at garden centres. They are almost always sold in pots so they can really be planted at any time, although early autumn or spring is preferable. Any species not stocked locally should be obtainable from one of the specialist nurseries either by mail order or a personal visit.

When planning your arrangement remember that although most alpines aren't too fussy some hate lime whereas others require it. These different tastes must be catered for either by sticking to one type, or by altering the soil conditions in the particular areas concerned. Keep your eyes open when visiting gardens and you can readily build up a list of species which appeal to your tastes. However, bear in mind that plants such as aubrieta and alyssum can become rampaging weeds so plant them with caution.

Easy alpines
Armeria maritima (thrift)
Campanula carpatica (dwarf campanula)
C. cochleariifolia
Dryas octopetala (mountain avens)
Erinus alpinus
Geranium subcaulescens
Hypericum dwarf species
Phlox douglasii
P. subulata
Primula alpine species
Saxifraga
Sempervivum

R. F. Beeston
294 Ombersley Road, Worcester,
Hereford and Worcester WR3 7HD
Tel Worcester (0905) 53245
Alpine specialist offering 200
varieties, concentrating on unusual
ones. Plants available by mail order.

Careby Manor Gardens
Careby, Stamford, Lincolnshire
PE9 4EA
Tel Castle Bytham (078 081) 220
Offer a wide range of alpines, small
plants and herbaceous perennials.
They also sell woody plants. Plants
available by mail order.

Castle Alpines
Castle Road, Wootton, Woodstock,
Oxford, Oxfordshire OX7 1EG
Tel Woodstock (0993) 812162
600 varieties of alpines,
lime-tolerant ones a particular
speciality. No mail order.

J. Cunnington
Engelberg Nursery, Bull Lane,
Brookmans Park, Hatfield,
Hertfordshire AL9 7AZ
Tel Potters Bar (0707) 58161
Alpine and rock plant specialist
with 400 varieties. Also offers 200
varieties of herbaceous perennials.
Plants available by mail order.

Edrom Nurseries
Coldingham, Eyemouth, Borders
TD14 5TZ
Tel Coldingham (039 03) 386
Alpine specialists offering 500
varieties. Concentrate on unusual
ones particularly primulas (90
varieties) and woodland plants.
Plants and seeds available by mail
order.

Jack Drake
Inshriach Nursery, Aviemore,
Highland PH22 1QS
Tel Kincraig (054 04) 287
Alpine specialist with 300 to 400
varieties – concentrating on hardy
varieties, in particular primulas (50
varieties) and rare plants. Plants,
seeds, corms and tubers available
by mail order.

Joe Elliott
Broadwell Alpines,
Moreton-in-Marsh, Gloucestershire
GL56 OTL
Tel Cotswold (0451) 30549
Specialises in lime-tolerant alpines
and alstroemeria 'Ligtu Hybrids'.
No mail order, except for seeds.

J. P. Geraghty
94 Avondale Road, South Croydon,
Surrey CR2 6JB
Specialises in Japanese alpines (300
varieties), also hardy and
half-hardy terrestrial orchids from
Australia, China, Japan and
Taiwan. 150 varieties of orchids.
Plants, corms and tubers available
by mail order.

Glenview Alpine Nursery
Quarryhill, by Forfar, Angus,
Tayside DD8 3TQ
Tel Foreside (030 786) 205
Alpine and rock plant specialist
stocking about 500 varieties.
Particular interest in lewisias,
gentians, meconopsis and Asiatic
primulas. Plants available by mail
order.

Halls of Heddon and Ovington
The Nurseries, Ovington, Prudhoe,
Northumberland NE42 6EE
Tel Prudhoe (0661) 32467
Alpines and herbaceous perennials
grown at this nursery, which is a
branch of Halls of Heddon. Plants
available by mail order.

Hartside Nursery Garden
Low Gill House, Alston, Cumbria
CA9 3BL
Tel Alston (0498) 81372
Alpine specialist with over 500
varieties. Aims to stock a wide
range of less common varieties
suitable for trough gardens and
alpine houses. Primulas are a
particular speciality, as are dwarf
shrubs (20 to 30 varieties), dwarf
conifers (30 to 50 varieties) and
20 to 30 varieties of dwarf
rhododendron. Also New Zealand
plants (10 to 20 varieties). Plants,
corms and tubers available by mail
order.

Holden Clough

Holden, Bolton-by-Bowland,
Clitheroe, Lancashire BB7 4PF
Tel Bolton-by-Bowland (020 07) 615
Alpine and herbaceous plants (over
1000 varieties). Also heathers (150
varieties), shrubs (300 varieties) and
dwarf conifers (200 varieties).
Plants available by mail order.

W. E. Th. Ingwersen

Birch Farm Nursery, Gravetye, East
Grinstead, W. Sussex RH19 4LE
Tel East Grinstead (0342) 810236
Alpine specialist with many
hundreds of varieties. Plants and
bulbs available by mail order.

Reginald Kaye

Waithman Nurseries, Silverdale,
Carnforth, Lancashire LA5 OTY
Tel Silverdale (0524) 701252
Alpine and rock plant specialist
with over 700 varieties including a
range of primulas. Also has
herbaceous perennials (260
varieties) and many trees and
shrubs eg dwarf conifers (50
varieties), dwarf trees (50 varieties),
azaleas and dwarf rhododendrons
(50 varieties). Hardy ferns (100
varieties) and aquatic plants (26
varieties plus waterlilies). Plants
available by mail order.

Mansfield Nurseries

Eastwood Rise, Eastwood, Essex
SS9 5DA
Tel Southend-on-Sea (0702) 525410
Specialise in pot-grown rock plants.
Also have a range of heathers and
dwarf conifers. Plants available by
mail order.

Martin Nest Nurseries

Victoria, Hepworth, Huddersfield,
W. Yorkshire HD7 1TW
Tel Huddersfield (0484) 686240
Alpines, especially those for cold
greenhouses, are the main
speciality. They also specialise in
primulas (at least 23 varieties) and
auriculas (at least 20 varieties –
show, alpines and fancy). Plants
available by mail order.

Oland Plants

Sawley Nursery, Risplith, Ripon,
N. Yorkshire HG4 3EW
Tel Sawley (076 586) 622
Specialise in alpines, ground cover
plants and perennials eg
ornamental grasses. They also have
a selection of ivies. Plants available
by mail order.

J. R. Ponton

Old Cottage Gardens, Legerwood,
Earlston, Borders TD4 6AS
Alpine specialist with 200 varieties.
Also offers 40 varieties of azaleas
and rhododendrons and 22
varieties of dwarf conifer. Plants
available by mail order.

Potterton and Martin

The Cottage Nursery, Moortown
Road, Nettleton, near Caistor,
Lincolnshire LN7 6HX
Tel Caistor (0472) 851792
Alpine specialists offering 700
varieties. They supply almost any
plant or dwarf bulb suitable for
rockery, bog or woodland.
Cyclamen (30 varieties), dwarf
conifers (50 varieties) and iris (50
varieties) are particular strengths.
Plants, corms and dry bulbs
available by mail order.

Rob Roy Nursery

Trossachs Road, Aberfoyle, Central
FK8 3SP
Tel Aberfoyle (087 72) 230
Specialises in alpines (80 varieties),
dwarf conifers (30 varieties), herbs
(30 varieties) and heathers (100 to
120 varieties). Plants available by
mail order.

Peter Trenear

Chantreyland, Chequers Lane,
Eversley Cross, Hampshire
RG27 0NX
Tel Eversley (0734) 732300
Specialises in rock plants, dwarf
conifers and trees for bonsai
training. Plants available by mail
order.

Also see:

HERBACEOUS PERENNIALS
Abbey Dore Court Gardens
Bressingham Gardens

FUCHSIAS
Fountains Nurseries

SHRUBS AND TREES
Brackenwood Nurseries
Chris Pattison

UNUSUAL PLANTS
County Park Nursery
Green Farm Plants

GOOD GARDEN CENTRES AND
GENERAL NURSERIES
Fishers Pond, Foulis Court Nursery
Waterperry, Waterperry Gardens
Wickwar, George Osmond
Widecombe-in-the-Moor,
Southcombe Gardens: rock plants

ASPARAGUS

Asparagus has the reputation of being rather a sophisticated vegetable. It occupies a permanent site and crops for just a few weeks each year. It will grow in most soils provided they are well drained, and a touch of lime is most welcome. The beds should be well dug and if possible plenty of well-rotted manure or compost incorporated in the autumn before planting. Asparagus plants don't usually need any fertiliser in subsequent years since they get all their nutrients through their deep roots. Two- or three-year-old crowns are often recommended. But one-year-old crowns are easier to establish, more likely to survive the first winter and will often provide a first harvest as soon as the older crowns. Wait two years before cutting.

Common-or-garden varieties are relatively easy to come by in the early spring at many garden centres. The crowns should feel moist and be free from dirt. If they are dry and wizened, the plants won't succeed. Check that there is a decent crown and no root damage and you should get a good plant. You are likely to get a bigger choice of varieties from specialists, and some continually try out new high-yield varieties and their own strains, so you have a chance of being at the forefront of asparagus growing! The variety 'Lucullus' does not produce female plants, so there is no problem with self-seeding.

Crowns seem to travel well so can safely be purchased by mail order. Order in January or February for despatch by April and planting in May. Seeds of common varieties can be obtained from general seedsmen.

Varieties to try

COMMON
'Connovers Colossal'
'Lucullus'

WORTH LOOKING FOR
'Limbras'
'Regal'

Gary Andrews
203 Pershore Road, Evesham,
Hereford and Worcester WR11 6NB
Tel Evesham (0386) 2882
Offers 'Lucullus' and his own
strain. Plans to import varieties
from France, America and Holland.

Plants sold in peat blocks in
summer and as dormant crowns in
winter. Supplied by mail order.

M. Bennett
Long Compton, Shipston-on-
Stour, Warwickshire CV36 5JN
Offers two varieties: 'Connovers
Colossal' and 'Lucullus'; also sells
globe artichokes. One-year-old
crowns supplied by mail order.

T. H. Bennet
Lisbon House, 62 Willersey Road,
Badsey, Evesham, Hereford and
Worcester WR11 5HB

Tel Evesham (0386) 830426
'Connovers Colossal' supplied as
one-, two- or three-year-old crowns
by mail order.

Crown Vegetables
Stock Corner Farm, Stock Corner,
Beck Row, Mildenhall, Bury St.
Edmunds, Suffolk IP28 8DW
Tel Burnt Fen (035 375) 377
Concentrate on 'Limbras' varieties,
although 'Lucullus' and 'Connovers
Colossal' also available. Sold as
first-year crowns by mail order.

E. Hubbold
25 Coniston Way, Bewdley,
Hereford and Worcester DY12 2QA
Tel Bewdley (0299) 404221
Own Evesham strain available as

one-, two-, or three-year-old
crowns. Available by mail order.

A. R. Paske and Co
The South Lodge, Gazeley Road,
Kentford, Newmarket, Suffolk
CB8 7QA
Tel Newmarket (0638) 750613
Offers 'Regal Pedigree' asparagus
crowns; also globe artichokes and
seakale. Available by mail order.

Also see:

SEEDS
S. M. McArd: crowns
Seeds-by-Size: seed

SOFT FRUIT
Ken Muir: crowns

AZALEAS AND RHODODENDRONS

The genus rhododendron encompasses both azaleas and rhododendrons.
Their colourful flowers are a common sight in formal gardens, woodlands
and parks in this country. Most of those grown are the species and varieties
that form large or medium-sized shrubs, but rhododendrons actually
include everything from tall trees to tiny shrubs – over 1000 species in all! –
and many more hybrids. In the wild they usually come from temperate
climates, but there are some sub-tropical species which will only survive as
pot plants or in the greenhouse.

Rhododendrons demand a free-draining soil in a semi-shaded position.
A few (for example *R. luteus*) will tolerate heavy clay, but hardly any will
grow in alkaline soils – although there are a few which will tolerate neutral
soil. Don't plant rhododendrons in frost pockets unless they're very
late-flowering varieties, nor where they might be exposed to the strong
morning sun – young plants are likely to be killed off during long periods of
sunshine if not properly shaded.

Before buying a rhododendron, it is sensible to decide what area you are
trying to fill. There will always be a wide range that will grow to the right
size and it would be a pity to plant those which will quickly outgrow their
welcome. Rhododendrons should, ideally, be planted in the autumn so
they can get established before the winter sets in. They have shallow,
compact, fibrous root systems and are easily moved from one site to
another providing they're not too big. It is possible to move them at any
time – however, if this is done in the late spring or summer it can be very
difficult to keep the soil adequately moist. Container-grown plants are
commonly available from garden centres but you may also find root-balled
plants. Rhododendrons and azaleas need careful watering initially as they
take time to establish. Don't be too alarmed if you discover your plant has
simply been containerised – that is, just put in the container ready for sale
rather than grown in it. The soil may crumble away from the rootball, but

this won't seriously damage the plant. Nurserymen often encourage rhododendrons to be well budded and in full flower when sold, and this means the plants can take a couple of years to recover their vigour, so you must be patient. Larger varieties are best bought with no buds. Buying older plants is not worth it – they are expensive, need extra care to establish and frequently do not develop as well as good young plants with several side-shoots ready to bush out. Specialist nurseries are the best source for the less widely available types.

Varieties worth trying

POPULAR

'Blue Diamond' small neat shrub, blue flowers
'Britannia' compact bush, large pinkish-scarlet flowers
'Coccinea speciosa' one of the best old azaleas, forms a neat shrub with orange red flowers
'Cynthia' deep rose-pink flowers
'Doncaster' dwarf spreading bush, dark red flowers
'Elizabeth' small neat shrub, red flowers
R. impeditum dwarf alpine with lavender blue flowers
R. hirsutum grows on alkaline soils
'Loder's White' large shrub, large white flowers
'Pink Pearl' large shrub, pink flowers
R. ponticum very common, naturalised in some parts of the country. Grows to a large shrub. Vivid mauve flowers
'Unique' pink buds opening ivory flushed with pink. Dense and shapely bush

WORTH LOOKING FOR

Deciduous azalea 'Sunte Nectarine' medium-sized, deep orange flowers with a yellow flame
Deciduous azalea 'Mixed Seedlings' medium-sized in a rainbow of colours from white through yellow and dark red.
'Fred Wynniatt' maize yellow with pink flush
R. falconeri grows to a large shrub or tall tree. Creamy-yellow flowers with purple markings. Very large leaves
R. macabeanum large shrub or tall tree, yellow flowers and large leaves
Hybrids of *R. yakushimanum* compact very rewarding plants with fine foliage

Exbury Gardens
Exbury, near Southampton, Hampshire SO4 1AZ
Tel Fawley (0703) 891203
Azalea and rhododendron specialists offering 420 varieties. They concentrate on the Rothschild collection of garden hybrid rhododendrons and the Exbury range of deciduous azaleas (including the new Solent range). They also offer a range of camellias. Plants and seeds available by mail order.

C. E. Henderson and Son
Leydens Nursery, Stick Hill, Edenbridge, Kent TN8 5NH
Tel Edenbridge (0732) 863318
Azalea and rhododendron specialist offering 140 varieties. Concentrates on Japanese evergreen azaleas and dwarf and giant-flowered rhododendrons. It also offers 90 varieties of conifers – mostly dwarf – and lawn grass seed mixtures for various purposes. It has over 30 varieties of wild flowers, mostly seeds but some plants. Mail order available.

Milton Hutchings
Pield Heath Nurseries, Hillingdon, Uxbridge, Middlesex UB8 3NP
Tel Uxbridge (0895) 31514
General garden centre, but specialises in the production of Cape heaths (26 varieties) and Japanese azaleas (30 varieties), both for indoor growing. No mail order.

Hydon Nurseries
Clock Barn Lane, Hydon Heath, Godalming, Surrey GU8 4AZ
Tel Hascombe (048 632) 252
Azalea and rhododendron specialists. They also specialise in trees and shrubs. Plants available by mail order.

King and Paton
Barnhourie Mill, Dalbeattie, Dumfries and Galloway DG5 4PU
Tel Southwick (038 778) 269
Azalea and rhododendron specialists with 80 varieties – they concentrate on species and their variants (not hybrids). Plants available by mail order.

Leonardslee Gardens
Lower Beeding, near Horsham, W. Sussex RH13 6PP
Tel Lower Beeding (040 376) 212
Rhododendron specialists with 500 varieties. They also offer other trees and shrubs. The gardens are open to the public in spring and autumn. Plants available by mail order.

Millais Nurseries
Crosswater Farm, Churt, Farnham, Surrey GU10 2JN
Tel Frensham (025 125) 2415
Azalea and rhododendron specialists with 200 varieties. Plants available by mail order.

G. Reuthe
Branch Nursery, Crown Point, Ightham, near Sevenoaks, Kent
Tel Farnborough (0295 89) 52249
Azalea and rhododendron specialist with over 450 varieties. Plants available by mail order, but correspondence to head office, at Foxhill Nurseries, Keston, Kent BR2 6AW.

Starborough Nursery
Starborough Road, Marsh Green, Edenbridge, Kent TN8 5RB
Tel Edenbridge (0732) 865614
Offers over 100 varieties of azaleas and rhododendrons – there is an extensive range of other shrubs, especially unusual ones. Plants available by mail order.

Trewithen Nurseries
Grampound Road, near Truro, Cornwall TR2 4DD
Tel St. Austell (0726) 882764
They specialise in rhododendrons for smaller gardens (35 varieties) and camellias (40 varieties). They also stock other shrubs. No mail order.

Wall Cottage Nursery
Lockengate, Bugle, St. Austell, Cornwall PL28 8RU
Tel Lanivet (0208) 831259
Azalea and rhododendron specialist with over 1000 varieties and a range of other plants that associate well with them. Plants available by mail order.

Also see:

ALPINES AND ROCK PLANTS
Hartside Nursery Garden
Reginald Kaye
J. R. Ponton

CAMELLIAS
Fairlight Camellia Nursery

HEATHERS
Hardwick Nursery

ROSES
Henry Street

SHRUBS AND TREES
Goscote Nurseries
C. J. Marchant
Nettletons Nurseries

UNUSUAL PLANTS
Ballalheannagh Gardens

GOOD GARDEN CENTRES AND
GENERAL NURSERIES
Glencarse, Glendoick Garden
Centre
Knaphill, Knaphill Nurseries

Tal-y-Cafn, Bodnant Garden
Nursery
Windlesham, L. R. Russell Nursery
Garden Centre

BEGONIAS

Lovely plants to add a splash of colour to tubs, window boxes and hanging baskets, while some are suitable for the border or as houseplants. There are large-flowered, tuberous begonias; fibrous-rooted types such as the many varieties of *B. semperflorens*, favoured for summer bedding and the Rieger begonias now widely sold as flowering indoor plants; also foliage varieties for indoors such as *B. rex*.

Semperflorens varieties are available from the major seed nurseries or as small plants. They are normally treated as annuals but can be overwintered indoors. Foliage varieties are sold as houseplants and are prized for their unusually coloured and textured leaves. Some also produce attractive yellow, pink, apricot or red flowers from March to October. Tuberous varieties are readily available in shops, markets and garden centres around the end of January. Though enthusiasts buy named varieties from specialist nurseries, they are usually sold according to colour. You can buy the upright sorts for tubs, window boxes or garden borders or the pendula (cascade) sort for hanging baskets and spilling over the edge of containers. Tuberous begonias bloom from mid July until the end of September. Mail order shopping will offer a wide and possibly better-quality choice, but the cost is high and tubers cannot be selected personally. In shops it's better to buy pre-packed tubers as those sold loose can quickly deteriorate in dry conditions. If you do buy them loose, get them as soon as they appear for sale, say early February. Check that tubers are not squishy or soft, but have about the same resistance as cork. Small swellings are signs of eelworms and any soft, sunken areas suggest rot. Choose tubers which show the remains of last year's roots rather than those which are smooth. Small shoots are not a problem, but if they are over 12mm (½in) long the tuber will be weakened.

Outdoors, begonias prefer light shade and they enjoy a moisture-retentive soil, but you can really grow them anywhere if the soil is carefully prepared.

Varieties

Begonias are usually sold by colour and type, not as named varieties, so choose them to suit your purpose, eg upright, colourful varieties for a window box, the pendula type for a hanging basket.

Blackmore and Langdon
Pensford, Bristol, Avon BS18 4JL
Tel Chew Magna (027 589) 2300
Begonia and delphinium specialists
with 40 and 50 varieties
respectively. They also offer 20
varieties of border phlox and
polyanthus. Predominantly mail
order.

Nielsen Plants
Danecroft Nurseries, Station Road,
Hellingly, E. Sussex BN27 4EU
Tel Hailsham (0323) 845186

Begonia specialists with 15 varieties. They concentrate on Rieger begonias. No mail order.

T. White and Son
Park Mains Nursery, Inchinnan, Renfrewshire, Strathclyde PA8 7AD
Tel 041-812 1246
Begonia specialists with about 25 varieties. They particularly specialise in named, double, tuberous varieties. Plants, seeds and tubers by mail order.

Also see:

BULBS

SEEDS

BONSAI

The 'art of bonsai' conjures up an image of tranquillity, harmony and grace. Curving branches, gnarled trunks, dramatic changes in shape and form, the mystery of bonsai relies on two words – time and training. Obviously an eye for line, skill at pruning techniques, and appreciation of trees are important elements, but without the patience to wait ten, twenty, fifty years for the specimen to reach its desired form they all come to nothing. You can, of course, buy mature bonsai trees but they are very expensive and won't give you the same satisfaction as creating a tree of your own.

Sources of starting material are numerous. When interest was first aroused in China and Japan the only source was to scour remote and mountainous terrain to obtain old trees dwarfed by the hardship of their surroundings. Now most of these have long gone and the modern bonsai enthusiast must seek other means. Some trees grow easily from seed, and a selection of the best seedlings will produce good starting material, although you will have to be patient. The plants may not have the same characteristics as the parent, but this is not always a disadvantage. An attractive little bonsai will take about five years to produce. A small seedling growing wild is another possibility, but do ask first before you start digging up people's land! Cuttings and layering are alternative methods of obtaining a good young plant especially for flowering species – seedlings of these may take many years before flowering. Shrub nurseries are often a good source of slightly older material, but avoid dwarf conifers as they are not suitable for training. Basically, one should choose a hardy plant which has the potential qualities of a good bonsai. Look for a sturdy trunk and plenty of nicely balanced branches, especially low down the trunk. A good fibrous root system is also important. The final source is to buy younger or partly trained trees from a specialist nursery. They should be able to provide saplings in a range of species as well as the correct ceramic pots and other accessories, and offer useful guidance as to how to treat your new acquisition. Price depends on age and quality (the cost increases as the bonsai ages). Non-specialists, florists and garden centres are worth trying but they probably won't be able to offer as much advice as a specialist. The drawback with buying from a shop or department store is that they may have kept the trees indoors. Most of the bonsai available in this country are of hardy varieties and must be kept outside – only brought in occasionally.

Many specialists stock a lot more plants than they list, so if you want something special, ask for it. You may be lucky.

Suitable trees

HARDY

Beech, autumn colour and bark
Birch, bark
Cotoneaster, flowers, berries and autumn colour
Crabapple, blossom and apples
Cryptomeria, bronze colour in winter, evergreen
Elm (Japanese, Chinese and English), autumn colour
Hawthorn, small flowers
Hornbeam, bark
Juniper, evergreen
Palmate maple, leaf shape, autumn colour
Pine, evergreen
Pyracantha, flowers, berries, evergreen
Quince, blossom
Willow, easy to obtain, grow, train and care for.

NON-HARDY

Pomegranate, scarlet flower

Bourne Bridge Nurseries

Oak Hill Road, Stapleford Abbots, near Romford, Essex RM4 1JL
Tel Romford (0708) 43203
Bonsai specialists with 20 to 30 varieties. Plants available by mail order.

Bromage and Young

Wildacre, Brookhurst Road, Cranleigh, Surrey GU6 7DW
Tel Cranleigh (0483) 232893
Bonsai specialists able to supply trees, seeds, bowls and other accessories. Mail order available.

Dawn and Peter Chan Bonsai

9 Riddlesdown Avenue, Purley, Surrey CR2 1JH
Tel 01-660 4002
Bonsai specialists with trees of all ages – from 2-year-olds to centenarians. The majority of the stock is locally raised. Pots, seeds and other sundries are available by mail order. Visits to the nursery by prior arrangement.

Greenwood Gardens

Ollerton Road, Arnold, Nottingham, Nottinghamshire NG5 8PR
Tel Nottingham (0602) 205757
Specialist bonsai nursery supplying trees and all accessories, books etc. Also run courses on bonsai. In addition, stock about 100 varieties of heather.

Potters Garden Bonsai Nursery

The Boat House, Potters Lane, Samlesbury, Preston, Lancashire PR5 OUE
Tel Samlesbury (077 477) 213
Bonsai specialist supplying plants, seeds, pots, tools and books. Only supply by mail order on request, but plan to produce a mail order catalogue.

Price and Adams

Cherry Trees, 22 Burnt Hill Road, Wrecclesham, Farnham, Surrey GU10 4RX
Tel Farnham (0252) 714266
A range of species but especially pines and maples. Tools and pots available by mail order, but not plants.

Seiyokan Bonsai

Buttercup Cottage, Corfe, near Taunton, Somerset TA13 7BY
Tel Taunton (0823) 42762
Approximately 20 species of trained bonsai including a selection of very old bonsai. Pots, seeds, books and other accessories available. Bonsai viewing by prior appointment only. Mail order from PO Box 87, London SW6 2HZ
Tel 01-731 5403

Also see:

ALPINES AND ROCK PLANTS
Peter Trenear

SHRUBS AND TREES
Glebe Nursery: seedlings for bonsai

GOOD GARDEN CENTRES AND GENERAL NURSERIES
Tansley, Matlock Garden Waterlife and Pet Centre

BROMELIADS

The unusual and exotic-looking bromeliads are well suited to cool greenhouse care, but can also make good houseplants. They are sometimes known as urn plants as the majority have leaves arranged in a rosette with a hollow centre which, in nature, fills with rainwater. Another common feature is that the main plant will die after flowering, but is usually replaced by one or more offsets. These grow quickly, but it can be difficult to induce some species, such as neoregelias and guzmanias, to flower. Many varieties have attractive leaves and make robust houseplants tolerating central heating, low light levels and irregular watering. They benefit from the occasional foliar feed when actively growing. Many tillandsias (air plants) will grow without any food or water except what they can absorb from the air and may be sold as room decorations mounted on coral or sea shells. A visit to the displays at the RHS Wisley Gardens, Kew Gardens or the Liverpool Botanic Gardens, or specialists' displays at shows, is a good way of acquiring familiarity with different species before buying.

Some bromeliads are very easy to find, and between Christmas and Easter the more popular varieties appear for sale in department stores, shops and florists, though you'll generally find a better quality and range in nurseries and garden centres which sell houseplants. You may wish to regard your bromeliad as disposable once it has flowered. In this case choose a large plant – the larger the plant, the quicker it will flower. Better still, buy one already in flower, but with the flower head just appearing from the rosette. (You are more likely to find plants at this stage at a nursery since shops tend to prefer to sell showy specimens in full flower.) If a flower has any brown tips this indicates it is nearing the end of its time, so avoid these. If you want to keep your bromeliad for several years, go for smaller, cheaper plants with attractive foliage, choosing ones which look fresh and unmarked. You may find bromeliads sold in unsuitable compost, and planted too deeply. The compost should be a quarter grit, and the base of the plant just below the surface. If necessary repot your plant, even if it's in flower, or you risk it rotting at the base. If you want an unusual variety, try the mail order specialists who send out bare-rooted plants all year round.

Species to try

POPULAR, EASY TO GROW

Aechmea fasciata (urn plant)
Ananas comosus 'Variegatus' (variegated pineapple)
Cryptanthus (earth star)
Tillandsia ionantha (air plant)

MORE DEMANDING

Guzmania lingulata
Neoregelia carolinae 'Tricolor'
Vriesea splendens (flaming sword)

Buckfast Nursery
Buckfast, Devon TQ11 0EA
Tel Buckfastleigh (0364) 42540

Approximately 25 varieties of tillandsia (airplants) – also many other exotic plants such as palms. Clubs and organisations are welcome to visit their display (just opposite Buckfast Abbey) by appointment. Plants available by mail order.

Vesutor Airplants
The Bromeliad Nursery,
Billingshurst Lane, Ashington,
W. Sussex RH20 3BA
Tel Ashington (0903) 892900
Bromeliad specialists concentrating

on tillandsia (airplants). Plants and seeds (the latter free when in stock) available by mail order.

Jacqueline Watts Plants
45 Sea Road, Abergele, Clwyd
LL22 7TE
Tel Abergele (0745) 825100

100 varieties of bromeliad available by mail order. Special interest in catering for the beginner.

Also see:

CACTI AND SUCCULENTS
Tamarisk Nurseries

BULBS

A bulb is essentially a storage house for the food which sustains a plant during its early growing period. The term is often used loosely to include corms, tubers and rhizomes and you will probably find that most bulb specialists include all of these in their catalogues. Bulbs can be suitable for naturalising in grass, growing in a mixed border or rockery, or in window boxes or pots indoors. Some bulbs are hardy enough to remain in the soil through the winter, while more tender bulbs need lifting in autumn and storing away from frosts. When planning bulb displays remember that not all bulbs are spring-flowering and you can have a colourful succession of blooms virtually throughout the year. It is also important to place your bulbs in a position where the fading leaves will not be an eyesore after flowering – they should be left at least six weeks to ensure they produce good bulbs for next year's flowering.

Buying bulbs can involve either a trip to a local shop, garden centre or nursery, or a browse through catalogues either from general bulb stockists, or those specialising in unusual bulbs. Although catalogues offer a great variety, the disadvantage of mail order shopping is that you can't check the bulb quality before buying. A good bulb should be solid, firm and a good size. It should be free from disease or pests, undamaged and not shrivelled. If buying locally, select bulbs when they are fresh and before they start to look dehydrated and plant them as quickly as possible after buying. When buying by post, order early so that you get the varieties requested and so there is time to return any sub-standard bulbs without missing the correct planting times. Spring-flowering bulbs, and summer-flowering ones which continue growing in winter, appear in shops, garden centres and catalogues in the summer. Summer-flowering bulbs which die down in winter are sold in the spring, either 'in the green' or as dry bulbs. Many general bulb stockists produce two mail order catalogues a year. When buying unusual bulbs you should insist on **cultivated** plants, not bulbs gathered from the wild, to avoid depleting natural populations.

Also see CYCLAMEN, DAFFODILS, GLADIOLI and IRIS

Bulbs to try

SPRING-FLOWERING
anemone
chinodoxa
crocus
fritillaria
galanthus (snowdrop)
hyacinth

muscari (grape hyacinth)
ornithogalum
scilla
tulip

SUMMER-FLOWERING
allium (ornamental onions)
amaryllis
camassia

crinum
eucomis
galtonia
ixia
nerine
ranunculus
tigridia

AUTUMN-FLOWERING
colchicum
crocus
sternbergia

WINTER-FLOWERING
crocus
eranthis
galanthus

General bulb suppliers

Jacques Amand
17 Beethoven Street, London
W10 4LG
Tel 01-969 9797

Appledore's Answer
Priory Lands, Appledore, Ashford,
Kent TN26 2DP
Tel Appledore (023 383) 285/393

Bakker Holland
Beeklaan, Hillegom, Holland
Tel 01031 252 0046
or PO Box 120, Miller Street,
Preston, Lancashire PR1 4RU

Walter Blom and Son
Coombelands, Leavesden,
Watford, Hertfordshire WD2 7BH
Tel Garston (0923) 672071/673767

P. de Jager and Sons (also trade as
Wallace and Barr)
The Nurseries, Marden, Kent
TN12 9BP
Tel Maidstone (0622) 831235

Groom Bros.
Pecks Drove Nurseries, Claylake,
Spalding, Lincolnshire PE12 6BJ
Tel Spalding (0775) 2421

Hortico (also trade as Spalding Bulb
Co and in shops as Geest)
Spalding, Lincolnshire PE12 6EB
Tel Spalding (0775) 5936

Kelways Nurseries
Langport, Somerset TA10 9SL
Tel Langport (0458) 250521
General bulbsmen, but also stock
180 varieties of iris in
summer/autumn catalogue.

Lowland Nurseries
St. Thomas's Road, Spalding,
Lincolnshire PE11 2TL
Tel Spalding (0775) 4871

J. Parker Dutch Bulbs
452 Chester Road, Old Trafford,
Greater Manchester M16 9HL
Tel 061-872 1700

Van Tubergen
Oldfield Lane, Wisbech,
Cambridgeshire PE13 2RJ
Tel Wisbech (0945) 64949

Suppliers of unusual bulbs

Avon Bulbs
Bathford, Bath, Avon BA1 8ED
Tel Bath (0225) 859495
Specialise in dwarf bulbs for the
garden or cold greenhouse.

R. Bowlby
PO Box 156,
Kingston-upon-Thames, Surrey
KT2 6AN
Specialises in unusual bulbs. Can
also supply more familiar bulbs in
large quantities.

Broadleigh Gardens
Barr House, Bishops Hull, Taunton,
Somerset TA4 LAE
Tel Taunton (0823) 86231
Specialise in small and unusual
bulbs; also offer unusual
herbaceous plants.

P. J. and J. W. Christian
Pentre Cottages, Minera,
Wrexham, Clwyd LL11 3PD
Tel 051-733 9889
Specialise in dwarf bulb species,
mostly rare or unusual.

Nerine Nurseries
Welland, Hereford and Worcester
WR13 6LN

Specialist nursery selling only nerines (Guernsey lily). Stock 10 hardy and about 70 tender species and varieties.

Paradise Centre
Twinstead Road, Lamarsh, Bures, Suffolk CO8 5EX
Tel Twinstead (078 729) 449
Growers of unusual bulbs and tuberous plants. Asiatic primulas, bog and shade plants also offered.

Also see:

ALPINE AND ROCK PLANTS
Potterton and Martin

HERBACEOUS PERENNIALS
J. and E. Parker-Jervis

UNUSUAL PLANTS
Cottage Garden Plants Old and New

CACTI AND SUCCULENTS

The world of cacti and succulents encompasses such bizarre and exotic shapes that their great popularity is not surprising. Easy and fun to grow, they are the favourites of children and beginners generally. Overwatering will quickly kill them, but other forms of neglect seldom result in casualties. But with a minimum of care these fascinating plants can produce marvellous displays. Grow them in a greenhouse where the sun is plentiful, but the frost is kept at bay; or alternatively in the house, away from warmth in winter and out on the patio in the summer. In general, the more light they are given, the better they will grow and flower.

Hundreds of species are available – specialist nurseries often have extraordinary ranges in their mail order catalogues. This is a good way to buy because of the choice and as the plants travel reliably. They will usually arrive bare rooted so be ready to pot them up. Prices are generally reasonable with rare and unusual species being sold surprisingly cheaply. Many shops, florists and garden centres also have interesting collections. Go for a plant you like the look of. If it's in flower, so much the better. Many flower freely and buying one this way is a sign that the plant has been cared for. Out of flower, avoid plants which seem starved of light or overwatered – these will have elongated, pale green growth. Make sure there are no wet, brown areas around the base of the stem. Check for stability – you don't want a plant with basal rot, or a poor root system. Finally, keep an eye out for pests – cacti and succulents are prone to mealy bug and scale insects.

Growing from seed is another option for those with a little patience. Specialists and large seed companies are two sources, and the relevant societies operate exchange schemes which can be handy and inexpensive. Most seeds retain their viability well. Whichever way you buy and whatever varieties you choose, give them plenty of light, don't overwater, and you should be well on your way to success.

Popular varieties
Euphorbia milii (crown of thorns) bright red bracts on shrub-like plant
Mammillaria zeilmanniana small, round with pink flowers
Schlumbergera buckleyi (Christmas cactus)
Crassula portulacea thick fleshy leaves with red tinge
Lithops (living stones) daisy-like flowers

A lot of specialists exhibit at shows and this can be a good place to buy plants.

Echeveria decorative leaves
Kalanchoe red, pink or orange flowers

Abbey Brook Cactus Nursery
Old Hacknay Lane, Matlock,
Derbyshire DE4 2QJ
Tel Matlock (0629) 55360
Cacti and succulent specialist with
over 2000 species and varieties in
total. Has a particular interest in
epiphytes and offers over 200
species and cultivars. Concentrates
on propagating endangered
species. Plants and seeds available
by mail order.

**Barleyfield Succulent Plant
Nursery**
Southburgh, Thetford, Norfolk
IP25 7TE
Tel Dereham (0362) 820457
Succulent specialist with several
hundred succulents listed, and
more in small numbers at the
nursery. Plants available by mail
order.

Cruck Cottage Cacti
Cliff Road, Wrelton, Pickering,
N. Yorkshire YO18 8PJ
Tel Pickering (0751) 72042
Cacti and succulent specialist with
150 and 120 species and varieties
respectively. The nursery organises
an annual cactus fair each year in
Harrogate – contact nursery for
details. No mail order.

The Exotic Collection
18 Franklin Road, Worthing,
W. Sussex BN13 2PQ
Tel Worthing (0903) 65789
Cacti and succulent specialists. A
general list is available to members
of the public, but plant offers and
an extensive seed list are only
available to subscribers of 'The
Exotic Collection' magazine.
Subscribers can also visit the
gardens. Sub-tropical plants, eg
frost-resistant palm trees, are also
offered. Plants and seeds available
by mail order.

Fold Garden
26 Fold Lane, Biddulph,
Staffordshire ST8 7SG
Tel Stoke-on-Trent (0782) 513028
Succulent specialist with 500
varieties, and some cacti (50
varieties). Also offers 200 varieties
of herbs. Plants available by mail
order.

Glenhirst Cactus Nursery
Station Road, Swineshead, Boston,
Lincolnshire PE20 3NX
Tel Boston (0205) 820314
Cacti and succulent specialist with
800 species and varieties. Specialise
in particular in sempervivums (100
or so species, cultivars and
hybrids), Christmas cacti,
epiphyllums and lithops. Plants
available by mail order.

Holly Gate Cactus Nursery
Billingshurst Lane, Ashington,
W. Sussex RH20 3BA
Tel Ashington (0903) 892930
Cacti and succulent specialist with
1500 to 2000 species and varieties,
including epiphyllums. Plants and
seeds available by mail order.

Jumanery Cacti
St. Catherines Lodge, Whaplode
St. Catherine, near Spalding,
Lincolnshire PE12 6SR
Tel Holbeach St. Johns (040 634) 373
Specialises in rare grafted cacti and
rare succulents. Plants and seeds
available by mail order.

Oakleigh Nurseries
Monkwood, Alresford, Hampshire
SO24 0HB
Tel Ropley (096 277) 3344
Specialists in epiphytic cacti (150
species and varieties), fuchsias (120
varieties) and pelargoniums (80
varieties). Plants available by mail
order.

The Plant Lovers
The Old Rectory, Candlesby,
Spilsby, Lincolnshire PE23 5RU

Tel Scremby (075 485) 256
Cacti and succulent specialists with
1000 species and varieties. No mail
order.

Southwest Seeds
200 Spring Road, Kempston,
Bedford MK42 8ND
Specialists able to supply both
plants and seeds. 100 varieties
available as plants – mostly South
African desert succulents. 1000
species of seed particularly desert
plant seed from South America and
Mexico. Plants and seeds available
by mail order.

Tamarisk Nurseries
Rumford, Wadebridge, Cornwall
PL27 75Y
Tel Rumford (084 14) 313
Cacti and succulent specialists with
340 species and varieties. They also
sell carnivorous plants (10
varieties), orchids (150 varieties)
and bromeliads, particularly
tillandsias (airplants), of which
they stock 40 varieties. Mail order
available.

Westfield Cacti
10 Shillingford Road, Alphington,
Exeter, Devon EX2 8UB
Tel Exeter (0392) 832921
Cacti and succulent specialist with

600 species and varieties. Plants
and seeds available by mail order.

Whitestone Gardens
Sutton-under-Whitestonecliff,
Thirsk, N. Yorkshire YO7 2PZ
Tel Thirsk (0845) 597467
Cacti and succulent specialists who
cover all aspects of the hobby –
plants, seeds, books etc. Over 2000
species and varieties. Mail order
available.

Roy Young
79 Pearcroft Road, Leytonstone,
London E11 4DP
Tel 01-556 8048
Cacti and succulent specialist who
concentrates on lithops and other
related genera. 500 and 2000 species
and varieties of plants and seed
respectively. Mail order only.

See also:

HERBACEOUS PERENNIALS
Abbey Dore Court Gardens:
sedums

SEMPERVIVUMS
Alan C. Smith

VIOLAS
R. E. Coombs

GOOD GARDEN CENTRES AND
GENERAL NURSERIES
Angmering, Manor Nursery

CAMELLIAS

Lovely spring-flowering evergreen shrubs for growing among other
shrubs, structuring a mixed border, training up walls or growing in
containers. They can also be used for a temporary display indoors.
Camellias have distinctive shiny dark green leaves and bushes will
eventually reach about 3.7 to 4.6m (12 to 15ft) but take many years to do so.
Some grow to as much as 9m (30ft) but all respond well to pruning just after
flowering. They can flower as early as Christmas, but spring is more likely.
Colours range from white, through pink to red, and flowers occur in many
shapes from single to the paeony and rose forms.

Camellias require an acid soil with a lot of humus. Good drainage is
important and shelter from wind. They like plenty of light but not hot, dry
conditions and will tolerate partial shade – but always ensure that the
plants are protected from the morning sun as this will destroy the buds if
there's been a frost.

When buying a camellia it is important to select a variety suited to your
part of the country. Although most camellias will survive easily outside,

only the *C. x williamsii* hybrids will flower well in the north of England and Scotland. A choice of varieties is easily found in garden centres across the country, usually *C. japonica* and *C. x williamsii* varieties. The best choice will be at Eastertime, and this is the ideal time for planting, although container-grown camellias can be planted out at any time of year except when it's very cold, very wet or hot and dry. A plant of about 25cm (10in) high is a good buy. A strong main stem with a number of side shoots, usually dark leaves and, when buying in spring, plenty of buds or flowers are points to check on. Avoid broken shoots or plants with roots exposed above the surface of the compost. Dried buds mean there has been frost damage, and mottled leaves suggest a virus disease. Prices and quality vary considerably so shopping around can pay off.

Varieties to try

OLD FAVOURITES, EASILY AVAILABLE

C. japonica 'Adolph Andersson' light red, semi-double
C. japonica 'Alba Simplex' white, single
C. japonica 'Contessa Lavinia Maggi' white, striped pink and red, double
C. japonica 'Grand Slam' dark red
C. x williamsii 'Anticipation' crimson, paeony form
C. x williamsii 'Debbie' rose pink, paeony form
C. x williamsii 'Donation' light rose pink, semi-double
C. x williamsii 'J. C. Williams' pale pink, single
C. x williamsii 'Leonard Messel' deep pink

WORTH LOOKING FOR

C. japonica 'Bobs Tinsie' crimson
C. japonica 'Haku-Rakuten' white
C. japonica 'Scentsation' pink
C. x williamsii 'Elegant Beauty' rose pink
C. x williamsii 'Innovation' rose crimson
C. x williamsii 'Mona Jury', apricot
C. x williamsii 'Satan's Rose' red
C. x williamsii 'Tiny Princess' shell pink

Fairlight Camellia Nursery
Three Oaks Village, Guestling, near Hastings, E. Sussex TN35 4NT
Tel Hastings (0424) 425371
Camellia specialist with over 200 varieties, specialises particularly in plants which are hardy and free-flowering in the open garden. Also has 50 varieties of rhododendrons, particularly modern hybrids. Plants available by mail order.

Marwood Hill Gardens
Barnstaple, Devon EX31 4EB
Tel Barnstaple (0271) 42528
Camellia specialists with 80 varieties, with particular emphasis on the japonica cultivars. Also specialises in clematis (30 varieties), hebes (60 varieties) and other trees and shrubs. No mail order.

Porthpean House Gardens
St. Austell, Cornwall PL26 6AX
Tel St. Austell (0726) 72888
Camellia specialists with 200 varieties concentrating on japonicas and sasanquas. Mail order available.

Stonehurst Nurseries
Stonehurst, Ardingly, E. Sussex RH17 6TN
Tel Ardingly (0444) 892436 (camellias) 892488 (orchids)
Camellia specialists with 110

varieties, mostly japonicas and their hybrids. They also specialise in orchids (69 varieties) mostly cymbidiums. Plants available by mail order.

Tregrehan Camellia Nurseries
Par, Cornwall PL24 2SJ
Tel Par (072 681) 2438
Camellia specialists with 300 varieties – they concentrate on japonicas. They also offer 80 to 100 varieties of rhododendrons. Plants available by mail order.

Trehane Camellia Nursery
Stapehill Road, Hampreston, Wimborne, Dorset BH21 7NE
Tel Wimborne (0202) 873490
Camellia specialist with over 400 varieties. Also offers companion plants for camellias and North American high bush blueberries. Plants available by mail order.

Trewidden Gardens
Trewidden, Penzance, Cornwall TR20 8TT

Tel Penzance (0736) 62087
Camellia specialists with 50 varieties including the more tender varieties. They also stock unusual plants suited to Cornwall, mostly trees and shrubs. Plants available by mail order.

Also see:

AZALEAS AND RHODODENDRONS
Exbury Gardens
Trewithen Nurseries

SHRUBS AND TREES
Everton Nurseries
C. J. Marchant
Nettleton Nursery

GOOD GARDEN CENTRES AND GENERAL NURSERIES
Glencarse, Glendoick Garden Centre: varieties suitable for Scotland
Gwennap, Burncoose and South Down Nurseries
Tal-y-Cafn, Bodnant Garden Nursery

CARNATIONS AND PINKS

The dianthus family can supply a range of plants from the elegant perpetual carnations to the dainty old-fashioned cottage garden pinks. The flowers are beautiful and often sweetly scented. Only the most acid or waterlogged soil gives them trouble, and neither pollution nor sea spray seem to cause difficulties. The carnation is much more of a specialist plant than the pink, and you are likely to find only annual bedding carnations in ordinary garden centres. For both hardy border carnations and perpetual-flowering carnations for greenhouse growing, virtually the only source is specialist nurseries. It is best to go for named young plants, as seed is difficult to find and the results unpredictable. Avoid long, leggy plants and buy those with foliage which is a good colour rather than a washed-out pale grey. Any plant which is brown or mottled will not be a good buy.

Pinks are more readily available at garden shops and centres and some rockery pinks can be bought as seed, though again the flower colour is a gamble. When buying plants it pays to have a close look since pinks can suffer badly from adverse weather and tend to go brown. If kept in pots outside excess rain might have caused rot. A stocky, green plant with lots of shoots is ideal. A good specialist nursery grows its plants under cover, but this is not always possible at garden centres. The other advantage of a specialist will be the greater choice available and, if you buy directly from the site, cheaper prices. Both carnations and pinks travel well, so you can safely buy by mail order. The best planting times are spring and autumn, but any time between April and October is reasonable.

Varieties to try

PERPETUAL-FLOWERING CARNATIONS
'Fragrant Ann' white
'Jacqueline Ann' white flecked with red
'Joanne' cerise
'Lavender Lady' lavender
'George Woodfield' yellow flecked with scarlet

BORDER CARNATIONS
'Clunie' apricot
'Harmony' soft grey flecked with cerise
'Zebra' crimson-maroon

PINKS
'Dad's Favourite' Tudor laced pink, white with chocolate lacing and dark eye, scented
'Diane' Allwoodii hybrid, salmon red
'Doris' Allwoodii hybrid, salmon pink, scented
'Mrs Sinkins' old-world garden pink, white, scented
'Prudence' Tudor laced pink, pale pink with purple lacing
'Valda Wyatt' hybrid pink, lavender with rose centre, scented

Allwood Bros.
Clayton Nurseries, Brighton Road, Hassocks, W. Sussex BN6 9LX
Tel Hassocks (079 18) 4229/2115
Carnation and pink specialists concentrating on perpetual-flowering, hardy border carnations, Allwoodii and garden pinks. Stock 163 varieties as plants and 41 varieties as seeds Also sell *Venidio arctotis* (South African sunshine flowers). Plants and seed available by mail order.

Steven Bailey
Silver Street, Sway, Lymington, Hampshire SO4 8ZA
Tel Lymington (0590) 682227
Carnation and pink specialist with 30 to 40 varieties of perpetual-flowering carnations including new introductions from Europe. 20 to 30 varieties of garden pinks with new introductions raised by the nursery. Plants and seeds available by mail order.

Barkers
Whipley Nurseries, East Whipley Lane, Shamley Green, near Guildford, Surrey GU5 OTD
Tel Cranleigh (0483) 274453

Carnation and pink specialists offering perpetual, spray and garden carnations (55 varieties in all) and 20 varieties of border pinks. Plants available by mail order.

Haywards Carnations
The Chace Gardens, Stakes Road, Purbrook, Portsmouth, Hampshire PO7 5PL
Tel Waterlooville (0705) 263047
Carnation and pink specialists concentrating on hardy border and perpetual-flowering carnations (total of 180 varieties). 60 varieties of pinks. Plants available by mail order.

Kingstone Cottage Plants
West-under-Penyar, Ross-on-Wye, Hereford and Worcester HR9 7NX
Tel Ross-on-Wye (0989) 65267
Specialise in old and unusual pinks and some old carnations – 80 varieties in total. 85 varieties of herbs also available. Plants available by mail order – but not the herbs.

Old Inn Cottage Nursery
Piddington, Bicester, Oxfordshire OX6 0PY

Tel Brill (0844) 238301
Holds the National Collection of old garden pinks (approximately 70 varieties) plus some old carnations. Also has other old cottage garden plants. Mail order not normally available, but if required contact the nursery.

Pinks and Carnations
22 Chetwyn Avenue, Bromley Cross, Bolton, Lancashire BL7 9BN
Tel Bolton (0204) 56273
Carnation and pink specialists concentrating on perpetual-flowering carnations for exhibition or cut flowers. 28 varieties of carnation and 25 varieties of pinks. Plants available by mail order.

Ramparts Nursery
Bakers Lane, Colchester, Essex CO4 5BD
Tel Colchester (0206) 852050
Pink and foliage specialists. Offer hybrid garden pinks (over 30 varieties), older pinks (over 40 varieties) and rockery pinks (over 20 varieties). Concentrate on grey and silver foliage plants (over 200 varieties). Plants available by mail order.

Swallows Villas Nurseries
147 Liverpool Old Road, Much Hoole, near Preston, Lancashire PR4 4GB
Tel Preston (0772) 613016

Carnation and pink specialists offering 50 varieties of perpetual-flowering carnations, 30 varieties of hardy border carnations and 10 varieties of garden pinks. Plants available by mail order.

Three Counties Nurseries
Marshwood, Bridport, Dorset DT6 5QJ
Tel Hawkchurch (029 77) 257
50 varieties of garden pinks, all types. Plants available by mail order only.

Woodfield Bros.
71 Townsend Road, Tiddington, Stratford-on-Avon, Warwickshire CV37 7DE
Tel Stratford-on-Avon (0789) 295779
Specialise in perpetual-flowering carnations (24 varieties). Also have 18 varieties of delphinium and are building up a collection of lupins. Plants and seeds available by mail order.

Also see:

DAHLIAS
Oscroft's Nurseries

HERBACEOUS PERENNIALS
J. and E. Parker-Jervis

PRIMULAS
Cravens Alpine Nursery

GARDEN CENTRES AND GENERAL NURSERIES
Angmering, Manor Nursery

CARNIVOROUS PLANTS

Carnivorous plants are so named because they have developed the ability to capture and digest insects. Although many of these plants look most extraordinary and exotic, a lot of them are much easier to grow than ordinary houseplants. However, you have to care for them differently – the rules commonly applied to indoor plants could be disastrous. Temperate carnivorous plants are happy to be grown on window sills, but they must have a humid atmosphere and wet compost. To achieve this, sit them in saucers of water 1 to 2.5cm (½ to 1in) deep – fatal to most houseplants, but ideal for the carnivorous species. During the dormant winter season, though, the compost should simply be kept moist. It's vital to use soft water (rain or distilled); hard tap water will quickly kill your new purchase. More and more garden centres are stocking carnivorous plants, but interested buyers should shop carefully. Mature plants will be expensive since they have been raised from seeds or cuttings and grown on for four to seven years. However, success from these will be more likely than from the little seedlings which are often just wild plants potted up. The size of a fully grown plant will vary depending upon what type it is, so do some reading beforehand. Avoid plants sold in boxes or under domes – they frequently don't survive. Look for a healthy plant growing in a pot and, unless the nursery has a very rapid turnover, the pots should be standing in soft water. Correct and detailed instructions should come with each specimen, but it can be worth checking these as they are sometimes wrong. Specialist nurseries stock the more unusual and sought-after varieties. Most will accept visitors, but this is often by appointment only. Mail order is the most common form of purchasing, and you can expect a mature plant to travel well any time of year as long as it has been carefully packed.

Plants to try

COMMON, EASILY AVAILABLE
Sarracenia flava (pitcher plant) yellow trumpet
Dionaea muscipula (venus fly trap) white flower
Drosera capensis (cape sundew) purple flower
Darlingtonia californica (cobra lily) crimson and green flower

MORE ADVANCED
Utricularia (terrestrial bladderworts) orchid-like flowers
Pinguicula (Central American butterworts) superb flowers summer and winter

Marston Exotics
Spring Gardens, Frome, Somerset
BA11 2NZ
Tel Street (0458) 42192 or Frome
(0373) 61665
Carnivorous plant specialist with
150 varieties. Plants, seeds and
books available by mail order.

Sarracenia Nurseries
Links Side, Courtland Avenue,
Mill Hill, London NW7 3BG
Tel 01-959 1570
Carnivorous plant specialists with
over 100 varieties concentrating on

sarracenia (pitcher plants) and their
hybrids and nepenthes. Plants
available by mail order.

See also:

ALPINES
Potterton and Martin

CACTI AND SUCCULENTS
Tamarisk Nurseries

GOOD GARDEN CENTRES AND
GENERAL NURSERIES
Kingswinsford, Ashwood
Nurseries and Aquatics

CHRYSANTHEMUMS

Chrysanthemums have long been a favourite of exhibition growers, but they are also attractive in the garden and specially dwarfed types have become very popular as pot plants.

They appreciate a slightly acid to neutral soil with good drainage and, being shallow-rooted, will benefit from the presence of some humus-making material in the top soil. In catalogues these plants are usually described in terms of their flower shape and flowering time, so when deciding on varieties you need to familiarise yourself with such terms as incurved, reflexed, spray, pompon and intermediate. A good way to do this is by a visit to a specialist nursery during the appropriate flowering period, or by going to trials such as those held every year at the RHS Gardens at Wisley, and at Peel Park in Bradford. Selecting a variety on the basis of show blooms can be misleading due to the extensive coddling these plants are given by their growers – a little wind and rain could soon leave a sorry sight. Local societies will have useful suggestions as to varieties suitable for the climatic and soil conditions of your neighbourhood.

Garden centres, general nurseries and specialist nurseries sell chrysanthemums usually as rooted cuttings. A choice plant will have healthy, rich-green leaves and be sturdy and short-jointed. Spindly growth showing washed-out, pallid foliage is a bad sign. Premature development of flower buds, loss of lower leaves or overcrowding in trays are other undesirable points. If you are buying by mail order and have a heated greenhouse, you can request the plants for as early as January or February. By early May – the time for direct planting – the optimum size for cuttings is between 15 to 20cm (6 to 8in). Whenever you want to receive your cuttings, it's best to order early otherwise it is likely that you will have to be satisfied with substitute varieties which aren't always comparable with your own selections.

Varieties to try
These are all outdoor early-flowering varieties.

'Anna Marie' spray, white double
'Lilian Hoek' spray, light orange/bronze double with red and yellow sports
'Margaret' spray, pink with many different sports
'Pennine Eagle' spray, rich gold double
'Pennine Gambol' spray, pink anemone
'Pennine Jade' spray, tangerine single with green eye
'Pennine Signal' spray, rich red single
'Pennine Wine' spray, ruby red double
'Alison Kirk' incurved, large white
'Peter Rowe' incurved, medium yellow
'Anne Dickson' intermediate, orange/bronze
'Cornish' intermediate, cream
'Mac's Delight' intermediate, large yellow
'World of Sport' intermediate, large white
'Bright Eye' pompon, golden yellow with red eye
'Fairie' pompon, pink with various sports
'Gambit' reflexed, large purple
'Joyce Stevenson' reflexed, medium, dark red
'Solitaire' reflexed, pink
'Venice' reflexed, medium pink with various sports

Beechview Nursery
Avery Lane, Waltham Abbey, Essex EN9 3QH
Tel Lea Valley (0992) 712186
Chrysanthemum specialist with a good range of sprays. Also more unusual types – spiders, charms, cascades and overseas introductions.

Collinwood Nurseries
Mottram St. Andrews, Macclesfield, Cheshire SK10 4QR
Chrysanthemum specialists listing

200 varieties – also offers exhibition onions as seedlings or plants. Plants available by mail order.

Dahlia Haven Plants
28 Hillside, Horsham, W. Sussex RH12 1NG
Tel Horsham (0403) 67792
Chrysanthemum and dahlia specialist. 70 varieties of exhibition and spray chrysanthemums. 110 varieties of dahlias. Plants available by mail order.

Dunshelt Nurseries
Ladybank Road, Dunshelt, Auchtermuchty, Fife KY14 7HG
Tel Auchtermuchty (033 72) 274
Chrysanthemum (90 varieties) and dahlia (110 varieties) specialists. Plants available by mail order.

Elm House Nurseries
Walpole St. Peter, Wisbech, Cambridgeshire PE14 7PJ
Tel Wisbech (0945) 780444
Chrysanthemum specialists offering 300 varieties. Also fuchsias (50 varieties). Plants available by mail order.

Hall Nurseries
Stretton Road, Lapley, Staffordshire ST19 9QQ
Tel Wheaton Aston (0785) 840281
Specialists with 500 varieties covering the whole range. Plants available by mail order.

Riley's Chrysanthemums
Alfreton Nurseries, Wooley Moor, Derby, Derbyshire DE5 6FF
Tel Chesterfield (0246) 590315 after 4pm
Chrysanthemum specialists offering 250 varieties, concentrating on hardy outdoor types. Plants available by mail order.

J. E. Roberts and Co
Ember Nursery, 50A Grove Way, Esher, Surrey KT10 8HL
Tel 01-979 3579
Specialises in spray chrysanthemums (200 varieties). Plants available by mail order.

H. Walker
Oakfield Nurseries, Huntingdon, Chester, Cheshire CH3 6EA
Tel Chester (0244) 20731
Specialist offering 300 to 400 varieties covering the whole range of types. Plants available by mail order.

Walkers
Belvedere Nurseries, Chapel Road, Hesketh Bank, near Preston, Lancashire PR4 6RX
Tel Hesketh Bank (077 473) 2135
Chrysanthemum specialists offering approximately 300 varieties. Plants available by mail order.

H. Woolman
Grange Road, Dorridge, Solihull, W. Midlands B93 8QB
Tel Knowle (056 45) 6283
Chrysanthemum specialist offering 200 varieties. Plants available by mail order.

Also see:

DAHLIAS
G. C. Titchard

PELARGONIUMS
Howard S. Waters and Son

GOOD GARDEN CENTRES AND GENERAL NURSERIES
Heddon-on-the-Wall, Hall's of Heddon Nursery Centre

CLEMATIS
The 'Queen of Climbers' is not difficult to please. They like alkaline soil but many will grow in neutral or moderately acid soils, provided they are fertile. They also like open, sunny places – roots in the shade, leaves in the sun – but some thrive on north-facing sites.

The best times for planting are spring and autumn. Many garden centres and shops stock clematis in the spring, and you should choose plants with good strong growth. If you are buying in late autumn or winter the tops will have died back, but look for plump new growth buds, particularly at the base. Specialist nurseries offer a much wider choice and send out their orders in the autumn and winter. Order early, say in March or April, to be sure of getting the varieties you want. Nurseries often run out of the popular varieties and may send substitutes, so it helps if you indicate a second choice. If you don't want a substitute, state this on your order. When choosing varieties, think about the flowering period as well as the size, shape and colour of the flowers, and also take into account the aspect and how vigorous the plants are – some of the species are very vigorous and make effective cover-up plants.

Varieties to try

POPULAR, WIDELY AVAILABLE

'Comtesse de Bouchard' easy to grow, quick to establish. Produces mauve-pink flowers July to August

'Ernest Markham' beautiful deep red flowers July to October

'Jackmanii Superba' rich purple flowers July to September

'Nelly Moser' flowers pale pink, carmine bar in May to June and August to September

'The President' deep purple-blue with reddish purple stamens, flowers June to September

C. alpina very hardy, produces small blue flowers in April to May

C. montana vigorous, trouble-free, produces small white flowers in May and June. Also several good varieties with different flower colours

MORE UNUSUAL

'Dr Ruppel' deep pink, carmine bar

'Lasurstern' lavender blue

'Niobe' dark red

'Madame Julia Correvon' red

C. macropetala lavender blue

C. tangutica yellow (silver seed heads)

John Beach Clematis Nursery
Thelsford Farm, Charlecote,
Warwickshire CV35 9EJ
Tel Barford (0926) 624173
Specialist with 100 hybrids and 50 species of clematis. Offers other climbers too. Plants available by mail order; postal enquiries to 9 Grange Gardens, Wellesbourne, Warwickshire CV35 9RL.

J. Bradshaw and Son
Busheyfields Nursery, Herne,
Herne Bay, Kent CT6 7LJ
Tel Herne Bay (022 73) 5415
25 large-flowered and 9 small-flowered varieties. Also specialise in climbing and wall plants and roses. No mail order.

Caddick's Clematis Plants
10 Richmond Avenue,
Grappenhall, Warrington,
Cheshire WA4 2ND
Tel Warrington (0925) 68357
Specialist with over 100 varieties. Plants available by mail order.

Fisk's Clematis Nursery
Westleton, near Saxmundham,
Suffolk IP17 3AJ
Tel Westleton (072 873) 263
Specialist with 150 varieties. Plants available by mail order.

Funnels Farm Nurseries
Maynards Green, Heathfield,
E. Sussex TN21 0DB
Tel Horam Road (043 53) 2367
Specialists with over 120 varieties.
Starting to offer other climbers too.
Plants available by mail order.

Great Dixter Nurseries
Great Dixter, Northiam, Rye,
E. Sussex TN31 6PH
Tel Northiam (079 74) 3107
Specialists with 116 varieties of
clematis. Also stock unusual
varieties of herbaceous perennials.

Peveril Clematis Nursery
Derril, near Holsworthy, Devon
EX22 6YA
Tel Bridgerule (028 881) 200
Specialist with 72 hybrids and 123
species of clematis. Concentrates on
species, including rare ones
unobtainable from any other source
(some only to order). Has
controlled breeding programme to
produce new varieties. Plants
available by mail order.

Priorswood Clematis
Priorswood, Widbury Hill, Ware,
Hertfordshire SG12 7QH
Tel Ware (0920) 61543
Specialist with over 60
large-flowered hybrids and 20
species. Plants available by mail
order (minimum order 3 plants).
Older and larger specimens are
available for collection only.

Also see:

CAMELLIAS
Marwood Hill Gardens

HERBACEOUS PERENNIALS
Bressingham Gardens
Fairview Nursery

HEATHERS
Little Heath Farm

GOOD GARDEN CENTRES AND
GENERAL NURSERIES
Lincoln, Pennells Garden Centre
Tenbury Wells, Treasures of
Tenbury

CYCLAMEN (HARDY)

The pink or white flowers of hardy cyclamen look like butterflies flitting
over the ground when these plants are naturalised under shrubs or in
woodlands. They do well in these conditions, and although they seem so
delicate they are surprisingly tough. They also succeed in rockeries or
planted in tubs and containers for balconies, courtyards and patios, and
need little attention being fairly free from pests and diseases.

The hardy varieties are sold as seed, or as dry or fresh tubers. Seed is
obviously the cheapest way of growing cyclamen, but there are problems.
The best seed is the freshest, and for good germination you really need to
plant it within a day of harvesting. This is obviously not possible with
bought seed, when you really have no idea how old it is. An alternative is
to obtain fresh seed in July or August either from friends or from the wide
range offered by the Cyclamen Society or the Alpine Garden Society. Plants
raised from seed will take at least two or three years before they flower.

Buying tubers can also be tricky. They go on sale in the autumn in shops
and garden centres but can be very dried out, having been out of the
ground for some time. Dry tubers are also less likely to be true to name, and
you might end up with a totally unexpected variety. Fresh tubers are the
best bet and these can be obtained by mail order from specialists in small
bulbs (check spring and winter catalogues). Here the tubers will have been
freshly lifted or potted and you can expect moist tubers with a bit of body
and roots. This form of buying is unfortunately the most expensive, but

you can be fairly sure that what you have purchased will grow and be true to name. If you choose your cyclamen carefully you can have blooms in the garden virtually all year round. The indoor varieties are derived from *C. persicum* which is not quite hardy but makes a lovely, scented plant for a cool greenhouse.

Species to try

POPULAR

C. hederifolium (C. neapolitanum) pink flowers, leaves are good ground cover through winter, flowers September to November

C. coum crimson, white or pink flowers from January to March

C. purpurascens (C. europaeum) scented flowers in shades of pink from July to September

C. repandum deep pink flowers with twisted petals, flowers April to May

RARER

C. cilicium white to pink, honey-scented

C. graecum white to dark pink with cerise mouth

C. mirabile dark pink mouth

C. intaminatum tiny flowers pale grey/white

Tile Barn Nursery
Standen Street, Iden Green,
Benenden, Kent TN17 4LB
Tel Cranbrook (0580) 240221
Specialist cyclamen nursery. Tubers available by mail order. If you wish to visit the nursery please telephone first.

Also see:

ALPINES AND ROCK PLANTS
Potterton and Martin

BULBS
Jacques Amand
Avon Bulbs
Walter Blom and Son
Broadleigh Gardens
P. J. and J. W. Christian
P. de Jager and Sons
Van Tubergen

SEEDS
Thompson and Morgan

DAFFODILS

Shelley called the narcissus 'the fairest flower of them all' and indeed their appearance across the country as the herald of spring is indicative of their great popularity. The narcissi include the familiar trumpet-shaped daffodil, but there are many other forms. A garden can spring to life with a collection of large-cupped narcissi, jonquils, the showy double-flowered narcissi or the dainty triandrus hybrids. With their wide choice of shape and colour, and an unfussy nature, this flower can find a place in any border or window box, or can even be naturalised in grass. A well-drained soil with some humus added will keep most varieties happy, and they will tolerate either sun or partial shade.

It is important to choose the right variety for the right situation – short varieties are ideal for tubs or rockeries. For lawns choose early-flowering varieties so that the leaves do not interfere with grass cutting for too long. A succession of varieties can provide flowers from the end of February until the end of April. Flower heads should be removed once they fade, but the leaves must be left for a further six weeks at least, in order to replenish the bulb.

Bulbs are readily available from supermarkets, hardware shops and garden centres and by mail order. Mail order suppliers include general bulb-merchants, specialists in dwarf and unusual bulbs, and daffodil specialists. Bulbs can be planted out as early as August, although it might be hard to find them in the shops at this time. The later you plant, the poorer your first display will be. When buying bulbs there are several things to look out for. You can find single and double-nosed bulbs (producing one or two stems) or mother bulbs (a main bulb with offsets). Generally, the fewer offsets or growing points the better the bulb will establish itself, and the larger a single-nosed bulb is, the better the flowers will be. A good bulb will be heavy and firm to the touch. If there is any softening at the base or the neck the bulb should be avoided. There should be no sign of any root or shoot growth when you purchase, and bulbs should be free from dirt and loose skin. Buying mixtures (unnamed varieties) or collections (named varieties) as opposed to individual varieties can be a saving. However, the mixtures are not always that varied and without knowing what you have, you cannot anticipate the flowering period. Garden centres are usually better bets than supermarkets for quality. Mail order gives far greater range of varieties – all the nurseries in the following list supply bulbs by mail order.

Varieties to try

OLD FAVOURITES

These varieties are easy to find in shops or catalogues of general bulb merchants:
'Carlton' yellow, large cupped
'Ceylon' yellow, large deep orange cup
'Edward Buxton' creamy-yellow petals and deep yellow, orange-rimmed cup
'Fortune' orange cup
'Golden Ducat' double yellow flowers
'Ice Follies' white petals and wide, pale yellow cup
'Mount Hood' white trumpet

UNUSUAL

Try a specialist nursery for these:
'Arctic Gold' yellow trumpet
'Dove Wings' white and yellow cyclamineus, small, dainty flower
'Kingscourt' imposing yellow trumpet
'Liberty Bells' yellow triandrus, small dainty flowers with drooping heads
'Merlin' white, small cup with vivid red rim
'Passionale' white, large pink cup
'Spellbinder' lime yellow, trumpet white with yellow rim
'Suzy' jonquilla sweet-scented with several flowers to a stem, yellow petals, orange cup
'Tête-à-Tête' dwarf-growing, light yellow, two heads per stem
'Tricolet' split corona (trumpet is split into three and opened out), white, with orange centre
'Unique' large white and yellow double

Many small specialists like you to send stamps when requesting a price list or catalogue.

J. Abel-Smith
Orchard House, Letty Green, near
Hertford, Hertfordshire SG14 2NZ
Tel Hatfield (07072) 61274/61585
Daffodil specialist with 140 varieties
listed.

Ballydorn Bulb Farm
Killinchy, Newtownards, Co.
Down, N. Ireland BT23 6QB
Tel Killinchy (0238) 541250
Daffodil specialist with 150 varieties
concentrating on new varieties,
especially their own hybrids.

Carncairn Daffodils
Broughshane, Ballymena, Co.
Antrim, N. Ireland BT43 7HF
Tel Ballymena (0266) 861216
Daffodil specialists, concentrate on
show varieties but also grow good
garden varieties. Approximately
280 varieties listed.

Clive Postles Daffodils
'The Old Cottage', Purshull Green,
Elmbridge, Droitwich, Hereford
and Worcester WR9 0NL
Tel Chaddesley Corbett
(056 283) 765
Daffodil specialist with 103
cultivars. Concentrates on breeding
hybrid daffodils.

Copford Bulbs
Dorsetts, Birch Road, Copford,
Colchester, Essex CO6 1DR
Tel Colchester (0206) 330008
Daffodil specialists with 250
varieties, primarily exhibitors' stock.

du Plessis Bros.
Marsh Farm, Landulph, Saltash,
Cornwall PL12 6NG
Tel Saltash (075 55) 3143
Daffodil specialists with 300
varieties listed.

Michael Jefferson-Brown
Maylite, Martley, Worcester,
Hereford and Worcester WR6 6PQ
Tel Wichenford (088 66) 518
Daffodil specialist with 400
varieties. Also offers 40 varieties of
lilies and 12 varieties of vines. Mail
order available for plants as well as
bulbs.

Rathowen Daffodils
'Knowehead', 15 Ballynahatty
Road, Omagh, Co. Tyrone,
N. Ireland BT78 1PN
Tel Omagh (0662) 42931
Daffodil specialists with 420
varieties. They concentrate on
hybridising and growing modern
varieties

Also see:

BULBS

GLADIOLI
Agincourt

DAHLIAS

Dahlias are flowers of great versatility with numerous flower shapes and a
colour range offering everything but pure blue. There are varieties suitable
for window boxes, the rockery, the back of herbaceous borders and most
places in between – be sure you are aware of all details of habit before
buying and planting so you buy the right type. Dahlias are happiest in a
sunny place. They will thrive in a wide range of soils from light sand to
heavy clay, but a well-prepared site will have its rewards.

To familiarise yourself with varieties before ordering or buying, visit local
shows in August and September or gardens which feature dahlias. Dahlias
are sold as seeds, tubers or rooted cuttings. The seeds can be obtained from
most of the main seed companies, but the colour, shape and height are not
guaranteed in the way they are with tubers and cuttings. Tubers (usually
pot-grown) become available from early in the year through to May in
shops and garden centres. Common varieties are sold in packs quite

cheaply, but don't be surprised if the flower you get is not true to the picture – mix-ups frequently occur. For a wide choice and a chance to try the modern varieties, the specialist nursery is the answer. However, because they concentrate on the most up-to-date show varieties, you'll find many specialists don't stock the old favourites – for these, try general bulb merchants.

The best tubers are firm and plump, and red or green eyes appearing on the crown are also a good sign. Plant them outside in early May (later in areas with late frosts). Rooted cuttings become available from specialist growers in late March. If you buy before they are potted it is cheaper, but you must have the facilities to care for the tender plants. The best plants to buy are those with a leaf spread equalling their height and a minimum of four sets of leaves. Don't buy plants which are spindly with a long stem between each leaf joint; also avoid plants with compost which is excessively wet or dry. Plant out about the end of May to avoid all chance of frost damage.

Varieties to try

POPULAR

'Cherry Wine' cherry-red decorative
'Doris Day' bright scarlet cactus
'Dr John Grainger' orange/bronze decorative
'Gerrie Hoek' silvery-pink decorative
'Glorie van Heemstede' butter-yellow decorative
'Klankstad Kerkrade' sulphur-yellow cactus
'Moor Place' rich purple pompon
'Nina Chester' white, flushed pink decorative
'Opal' pink and white ball

MORE UNUSUAL

'Border Princess' dwarf bronze cactus
'Giraffe' bronze and yellow orchid-flowered
'Hamari Fiesta' orange-red and yellow decorative
'Holland Festival' orange and white giant decorative
'Mariposa' lilac pink, cream inner petals, collerette
'Topmix' miniature varieties in various colours
'Willo's Surprise' dark red pompon
'Wooton Cup' pink pompon

G. Beatty
186 Mayors Walk, Peterborough, Cambridgeshire PE3 6HQ
Tel Peterborough (0733) 61736
Market gardener specialising in dahlias (73 varieties) and fuchsias (38 varieties). Only tubers available by mail order.

Tom Bebbington Dahlias
Lady Gate Nursery, 47 The Green, Diseworth, near Derby, Derbyshire DE7 2QN
Tel Derby (0332) 811565

Dahlia specialist offering 150 varieties of all types. Plants and tubers available by mail order.

Butterfields Nursery
Harvest Hill, Bourne End, Buckinghamshire SL8 5JJ
Tel Bourne End (062 85) 25455
Specialists offering 130 varieties of dahlias as rooted cuttings. They also specialise in pleiones and delphiniums. Only delphinium seeds and pleione pseudo-bulbs available by mail order.

Terry Clarke Nurseries
Beccles, Suffolk NR34 7RL
Tel Beccles (0502) 715728
Dahlia specialist offering 50
varieties. Plants available by mail
order.

F. Currie
20 Rydal Mount, Kendal, Cumbria
LA9 4RS
Tel Kendal (0539) 25410
Dahlia specialist offering 80
varieties in the form of rooted
cuttings. Available by mail order.

Oscroft's Nurseries
Sprotboro Road, Doncaster,
S. Yorkshire DN5 8BE
Tel Doncaster (0302) 785026
Dahlia specialists with over 200
varieties concentrating on
decorative, cactus and pompon
types. Also offer border pinks,
carnations and pelargoniums (80
varieties). Plants and tubers
available by mail order

R. Porter
'Willowbrook', 58 Stanley Road,
Halstead, Essex CO9 1LA
Tel Halstead (0787) 476690
Dahlia specialist with 80 varieties of
all types but with emphasis on
exhibition varieties. Plants available
by mail order.

Sedgewood Nurseries
14 Sedge Close, Bramley,
Rotherham, S. Yorkshire S66 OSY
Tel Rotherham (0709) 549594
Dahlia specialists with 75 varieties,

mostly exhibition but some cut
flower. They also offer gladioli (40
varieties) and pelargoniums (50
varieties). Plants and tubers
available by mail order.

G. G. Titchard
Meadowsweet Nursery,
Uppingham, Rutland,
Leicestershire LE15 9TU
Tel Uppingham (0572) 822451
Dahlia specialist offering 175
varieties of all types. Also sells
spray chrysanthemums, though
they are not listed in the catalogue.
Plants and tubers available by mail
order.

Philip Tivey and Son
28 Wanlip Road, Syston,
Leicestershire LE7 8PA
Tel Leicester (0533) 692968
Dahlia specialists with about 150 to
160 varieties. Plants and tubers
available by mail order.

Also see:

BULBS
for dahlia tubers

CHRYSANTHEMUMS
Dunshelt Nurseries

FUCHSIAS
Markham Grange Nurseries

GOOD GARDEN CENTRES AND
GENERAL NURSERIES
London Colney, Ayletts Nurseries
Heddon-on-the-Wall, Hall's of
Heddon Nursery Centre

DELPHINIUMS

These popular blue, mauve and white spires are understandably known as
the Queen of the Border. If planted in deep, rich soil and protected from
the wind they will provide a beautiful display at the back of the border or in
a bed of their own (but don't plant them under trees). Perennial garden
delphiniums have been bred from crosses between many wild species,
particularly *D. elatum* and *D. grandiflorum* . There are three main groups –
the large-flowered or Elatum type, which are the classic delphiniums; the
Belladonna type which are shorter, more branched, graceful plants; and the
seed-raised hybrids which are only short-lived perennials in Britain, such
as 'Pacific Hybrids'. *D. consolida*, usually known as larkspur, is an annual.

The truly perennial varieties are propagated by cuttings, best bought as small plants in late spring – you will probably have to go to a specialist nursery for these. You can purchase by mail order – plants are sent out when they are small so travel well. Even if the tops get broken off in transit, new growth will quickly spring up. It's wise to order in the early spring to make sure you get what you want, and delivery will usually be at the beginning of May. Most plants sold in garden centres will be seed-raised. Delphinium seeds are widely available, but they quickly lose their viability so buy early and store in a cool, dry place before sowing. Better still, collect seed fresh from other growers or buy from the Delphinium Society (see page 399).

Varieties to try

OLD FAVOURITES

'Blue Nile' mauve, white eye
'Chelsea Star' rich violet, small white eye
'Christella' bright mid-blue, white eye
'Fanfare' silvery pastel mauve
'Loch Levan' mid-blue, white eye
'Michael Ayres' rich violet

NEW VARIETIES

'Faust' ultramarine blue and indigo
'Fenella' gentian blue, black eye
'Gillian Dallas' slate blue, white eye
'Mighty Atom' deep lavender

See

BEGONIAS
Blackmore and Langdon

CARNATIONS AND PINKS
Woodfield Bros.

DAHLIAS
Butterfields Nursery

DWARF CONIFERS

The joy of growing dwarf conifers is that they add an array of texture, shape and winter colour to even the smallest garden. Silver, prostrate, feathery, copper-bronze, and columnar are just some of the adjectives describing these evergreens – and with skilful placing there's really no limit to the picture an imaginative gardener can create.

A dwarf conifer should not exceed 1.5m (5ft) in 10 years but some may grow to 3 or 4m (10 or 13ft) eventually. Their dwarf nature is a result of seed or bud mutations, selective cuttings or simply being alpine forms of larger species. Suitable sitings would be around ponds, in small groups in a corner of the garden or in an island bed, as an integral element of a heather garden, or in tubs and troughs on the patio. An open, sunny position and good drainage are the main requirements for a happy plant.

A major problem is to decide which varieties to grow from the multitude on sale. Garden centres sell quite a range; you should usually find at least 20 to 30 varieties. Prices vary a lot between one garden centre and another, in variety and of course size. Remember that large plants won't be so easy to establish. Overall the quality tends to be very good; nevertheless you should steer clear of any weak, spindly plants or those with brown patches. Don't buy anything which is pot-bound, has its roots protruding from the base of the container, or with a lot of moss or weeds on the compost surface.

Mail order requests should be made before the end of November. Dealing with specialists will open up a greater choice and will enable you to get any variety you can't find locally. Most plants are sent in their containers and arrive within a few weeks of ordering, generally in satisfactory condition. The best planting times are early autumn or late spring.

Species to try

EASILY AVAILABLE
Chamaecyparis pisifera 'Boulevard'
Juniperus sabina 'Tamariscifolia'
J. squamata 'Blue Star'
Thuja occidentalis 'Rheingold'
Picea glauca 'Albertiana Conica'

WORTH LOOKING FOR
Cedrus libani 'Sargentii'
Cyptomeria japonica 'Vilmoriniana'
J. communis 'Compressa'
P. abies 'nidformis'
Pinus mugo (dwarf varieties)
Pinus sylvestris 'Beuvronensis'
T. orientalis 'Aurea Nana'

Hull Farm
Spring Valley Lane, Ardleigh, Colchester, Essex CO7 75B
Tel Colchester (0206) 230172
Conifer specialist with 270 varieties including dwarf conifers. No mail order.

Kenwith Castle Nurseries
Kenwith Castle, Bideford, Devon EX39 5BE
Tel Bideford (023 72) 3712
Specialise in dwarf and slow-growing conifers with 570 varieties. Available by mail order.

Orchardleigh Nursery
Botley Road, Bishop's Waltham, Southampton, Hampshire SO3 1DR
Tel Bishops Waltham (048 93) 2687
Specialises in dwarf and slow-growing conifers (60 varieties) as well as heathers (100 varieties). No mail order.

Pine Cottage Arboretum
Gibbs Lane, Morcombelake, Bridport, Dorset DT6 6DT
Tel Chideock (0297) 89455
Dwarf and slow-growing conifer specialist with 150 to 200 varieties. Concentrates on the rarer varieties including grafted plants. No mail order now but possibly at the end of 1985.

Robinsons Gardens
Rushmore Hill Nurseries, Knockholt, Sevenoaks, Kent TN14 7NN
Tel Knockholt (0959) 32269
Dwarf conifer specialists with 170 varieties. Also stock about 1000 varieties of trees and shrubs. No mail order.

Walker's Nursery
Blaxton, near Doncaster, S. Yorkshire DN9 3BA
Tel Doncaster (0302) 770325
Offers nearly 300 varieties of dwarf and slow-growing conifers as well as taller conifers, ornamental trees and shrubs. Plants available by mail order.

The Wansdyke Nursery
Hillworth Road, Devizes, Wiltshire SN10 5HD
Tel Devizes (0380) 3008
Specialises in dwarf conifers, selling about 350 varieties including many rare and unusual ones. Operates in conjunction with The Pigmy Pinetum established in 1959 and displaying over 1200 varieties of dwarf and slow-growing conifers. Mail order available.

Wessex Nurseries
Great Hinton, Trowbridge, Wiltshire BA14 6BY
Tel Keevil (0380) 870427
Specialise in dwarf conifers (50 to 60 varieties) and miniature roses (75 varieties). They also have 30 to 40 varieties of heather. Plants available by mail order.

Also see:

ALPINES AND ROCK PLANTS
Holden Clough Nursery
W. E. Th. Ingwersen
Mansfield Nurseries
Potterton and Martin
Peter Trenear

AZALEAS AND RHODODENDRONS
C. E. Henderson and Son

FUCHSIAS
John Smith and Son

HEATHERS
Barncroft Nurseries
Blairhoyle Nursery
Four Acres Nursery
The Heather Garden
Longdale Heathers
Okell's Nurseries
Wingates

HERBACEOUS PERENNIALS
Bressingham Gardens

SHRUBS AND TREES
Binks Nurseries
Goscote Nurseries
MacFarlanes Nurseries and Garden Centre

GOOD GARDEN CENTRES AND GENERAL NURSERIES
Sheffield, Abbey Lane Nurseries

FERNS

Although ferns are one of the oldest known plants on earth, stretching back some 400 million years, they are rather neglected in today's gardens. They tend to get pushed into inhospitable corners because they thrive where other plants cannot, but here they fail to reach their full potential. Given full or dappled shade, protected from strong winds and not subjected to heavy and poorly drained soil, ferns will create a delightfully cool spot with arching fronds of all shapes and sizes and a surprising variety of hues. To complement their foliage, you can plant such things as scillas, epimediums, hellebores, hostas, chionodoxas, primroses, snowdrops or bleeding heart, all suited to shady conditions.

Some ferns are hardy, while others have to be kept in the greenhouse or as pot plants. The indoor types are commonly seen for sale in florists, department stores or garden centres, and some of the big houseplant suppliers stock quite a wide range. Size is unimportant when buying indoor ferns because even the small ones will grow quickly if the conditions are right. Buy a fresh green plant with no dry or shrivelled foliage, and no signs of mealy bugs or scale insect. Hardy ferns are less widely available. Garden centres will occasionally stock them, but the choice is generally limited to the more common varieties. They tend not to be popular with garden centres since they can easily look tired and straggly and need a good spot in the shade if they are not to suffer. It is important to buy a good-sized plant, so that it will establish well. For most varieties this means one in a 10 to 13cm (4 to 5in) pot. Dwarf varieties will naturally be smaller but should still show plenty of growth. Pests and diseases are rarely a problem. Specialist nurseries stock a greater variety and since ferns are mostly container-grown, they can be planted at any time (bare-rooted stock should be planted October to March). Mail order is another way of obtaining unusual varieties since ferns travel well, especially in the dormant season.

Species to try

POPULAR, HARDY
Dryopteris filix-mas (male fern)
Osmunda regalis (royal fern)
Phyllitis scolopendrium (hart's tongue fern)

Polystichum setiferum (P. angulare) (soft shield fern)

POPULAR, INDOOR
Adiantum raddianum (A.cuneatum) (maidenhair)
Nephrolepis exaltata (Boston fern)

WORTH LOOKING FOR, HARDY
Asplenium scolopendrium
Athyrium filix-femina (lady fern)
Blechnum spicant (hard fern)
Cyrtomium fortunei
D. pseudomas (king fern)

WORTH LOOKING FOR, INDOOR
C. falcatum (Japanese holly fern)
Davallia
Platycerium hillii (stag's horn fern)

Fibrex Nurseries
Harvey Road, Evesham, Hereford
and Worcester WR11 5BQ
Tel Evesham (0386) 6190
100 varieties of hardy and tender
ferns. They also offer ivies (100
varieties), pelargoniums (800
varieties) and streptocarpus (30
varieties). Plants available by mail
order.

J. K. Marston
'Culag', Green Lane, Nafferton,
near Driffield, Humberside
YO25 8SU
Tel Driffield (0377) 44487
Specialist grower of ferns for the
garden and greenhouse.
Approximately 100 varieties. Plants
available by mail order.

Also see:

ALPINES AND ROCK PLANTS
Reginald Kaye

FOLIAGE PLANTS
Dunstan Garden Design

HERBACEOUS PERENNIALS
Abbey Dore Court Gardens
Bressingham Gardens

FOLIAGE PLANTS

The beauty of plant leaves is often overlooked in favour of a bright,
colourful show of flowers, but by doing this gardeners can be missing out
on an intrinsic part of garden design. The subtle changes in foliage from
season to season can enrich lifeless areas, and the many contrasting shapes
and textures can act as a perfect backdrop to flowers with less exciting
foliage. Some leaves have a covering of fine hairs which reflect the light and
turn them to shimmering silver, others are variegated, while some will turn
into brilliant golds, bronzes and reds in the autumn months. The curving
fronds of ferns can add grace to a garden, while ivies will change the
character of a house. Choose a species which will be seen at its best where
you want to plant it – for example, the silver-leaved plants will appear very
dull in a shaded spot. You must also take into account the conditions the
plants prefer – most dislike heavy clay and dense shade, and will
appreciate a sheltered position, but there are exceptions. Sensibly and
imaginatively planted foliage plants will both complement surrounding
flowers and extend the appeal of the garden throughout the year.

Few nurseries specialise solely in foliage plants, but there are quite a
number which take a keen interest in variegated or silver-leaved plants, or
simply offer a wide range of plants which include many with attractive
foliage. It's impossible to generalise about what to look for in such a diverse
group of plants, though obviously it is wise to avoid excessively pot-bound
specimens, or those with signs of pests or diseases. However, it's worth
noting that variegated plants are generally smaller than their normal
counterparts – some only half the size. Some nurseries sell by mail order,
despatching in either autumn or spring,

A lot of specialists exhibit at shows and this can be a good place to buy plants.

Some good foliage plants

GREEN

Acanthus mollis
A. spinosus
Alchemillas
Astilbe
Bergenia
Crambe cordifolia
Dicentra
Gunnera manicata
Kirengeshoma
Macleaya microcarpa
Peltiphyllum peltatum

VARIEGATED

Arundinaria viridistriata
Arum italicum 'Pictum'
Brunnera macrophylla 'Variegata'
Hosta 'Albopicta'
Iris foetidissima 'Variegata'
Miscanthus sinensis
Phormium tenax 'Variegatum'
Pulmonaria saccharata

BRONZE OR PURPLE

Ajuga reptans 'Purpurea'
Epimedium x rubrum
Foeniculum vulgare 'Purpureum'
Melica altissima 'Atropurpurea'
Rheum palmatum 'Rubrum'
Rodgersia podophylla
Saxifraga fortunei 'Wada's variety'
Sedum maximum 'Atropurpureum'

BLUE/GREY/SILVER

Avena candida
Achillea
Anaphalis
Artemisia
Ballota
Eryngium
Festuca glauca
Hosta sieboldiana 'Glauca'
Ruta graveolens 'Jackman's Blue'
Stachys olympica (S. lanata)

Dunstan Garden Design
Maperton, Wincanton, Somerset
BA9 8EJ
Tel Wincanton (0963) 32521
Garden designers who specialise in
foliage plants – 75 varieties with
emphasis on shade plants, hardy
ferns (26 varieties) and green
flowers. In the future they hope to
offer hellebores. Mail order only.

Floreat Garden
148 Albert Road, Parkstone, Poole,
Dorset BH12 2HA
Tel Poole (0202) 746372
Stocks quite a range of unusual
foliage concentrating on hostas
(over 30 varieties). No mail order.

Gold Brook Plants
Hoxne, Eye, Suffolk IP21 5AN
Tel Hoxne (037 975) 770
This nursery aims to offer unusual
plants with particular emphasis on
foliage, especially gold and
variegated plants, architectural
plants and plants for shade.
National Collections of astrantia
and elaeagnus are being
established. No mail order.

Hopleys Plants
Much Hadham, Hertfordshire
SG10 6BU
Tel Much Hadham (027 984) 2509
250 varieties of foliage plants listed
– nearly half of which are
variegated. They also offer
herbaceous perennials, shrubs
(especially potentillas and
pyracantha) and unusual conifers.
Over 40 varieties of double
primrose are also listed. Plants
available by mail order.

Also see:

CARNATIONS AND PINKS
Ramparts Nursery

HERBS
Wells and Winter

SHRUBS AND TREES
Norcroft Nurseries

---

*Many specialists sell plants by mail order, but it's always better to visit the nursery
if you can to select your own plants and discuss your problems and requirements
with the proprietors. Many are only too keen to share their knowledge.*

FRUIT TREES

Every gardener must have thought about the pleasures of eating fruit straight from the tree, but many have given up the idea due to lack of space. In fact, you don't need an entire orchard to realise this wish, and even a small garden will accommodate a tree grafted on to the appropriate rootstock, or one trained against a fence or wall.

The vigour of a fruit tree is controlled by the rootstock on to which it is grafted. These roots directly influence the size and fruiting capacity of the tree – so if you want a tree with a dwarf habit you must be sure it is grafted on a rootstock which will encourage this type of growth. Unfortunately garden centres and even nurseries do not always tell you what rootstock a tree is growing on – if this is the case don't buy.

When choosing a tree check that the point at which it is grafted has formed a strong union – there shouldn't be too sharp a kink or any dead bits of old stem sticking up, and the layer of bark around the stem should be reasonably even. Also look for a strong, straight central stem and vigorous shoots. Growth should not be one-sided, and container-grown trees must not be root-bound showing lots of roots above the soil. Besides choosing a tree on the right rootstock, you must decide what shape of tree you want to end up with and what age to purchase. Standard, half-standard, bush, cordon, espalier, fan or dwarf pyramid are some of the options. If you buy a maiden (year-old tree) it will consist of a single stem, perhaps with a few side shoots known as 'feathers', and must be trained entirely by you. Maidens are relatively cheap but not that easy to come by in garden centres or general nurseries. Specialists sell maidens but, in general, two-year-old, partly trained trees are much more common. Once a tree reaches four years old it becomes hard to establish and is not a good buy. Bush and half-standard are the most widely available forms of partly trained trees both in garden centres and specialist suppliers. You may find cordons, fans, espaliers and full standards but you must shop around. You shouldn't find it difficult to buy a good-quality tree at a garden centre if you know what you're looking for. Specialist nurseries offer a wider choice of variety and form, but you may have to pay more and if you have to buy by mail order the carriage costs are high. Moreover, you can't select the trees yourself. Remember that fruit trees need pollination to produce good crops, so unless your choice is self-fertile there must be another variety of the same fruit with a similar flowering time in the neighbouring area.

Widely available varieties

EATING APPLES

'Cox's Orange Pippin' very well known and stores until January but not easy to grow. Eat October to January. 'Sunset' is a good alternative

'Golden Delicious' sweet and juicy but not much flavour. Needs a warm climate to ripen properly. Eat October to February

'James Grieve' very juicy, sharp at first then sweeter. Ripens early but bruises easily and doesn't keep. Eat September

'Laxton's Superb' sweet and juicy with thickish skin. Crops biennially but stores well. Eat October to February

'Lord Lambourne' sweet and juicy with thickish skin that becomes sticky in store. Crops regularly. Eat mid September to November

'Worcester Pearmain' sweet and dry with tough skin but a 'perfumed' flavour. Eat September to October

COOKING APPLES

'Bramley's Seedling' good reliable, useful apple from October to February

PEARS

'Conference' self-fertile and very reliable but not outstanding flavour. Stores from October until November or December
'Doyenne du Comice' delicious juicy fruit of excellent flavour but needs warm climate or position. Eat November to December
'Williams Bon Cretien' good flavour for a pear that ripens in September, but season over in a few weeks

PEACH

'Peregrine' the most reliable variety for warm areas out of doors and superb to eat

PLUM

'Victoria' self-fertile and the most reliable

CHERRIES

'Stella' the first and only self-fertile variety
'Morello' good for jam. Tolerates a north position

Varieties worth looking for:

EATING APPLES

'Greensleeves' juicy eating apple, moderately acid, good flavour, eat September to November
'Katy' juicy eating apple, sweet flavour, similiar to 'Worcester', eat September to October
'Sunset' almost as good as 'Cox's' but easier to grow. Eat September to December

PEARS

'Beth' early pear, free cropping, excellent flavour
'Onward' late pear, very sweet and juicy

J. C. Allgrove
The Nursery, Middle Green, Langley, Slough, Berkshire SL3 6BU
Tel Slough (0753) 20155
Fruit tree and soft fruit specialist. Has over 200 varieties of fruit trees and a wide range of soft fruit including 15 to 20 varieties of gooseberries, 20 varieties of currants and 12 varieties of raspberries. Also provides a bud or graft service. Plants available by mail order.

Bentley's Nurseries
331 Benfleet Road, South Benfleet, Essex SS7 1PW
Tel South Benfleet (037 45) 50874

Fruit tree specialists with over a dozen varieties; their particular speciality is fruit trees on dwarfing root stock. Plants available by mail order.

Chris Bowers
Whispering Tree Nursery, Wimbotsham, Norfolk PE34 8QB
Tel Downham Market (0366) 388752
Fruit tree and soft fruit specialist. Also sells 10 varieties of rhubarb available as crowns. Mail order available.

Dayspring Nursery
Quarr, Buckhorn Weston, Gillingham, Dorset SP8 5PA
Tel Gillingham (074 76) 3030

Fruit tree and soft fruit specialist with 100 varieties of fruit trees. Offers a grafting service for customers where varieties of fruit trees can be grafted on to selected rootstocks. No mail order except for grafting service.

Deacons Nursery
Moor View, Godshill, Isle of Wight PO38 3HW
Tel Isle of Wight (0983) 840750
Fruit tree and soft fruit specialist. Nearly 200 varieties. Family trees are a speciality. A range of many types of soft fruit. Trees available by mail order.

Family Trees
Summerlands, Curdridge, Botley, Southampton, Hampshire SO3 2HB
Tel Botley (048 92) 6680
Fruit tree specialist with over 100 varieties. Trees available by mail order.

C. W. Groves and Son
West Bay Road, Bridport, Dorset DT6 4BA
Tel Bridport (0308) 22654
Fruit tree and soft fruit specialists – concentrating particularly on strawberry plants. They also specialise in English violets – especially parma violets. Plants available by mail order.

Keepers Nursery
446 Wateringbury Road, East Malling, Maidstone, Kent ME19 6JJ
A small nursery with 100 varieties of apples, 20 varieties of pears and 30 varieties of plums. Many old varieties. Also sells soft fruit. Can supply fruit rootstocks and will do budding and grafting to order.

New Tree Nurseries
2 Nunnery Road, Canterbury, Kent CT1 3LS
Tel Canterbury (0227) 61209
Fruit tree specialists with over 1,000 varieties in total. They concentrate on old historic and new varieties of apple. But they are also interested in pears and peaches. Trees available by mail order.

T. A. Redman
Elms Farm, Ancton Lane, Middleton-on-Sea, Bognor Regis, W. Sussex PO22 6NJ
Tel Middleton-on-Sea (024 369) 694447
Fruit tree specialist with 150 varieties in total. Concentrates on trained forms. No mail order.

Also see:

ROSES
Knights Nurseries

SHRUBS AND TREES
Binks Nurseries
Brackenwood Nurseries
Buckingham Nurseries and Garden Centre

UNUSUAL PLANTS
Clive Simms: unusual and sub-tropical fruiting plants

GOOD GARDEN CENTRES AND GENERAL NURSERIES
Ashby-de-la-Zouche, Staunton Harold Nurseries
Exeter, St Bridget Nurseries
Knutsford, Caldwell and Sons
Merriott, Scotts Nurseries
Pickering, The Roger Plant Centre
Topsham, Yeoman Gardeners: old varieties
Whitminster, Highfield Nurseries

FUCHSIAS

Fuchsias are easy plants to grow and they reward the enthusiast with a long flowering period from May through until the end of October. They are available in a variety of colours from white through pink, rose, violet and orange, to the deepest reds and purples. They are easily trained as bush plants or standards, while the basket types take on lovely pendulous shapes.

Many varieties will do well in the garden if treated as hardy perennials. Each year the dead top growth will be replaced by new shoots from the ground in the spring. Fuchsias generally like a sunny spot with some shelter, although they tolerate partial shade and some varieties actually prefer it. The less hardy varieties are best overwintered indoors either in a greenhouse or shed that is kept frost free, or even a spare room in the house – but make sure the plants don't dry out completely.

When buying fuchsias you're likely to be spoilt for choice because there are so many varieties to choose from. Plants start to appear on sale at the end of April at almost every market, garden shop, florist and garden centre. Many amateur growers sell from home and they, along with specialist nurseries, advertise in papers and magazines in the spring. If you are near to a specialist nursery or fuchsia enthusiast it's worth a visit while the plants are in flower. However, unless you want a very unusual variety, you should find something to suit you at an ordinary garden centre or nursery.

For good value, buy rooted cuttings in 8cm (3in) pots in early spring, or larger plants towards the end of June. Choose a plant which will develop a good, well-balanced shape. Look for sturdy plants with green rather than woody stems (a sign of irregular watering), a well-developed system of roots, and a least five side shoots starting from the base of the main stem. Obviously you should avoid damaged plants or those which are very pale and spindly. You should also look under the leaves to check for aphids or whitefly and avoid plants which are in pots that are too small – these may be root-bound and have lost their vigour. With some careful training you can achieve a beautiful display in your borders, on the patio or in baskets. Many nurseries will sell by mail order, but plants can be damaged easily if they are not securely packed and protected from drying out in transit.

Varieties to try

WIDELY AVAILABLE

'Dollar Princess' flowers early, makes a good standard, red and purple flowers

'Lady Thumb' a red and white version of 'Tom Thumb'

'Marinka' basket type, good as weeping standard, red and dark red, one of the best and easiest to grow

'Mrs Popple' bushy and upright with large red and purple flowers on arching branches, one of the hardiest

'Riccartonii' arching stems produce late red and purple flowers, one of the hardiest

'Snowcap' bushy, upright with red and white flowers very freely produced

'Swingtime' basket type producing large red and white blooms, spreading growth

'Tom Thumb' dwarf, bushy, red and purple flowers

WORTH LOOKING FOR

'Gracilis Tricolour' very hardy with attractive green, white, and pink foliage

'Ting-a-Ling' one of the best whites, naturally bushy

'La Campanella' pink, white and purple flowers, makes a good weeping standard

'Lyes Unique' white and orange, dainty flowers, bushy

'Pink Galore' basket type, one of the best pinks with large, fluffy flowers

B. and H. M. Baker
Bourne Brook Nurseries,
Greenstead Green, Halstead,
Essex CO9 1RJ
Tel Halstead (0787) 472900
Fuchsia specialists with over 600
varieties. Rooted cuttings available
by mail order.

Bromesberrow Place Nurseries
Bromesberrow, near Ledbury,
Hereford and Worcester HR8 1RZ
Tel Bromesberrow (053 181) 348
Fuchsia specialists with 50 varieties.
Their varieties are chosen for
hanging baskets and patio
containers. There is a private
collection of orchids for view by
appointment only but none for sale.
No mail order.

Conroy Fuchsias
8 Kingfisher Crescent, Cheadle,
Stoke-on-Trent, Staffordshire
ST10 1RZ
Tel Cheadle (0538) 755845
Fuchsia specialist with 260 varieties
listed and more in stock. Plants
available by mail order.

Fountains Nurseries
by Fountains Abbey, Ripon,
N. Yorkshire MG4 3DZ
Tel Sawley (076 586) 623
Fuchsia specialists with over 300
varieties. They also have alpines (50
to 100 varieties) and some hardy
perennials (over 50 varieties). Only
rooted cuttings of fuchsias available
by mail order.

W. and M. Fuchsias
97 The Avenue, Nunthorpe,
Middlesborough, Cleveland
TS7 0AF
Tel Middlesborough (0642) 316950
Fuchsia specialists with over 200
varieties. Plants available by mail
order.

Fuchsiavale Nurseries
Stanklyn Lane, Summerfield,
Kidderminster, Hereford and
Worcester DY10 4HS
Tel Kidderminster (0562) 694444

Fuchsia specialists with 300
varieties. Plants available by mail
order.

D. and P. Gardens
18 Walthamstow Avenue,
Chingford, London E4 8ST
Tel 01-530 3178
Fuchsia specialist with 200 varieties.
Plants available by mail order.

High Trees Nurseries
Buckland, Reigate, Surrey RH2 9RE
Tel Reigate (073 72) 47271
Fuchsia specialists stocking over
300 varieties available by mail order
as rooted cuttings. Also specialise
in summer bedding plants.

Hill Top Fuchsia Nursery
Gladsmar, 20 Hill Top, Baddesley
Ensor, Atherstone, Warwickshire
CV9 2BQ
Tel Atherstone (082 77) 2502
Fuchsia specialist with 220 varieties.
Plants available by mail order.

D. T. and J. A. Hobson
130 Aughton Road, Swallownest,
Sheffield, S. Yorkshire S31 0TH
Tel Sheffield (0742) 872532
Fuchsia specialists with 400 to 500
varieties. They also keep 40
varieties of regal pelargoniums.
Plants available by mail order.

Jackson's Nurseries
Clifton Campville, near Tamworth,
Staffordshire B79 0AP
Tel Clifton Campville (082 786) 307
Fuchsia specialist with 200 varieties.
Plants available by mail order.

Kerrielyn Fuchsias
39 Holbrook Road, Cambridge,
Cambridgeshire CB1 4SX
Tel Cambridge (0223) 243862
Fuchsia specialist with 1,020
varieties, mostly greenhouse
varieties but also 124 hardy varieties
and 26 species. Rooted cuttings
available by mail order. A 'search
and acquire' service available for a
small extra charge.

C. S. Lockyer
'Lansbury', 70 Henfield Road, Coalpit Heath, Bristol, Avon BS17 2UZ
Tel Winterbourne (0454) 772219
Fuchsia specialist with 320 varieties. Plants available by mail order.

Markham Grange Nurseries
Long Lands Lane, Brodworth, near Doncaster, S. Yorkshire DN5 7XB
Tel Doncaster (0302) 722390
Fuchsia specialists with 300 varieties. Rooted cuttings available by mail order.

Oldbury Nurseries
Brissenden Green, Bethersden, Kent TN26 3BJ
Tel Bethersden (023 382) 416
Fuchsia specialists with 400 varieties. Plants available by mail order.

R. and J. Pacey
Fuchsia Nurseries, Stathern, Melton Mowbray, Leicestershire LE14 LHE
Tel Harby (0949) 60249
Fuchsia specialists with 240 varieties. Plants available by mail order

Porter's Fuchsias
12 Hazel Grove, Southport, Merseyside PR8 6AX
Tel Southport (0704) 33902
Fuchsia specialist with 200 varieties listed and a further 300 available on request. Plants available by mail order.

Silver Dale Nurseries
Shute Lane, Combe Martin, Ilfracombe, Devon EX34 OEU
Tel Combe Martin (027 188) 2539
Fuchsia specialists with over 200 varieties. They grow the plants on to a larger size than normal and the basket varieties are sold in hanging baskets throughout the summer. No mail order.

John Smith and Son
Hilltop Nurseries, Thornton, Leicestershire LE6 1AN
Tel Bagworth (053 021) 331
Fuchsia specialists with 210 varieties. Also have 65 varieties of dwarf conifers and 15 varieties of modern ivy-leaved pelargoniums. Plants available by mail order.

T. G. D. Nurseries
25 Bellars Lane, Barnards Green, Malvern, Hereford and Worcester WR14 2DJ
Tel Malvern (068 45) 62693
Fuchsia specialists with 500 varieties. 'Pacific Giant' polyanthus available in mixed colours grown from seed. Plants available by mail order.

Ward Fuchsias
5 Pollen Close, Sale, Cheshire M33 3LP
Tel 061-973 6467
Fuchsia specialist with 110 varieties. Concentrates on basket and exhibition varieties. Cuttings available by mail order.

Willis Fuchsias
Chapel Lane, West Wittering, Chichester, W. Sussex PO20 8QG
Tel Chichester (0243) 513065
Fuchsia specialist with 300 varieties. No mail order.

See also:

CACTI AND SUCCULENTS
Oakleigh Nurseries

CARNATIONS AND PINKS
Barkers

CHRYSANTHEMUMS
Elm House Nurseries

PELARGONIUMS
The Vernon Geranium Nursery
Howard S. Waters and Son

Many specialists stock a lot more plants than they list, so if you want something special, ask for it. You may be lucky.

GLADIOLI

There are more than 300 species of gladioli or sword lily – both names coming from the sword-like shape of its leaves. Most were originally natives of South Africa, and have been known in Britain since 1596. After years of crossing and selection, hybrids have outstripped the species in popularity, although some of the species are very lovely.

Gladioli are not at all difficult to grow and they make beautiful cut flowers for the home, as well as excellent flower-arranging and exhibition material. The flowers come in a wide variety of colours and a surprising number of shapes and sizes, from the familiar large-flowered varieties to miniatures, butterfly and primulinus gladioli with unusual markings and often with ruffled or frilled petals.

Gladioli thrive in sunny positions and prefer a neutral soil. Good drainage is most important. Early-flowering types such as *G. colvillei* and *G. nanus* should be planted in pots in early October and kept free of frost. In the south and west *G. byzantinus* can be planted outdoors in autumn. Other varieties can be planted in open ground from the end of March until the last week in May – if corms are planted every couple of weeks throughout this period you will be assured of a continuous display right through August and September. Planting deep – 10 to 15cm (4 to 6in) – ensures that the long stems will be held firmly, although for exposed or windy sites staking will be necessary. Well-prepared soil and ample food and water should ensure high-quality blooms.

Corms of popular varieties are stocked by most garden centres and nurseries as well as supermarkets, garden shops and florists. A wider range is sold by mail order by general bulb companies and specialists – they usually appear in the spring catalogues. Species gladioli are often listed by specialists in unusual bulbs.

When buying corms, choose those which are high-shouldered and deep rather than thin or flat. When squeezed they should not be soft, but offer some resistance – any corm with a hollow top or base should be discarded. A small base plate indicates a vigorous corm. Corms which are 10 to 14cm (4 to 5½in) in circumference are best – larger and they are past their prime, smaller and they are not ready to flower.

Varieties to try

POPULAR

'Flos Florium' large-flowered, light salmon
'Flower Song' large-flowered, deep golden yellow
'Green Woodpecker' medium-flowered green-yellow, scarlet throat
'Oscar' giant-flowered, deep red
'Peter Pears' large-flowered, tangerine with scarlet tongue
'Rose Supreme' giant-flowered, pink and white
G. colvillei 'The Bride' white

G. nanus 'Amanda Mary' salmon red
G. nanus 'Peach Blossom' delicate pink

MORE UNUSUAL

'Capriccio' small-flowered, lilac, red blotch
'Indian Maid' small-flowered, deep tan
'Little Jade Green' small-flowered, ruffled jade green
'Misty Eyes' large-flowered, plum red with yellow throat, plum and apricot blotch
'Nirvana' small-flowered light salmon-pink, red rim and lower petals

Agincourt
Coombe Cottage, Heckfield, near
Basingstoke, Hampshire RG27 0LJ
Tel Heckfield (073 583) 392
Gladioli specialist with about 90
varieties, concentrating on
exhibition varieties. Also offers over
25 varieties of daffodils. Bulbs and
corms available by mail order.

Rainbow Glads
6 Woodland End, Lepton,
Huddersfield, W. Yorkshire
HD8 0HY
Specialises in exhibition gladioli
with particular emphasis on small-
flowered and primulinus types. 200
different cultivars. Mail order only
(supply corms).

Showglads
3 Baddeley Drive, Wigston,
Leicester, Leicestershire LE8 1BF
Tel Leicester (0533) 811075
Specialises in gladioli for exhibition
and floral art. Between 110 to 120
varieties. Corms available by mail
order.

Also see:

BULBS (GENERAL)
for named varieties

BULBS (UNUSUAL)
for species

SEEDS
Samual Dobie and Son
Suttons Seeds
Unwins Seeds

GROUND COVER PLANTS

The object of ground cover is to smother weeds and create interest in
otherwise bare patches: the deep shade of an overhanging tree, a dry
sloping bank or between bushes in the shrubbery – all areas where weeds
happily establish themselves to the detriment of the rest of the garden.
Some form of ground cover can keep these at bay and add colour and shape
to an otherwise dull scene. It pays to prepare the site well, since a good
fertile soil will encourage vigorous growth, and the quicker the ground
cover plants spread the better they will be able to stifle new weeds.
Remember that ground cover will not eradicate weeds – these must be
destroyed before planting – but once it is established it will dominate an
area and provide much more inhospitable conditions for the invaders.
When planting, you must take account of the rate of growth of the chosen
plants when deciding how closely to plant them. You must also consider
the growth habit – whether you want spreading runners, a dense mat of
foliage or clumps and mounds – and finally what will grow well and look
good in the chosen site.

If you want ground cover as an alternative to grass, it must be able to
withstand hard wear; camomile or thyme, for example, are suitable.
Generally speaking the plants most suitable for ground cover offer some
attractive leaf feature, either in colour, or texture, or shape, need little
attention once established, are fast growers and are reasonably permanent.

A lot of ground cover plants are available at run-of-the-mill garden
centres, but specialist nurseries which concentrate on herbaceous plants
offer the widest choice and the most unusual varieties. Many sell by mail
order and usually despatch plants between October and March. In some
shops and garden centres you may see plants for sale covered in blooms or
berries to entice buyers – it is sensible to leave these since they have passed
their young and vigorous stage and will grow much more slowly than the

smaller specimens. Lots of young plants are a much better buy than a few older ones. Container-grown plants should not be pot-bound nor have brown leaves – they will take time to recover and won't spread so rapidly as healthy plants. Bare-rooted stock must have a good healthy root system which should be moist and not frosted. With a bit of thought and planning you can turn a featureless space into a mosaic of foliage which is not only a delight to the eye, but also serves a useful function.

Plants to try

COMMON, EASILY AVAILABLE
Euonymus fortunei spreading evergreen
Hebe pinguifolia 'Pagei' white flowers, silver foliage, produces mounds
Hedera helix (common ivy) spreads rapidly, many different varieties including variegated forms
Helianthemum spp (sun rose, rock rose) colourful, summer-flowering, spreads into wide mats
Saxifraga umbrosa (London pride) evergreen, clumps, pale pink/white flowers in spring
Vinca minor (lesser periwinkle) pale blue, white or purple flowers, spreading

LESS COMMON
Acaena microphylla semi-evergreen, bronze, mat-forming
Asarum europaeum forms dense, evergreen cover
Rubus calycinoides evergreen, forming a ground-hugging mat
Tellima grandiflora green-white flowers, hairy leaves
Vaccinium vitis-idaea evergreen, pink flowers, orange fruits
Vancouveria hexandra white flowers, dense evergreen cover

Growing Carpets
The Old Farmhouse, Steeple Morden, near Royston, Hertfordshire SG8 0PP
Tel Royston (0763) 852417
Ground cover specialists with about 150 varieties. The plants range from prostrate alpines to shrubs. Plants available by mail order.

Morehavens
Sway, Hampshire SO4 0EG
Tel Lymington (0590) 682603

Camomile specialists offering 'Treneague', a non-flowering variety that can provide you with a lawn that never needs mowing. Plants available by mail order.

Also see:

ALPINES AND ROCK PLANTS
Oland Plants

FOLIAGE PLANTS
HERBACEOUS PLANTS
UNUSUAL PLANTS

HEATHERS
The three groups of heathers, callunas, ericas and daboecias, are easy-care plants which, with careful selection, will give a display of colour from both flowers and foliage throughout the year. One of their best-known characteristics is that they hate lime, but most of the winter-flowering ericas (*E. carnea*, *E. darleyensis* and *E. erigina*) are lime-tolerant. Less well known is their strong dislike of heavy, clay soil – though the addition of plenty of peat can improve this.
Heathers are beautiful ground cover plants, fit well in rockeries and

greatly enhance mixed borders – though their full beauty can best be seen in a special heather garden. Sweeps of colour gently offset by the greenery of select dwarf conifers make a beautiful sight. When planting heathers it is a good idea to plant them in groups since a single heather can look most unimpressive. An open position will encourage compact growth and good flowering – a shady site gives little reward, and full sun is essential for foliage varieties. An annual trim removing the dead flowers and most of that year's growth is essential to retain a compact shape.

When buying heathers, decide first whether you want winter- or summer-flowering ones – there is no point buying 'on spec' as the pretty plant you choose may be entirely unsuitable for your site. Container-grown heathers may be planted at any time, and if you buy them this way damage to the roots will be minimal. Young, bushy plants are the best choice, but check that the plants are not pot-bound. The ideal time to purchase bare-root stock is from October to March. If planted in the autumn they have plenty of time to become established before any dry and windy weather. If you are particularly interested in the more unusual varieties try one of the specialist nurseries listed. If possible go to the nursery in person since heathers may suffer in the post.

Varieties to try

WIDELY AVAILABLE
Calluna vulgaris
   'Beoley Gold' bright golden foliage, white flowers
   'Darkness' compact plant, crimson flowers
   'Peter Sparkes' deep rose-pink, double flowers
   'Robert Chapman' gold foliage, orange/red in winter
   'Silver Queen' silver-grey foliage, pale mauve flowers
   'Elsie Purnell' shell-pink flowers with silvery sheen

E. carnea
   'Aurea' golden foliage, darker in winter
   'King George' compact plant, pink flowers
   'Myretoun Ruby' deep purple flowers
   'Pink Spangles' flowers shell-pink with deep pink tips
   'Springwood White' clear white flowers
   'Vivellii' dark bronze-green foliage, deep pink flowers

WORTH LOOKING FOR
C. vulgaris
   'Drum-Ra' one of the best whites
   'Johnson's Variety' compact plant, lavender flowers, very late

E. carnea
   'Adrienne Duncan' dark bronze foliage, crimson flowers
   'R. B. Cooke' clear pink with lilac tinge

E. cinerea
   'Atrosanguinea Smith's Variety' free-flowering, ruby red flowers
   'C. D. Eason' bright magenta flowers
   'Eden Valley' white flowers with lavender tips
   'Golden Hue' pale yellow foliage

E. erigina
'Golden Lady' golden foliage
'W. T. Rackliff' dark green foliage, white flowers

E. darleyensis
'Furzey' very dark foliage, deep lilac pink flowers
'Silberschmelze' white flowers, new shoots creamy-pink

Angus Heathers
10 Guthrie Street, Letham, Forfar,
Angus, Tayside DDB 2PS
Tel Letham (033 781) 504
Heather specialist with 137
varieties. No mail order.

Barncroft Nurseries
Dunwood Lane, Longsdon,
Stoke-on-Trent, Staffordshire
ST9 9QW
Tel Leek (0538) 384310
650 varieties of heathers and over
300 varieties of trees and shrubs
suitable for inclusion in heather
gardens. In addition they offer a
range of 400 varieties of garden
conifers. No mail order.

Blairhoyle Nursery
Port of Menteith, Stirling, Central
FK8 3LF
Tel Port of Menteith (087 75) 669
Heather specialist with 130
varieties. Dwarf and slow-growing
conifers also available. No mail
order.

Brynhyfryd Nurseries
Brynhyfryd, Rhydycroesau,
Oswestry, Shropshire
Heather specialist with
approximately 250 varieties.

P. G. Davis
Timber Tops, Marley Common,
Haslemere, Surrey GU27 3PT
Tel Haslemere (0428) 2825
Specialises in heathers – all open
ground plants – about 100 varieties
offered. No mail order.

Denbeigh Heather Nurseries
All Saints Road, Creeting St Mary,
Ipswich, Suffolk IP6 8PJ
Tel Stowmarket (0449) 711220
Heather specialists with 450
varieties, they have a range of

heathers from South Africa. They
offer rooted cuttings for mail order
and plants for collection from the
nursery.

D. and M. Everett
Greenacres Nursery, Bringsty,
Worcester, Hereford and Worcester
WR6 5TA
Tel Bromyard (0885) 82206
Heather specialists with 200
varieties; also building up a range of
conifers. No mail order.

Felsberg Nurseries
Dobwalls, near Liskeard, Cornwall
PL14 6JB
Tel Liskeard (0579) 20333
Have a range of 200 to 300 varieties
of heathers. They also offer grafted
tomatoes in 10 varieties. No mail
order.

Four Acres Nursery
Cosheston, Pembroke Dock, Dyfed
SA72 4SC
Tel Pembroke (0646) 683178
Heather specialist with about 80
varieties, concentrates on lime-
tolerant varieties. Also specialises
in conifers (110 varieties). No mail
order.

M. G. Frye
The Willows, Poors Lane (North),
Daws Heath, Thundersley, Essex
SS7 2XF
Tel Southend-on-Sea (0702) 558467
Heather specialist with 140
varieties. Plants available by mail
order.

The Heather Garden
139 Swinston Hill Road,
Dinnington, Sheffield, S. Yorkshire
S31 7RY
Tel Dinnington (0909) 565510
Heather specialist with 110

varieties; also offers 45 to 50 varieties of dwarf and slow-growing conifers suitable for small heather gardens. No mail order.

Hardwick Nursery
18 Western Road, Newick, Lewes, E. Sussex BN8 4LF
Tel Newick (082 572) 2024
Heather specialist offering 170 varieties. Also offers over 200 varieties of shrubs and 50 varieties of Japanese azaleas. In addition there is a range of unusual plants. No mail order.

Desmond G. John
366 Wallisdown Road, Bournemouth, Dorset BH11 8PS
Tel Bournemouth (0202) 517139
Heather specialist with 130 to 140 varieties. A range of 30 varieties of dwarf conifers also offered. Plants available by mail order.

Kingfisher Nursery
Gedney Hill, Spalding, Lincolnshire PE12 OPP
Tel Holbeach (0406) 330503
Heather specialist with 120 varieties. No mail order.

Little Froome Heathers
Drayton Lane, Fenny Drayton, Nuneaton, Warwickshire CV13 6AZ
Tel Atherstone (082 77) 3382
Heather specialist offering over 120 varieties. Plants available by mail order only.

Little Heath Farm
Little Heath Lane, Potten End, Berkhamsted, Hertfordshire HP4 2RX
Tel Berkhamsted (044 27) 4951
Heather specialist with over 120 varieties. Also specialises in clematis (70 varieties), dwarf conifers (20 varieties) and hardy plants. Plants sometimes available by mail order.

Longdale Heathers
Longdale Lane, Ravenshead, Nottinghamshire NG15 9FG
Tel Mansfield (0623) 792756
Heather specialists with 350 varieties of heathers including 'collectors'' varieties and well-known ones. Will grow any commercially available variety to meet special order if given 18 months' notice. They also offer 100 varieties of slow-growing conifers and 100 varieties of herbs. Mail order on request.

Norwich Heather and Conifer Centre
54A Yarmouth Road, Thorpe, Norwich, Norfolk NR14 6PU
Tel Norwich (0603) 39434
Heather and conifer specialists with 650 and 430 varieties respectively. Plants available by mail order.

Oliver and Hunter
Moniaive, Thornhill, Dumfries and Galloway DG3 4HH
Tel Moniaive (084 82) 291
Heather specialists with 200 varieties (not all listed in their catalogue). Plants available by mail order.

Okells Nurseries
Duddon Heath, near Tarporley, Cheshire CW6 OEP
Tel Tarvin (0829) 41512
Heather specialists with 200 varieties concentrating on those that give all-year interest and are suitable for a range of soil types. They also offer 150 varieties of conifers – mainly dwarf and slow-growing ones. Plants available by mail order.

Otter's Court Heathers
Otter's Court, West Camel, near Yeovil, Somerset BA22 7QF
Tel Marston Magna (0935) 850285
Heather specialists that only grow lime-tolerant heathers – they offer 80 varieties. There is also a small range of dwarf conifers. Plants available by mail order.

Pennyacre Nurseries
Station Road, Springfield, Fife
KY15 5RU
Tel Cupar (0334) 55852
Heather specialists with 174
varieties. Also a few dwarf conifers.
Plants available by mail order –
although the full range of plants
will not be available by mail order
until September 1985.

Polden Acres Gardens
Edington, Bridgwater, Somerset
TA7 9HA
Tel Chilton Polden (0278) 722331
Heather specialists with 120
varieties, specialise in lime-tolerant
varieties. Also offer nearly 200
species and varieties of hebe. No
mail order except for small
quantities of hebe cuttings.

Rideway Heather Nursery
Horderley Farm, Horderley, near
Craven Arms, Shropshire SY7 8HP
Tel Craven Arms (058 82) 2248
Heather specialist with 120 varieties
– container-grown. No mail order.

Speyside Heather/Garden Centre
Dulnain Bridge, Highland
PH26 3PA
Tel Dulnain Bridge (047 985) 359
Heather specialist with 128 varieties
listed in catalogue and many others
not listed. There are about 300

varieties in the show gardens. Also
offers some conifers and shrubs
that associate well with heathers.
Heather plants and seed available
by mail order.

Wingates
62A Chorley Road, Westhoughton,
Bolton, Lancashire BL5 3PL
Tel Westhoughton (0942) 813357
Heather specialist with 200 varieties
of heather and a range of dwarf
conifers (50 varieties). No mail
order.

Also see:

ALPINES AND ROCK PLANTS
Holden Clough
Mansfield Nurseries
Rob Roy Nursery

AZALEAS AND RHODODENDRONS
Milton Hutchings: Cape heaths

BONSAI
Greenwood Gardens

DWARF CONIFERS
Orchardleigh Nursery

HERBACEOUS PERENNIALS
Bressingham Gardens

UNUSUAL PLANTS
Corran Garden

GOOD GARDEN CENTRES AND
GENERAL NURSERIES
Wickwar, George Osmond

HERBS

Everyone is familiar with the aromatic scents and distinctive tastes of the
culinary herbs. Their medicinal properties and use as dyes or cosmetics are
less well known. Herbs have waxed and waned in popularity through the
ages and we are just at the beginning of a new surge in interest, contrasting
with an almost total dismissal which characterised the Victorian attitude.

Herbs can enhance your garden as well as your cooking. Try them in
flower borders, in pots outside the kitchen door, or set out a complete
formal herb garden. Some have pretty flowers and foliage and others such
as lavender and thyme produce heady smells.

The principal battle today is the establishment of more rigid standards in
naming varieties. Even the specialist suppliers are guilty of selling sweet
marjoram as pot marjoram, or spearmint as peppermint, and garden
centres are even worse. Steps are being taken to improve this state of affairs
by the British Herb Trade Association who are setting up reference
collections, but for the time being customers must often rely on their own

knowledge and judgement. A good garden centre with lots of different, well-displayed herbs is a reasonable bet – particularly if you can identify plants yourself. For unusual varieties you must turn to the specialists. It is better by far to shop in person since mail order plants may not survive a delayed journey. Buying plants can give you a quick harvest, but many herbs can be grown from seed and some, such as basil and dill, do better this way. A number of general seed merchants can supply many types of herbs, both culinary and medicinal.

Plants to try

Allium schoenoprasum (chives) Mild onion flavour. Easy to raise from seed
Anethum graveolens (dill) Aromatic leaves, good with fish and beans. Best grown from seed
Angelica archangelica (angelica) Large, decorative plants. Young stems can be candied. Raise from seed sown in late summer, or buy plants in spring
Artemisia dracunculus (French tarragon) Bitter-sweet flavour, used in savoury dishes and for tarragon vinegar. Make sure you buy French tarragon plants rather than the Russian type
Foeniculum vulgare (fennel) Two types used in cooking: vegetable (or Florence) fennel whose stem is used, and the herb fennel of which the foliage is used with fish, salads, eggs and cheese. Easily raised from seed
Laurus nobilis (sweet bay) Shrub or small tree with aromatic leaves used in meat dishes. Buy small plants for economy, large ones can be costly. Cuttings can be difficult to root
Levisticum officinale (lovage) Perennial with aromatic leaves used in savoury dishes. Sow seeds as soon as they are ripe, or buy plants in spring
Mentha spp. (mint) Many different types with different aromas. Very vigorous and invasive. Buy plants initially, divide established roots
Melissa officinalis (lemon balm) Bushy plant with lemon-flavoured leaves used in drinks and with pork and fish. Very easy to raise from seed
Myrrhis odorata (sweet cicely) A large plant with aniseed-flavoured leaves used with tart fruit dishes. Not difficult to raise from seed
Ocimum basilicum (sweet basil) Bushy little plant, a half-hardy annual with strongly aromatic leaves used in egg and cheese dishes, fish soup and with tomatoes. Best raised from seed
Origanum spp. (marjoram) Three types commonly used in cooking: pot marjoram, sweet or knotted marjoram and wild marjoram (oregano). Used in many savoury dishes. Grow sweet marjoram from seed. Pot and wild marjoram are usually grown from cuttings or division
Petroselinum crispum (parsley) Hardy biennial, many uses. Easy to grow from seed though germination may take several weeks
Rosmarinus officinalis (rosemary) Evergreen shrub, pungent leaves used with fish and meat. Buy plants or take cuttings
Satureja montana (winter savory) Hardy, semi-evergreen shrub. Spicy flavour, good with beans. Grow from seed, take cuttings or divide existing plants
Thymus spp. (thyme) Small evergreen shrub used in savoury dishes. Raise from seed or buy plants for a quicker start. Lemon thyme is strongly lemon-scented

Arne Herbs
The Old Tavern, Compton
Dundon, Somerton, Somerset
TA11 6PP
Tel Somerton (0458) 42347
Over 250 varieties. No mail order.

Barns Garden Centre
Alcester Road, Burcot, Bromsgrove,
Hereford and Worcester B60 1PU
Tel 021-472 0303
Specialises in herbs (80 varieties).

Candlesby Herbs
Cross Keys Cottage, Candlesby,
Spilsby, Lincolnshire PE23 5SF
Tel Scremby (075 485) 211
Specialise in herbs (200 varieties),
wildflowers (50 varieties) and
herbal products. Plants and herbal
products available by mail order.

The Cottage Herbery
Mill House, Boraston, near Tenbury
Wells, Hereford and Worcester
Over 120 varieties of herbs. No mail
order.

Daphne Ffiske Herbs
Rosemary Cottage, Bramerton,
Norwich, Norfolk NR14 7DW
Tel Surlingham (050 88) 8187
Specialises in herbs (over 100
varieties) concentrating on culinary,
fragrant and medicinal ones. Plants
available by mail order.

Hatfield House Garden Shop
Hatfield House, Hertfordshire
AL9 5NQ
Tel Hatfield (07072) 64412
Specialises in herbs (60 to 80
varieties). No mail order.

The Herb Garden
Brynteg, Anglesey, Gwynedd
Tel Tynygongl (0248) 853407
Specialises in herbs, selling over 400
varieties. Also stocks herbaceous
perennials (100 varieties), cottage
garden plants (100 varieties) and
wild flowers (100 varieties). Plants
and seeds available by mail order.

Highlands Herbs Nursery
Tigh-an-Allt, Tomatin, Highland
IV13 7YP
Tel Tomatin (080 82) 295
Specialises in culinary herbs (over
60 varieties). Plants available by
mail order.

Hollington Nurseries
Woolton Hill, Newbury, Berkshire
RG15 9XT
Tel Highclere (0635) 153908
Specialise in herbs suitable for
growing as decorative plants, as
well as the more usual ones. They
have 400 species and varieties. Also
a range of plants for the cool
conservatory. Plants available by
mail order.

Iden Croft Herbs
Frittenden Road, Staplehurst,
Kent TN12 0DH
Tel Staplehurst (0580) 891432
Specialise in herbs and aromatic
plants with 450 varieties. They also
have herb products, demonstration
gardens and the National Collection
of origanum. Plants, seeds and
herbal products available by mail
order.

Laundry Farm Herbs
Nesscliffe, Shrewsbury, Shropshire
SY4 1AX
Tel Nesscliffe (074 381) 406
Specialise in medicinal herbs
(approximately 200 varieties). They
also grow flowers for dried flower
arrangements and have a range of
herbal products. No mail order.

Lympne Market Garden
Lympne Place, Lympne, Kent
CT21 4PA
Tel Hythe (0303) 66183
Specialises in herbs (over 90
varieties). Also sells organic
vegetables, free-range eggs and
goats' milk. Plants available by
mail order.

E. Macleod Matthews
The Manor House, Chenies,
Buckinghamshire WD3 6ER
Tel Little Chalfont (024 04) 2888

Specialises in culinary herbs (50 varieties). No mail order.

Netherfield Herbs
Netherfield Cottage, Nether Street, Rougham, Bury St. Edmunds, Suffolk IP30 9LW
Tel Beyton (0359) 70452
Specialise in herbs (150 varieties available and another 50 varieties to order). Concentrate on the aromatic sub-shrubs, and offer a garden design service for herb and cottage gardens. No mail order.

Norfolk Lavender
Caley Hill, Heacham, King's Lynn, Norfolk PE31 7JE
Tel Heacham (0485) 70384
Lavender specialist offering plants and lavender products. Plants and products available by mail order.

Oak Cottage Herb Farm
Nesscliffe, near Shrewsbury, Shropshire SY4 1DB
Tel Nesscliffe (074 381) 262
Specialises in culinary herbs and old-fashioned flowers. Also offers medicinal herbs, ground cover plants and plants for flower arranging. Plants and seed available by mail order.

The Old Rectory Herb Garden
Ightham, Kent TN15 9AL
Tel Borough Green (0732) 882608
Specialises in herbs and herb products. No mail order.

Poyntzfield Herb Nursery
Black Isle, by Dingwall, Cromarty, Highland
Tel Poyntzfield (038 18) 352
Specialises in herbs (280 varieties). Offers a full range but specialises in European and North American medicinal herbs. Plants available by mail order.

Stoke Lacy Herb Garden
Bromyard, Hereford and Worcester HR4 7JH
Tel Burley Gate (043 278) 232
Specialises in less common herbs (200 varieties). Plants and seeds available by mail order.

Suffolk Herbs
Sawyers Farm, Little Conrad, Sudbury, Suffolk CO10 0NY
Tel Sudbury (0787) 227247
Herb specialists supplying wide selection of plants and seeds. They also publish a seed-growers guide to herbs and wild flowers. Plants and seeds available by mail order; the nursery is open only on Saturday (9am to 5pm).

The Weald Herbary
Park Cottage, Frittenden, Cranbrook, Kent TN17 2AU
Tel Frittenden (058 080) 226
Specialises in herbs (250 varieties). Plants and seeds available by mail order.

Wells and Winter
Mere House, Mereworth, Maidstone, Kent ME18 5NB
Specialise in herbs (85 varieties) and variegated plants (60 varieties). No mail order.

Wilton Park Nursery
Park Lane, Old Beaconsfield, Buckinghamshire HP9 2HT
Tel Beaconsfield (049 46) 3418
Specialises in herbs (80 varieties) concentrating on culinary ones. Also have unusual shrubs (50 varieties) and patio plants. Herbs available by mail order.

Also see:

ALPINES AND ROCK PLANTS
Rob Roy Nursery

CACTI AND SUCCULENTS
Fold Garden

CARNATIONS AND PINKS
Kingstone Cottage Plants

HEATHERS
Longdale Heathers

HERBACEOUS PERENNIALS
Glen Haven Gardens

UNUSUAL PLANTS
Eastgrove Cottage Garden Nursery

WILDFLOWERS
John Chambers

HERBACEOUS PLANTS

The herbaceous border has traditionally been the backbone of many country gardens. Fronted by lawns, against a foil of hedging or walls, the spectacular colours entertain the viewer through the summer. There are, of course, practical problems in maintaining an impressive border. Adequate space is most important (a width of at least 1.5m (5ft) is desirable); there are gaps to deal with when plants die back; taller species need staking; and during the winter and spring months the herbaceous border can look rather scrappy. For those willing to take on the tasks of planning and maintenance, its beauty can be unrivalled. Herbaceous perennials can also be grown in 'island beds', along the sides of paths, amidst the shrubbery, scattered along the waterside or even in a wild garden.

Before buying or raising plants it is a good idea to make a plan and decide which flowers will be suitable in terms of their spread, colour, flowering period, soil requirements, and height. With a list in hand, your local garden centre should be the first port of call. Spring and autumn are the best periods for planting. Make sure you buy new plants – old ones may be root-bound, weedy and short of nutrients. A helpful clue as to whether the plant has been around all summer will be the state of its label and price tag – the one time where tatty labelling serves a useful purpose! Many garden centres tend to be unimaginative and unadventurous in the varieties of perennials they stock, so if you have specific ideas or want something un- usual, try the specialist nurseries. About half those listed sell by mail order.

Also see FOLIAGE PLANTS AND UNUSUAL PLANTS

Plants to try

WIDELY AVAILABLE
Achillea 'Moonshine'
Aster novi-belgii 'Lady-in-Blue'
Astilbe
Campanula persicifolia
Euphorbia polychroma
Geranium 'Johnson's Blue'
Helleborus foetidus
Sedum 'Autumn Joy'
Potentilla nepalensis 'Miss Willmott'
Pulmonaria rubra 'Bowles Variety'
Salvia nemorosa 'Friesland'

WORTH LOOKING OUT FOR
Anemone 'Honorine Jobert'
Aster amellus
Astrantia major 'Rubra'
Dicentra spectabilis 'Alba'
E. grifithii 'Fireglow'
E. robbiae
Helleborus orientalis
Paeony 'Bowl of Beauty'
Nepeta 'Six Hills Giant'
Rudbeckia 'Goldsturm'

Abbey Dore Court Gardens
Abbeydore, near Hereford,
Hereford and Worcester HR2 OAD
Tel Golden Valley (0981) 240419
Unusual herbaceous plants are the main feature of the garden – there are approximately 300 varieties. They have the National Collection of sedums (250 varieties) and a selection of ferns. No mail order.

Bressingham Gardens
Diss, Norfolk IP22 2AB
Tel Bressingham (037 988) 464
Famous for herbaceous perennials, and dwarf conifers, they also stock a good range of ferns, alpines, shrubs and heathers. Mail order only.

Fairview Nursery
Newmans Lane, Westmoors,
Dorset BH22 OLW
Tel Ferndown (0202) 877745
Herbaceous perennial specialist – over 1000 varieties usually in stock. Also stocks 200 varieties of heather, half as many shrubs (some rare), 36

varieties of clematis and a selection
of other climbers. No mail order.

Glen Haven Gardens
21 Dark Lane, Backwell, Bristol,
Avon BS19 3NT
Tel Flax Bourton (027 583) 2700
300 varieties of herbaceous
perennials available. They also have
about 100 varieties of rare plants
and a range of herbs. Plants
available by mail order.

Lye End Nursery
Woking, Surrey GU21 1SW
Tel Woking (048 62) 69327
125 varieties of herbaceous
perennials, available by mail order.

J. and E. Parker-Jervis
Marten's Hall Farm, Longworth,
near Abingdon, Oxfordshire
OX13 5EP
Tel Longworth (0865) 820376
Offer 200 varieties of herbaceous
perennials for small gardens
concentrating on old-fashioned,
scented and flower-arranging
plants including a collection of 20
old-fashioned pinks. Also 75
varieties of unusual bulbs, mostly
grown in pots. No mail order at
present.

Plants for Pleasure
2 The Cottage, Maybourne Rise,
Mayford, Woking, Surrey
GU22 0SQ
Tel Woking (048 62) 64958
Over 100 varieties of herbaceous
perennials (including ground cover
and herbs). Also specialises in
white-flowered plants. Plants
available by mail order. Visitors
only by appointment.

Plants from the Past
The Old House, 1 North Street,
Belhaven, Dunbar, Lothian
EH42 1NU
Tel Dunbar (0368) 63223
Concentrate on old cultivars of
herbaceous perennials – about 400
in stock – especially aquilegias,
bellis, cheiranthus, dianthus,
fragraria, violas.

The Thatch Nurseries
Whitley Hill, Henley-in-Arden,
Solihull, W. Midlands B95 5DL
Tel Henley-in-Arden (056 42) 2327
Stock a range of herbaceous
perennials, including unusual
varieties. Their speciality is plants
and shrubs for flower arrangers. No
mail order.

Tomperrow Farm Nurseries
Tomperrow Farm, Threemilestone,
Truro, Cornwall TR3 6BE
Tel Truro (0872) 560344
Herbaceous perennial specialists
with over 200 varieties. The
emphasis is on plants not normally
available. Plants available by mail
order.

M. C. Wickenden
Well Meadow, Crawley Down,
W. Sussex R10 4EY
Approximately 700 varieties of
herbaceous perennials;
concentrates on ones that are not
easy to obtain, including old
varieties. Has a good range of
ornamental grasses. Plants
available by mail order.

Also see:

ALPINES AND ROCK PLANTS
BEGONIAS
Blackmore and Langdon: border
phlox

CARNATIONS AND PINKS
Woodfield Bros: lupins (seed only
at present)

FOLIAGE PLANTS
Hopleys Plants

SHRUBS AND TREES
Brackenwood Nurseries
Goscote Nurseries
MacFarlanes Nurseries and Garden
Centre

UNUSUAL PLANTS
GOOD GARDEN CENTRES AND
GENERAL NURSERIES
Bournemouth, Saxonbury
Nurseries
Fishers Pond, Foulis Court Nursery
Startley, Startley Hill Nurseries
Waterperry, Waterperry Gardens

IRIS

The iris family offers flowers ranging from the tiny 10cm (4in) dwarf varieties to those at 1 to 1.3m (4 to 5ft). They come in all the colours of the rainbow from white through yellow, brown, mauve, purple, blue to black – the subtleties of shade are endless. Of the 200 or more species, a few need specialist care, but most are easy to grow. A sunny, well-drained position will suit the majority, but there are species for both shade and waterside. The small, bulbous types flower in the early spring and look well in the rock garden, naturalised under the dappled shade of trees, or planted as edging. Larger bulbous types flower a little later, and include the well-known 'Dutch' varieties ideal for cutting. Most popular are the bearded irises, available in a range of sizes – dwarf, intermediate and tall. All are very easy to grow and are completely hardy. They flower in May and June and are best planted in a mixed border or where space permits in a border of their own. They will tolerate the grime and pollution of town surprisingly well, and will flourish if given a lot of sun, a well-drained soil and some lime.

Irises are best planted in the autumn and mail orders from specialist nurseries will start to arrive from July to September. Buying from a specialist nursery is usually the best way of obtaining a wide choice of iris. If possible, visit the nurseries at flowering time to choose the varieties you like. Garden centres occasionally sell container-grown plants of both bearded and species iris. However, nurseries tend to stock only the older and well-tried varieties. The best way to obtain modern varieties is through the special sales list put out by the British Iris Society. Members often import new varieties from America which British nurseries don't stock, and these are sold between society members.

Bulbous irises are more easily available from garden centres or from the same mail order sources as other garden bulbs.

Popular species and varieties to try

DWARF BEARDED

'Blue Denim' blue, white beard
'Green Spot' pure white, brilliant green spot
'Tinkerbell' blue, ruffled

TALL BEARDED

'Blue Rhythm' cornflower blue, overlaid with silver
'Cliffs of Dover' milk-white
'Dancer's Veil' white with blue-purple etching
'Jane Phillips' bright blue
'Ola Kala' brilliant orange-yellow
'Party Dress' flamingo pink, ruffled
'Starshine' creamy yellow with gold
'Staten Island' gold and velvety red
'White City' porcelain white with a flush of blue

LARGE BULBOUS

Dutch iris eg
'Golden Harvest' yellow
'Ideal' blue
'Imperator' navy blue
'White Excelsior' white

SMALL BULBOUS

I. reticulata purple or blue eg
  'Cantab'
  'Clairette'
  'Joyce'
I. danfordiae yellow
I. histriodes 'Major' deep blue

OTHERS

I. bucharica yellow, Juno
I. magnifica bluish white, Juno
I. unguicularis (*I. stylosa*) pale mauve, winter-flowering, November to March

V. H. Humphrey
8 Howbeck Road, Arnold, Nottingham, Nottinghamshire
NG5 8AD

Tel Nottingham (0602) 260510
Specialist with 150 bearded varieties
and also a range of species, siberica,
spuria and Pacific Coast types.
Plants and seeds available by mail
order.

Also see:

ALPINES AND ROCK PLANTS
R. F. Beeston

Potterton and Martin
BULBS (GENERAL)
Kelways Nurseries

BULBS (UNUSUAL)
FOLIAGE PLANTS
Gold Brook plants

HERBACEOUS PERENNIALS
Bressingham Gardens
Glen Haven Gardens

===

IVY

Ivy is a native of Britain, and has a very long history of cultivation in this
country. It has become a familiar sight on cottage walls, climbing up trees,
covering old sheds or as ground cover. Some plants are on record as
surviving some four hundred years, and because of its longevity ivy has
acquired a unique place in folklore and mythical tradition. Ivies are often
accused of causing damage to buildings, but in fact they seem to have little
ill effect provided the basic structure is sound. They prefer light shade to
full sun and are particularly happy growing up walls since they enjoy the
alkaline soil at the base. If grown as houseplants they require a spot with
light shade, a moderate temperature and a moist medium – they will suffer
stress if subjected to hot and dry conditions.

The choice of variety must be made after considering what role it is to
play. For an ivy to cover a large area it should be vigorous, with large
leaves, while if it is to be used for ground cover it must be tough and frost
resistant. The colour of the leaves can be chosen to harmonise with
surrounding flowers and foliage or contrast with a brick wall. Some colours
will blend into the background and help unsightly objects disappear,
others will call out to the passer-by.

The popular hardy varieties will be found at most garden centres. They
are grown up canes and can be up to three years old when sold. There is no
advantage in buying tall plants as only new growth will produce aerial
roots which can cling and enable the ivy to climb. The best value is in 7 to
9cm (3in) pots with several 10 to 15cm (4 to 6in) trails of about a year old
and plenty of roots. Hardening-off young ivies sold as houseplants will
extend the range of varieties, but they can be subject to winter problems.
Because ivies are readily propagated they are available throughout the
year, and planting is possible in all but the dead of winter.

Species and varieties to try

EASILY AVAILABLE
Hedera helix English or common ivy
    'Goldheart' small dark leaves, gold centre
    'Glacier' grey-green, white margin
    'Deltoidea' attractive-shaped green leaves
H. canariensis (Canary ivy)
    'Gloire de Marengo' grey-green leaves, bordered with white
H. colchica (Persian ivy)
    'Dentata Variegata' large shining leaves with variable yellow edge

WORTH LOOKING FOR

H. helix

'Adam' indoor variety, small white-edged leaf
'Buttercup' small yellow leaves, slow-growing
'Green Ripple' for ground cover, attractive
'Hibernica' (Irish ivy) fast ground cover
'Ivalace' lacy, dark green leaves, purple stems
'Lutzii' indoor variety, flecked with cream
'Manda's Crested' bright green, crinkled and frilled
'Pedata' (bird's-foot ivy) slim-lobed leaves

H. canariensis

'Aurea Maculata' creamy-white mottling

H. colchica

'Sulphur Heart' bright green leaves, cream centre

Tynedale Nurseries
Green Side Road, Ryton, Tyne and Wear NE40 4LF
Tel Tyneside (091) 413 2131
They offer 70 varieties of ivy and also about 30 types of hebe. No mail order.

Whitehouse Ivies
Hylands Farm, Rectory Road, Tolleshunt Knights, Maldon, Essex CM9 8EZ
Tel Maldon (0621) 815782
Ivy specialist with 300 varieties available by mail order in 7 to 9cm (3in) pots.

Also see:

ALPINES AND ROCK PLANTS
Oland Plants

FERNS
Fibrex Nurseries

JAPANESE MAPLES

The delicately cut foliage of these attractive trees makes them ideal either as specimen plants with a space to themselves or to add variety and interest among other shrubs. They vary from tiny shrubs to small trees, and their habit ranges from upright to spreading or even pendulous. Their small size but range of habit and leaf shape together with striking variations of foliage colour make them ideal for many positions in even the smallest garden. They look lovely in the rock garden, planted in a tub on the patio or arranged with other Japanese maples in a special display. Their often horizontal, tiered habit and feathery leaves are seen to advantage if set against a foil of other shrubs with dense foliage. They'd contrast well with upright conifers while those with pale leaves will show up against a dark-leaved background and those with dark leaves against shrubs with pale foliage. They can be wasted if planted into a mixed border without careful thought – their subtle beauty just gets lost.

The Japanese maple is not very demanding about soil conditions. It does not like to be waterlogged, but apart from that, if given a good amount of organic matter when planted and a yearly mulch it should be contented. They need some shelter from the wind, and a site which is protected from frosts late in the spring. Dappled shade or full sun is suitable for most varieties, but those with variegated, yellow or dark purple leaves can be scorched in full sun so are best in dappled shade. The root system is shallow growing and benefits from a surface mulch; it is also fibrous and

355

compact so that reasonably young trees transplant easily.

Most garden centres stock a few varieties and if you shop around and can find a good, healthy plant of the type you require locally it should be reasonable value for money. Look for a well-shaped, vigorous specimen with a good root system. The graft should be strong and low down so that it does not spoil the shape of the tree (except for weeping standards where the graft will be high up). Avoid trees with dead shoot tips or any signs of die back.

Unusual varieties will have to be obtained from a large nursery or specialist, many of whom do mail order. This is generally a reliable way to buy rare and unusual varieties.

Species and varieties to try

EASILY AVAILABLE

Acer palmatum atropurpureum upright variety, 2m (6ft) in 10 years. Leaves open bright red, then fade to bronze – some turn green by summer. Good autumn colours

A. palmatum 'Osakazuki' upright variety, 2.5m (8ft) in 10 years. Leaves plain green but dazzling scarlet in autumn. Hanging bunches of red-winged seeds appear in summer

A. palmatum dissectum slow, mound-forming, taking many years to grow above 1.5m (5ft). Fresh green, finely divided leaves turn shades of yellow, orange and scarlet in autumn

A. palmatum dissectum atropurpureum finely dissected leaves open red, turn purple, then bright scarlet in autumn

A. japonicum 'Aureum' upright growth to 2m (6ft) in 10 years. Leaves open a pale yellow, turn gold, then green in summer. Needs some shade to prevent scorch

WORTH LOOKING FOR

A. palmatum 'Butterfly' upright to 2m (6ft) in 10 years. Pale green and white variegated leaves, white parts turn magenta in autumn

A. palmatum 'Senkaki' upright to 2.5m (8ft) in 10 years. Called the coral bark maple because of the young shoots which are bright pinkish-red through winter

A. palmatum 'Coralinum' upright but only to 0.5m (1.6ft) in 10 years so almost a natural bonsai. Leaves open shrimp pink

A. japonicum 'Aconitifolium' large open bush to 2.5m (8ft) in 10 years, deeply divided, deep green leaves turn scarlet in autumn

Mallet Court Nursery
Mallet Court, Curry Mallet, Taunton, Somerset TA3 6SY
Tel Hatch Beauchamp (0823) 480748
Japanese maple specialist with about 100 to 120 varieties. Also has some rare and unusual trees and shrubs including over 50 species of oak. Plants available by mail order.

Seed Lee Nursery
Brindle Road, Bamber Bridge, Preston, Lancashire PR5 6AP

Tel Preston (0772) 311174
Japanese maple specialist with 180 varieties. Has a range of mature landscape specimens 6 to 10 years old. No mail order.

Also see:

SHRUBS AND TREES
C. J. Marchant
Nettleton Nurseries

LILIES

The stately lily is a most beautiful ornamental flower which is excellent for cutting, as well as providing a striking display in the garden. For preference it should be sited in a border, since the roots are happy in the shade, while the flowers generally thrive in sun. This is not a steadfast rule though, because lilies vary enormously and you will find some varieties which like sun while others prefer shade. They also vary in soil requirements – all need good drainage but some thrive in calcareous soil, others like a lime-free site. Check on the individual requirements of any species you buy. Most are completely hardy but a few are only suitable for growing under glass, notably *Lilium longiflorum*, sometimes seen as cut flowers. It is also important to note details about height since this can range from 60cm to 1.8m (2 to 6ft).

Lilies look best when planted in groups – the larger the better – and all of one variety. Even when growing in containers, try to keep to a minimum of three.

Flowers appear from the end of May right through until September. The best time for planting is early autumn, but you may not be able to buy lilies this early. The soil in winter is usually too cold and wet for planting, so it's best to pot them up as soon as you buy them, grow them in a cold greenhouse and plant out in spring. Lilies are widely available in garden centres and by mail order from general bulb companies, lily specialists and some seedsmen.

Lily bulbs are covered in scales attached to a basal plate. The scales can easily get broken so take care in handling and when choosing bulbs in garden centres avoid any which are damaged. Don't purchase bulbs either where the scales are dried out, withered, soft or loose. Also look for plenty of white, fleshy roots. If you can't plant or pot up your bulbs immediately, pack them in peat to stop them drying out. The shorter the bulbs are out of the soil the better.

Species and varieties to try

POPULAR

'Connecticut King' yellow, upright-facing, 1m (3ft), July
'Destiny' golden-yellow, brown spots, upright-facing, 1m (3ft), July
'Enchantment' orange-red, upright-facing, 1m (3ft), June
'Golden Splendour' yellow trumpet with wine-coloured stripe on outside of each petal, 1.2m (4ft), July
L. regale white with yellow throat, 1.5 to 2m (5 to 6.5ft), July
L. speciosum 'Rubrum' white flushed pink or red, 1.2 to 1.5m (4 to 5ft), August

MORE EXOTIC/EXPENSIVE

L. amabile dainty, pomegranate red, Turk's cap flowers, rare, 1.2m (4ft), June and July
L. auratum white, spotted large flowers. Several different varieties available, all expensive but all lovely, 1.2 to 2m (4 to 6.5ft), August
L. cernuum rare and dainty, pinkish-purple, purple spots, 1.2m (4ft), June to July
L. martagon white or purple to pink, Turk's cap flowers – scarce but easy to

grow and good for naturalising, 0.6 to 1m (2 to 3ft), June to July
L. pyrenaicum bright greenish-yellow, Turk's cap flowers. Tolerates lime, 0.6 to 1m (2 to 3ft), June

Bullwood Nursery
54 Woodlands Road, Hockley,
Essex SS5 4PY
Tel Southend-on-Sea (0702) 203761
Lily specialist with 124 species and varieties. Concentrates on producing hybrids of Western American species and on Liliaceae which are suited to shady and woodland conditions. Also has a range of uncommon hardy or near-hardy plants that are not listed in the catalogue. Bulbs available by mail order.

Also see:

BULBS (GENERAL)

DAFFODILS
Michael Jefferson-Brown

GOOD GARDEN CENTRES AND
GENERAL NURSERIES
Kiltarlity, Highland Liliums

ORCHIDS

Those gardeners who specialise in orchids will never be without new plants to challenge and excite them – the choice of fascinating and beautiful plants is almost endless. To help you embark on this hobby, consult books and catalogues, visit flower shows and botanic gardens and make contact with your local society (list available from the British Orchid Council, R. Buxton, 41 Whitbarrow Road, Lymm, Cheshire WA13 9AW). Orchids have a reputation for being very difficult to grow and for needing detailed specialist knowledge, but in fact a conscientious amateur can do very well. One of the prerequisites of successful growing is a greenhouse which offers you easy control of heat and humidity. Good ventilation and a means of providing shade are also essential.

When buying orchids make sure they are of a variety suited to the temperature of your greenhouse. An orchid which consistently suffers temperatures below its optimum will fail.

When buying, it's best to go to one of the dozen or so specialist nurseries across the country and see the plants in flower, choose what you like and ask about individual growing instructions. Some specialists concentrate on a particular genus, others on groups with particular temperature requirements. It is not advisable to buy seedlings because although they are cheaper, they will not flower for five to seven years and the young seedlings require very special conditions. Many people order mixed collections and find that, after the long wait for them to flower, they don't really like them, so it's best to start with individually named plants.

Some garden centres also sell orchids, but they are unlikely to have the expertise of the specialists, so plants may have been kept in less than ideal conditions. They are also unlikely to be able to offer much advice on caring for the plants. You can buy at any time of year: different plants bloom at different times. Orchids are not cheap and you may have to pay £15 or more for a reasonable specimen, although prices start at around £5.

When buying, look for a good root system and foliage that has a good, deep green colour, avoiding specimens with blemishes on the foliage. If buying pseudo-bulbs, from which many orchids grow, they should be firm and hard.

Genera to try

POPULAR, EASY STARTERS

Cymbidium, hybrids of different colours, long-lasting flowers

Masdevallias, a very variable genus with relatively few hybrids. Examples that are easy to grow are *M. coccinea* and *M. barlaeana*

Odontoglossums, so called 'Butterfly orchids', are very popular cool-growing hybrids producing many different colours

Paphiopedilum, many hybrids, evergreen

EXOTIC

Phalaenopsis, many beautiful hybrids. Tender, with flowers produced on slender, arching stems

Cattleya, tender, evergreen with good species and many hybrids. Many have showy flowers 15 to 20cm (6 to 8in) across

Bardfield Orchids

Great Bardfield Hall, Great
Bardfield, near Braintree,
Essex CM7 4RZ
Tel Great Dunmow (0371) 810066
Specialises in cymbidiums. No mail order.

Burnham Nurseries

Orchid Avenue, Kingsteignton,
Newton Abbot, Devon TQ12 3HQ
Tel Newton Abbot (0626) 2233/4
Specialise in all orchids for cool to hot greenhouses. Plants available by mail order.

Cley Orchids

Rectory Hill Nursery, Holt Road,
Cley-next-the-Sea, Norfolk
NR25 7TX
Tel Cley (0263) 740892
Orchid specialist offering 200 species and 200 hybrids. Also a selection of modern and old-fashioned roses (130 varieties approximately). Plants available by mail order.

D. J. Harberd

29 Foxhill Crescent, Weetwood,
Leeds, W. Yorkshire LS16 5PD
Tel Leeds (0532) 784684
Specialises in pleiones and maintains a collection of all forms in cultivation. Also breeds new forms and collects and imports from China, Burma, India. Pseudo-bulbs supplied by mail order.

A. J. Keeling and Son

Grange Nurseries, Westgate Hill,
near Bradford, W. Yorkshire
BD4 6NS
Tel Bradford (0274) 682120
Orchid specialist concentrating on masdevallias and species. Plants available by mail order.

Mansell and Hatcher

Cragg Wood Nurseries, Rawdon,
Leeds, W. Yorkshire LS19 6LQ
Tel Leeds (0532) 502016
Orchid specialist concentrating on odontoglossums. Plants available by mail order.

Randalls Orchids

Highlands Hall, Monks Eleigh, near
Ipswich, Suffolk IP7 7QS
Tel Bidleston (0449) 740780
Specialise in large and miniature cymbidiums. Orchid flowers supplied by mail order.

Ratcliffe Orchids

Chilton, Didcot, Oxfordshire
OX11 0RT
Tel Didcot (0235) 834385
Orchid specialists – breed paphiopedilum varieties but also offer phalaenopsis and odontoglossum. Plants available by mail order.

St. Dunstan's Nursery

Ham Street, Baltonsborough,
Glastonbury, Somerset BA6 8AL
Tel Glastonbury (0458) 50037
Specialises in cymbidiums (offers

150 to 200 varieties) and orchids as houseplants. Plants available by mail order.

T. Simmons and Son
166 Nether Street, Finchley, London N3 1PF
Tel 01-346 2245
Specialises in species orchids for cool/intermediate conditions. Plants available by mail order.

David Stead Orchids
Leeds Road Nurseries, Lofthouse, near Wakefield, W. Yorkshire WF3 3QF
Tel Wakefield (0924) 822011
A variety of orchid stock, but with the breeding and raising emphasis on intergeneric odontoglossum hybrids and endangered species. Plants and orchid compost available by mail order

Wellbank Orchids
Pardown, Oakley, Hampshire RG23 7DY

Tel Basingstoke (0256) 780386
Specialise in orchid seedlings of all genera. Mail order available.

Wyld Court Orchids
Hampstead Norreys, Newbury, Berkshire RG16 OTN
Tel Hermitage (0635) 201283
Specialise in lycaste and species orchids. Plants available by mail order.

Also see:

ALPINES AND ROCK PLANTS
J. P. Geraghty

CACTI AND SUCCULENTS
Tamarisk Nurseries

CAMELLIAS
Stonehurst Nurseries

DAHLIAS
Butterfields Nursery: pleiones

GOOD GARDEN CENTRES AND GENERAL NURSERIES
Startley, Startley Hill Nurseries

PELARGONIUMS

The pelargoniums are a large group of plants including not just zonal pelargoniums – the familiar bedding plants most of us call 'geraniums' – but also regal, scented-leaved, ivy-leaved and miniature pelargoniums. They should not be confused with the real geranium or cranesbill. Zonal pelargoniums have attractive leaves and bright flowers in many shades of red, pink, coral and salmon as well as white. Apart from being used for bedding, they are ideal plants for pots, tubs, window boxes and hanging baskets. Regal pelargoniums make good specimen plants for the house, conservatory or greenhouse. They have large flowers often blotched with one colour on another.

Ivy-leaved pelargoniums tend to trail or climb and make particularly good plants for hanging baskets and window boxes. Scented-leaved pelargoniums are often used as houseplants. Their flowers are usually rather small, and both the flowers and leaves lack the vivid colours of most pelargoniums. Miniature geraniums are particularly good in window boxes. They usually form bushy plants and many have double or semi-double flowers. They can be overwintered in the house where they will continue to grow and flower. Pelargoniums are not fussy plants and can be grown in most types of soil or compost. They can be propagated easily from cuttings.

In the spring you will find zonal pelargoniums sold for bedding on almost every street corner, market stall and shop shelf. However, many of these will be un-named so you can't be sure of what you are getting. Some garden centres sell named varieties and also other types of pelargonium, such as the scented-leaved and ivy-leaved varieties. Choose a plant with deep green (or brightly coloured) leaves and no yellowing leaves at the base of the stem. Look for strong, healthy growth with stout stems and short joints. If planting outside, it is a good idea to harden plants off yourself as this has often not been done properly.

Zonal pelargoniums used to be grown almost entirely from cuttings, but nowadays there are many varieties you can raise from seed. The best time to sow is early autumn or January. Seed-raised plants have some disadvantages – they tend to be leggy and late-flowering – but save you the problems of overwintering stock plants. Most seedsmen sell a limited number of varieties and mixtures of zonal pelargonium seed and some also sell seed of the other types of pelargonium.

Varieties to try

ZONAL FROM SEED
'Lyric' very attractive, deep green leaves with marked zoning, pink flowers
'Paintbox Mixed' tall but shapely and well branched, mixed colours
'Red Elite' attractive plants with red flowers
'Startel' unusual variety with jagged edges to the flowers and leaves. Various colours
'Sonnet' handsome plants, dark green leaves, light salmon flowers

ZONAL FROM CUTTINGS
'Blue Fox' double flower, blue/purple
'Highfields Festival' double flower, pale pink with white eye
'Pearl Necklace' pure white, semi-double
'Regina' double flower pink/salmon

REGALS
'Aztec' white with strawberry marking on each petal
'Beau Geste' pale lavender, maroon markings
'Carisbrooke' large rose-pink flowers, cerise blotches
'Lavender Grand Slam' silvery-mauve
'Rembrandt' purple with white throat
'Sunrise' large salmon-orange flower with white throat

SCENTED-LEAVED
'Attar of Roses' rose-scented, pale mauve flower, branched foliage
'Citrodorum' orange-scented, deep green foliage
'Odoratissimum' apple-scented, grey leaves, small white flowers
'Variegated Fragrans' pine-scented, small white flowers, green and cream foliage

IVY-LEAVED
'Lilac Gem' masses of pale lilac blooms, scented
'Mini Cascades' with red or pink flowers
'Rouletta' white, edged with crimson

MINIATURE
'Davina' salmon pink, double
'Diane' dawn pink
'Jane Eyre' deep lavender, double flowers, dark leaves
'Pink Fondant' pink, brightly zoned foliage

Beckwood Nurseries

New Inn Road, Beckley, near Oxford, Oxfordshire OX3 9SS
Tel Stanton St. John (086 735) 780
Pelargonium specialist with about 500 varieties. Plants available by mail order.

Clifton Geranium Nursery

Cherry Orchard Road, Whyke, Chichester, W. Sussex PO19 2BX
Tel Chichester (0243) 782010
Pelargonium specialist with 400 varieties. Plants and seeds available by mail order.

Cypress Nursery

Powke Lane, Blackheath, Birmingham, W. Midlands B65 0AG
Tel 021-559 1495
Pelargonium specialist with over 170 varieties. Particularly interested in hybridising, and in export and import to and from America. Also have 50 varieties of conifers. No mail order.

Finnside Nurseries

The Street, Martlesham, Woodbridge, Suffolk IP12 4RG
Tel Woodbridge (039 43) 7463
Pelargonium specialists with 600 varieties – concentrate on miniatures. Plants and seeds available by mail order.

D. Gamble and Son

Highfield Nurseries, Longford, Derbyshire DE6 3DT
Tel Great Cubley (033 523) 238
Pelargonium specialist with 400 varieties, specialising in zonal pelargoniums. Plants available by mail order.

F. W. Mepham

11 Chestnut Avenue, Northwood, Middlesex HA6 1HR
Tel Northwood (0972) 21284
Pelargonium specialist with 183 varieties listed, but over 400 in stock. Concentrates on miniature and dwarf types. Plants sold as rooted cuttings by mail order only.

Redvale Nurseries

St. Tudy, Bodmin, Cornwall PL30 3PX
Tel Bodmin (0208) 8503
Pelargonium specialists with 600 varieties. Plants available by mail order.

Thorp's Nurseries

257 Finchampstead Road, Wokingham, Berkshire RG11 3JT
Tel Wokingham (0734) 781181
Pelargonium specialists with 400 varieties. Plants available by mail order.

The Vernon Geranium Nursery

Hill End Road, Harefield, Uxbridge, Middlesex UB9 6LH
Tel Harefield (089 582) 2369
Pelargonium and fuchsia specialist with 270 and 200 varieties respectively. Rooted cuttings available by mail order.

Howard W. Waters and Son

Beech Hill Nurseries, Swanland, North Ferriby, Humberside HU14 3QY
Tel Hull (0482) 633670
Pelargonium and fuchsia specialist with 600 and 200 varieties respectively. Also stocks a few chrysanthemums. Plants available by mail order.

Westdale Nursery

Holt Road, Bradford-on-Avon, Wiltshire BA15 1TS
Tel Bradford-on-Avon (022 16) 3258
Pelargonium specialist with over 600 varieties. No mail order.

Also see:

CACTI AND SUCCULENTS
Oakleigh Nurseries

DAHLIAS
Oscroft's Nurseries
Sedgewood Nurseries

FERNS
Fibrex Nurseries

FUCHSIAS
D. T. and J. A. Hobson

POTATOES

There are a lot more types of potato than the 'whites' or 'reds' you buy from the greengrocer. Growing your own allows you to try different varieties until you find those that suit your garden and that you enjoy eating. Grow an early and second early variety to provide new potatoes through the summer. If space is limited, concentrate on early potatoes, when they are expensive to buy. Main crop varieties can be stored into the winter.

Potatoes like an open site and a fertile well-drained soil, on the acid side. Work in plenty of compost or manure the previous autumn to retain moisture, and water well when the tubers are forming (when the plants are in flower). Practise crop rotation to prevent pests and diseases.

You can buy seed potatoes either loose or prepacked in bags, usually 3 or 6kg (6.6 or 13lb). You should have a reasonable choice of varieties. For unusual varieties you may have to buy by mail order.

Seed potatoes are tubers grown under strictly controlled conditions – government regulations are designed to prevent the spread of serious pests and diseases. When buying tubers, look for a blue label stating that they are certified seed, class CC. If the individual packs aren't labelled, the shop should display the label from the sack which gives the country of origin, the producer's number, the grade (the size of the tubers) and the month and year they were packed. If they're sold loose, avoid diseased or damaged tubers and choose well-graded seeds. Ideally they should be 35 to 50mm (1.4 to 2in) in diameter for main crop potatoes. Early potatoes will crop earlier if the tubers are a bit bigger. You should get 12–16 tubers in a kilogramme (2.2lb). Buy seed potatoes early and store them in a cool (but frost free) well-lit place to 'chit' (encouraging sprouts to appear). If you buy in March or April each tuber should have at least two sturdy green sprouts.

Varieties to try

EARLY
'Pentland Javelin'
'Vanessa'
'Duke of York'
'Maris Bard'
'Foremost'
'Arran Comet'

SECOND EARLY
'Romano'
'Maris Peer'
'Wilja'

MAIN CROP
'Desiree'
'King Edward'
'Maris Piper'
'Drayton'

D. Maclean
Dornock Farm, Crieff, Tayside PH7 3QN
Specialist with 300 varieties. In addition to early, second early, main crop and exhibition, there are many rare and foreign varieties that are hard to obtain elsewhere. Tubers available by mail order.

Scotston Seed Potatoes
Scotston, Laurencekirk, Grampian AB3 1ND
Tel Laurencekirk (056 17) 447
Seed potato specialists with 32 varieties. They concentrate on first early varieties but also offer second early, main crop, exhibition and old varieties. Tubers available by mail order.

Also see:

SEEDS
Samuel Dobie and Son
S. E. Marshall and Co
Thompson and Morgan

PRIMULAS

Primulas provide colourful clumps of flowers in the border or rockery from March until July. The range available includes anything from tiny alpines to large plants with imposing 1m (3ft) flower spikes, while colour can be either subtle shading or showy brilliance. They like a well-drained but water-retentive soil, and prefer light shade rather than full sun.

Garden centres stock the popular polyanthus, as well as *P. rosea* and *P. denticulata*, but once you move into the realm of auriculas, species, Asiatics and Europeans you'll either need to raise them from seed or buy plants from a specialist nursery. Seed is obviously cheaper, but it is essential that it is fresh since viability is very quickly lost and the alpine sorts are often very tricky to raise this way. Buy seed by mail order or as soon as it appears in the shops. The best all-round time for sowing bought seed is March. If it arrives, or if you buy it, before this, mix it with a little damp sand and peat and store it in the salad compartment of your fridge. This helps to maintain its viability. Once the seedlings are growing, never let them dry out and protect them from direct sunlight.

Results are more immediate, and less risk is entailed, if you buy plants. The best time to buy is April or May, certainly not much after June. Look for sturdy plants with good crowns preferably several per pot and crisp green leaves. Those with fleshy roots should be potted to the correct depth and not have any roots exposed at the surface. If you're buying mail order plants, order in autumn for spring delivery, but if possible make a personal visit to the nursery so you can examine the plants yourself and possibly find varieties not listed in the catalogue.

Species to try

EASILY AVAILABLE AS PLANTS

Auricula hybrids – mixed colours

Coloured primroses

Polyanthus – mixed colours

P. denticulata (drumstick primrose) lilac or white flowers in spring, 30cm (12in)

P. japonica (candelabra primrose) crimson or magenta flowers early summer, 45cm (18in)

P. juliana (P. x pruhoniciana) numerous varieties in many colours

P. rosea deep rose flowers in spring, 13cm (5in)

WORTH LOOKING FOR

P. aureata creamy-yellow flowers, orange centre, flowers in spring

P. florindae (giant cowslip) yellow flowers in summer, 60cm (24in)

P. frondosa pink flowers in spring, 15cm (6in)

P. gracilipes lavender-pink with white eye, early spring

P. marginata varieties, for raised alpine bed or rockeries

P. viallii like miniature mauve red hot pokers, early summer

Barnhaven
Brigsteer, Kendal, Cumbria
LA8 8AU
Tel Crosthwaite (044 88) 386

Primrose seed specialist, particularly polyanthus and primroses (61 varieties) and *Primula sieboldii* (6 varieties). Seeds available by mail order.

Cravens Alpine Nursery
1 Foulds Terrace, Bingley,
W. Yorkshire BO16 4LZ
Tel Bradford (0274) 561421
Show auricula and primula
specialist with 200 varieties. Also
propagates named, old-fashioned
pinks along with newer varieties.
Plants and seeds available by mail
order.

G. Douglas
67 Church Road, Great Bookham,
Surrey KT23 3EG
Tel Bookham (31) 58182
Auricula specialist with a particular
interest in show and alpine
varieties. Mail order for seeds only.

P. H. Gossage
Oakenlea, West Coker Hill, Yeovil,
Somerset BA22 9DG
Tel West Coker (093 586) 2605
Private garden – holds National
Collection of *Primula vulgaris*
cultivars. Plants sometimes
available by mail order.

Brenda Hyatt Auriculas
1 Toddington Crescent, Bluebell
Hill, near Chatham, Kent ME5 9QT
Tel Medway (0634) 63251
Auricula specialist with 250 to 300
varieties. Rosette and duet double
impatiens (about 20 varieties) are
also offered. Plants and seeds
available by mail order.

Laurels Double Primroses
Tralodden Cottage, by Girvan,
Strathclyde KA26 0TX

Primula specialist with over 800
varieties. The particular speciality
is, as the name suggests, double
primroses. Plants and seeds
available by mail order.

West Blackbutts Nursery
West Blackbutts, Stonehaven,
Grampian AB3 2RT
Tel Newtonhill (0569) 30430
Primula specialist with 45 varieties
concentrating on dwarf, hardy
primulas and double primroses.
Plants available by mail order.

Also see:

ALPINES AND ROCK PLANTS
Careby Manor Gardens
Edrom Nurseries
Glenview Alpines
Hartside Nursery Garden
Reginald Kaye
Martin Nest Nurseries
BULBS
Paradise Centre

FOLIAGE PLANTS
Hopleys Plants

SEEDS (GENERAL)
SEEDS (UNUSUAL)
UNUSUAL PLANTS
Ballalheannagh Gardens
Cottage Garden Plants Old and
New
Yew Tree Nursery

WATER AND WATERSIDE PLANTS
Longstock Park Nursery

RHUBARB

The history of rhubarb can be traced back to China at around 3000 BC,
though until the early 19th century it was used in this country mostly for its
medicinal properties. Now it is a common sight tucked into the corner of
allotments and vegetable patches, where it is left to get on by itself and
supply the first fresh spring puddings. Given a bit of help though, in the
form of a rich, well-drained soil and a sunny spot, this old favourite will
provide some real surprises.

Rhubarb is sold as seed, in containers or as bare-rooted stock. Seeds are
well worth trying as you can obtain a wider range of healthy varieties this
way, and will only have to wait another two or three years to harvest the

crop. Seed-raised plants are more variable than divided crowns, but most plants will still retain their true characteristics. If buying sets (divided crowns) there will be a limited choice available at garden centres and general nurseries, perhaps a couple of varieties. If you want more choice you will have to try a specialist supplier. Container-grown plants can be planted any time, but the bare-rooted sets should go in when the roots are dormant, preferably in autumn.

A good plant will show fresh, healthy leaves and sturdy roots and buds. Any spots on the leaves could be a sign of virus infection which if slight may not hurt the rhubarb, but a heavy infection will cause serious deterioration in the crop. It also might affect other crops in the garden. Virus-free stock is available through the Nuclear Stock Association (Rhubarb), 4 St. Mary's Place, Stamford, Lincolnshire PE9 2DN so you might feel it is worth while buying this.

Rhubarb is commonly forced to supply a very early crop. Use a crown which is at least two or three years old (according to variety) and discard it after forcing as it won't produce again for a few years. Avoid buying old forced crowns.

Varieties to try

EASILY AVAILABLE
'Champagne Early' vigorous
'Cherry' cherry flavoured
'Prince Albert' good for forcing
'Timperley Early' earliest, suitable for forcing from two-year-old crowns
'Victoria' good from seed

OTHERS
'Cawood Delight' new variety, red flesh
'Glaskin's Perpetual' reliable from seed
'Holstein Bloodred' reliable from seed
'Reeds Early Superb' very heavy cropping
'Stockbridge Arrow' new variety, suitable for forcing from two-year-old crowns
'Stockbridge Harbinger' second early, red stick, suitable for forcing

See:

FRUIT TREES
Chris Bowers
SEEDS (GENERAL)
SEEDS (UNUSUAL)
Seeds-by-Size

ROSES

Growing wild in much of the northern hemisphere, the rose also has a long and noble history in cultivation. Paintings of roses appear on Cretan palaces and Egyptian tombs; they were admired by the Greeks and loved by the Romans. In the Middle Ages they were treasured mostly for their herbal properties, but from Tudor times took on a wider significance as a royal symbol and as a garden plant. In the centuries that followed, collectors, gardeners and plant breeders developed the rose, building up the number of petals, extending the flowering season, introducing new colours and forms until today the rose is perhaps the most versatile and best loved of all our garden flowers.

Roses are now available in a great range of shades and colours, both subtle and dazzling, and in all shapes and sizes from the low, ground-hugging types and miniatures to some of the biggest climbers which can smother a tree in fragrant blossom. Most popular are the bush roses, traditionally called hybrid teas and floribundas but now more descriptively known as large-flowered and cluster-flowered roses.

Roses will grow in most garden conditions except shade, and a careful choice of variety can give blooms from May to October or even later. Before buying, choose varieties to suit their situation. In particular, check carefully on their likely size: there are many miniatures and low-growing floribundas which will flower profusely at 60cm (2ft) or less and are ideal for small gardens, patios or tubs. Conversely, many old-fashioned varieties and shrub roses can form bushes 2.5m (8ft) high and wide so need a garden with space to spare

The best way to choose is to see the roses growing – catalogues rarely show more than a close up of the flower. If possible visit the Gardens of the Rose, the headquarters of the Royal National Rose Society, in St. Albans (see specialist societies). Alternatively, many parks and gardens have large rose displays and most rose nurseries are open to the public in the flowering season.

There are three main ways to buy plants: bare-rooted, root-balled or container-grown. Bare-rooted and root-balled roses are only available in the dormant season, container-grown roses all year round. The best times to plant are autumn and spring. Bare-root roses are widely available from specialists by mail order or may be lifted for you at garden centres and nurseries. Stems should be smooth, green and firm, have two or three main stems of at least pencil thickness and be about 20cm (8in) long. Roots should have a reasonable number of fibrous branches and be moist, not waterlogged or dried out.

Root-balled roses have soil or peat packed round the roots and covered with polythene or sacking secured with string. They will survive out of the ground longer than bare-root roses but are not container-grown and should only be moved when dormant. Pre-packed roses sold in shops are similar – their roots are protected from drying out then the whole plant sealed in a plastic bag. They tend to be smaller than good bare-root roses, but a more serious problem is the risk of drying out or premature growth in the warm shop atmosphere – avoid plants with shrivelled stems, any signs of mould or rot, or any new shoots.

If choosing a container-grown plant look for one with evenly balanced branches and make sure it is container-grown, not just recently containerised – a few weed seedlings on the surface, and a few roots beginning to emerge at the base of the pot are good signs.

'The Rose Directory', sent free to Royal National Rose Society members, contains useful details of a large number of rose varieties
'Find that Rose', published by the Rose Growers Association and costing 30p, will help you find nurseries selling the variety you want.

Recommended varieties

LARGE-FLOWERED

'Alec's Red' cherry red, scented
'Alexander' vermilion
'Blessings' rose pink
'City of Gloucester' deep yellow
'Fragrant Cloud' dull red, scented
'Grandpa Dickson' lemon yellow
'Just Joey' orange/buff
'Pascali' white
'Peace' creamy yellow, tinged pink
'Silver Jubilee' cream, pink, peach

CLUSTER-FLOWERED

'Allgold' butter yellow
'Anna Ford' deep red-orange
'Clarissa' apricot
'Fragrant Delight' orange-salmon, scented
'Iceberg' white
'Kim' yellow and red
'Korresia' bright yellow
'Margaret Merril' ivory, scented
'Matangi' orange-red, white eye
'Queen Elizabeth' sugar pink

MINIATURES

'Angela Rippon' coral pink
'Baby Masquerade' yellow buds turning pink then red with age
'Easter Morning' ivory
'Magic Carrousel' cream with pink edge
'Rosina' yellow

MODERN SHRUBS

'Buff Beauty' light apricot
'Chinatown' bright yellow, pink flushes
'Nevada' pale yellow
'Penelope' creamy pink
'Roseraie de l'Hay' purple

OLD-FASHIONED

'Cécile Brunner' light pink, China
'Common Moss' pink, Moss
'Fantin-Latour' pink, Centifolia
'Madame Hardy' white, Damask
'Rosa Mundi' pink and white stripes, Gallica

CLIMBERS

'Aloha' rich pink
'Compassion' pink
'Golden Showers' bright yellow
'Handel' cream, flushed rose
'New Dawn' pale pink

All these rose nurseries supply plants by mail order:

Anderson's Rose Nurseries
Friarsfield Road, Cults, Aberdeen, Grampian AB1 9QT
Tel Aberdeen (0224) 868881
Rose specialists with 110 varieties.

Apuldram Roses
Apuldram Manor House, Chichester, W. Sussex PO20 7EF
Tel Chichester (0243) 785769
Rose specialist with 150 varieties.

David Austin Roses
Bowling Green Lane, Albrighton, Wolverhampton, W. Midlands WV7 3HB
Tel Albrighton (090 722) 2142/4659
Rose specialist listing over 700 varieties with particular emphasis on old-fashioned roses.

Peter Beales Roses
London Road, Attleborough, Norfolk NR17 1AY
Tel Attleborough (0953) 454707
Rose specialist with 920 varieties – specialises in old-fashioned varieties.

Cants of Colchester
The Old Rose Gardens, Stanway, Colchester, Essex CO3 5UP
Tel Colchester (0206) 210176
Rose specialist with over 200 varieties.

James Cocker and Sons
Whitemyres, Lang Stracht, Aberdeen, Grampian AB9 2XH
Tel Aberdeen (0224) 33261
Rose specialist with 200 varieties.

W. H. Collin and Sons
Manor House, Knossington, Oakham, Leicestershire LE15 8LX
Tel Somerby (066 477) 323
Rose specialist with nearly 300 varieties.

Mark Court Thanet Roses
Pyson's Road, Broadstairs, Kent CT10 2LA
Tel Thanet (0843) 592521

Rose specialist with 100 varieties – concentrates on exhibition varieties.

Gandy's Roses
North Kilworth, near Lutterworth, Leicestershire LE17 6HZ
Tel Market Harborough (0858) 880398
Rose specialist with 600 varieties.

Greenhead Roses
Greenhead Nursery, Old Greenock Road, Inchinnan, Strathclyde PA4 9PH
Tel 041-886 3430
Rose specialist with 200 varieties.

C. Gregory and Son
The Rose Gardens, Toton Lane, Stapleford, Nottinghamshire NG9 7JA
Tel Nottingham (0602) 395454
Rose specialist with 125 varieties. Concentrates on modern garden roses and miniatures.

F. Haynes and Partners
10 Heather Road, Kettering, Northamptonshire NN16 9TR
Tel Corby (053 63) 4382 daytime, Corby (053 63) 85660 evenings
Rose specialists with 200 varieties.

Headon Roses
Fleecethorpe Farm Cottage, Bilby, Retford, Nottinghamshire D22 8JG
Tel Blyth (090 976) 296
Rose specialist with 105 varieties.

R. Hill and Son
The Nurseries, Appleton, Abingdon, Oxford, Oxfordshire OX13 5QN
Tel Oxford (0865) 8652081
Rose specialist with 385 varieties. Also offer 12 varieties of standard grafted gooseberry trees. Plants available by mail order.

C. and K. Jones
1 North Street, Sandycroft, Deeside, Clwyd CH5 2PP
Tel Tarvin (0829) 40663
Rose specialist with 300 varieties of mainly modern roses.

The Limes Rose Nursery
Kelly, Lifton, Devon PL16 0HQ
Tel Milton Abbot (082 287) 292
Rose specialist with 78 varieties. A breeding nursery specialising in new roses from around the world and its own introductions.

James McIntyre Roses
Rose Cottage, Main Street, North Leverton, Retford, Nottinghamshire DN22 OAN
Tel Gainsborough (0427) 880673
Rose specialist with 100 varieties – concentrates on old-fashioned shrub roses.

John Mattock
Nuneham Courtenay, Oxford, Oxfordshire OX9 9PY
Tel Nuneham Courtenay (086 738) 265/454
Rose specialist with over 360 varieties.

Nostell Priory Rose Garden
Nostell, near Wakefield, W. Yorkshire WF4 1QF
Tel Wakefield (0924) 862248
Rose specialist with over 400 varieties. Offers the whole range but concentrates particularly on scented varieties.

Rearsby Roses
Melton Road, Rearsby, Leicestershire LE7 8YP
Tel Leicester (0533) 601211
Rose specialist with 200 varieties.

Rosemary Roses
The Nurseries, Stapleford Lane, Toton, Nottinghamshire NG9 5FD
Tel Nottingham (0602) 226877
Rose specialist with 137 varieties – also sells Nottingham lace.

Roses du Temps Passé
Woodlands House, Stretton, near Stafford, Staffordshire ST19 9LG
Tel Wheaton Aston (0785) 840217
Rose specialist concentrating on old-fashioned and rare roses with 90 varieties listed.

John Sandy Roses
Over Lane, Almondsbury, Bristol,
Avon BS12 4DA
Tel Almondsbury (0454) 612195
Rose specialist with 150 varieties of
roses.

Sealand Nurseries
Sealand, Chester, Cheshire
CH1 6BA
Tel Chester (0244) 880501
Particularly well known for roses;
also sell a wide general range of
bulbs, and herbaceous perennials
as well as some fruit and shrubs.

Henry Street
Surrey Rose Nurseries, West End,
Woking, Surrey GU24 9HP
Tel Brookwood (048 67) 3253
Rose specialist with 200 varieties.

Timmerman's Roses
Lowdham Lane, Woodborough,
Nottingham, Nottinghamshire
NG14 6DN
Tel Nottingham (0602) 663193
Rose specialist with 140 varieties.

Watkins Roses
Kenilworth Road,
Hampton-in-Arden, Solihull,
W. Midlands B29 0LP
Tel Hampton-in-Arden (067 55) 2866
Rose specialist with 200 varieties.

Wisbech Plant Co
Walton Road, Wisbech,
Cambridgeshire PE13 3EF
Tel Wisbech (0945) 582588/9
Rose specialist with 190 varieties.

Also see:

CLEMATIS
J. Bradshaw and Son

DWARF CONIFERS
Wessex Nurseries: miniature roses

ORCHIDS
Cley Orchids

SHRUBS AND TREES
Knights Nurseries

UNUSUAL PLANTS
Yew Tree Nursery: miniature roses

GOOD GARDEN CENTRES AND
GENERAL NURSERIES
Chiswell Green, Burston-Tyler Rose
and Garden Centre
Donnington, Sherrards, The
Garden Centre
Edwalton, Wheatcroft Garden
Centre
Exeter, St. Bridget Nurseries
Great Warley, Warley Rose
Gardens
Hitchin, Harkness Rose and Plant
Centre
Knutsford, Fryers Nurseries
Merriot, Scotts Nurseries
North Walsham, E. B. Le Grice
Pamber End, Elm Park Garden
Centre and Nursery
Pickering, The Roger Plant Centre
Romsey, Hilliers Garden Centre
and Hillier Plant Centre
Stapleford, Bardill's Roses Garden
Centre
Whitminster, Highfield Nurseries
Winchester, Hillier Garden Centre
Woodbridge, Notcutts Garden
Centre

SAINTPAULIAS

The African violet or *Saintpaulia ionantha* is one of the most popular
flowering houseplants in this country. However, it can be a demanding
guest, as it needs plenty of light (but not direct sun) and a steady
temperature. Between 18 and 24°C (64 and 75°F) is usually recommended,
though many varieties will thrive at 16°C (60°F). It is important not to
overwater – add tepid water only when the compost begins to dry out. The
standard store-bought plants are compact with a dense rosette of leaves.
However, there are more unusual varieties with trailing stems, double
flowers, variegated leaves and even miniatures. Florists and garden shops
and centres usually offer flowering plants in 7 to 10cm (3 to 4in) pots and

the quality can be variable. When buying an African violet choose a specimen with a few blooms and lots of buds. The plant should comfortably fill the pot, but the crown, or centre, should be open, not crowded with small leaves and shoots – congestion will reduce flowering. The leaves should be firm, crisp and green. Blemishes on leaves are usually caused by water drops. The leaf stalks are brittle and easily damaged so check your plant is not broken or torn. Finally it is sensible not to buy plants from cold premises or where they have been left outside.

When purchasing from a specialist nursery you will obviously have a greater range of varieties to choose from and there is the added advantage of being able to buy young plantlets, usually at a cheaper price.

Varieties to try

'Chiffon Gipsy' deep rose pink
'Chiffon Harmony' fluted pale pink
'Chiffon Raspberry Crush' fringed rose pink
'Classic Pink' pink
'Colorado' frilled red
'Easter Trail' double mauve trailer
'Rose Ember' rose
'Silver Milestone' magenta edged with white
'Snow Ballet' white
'Wonderland' light blue

African Violet Centre

Station Road, Terrington St. Clement, King's Lynn, Norfolk PE34 4PL
Tel King's Lynn (0553) 828374
Specialist with 50 varieties listed and others available on request – concentrates on bi-colours and micro-miniatures. Plants and seeds available by mail order.

Jonjo Violets

Whitchurch, Shropshire SY13 1DA
Tel Whitchurch (0948) 2545
Specialist with 230 varieties listed. They grow a number of their own hybrids as well as some from North America. Mail order only – unrooted leaf cuttings May until end of October.

SEEDS

Raising plants from seeds yourself is certainly a cheap way of establishing a garden display or vegetable plot, but to achieve good results it needs a fair amount of planning, some skill, the appropriate equipment and facilities (which can be very modest) and a fair degree of patience. You also need to choose suitable varieties for your needs, whether to produce flowers for cutting, plants for bedding out, or vegetables for the kitchen. Luckily this is an area where plenty of advice is available, though sometimes you must read between the lines. It can be difficult to assess the true characteristics of a certain variety from a catalogue picture or description so it is well worth visiting seed trials held by horticultural societies, parks departments or the seedsmen themselves. Try to choose varieties geared to the domestic gardener rather than the commercial grower, otherwise you might end up with a new variety of bean which scores well in uniformity and shelf-life, but tastes fairly nondescript.

There are many ' brands' of seeds, about half of which are only found in shops or garden centres. These are Bees, Carters, Cuthbert (only in Woolworth and Woolco shops), Hurst, Johnson's, J. Arthur Bowers, Webbs and Wilko (only in Wilkinson Stores). Many shops also sell seeds specially packeted for them with their own name printed on the packet.

Several seedsmen sell only by mail order and others do both – all these are listed below. Another source of seeds is through exchange and distribution schemes run by various specialist societies (see SOCIETIES AND ORGANISATIONS, page 395).

Generally speaking the best time to buy seeds is early, about the end of November, when they have just appeared in shops and when the catalogues start to come out. This is particularly important when buying over the counter, since conditions away from the seedsmen's stores are not conducive to the storage of seeds and the longer they are left the less likely they are to germinate. However, if you store them in a cool and dry place many will last two or three years. Seeds in unopened foil packets will keep better than those in paper packets. Ordering by mail order from a specialist opens up a wide area of choice, but don't forget the cost of postage and packing can be considerable, relative to the cost of the seed, if you only want a few packets.

General seedsmen

J. W. Boyce
67 Station Road, Soham, Ely, Cambridgeshire CB7 5ED

D. T. Brown and Co
Station Road, Poulton-le-Fylde, Blackpool, Lancashire FY6 7HX
Tel Poulton-le-Fylde (0253) 882371

Arthur Cole and Co
17 Victoria Place, Brightlingsea, Colchester, Essex CO7 0BX
Tel Brightlingsea (020 630) 2654/4222

Samuel Dobie and Son
Upper Dee Mills, Llangollen, Clwyd LL20 8SD
Tel Llangollen (0978) 861212
Also sold in shops and garden centres.

Mr Fothergill's Seeds
Gazeley Road, Kentford, Newmarket, Suffolk CB8 7QB
Tel Newmarket (0638) 751161
Also sold in shops and garden centres.

S. E. Marshall and Co
Regal Road, Wisbech, Cambridgeshire PE13 2RF
Tel Wisbech (0945) 583407

Suttons Seeds
Hele Road, Torquay, Devon TQ2 7QJ
Tel Torquay (0803) 62011

Also sold in shops and garden centres.

Thompson & Morgan
London Road, Ipswich, Suffolk IP2 0BA
Tel Ipswich (0473) 214226
Also sold in shops and garden centres.

Unwins Seeds
Histon, Cambridgeshire CB4 4LE
Tel Histon (022 023) 2270/2308
Also sold in shops and garden centres.

Unusual seedsmen

Bristol University Botanic Garden
Bracken Hill, North Road, Leigh Woods, Bristol, Avon BS8 3PF
Tel Bristol (0272) 733682
Offers seeds of plants that are threatened in the south-west, particularly wildflowers. Seed distribution scheme costs £4/year to join including 10 free packets of seeds from their list.

Chase Organics
Gibraltar House, Shepperton, Surrey TW17 8AQ
Tel Walton-on-Thames (0932) 221212
Seeds for organic gardens and farms – concentrate mainly on vegetable seed (160 varieties). Also do a range of seaweed products.

Chiltern Seeds
Bortree Stile, Ulverston, Cumbria
LA12 7PB
Ornamental plants – many unusual
ones, some from as far afield as
Australia and Japan – wildflowers
and unusual vegetables.

Down-To-Earth Vegetable Seeds
Cade Horticultural Products,
Streetfield Farm, Cade Street,
Heathfield, E. Sussex TN21 9BS
Commercial vegetable varieties.

H. D. R. A. Sales
20 Convent Lane, Bocking,
Braintree, Essex CM7 6RW
Tel Braintree (0376) 24083
Traditional and good modern
varieties.

C. W. Hosking
Exotic Seed Importer/Exporter, PO
Box 500, Hayle, Cornwall TR27 4BE
Tropical seed specialist with 800 to
1000 species – mainly exotic
flowering trees and shrubs. There
are plans to introduce
pre-germinated seeds and
palm seedlings.

S. M. McArd (Seeds)
39 West Road, Pointon, Sleaford,
Lincolnshire NG34 0NA
Tel Sleaford (0529) 240765
Offers agricultural seed in small
amounts for smallholders etc. Also
stocks vegetable, herb, houseplant,
rockery, flower, tree and shrub
seed and offers plants of unusual
vegetables, eg asparagus crowns,
Jerusalem artichokes.

W. Robinson and Sons
Sunny Barn, Forton, near Preston,

Lancashire PR3 0BN
Tel Forton (0524) 791210
Specialises in exhibition vegetables
including the 'Mammoth' range of
onions and leeks. Also a range of
unusual tomatoes (7 varieties).

Seeds-by-Post
Suffolk Herbs, Sawyers Farm,
Little Cornard, Sudbury, Suffolk
CO10 0NY
Tel Sudbury (0787) 227247
Offer seeds of herbs, wild flowers,
cottage garden flowers, unusual
vegetables and wild flower/grass
mixtures. In addition, herbs and
wild flowers are available as plants.

Seeds-by-Size
60 Glenview Road, Boxmoor,
Hemel Hempstead, Hertfordshire
HP1 1TB
Tel Hemel Hempstead (0442) 51458
Seed specialist selling seed in any
quantity requested (minimum
1 gramme), both flowers and
vegetables. Large range of varieties
in some areas, eg sweet peas 150
varieties, begonias 43 varieties,
primula 33 varieties and rhubarb
6 varieties.

Many other suppliers sell seeds
relevant to their speciality – see
under the appropriate sections.

Also see:

GOOD GARDEN CENTRES AND
GENERAL NURSERIES
Croydon, Thomas Butcher
Great Amwell, Van Hage's
Nurseries and Garden Centre

SEMPERVIVUMS
It is not difficult to see why the name of this plant means 'to live forever';
less obvious is the origin of its popular names of house leek and
'welcome-home-husband-however-drunk-you-be'! Sempervivums or their
close relatives, jovibarbas, can be seen growing on houses and along walls
in many parts of the country. The plant consists of tightly packed rosettes
of evergreen, fleshy, succulent leaves which vary in colour from pale grey
green through bright greens and reds to deep purple. The flower spikes

with red or yellow star- or bell-shaped flowers can be spectacular.

They prefer sunny positions, but are very adaptable as to growing medium. They survive in brick rubble, on dry walls, in sandy soil and screes. Good drainage is important and some humus is required. Most require little attention and survive droughts well.

New purchases may be planted any time from April until September. Most large garden centres stock a few varieties of sempervivum, but you must deal with specialist nurseries for the more unusual varieties. Descriptive catalogues are available from the nurseries so ordering by post is possible. If you want to see the plants first, phone and arrange a time with the nurseryman.

When choosing a specimen, select a healthy and undamaged plant and look for a pot with a mixture of mature rosettes and younger offsets, as the central rosette will die after flowering. They vary in rate of growth, producing from one to eight offsets a year – the varieties available at garden centres can generally be propagated easily and rapidly.

Some species and varieties to try

COMMON SPECIES

S. arachnoideum (cobweb house leek) deep pink flower, small ball-shaped rosettes with green or red leaves, according to variety, covered in hairs
S. galicum small yellow flowers, tiny, hairy rosettes of leaves, plum-red in summer
S. thompsonianum pale red flowers

COMMON VARIETIES

'Black Prince' pale pink flowers, dark purple-black leaves, silver hairs
'Lavender and Old Lace' pale pink flowers, leaves have silver hairs
'Night Raven' pale pink flowers, large green rosette, deep purple marks

UNUSUAL SPECIES

Jovibarba heuffelii yellow-fringed flowers, leaves in many colours according to variety
S. cantabricum yellowy-pink flowers, green, purple-tipped leaves

Mary and Peter Mitchell
11 Wingle Tye Road, Burgess Hill,
W. Sussex RH15 9HR
Tel Burgess Hill (044 46) 6848
Sempervivum specialists with about 300 species, hybrids and cultivars. Concentrate on jovibarbas and rosularias in particular. Plants available by mail order.

Alan C. Smith
127 Leaves Green Road, Keston,
Kent BR2 6DG
Tel Biggin Hill (0959) 725312
Sempervivum and jovibarba specialist with over 150 species, hybrids and cultivars. Also has 50 varieties of sedums. Plants available by mail order.

H. and J. Wills
2 St. Brannocks Park Road,
Ilfracombe, Devon EX34 8HU
Tel Ilfracombe (0271) 63949
Sempervivum and jovibarba specialists with over 250 species, hybrids and cultivars. Plants available by mail order.

Also see:

CACTI AND SUCCULENTS
Glenhirst Cactus Nursery

Many specialists stock a lot more plants than they list, so if you want something special, ask for it. You may be lucky.

SHRUBS AND TREES

Many people see these plants as the foundations and backbone of a garden. They offer the scale, perspective, shape and texture around which you can introduce smaller and less permanent plants. Because of their importance, careful consideration needs to be taken before embarking on any shopping trip. Firstly, will your choice fit into the size and mood of your garden without clashing with its surroundings? There's no point choosing a tree or shrub that won't be happy with the soil conditions or will grow too big for the space available. Take into account the ultimate height and spread of the plant and try to visualise its shape – weeping, columnar, round – where you plan to put it.

Also think about when and how much interest it will add to your garden and how it will complement other plants. The ideal tree or shrub should offer interest all-year-round in the form of flowers, berries, colourful foliage, and attractive bark – few species provide all these features, but in a small garden you should pick those with more than one period of interest – say autumn colour in addition to spring flowers. Try also to get a balance between evergreen and deciduous types.

Plants are sold either bare-rooted, root-balled or more usually container-grown. Container-grown plants may be planted any time of year; however, bare-rooted or root-balled deciduous plants are best planted from November to March, while the evergreens should go in between late September and the end of October or April to early May.

When buying container-grown plants make sure they are just that and haven't been popped into a pot at the last minute – a few weed seedlings and roots just showing through the bottom of the container are good signs. However, any container-grown plant with a root-bound mass should always be avoided as it may never grow well. As far as possible, always choose young vigorous plants in preference to larger or older ones. They will establish more easily, are cheaper and will probably outgrow older specimens after a few years. Avoid plants which have dry roots, especially if bare-rooted, or those that have been waterlogged. Steer clear of brown-edged leaves, lop-sided growth and any signs of pests or disease. Trees should have a strong central shoot; shrubs want branches growing right down to ground level. Most garden centres offer a fair range of shrubs and trees, generally container-grown. If you don't live near a nursery, or can't find the species you want at the local garden centre, buying by mail order from a specialist opens up a huge choice. Remember, though, the cost for mail order can be almost double the price for a single tree – and you are buying blind. However, the quality of plants from some suppliers can be very good and the prices reasonable, especially for rare trees and shrubs that garden centres seldom stock.

Binks Nurseries
Darlington Road, Northallerton,
N. Yorkshire DL6 2PW
Tel Northallerton (0609) 3992
Shrub and tree specialists with 600 varieties. They also offer fruit trees (80 varieties), dwarf conifers (60 varieties) and herbs (60 varieties). No mail order.

Brackenwood Nurseries
131 Nore Road, Portishead, near Bristol, Avon BS20 8DU
Tel Bristol (0272) 843484

Shrub and tree specialists with over 1000 varieties. They also offer alpines (50 to 200 varieties), herbaceous perennials (over 200 varieties), fruit trees (over 50 varieties) and aquatic and bog plants (over 100 varieties). No mail order.

Buckingham Nurseries and Garden Centre

Tingewick Road, Buckingham, Buckinghamshire MK18 4AE
Tel Buckingham (0280) 813556
Hedging is their main speciality but they also stock fruit trees. Mail order available.

Durston (Somerset) Woodlands

Elmfield, Higher Durston, Taunton, Somerset TA3 5AQ
Tel West Monkton (0823) 412387
Shrub and tree specialists with over 300 varieties. In addition they have a range of conifers, roses, fruit trees and hedging. No mail order.

Everton Nurseries

Everton, near Lymington, Hampshire SO4 0JZ
Tel Lymington (0590) 42155
Shrub and tree specialists with over 100 varieties. They also offer alpines (160 varieties), herbaceous perennials (300 varieties) and fruit trees (60 varieties). No mail order.

Fyne Trees

Cairndow, Argyll, Strathclyde
Tree specialist with about 600 species available. The emphasis is on conifers, but rare broadleaves and species of shrubs also available. Plants available by mail order.

Glebe Nursery

Aboyne, Grampian AB3 5JB
Tel Aboyne (0339) 2919
Forest tree nursery specialising in trees for shelter and amenity (40 varieties) and hedging (15 varieties). Bonsai starters also supplied. Plants available by mail order.

Goscote Nurseries

Syston Road, Crossington, Leicestershire LE7 8NZ
Tel Sileby (050 981) 2121
Tree and shrub specialists with over 600 varieties including azaleas and rhododendrons. They also have conifers (150 varieties; about half are dwarf conifers) and herbaceous plants (70 varieties). In particular they specialise in hardy plants suitable for growing in the Midlands and the north of the country. Plants available by mail order.

Michael Haworth-Booth

Farall Nurseries, Roundhurst, near Haslemere, Surrey GU27 3BN
Tel Haslemere (0428) 53024
Flowering shrub specialist with about 300 varieties. There is a demonstration garden where the shrubs can be seen. No mail order.

P. H. Kellet

Laurels Nursery, Benenden, Cranbrook, Kent TN17 4JU
Tel Cranbrook (0580) 240463
Shrub and tree specialist with 300 varieties. Concentrates on flowering cherries (30 varieties), crab apples (30 varieties) and conifers (60 varieties). No mail order.

Kingsfield Tree Nursery

Broadenham Lane, Winsham, Chard, Somerset TA20 4JF
Tel Winsham (046 030) 697
Specialises in native shrubs and trees (50 species) and native wild flowers (250 species and varieties). Plants available by mail order.

Knights Nurseries

3 Ernsham Road, Hailsham, E. Sussex BN27 3LD
Tel Hailsham (0323) 842454
Specialise in container-grown shrubs, climbers and conifers – over 1500 varieties. They also stock 160 varieties of roses. Plants available by mail order.

MacFarlane's Nurseries and Garden Centre
Swingfield, Dover, Kent CT15 7HX
Tel Selsted (030 383) 244
Shrub and tree specialists offering over 60 varieties of semi-mature ornamental trees and 150 varieties of conifers. They also have 450 varieties of herbaceous plants, grasses and ferns. No mail order.

C. J. Marchant
Keeper's Hill Nursery, Stapehill, near Wimborne, Dorset
BH21 7NE
Tel Ferndown (0202) 873140
Specialises in shrubs and trees including azaleas and rhododendrons (60 varieties), camellias (40 varieties) and Japaneses maples (40 varieties). Trees available by mail order.

Mount Pleasant Trees
Rockhampton, Berkeley, Gloucestershire GL13 9DU
Tel Falfield (0454) 260348
Tree specialist with about 200 species and varieties of trees. Concentrates on less-usual trees especially for woodlands, shelter belts and forestry. Also has hedging plants, especially for topiary. Trees available by mail order. Callers by appointment only.

Newlands Conifer Nurseries
Myerscough Hall Drive, Garstang Road, Bilsborrow, Preston, Lancashire PR3 0RE
Tel Brock (0995) 40304
Specialise in hedge plants, particularly conifers. Plants available by mail order.

Nettletons Nursery
Ivy Mill Lane, Godstone, Surrey RH9 8NH
Tel Godstone (0883) 842426
Shrub and tree specialist with 150 varieties of conifer (including 60 varieties of dwarf conifer), camellias (30 varieties) rhododendrons (70 varieties), Japanese maples (25 to 30 grafted forms). No mail order.

Norcroft Nurseries
Norcroft Lane, Cawthorne, Barnsley, S. Yorkshire S75 4DY
Tel Barnsley (0226) 206102
Shrub and tree specialists with 150 species and varieties. They concentrate on slow/medium conifers, trees for colourful foliage and/or fruit blossom. Plants and bulbs available by mail order.

Oakover Nurseries
Potters Corner, Ashford, Kent TN25 4NP
Tel Ashford (0233) 20390
Shrub and tree specialists with 300 species and varieties. They concentrate on raising trees and shrubs from seed to produce seedlings for the trade, but also they have retail sales though no mail order.

Old Presbytery Conifer and Heather Gardens
Stoke Ferry Road, Oxborough, King's Lynn, Norfolk PE33 9PS
Tel Gooderstone (036 621) 229
Conifer specialists with over 400 varieties including slow-growing and rare ones. They also have over 70 varieties of heather. There is an established garden. No mail order.

Chris Pattison
Brookend, Lower Pendock, Gloucestershire GL19 3PL
Tel Bromesberrow (053 181) 480
Shrub specialist with over 200 varieties; 60 to 80 varieties of alpines also available. No mail order.

Perrie Hale Nursery
Northcote Hill, Honiton, Devon EX14 8TH
Tel Honiton (0404) 3344
Specialises in shrubs, amenity trees and hedging: 50 species and varieties in total. Plants available by mail order.

Pickards Magnolia Gardens
Stodmarsh Road, Canterbury, Kent CT3 4AG
Tel Canterbury (0227) 63951

Magnolia specialists with 29 varieties. They concentrate on *M. soulangeana*, *M.stellata*, *M.grandiflora*, *M.liliflora* and their hybrids. No mail order.

Ben Reid and Co
Pinewood Park, Countesswells Road, Aberdeen, Grampian AB9 2QL
Tel Aberdeen (0224) 38744
Shrub and tree specialist with over 300 varieties of ornamental trees and shrubs, over 50 varieties of forest trees and 60 varieties of hardy ornamental conifers. Plants available by mail order.

G. Reuthe
Foxhill Nursery, Jackass Lane, Keston, Kent BR2 6AW
Tel Farnborough (029 589) 52249
Shrub and tree specialist; also offers conifers. Mail order available.

Roskellan Nursery
Maenlay, Helston, Cornwall TR12 7QR
Specialises in rooted shrub cuttings (over 360 varieties). Plants available by mail order.

Weasdale Nurseries
Newbiggin-on-Lune, Kirkby Stephen, Cumbria CA17 4LX
Tel Newbiggin-on-Lune (058 73) 246
Tree specialists with 350 to 400 hardwood and 250 to 270 coniferous varieties. They also offer hedging. Mail order available.

Also see:

ALPINES AND ROCK PLANTS
Careby Manor Gardens: woody plants
Reginald Kaye

AZALEAS AND RHODODENDRONS
Hydon Nursery
Starborough Nursery: unusual shrubs

CAMELLIAS
Marwood Hill Gardens: shrubs

DWARF CONIFERS
Hull Farm: conifers

Robinsons Gardens
Walker's Nursery

FOLIAGE PLANTS
Hopley's Plants: shrubs and unusual conifers

HEATHERS
Barncroft Nurseries: trees and shrubs to associate with heathers, especially conifers
Hardwick Nursery: shrubs
Norwich Heather and Conifer Centre: conifers

HERBACEOUS PERENNIALS
Fairview Nursery: shrubs

HERBS
Wilton Park Nursery: unusual shrubs

IVY
Tynedale Nurseries: hebes

ROSES
Henry Street

UNUSUAL PLANTS
Ballalheannagh Gardens
Country Park Nursery: hebes
Knightshayes Garden Trust
The Knoll Gardens
The Palm Farm
Rosemoor Garden Trust

WATER AND WATERSIDE PLANTS
Longstock Park Nursery: shrubs

GOOD GARDEN CENTRES AND GENERAL NURSERIES
Donnington, Sherrards, The Garden Centre
Exeter, St. Bridget Nurseries
Great Warley, Warley Rose Gardens
Knutsford, Caldwell and Sons Garden Centre
Pickering, The Roger Plant Centre
Romsey, Hillier Garden Centre and Hillier Plant Centre
Tal-y-Cafn, Bodnant Garden Nursery: magnolias
Washington, A. Goatcher and Son
Whitminster, Highfield Nurseries
Wickwar, George Osmond
Windlesham, L. R. Russell Nursery Garden Centre
Woodbridge, Notcutts Garden Centre

SOFT FRUIT

Growing your own soft fruit means you can choose varieties with a better flavour than those you'll find in the greengrocers or supermarket and, because you can eat them just after picking, their flavour will be at its peak. You can also grow types of soft fruit such as loganberries that you'll seldom find in the shops. However, there are a few problems that you have to overcome, not least of which are the hungry neighbourhood birds. Some sort of netting will usually be necessary, but the returns are worth the effort. A sunny, sheltered spot and water-retentive but well-drained soil suit most soft fruits. The only really fussy fruits are blueberries and cranberries which need an acid soil.

In choosing the type of fruit and the varieties you want to grow, there are many factors to consider: how much work is involved in training and pruning? Is the fruit suitable for eating fresh, bottling or freezing? What is the yield? What is the quality and size of the fruit? And not least, is it suitable for your garden? Specialist fruit nurseries and some general nurseries list a wide range of soft fruits, which they sell by mail order, and some have informative catalogues which may help you choose the right plants.

When buying by mail order, unpack the plants as soon as they arrive. If you find they have been badly packed and are obviously dried out, return them immediately – there is no point trying to revive them. One disadvantage of buying this way is that there may be a minimum order. When buying raspberries, blackcurrants and strawberries, look for certified plants – these will have been raised from selected, healthy plants that have been checked for levels of virus infection and general health.

Garden centres can also be a good source of soft fruits. The choice may not be as wide as from mail order suppliers, but the advantage is you can check the quality of the plants before buying and if you find good ones they'll probably be a cheap alternative to mail order. Check whether plants have been certified then look for well-developed root systems that have not been allowed to dry out; also look for strong healthy-looking stems and shoots (if you scratch the surface of the stems of soft fruit bushes or canes they should be green underneath); avoid damaged plants, those suffering from disease or pests and any which look as if they've been sitting around in the garden centre for a long time (faded labels are a good giveaway). If you live close to a good specialist nursery it is worth going there directly and picking your plants.

Varieties to try that are widely available

BLACKBERRY
'Himalaya Giant'
'Oregon Thornless'

BLACKCURRANT
'Baldwin'
'Boskoop Giant'
'Wellington XXX'

GOOSEBERRY
'Careless'
'Leveller'

'Winham's Industry'

LOGANBERRY (THORNLESS)
'LY 654'

RASPBERRY
'Glen Clova'
'Malling Jewel'
'Zeva'

REDCURRANT
'Laxton's No. 1'

STRAWBERRY
'Cambridge Favourite'
'Cambridge Vigour'
'Red Gauntlet'
'Royal Sovereign'

Varieties worth looking for

BLACKBERRY
'Ashton Cross'
'Smoothstem'

BLACKCURRANT
'Ben Lomond'
'Blackdown'

BLUEBERRY
'Earliblue'
'Berkeley'
'Bluecrop'
'Jersey'

GOOSEBERRY
'Golden Drop'
'Invicta'
'Whitesmith'

HYBRID BERRIES
Tayberry

RASPBERRY
'Malling Admiral'
'Malling Delight'
'Malling Leo'
'Fallgold'

REDCURRANT
'Red Lake'

STRAWBERRY
'Aromel'
'Domanil'
'Pantagruella'
'Tamella'

Ashleigh Nursery
Bourne Road, Closterworth,
Grantham, Lincolnshire NG33 5JN
Soft fruit specialist with 15 varieties.
Plants available by mail order.

Kingsley Strawberries
Headley Hill Farm, Bordon,
Hampshire GU35 8RH
Tel Bordon (042 03) 2322
Strawberry specialist with 20
varieties of plants and alpine
strawberry seed. Plants and seeds
available by mail order.

Ken Muir
Honeypot Farm, off Rectory Road,
Weeley Heath, Clacton-on-Sea,
Essex CO16 9BJ
Tel Weeley (0255) 830181
Soft fruit specialist with 20 varieties
of strawberries and 40 varieties of
cane and bush fruits. Also some
stone fruits and apples. Two
varieties of asparagus. Plants
available by mail order.

Also see:

BULBS
Bakker Holland

FRUIT TREES

GOOD GARDEN CENTRES AND
GENERAL NURSERIES
Blairgowrie, James McIntyre and
Sons
Knutsford, Caldwell and Sons
Topsham, Yeoman Gardeners

STREPTOCARPUS

Streptocarpus or the Cape primrose is an evergreen plant with large leaves
and an abundance of large flowers which bloom for up to six months of the
year. The flowers come in shades of pink, red, white, blue, mauve or rose,
and the beauty and ease of care of this plant make it an up-and-coming rival
to the African violet. It can be grown as a greenhouse plant, but only really
needs to be protected from frost in the winter so will keep in the house or a
cool conservatory quite well. Streptocarpus are not put off by a dry
atmosphere or draughts and in fact are difficult to kill off altogether.

Garden centres which buy small plants and grow them on will often
stock streptocarpus, mainly the modern hybrids which have taken over in
popularity from the species. The John Innes and Dutch named varieties are
the most common. When buying a plant it is best to select one in flower
(not difficult since they are in flower so long). Try to find a specimen with

several flowers on each stem, say seven or eight. Look for a good set of leaves all coming up from the base and forming a nice rosette. After that the choice is a personal one – large or small leaves, flowering time, colour and size of flower.

Garden centres sometimes sell streptocarpus grown from seeds which are generally not as good as named varieties. They have fewer stems, fewer flowers per stem and rather wishy-washy colours tending towards the blue. If there is a batch of similar plants at a garden centre these are likely to be named varieties; if the selection is more mixed they are probably seedlings. If you can't find a suitable plant locally, or want something specific, a specialist nursery will supply by mail order. They send out young plants with small shoots and a root-ball which travel well.

Varieties worth trying
Varieties are rarely labelled in garden centres, but these are worth looking out for:
'Albatross' white
'Cynthia' magenta red, yellow throat
'Neptune' deep blue
'Paula' blue
'Sandra' blue, purple veining
'Tina' pink

Efenechtyd Nursery
Cefn Rhydd, Llanelidan, Ruthin, Clwyd LL15 2LG
Tel Llandegla (097 888) 677
Specialises in named varieties and species – 27 varieties altogether. Plants available by mail order.

Also see:

FERNS
Fibrex Nurseries

SWEET PEAS

Its rainbow of colours, heady fragrance and continuous flowering from May or June until late autumn make this hardy annual a great favourite with gardeners and exhibitors alike. There are several alternative forms, from the dwarf sweet pea, which looks lovely as border edging or in pots and tubs, to the tall 1.8m (6ft) varieties which are suitable trained up fencing or along a wall. The semi-dwarf sweet pea will make itself at home in any of these situations besides looking just right in the herbaceous border. The delicate but long-lasting blossom on its long stem makes this flower an ideal candidate as a cut flower, and what is more it is very prolific – the more the blooms are cut the more more new blooms spring into growth.

Sweet peas prefer an unshaded and open site which has been well dug over and manured. Double-digging is only necessary if you are after 'show' blooms. They are most at home in a pH of 6.5 to 6.7, so add some carbonate of lime if your soil is unduly acid. A moist root run is very welcome so don't sit by while the ground dries out – it is worth putting down a mulch of straw or peat to retain moisture in the ground. A balanced liquid feed will encourage your sweet peas to flower well into the autumn.

In the spring young plants start to appear for sale at shops and garden centres along with bedding plants. Packets of mixed seed are available almost everywhere that sells flower seeds. However, if you are keen on a more interesting selection of named varieties or single colours, seed bought by mail order from general or specialist seed companies is the answer. Some of the big flower shows also have stands for specialists where seed is available. The best time for sowing in the south is autumn – either straight into the ground or in pots ready for planting out in spring. Good results can also be obtained by sowing in pots in spring – although flowering will start 2 or 3 weeks later. In the north, autumn sowing is inadvisable – even the experts wait until spring.

Varieties to try

TALL SPENCER VARIETIES
'Alice Hardwicke' cerise
'Cream Southborne' cream
'Mrs Bernard Jones' pink
'Noel Sutton' blue
'Red Ensign' red
'Southampton' lavender
'White Leamington' white

OTHERS
'Bijou' dwarf
'Galaxy' tall
'Jet Set' semi-dwarf
'Patio' dwarf
'Snoopea' semi-dwarf

R. S. and R. Bailey
Red Gables, Preston Wynne, Hereford, Hereford and Worcester HR1 3PE
Tel Sutton St. Nicholas (043 272) 410
Sweet pea specialists with 48 Spencer varieties listed. They have over 50 other varieties including 'Galaxy' and 'Jet Set' (both mixed and separate colours) as well as grandiflora and early multiflora gigantea types. Plants and seeds available by mail order.

S. and N. Brackley
117 Winslow Road, Wingrave, Aylesbury, Buckinghamshire HP22 4QB
Tel Aylesbury (0296) 681384
Sweet pea specialists with 50 Spencer varieties and 14 others. They also offer 26 varieties of exhibition vegetables. Plants and seeds available by mail order.

L. J. Everitt
Meadow Cottage Nursery, Little Clacton, Clacton-on-Sea, Essex CO16 9QZ
Tel Clacton-on-Sea (0255) 424310
Sweet pea specialist with 40 Spencer varieties. Seeds available by mail order.

S. E. Gaisford and Sons
The Nurseries, Colerne, Chippenham, Wiltshire SN14 8EH
Tel Box (0225) 742415
Sweet pea specialist with 70 varieties. Plants are available by mail order (does not sell seeds).

W. G. and D. M. Maishman
Niton Nursery, Parkers Road, Cotton, Stowmarket, Suffolk IP14 4QQ
Tel Bacton (0449) 781596
Sweet pea specialists with 35 varieties, particularly Spencers. Seeds available by mail order.

Les Marchant Sweet Peas
17 Old Road, North Petherton, Somerset TA6 6TF
Tel North Petherton (0278) 662813
Sweet pea specialist with 50 varieties plus 10 mixtures. Concentrates on new varieties for the exhibitor. Seeds available by mail order.

Also see:

SEEDS
Seeds-by-Size
Suttons Seeds
Unwins Seeds

GOOD GARDEN CENTRES AND GENERAL NURSERIES
Birdbrook, Boltons Garden Centre

Specialist nurseries in this part of the Guide *have not been tested or inspected by us, so their inclusion does not amount to a recommendation and is no indication of the quality of the plants they sell. It's always best to visit the nursery yourself to check the quality of the plants and make your own selection.*

TURF

Laying turf is the quickest way of providing yourself with a brand new lawn, but it is expensive – and you have to prepare the ground just as thoroughly as you do for sowing seed. Turf is best laid between October and February, weather permitting. In spring and summer you would need to keep it watered during dry spells until it is established. Prepare the site well in advance to give it time to settle.

When shopping for turf there are two main types you will come across: meadow turf cut from pastures or meadows, and cultivated (seeded) turf grown specifically for lawns. Suppliers sometimes describe meadow grass as cultivated because it was seeded at the outset but with grasses suitable for pastures, not lawns – a point worth checking when you buy. Cultivated turf can be hard to find locally and most suppliers will not deliver the small amounts needed for domestic lawns over long distances – the transport costs are too high. But a few turf specialists such as Bravura Rolawn and Turfland will deliver anywhere in the country, so are worth approaching if you can't buy good turf locally.

Meadow turf is generally much easier to get hold of than cultivated turf, and cheaper too – about 70p a sq m (1.2 sq yd) compared with £1.70 or more for cultivated turf – but your choice should depend on the type of lawn you want as well as the price. For an ornamental lawn – one suitable for close cutting and little hard wear – you'll have to buy cultivated turf containing fine-leaved grasses such as bents and fescues. Don't opt for a fine lawn unless you're prepared to look after it – it will soon deteriorate if neglected.

If your lawn will be subjected to everyday family use, then a hard-wearing turf is essential. Here you can choose between a good-quality meadow grass or a cultivated turf containing some ryegrass. Meadow turf is your best option if you can find a good supplier locally, but only buy if you can inspect it first. Quality varies a lot – look for well-cut turves of uniform thickness with no clumps of coarse grasses or weeds – most meadow turf is weed-treated before cutting. The grass should be a healthy green colour, uniform and densely growing. Avoid any turf which has a lot of thatch (a tangle of dead grass on the soil surface), or is on stony, silty soil or a heavy clay. Make sure you can pick the turves up without them falling apart.

Many suppliers will let you inspect turf before buying, but some garden centres only sell to order so you take a chance when buying this way. Check that the supplier will deliver the amount of turf you need. Also check what you will have to pay for delivery and how long you will have to wait – the distributors may not deliver until they have several orders in the same area. Having chosen your turf make sure you are ready to lay it when it arrives since turf deteriorates rapidly. If you must store it for a day or two, unroll the turves and water them lightly to keep them moist.

Bravura Turf
Elborough Nursery, Hutton,
Weston Super Mare, Avon
BS24 9UB
Tel Bleadon (0934) 814376

National turf supplier selling Bravura turf, a non-ryegrass ornamental mixture in 45cm (1½ft) wide strips.

Rolawn
Elvington, York, N. Yorkshire
YO4 5AR
Tel York (0904) 85661
National turf supplier with three
types available for lawns: R1
Tournament (extra fine), R2
Olympic (fine), R3 Medallion
(hardwearing and shade-tolerant).
In addition it produces one for
bowling and golf clubs.

Turfland
Redhouse Farm, Dutton,
Warrington, Cheshire WA4 1BR
Tel Aston (092 86) 340
National turf supplier with four
types available for lawns: Crown
Green (fine ornamental), Bonny
Blue (hardwearing, shade tolerant),
the Sportsman (hardwearing,
ornamental, dwarf varieties) and
Lady Ruby (fine).

UNUSUAL PLANTS

If you're looking for an unusual rose, daffodil or variegated shrub, your
first port of call will usually be the appropriate specialist nursery. However,
there is a range of nurseries whose speciality is **unusual plants**. Here you
will find catalogues featuring plants with green flowers, plants from New
Zealand, rare old-fashioned flowers, unusual hedging plants and so on.

We've also grouped here nurseries with a particular speciality not listed
elsewhere such as achimenes, tropical foliage plants or palms.

A browse through this section may help you find a plant you've long
been searching for, or start you off in a whole new direction.

I. Allen and J. Huish
Belmont House, Tyntesfield,
Wraxall, Bristol, Avon BS19 1NR
Tel Flax Bourton (027 583) 2756
A private garden which holds the
National Collection of asters. About
300 varieties of Michaelmas daisy
and 30 species of aster available for
sale, with a range of other plants.
Plants sold by mail order; visitors
welcome.

Alpine Nursery
Gareth, off Tower House Lane,
Wraxall, Bristol, Avon BS19 1JX
Tel Nailsea (0272) 855831
Hellebore specialist with 7 varieties.
Small numbers of alpines and dwarf
conifers available, but this side of
the nursery is being run down. No
mail order.

Anmore Exotics
4 The Curve, Lovedean,
Portsmouth, Hampshire PO8 9SE
Tel Horndean (0705) 596538
Stocks about 800 genera of tropical
foliage plants, especially rare and
exotic ones. Available by mail
order.

Ballalheannagh Gardens
Glen Roy, Lonan, Isle of Man
Tel Laxey (0624) 781875
Sell trees and shrubs (including
azaleas and rhododendrons),
conifers, climbers, heathers,
primulas, herbaceous and alpine
plants, ornamental grasses and
ferns. Concentrate on species and
varieties not generally available.
Mail order service.

Helen Ballard
Old Country, Mathon, Malvern,
Hereford and Worcester WR13 5PS
Hellebore specialist with over 30
varieties and species. Also stocks
snowdrops. Mail order available.

Corran Garden
Onich, Fort William, Highland
PH33 6FE
Tel Onich (085 53) 246
Specialises in lime-hating plants,
especially heathers (150 to 200
varieties) and azaleas and
rhododendrons.

Cottage Garden Plants Old and New
Yardewell Cross, North Molton, Devon EX36 3HA
Tel Brayford (059 88) 530
Sells a wide range of cottage garden plants, especially primulas and violas, together with unusual bulbs. Mail order available.

County Park Nurseries
Essex Gardens Road, Hornchurch, Essex RM11 3BU
Tel Hornchurch (040 24) 45205
Specialise in rock plants and alpines, particularly plants from New Zealand – 350 varieties including 160 hebes. No mail order.

Court Farm Nursery
Honeybourne Road, Pebworth, near Stratford-on-Avon, Warwickshire CV37 8XP
Hellebore specialist with 12 to 15 named varieties. Plants available by mail order.

Eastgrove Cottage Garden Nursery
Sankyns Green, Little Witley, Hereford and Worcester WR6 6LQ
Tel Great Witley (029 921) 389
Specialises in cottage garden plants – about 600 varieties, many grown to order. Has a selection of herbs (60 varieties). No mail order.

Green Farm Plants
Bentley, Farnham, Surrey GU10 5JX
Tel Bentley (0420) 23202
Sell uncommon plants chosen for suitability in low-maintenance and cottage gardens.

Herterton House Garden Nursery
Hartington, Cambo, Morpeth, Northumberland NE61 4BN
Tel Scots Gap (067 074) 278
Specialises in old country garden perennials – up to 400 varieties. No mail order.

Knightshayes Garden Trust
Knightshayes, Tiverton, Devon EX16 7RG
Specialises in unusual garden plants, many propagated to order.

Includes trees, shrubs, climbers and herbaceous plants. No mail order.

The Knoll Gardens
Stapehill Road, Stapehill, Wimborne, Dorset BH21 7ND
Tel Wimborne (0202) 873931
Specialise in three areas: unusual herbaceous plants (150 varieties); unusual trees and shrubs, especially Australian and marginally hardy plants (600 varieties); plants for conservatories. No mail order.

Long Man Gardens
Lewes Road, Wilmington, Polegate, E. Sussex BN26 5RS
Abutilon specialist.

Stanley Mossop
36 Thorny Road, Thornhill, Egremont, Cumbria CA22 2RZ
Tel Egremont (0946) 821817
Specialises in achimenes (hot-water plant) of which he lists 100 varieties. Also 24 varieties of smithiantha (temple bells). Rhizomes by mail order.

The Palm Farm
Thornton Hall Gardens, Ulceby, Humberside DN39 6XF
Tel Barrow-on-Humber (0469) 31232
Lists a range of hardy, half-hardy and exotic palms (about 50 varieties) plus a dozen varieties of meconopsis (blue poppy). Also stocks 200 to 300 varieties of trees and shrubs (not listed). All available by mail order.

The Palm House
22 Guildford Road, London SW8 2BX
Tel 01-720 8635
Grows about 100 varieties of palm, particularly tropical ones, but only 15 to 20 available for sale at any one time. Also other tropical plants. Available by mail order.

Robinsons Hardy Plants
Greencourt Nurseries, Crockenhill, Swanley, Kent BR8 8HD
Tel Swanley (0322) 63819

Specialises in dwarf and unusual perennials with 1000 varieties. Plants available by mail order in autumn and winter only.

Rosemoor Garden Trust
Torrington, Devon EX38 7EG
Tel Torrington (080 52) 2256
Unusual plants, including trees and shrubs, herbaceous plants and a few alpines are the speciality. Available by mail order.

Clive Simms
Woodhurst, Essendine, Stamford, Lincolnshire PE9 4LQ
Tel Stamford (0780) 55615
Specialises in sub-tropical and otherwise unusual fruiting plants but also sells a small range of interesting plants for greenhouse or conservatory. Available by mail order.

Stone House Cottage Nursery
Stone, near Kidderminster, Hereford and Worcester DY10 4BG
Tel Kidderminster (0562) 69902
Based in a walled garden this nursery specialises in climbers, wall shrubs and unusual herbaceous perennials. No mail order.

E. Strangman
Washfield Nursery, Horns Road, Hawkhurst, Kent TN18 4QU
Tel Hawkhurst (058 05) 2522
Specialises in unusual plants, particularly for shade and woodland conditions. Often has small quantities of unusual plants not listed. Plants available by mail order.

Torbay Palm Farm
St. Marychurch Road, Coffinswell, near Newton Abbot, Devon TQ12 4SE
Tel Kingskerswell (080 47) 2800
Sells *Cordyline australis* in a range of sizes, and *Trachycarpus fortunei* (Chusan palm) by mail order.

K. J. Townsend
17 Valerie Close, St. Albans, Hertfordshire AL1 5JD
Tel St. Albans (0727) 34753
Lists 150 varieties of achimenes (hot-water plants). Includes some Victorian rarities and rare species. Tubers and plants available by mail order.

Valleyhead Nursery
Dihewid, Lampeter, Dyfed SA48 7PJ
Tel Lampeter (0570) 470591
Holds the National Collections of aquilegia, ashphodelus and ashphodeline. Also lists unusual plants of all kinds, especially herbaceous perennials and plants for seaside or mild areas. No mail order available.

Yew Tree Nursery
Lydart, Monmouth, Gwent NP5 4RJ
Tel Monmouth (0600) 2293
Specialises in rare plants, choice varieties and unusual plants of interest. In particular stocks about 20 less-common primulas and an increasing range of miniature roses. No mail order.

Also see:

ALPINES AND ROCK PLANTS
Hartside Nursery Garden: New Zealand Plants

ASPARAGUS
M. Bennett: globe artichokes
A. R. Paske and Co: globe artichokes and seakale

BULBS
Paradise Centre: shade plants

CACTI AND SUCCULENTS
The Exotic Collection: sub-tropical plants

CARNATIONS AND PINKS
Old Inn Cottage Nursery: old-fashioned plants

FOLIAGE PLANTS
Dunstan Garden Design: plants for shade
Goldbrook Plants: plants for flower-arrangers

HERBACEOUS PERENNIALS
Plants for Pleasure: white-flowered plants

HERBS

The Herb Garden: bee- and
butterfly-attracting plants
Hollington Nursery: plants for the
cold conservatory
Laundry Farm Herbs: flowers for
drying
Iden Croft Herbs: aromatic plants
Netherfield Herbs: aromatic
sub-shrubs

GOOD GARDEN CENTRES AND
GENERAL NURSERIES

Breage, Trevena Cross Nursery:
coastal, semi-tropical and New
Zealand plants
Elmstead Market, Unusual Plants
Lymington, Spinners: rare and
shade plants
Pewsey, Peter Jones: old-fashioned
plants

VINES

Our wet and cloudy summers may seem a sad alternative to the dry,
sun-baked climate of the European wine-producing areas. However, vines
are completely hardy and you can get good crops outdoors in the warmer
parts of the country though you'll need a greenhouse in the north. The
outdoor varieties are principally raised to produce wines, and the
likelihood of success with these diminishes the further north and the
higher up you live. Grown outdoors, vines will need sun and shelter, and a
well-drained soil is essential. In less favourable areas choose the earliest
varieties. They can be planted in an unheated greenhouse between
November and March, but outside the months of March/April or
October/November are best. Garden centres usually have vines for sale, but
are unlikely to offer a great choice of varieties. Because you will be buying a
dormant plant, assessing its quality is a little tricky. Look for those which
are vigorous and have been trained to produce just one strong shoot at least
5mm (¼in) in diameter. Avoid those with several stems and those with thin
or weak shoots.

To obtain a particular variety not sold locally you will have to buy by mail
order from a specialist. If you send your orders in late summer or early
autumn, nurseries should post off your plants in time for autumn planting
though some outdoor vines are imported and these may not arrive until
spring. The standards for a good vine still apply here, and some specialist
nurseries can be guilty of sending out weak or poorly trained plants which
will need additional time and attention before they reach their full
potential. Growing vines, whether for the wine or eating fresh grapes, can
give great enjoyment: the sight of a gnarled vine criss-crossing the roof and
walls of the conservatory is not unknown in this country and the pleasure
of picking the plump, fresh fruit is unsurpassed.

Varieties most readily available

INDOOR

'Black Hamburg' large, dark maroon, fair flavour

OUTDOOR

'Brandt' semi-ornamental, not good for wine but small, black grapes good
for eating fresh. Good autumn colour
'Madeleine Angevine' reliable, heavy crops
'Madeleine Sylvaner' reliable and early but only light yields
'Müller-Thurgau' not too easy to grow and only moderate yields but
excellent for wine

Varieties worth looking for

INDOOR

'Muscat of Alexandria' large golden-yellow, very good flavour
'Muscat Hamburg' large dark red or maroon, very good flavour
'Chasselas Rose Royale' medium pinkish gold or amber, good flavour

OUTDOOR

'Seyval Blanc' high yielding, light fruity white wine
'Siegerrebe' very early, good for less favourable areas. Spicy, white wine
'Seibel 13053' easy to grow and high yields for a good red or rosé wine
'Triomphe d'Alsace' very vigorous and high yields for a Beaujolais-type wine

Cranmore Vine Nursery
Yarmouth, Isle of Wight PO41 OXY
Tel Yarmouth (0983) 760080/760561
Vine specialist with 27 varieties.
Concentrates on outdoor varieties
but has 5 varieties suitable for cold
greenhouses. Plants available by
mail order.

Greenland Vines
5 Greenland Cottages, High
Hoyland, Barnsley, S. Yorkshire
S75 4AZ
Tel Barnsley (0226) 385665
Vine specialist with 16 varieties
listed. Indoor and outdoor vines
supplied with the emphasis on
early outdoor varieties suitable for
the Midlands and parts of northern
England. Plants available by mail
order.

S. E. Lytle
1A Park Road, Formby, Merseyside
L37 4FH
Tel Formby (070 48) 73807
Vine specialist with over 20
varieties of indoor and outdoor
vines listed. Plants available by mail
order.

Pilton Manor Vineyard
Manor House, Pilton, Shepton
Mallet, Somerset BA4 4BE
Tel Pilton (074 989) 325
Vine specialist with 8 varieties for
wine making. No mail order.

Reads Nursery
Hales Hall, Loddon, Norfolk
NR14 6QW

Tel Raveningham (050 846) 395
Vine specialist with 80 varieties.
Also specialises in certain fruits, eg
citrus (15 varieties), figs (10
varieties) and has 30 varieties of
climbing and conservatory plants.
Plants available by mail order.

G. E. Williams Associates
2 Heath Villas, Appledore,
Ashford, Kent TN26 2BB
Tel Appledore (023 383) 434
Vine specialist with over 40
varieties of both outdoor and
indoor types. Plants available by
mail order. Visitors welcome by
appointment.

Yearlstone Vineyard
Chilton, Bickleigh, Tiverton,
Devon EX16 8RT
Tel Bickleigh (088 45) 450
Vine specialist with 20 outdoor
varieties. Concentrates on hardy,
early-ripening wine grapevines.
Courses available for wine growers.
Plants available by mail order.

Also see:

DAFFODILS
Michael Jefferson-Brown

FRUIT TREES
Deacons

GOOD GARDEN CENTRES AND
GENERAL NURSERIES
Sawbridgeworth, Greenscape
Garden Centre
Whitminster, Highfield Nurseries

VIOLAS

The familiar face of the pansy is the best known of this attractive family which also includes violas, violettas and violets. All the species generally raised here are both hardy and perennial. However, bedding pansies, in particular, are often treated as annuals as they tend to become straggly and produce fewer flowers as they age. Violas and their smaller counterpart violettas are distinguished from pansies by their more tufted habit of growth, longer life and proportionately longer flower stems. Many are plain-coloured but others show subtly blended combinations of shades and tints, and some even carry the blotches typical of pansies. Most cultivated violets are derived from the wild sweet violet (*Viola odorata*), and occur in a surprising range of colours from cream through pink to purple.

All members of the family like a cool root run in a moist but free-draining soil. Most are shade-tolerant, but pansies in particular need sunshine to give of their best. Although they are all suitable for growing in borders or rockeries, enthusiasts like to grow them in shallow pots to enjoy the flowers, and scent, at close quarters.

When it comes to buying violas, you will need to try different suppliers according to what you want. Bedding pansies for winter and spring or summer flowering are very widely available both as seeds and plants. When buying plants choose dark green, compact plants with no sign of slug damage. It does not matter if they are in flower, but see there are plenty more buds to come. Garden centres may sell a few popular violas and violets but for a real choice turn to the mail order specialists. Violets flower in early spring, violas and violettas more or less continually from March to November.

Varieties to try

SUMMER-FLOWERING PANSIES
'Clear Crystals' mixed colours, no marking
'Majestic Giants' mixed colours
'Swiss Giants' mixed colours, some individual colours also sold,
eg 'Ullswater' a rich, light blue

WINTER-FLOWERING PANSIES
'Floral Dance' mixed colours
'Universal' mixed colours

BEDDING VIOLAS
'Admiration' purple-blue, yellow eye
'Betty' mauve, edged with purple
'David Wheldon' yellow
'Gladys Findlay' deep violet-blue, white centre
'Grey Owl' grey-mauve, yellow centre
'Irish Molly' copper-yellow
'Inverurie Beauty' violet-mauve
'James Pilling' white with violet-blue
'Maggie' yellow-green, suffused with pale blue
'Maggie Mott' silver-mauve

BEDDING VIOLETTAS
'Buttercup' deep yellow

'Little David' creamy-white, frilled
'Rebecca' creamy-white, violet flecks

VIOLETS

'Coeur d'Alsace' dusty rose pink
'John Raddenbury' blue, white eye
'Lianne' purple-red
'Opera' lavender-mauve, rose shading
'Princess of Wales' deep blue, highly scented
'Rawsons White' white
'Rosina' deep pink
'Sulphurea' pale orange-yellow

R. G. M. Cawthorne
28 Trigon Road, London SW8 1NJ
Nursery itself is in Kent. Specialist
selling 350 varieties of bedding
violas, violettas and viola species –
the largest collection in Europe.
Trying to conserve both old and
new varieties. Plants available by
post, minimum order 12 plants.

R. E. Coombs
'Pippins', Weston, Honiton, Devon
EX14 0NZ
Tel Honiton (0404) 3668
Specialises in double violets,
cottage garden plants and some
cacti, eg *Mammillaria elongata*, and
Chamaecereus hybrids. Plants
available by mail order.

Rodney Fuller
Clematis Cottage, Deanway,
Chalfont St. Giles,
Buckinghamshire HP8 4JH
Specialist selling 23 named varieties
of sweet violet (*V. odorata*), 27
bedding violas and 5 violettas. Sells
both old, established varieties,
some of which are becoming scarce,
and new introductions. Mail order
only.

Joseph S. Jackson and Son
Post Office Nurseries,
Kettleshulme, Stockport, Cheshire
SJ12 7RD
Tel Whaley Bridge (066 33) 2623
Viola specialist with over 80
varieties including exhibition
pansies and violas, bedding violas
and violettas. Plants available by
mail order.

E. Smith
Downside, Bowling Green,
Constantine, near Falmouth,
Cornwall TR11 5AP
Small-scale enterprise, specialising
in named violets, 18 varieties listed,
others grown to order. Mail order
only.

Also see:

ALPINES AND ROCK PLANTS
Careby Manor Gardens

FRUIT TREES
C. W. Groves & Son: English violets

HERBACEOUS PERENNIALS
Plants from the Past

UNUSUAL PLANTS
Cottage Garden Plants Old and
New
Herterton House Garden Nursery

WATER AND WATERSIDE PLANTS

The fascination of water gardening must largely be a result of the hypnotic
effect of floating foliage, or ever-moving fish and the relaxing, peaceful
nature of the water. However, before indulging, there are a few hard facts
to be faced. A water garden requires careful siting, preferably in full sun – a
pond placed under a tree will be a sad disappointment – and the pool itself
must be designed with varying depths of water for the different plant

types, from the marginals to the deep-rooting varieties.

Once the position and shape of the pool are decided, the best options for the lining are concrete, rigid pre-shaped fibreglass or reinforced PVC or butyl rubber sheet.

A bog garden may be easily established at the same time as installing a pool by extending the pool lining at about 30cm (1ft) depth and covering it with a water-retentive combination of peat and heavy soil over a bed of gravel for good drainage. It's important to remember that all bog plants need lots of moisture, but few can survive being waterlogged. Of course, if you have a naturally moist area in your garden the job is done for you, although before introducing your waterside plants, ensure the site is free of weeds as hand-weeding in an established bog garden is both cold and unpleasant. An alternative way to control weeds is to introduce large, vigorous plants into enriched pockets of soil – they should soon spread and smother the culprits. Water plants, both submerged and floating, are best put in position in April and May. The purpose-built containers which allow water to move freely around the roots, and give you some control over position and spreading, are a good investment.

Garden centres have expanded their dealings in aquatics over the past few years, but mail order is still cheaper and gives you a wider choice. If you order at the beginning of March you can expect to start receiving plants in April. Availability at garden centres is generally restricted to the peak months of May, June and July. Always choose plants which look fresh and healthy with new growing shoots and few old or damaged leaves. Don't buy anything weedy or lanky, and always check for signs of pests and diseases.

Waterside and other moisture-loving plants appear in garden centres and specialist nurseries in the spring and are sometimes available until early autumn, though it is best to buy them early so they have time to establish before the winter. The more common varieties can be bought at many garden centres, but for the rare types you'll need to go to a specialist – many supply plants by mail order.

Varieties to try

WATERLILIES
(the figures give the depth of water needed)
Nymphaea pygmaea 'Helvola' (15cm to 30cm, 6 to 12in)
N. odorata 'William B. Shaw' (30cm to 45cm, 12 to 18in)
N. 'Albatross' (45cm to 60cm, 18 to 24in)
N. odorata sulphurea (45cm to 60cm, 18 to 24in)
N. marliacea 'Albida' (60cm to 90cm, 24 to 35in)
N. 'Conqueror' (60cm to 90cm, 24 to 35in)
N. gladstonia (over 90cm, 35in)

DEEP-WATER AQUATICS
Apnogeton distachyus (water hawthorn)
Nymphoides peltata (water fringe)

FLOATING PLANTS
Hydrocharis morsus-rana (frogbit)
Stratiotes aloides (water soldier)
Trapa natans (water chestnut)

SUBMERGED OXYGENATORS
Ceratophyllum demersum (hornwort)
Hottonia palustris (water violet)
Ranunculus aquatilis (water crowfoot)

MARGINAL PLANTS
Myosotis scorpiodes (water forget-me-not)
Acorus calamus 'Variegatus'
Butomus umbellatus (flowering rush)
Calla palustris (bog arum)

Caltha palustris (marsh marigold)
Glyceria aquatica 'Variegata'
Iris laevigata
Menyanthes trifoliata (bog bean)
Pontederia cordata (pickerel weed)
Sagittaria japonica (arrowhead)

MOISTURE LOVERS
Aconitum napellus (monkshood)
Asclepias incarnata (swamp milkweed)
Astilbe hybrids
Hosta undulata medio 'Variegata'
Parnassia palustris (grass of Parnassus)
Primula japonica (candelabra primula)
Rheum palmatum
Trollius europaeus (globe flower)

Bennett's Water Lily Farm
Putton Lane, Chickerell, Weymouth, Dorset DT3 4AF
Tel Weymouth (0305) 785150
Water garden specialist with over 170 varieties of bog and water plants. Mail order available.

Blagdon Water Garden Centre
Church Street, Blagdon, Avon BS18 6RZ
Tel Blagdon (0761) 62344
Specialises in water-gardening plants, lilies and marginals. Plants available by mail order.

Higher End Nursery
Hale, Fordingbridge, Hampshire SP6 2RA
Tel Downton (0725) 22243
Water-garden specialist with 50 varieties of water lilies and aquatics, 80 varieties of bog plants. No sundries or equipment. Has over 200 varieties of herbaceous perennials. Also plants for shade, eg hellebores (10 varieties) and bergenias (13 varieties). No mail order.

Honeysome Aquatic Nursery
The Row, Sutton, near Ely, Cambridgeshire CB6 2PF
Tel Ely (0353) 778889
Water-gardening and bog plant specialist with 170 varieties. Plants available by mail order.

Longstock Park Nursery
Stockbridge, Hampshire SO20 6EH
Tel Andover (0264) 810894
Water-plant specialist with 200 varieties. Also sells 300 to 400 varieties of container-grown shrubs and 50 to 60 varieties of herbaceous perennials. In addition, over 20 species and cultivars of Asiatic primulas. No mail order.

Maydencroft Aquatic Nurseries
Maydencroft Lane, Gosmore, Hitchin, Hertfordshire SG4 7QD
Tel Hitchin (0462) 56020
Water-garden specialist with water lilies (60 varieties), marginal plants (70 varieties) and bog plants (40 varieties). Plants available by mail order.

Orchards Cottage Garden Centre
Scalby Lane, Brough, Gilberdyke, Humberside HU15 2UJ
Tel Howden (0430) 40169
Bog plant specialist (50 varieties) and water-gardening equipment. Mail order available.

Peters Gardens
Stoke Road, Stoke D'Abernon, Cobham, Surrey KT11 3PU
Tel Cobham (0932) 62530
Water-garden plant specialist with the emphasis on marginal types. They offer 40 varieties of water garden plants, bog plants (30 varieties) and fish. They also have a range of herbaceous perennials and rock garden plants. No mail order.

Waveney Fish Farm
Park Road, Diss, Norfolk IP22 3AS
Tel Diss (0379) 2697
Water-garden plant specialist with over 130 varieties listed. Mail order available.

Wayside Water Garden
Doncaster Road, Oldcotes, near Worksop, Nottinghamshire S81 8HT
Tel Worksop (0909) 731367
Water-garden specialist with about 70 varieties of bog and aquatic plants. No mail order.

Wildwoods Water Gardens
Theobalds Park Road, Crews Hill,
Enfield EN2 9BP
Tel 01-366 0243/4
Water-garden specialist with water
lilies (40 varieties), marginal plants
(80 varieties). Plants available by
mail order.

Also see:

ALPINES AND ROCK PLANTS
Jack Drake
Reginald Kaye

BULBS
Paradise Centre

SHRUBS AND TREES
Brackenwood Nurseries

GOOD GARDEN CENTRES AND
GENERAL NURSERIES
Chorleywood, Highlands Water
Garden Nursery
Nantwich, Stapeley Water Gardens
Southwell, New Minster Water
Gardens and Garden Centre
Tansley, Matlock Garden Waterlife
and Pet Centre

WILD FLOWERS

Commercially produced wild flowers have dramatically increased in
popularity over the last few years. Conservation-minded gardeners may
like to turn over an entire area for native plants to grow and spread at will,
but some wild flowers also fit well in the herbaceous border.

Many garden centres now sell wild flower seeds, though the range is
usually limited to the most popular sellers. You may also find young plants
of popular species. If you're keen it's probably worth contacting the
specialist mail order suppliers – some now offer several hundred wild
flowers and grasses. Again, most of the trade is done in seeds but some
suppliers are starting to sell container-grown or bare-rooted plants by mail
order. Container-grown plants can be ordered any time of the year; seeds
are best ordered for early autumn despatch. Early autumn sowing allows
you to take advantage of freshly harvested seed and many will have the
chance to germinate and establish before winter.

Wild flower seeds are started off in much the same way as their
cultivated counterparts – sown directly into the ground or germinated in
containers in the greenhouse to be planted out later. Since most wild flowers
are generally perennials they can be left alone and with any luck they will
reappear every year with the addition of new seedlings – though they need
to be well suited to the conditions in your garden to do this. Bear in mind
that many wild flowers are very finnicky about growing conditions and
may not necessarily thrive in your garden. Most seed companies also sell
seed mixtures, which can be a good idea if you are unclear about what
species to select. These mixtures will be designed according to planting
position or special characteristics, for example, sandy soil, shade, wetland,
butterfly and bee attracting. Out of a wide range of plants you stand a good
chance, this way, of finding at least some that will do well. Some nurseries
will see customers, but by appointment only. Many herb specialists carry a
range of wild flowers as the boundary between these two areas is not very
distinct.

*If you have trouble finding the plants you want, try contacting appropriate societies
and organisations – see Chapter 3; they may be able to direct you to specialist
growers in your area.*

Plants to try

EASILY AVAILABLE
cowslip
primrose
wild pansy
foxglove
ox-eye daisy

WORTH LOOKING FOR
harebell
meadow cranesbill
ragged robin
red campion
small scabious
toadflax

John Chambers

15 Westleigh Road, Barton
Seagrave, Kettering,
Northamptonshire NN15 5AJ
Tel Wellingborough (0933) 681632
(daytime), Kettering (0536) 513748
(evenings)
Specialises in many unusual seeds
including wild flowers, wild
flower/grass mixtures, herbs,
everlasting flowers, flowers for
wildlife, ornamental grasses.

Naturescape

Little Orchard,
Whatton-in-the-Vale,
Nottinghamshire NG13 9EP
Tel Whatton (0949) 51045
Wild flower specialist with about 50
varieties of seed and 24 varieties
available as plants. Also offers
conservation blends of wild flower
and grass seed. Plants and seeds
available by mail order.

Also see:

ALPINES AND ROCK PLANTS
Careby Manor Gardens

AZALEAS AND RHODODENDRON
C. E. Henderson and Son

HERBS
Candlesby Herbs
The Herb Garden

SHRUBS AND TREES
Kingsfield Tree Nursery

SEEDS (GENERAL)

SEEDS (UNUSUAL)
Bristol University Botanic Garden
Seeds-by-Post

3 Societies and organisations

Alpine Garden Society
Lye End Link, St. Johns, Woking, Surrey GU21 1SW
Tel Woking (04862) 69327
Established 1929. Membership 8,400. Subcription £9, family £11. Life membership £180.
Publish and supply books/booklets, quarterly bulletin. Library and slide library. Has a seed distribution scheme, arranges overseas tours to mountain areas and has a panel of experts to advise members. 45 local branches provide visiting lecturers and operate plant exchanges. Bi-annual conference. Holds own show, exhibits at others.

The Amateur Rose Breeders Association
48 Shrewsbury Fields, Shifnal, Shropshire TF11 8AN
Tel Telford (0952) 461333
Established 1975. Membership 100. Subscription £2, family £2.50.
Aims to improve the skill, knowledge and status of the amateur rose breeder. Produces a newsletter three times a year. Has a pollen exchange scheme and its own seedling trial garden. Exhibits at Royal National Rose Society shows. Holds annual general meeting.

Arboricultural Association
Ampfield House, Ampfield, Romsey, Hampshire SO5 9PA
Tel Braishfield (0794) 68717
Established 1964. Membership 1,000. Subscription; associate £18, ordinary £12, student £8, corporate £22.
Semi-professional organisation which aims to advance the study of arboriculture – the care, culture, management and improvement of trees. Also hopes to encourage interest in trees through publications, exhibitions, and to stimulate research and experiment. Issues quarterly journal and newsletter, booklets and technical notes. Has a directory of consultants and contractors. Holds conferences, seminars, local meetings and exhibits at shows.

Association of British Herb Growers and Producers
2 Manor Farm Cottage, Cothelstone, Thornton, Somerset TA4 3DS
Tel Thornton (0823) 54900
Established 1975. Membership 60 companies. Subscription £30.
Professional trade association for commercial growers. A special service to the public is an information pack consisting of illustrated fact sheets on various aspects of herb growing and use, plus a book list. Available at £2.90 from 'A Scented Corner', 46 Church Street, Buckden, Cambridgeshire PE18 9SX.
Tel Huntingdon (0480) 810818.

Bristol and West of England Orchid Society
17 Freemantle Road, Eastville, Bristol B35 6SY
Tel Bristol (0272) 512212
Established 1949. Membership 145. Subscription £3, family £4.50.
Aims to encourage and extend the cultivation of orchids. Issues monthly newsletter and provides book and slide library. Monthly meetings offer lectures, discussions and slide shows. Arranges party visits to orchid nurseries. Holds annual exhibition.

British Agricultural and Garden Machinery Association
Church Street, Rickmansworth, Hertfordshire WD3 1RQ
Tel Rickmansworth (0923) 720241
Established 1917. Membership 850. Subscription £93 plus VAT, £40 plus VAT for additional places of business.
Promotes and protects the interests of dealers in the agricultural and garden machinery industry. Issues monthly magazine, handbook, market guide, technical guide. Annual conference, regional branch meetings held monthly. Offers advice and information to members. Refers members of the public to appropriate companies for advice on garden machinery.

British Agrochemicals Association
Alembic House, 93 Albert Embankment, London SE1 7TU
Tel 01-735 8471
Established 1926. Membership 51 companies.
Aims to encourage responsible manufacture, distribution and use of agrochemicals. Represents industry to government, consumers, and press. Publishes leaflets, annual handbook and code of practice. Publishes Directory of Garden Chemicals, available to gardeners for £1 (includes postage) from above address, but does not deal with other enquiries from the public.

British Bonsai Association
23 Nimrod Road, London SW16 6SZ
Tel 01-667 9065
Established 1974. Membership 500. Subscription £2.50, family £3, plus 50p entry fee. Affiliated to RHS.
Publishes a quarterly magazine. Has a library and advice-giving service. Regular meetings and tree sales take place in London. Exhibits at Chelsea Flower Show and elsewhere.

British Bromeliad Society
c/o Mr Lucibell, Dept of Plant Biology, Queen Mary College, London E1 4NS
Established 1968. Membership 350. Subscription £2.50. Affiliated to RHS.
Supplies books and booklets, some at reduced rates. Issues quarterly bulletin. Has a book and slide library. Operates seed distribution scheme. Exhibits at shows.

British Cactus & Succulent Society
43 Dewar Drive, Sheffield S7 2GR
Tel Sheffield (0742) 361649
Established 1983. Membership 5,000. Subscription £6, OAPs and juniors £3.50.
The Society publishes a quarterly journal and has a slide library. Local branch meetings are held monthly which involve plant auctions, lectures, and discussions. Seed distribution scheme. Arranges inter-branch competitions and quizzes. Organises visits to nurseries, public and private collections and shows. Holds annual course for qualifications as exhibition judge.

British and European Geranium Society
'Morval', The Hills, Bradwell, Sheffield S30 2HZ
Tel Hope Valley (0433) 20459
Established 1970. Membership 2,000. Subscription £2, family £2.60. Life membership £40.
Aims to promote and further interest in cultivation and hybridisation of Pelargoniums and Geraniums. Publishes a year book and three gazettes each year nationally, plus newsletters from regions. Has a slide library and an advisory panel to give guidance to members. Local branch meetings and outings. National and regional shows.

The British Fuchsia Society
29 Princes Crescent, Dollar, Clackmannanshire, Central FK14 7BW

Tel Dollar (025 94) 3180
Established 1938. Membership 6,000. Subscription £4, family £5. Life membership £50. Affiliated to RHS.
Publishes an annual book and two bulletins. Slide collection for hire. Has trials at Harlow Car Gardens. Holds a general meeting each year, plus eight national shows. Local affiliated groups hold monthly meetings and annual show.

British Gladiolus Society
10 Sandbach Road, Thurlwood, Rode Heath, Stoke-on-Trent, Staffordshire ST7 3RN
Tel Alsager (09363) 2530
Established 1926. Membership 500. Subscription £1.50–£5 depending on age and situation. Affiliated to RHS.
Publishes and supplies books, yearbook and bi-annual bulletin. Has both book and slide library. Operates cormlet distribution scheme. Holds shows, exhibits at others. Has trial grounds.

British Hosta and Hemerocallis Society
42 Fairoak Drive, Eltham, London SE9 2HQ
Tel 01-850 9324
Established 1979. Membership 150. Subscription £5, family £8.
Publishes bulletin and two newsletters annually. Provides library service for books and slides. Gives advice and answers queries. Records new varieties and traces lost species. Has use of trial ground, seed and plant exchange. Organises shows, lectures and garden visits. Annual general meeting.

The British Iris Society
197 The Parkway, Iver Heath, Iver, Buckinghamshire SL0 0RQ
Established 1922. Membership 800. Subscription £7, family £7 and £1.40 each additional family member, juniors £1.40.
Publishes a year book and newsletters. Has both a book and slide library. Offers a plant and seed sales scheme. Holds four

shows each year. Arranges visits to members' gardens during the season.

The British Ivy Society
Woodlands, Gravel Path, Berkhamsted, Hertfordshire HP4 2PF
Tel Berkhamsted (04427) 73010
Established 1974. Membership 150. Subscription £5.
Aims to unite those interested in the genus Hedera and to provide information and sources of supply. Publishes a quarterly journal and two newsletters each year. Has a slide library and holds a national collection at trial ground at Erddig, Clwyd. Operates a plant and cuttings exchange scheme. Gives cultural advice and has advisory panel to help members.

British National Carnation Society
61 Carmodale Avenue, Perry Barr, Birmingham B42 1PN
Tel 021-356 9887
Established 1948. Membership 750. Subscription £5, family £5.50.
Publishes two newsletters a year. Prints three up to date 'How to grow' books. Has slides for hire. Keeps a trial ground at Wisley in conjunction with the RHS. Plant exchange scheme. Provides information and advice service and lectures. Annual general meetings. Exhibits at shows.

British Pelargonium and Geranium Society
2/108 Rosendale Road, West Dulwich, London SE21 8LF
Tel 01-670 9144
Established 1951. Membership 1,800. Subscription £3. Life membership £40. Affiliated to RHS.
Issues four publications each year covering society affairs and a range of subjects relevant to the plants. Has a selection of books which can be purchased by post. Advice and information service. Arranges lectures, discussions and visits. Exhibits at shows, holds annual competition and annual conference.

The British Pteridological Society
42 Lewisham Road, Smethwick,
Warley, West Midlands B66 2BS
Tel 021-558 4481
Established 1891. Membership 700.
Subscription £7, family £5.
Promotes the study, cultivation and
conservation of ferns and fern
allies. Three publications a year.
Organises new and second-hand
book sales, and spore and plant
exchange scheme. Arranges field
meetings, garden visits and local
group meetings. Alternative contact
address: BPS, c/o British Museum
(Natural History), Cromwell Road,
London SW7 5BD.

British Trust for Conservation Volunteers
36 St. Mary's Street, Wallingford,
Oxfordshire OX10 0EU
Tel Wallingford (0491) 39766
Established 1959. Membership 4,000,
volunteers 20,000. Subscription £5.
Aims to involve volunteers in
practical conservation work.
Publishes handbooks on footpaths,
coastlands, woodlands, wetlands
and waterways, dry stone walling,
hedging. Has photograph library.
Organises conservation working
holidays, regional mid-week
projects and training courses.
Offers advice and practical help on
conservation projects. Scotland is
covered by Scottish Conservation
Projects Trust, 70 Main Street,
Doune, Tayside.

Bulb Information Desk
Stubbings House, Henley Road,
Maidenhead, Berkshire SL6 6QL
Tel Maidenhead (0628) 825422
Established 1958.
Service organisation supplying
information and guidance to the
horticultural trade, the media and
the public on all aspects of flower
bulbs. Provides leaflets and advice
service. Free film and slide service
to societies and organisations.

Carnivorous Plant Society
174 Baldwins Lane, Croxley Green,
Hertfordshire WD3 3LQ
Established 1978. Membership 350.
Subscription £4.50, overseas £6,
juniors £2.50. Affiliated to RHS.
Publishes four newsletters and two
journals each year. Has a book and
slide library. Operates a seed and
plant exchange scheme linked with
growers from all over the world.
Arranges outings, holds monthly
meetings in London and exhibits at
the Chelsea Flower Show.

The Central Orchid Society
48 Ashmead Road, Chase Terrace,
nr Walsall, Staffordshire WS7 8DG
Tel Burnt Wood (054 36) 75531
Established 1958. Membership 100.
Subscription £3, family £5.
Promotes the culture of orchid
plants. Issues quarterly newsletter.
Offers advice service. Holds
monthly meetings. Runs two shows
each year and exhibits at others.

The Cottage Garden Society
15 Faenol Avenue, Abergele,
Clwyd LL22 7HT
Tel Abergele (0745) 822059
Established 1982. Membership 700.
Subscription £2.
A society geared to keeping alive
the tradition of old-fashioned
flowers and cottage gardening.
Issues four newsletters a year,
leaflets and lists of helpful
nurseries. Arranges visits to private
gardens and those of their own
members. Gives advice and holds
branch meetings.

Council for the Protection of Rural England
4 Hobart Place, London SW1W 0HY
Tel 01-235 9481
Established 1926. Membership 30,000.
Subscription £10. Life membership
£250.
Independent conservation pressure
group for the protection of the
English countryside as a whole.
Quarterly journal and in-house
publications list. One or two
conferences a year. 43 branches
represent local conservation
interests and act as watchdogs for
area. Branch groups also arrange

meetings, lectures, exhibitions and campaigns.

The Cyclamen Society
Tile Barn House, Standen Street, Benenden, Kent PN17 4LB
Membership 560. Subscription £3, family £4.
Publishes a journal and has both a slide and book library. Operates a seed distribution scheme as well as plant sales and exchanges. Gives advice on pests, diseases and cultivation. Attends shows as a society. Holds meetings and arranges talks by experts. Annual conference.

The Daffodil Society
32 Montgomery Avenue, Sheffield S7 1NZ
Tel Sheffield (0742) 550559
Established 1898. Membership 500 individuals, 130 affiliated societies. Subscription £3.
Publishes a journal, newsletter and a 'show handbook'. Produces daffodil seed available to members. Each member group holds special events and bulb sales. Annual show and specialist section at Harrogate Spring Show. Maintains list of approved judges.

The Delphinium Society
11 Long Grove, Seer Green, Beaconsfield, Buckinghamshire HP9 2YN
Tel Beaconsfield (049 46) 6315
Established 1928. Membership 1,500. Subscription £2. Affiliated to RHS.
Issues 120-page year book and cultural booklets. Provides advice service and arranges social events. Gifts of seed to overseas members. Species and hybrid seed available at modest cost. Holds three annual shows.

English Vineyards Association
The Ridge, Lamberhurst Down, Kent TN3 8ER
Tel Lamberhurst (0892) 890734
Established 1967. Membership 570. Subscription details from association.
Aims to help both commercial and non-commercial growers. Acts as liaison between growers and government. Gives advice and issues list of vine suppliers. Publishes leaflets and newsletter. Has four local branches. Holds annual general meeting.

Epiphytic Plant Study Group
1 Belvidere Park, Great Crosby, Merseyside L23 0SP
Tel 051-928 2770
Established 1968. Membership 150. Subscription £2.60.
Aims to promote an interest in and a knowledge of epiphytic plants. The general bias is toward epiphytic cacti, but information is also provided about other epiphytic plants. Publishes quarterly newsletter. Offers free seed distribution scheme. Members may exchange, sell or advertise for plants.

Gardens for the Disabled Trust
Church Cottage, Headcorn, Kent TN27 9NP
Tel Headcorn (0622) 890467
Established 1968. Membership 250. Subscription £1, family £2. Life membership £15.
Helps individual gardeners in their own homes. Assists hospitals and institutions which deal with horticultural therapy. Its 'Garden Club' publishes a quarterly newsletter with articles of special interest to the disabled gardener. The club endeavours to deal with queries, offers a plant and seed exchange scheme and encourages members to share problems and experiences. Grants are made available for adapting gardens to specific needs.

Garden History Society
66 Granville Park, London SE13 7DX
Tel 01-852 1818
Established 1965. Membership 1,600. Subscription £12, family £15.
Aims to assemble those interested in all aspects of garden history – landscape design and its relation to

art, architecture, philosophy and society; plant introduction, propagation and taxonomy; estate and woodland planning and maintenance. Acts as a pressure group for the conservation of historic gardens. Issues a magazine and newsletters and has slide lecture for hire. Offers day visits to gardens normally closed to the public, foreign tours to gardens and lectures. Four-day conference held annually.

Gardeners' Sunday
White Witches, 8 Mapstone Close, Glastonbury, Somerset BA6 8EY
Established 1956.
A fund-raising organisation founded specifically to help two old, established charities – The Gardeners' Royal Benevolent Society and The Royal Gardeners' Orphan Fund. A booklet 'Gardens to Visit' is published annually giving details of gardens which are opened to the public in aid of the two charities. Available for 50p from bookshops, 70p including postage from above address.

Gladiolus Breeders Association
Chelsea Avenue, Thorpe, Southend-on-Sea, Essex SS1 2YL
Tel Southend-on-Sea (0702) 68779
Established 1971. Membership 65. Subscription £1 (UK), £1.50 (overseas). Affiliated to RHS via British Gladiolus Society.
Promotes the breeding of new Gladiolus cultivars by amateur British growers. Publishes two newsletters each year. Encourages seed and corm exchange. Gives advice to members. Holds occasional meeting. Exhibits at shows.

The Good Gardeners' Association
Arkley Manor Farm, Rowley Lane, Arkley, Barnet, Hertfordshire EN5 3HS
Tel 01-449 7944
Established 1966. Membership 550. Subscription £7.50.

Attempts to help gardeners with all aspects of organic, minimum work gardening (no purely chemical fertilisers used, no digging). Publishes a bi-annual handbook and a bi-monthly newsletter. Supplies organic garden sundries and organically grown produce. Has a trial ground open to the public. Open day and lecture several times a year.

The Gooseberry Society
Woodview Lodge, 14 Hillary Rise, Barnet, Hertfordshire EN5 5A2
Tel 01-441 3120
A society for professional growers which promotes and protects old and new gooseberry cultivars and varieties. Publishes leaflets and newsletters. Has trial ground. Interested in hearing from people with genuine old varieties in their gardens. Distributes surplus plants to general public at reasonable cost.

The Hardy Plant Society
10 St Barnabas Road, Emmer Green, Caversham, Reading, Berkshire RG4 8RA
Tel Reading (0734) 472816
Established 1957. Membership 2,500. Subscription £4, joint £5. Affiliated to the RHS.
Aims to stimulate interest in hardy herbaceous plants both old and new and to encourage the propagation and distribution of such plants. Issues bi-annual bulletin and four monthly newsletters. Has slide library. Publishes 'Hardy Plant Directory' which lists 3,000 rarer hardy plants and the nurseries that distribute them. Operates plant propagation scheme and seed exchange. Holds both local and national meetings. Exhibits at RHS and other shows.

The Heather Society
7 Rossley Close, Highcliffe, Christchurch, Dorset BH23 4RR
Tel Highcliffe (04252) 72191
Established 1963. Membership 1,500. Subscription £3, family £4.

Publishes a book, plus three news bulletins each year. Has a slide library and holds trials at Harlow Car. Offers free advice to members on cultivation problems. Exhibits twice a year at RHS shows. Local branch meetings; annual conference.

Henry Doubleday Research Association
Convent Lane, Bocking, Braintree, Essex CM7 6RW
Tel Braintree (0376) 24083
Established 1958. Membership 7,000. Subscription £8; unwaged, retired, students £4. Life membership £80.
Researches into, and promotes interest in, organic gardening. Publishes and supplies books and booklets. Offers mail order service for seed, fertilizer, books and safe pesticides. Quarterly newsletter, seed library of unlisted seeds and free advice service available to members. Trial garden open to public. Local branch meetings.

The Herb Club
The Herb Shop, Riverside Place, Thornton, Somerset TA1 1JH
Tel Thornton (0823) 54900
Established 1983. Membership 1,000. Subscription free (£3.50 for newsletter).
Promotes a wider understanding of the cultivation and use of herbs among all those interested in herbs and their related products. Issues a quarterly newsletter. Runs two-day courses on growing and using herbs. Exhibits at agricultural and horticultural shows in the south west of England.

The Herb Society
77 Great Peter Street, London SW1P 2EZ
Tel 01-222 3634
Established 1927. Membership 2,400. Subscription £9.50, overseas £15, under 18 and senior citizens £6.50. Life membership £150.
Promotes the development and continued use of herbs. Disseminates information on herbs

and their history to members. Issues quarterly journal, 'The Herbal Review'. Provides use of library, museum, information service and practical courses to members. Products available from herb farmers and suppliers at preferential discounts. Arranges meetings, lectures, excursions and weekend seminars.

The Institute of Groundsmanship
The Pavilion, Woughton-on-the-Green, Milton Keynes, Buckinghamshire MK6 3EA
Tel Milton Keynes (0908) 663600
Established 1934. Membership 4,000. Subscription £10.
Aims to improve the status of professional groundsmen and to encourage good grass and turf everywhere. Publishes a monthly journal as well as technical/advisory literature. 50 local branches arrange visits, film shows and lectures. Offers training courses and an examination syllabus. Organises annual conference and exhibition. Provides advisory service to general public.

The International Asclepiad Society
10 Moorside Terrace, Drighlington, Bradford BD11 1HX
Tel Drighlington (0532) 852949
Established 1974. Membership 300. Subscription £6.
Promotes the study and propagation of all plants of the Asclepiadaceae. Members receive a journal three times a year. Has a slide library and a seed and plant distribution scheme. Holds annual general meeting. Exhibits at shows.

International Camellia Society
Acorns, Chapel Lane, Bransford, Hereford & Worcester WR6 5JG
Tel Leigh Sinton (0886) 32610
Established 1962. Membership 1,400. Subscription £4.50, family £6. Life membership £90.
Publishes a journal and two

newsletters each year, as well as a 'Beginner's Guide'. Provides advice on cultivation, nomenclature and registration of camellias. Sponsors growing trials and exhibits at RHS shows. Collaborates in establishing National Reference Collection. Holds annual conference and an International Congress every other year.

The International Clematis Society
Burford House, Burford, Tenbury Wells, Hereford & Worcester WR15 8HQ
Established 1984. Membership 250. Subscription £5.
Promotes the exchange of knowledge world-wide on the genus clematis and the distribution of rare species and cultivars. Issues two newsletters each year. Has a seed exchange scheme. Holds a world conference every two years.

International Dendrology Society
Whistley Green Farmhouse, Hurst, nr Reading, Berkshire RG10 0DU
Established 1952. Membership 1,000. Subscription £10. Life membership £100.
Promotes the study and cultivation of woody plants. Aims to preserve and conserve those that are rare, endangered and not commercially available. Publishes a book and two newsletters each year. Holds 4–5 specialised tours a year for members. Has an annual dinner.

Irish Garden Plant Society
c/o National Botanic Gardens, Glasnevin, Dublin 9, Republic of Ireland
Established 1981. Membership 250. Subscription £10 (IR) £8.50 (UK), family £15 (IR) £12.50 (UK).
Aims to conserve Irish garden plants and promote other good garden plants. Publishes a quarterly newsletter, annual journal and occasional other publications. Arranges garden visits, offers seed exchange and plant sales scheme. Holds lectures and annual general meeting. Affiliated to the National

Council for the Conservation of Plants and Gardens. Alternative contact address: c/o Baronscourt, Newtownstewart, Co Tyrone, Northern Ireland.

Lancashire and Cheshire Carnation Society
258 Mosley Common Road, Worsley, Manchester M28 4BP
Tel 061-790 8462
Established 1972. Membership 360. Subscription £1, family £1.50. Affiliated to the RHS.
Promotes new strains of the dianthus group. Largest of the national society's affiliated groups. Exhibits at London, Southport and Harrogate shows among many others.

London Association of Recreational Gardeners
45 The Ridgeway, Kenton, Harrow HA3 0LN
Tel 01-907 2040
Established 1974. Membership 70 organisations and 70 individuals. Subscription individual £2, organisation £10.
Aims to improve the lot of recreational gardens and allotments through campaigns and improved legislation. Publishes four journals a year and information sheets. Has substantial slide library of gardens in UK and Western Europe. Holds symposiums.

The Mammillaria Society
Bramble Cottage, Milton Street, Polegate, East Sussex BN26 5RN
Tel Alfriston (0323) 870630
Established 1960. Membership 600. Subscription £4, family £4.50.
Promotes a wider horticultural and scientific interest in Mammillaria and related genera. Publishes a bi-monthly journal and several booklets. Has an annual offer of seeds. Arranges study groups and has open days to visit members' collections.

The Men of the Trees
Turners Hill Road, Crawley Down,
Crawley, West Sussex RH10 4HL
Tel Copthorne (0342) 712536
*Established 1922. Membership 4,500
(UK). Subscription £8, family £12. Life
membership £100.*
Promotes the planting of trees and
their protection. Publishes journal
twice a year and branch
newsletters. Has a slide library and
an advisory service. Annual general
meeting and lecture. Holds local
branch meetings quarterly.

The Midland Geranium,
Glasshouse and Garden Society
179 Poplar Avenue, Edgbaston,
Birmingham B17 8EJ
Tel 021-429 1947
*Established 1969. Membership 94.
Subscription £1.50.*
Issues newsletters and has monthly
lectures. Holds local branch
meetings. Organises geranium
show in July and fuchsia show in
August.

National Association of Flower
Arrangement Societies of Great
Britain
21 Denbigh Street, London
SW1V 2HF
Tel 01-828 5145
*Established 1959. Membership
100,000. Subscription 50p plus local
club fee.*
Co-ordinates the activities of flower
arrangers and gives advice and
information whenever possible.
Promotes wider interest in flower
arranging, gardening and
knowledge of plants. Publishes
quarterly magazine,
correspondence cards and
instruction leaflets. Has slides for
hire. 1350 local clubs and societies
meet monthly. Practical courses,
competitions, lectures and visits
organised. Annual flower festival
and conference.

National Auricula and Primula
Society (Northern)
146 Queens Road, Cheadle,
Cheshire SK8 5HY
Tel 061-485 6371
*Established 1872. Membership 400.
Subscription £3, family £3.50.*
Encourages the growing and
showing of auriculas and primulas.
Publishes a year book and
newsletter. Exhibits at shows.

National Auricula and Primula
Society (Southern)
67 Wareham Court Road,
Carshalton Beeches, Surrey
SM5 3ND
*Established 1876. Membership 550.
Subscription £2, family £3. Affiliated
to RHS.*
Aims to encourage, improve and
extend the breeding and cultivation
of auriculas and hardy primulas.
Publishes a year book and
newsletter. Offers illustrated
lectures to horticultural societies in
the south of England. Holds plant
sales. Has two spring shows and
exhibits at RHS Westminster Show.
Annual autumn meeting.

National Begonia Society
3 Gladstone Road, Dorridge,
Solihull, West Midlands B93 8BX
Tel Knowle (056 45) 6323
*Established 1948. Membership 1,000.
Subscription £2, family £3. Affiliated
to RHS.*
Publishes three bulletins and three
newsletters each year. Cultural
handbook issued to new members.
Keeps a large number of slides and
has produced a film on begonia
culture. Arranges lectures,
shows and exhibits.

National Bonsai Society
24 Bidston Road, Liverpool L4 7XJ
Tel 051-263 5259
*Established 1973. Membership 1,500.
Subscription £2.*
Publishes booklets and a quarterly
journal. Issues a handbook on
joining. Has both a book and slide
library. Holds monthly meetings
and demonstrations. Organises
own shows and exhibits at others.

National Chrysanthemum Society
2 Lucas House, Craven Road,
Rugby, Warwickshire CV21 3HY
Tel Rugby (0788) 69039
Established 1846. Membership 8,000.
Subscription £9, family £11. Affiliated
to RHS.
Aims to develop the raising of
chrysanthemums and advise
growers on registration and
classification. Publishes a year book
and several bulletins. Has slides for
hire. 1,200 affiliated societies. Has
use of trial grounds at Wisley. Large
national shows, annual
conferences.

National Council for the
Conservation of Plants and
Gardens
Wisley Garden, Woking, Surrey
GU23 6QB
Tel Guildford (0483) 224234
Established 1978. Membership 3,000.
Subscription: arranged by local branch
group.
Aims to conserve and promote
good garden plants – those which
are rare in the wild, are historically
important, have distinctive
properties or are important for
future breeding. Encourages public
awareness of threats to cultivated
plants and gardens. Publishes
newsletter twice a year. 34 local
groups issue own newsletters and
arrange own activities; carry out
surveys of nurseries and particular
plants; propagate and distribute
unusual plants; arrange lectures,
garden visits and social events for
members. Encourages the setting
up of National Collections of
plants.

National Dahlia Society
26 Burns Road, Lillington,
Leamington Spa CV32 7ER
Tel Leamington Spa (0926) 22097
Established 1881. Membership 3,000.
Subscription £5.98, family £6.50. Life
membership £40.
Issues two books each year. Holds
shows, trials and conferences.
Maintains judges list.

National Gardens Scheme
(Charitable Trust)
57 Lower Belgrave Street, London
SW1W 0LR
Tel 01-730 0359
Arranges for gardens to open to the
public – all proceeds go to the
four charities the scheme supports:
the National Trust, Queen's
Nursing Home, Cancer Relief,
Nurses' Welfare Service. Annual
publication 'Gardens of England
and Wales open to the public' is
published in March. It lists
participating gardens and is
available at newsagents for 80p, or
direct from above address for £1.35,
including p&p.

National Pot Leek Society
23 Beanley Place, High Heaton,
Newcastle-upon-Tyne NE7 7DQ
Tel Newcastle-upon-Tyne
(0632) 811782
Established 1978. Membership 400.
Subscription £5.
Encourages the culture of leeks
through competition and
exhibition. Publishes occasional
newsletters, plus a year book. Has a
slide library. Provides advice
service by phone to interested
members of the public. Holds
'talk-ins' and committee meetings.

National Society of Allotment and
Leisure Gardeners
22 High Street, Flitwick, Bedford
MK45 1DT
Tel Flitwick (0525) 712361
Established 1930. Membership 1,300
individuals, 1,500 allotment
associations, 200 local authorities and
schools. Subscription: individuals £4,
local authorities £6, associations 25p a
member; plus 10p for each individual or
association. Life membership £10.50.
Aims to help everyone enjoy the
recreation of gardening by
encouraging the formation of
gardening associations,
safeguarding their interest through
improved legislation and generally
assisting amateur gardeners.
Publishes a quarterly bulletin and

horticultural leaflets. Has a seed scheme. A conference report is published annually.

The National Sweet Pea Society
Acacia Cottage, Down Ampney, Cirencester, Gloucestershire GL7 5QW
Tel Swindon (0793) 750385
Established 1901. Membership 1,500. Subscription £7, family £10. Life membership £100.
Publishes year book, spring and autumn bulletins, 'How to Grow Sweet Peas' booklet. Slides available for hire. Lectures given to affiliated societies. Sweet Pea trials held at RHS Trial Grounds, Wisley. Holds national and provincial shows and exhibits at other shows. Annual general meeting.

The National Trust for Places of Historic Interest or Natural Beauty
36 Queen Anne's Gate, London SWIH 9AS
Tel 01-222 9251
Established 1895. Membership 1.13 million. Subscription £12.50, family £25.00. Life membership £300.
Aims to conserve places of historic interest or natural beauty. Issues leaflets and newsletters and has a slide library. 130 local centres organise lectures and functions. Membership allows free admission to properties, including over 100 gardens and 20 national plant collections.

The National Trust for Scotland
5 Charlotte Square, Edinburgh EH2 4DU
Tel 031-226 5922
Established 1931. Membership 126,000. Subscription £12, family £20. Life membership £170.
Aims to conserve places of historic interest or natural beauty. Issues a year book and a quarterly magazine. Membership includes free admission to all properties and gardens. Their 'Gardening Advice Centre', Greenbank House, Clarkston, Glasgow G76 8RB, offers

an advice service, plant sales and courses in gardening and plant identification.

National Vegetable Society
29 Revidge Road, Blackburn, Lancashire BB2 6JB
Tel Blackburn (0254) 64989
Established 1960. Membership 3,000. Subscription £3, family £4. Affiliated to RHS.
Aims to advance the culture, study and improvement of vegetables. Publishes a year book, leaflets and a quarterly newsletter. Has book and slide library. Has trial grounds at Harlow Car, Harrogate and Cardiff. Organises lectures and visits to places of interest. Local branch meetings. Stages local competitions and a yearly national championship.

National Viola and Pansy Society
16 George Street, Handsworth, Birmingham B21 OEG
Established 1907. Membership 150. Subscription 75p.
Promotes the growing of exhibition violas and pansies, show pansies, bedding violas and pansies, and violettas. Publishes leaflets, gives first-class and award of merit certificates to new varieties. Holds meetings in Birmingham.

North of England Orchid Society
41 Whitbarrow Road, Lymm, Cheshire WA13 9AW
Tel Lymm (092 575) 3662
Established 1897. Membership 150. Subscription £5, family £5.
Publishes quarterly news sheet. Has library plus slides. Holds monthly meetings (includes shows and talks). Has own system of awards. Arranges visits and offers free expert advice. Exhibits at some public shows and British Council Congresses.

The North of England Pansy and Viola Society
27 Fir Avenue, Ravensthorpe, Dewsbury, West Yorkshire WF13 3B

Tel Mirfield (0924) 492621
Established 1915. Membership 80.
Subscription £1.
Promotes the growing and showing of pansies and violas. Introduces new varieties and conserves old varieties. Publishes yearly journal. Helps members obtain stock. Holds annual show in Bradford.

North of England Rose, Carnation and Sweet Pea Society
'Rosecarpe', 17 Low Gosforth Court, Newcastle-upon-Tyne NE3 5QU
Tel Newcastle-upon-Tyne (0632) 366983
Established 1938. Membership 300.
Subscription £1.
Holds monthly meetings with lectures and slide shows; organises trips. Produces newsletters and an annual. Free advice to members. Annual show in conjunction with Tyneside Summer Exhibition.

North Wales Horticultural Society
Zanadu, 2 Bryn Eglwys, Flint Mountain, Flint, Clwyd CH6 5SN
Tel Flint (035 26) 91346
Established 1962. Membership 200.
Subscription £1 or £2. Affiliated to RHS.
Encourages interest in horticulture and publishes items relating to horticulture in North Wales in an occasional journal. Produces newsletter and holds monthly meetings. Has panel of experts to solve problems.

Northern Horticultural Society
Harlow Car Gardens, Crag Lane, Harrogate HG3 1QB
Tel Harrogate (0423) 65418
Established 1948. Membership 7,000.
Subscription £10. Life membership £150.
Publishes leaflets and a quarterly magazine 'The Northern Gardener'. Has study centre and library. Has trial ground and seed exchange scheme. Offers educational facility which organises demonstrations

and exhibitions. Membership allows free entrance to Harlow Car Gardens. Specialist groups organise meetings and excursions.

The Orchid Society of Great Britain
28 Felday, Lewisham, London SE13 7HJ
Tel 01-690 4519
Established 1951. Membership 1,500.
Subscription £5.50. Affiliated to RHS.
Publishes a quarterly journal and new members receive a cultural handbook. Has a book and slide library and operates a plant distribution scheme. Holds ten meetings each year. Organises demonstrations and shows, gives awards.

Royal Caledonian Horticultural Society
3 West Newington Place, Edinburgh EH9 1QT
Tel 031-667 0654
Established 1809. Membership 1,000.
Subscription individual £5, business £10, students at horticultural college £1, juveniles 50p. Affiliated to RHS.
A horticultural society geared mainly to the amateur. Supplies books, booklets and an annual journal. Has use of library at Royal Botanic Gardens, Edinburgh. Organises five outings each summer. Has two meetings a month from September–April. Holds own shows, exhibits at others.

Royal Forestry Society of England, Wales and Northern Ireland
102 High Street, Tring, Hertfordshire HP23 4AH
Tel Tring (044 282) 2028
Established 1882. Membership 4,500.
Subscription non-professional £8.
Aims to advance knowledge and practice of forestry and arboriculture. Publishes quarterly journal. Library and slide library. 19 local groups. Holds meetings at home and abroad and arranges visits. Annual study tour.

The Royal Horticultural Society

80 Vincent Square, London
SW1P 2PE
Tel 01-834 4333
Established 1804. Membership 80,000.
Subscription £24 including two tickets
to Chelsea Flower Show, or £14 with
one ticket, plus £5 enrolment fee.
Publishes books, booklets,
yearbooks on daffodils and
rhododendrons and monthly
journal. Has library, lecture set of
slides, seed distribution scheme,
gardens and trial grounds at
Wisley, Surrey. Gives lectures at
shows, arranges demonstrations,
holds shows and presents awards.
Lily, rhododendron and fruit
groups. Affiliated societies receive
6 free tickets to Chelsea and
Westminster Flower Shows, copy of
monthly journal and reduced rates
to Wisley Gardens.

Royal Horticultural Society of Ireland

Thomas Prior House, RDS,
Merrion Road, Dublin 4
Tel Dublin (0001) 684358
Established 1830. Membership 1,250.
Subscription £12.50. Life membership
£150. Affiliated to RHS.
Promotes good gardening.
Arranges garden tours at home and
abroad. Holds illustrated talks,
shows and plant sales.

The Royal National Rose Society

Chiswell Green, St Albans,
Hertfordshire AL2 3NR
Tel St Albans (0727) 50461
Established 1876. Membership 25,000.
Subscription £7, students £5,
family £9.
Issues a quarterly journal and
publishes several handbooks. Has
slide, film and book library. Holds
own shows and exhibition. Branch
meetings held by 1,000 affiliated
horticultural societies.
Headquarters at St Albans has
show gardens and trial grounds
open to members and general
public.

Royal Scottish Forestry Society

1 Rothersay Terrace, Edinburgh
EH3 7UP
Tel 031-226 3157
Established 1854. Membership 1,800.
Subscription non-professional £7.
Encourages the advancement of
forestry in all branches. Publishes
quarterly journal. Has library and
employment register for members.
Hold annual conference and
occasional visits overseas. Six
regional groups hold meetings and
excursions. Exhibits at Royal
Highland Show and other local
shows.

Royal Society for Nature Conservation

The Green, Nettleham, Lincoln
LN2 2NR
Tel Lincoln (0522) 752326
Established 1912. Membership
155,000. Subscription varies between
local groups (£4–£10).
Promotes nature conservation.
Comprises 46 local Nature
Conservation Trusts which own
and manage nature reserves. They
publish newsletters, hold meetings,
advise on conservation problems,
sell wild flower seeds. Central body
will supply addresses for local
trusts and produces thrice yearly
magazine.

Saintpaulia and Houseplant Society

82 Rossmore Court, Park Road,
London NW1 6XY
Established 1968. Membership 600.
Subscription £2, family £2.50.
Affiliated to RHS.
Aims to bring together people
interested in growing and caring for
Saintpaulias and other houseplants.
Issues quarterly bulletin, list of
Saintpaulia varieties and pamphlets
on specialised subjects. Has library
and exchange scheme for
propagating material. Organises
society outings.

Scottish Begonia Society

Clydebridge Lodge, Greenacres
Estate, Motherwell ML1 3BH
Tel Motherwell (0698) 51033
*Established 1936. Membership 320.
Subscription £2.*
Publishes four newsletters each
year. Issues leaflets for beginners.
Has a slide library and a video on
growing begonias. Named varieties
available at reasonable prices.
Holds four public meetings with
lectures. Exhibits at shows.

Scotland's Gardens Scheme

31 Castle Terrace, Edinburgh
EH1 2EL
Tel 031-229 1870
Established 1931.
Opens gardens throughout
Scotland for charity. Annual
booklet of details. All size gardens
welcome.

Scottish Gladiolus Society

63 Gardiner Road, Edinburgh
EH4 3RL
Tel 031-332 3681
*Established 1972. Membership 75.
Subscription £1.*
As part of British Gladiolus Society
supplies a journal and slide library
as well as participating in national
shows and international trials.
Locally, produces newsletter and
provides lectures and advice.
Distributes cormlets and arranges
bulk order of gladioli. Holds own
show and takes part in others.

Scottish National Sweet Pea, Rose and Carnation Society

'Rosebank', 7 Brown Street,
Motherwell, Strathclyde ML1 1LJ
Tel Motherwell (0698) 61655
*Established 1893. Membership 200.
Subscription £1.50.*
Produces newsletter. Slide library
and seed exchange. Holds branch
meetings and annual conference.
Exhibits at shows. Has trial ground
for sweet peas at Bellahouton Park,
Glasgow, testing seed from many
countries.

Scottish Rock Garden Club

21 Merchiston Park, Edinburgh
EH10 4PW
Tel 031-229 8138
*Established 1933. Membership 3,500.
Subscription £5, family £6. Life
membership £100. Affiliated to RHS.*
Promotes interest in and
knowledge of alpine plants and
shrubs from world wide locations.
Publishes bi-annual journal and
newsletter. Has a slide library and
seed exchange scheme. Holds
art/photographic competition twice
yearly. Holds other shows as well
as exhibiting generally. Local
branch meetings, annual
conference.

Seed Exchange

44 Albion Road, Sutton, Surrey
SM2 5TF
*Established 1978. Membership 200.
Subscription £2, unemployed £1.50,
organisations £2.50.*
Promotes survival and use of wild
plants in modern world. Annual
newsletter and list of seeds
available for exchange and
purchase. Seed search available.
Seed stored in Seed Bank.

Sempervivum Society

11 Wingle Tye Road, Burgess Hill,
West Sussex RH15 9HR
Tel Burgess Hill (04446) 6848
*Established 1970. Membership 400.
Subscription £5.50, institutions and
colleges £12.50 (receive three sets of
publications). Affiliated to RHS.*
Publishes and supplies books and
booklets, some at reduced rates.
Issues four journals a year and
occasional newsletters. Has book
and slide library and plant
distribution scheme. Trial ground at
Burgess Hill. Holds shows and has
open days at members' gardens.

Society for Horticultural Therapy

Goulds Ground, Vallis Way,
Frome, Somerset BA11 3DW
Tel Frome (0373) 64782

Established 1978. Membership 800. Subscription £8.
Helps the disabled and handicapped to enjoy and benefit from gardening and horticulture. Publishes quarterly magazine. Offers library, information and advice services, as well as short courses and training. Land use volunteers run special projects. Demonstration gardens at Syon and Battersea Parks. Local voluntary gardening advisers.

The Soil Association
Walnut Tree Manor, Haughley, Stowmarket, Suffolk IP14 3RS
Tel Stowmarket (0449) 673235
Established 1946. Membership 4,500. Subscription £10, family £15. Life membership £200. Affiliated to RHS.
Promotes organic farming and gardening, care for the soil, as well as general nutrition and health. Publishes a quarterly review, membership news and booklist. Has a bookshop and reference library. Exhibits at various shows and holds annual general meeting.

The Tradescant Trust
Museum of Garden History, St Mary-at-Lambeth, Lambeth Palace Road, London SE1 7JU
Tel 01-261 1891
Established 1977. Membership 2,000. Subscription £2. Affiliated to RHS.
Promotes interest in the history of gardening. Produces quarterly newsletter. Holds talks, fairs, slide-shows and exhibitions.

The Tree Council
Agriculture House, Knightsbridge, London SW1X 7NJ
Tel 01-235 8854
Established 1974. Membership 30 organisations. Subscription not applicable. £10 plus donation to become 'Friend of the Tree Council'.
Promotes planting and care of trees.

Organises National Tree Week and supports local groups. Monitors national tree problems. Produces newsletter.

Wakefield and North of England Tulip Society
67 Beverley Road, South Cave, Brough, North Humberside HU15 2BB
Tel North Cave (043 02) 3384
Established 1835. Membership 100. Subscription £1.
Aims to cultivate and exhibit the English Florist Tulip. Produces newsletter. Holds meetings and an annual show. Occasional bulb distribution.

Women's Farm and Garden Association
175 Gloucester Street, Cirencester, Gloucestershire GL7 2DP
Established 1899. Membership 300. Subscription £5, students £2.50.
Aims to unite all women involved or interested in agriculture, horticulture and allied subjects. Produces newsletter and leaflets. Holds residential conferences and regional meetings. Annual travel bursary. Men welcome to join.

The Woodland Trust
36 Westgate, Grantham, Lincolnshire NG31 6LL
Tel Grantham (0476) 74297
Established 1972. Membership 40,000. Subscription £5. Life membership £100. Affiliated to RHS.
Aims to safeguard native woodlands through acquisition and to plant trees and create woods. Operates 'Plant a Tree' scheme, whereby a tree is planted specifically on behalf of a member of the public. Issues a booklet, a directory of Trust Woodlands (including maps), and regular newsletters.

4 Buying tools and equipment

Introduction

The advertising industry has made most of us keenly aware that there are lots of differences between different makes and types of lawnmower. But the more mundane tools are frequently taken for granted – one garden fork seems much like the next at first glance, and what could be more down-to-earth and uncomplicated than a spade?

When you look at the price tags and see that you can pay more than twice as much for one spade than for another, and that the biggest difference between some of the trowels seems to lie in the packaging and the price, it's natural to wonder whether many of the differences lie more in presentation and visual appeal than in the efficiency of the tool.

It does pay to choose your tools carefully though. **Quality** of materials will show in the length of time they last – spades and forks may last for your gardening lifetime, while tools such as secateurs will last for decades with care and maintenance. **Good design** will show itself in ease and comfort of use, especially during a long spell of gardening, and in how well the tool actually does the job. Stainless steel tools cost a lot more than ordinary carbon steel, but may be worth considering if appearance is important to you – they don't rust, are easy to clean and may retain their edge a bit longer than ordinary steel.

Some tools are more vital than others of course – you can garden for a lifetime and never possess a dibber, yet you could hardly manage without a spade, and it might be better to buy a few good quality, really useful tools if resources are limited than to buy a lot of tools that may be of more doubtful benefit. In the following section we have suggested a basic tool kit, and what you are likely to have to pay for it. And in the pages that follow we have grouped the tools by use wherever possible. For instance you'll find digging and cultivating tools together, and lawncare aids grouped so that you can decide on the best tool for the job – sometimes one tool might be adequate instead of two.

In the description for each tool it is only possible to give a brief account of what's available, and sufficient guidelines to tell you what to look for. Often, however, it will be impossible to know how well a particular brand will perform in use: you won't be able to tell how hard the steel is (and therefore how long a blade is likely to remain sharp), or how strong a handle is (you can hardly test it to breaking point in the shop!). You can really only make this sort of judgement by testing, and where **Gardening from Which?** has done comparative testing, we have indicated this at the end of each section, giving the issue in which the report appeared.

Back numbers are available but only to subscribers to **Gardening from Which?**. Write stating which month you'd like and enclosing £2.50 (cheque/PO payable to Consumers' Association) to **Gardening from Which?**, 2 Castlemead, Gascoyne Way, Hertford SG14 1LH. Where we mention gardeners' preferences or results of trials, these are based on testing carried out for **Gardening from Which?**

SHOPPING AROUND FOR TOOLS

You will usually find the largest range of tools in garden centres, but it's also worth looking in good ironmongers' shops, supermarkets and DIY superstores, as well as discount houses. These often have very competitively priced tools, albeit a limited range. Many of them offer power tools at a substantial discount over the manufacturer's suggested price.

'Own brand' tools made for supermarkets and chain stores may be well worth considering. **Gardening from Which?** tests have often shown these to be good value for money.

The basic toolkit

In this part of the Guide, we've tried to cover most of the tools that you are likely to find in shops and garden centres, but you only **need** a small proportion of these in most gardens. Many of the tools are useful, but you can manage without them if you want to avoid a heavy expenditure, and some are very specialised and required only if you have a specific need. For specialised items used only very occasionally (such as a post-hole borer) you are probably better off hiring.

To give you an idea of how much it is likely to cost you to build up a basic toolkit, we've given an approximate price that you may have to pay for each tool. We have based the figures on the cost of the cheapest recommended brand or the 'best buy' where **Gardening from Which?** has reviewed the tools; and an average price for tools not yet tested. You may, of course, have to pay more for a particular feature that you like. The figures are based on 1985 prices; don't forget to allow for inflation.

Compression sprayer £11
Digging fork £16.50
Dutch hoe £7.50
Gardening gloves £3.50
Hedging shears £11
(can also be used for lawn edging)

Lawnmower
   Hand £35
   Electric cylinder £100
   Electric rotary £90

Lawnmower *cont.*
   Electric hover £84
   Petrol cylinder £270
   Petrol rotary £176
   Petrol hover £230

Rake £7.50
Secateurs £11.50
Spade £15
Trowel £2.50
Watering can, 2 gallon £5

Likely cost of basic toolkit £126 to £361 (depending on type of mower chosen).

PRIORITY EXTRAS

You will probably be able to manage without the following tools, but they should make life a lot easier and may be essential in a large garden.

Hose pipe with fittings £7.50
Lawn rake £7 (powered £50)
Nylon line trimmer £53.50
Electric hedgetrimmer £64
Pruning saw £11 or loppers £17
Sprinkler £10
Wheelbarrow £13

Likely cost of priority extras £166 to £215.

Tools for the less able gardener

Do you have trouble gripping tools? Or perhaps your back isn't as strong as it used to be. Gardening can be a strenuous hobby, but using appropriate tools and techniques can make a lot of difference. In fact it is a hobby enjoyed by even the most severely disabled as well as gardeners who are not as fit as they would like to be.

Many of the tools mentioned in this book can be used by less able gardeners, though in some cases special tools or adaptations are required.

If you need help or advice in deciding which tools might be suitable, and what special aids there are available, it is worth contacting one of the following organisations:

Mary Marlborough Lodge *Nuffield Orthopaedic Centre, Headington, Oxford OX3 7LD.*

The Society for Horticultural Therapy *Goulds Ground, Vallis Way, Frome, Somerset BA11 3DW.*

After many years of research, Mary Marlborough Lodge has produced a book, **Leisure and Gardening,** *one in a series on equipment for the disabled. The gardening section starts with garden design which suggests ways of simplifying work and providing easy access in your garden. It then deals with techniques and tools and accessories – mostly everyday equipment, but with some tools which are specially designed and other do-it-yourself ideas for adapting tools to make them easier to use. Recommendations concerning tools to buy are related to different types of disability.*

Leisure and Gardening *can be obtained for £3.50 plus packing and postage from Equipment for the Disabled, Mary Marlborough Lodge, at the address given above. Do not send any money with your order; you will be sent an invoice. A leaflet is also available free of charge listing suggested gardening tools for disabled people and giving the names and addresses of the manufacturers. Write stating what your problem is, enclosing a stamped addressed envelope, and you will be sent the appropriate list.*

Digging and cultivating tools

SPADES

Digging spades have a blade about 29cm x 19cm (11½in x 7½in), but you can also buy smaller types such as border spades. These generally dig about 20 to 23cm (8 to 9in) deep, and are intended for digging in borders or around shrubs, but if you find an ordinary spade hard to handle it might be worth considering one of these for general digging. You may also find 'junior' or 'medium' spades, which come somewhere between the other two in size.

Weight and balance are both important but this is often a matter of personal taste. Try handling various spades in the shop, and avoid any that feel too heavy or too light at the blade end. Hold them as if you were digging. If you want a blade with a tread (trials have shown that treads are usually preferred), this will narrow your choice. If you want a stainless steel spade you will have to accept one without a tread.

Years ago there were many different forms of hilt, most of them regional variations, but nowadays you are unlikely to have any option other than the D or Y type. In practical terms these are similar to use. It is the materials used, and the dimension of the hilt that will affect comfort most. The real test is to make sure that the grip is wide enough for your hands. If you wear gloves while digging in the winter, try to hold the grip while wearing a pair of gloves.

Finally, slide your hand down the shaft to make sure the rivets are flush with the socket and that there are no sharp edges at the top of the socket to catch your fingers.

You will not be able to judge the strength of the spade very easily just by looking at it. In tests, wooden handles have generally done less well than metal ones, but the best have been as good as metal.

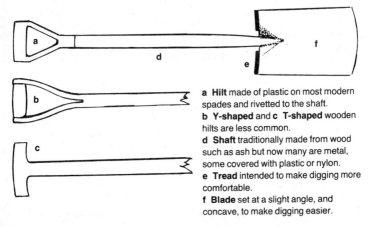

a **Hilt** made of plastic on most modern spades and rivetted to the shaft.
b **Y-shaped** and c **T-shaped** wooden hilts are less common.
d **Shaft** traditionally made from wood such as ash but now many are metal, some covered with plastic or nylon.
e **Tread** intended to make digging more comfortable.
f **Blade** set at a slight angle, and concave, to make digging easier.

The least expensive spades are usually made from pressed steel. These are unlikely to last as long as those made from hardened or toughened steel. Stainless steel reduces the friction as you dig, and resists rust; whether you think these advantages are worth the considerably higher price probably depends on how much digging you do.

Ordinary spades were reviewed in **Gardening from Which?** *November 1983. Unusual spades and forks are also available, for example, those with long handles or some sort of lever arrangement designed to reduce back-strain, but these have not been tested.*

FORKS

There are special forks for lifting potatoes (these have flat, broad tines) and border forks with a head as small as 22cm x 14cm (8¾in x 5½in), but the normal digging fork with a head at least 29cm (11½in) long and 20cm (8in) wide is the most useful one. As with the spades, however, it may be worth considering a border fork, or one of the intermediate 'medium', or 'youth' forks if you find that digging with the normal size is too heavy.

It's worth handling as many different forks as possible in the shop. Some will feel better to you than others, though as far as weight and balance are concerned you are not likely to find any great differences.

Traditionally the shaft of forks was made from ash or hickory, but now they are often plastic-coated metal. The choice between a wooden or metal shaft is a matter of personal preference. Metal shafts are not necessarily stronger than wooden ones and at least you can replace a wood one easily if it breaks. However if you leave a wooden one out in the rain a lot, it may become less comfortable to use where the lacquer cracks or flakes off.

Check that the joint between the socket and shaft is flush, with no sharp edges or projecting rivets. With a wooden handle watch out for any rough areas.

The hilt (where you put your hand) should be comfortable – if you garden in gloves, don't forget to allow for these.

If you want a fork for occasional light digging, strength is not very important, and a normal carbon steel head should be perfectly adequate and will last a lifetime with care. Stainless steel penetrates the soil more easily but you will be paying perhaps twice the price for it.

Garden forks were reviewed in **Gardening from Which?** *December 1982.*

RAKES

Part of the basic toolkit, a rake is essential for forming a level surface for sowing seeds or planting. It won't be used a lot, but you still need one that will do an efficient job and be comfortable to use.

Quality rakes generally have angular rather than rounded teeth – about a dozen in number. You can buy stainless steel rakes, but unless you want to indulge in a little luxury it is better to put the extra money towards other garden tools.

As with hoes, you will probably find plastic-coated tubular aluminium handles the most comfortable to use. It is worth handling a few rakes in the shop to see which length of handle causes the least stooping and feels most comfortable.

HOES

Hoes seem to attract the attention of designers more than most tools – if you look around you'll find lots of variations on the traditional hoes. Generally they have only marginal, if any, benefits over the long-established Dutch and draw hoes.

Dutch hoes are designed primarily for slicing off weeds at ground level, or for breaking up the soil surface and hoeing in fertilisers. The traditional Dutch hoe has a flat blade attached to two arms. The blade is usually angled slightly so that it works more or less parallel to the soil surface, and is sharpened on the pushing edge. It is ideal for hoeing but no use for earthing up, and a little awkward for taking out seed drills.

Push-pull hoes are used in much the same way as a Dutch hoe but they have two cutting edges (three in the case of the Wilkinson Sword Swoe), sometimes with a wavy edge which is supposed to increase the cutting surface. As you normally hoe with a push-pull movement the second cutting edge gives you another slice at the soil on the return stroke. However, if you have not let the weeds become too large, they should already have been sliced off on the push stroke.

Draw hoes are intended mainly for earthing up (drawing the soil up into ridges) around crops such as potatoes and celery. They are also good for making seed drills, covering seeds and thinning out unwanted seedlings.

You can use a draw hoe for weeding by using a chopping motion, but since you have to move forwards as you work, you either have to stand to one side of the ground you have just hoed or trample on it, so a Dutch hoe is better.

Variations include hoes with a **triangular** blade, and those with a **mattock-type** head, some of which have prongs on the opposite side which you can use for breaking up soil. The triangular type is particularly useful for taking out drills, and the mattock-type with prongs for breaking up hard ground.

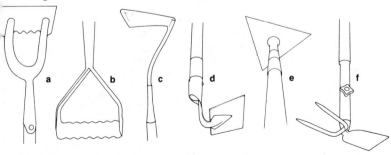

a Dutch hoe   b Push-pull hoe   c Wilkinson Sword Swoe   d Draw hoe
e Triangular hoe   f Mattock-type hoe

An **onion hoe** is like a swan-necked draw hoe on a short handle about 75cm (2ft 6in) long. It is intended for use with one hand and was used extensively in the past for weeding around onions.

There are plenty of other hoe designs which can look attractive, but we suggest that you try one out first if possible before buying. Gardeners generally find that a conventional hoe is just as easy to use, and in many cases is more efficient.

What to look for

First decide which **type** of hoe you need. It's worth investing in a good Dutch hoe for hoeing, though gardeners have also found the Wilkinson Sword Swoe good for weeding. Occasional earthing up can always be done with a spade, but if you grow potatoes regularly, or other crops that need earthing up, it is also worth investing in a draw hoe.

Do not be influenced by minor uses such as how easy it will be to take out seed drills – a job for which you can use a rake or even a stick.

Blades For hoeing between rows or among plants the width of blade can be important. If you want to cover as much ground as possible along straight, wide rows (perhaps in the vegetable plot), a wide blade will be quicker; but for hoeing around plants that are close together, perhaps in beds or borders, a narrow blade will be easier to use.

The Swoe is particularly good for weeding among plants because it has three cutting edges and its small head on an angled neck makes it very manoeuvrable.

Most blades are made from carbon steel, which is perfectly adequate. Stainless steel blades are available, and these may make a hoe slightly easier to use and to keep clean, although the benefits for a hoe are not great.

Handles A few hoes are sold without handles, but an ordinary broom handle should fit. Some ranges are designed to fit a special handle that can be used with other tool heads (see COMBINATION TOOLS, page 421).

The vast majority of hoes come complete with a handle which is likely to be between 1.3 and 1.7m (4ft 4in and 5ft 7in) long. The right height will depend on two things: your height and the angle of the blade. Give the hoe a 'dry run' in the shop. It should feel comfortable, and you should not have to stoop to use it.

The handle is likely to be either wooden or coated tubular aluminium or aluminium alloy. You will probably find the plastic-coated tubular aluminium handles the most comfortable to use, but a plastic handgrip is unlikely to be a great asset. If left outside, varnished wooden handles are likely to deteriorate in appearance and become less pleasant to handle once the varnish starts to flake.

Hoes were reviewed in **Gardening from Which?** *June 1984.*

Stainless steel tools cost a lot more than ordinary carbon steel, but may be worth considering if appearance is important to you – they don't rust, are easy to clean and may retain their edge a bit longer than ordinary steel.

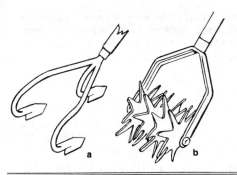

a Hand cultivators usually have three or five prongs. With some you can remove the central prongs to straddle a row of plants.
b Soil surface cultivators are intended only for producing a fine tilth, for sowing seeds for instance.

HAND CULTIVATORS

You should not need a hand cultivator unless you have an area of open soil to cultivate, such as a vegetable plot. It is unlikely to solve as many problems as you expect. On heavy soil they are useful for breaking down clods and loosening compacted soil, but it's very hard work. And on light soil they should not be necessary. Most hand cultivators have a head with three or five curved prongs (tines) but with some you can remove or add tines to make the tool more adaptable. By removing the middle one or three tines, for instance, it is possible to straddle a row of seedlings to cultivate the soil either side.

Tools with star-shaped rotors are sometimes called cultivators, but they are only intended for surface preparation, and are unnecessary on many soils. They break the soil down into a fine tilth for sowing, but you can achieve the same result with a rake and hoe.

Wheeled cultivators consist of a wheel-mounted toolbar with long handles. You can attach cultivating tines, hoe blades, or a small plough. This type of cultivator is really only necessary on, say, a large vegetable plot, and even then usually works best on light or well-cultivated soil. In the right conditions they can be useful for ridging or hoeing between rows.

MECHANICAL CULTIVATORS

Before you buy a cultivator, consider whether hiring one might be a better idea (see page 456); it's an expensive item if you are only going to use it for a couple of days a year. Even if you think it is probably worth the investment, think about hiring one for a day to see how you get on with it if you haven't used a cultivator before – even the versatile types have limits to what they can do for you, and they can be heavy and tiring to use.

Petrol or electric?

Electric-powered cultivators are generally cheaper than those with a petrol engine, and are quieter and cleaner to use. Maintenance is also easier. The drawbacks are lack of power and the problem of a trailing cable: not only must you keep it behind you, but also prevent it pulling diagonally across the plot where it might damage plants. And, of course, you need to be near a power supply.

417

A petrol-powered cultivator can be used where there is no power supply, and there is a much wider choice of models, which are likely to be more powerful and offer a bigger range of attachments. The price you pay is an increased initial financial outlay, and the inconvenience of more maintenance, noise, and fumes.

Where should the engine be?

Mid-engine cultivators have the engine directly over the rotors and are the most common type. The weight over the rotors helps them to penetrate the ground. But because the rotors have to haul the cultivator along as well as cultivate the soil, controlling the machine can be difficult.

Rear-engined cultivators have wheels on the back and the rotors are attached to a boom-like extension. You use these by sweeping the boom from side to side as you push the cultivator forward. The narrow shape makes them particularly useful for cultivating between rows. You can also dig a hole with this type.

Front-engined cultivators have powered wheels below the engine and cultivating tines at the rear. This makes them easy to control and less tiring to use, but only the more expensive models (starting at around £500) are of this type.

What jobs do you want to do?

Be clear about what you want your cultivator to do: whether you want it primarily for cultivating (remember it won't do such a good job as a spade, as it will only turn over and mix the top 10 to 20cm/4 to 8in or so of soil), for

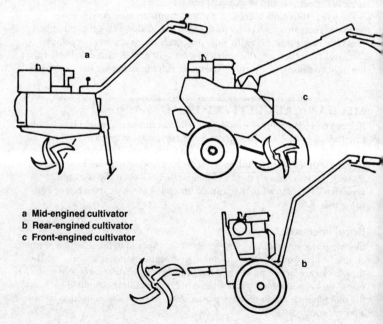

a **Mid-engined cultivator**
b **Rear-engined cultivator**
c **Front-engined cultivator**

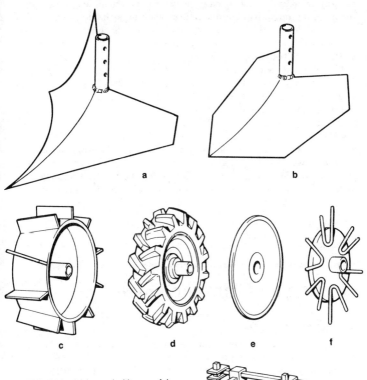

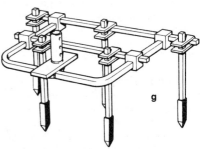

a **Ploughs** are only used with powerful machines, and are only needed for a large garden where you want to turn over the soil for the winter.

b **Ridgers** (furrowers) look like twin-bladed ploughs and are used for earthing up, or for taking out a wide drill or trench.

c **Spade-lug wheels** grip wet ground or snow – fitted in place of rotors when using tool frame, plough, snow blade etc.

d **Rubber-tyred wheels** fitted in place of rotors when using tool frame, ridger etc.

e **Plant guard** (crop shield) fitted outside rotors to protect plants when cultivating between rows.

f **Finger rotor** (fine rotor) replaces standard rotors to produce fine tilth for seeds or for shallow mixing of fertilisers.

g **Tool frame** fitted in place of rear skid, may be a single bar or more complex – usually supplied with a range of tools for harrowing, hoeing etc.

Digger blades (slasher rotors) break up the ground initially.

Hoe blades are intended for keeping the ground clear of weeds.

Pick blades with flat, arrow-like heads are used for breaking up a hard, compacted surface.

Weeders (usually found on the smaller machines with a boom) break up the soil and can be used for keeping the ground clear of weeds.

cultivating between growing crops (using it as a mechanical hoe), for turning over rough, hard ground or to provide a fine tilth for sowing seeds. Don't be influenced by attachments that you are unlikely to use.

If you want to cultivate right up to a fence, or where there is no turning space, the ability to reverse might be useful.

The handles should be adjustable, but if you are trying out the 'feel' in a shop, bear in mind that the head will drop as the rotors bite into the ground in use. If you want to cultivate alongside a fence, the ability to offset the handles at an angle could be useful.

Safety

The clutch should have a deadman's handle control. If it is one that can be locked on, we advise you not to use this facility – if you slip and let go, the cultivator would continue running. Sometimes the clutch lever can be awkwardly placed or stiff to hold on, in which case there would be a temptation to lock it in position, so make sure the clutch is comfortable to use.

Powered cultivators were reviewed in **Gardening from Which?** *November 1982 and small electric cultivators in October 1983.*

Pruning and trimming tools

HEDGETRIMMERS

A hedgetrimmer will save both time and effort, and the longer and larger the hedge you have to cut, the more important these considerations become. At a cost of something between £40 and £70 for an electric hedgetrimmer (though you can pay more than £150) and £120 to £250 for a petrol version, you will need to make sure that it will do the job you want efficiently and safely.

Petrol or electric?

If you have a relatively short garden and all the hedges are within reasonable reach for a power cable, an electric trimmer has a lot of advantages: it will be much cheaper than a petrol trimmer, quieter and cleaner (no fumes), and because it will weigh less, it will be less tiring to use. Some petrol trimmers are twice the weight of electric ones.

Petrol trimmers are worth considering if you have a large garden with hedges some distance from a power supply.

Electric hedgetrimmers

For most people, a blade between 405mm and 420mm (about 16in) in length will be about right. Some of the key points to look for when choosing are listed below, but comfort is something that you will have to judge by holding the trimmer for as long as possible, preferably in the position in which you will use it. To know how well it will cut, and to check on electrical safety, it's best to see whether the model has been tested in a **Gardening from Which?** report.

Combination tools

It will be clear from the vast array of tools described in this book that you could easily amass a shed full of them – costly and space-consuming. The idea of 'combination' tools therefore has some appeal; one tool with attachments for many jobs sounds a good idea.

Hand tools *Several manufacturers produce a combination system of hand tools consisting of a single handle with lots of interchangeable heads. They undoubtably save you storage space, but do have drawbacks, and you should think carefully before committing yourself to this type of system. You have to offset the inconvenience of perhaps having to keep changing heads against any saving in space. One type of attachment may be good (and it could be worth buying the tool for that alone), another may not be as efficient as a separate, conventional tool. You may not save anything on cost either, because a separate tool complete with handle may be no more expensive than one interchangeable head. Think carefully about which heads you are likely to use a lot, and compare the cost of these plus a handle with the cost of conventional tools.*

The Gardena and Wolf combination systems were reviewed in **Gardening from Which?** *August 1984.*

Power tools *There are several multi-purpose power tools available which will do a variety of different tasks. The Black and Decker Gardenworker, for example, is capable of shallow cultivation and weeding, and has an attachment for lawn aeration; the Flymo DME is basically a small cultivator with various attachments, for example, for weeding and ridging.*

The problem with tools like this is that they are unlikely to do all the jobs as fast and efficiently as more specialised power tools, and you could find this frustrating. They cost a lot – from around £50 to £90 – though possibly less than buying several specialised power tools to do the same jobs.

Electric multi-tools were reviewed in **Gardening from Which?** *October 1983.*

Blades Two moving blades are preferable to one moving and one fixed – they vibrate less. The number of teeth can affect performance: more teeth may help to achieve a smoother finish on a fine, close-clipped hedge; fewer, more widely spaced teeth should be able to tackle larger branches. Don't worry about whether they look sharp; hedgetrimmers do not usually have sharpened teeth.

Some hedgetrimmers have teeth on both sides of the blades, others on only one. Which you get on with best is probably a matter of which you're used to using, but double-sided blades are generally preferred.

Handles A large D-shaped handle at right-angles to the blade is likely to increase comfort, and a hand shield on the blade side of the handle will reduce the chance of scratches from the hedge – but make sure it is not too close to be able to insert your hand comfortably. If you have large hands, the clearance within the handles can be crucial – make sure you can hold the tool comfortably.

Power drill trimmer attachments can be particularly awkward to hold because of the position of the handle in relation to the blade.

Length of cable The flex attached to the trimmer is sometimes short – this can be an advantage as it keeps the connector off the ground, and if you do have the misfortune to cut through the flex it will probably be on the extension lead and the trimmer will not have to be opened to make the repair. On the other hand, a very short lead may mean the connector gets in the way. An ideal position for the connection would be between waist level and the ground.

The switches The type of switch is important. A lock-on switch (you can lock the switch in the *on* position by pushing a locking button) can be dangerous because the blades will continue to run even if you have an accident and you let go of the switch. Push-on switches are safer because the trimmer stops when you let go of the switch. Lock-off switches are the safest of all – you have to press a release button before the switch will work, so the trimmer can't be turned on accidentally.

Electrical safety Even though the trimmer should meet the British Standard for electrical safety, and be double insulated, the danger presented by a live wire if you cut the cable accidentally makes it well worth while investing in a residual current device (earth leakage circuit breaker) to protect against the possibility of electrocution.

Petrol hedgetrimmers

Petrol hedgetrimmers have 2-stroke engines and run on a mixture of petrol and oil (the ratio can vary with the model, so check).

The trimmer is likely to have reciprocating blades (both move) to even out the vibration. Some have teeth on one side only, which many gardeners find restricting – teeth on both sides of the blade are likely to be more useful.

Weight and balance are even more important with a petrol hedgetrimmer than with an electric model because of the extra weight.

Safety Look for a model with a dead man's throttle lever (so that the blade will stop moving quickly if you drop the trimmer). Most have this feature. It is not a good idea to buy one with a throttle lever that can be locked into the *on* position.

Before you buy think about hiring a petrol trimmer for a day to see how you get on with one – you might find it too heavy to use. If you decide to buy one, you may need to go to a garden machinery specialist for a good range. Look in the Yellow Pages under *Garden equipment and tool retailers* or *Lawnmower and garden machinery dealers*.

If the hedgetrimmer is not already assembled, ask the retailer to assemble it for you.

Electric hedgetrimmers were reviewed in **Gardening from Which?** *September 1982, and petrol hedgetrimmers in August 1983.*

HEDGE SHEARS

Hedge shears are intended primarily for cutting hedges, but you may want to use them for small areas of long grass (though there are long-handled shears intended specifically for grass – see LAWNCARE TOOLS) and for trimming shrubs and, say, the dead heads off heathers.

Short-term tests suggest that more expensive shears show no particular advantages over many of the cheaper models. Three things influence how easy shears are to use: the sharpness of the blades, how tightly they are adjusted, and the weight and balance of the shears. The harder the steel, the longer the blade will stay sharp, but unfortunately you have no way of telling how hard the steel is just by looking at it; blades adjusted too tightly will be hard to use, too slack and they won't cut properly, so check how easy they are to adjust (some need special tools); weight and comfort you can judge most easily by holding the shears.

Blades on most shears have straight or slightly curved cutting edges. Some have a wavy or serrated edge and these can be tricky to re-sharpen, but tend to cut through mature wood more easily. Wavy-edged blades also trap twigs for cutting while straight-edged blades tend to push them out. For normal hedges trimmed frequently these differences are unlikely to be important, but it might be an advantage if you have a lot of mature wood to cut.

All the shears you find in the shops are likely to have a notch in one or both blades, towards the handles, for cutting through thick twigs. Tests have shown no preference by gardeners for a notch on one or both sides.

Handles are normally either plastic or wood, and again trials have shown no marked preference, so it's just a matter of deciding whether you prefer the feel of one type better than another. The handles are usually shaped so you can use the shears flat against a hedge or close to the ground without scraping your knuckles.

Some brands have shock absorbers to reduce the jarring your hands receive while cutting, but in trials gardeners have not found them a particular advantage.

Size and weight Most manufacturers make shears in a range of different sizes. Generally speaking, the larger the shears the tougher the material they will tackle, but you may find larger models tiring to use.

Hedge shears were reviewed in **Gardening from Which?** *July 1984.*

SECATEURS

Secateurs vary widely in price – from less than £5 to over £20. There are some 'Rolls-Royces' which are probably worth the investment if you do a lot of pruning, but if you only need to prune the roses once a year a more modest pair may be perfectly adequate.

Most of the secateurs that you will find in shops are 'general-purpose' and these should be adequate for most gardeners. For less demanding jobs you could manage with 'light duty' and for a lot of fruit tree pruning it might be worth looking for 'heavy duty' secateurs.

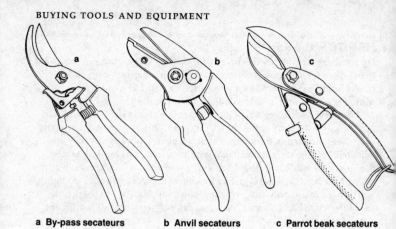

a By-pass secateurs   **b** Anvil secateurs   **c** Parrot beak secateurs

The cutting action

Secateurs cut in one of three ways:

Bypass secateurs (sometimes called curved secateurs) work like a pair of scissors, a convex sharpened blade cutting against a squared, concave blade. This is the most common type.

Anvil secateurs have a straight, sharp blade that cuts against a flat platform called an anvil. There are variations, and in some there is a groove down the centre of the anvil, which is to allow sap to run off. **Swing anvil** secateurs have an anvil that is pivoted at the forward end so that it remains more parallel with the cutting blade which slices through the wood rather than pressing through it.

One elaborate type, the Ceka Ratchet 5673, has a ratchet action and as you squeeze the handle several times the blade angle tightens and cuts through the wood in a series of bites – useful if you have a weak grip.

Parrot beak secateurs are less common. They work on the scissor principle, but both blades are usually sharpened and convex, so that the wood is forced backwards to the mid point as they close.

All three types will work well, and trials showed that brand is generally more important than the type of cutting action, though a good, sharp pair of bypass secateurs should damage the cut end of the stem less than the anvil type.

What to look for

Overall size and the angle of the handles when the blades are fully open will affect comfort. An overall length of 20 to 22cm (about 8in) is a good size, with a handle length of 14cm (5½in) or more. See if you think they open too wide for comfort, especially if there is a strong spring.

Secateurs can become uncomfortable and tiring to use after a while, so try holding them in the shop. Choose a pair which fit neatly into your hand and are not too heavy, or unbalanced.

The spring should return the secateurs to the open position quickly and smoothly when you release your grip, but should not be so strong that you feel as if you're fighting against it.

The safety catch is also important – check for both safety and comfort. You should be able to put the catch on quickly and easily with one hand.

If you are left-handed you should be able to use most secateurs comfortably, though the catch may be at the back where you cannot operate it with your thumb. Felco make true, left-handed secateurs.

Handles used to be metal, but most are now plastic, or at least plastic-coated. Metal handles are likely to be too cold for comfort without gloves in winter.

Blades which did best in trials were thin and well supported away from the cutting edge to prevent distortion. If you will be using the secateurs a lot, check that they are easy to resharpen – can the blade be removed? Find out if spare parts or a repair service are easily available, and look to see if the secateurs are guaranteed.

Secateurs were reviewed in **Gardening from Which?** *October 1982.*

LONG-HANDLED PRUNERS

Long-handled shrub pruners, sometimes described as branch cutters, look like large secateurs with long handles. The handles give you lots of leverage so you can cut through most stems very easily, even quite thick ones, much thicker than you could manage with secateurs. The long handles also enable you to reach branches well above your head and help you avoid the scratches when tackling prickly shrubs. Overall they can be a very useful addition to your range of hand tools.

Tree loppers work on a different principle. The blade is operated by a lever and they may be assembled from two or three sections to give a reach of say 1.8 or 3m (6 or 9ft). They're only worth thinking about if you have a lot of tree pruning to do.

When buying tree loppers or long-handled shrub pruners, check the size and weight. Shorter models might not give you enough leverage to cope with really thick branches, while those with much longer handles could prove unwieldy and tiring to use. Also check that the handle grips are comfortable and provide sure firm grip. Flimsy plastic grips that can slide or twist round in use can be irritating.

Long-handled pruners were reviewed in **Gardening from Which?** *December 1984.*

PRUNING SAWS

If you only want to remove an odd branch, and have a bow saw, use that. If you have an orchard, or lots of trees to prune, then a pruning saw is worth considering.

English pruning saws usually have a wooden handle and straight blade. Some have fine teeth on one edge and coarse teeth on the other. These have to be used with care as the upper teeth can damage other branches when cutting in a confined area.

Grecian saws are worth looking for. They have a curved, pointed blade which makes them easy to use in confined and awkward places, and the teeth are on one side only and point backwards, so you can use the saw above your head, pulling it down towards you.

You can buy pruning saws that fold into the handle. This is convenient for storage, but no advantage while you are working.

Long-handled pruning saws are useful for branches otherwise out of cutting reach, but make sure the cutting head is well secured to the handle – if it bolts on you may need to check regularly to see that it is secure.

GARDEN KNIVES

A garden knife is one of those tools that you can manage perfectly well without for years, but find dozens of uses for once you have one. And there are a few specialist gardening jobs, such as budding and grafting, where a suitable knife becomes essential.

A pruning knife (occasionally called a peach pruner) has a large curved blade and sometimes a curved handle too.

A grafting or **cuttings knife** has a straight blade.

A budding knife may have a piece cut out of the top of the blade (this is known as a clip point blade) and possibly a projection on the top of the blade, and a tapered handle or a metal projection on the end of the handle, all of which are intended to open up the cut to insert the bud.

A general garden knife may have a curved or straight blade.

Most gardeners will use secateurs for pruning rather than a knife, so it is probably more important to choose a knife that is suitable for other garden jobs such as taking cuttings (a blade that is too thick and too broad may be a drawback for this), harvesting vegetables, and cutting string.

Budding knives are likely to be unsuitable for general use – the protrusions that are useful for budding are likely to get in the way. But don't dismiss one described as a grafting knife – it may be a good all-round knife too.

A stainless steel blade will not rust or corrode like carbon steel, and should retain its edge longer than a carbon steel blade of the same

a Pruning knife

b Grafting or cuttings knife

c Budding knife

hardness. But it is not difficult to keep an ordinary blade sharp with a fine sharpening stone.

Trials have shown that the choice of handle type is determined by personal preference, and perhaps the job the knife is being used for. You might have a choice of plastic, wood, metal, and possibly horn, handles. In trials wooden handles were popular, and metal ones generally unpopular. Among the plastic handles, slim, straight ones were favoured.

Garden knives were reviewed in **Gardening from Which?** *September 1984.*

FLOWER PICKERS

Unless you do a lot of flower-gathering there isn't much point in buying a special tool for flower picking – secateurs or scissors will be perfectly adequate. If you are keen on flower arranging, however, you may want to invest in one of the various tools designed for the job.

Flower pickers are basically scissors or shears that grip the stem once it's been cut. These do not really have advantages over tools that don't hold the stem unless you have a problem reaching. You can buy a long-handled flower gatherer, but they are expensive and probably only worthwhile if you are disabled or unable to reach across a border.

Pocket pruners (small secateurs) can be your best bet, but floral art scissors may be even more useful – although they won't hold the stem, they are generally cheap and will probably have a cutting notch for florists' wire and a stem crusher between the handles.

What to look for

Try the flower pickers in the shop to make sure they are comfortable to use. Secateur-type handles are generally preferred to scissor-type handles. If they have a safety catch, make sure it is easy to use – especially if you are left-handed (remember, although secateurs can be used either way up, those that hold the stem must be used the right way up).

Tools that cut the stems best without crushing are those with a sprung gripper that holds the stem **before** it is cut. Those with a gripper attached to the side of the blade tend to grip the stem only after it has been cut, and may crush the stem if squeezed too hard.

Flower pickers were reviewed in **Gardening from Which?** *July 1984.*

Prices vary a lot at garden centres and nurseries. We've calculated a basket price for plants and given ratings from £ to ££££££ – very cheap to very expensive.

You will usually find the largest range of tools in garden centres, but it's also worth looking in good ironmongers' shops, supermarkets and DIY superstores, as well as discount houses. These often have very competitively priced tools, albeit a limited range. Many of them offer power tools at a substantial discount over the manufacturer's suggested price.

'Own brand' tools made for supermarkets and chain stores may be well worth considering. **Gardening from Which?** *tests have often shown these to be good value for money.*

Lawncare tools

LAWNMOWERS

A lawnmower is perhaps one of the most difficult tools to choose – there are so many types and models, and so much pressure from advertisements with apparently conflicting claims, that the whole business can be bewildering.

Perhaps the best way to decide which is likely to be the right type for you is to decide exactly what you want from your mower – this eliminates some options immediately.

Is ease of mowing more important than price?

If the answer is yes: go for a powered mower. If the lawn is large, choose a self-propelled one, that is one with a powered drive and not just powered cutting cylinders or blades.

If the answer is no: think about a hand mower – they still have a role to play, especially if the area is small (though for a large area it's still worth considering a powered mower just to save time).

Do you object to a noisy mower?

If the answer is yes: avoid a petrol mower. Electric mowers are usually quieter, although some electric hover mowers and cylinder mowers can be noisy. A well-maintained hand mower should not make an objectionable noise.

If the answer is no: your choice is unrestricted. Concentrate on other qualities.

Is your lawn over 250sq m (300sq yd)?

If the answer is yes: it's worth considering an electric mower – if it's the size of say a bowling green then you will probably need something more substantial, such as a petrol mower.

If the answer is no: you should be able to manage with a hand mower unless you want to avoid the physical effort.

Do you want 'stripes' in your lawn?

If the answer is yes: you'll have to choose a cylinder mower or a rotary mower with rear rollers to produce the stripes.

If the answer is no: any of the rotary or hover mowers will be suitable, or a side-wheeled hand-pushed cylinder mower for a small area.

Do you want a mower simply to cut long grass (in say an orchard)?

If the answer is yes: a rotary mower will do the job, though you'll need a powerful machine if the grass is very long.

If the answer is no: it's best to choose a mower that will give quality finish, such as a cylinder mower or perhaps a hover mower.

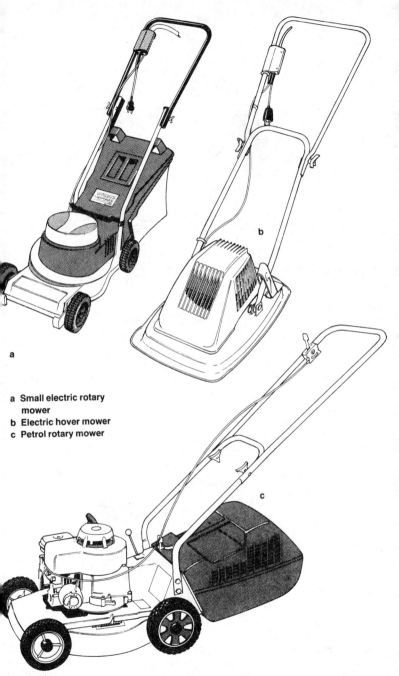

a Small electric rotary
mower
b Electric hover mower
c Petrol rotary mower

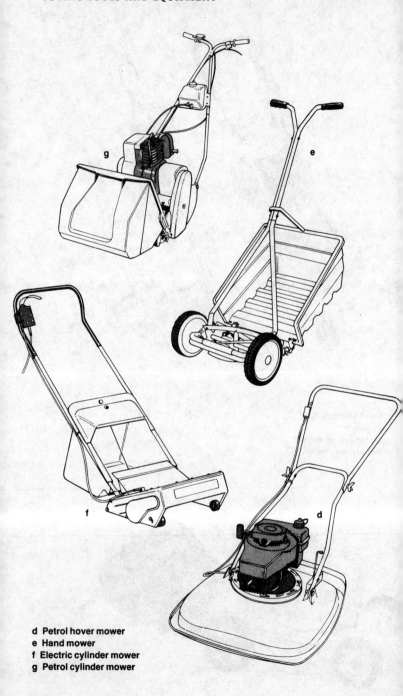

d Petrol hover mower
e Hand mower
f Electric cylinder mower
g Petrol cylinder mower

Are neat edges important?

If the answer is yes: choose a cylinder mower or a rotary mower with inset wheels or a roller. A hover mower will probably lose its cushion of air if you push it too far over the edge, and the blade may then carve up the turf.

If the answer is no: any mower type should be satisfactory.

Points to watch for

Width of cut For a small lawn, a cutting width of 31cm (just under 13in) should be adequate. But if your lawn is over say 100sq m (120sq yd), you will need a wider cut to make the job less tedious.

Cylinder mowers have blades on a rotating cylinder. Cylinders with the fewest blades generally cut long grass the best, but give a ribbed effect to the mown grass. More blades produce a finer and more even finish.

Mower safety

Powered mowers are potentially dangerous tools to handle. Many accidents are caused by carelessness, but there are design features that make some mowers safer than others. It is worth paying a bit more for a model with good safety features (provided it also performs well) than to accept a cheaper one with hazards.

The safety features to look for are summarised below:

Foot protection *Rotary mowers of all types should have the blade completely enclosed by the hood (housing) and deflector plate, so that it is only exposed underneath. And the rear of the hood should be 3mm (1/6in) below the blade and provide enough protection to stop anyone's foot touching the blade. Alternatively the handle should be long enough to stop you getting too close.*

Danger to hands *The mower should have a safe and efficient means of stopping the engine. And the blade should stop quickly from its maximum speed – ideally within two or three seconds. You probably won't be able to determine this without a trial first, but if the mower has been tested by* **Gardening from Which?** *this and other safety aspects will have been covered.*

Flying stones *A deflector plate should effectively prevent stones being thrown out when the mower is being used without the grasscatcher.*

Electric mowers *should have an on/off control based on the deadman's handle principle, where you have to hold the switch on to keep the motor running. A lock-off device is an additional advantage – this prevents the mower being turned on accidentally (the lock-off switch has to be turned on before the deadman's control works).*

If you're buying an extension lead for your mower, choose a brightly coloured one so that you can see it easily on the lawn.

It is well worth using a residual current device (you may also know it as an earth leakage circuit breaker) in the circuit for peace of mind.

Cylinder mowers that have a rear roller to flatten the grass will produce alternating 'stripes' if you mow neatly.

The more expensive powered models will be self-propelled, but the cheaper ones still have to be pushed along.

Rotary mowers have a single horizontal blade that rotates at high speed under a protective cover. In the past some of these have performed poorly in tests, but there are some models that will perform as well as other types. It pays to check on recent test reports if possible.

Petrol rotaries are usually noisy, but are worth thinking about for a large lawn. If you have a lot of grass to cut, it may be worth considering a self-propelled model, though you may have to pay £30 to £100 more than for a similar hand-propelled mower.

Hover mowers cut like rotary mowers but are supported on a cushion of air. This makes them very easy to push on short and medium length grass, and they are capable of producing a good finish. Unfortunately many will not collect the clippings for you.

Hand and small electric mowers were reviewed in **Gardening from Which?** *Preview issue, petrol rotaries in April 1983, small electrics in April 1984, and petrol cylinder mowers in April 1985.*

TOOLS FOR TRIMMING A LAWN EDGE

If you want a neat lawn, the grass at the edges has to be trimmed regularly and doing it on hands and knees with hedge shears is laborious. Traditionally this job was done with long-handled lawn edgers, often called border shears, though you can also buy trimmers with a rotating blade designed for this purpose. Alternatively you can use a nylon line trimmer

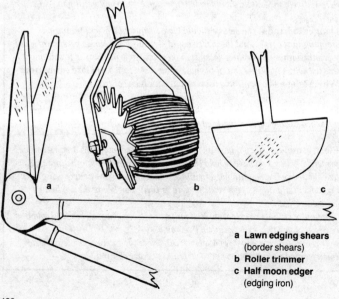

a **Lawn edging shears**
(border shears)
b **Roller trimmer**
c **Half moon edger**
(edging iron)

(see TRIMMERS AND BRUSHCUTTERS) though you have to take care not to gouge lumps out of your lawn edge. Models with a tilting head are particularly suitable because the head can be set at the right angle to tackle the lawn edge. If you want to recut the edge of your lawn you will also need a half moon edger (edging iron).

Lawn edging shears

Although you won't have to bend, these shears can still be tiring to use because you have to support the weight (sometimes over 1.8kg/4lb) in the right position off the ground. Balance and total weight can both make a difference, so have a 'dry run' in the shop to see whether the tool feels right.

Nowadays the handles are almost certain to be coated tubular steel or aluminium. They should be strong, but a little 'spring' in them will make them less tiring to use. If you find the conventional handles awkward to hold, you might get on better with a D-shaped handle.

Unless you are prepared to wipe the blades clean and oil them after use, it will be worth paying a little more for a rust-resisting finish (treatments include chrome-plating and galvanising).

Edge trimmers

Tools like the Wolf Lawnline Edge Trimmer work on an entirely different principle. The trimmer is pushed along the edge of the lawn and a rotating blade trims the grass. Try to use a friend's or have a demonstration before you buy; you may not find it any easier to use than border shears.

Powered versions like the Black and Decker Lawn Edger are also available. These will give a neat finish, and may be worth considering if you have a large amount of lawn edge to trim regularly and don't have a nylon line trimmer that will cope.

Half moon edgers

Likely to be described as either a half moon edger or an edging iron, this is a tool more talked about than used. Its purpose is to cut the edge of a lawn in a straight line – invaluable for a newly established lawn but to be used with restraint as a regular treatment for tidying up a lawn, otherwise the beds will become steadily larger and the lawn smaller.

There's a temptation to use a spade for the same job, but the blade will be slightly curved, and leave a scalloped effect. Used against a straight-edge, a half moon edger will produce a straight, neat edge. Designs vary little.

LONG-HANDLED GRASS SHEARS

The forerunner of the nylon line trimmer, long-handled grass shears are still useful if you don't want to use a power tool but have to cut a lawn close to trees or a fence, where the mower can't reach.

They are similar to lawn edging shears (except that the blades cut parallel to the lawn surface rather than vertically) and the general points made about buying lawn edging shears also apply to these.

TRIMMERS AND BRUSHCUTTERS

There are now lots of nylon line trimmers and brushcutters on the market, some costing as little as £20, others more than £100. Generally your choice will depend on what you want the machine to do.

What's the difference?

Most of the tools sold to amateurs for cutting down grass and weeds in awkward places are called trimmers and have nylon cutting line; the more powerful models, suitable for cutting through tough growth such as brambles, are likely to be called brushcutters and are usually fitted with blades. But the borderline is not clear cut and one manufacturer's brushcutter may be another's trimmer. When deciding what to buy, be guided by the features the machine possesses and what it can do, not by the name given to it.

Petrol or electric?

If you have a small garden and just want a trimmer to cut lawn edges and awkward patches of grass, a small electric trimmer is probably the best choice. Larger, more powerful electric trimmers, costing say over £40, can be more comfortable and convenient to use if you want to cut large amounts of rough weeds. Petrol models are the most expensive, costing over £100. They are also noisier, heavier, tiring to use, and more difficult to manoeuvre for small or delicate jobs; their merit lies in their ability to cope with tougher jobs such as hacking down rough vegetation. Brushcutters which can be fitted with metal blades can even tackle heavy undergrowth.

There are a few battery-powered trimmers around which could be worth considering if you find trailing cable an inconvenience (however, you will have to shop around a lot more for one of these).

What to look for

See illustrations on page 435.

Trimmers and brushcutters were reviewed in **Gardening from Which?** *August 1984.*

Safety

Electric trimmers *should be fitted with a deadman's handle – once you let go the motor stops. Some are tiring to hold down, so see how comfortable it feels.*

Even safer is a lock-off deadman's handle – once you let go you have to operate a second switch to start it again (this reduces the chance of the trimmer being started accidentally).

A cable clamp is also a good feature – it keeps the electric cable clamped to the handle and so out of the way while you are cutting.

Petrol trimmers *or brushcutters will have some device for stopping the engine. A toggle or sliding switch is better than a button that you have to hold down for several seconds (this could be difficult in an emergency).*

A clutch is also a good feature – this means the cutting head will not move until you build up the engine speed. It makes the machine easier to control and means you can't bump start the engine by accident.

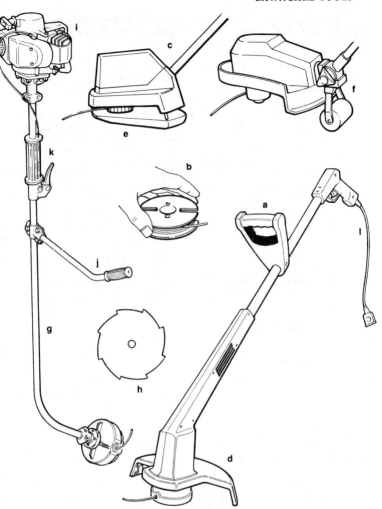

a Second handle or grip makes the job less tiring and the tool easier to manoeuvre (most of the smaller models have only one handle).

Heavy brushcutters may have an adjustable harness to put round your shoulders – this will help to take most of the weight of the machine.

Try holding the machine in the shop, first adjusting the harness and handles (if possible), and moving the head from side to side in a swinging motion.

Automatic line feed is a useful feature – it saves you having to stop the motor and bend down to pull out more nylon line every time the line wears and/or snaps off. There are various systems – with some you tap the bottom of the spool on the ground, with others you may have to press a button or lever in the handle. On a few trimmers, you have to press your foot down on the trimmer casing – not such a convenient method as the nylon line tends to gouge a hole in your lawn while you are doing it.

b Replacement spools are often

435

supplied with the trimmer. Changing spools is usually an easy task.

Double cutting lines are not necessarily more efficient at cutting than a single line.

c Adjustable head: on some trimmers you can tilt the head backwards, forwards and sideways. This is very useful for cutting along a lawn edge, on a bank or slope, or under overhanging bushes.

d Shield or guard covering part or the whole of the cutting head helps to prevent debris being thrown up at you. Look for a shield that also allows you to see where you are cutting.

e Skid or sledge takes the weight of the machine, and is useful when pushing the trimmer under overhanging bushes. It may also be worth looking for if you think you will find a trimmer tiring to use, though it's not much use over rough ground.

f Steering roller acts in much the same way as a skid.

g Drive shafts on petrol trimmers: a flexible drive shaft is more prone to damage, but rigid shaft models are more expensive.

h Interchangeable heads are a feature of some of the larger machines – the nylon line can be replaced by a plastic or metal blade. Metal blades are useful for cutting through undergrowth and brushwood. Plastic blades will not cut better than a nylon line, buy may suffer less damage when you hit an obstacle.

i Diaphragm carburettor: machines with this type of carburettor can be used at a steep angle, say for cutting back hedges and undergrowth, without the engine stalling. On some machines the whole engine swivels to keep it vertical.

j Tiller arm is a second handle in the form of an arm which sticks out from the main shaft. It is designed to help you guide and manoeuvre the machine.

k Vibration dampeners are fitted to some machines and should reduce vibration and make the trimmer more comfortable to use.

l Cables and connectors: many electric trimmers have no cable, so you will need to buy an extension lead. Most are supplied with waterproof connectors. Make sure the two-pinned connector is attached to the trimmer and the socket to the extension lead, so you will be in no danger of touching live pins.

LAWN RAKES

Be clear about what you expect your lawn rake to do – simply gather up leaves and perhaps grass cuttings, scratch out moss, or to scarify, removing 'thatch' and moss.

For removing leaves and grass cuttings, there are a number of different types of lawn rakes: flat-tined leaf rakes, leaf rakes with rubber prongs or plastic heads, and gatherer rakes which are like soil rakes but have longer tines. There are also grabber rakes with which you can rake and pick up the leaves. For raking out the moss too, you need a rake with some natural spring in it. Wire spring-tine rakes are the most common type, but you can also get similar, fan-shaped rakes made of plastic or bamboo. For a small lawn, a spring-tine rake will be adequate for most purposes, but for a larger lawn you will need to think about buying a special leaf rake as well.

If you are mainly interested in removing the thatch (matted dead grass), and opening up the grass, a rake with small, curved metal blades which hook downwards through the thatch (sometimes called an aerator or slitter rake) might be better. But these can be hard work to use and if you have a large area of mossy lawn, it is worth thinking about a powered lawn rake.

Powered lawn rakes sometimes called scarifiers/aerators do generally work effectively. The popular types have spring tines which remove moss and dead grass, but there are some that have solid swinging tines (these are designed for tougher work and it may be worth hiring a tool of this kind). The Black and Decker Lawnraker is the most widely available powered

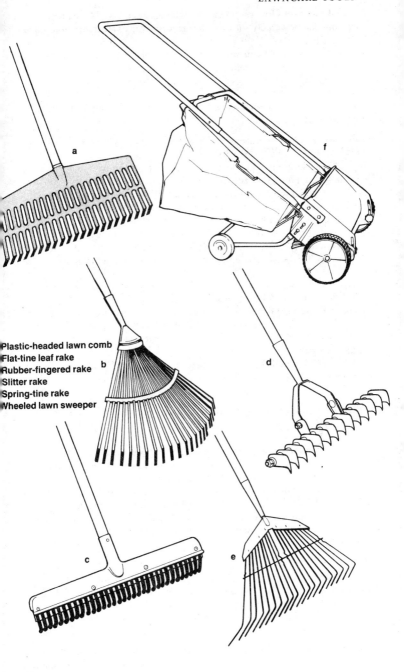

Plastic-headed lawn comb
Flat-tine leaf rake
Rubber-fingered rake
Slitter rake
Spring-tine rake
Wheeled lawn sweeper

a

b

c

d

e

f

437

lawn rake and sells for around £60 though you should be able to find it discounted substantially – it's worth comparing prices at supermarkets and DIY stores.

Clearly expensive if you have only a small lawn, but it will save a lot of time and effort (it should take perhaps a third the time in comparison with manual raking).

Powered lawn rakes and slitter rakes were reviewed in **Gardening from Which?** *September/October 1984.*

WHEELED LAWN SWEEPERS

If you have a large lawn and lots of trees in close proximity, it may be worth considering a wheeled lawn sweeper – it's possible to buy one that you tow behind a small tractor or ride on mower, if you have a very large lawn, but for most gardeners something more modest is perfectly adequate. Even so, you can expect to pay between about £50 and £100 for one.

The wider the sweep, the more quickly you will cover the lawn.

This is a tool that you will use for a comparatively short period each year, so you may also be influenced by how bulky the equipment is to store.

LAWN AERATORS

You can aerate a lawn by inserting the prongs of a fork at frequent intervals, to a depth of about 10cm (4in). It will do the job just as well, often better, than most proper lawn aerators. But it's hard work and time-consuming.

Aerators fall into three distinct types: those that simply make shallow slits, those with solid tines, and those with hollow tines that remove a core of soil.

Slitter aerators are useful for shallow aeration, and may stimulate the grass, but do not penetrate deeply enough to have much impact on compacted soil.

Most are pushed along on wheels and have spiked discs which rotate (they may have a platform for weights to improve penetration), but they need a lot of effort to use. If you buy one of those with weights, make sure they can be fixed on properly otherwise you may have trouble with them falling off. There are slitter attachments that you can fit to powered mowers, and these may be worth considering for a large lawn. You will have to find one that fits your particular mower. Don't expect too much from these slitters.

Solid-tine aerators usually have rows of spikes set around a cylinder or frame. They are pushed along like a mower, but they are difficult to use properly – they need a lot of pressure to push the tines into the ground.

Aerator sandals can be strapped to your ordinary shoes to spike the lawn as you mow. But the tines don't penetrate very well, and they are tiring to use.

Hollow-tine aerators are the most efficient at aerating compacted ground. The hollow tines are pushed into the ground to remove a core of earth, and

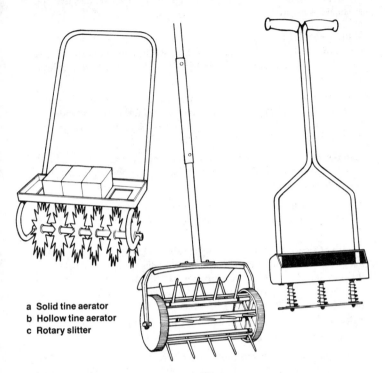

a Solid tine aerator
b Hollow tine aerator
c Rotary slitter

pulled out again. Some models have a collection box for catching the cores of soil, which saves you sweeping them up. Look for a model with large sturdy tines at least 10mm (about ½in) in diameter and 90mm (3½in) deep. If the tines are too narrow, they tend to clog. These aerators can be difficult to use on hard, stony ground.

Lawn aerators were reviewed in **Gardening from Which?** *September 1984.*

LAWN FERTILISER SPREADERS

Fertiliser spreaders can be used to spread fertiliser and sometimes seed over any level ground, but usually they are used for lawns because this provides the most suitable surface for a wheeled spreader. You can, of course, scatter fertiliser by hand, but this can be tedious if you have a large lawn. You might encounter non-wheeled spreaders of various kinds, but **Gardening from Which?** tests have shown wheeled spreaders to be superior.

Some spreaders are more versatile than others – all should spread lawn fertiliser, but not all will deal with grass seed or lawnsand. Some will not cope with a general fertiliser such as Growmore, and some might only work effectively with specific brands of lawn fertiliser. So if you want a

439

versatile spreader, make sure the one you buy will cope with all that you are likely to use in it.

What to look for

Spreading width If it's too narrow the job will be tedious. Go for at least 40cm (16in) for an average lawn, but for a large lawn look for one at least 45cm (18in) wide.

Weight when empty can be significant if you are not very strong – you may want to hang it up for storage, or tip it up to clean. When filled with fertiliser some can be very heavy – as much as 26kg (½ cwt) – something to bear in mind if you have to lift it over flower beds, for instance.

Handles may be single, or the pram-handle type, preferred by many people. If you need to use the spreader for long periods, make sure it's comfortable to push.

Stopping the flow Make sure there is some way of stopping the flow when you are wheeling the spreader to where you want to use it – otherwise you'll have to carry it.

Choice of settings A wide range will enable you to apply a bigger choice of materials at different rates. This usually provides the option of delivering the complete dose in one go or applying half the rate for the first pass and the rest at a second pass at right-angles to be sure of a more even spread. Make sure the settings are easy to adjust.

Capacity A large capacity is not necessarily a significant advantage – it will simply be heavy to lift and to push.

A word of warning: always check how much the spreader is delivering before you use it on the lawn – some may deliver several times too much or too little of some fertilisers, etc. Roll it over a couple of measured sheets of newspaper on the ground, then weigh how much has been delivered.

Lawn fertiliser spreaders were reviewed in **Gardening from Which?** *March 1984.*

Watering equipment

HOSE-PIPES

Most conventional hose-pipes are made of PVC and come in lengths of about 15m or 30m (50ft or 100ft), though some makes are also sold in 50m or 75m (about 170 or 250ft) lengths if you need a particularly long run and don't want to join shorter pieces together.

Single-walled hoses are made from just a single layer of PVC and are likely to lack strength.

Double-walled hoses should be strong enough for general garden use, although some makes have a rather low bursting strength.

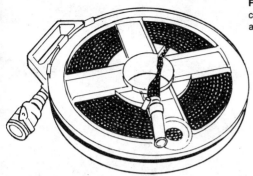

Flat hoses wind into a cassette for easy storage and carrying.

Reinforced double-walled hoses have a fibre reinforcement between the layers. They are the most reliable type. They are strong and also less likely to kink (kinking is frustrating and it also leads to weak spots that can eventually leak once the hose gets old). **Gardening from Which?** tests showed little to choose between the various brands of reinforced hose, so you will probably be happy with the cheapest you can find.

Smooth or ribbed? Some hoses have a ribbed finish. This gives you a better grip on the hose.

Flat hoses wind up into a cassette for easy storage. They have several disadvantages: they are more expensive than conventional hoses of the same length, but they are usually sold with fittings and you won't have to buy a hose reel; they come in fixed lengths (though you can buy extensions), and they have to be completely unwound before use. You may be prepared to accept these disadvantages for the convenience of easy storage and carrying.

There are two types: fibre reinforced PVC, and those with a fabric outer layer and inner plastic tube. The PVC type are generally heavier, more difficult to rewind, and come with universal adaptors that have shortcomings. The fibre type seem to have most to offer.

Also think about the fittings. Some makes have a universal fitting that you can use on different types of tap, and others have a threaded fitting permanently attached to the end of the hose – these can be connected to a threaded tap or screwed on to other fittings. Many are also supplied with spray nozzles and connections for use with other accessories. Bear in mind a threaded connector may not fit the thread on your outside tap.

Extensions are not available for all makes, so check this point if you are likely to want to extend the hose later.

Hoses were reviewed in **Gardening from Which?** *June 1983.*

HOSE FITTINGS

All hose fittings fall into one of two categories:

Standard hose fittings usually screw on to the hose and whatever you are connecting them to – a tap, sprinkler, or another length of hose, for example. If you want to detach the fitting you have to unscrew it.

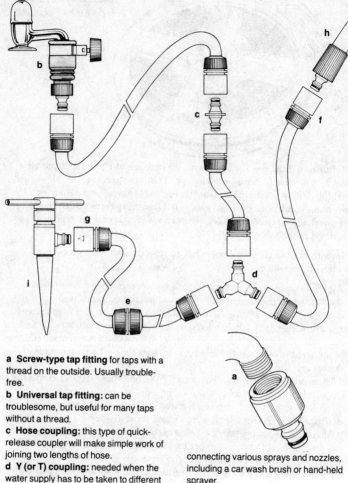

a **Screw-type tap fitting** for taps with a thread on the outside. Usually trouble-free.

b **Universal tap fitting:** can be troublesome, but useful for many taps without a thread.

c **Hose coupling:** this type of quick-release coupler will make simple work of joining two lengths of hose.

d **Y (or T) coupling:** needed when the water supply has to be taken to different points – perhaps for a trickle irrigation system.

e **Hose repair connector:** useful for repairing a hose or joining two lengths.

f **Female connector:** useful for connecting various sprays and nozzles, including a car wash brush or hand-held sprayer.

g **Female connector with waterstop:** when the male fitting is unplugged the flow of water is shut off.

h **Hand-held spray nozzle**

i **Rotating sprinkler**

Quick-release fittings are designed so that one part can be permanently attached to the hose, and whatever you are using can then be plugged into it. If you are likely to need to change fittings frequently, it is worth buying the quick-release type.

Universal tap connectors are not as universal as they sound – you are likely to have trouble with some mixer taps and round taps without sufficient straight length of pipe to tighten the fitting on to. If you have this sort of problem it is better to fit a special outside tap than to hope for a dependable leak-proof fitting.

If you install an outside tap, choose a threaded one – threaded connectors are more reliable than universal connectors.

There are many other fittings for joining hoses and attachments, and these are likely to be more trouble-free than the tap connectors. The illustration on page 442 shows some of the fittings that might be useful.

Hose fittings were reviewed in **Gardening from Which?** *June 1983.*

SPRINKLERS

Sprinklers range widely in price (from about £2 to over £50) and in the area they cover (less than 50sq m/60 sq yd to over 500sq m/600 sq yd).

Measure the area of your lawn before choosing a sprinkler. If you have a big lawn, you can obviously move the sprinkler about, but this isn't something that you'd want to do more than say half a dozen times at one session. If the garden is very small, you will also need to check the minimum area that is covered by the equipment – some of the very powerful ones could cause annoyance to your neighbours by sending the jet over the garden fence.

Check whether you can adjust the area covered.

There are four types of sprinklers (excluding 'travelling' sprinklers which you are unlikely to find in shops), and you can also use a sprinkler hose or seep hose for watering your lawn.

Static sprinklers have no moving parts – the water is forced out through a hole (or holes) and is broken up into a spray in the process. Some have a spike on the bottom for sticking into the lawn. Others have a flat base and just sit on the ground. Static sprayers are usually cheap (they can cost as little as £2 or £3) and are generally perfectly adequate for a small lawn. On some you can adjust the area sprayed.

Most static sprinklers spray from just above ground level, but some have a long stalk so that the head is held clear of growing plants – these are useful for sprinkling vegetables and flowers.

Oscillating sprinklers have a tube or barrel which slowly oscillates to and fro. They cover a rectangular area and normally you can alter the setting to treat a narrow or wide strip at one or both sides of the sprinkler. These are generally more expensive than the static type, costing from around £8, but cover a bigger area and the rectangular pattern makes it easier to water the lawn evenly without overlap.

Rotating sprinklers generally have two or three arms that rotate about a central column. Some are mounted on a spike. They are similar in price to static sprinklers and usually cover a larger area, but otherwise have no advantage over static sprinklers.

Pulse-jet sprinklers produce a circular spray pattern but rotate in steps or pulses rather than smoothly. They are generally the most expensive type,

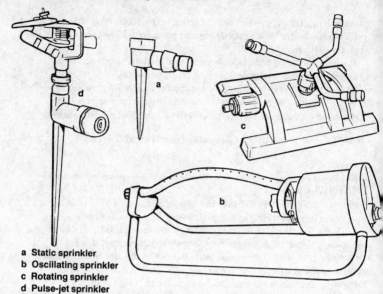

a Static sprinkler
b Oscillating sprinkler
c Rotating sprinkler
d Pulse-jet sprinkler

costing from around £9 to more than £50, but they cover the largest area and you can adjust the shape and size of the area and usually the fineness of spray too.

Some models sit on a long stalk or tripod so that the head is clear of growing plants, and these are ideal for watering flower beds and vegetables. For a lawn, a low head is perfectly satisfactory. Some models have a spike, others have broad bases for stability. Worth thinking about for a large area of lawn.

Sprinkler hoses are basically hoses with holes in them. They can be snaked over a rectangular lawn or used to cover a long, sweeping area such as a broad grass path.

Seep hoses are usually made from plastic or polythene tubing. You can buy versions with small holes already pierced, or watertight tubing in which you can make pinpricks at the right positions for your needs. These are useful for watering vegetable crops in rows, but of limited application for more general watering.

Lawn sprinklers were reviewed in **Gardening from Which?** *May 1984.*

WATERING-CANS

Be clear what you want from your watering-can. If you want to water garden plants, houseplants, and the greenhouse, you really need three.

Small cans for watering houseplants don't have to hold much water, just pour well and perhaps look attractive. Long spouts are no particular advantage unless you have plants that you have difficulty in reaching. Don't worry about the rose; it's more important to have a narrow-necked spout that pours well.

For general garden use, a 2-gallon plastic or galvanised metal can is the most useful. Although galvanised cans are less popular now, they should last as long as a plastic can, probably longer.

The problem with many plastic cans is the inefficiency of the plastic rose, but you can replace them with brass roses. These will become clogged, of course, unless you have a filter or strainer to keep back the largest pieces of dirt.

For watering in a greenhouse you will probably need a can with a long spout so that you can easily reach pots at the back of the staging. The can should also be small enough to lift comfortably to the level required for watering plants on staging. For watering seedlings a fine rose is essential.

A test for any watering-can is how well it pours. The shop may not be happy about letting you put it to the test, but if you know someone with a particular watering-can that you are interested in, ask if you can try using it. See how well it pours, how comfortable it feels, and whether it produces a lot of coarse drips or dribbles when you start or finish watering (a particular problem if you are watering seeds or seedlings).

Weeding and spraying equipment

PRESSURE SPRAYERS

Pressure sprayers are useful for a variety of jobs – from applying pesticides to misting plants for increased humidity, and even applying greenhouse shading.

For misting houseplants and applying pesticides to just a few plants, a small trigger-pump sprayer will be adequate. For the garden, and especially if you need to spray say a bed of roses, one of the bigger compression sprayers will be necessary.

Trigger-pump sprayers

Most of these are made from semi-rigid translucent polythene. This is less likely to break if dropped than those made of a very hard, rigid plastic.

Most have a plastic nozzle too, but sometimes brass is used. The plastic ones can work just as well. It's useful to have one that is not too opaque – it helps to be able to see how much liquid is inside.

Make sure there is a filter on the dip tube – clogged nozzles can be difficult to clear.

You are as likely to be satisfied with one of the cheaper sprayers as an expensive one. But hold the sprayer and operate the trigger before you buy. See that it fits your hand comfortably and that the trigger is not tiring to use (a long trigger is likely to be more comfortable than a short one).

Compression sprayers

There are larger sprayers, usually of the knapsack type, but a 5 litre (1 gallon) size is likely to be adequate for all normal garden jobs.

Almost all of the compression sprayers you are likely to find in the shops

Dribble bars for watering-cans

It's not a good idea to use a compression sprayer to apply a weedkiller. Even a light breeze can cause the fine droplets to drift on to nearby plants. It is better to use a watering-can with a dribble bar attachment.

will be plastic (it is possible to buy metals ones which should last longer, but these will be much more expensive and may not do the job as well as many much cheaper plastic ones). If you do buy a metal one, bear in mind that the weedkiller glyphosate can attack galvanised steel.

Look for one with an adjustable nozzle, and a see-through, ideally graduated, case. A trigger lock-off is desirable (this reduces the risk of turning the sprayer on accidentally) but it is an uncommon feature. A curved lance will make it easier to spray round plants and under leaves.

Pressure sprayers were reviewed in **Gardening from Which?** *May 1984.*

SPOT WEEDERS

A spot weeder will enable you to apply glyphosate (a weedkiller that will kill the roots of the plants even though it is applied to the leaves) to selected plants.

It is more economic than using a spray, but more importantly it is safer to use among plants you value because there is no risk of spray drift (though you'll have watch out for drips). Tests have shown that these weeders are not without problems and you may be better off with a sprayer fitted with a shield. If you want to try a spot weeder you are most likely to be satisfied with one that takes a Tumbleweeder cartridge.

Spot weeders were reviewed in **Gardening from Which?** *July 1983.*

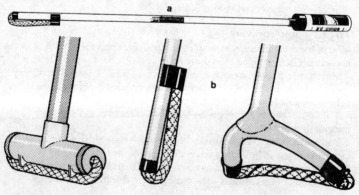

a **Spot weeder**
b **Different types of head:** weedkiller soaks into the wick from a reservoir in the handle.

FLAMEGUNS

Flameguns control weeds but they generate only enough heat to kill annuals, weed seeds on or near the surface, and the tops of perennials, unless you use them repeatedly. Flameguns are slow to use and can't be used close to desirable plants. A gun with a shield will be safer to use near plants.

Planting tools and aids

HAND TROWELS AND FORKS

If you look around, you'll be confronted by a wide range of different hand trowels and forks, perhaps because they make useful gifts for gardeners. They are sometimes sold as boxed sets – these look nice, but compare the prices of the individual tools first, and question whether you really need the complete set (it may contain additional tools such as a narrow trowel, which you may not need).

There are a number of unconventional designs, but unless you have had chance to try these out you will probably be wise to stick to the traditional shapes.

How useful and pleasant to handle a trowel or fork is, will depend partly on the 'working end' – the prongs or blade – and partly on the handle.

Handles Round wooden handles, usually painted or lacquered, should be perfectly satisfactory, but watch out for rough ends produced by the lathe. You may find those shaped to provide finger grips are uncomfortable and irritating to use.

Whether you get on with plastic handles will be a matter of personal preference – gardeners are usually divided about them. The two other types of handles that you may not like are wooden ones with a socket joint for the head, and those on all-in-one metal tools.

Some long-handled trowels and hand forks are available, but these are only worth considering if you find bending difficult. The forks with a full hoe-length handle can be useful for loosening the soil around plants, but it's a job you can also do with a hoe.

Fork heads The most popular type of head has three flat prongs joined to a kinked stalk (tang) which fits into the handle. Those made from thin pressed metal to give a curved cross-section are generally less satisfactory and you may find them more difficult to clean. Heads with four twisted prongs joined to the handle by a socket are also less popular.

Trowel heads are all fairly similar to use, and there is little to choose between the types. There are a few unusual trowel head designs, but you are unlikely to find these more convenient to use than an ordinary trowel.

Narrow trowels, also known as rockery or transplanting trowels, are useful for working in a confined space, such as a rock garden.

Some trowels have a depth gauge stamped into the metal, and you may find this helpful when planting bulbs, for instance. It can be a convenient guide for planting distances too.

The blade or prongs may be made from aluminium alloy, chrome-plated steel, ordinary steel, or stainless steel. Trials have shown no particular preference for any of these materials, though stainless steel always looks good – especially if the tools are being given as a present.

Trowels and hand forks were reviewed in **Gardening from Which?** *December 1983.*

DIBBERS AND BULB PLANTERS

A dibber is a tool used for making holes in the soil – pencil-like ones are suitable for inserting cuttings or when pricking out seedlings, and those the thickness of a spade handle are useful for making holes for leeks and for firming in plants such as cabbages and wallflowers. They are no substitute for a trowel for general planting – making holes with a dibber consolidates the soil too much. They are not suitable for planting bulbs either as they are likely to leave a pocket of air beneath the bulbs.

You can make a dibber from an old spade or fork handle by cutting it down and rounding the end with a plane or file.

If you want to buy one, choose one with a rounded rather than pointed end. A steel-tipped one will be more serviceable.

A bulb planter will take out a core of soil and return it once you have planted the bulb in position. Unlike a dibber it does not compact the soil.

Refinements that you may find useful are a depth gauge marked on the metal, and the ability to release the core of soil with a trigger-like action that causes the planter to open like jaws.

You can buy long-handled bulb planters, which could be useful if you plant a lot of bulbs and find bending a problem.

GARDEN LINES

A garden line is most useful in a vegetable garden, but is worth using in all parts of the garden to make sure seeds or plants are set out neatly. A reel-mounted type is easy to manage, and a polypropylene cord will last a long time. A bright colour, such as orange, will enable the line to be seen more easily against the ground.

You will usually find the largest range of tools in garden centres, but it's also worth looking in good ironmongers' shops, supermarkets and DIY superstores, as well as discount houses. These often have very competitively priced tools, albeit a limited range. Many of them offer power tools at a substantial discouunt over the manufacturer's suggested price.

If you have trouble buying more unusual gardening equipment, contact the British Agricultural and Garden Machinery Association (see SOCIETIES AND ORGANISATIONS*) – they will be able to refer you to appropriate manufacturers.*

Other gardening aids

GLOVES

Gardening gloves are sensible protection against cuts, scratches, and other injuries. But the type of gloves that you need will depend on the job you need them for – what's right for pruning roses might not be adequate for concrete mixing and construction jobs.

All-leather gloves are usually made from an inexpensive type of leather, but are ideal for heavy work and very prickly jobs such as pruning roses. Although they'll last well, they will probably make your hands hot and sweaty.

All fabric (usually cotton or cotton and synthetic fibres) are only suitable for light work, perhaps where you want to avoid friction or the risk of blisters, and afford little protection against thorns and dirt. They are unlikely to wear well either, but will let your hands 'breathe'.

Leather and fabric gloves with leather palms and fabric backs are reasonably hard-wearing and give your palms protection from thorns. They're not as weatherproof as all-leather gloves, but are likely to be less sweaty and uncomfortable to wear.

Vinyl-impregnated fabric gloves look rather like imitation suede (you will probably see the grain of the fabric on the surface). They should wear better and give your hands better protection than all-fabric gloves.

Vinyl-coated fabric gloves are shiny and look like plastic. They are the ones to choose for very dirty jobs, perhaps during construction work or when handling chemicals (they are waterproof). They will be hot to wear, however, and will probably make your hands sweaty.

Getting a good fit

Only rarely are the sizes of gardening gloves given in correct glove sizing units – usually they will simply be described as 'men's' or 'ladies' ', though sometimes there are additional sizes. However, these are generally little use as the actual size is likely to vary from manufacturer to manufacturer, and can be variable even for the same brand. Try on several pairs to see which fits the best.

Open cuffs can allow soil or debris to fall inside the gloves, but a knitted wrist may make your hands hot. The gauntlet type provide better protection for your wrists and may keep your sleeves cleaner.

Gardening gloves were reviewed in **Gardening from Which?** *December 1983.*

WHEELBARROWS

For most gardeners, a good wheelbarrow will cope with most tasks around the garden. For heavy construction work, a builder's wheelbarrow is best (you can usually buy these from a builders' merchant or DIY superstore), but these are too heavy for everyday gardening jobs.

Most wheelbarrows have zinc-coated steel bins, though some are plastic. Either will do the job.

Solid rubber tyres are common, but they have little cushioning effect on rough ground. For soft ground, the wider the wheel the better. The pneumatic ball type are particularly good on soft ground.

The capacity of the barrow is not as important as one might assume. A large barrow may hold more soil than you can manage comfortably. Width can be important. Make sure it's not too wide to go through the narrowest gap.

If you are likely to want to tip the contents out, a tipping bar will be an advantage (otherwise the barrow may tend to run back as you tip).

Test for comfort: try pushing and pulling an assembled barrow (many come as a kit, but the shop should have one that's assembled). You may find that you catch your shins on the back of the barrow, or that the legs get in the way of your feet. You don't want to stoop too low to pick up the barrow, yet you don't want its legs to trail on the ground. For comfort, your arms should be straight down by your sides when you walk.

Wheelbarrows were reviewed in **Gardening from Which?** *December 1982.*

CARTS AND TROLLEYS

If you do decide on one of the alternatives to a wheelbarrow, there are three main options:

Garden carts are much more stable than wheelbarrows, and because many of them have a pram-type handle you can push or pull them with one hand. For this reason they are a good choice for anyone elderly or disabled. But generally they are less manoeuvrable than wheelbarrows. Check that the clearance above the ground is sufficient to clear obstacles and will not

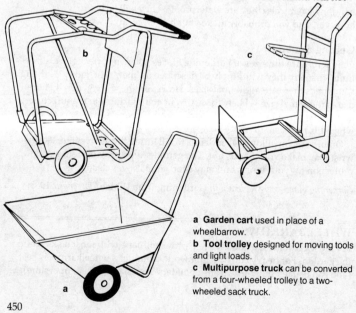

a Garden cart used in place of a wheelbarrow.
b Tool trolley designed for moving tools and light loads.
c Multipurpose truck can be converted from a four-wheeled trolley to a two-wheeled sack truck.

present problems on steps, for instance. Check that the handle is at a convenient height. If storage space is a problem, it might be worth considering one that has a folding metal frame and detachable canvas bag, for example, the Boscart.

Tool trolleys are intended mainly for moving tools around, and for light loads, but are no substitute for a barrow. You will need to question carefully whether a tool trolley will do the particular job you want – carry the right tools or load. They can be useful if you have a large garden and have difficulty getting around.

Multi-purpose trucks can convert from a two-wheeled sack truck to a four-wheeled truck or platform. These are most likely to be useful for construction jobs – moving sacks of cement, bricks, paving slabs, and so on – and most can also be fitted with a rubbish sack. Check how much work is involved in converting it from one form to another – if it's too involved you may find that you don't use the feature. See how heavy it is to move about when empty, question whether the clearance beneath the truck will be sufficient to cope with steps and so on, and if storage space is a problem check how small it will fold down to.

Upright 'porters' trolleys' or 'sack trucks' are also available. These do not convert into four-wheeled trucks.

Garden carts and trucks were reviewed in **Gardening from Which?** *November 1984.*

COMPOST BINS

You can make perfectly good compost in a heap, but you may prefer a bin because it generally looks neater. A compost bin is no substitute for following the basic principles of compost making, and you cannot rely on it to make good compost unless conditions are right.

Tests have shown little difference in performance between makes, but you will probably be strongly influenced by appearance and how easy they are to use. The basic types are:

Metal frames usually plastic coated wire meshing, round or rectangular in shape (some have a plastic liner).

Wooden bins of traditional shape using sections that slot together.

Plastic bins of various shapes, often round or cone-shaped, sometimes rectangular. Some have to be assembled from plastic panels, others come ready-made.

You can, of course, make your own bin from materials such as bricks, wood, wire netting or even corrugated iron or plastic.

A good bin, whether bought or made, should have:

- soil contact for the compost material at the base
- adequate ventilation, either from the base or sides
- a cover (though you could easily make a lid yourself)
- good capacity – the larger the bin, the better the compost is likely to be, as long as you have enough material to keep it filled

For convenience, look for:

- the ability to get at the compost – it is sometimes useful to be able to remove some compost without having to dismantle the whole bin, or remove a lot of unrotted material first
- if you are likely to keep dismantling to store or move it, ease of assembly may be important. Ideally though, your compost bin should always be in use

Compost bins were reviewed in **Gardening from Which?** *December 1982.*

PROPAGATORS

Propagators will help you to get your seeds off to a good start, and probably enable you to root many cuttings more successfully. But they vary enormously in both price and sophistication, so it's important to be clear about what you want from your propagator.

If you simply want to raise a few seedlings indoors you may not need a heated propagator at all. Your home may well be warm enough for germination, and you could be better off spending your money on some form of supplementary lighting to prevent the seedlings becoming too drawn once they germinate. If you want to buy a propagator for indoors, an unheated one may be adequate (it will provide a convenient, closed environment that will reduce fluctuations in temperature and help to provide the humidity that's useful for rooting cuttings).

For a greenhouse or unheated room, however, you will need a heated propagator. You can buy propagators to set over a paraffin heater, but most of them are electric.

Heating pads are the cheapest and simplest way to turn an unheated propagator (a seed tray and plastic top) into a heated one. These are simply a heating element in the form of a metal plate. The plate fits into the seed tray and is covered with compost. If you only want to raise a few seedlings, it should be adequate and will cost little more than 10p a week to run continuously. But you will find its scope limited and it will be tied up until you prick out the seedlings. It is unlikely to provide more than a few degrees lift in temperature.

Heated bases consist of a heating element in a sealed plastic base on which you stand one or two standard seed trays or an unheated propagator. Some come with a top to provide a sealed environment over the trays. Although not a very efficient method of heating, it is cheap to run, say 15p to 20p a week, and you can use the base for a succession of boxes once the seeds have germinated, without having to wait until the pricking-out stage.

Heated trays have a heating element sandwiched between two plastic skins of a seed tray, and usually a moulded plastic or flexible polythene top. Most are supplied with small seed trays to fit inside the larger one.

Those without a thermostat can prove useful, and cost between 15p and 20p a week to run. The lack of a thermostat can be a disadvantage if room or greenhouse temperatures are high or rise rapidly during the day.

Those with a fixed thermostat (it cuts off the heater at a certain

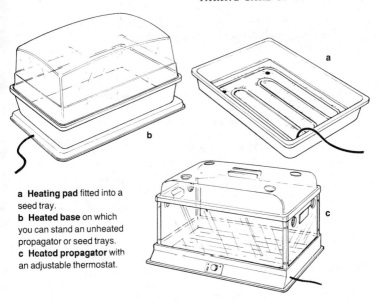

a Heating pad fitted into a seed tray.
b Heated base on which you can stand an unheated propagator or seed trays.
c Heated propagator with an adjustable thermostat.

temperature, but you can't adjust that temperature) generally have a more powerful heating element. If the room is warm anyway, it may not have many advantages over a propagator without a thermostat (though it will avoid overheating) and in a cool environment may cost over 50p a week to run.

Propagators with an adjustable thermostat are generally larger, taking say three full-sized trays, and offering a choice of tops. They're more expensive than other propagators, costing from about £28 to as much as £85, and tests have shown that many models do not let you control the temperature of the compost very well, especially at low room or greenhouse temperatures. Running costs will depend on the setting and the temperature of your greenhouse or room.

Electric propagators were reviewed in **Gardening from Which?** *March 1983.*

Taking care of your tools

It pays to take care of your tools – besides looking better, they will work better and last longer. Most handtools should last a lifetime.

There are some general rules that apply to all tools:

- don't put them away dirty. Wash them or hose them down if necessary
- don't leave them out. Put them away after use – it's a routine that eventually becomes automatic if you discipline yourself – like cleaning your teeth

453

- try to put them away dry, and keep an oily rag handy to wipe over unprotected metal (stainless steel only needs dipping in water and wiping dry with a cloth)

There are other things that you can do for specific tools.

WHEELBARROWS

You can protect the bottom of the legs, and the tipping bar, by slitting a small piece of plastic hose and pushing it over the frame. Alternatively, you could bind the frame with plastic tape.

To reduce the risk of the bolt holes rusting through, use wide washers to bolt the bin to the frame, and paint round the holes with zinc-based paint.

If you have to leave a metal barrow outside, stand it on end so that water doesn't collect in it.

HEDGETRIMMERS

Clean sap and debris off the blade. Use paraffin or soapy water and a stiff brush. Dry, then oil lightly. Clean outer casing, especially fins.

For petrol trimmers, after 10 hours of use or once a year, whichever is sooner:

- check that the bolts securing the blades are correctly tensioned
- make sure the fuel strainer is clear
- add grease to the gear housing if necessary
- check the spark plug. Clean; reset gap if necessary
- clean out the silencer
- sharpen the blade with a flat file

HEDGING AND LAWN SHEARS, AND SECATEURS

- oil the pivot occasionally
- keep blades sharpened
- adjust tension if necessary

MOWERS

Follow the manufacturer's maintenance instructions. In general, you should:

- remember to check the blade clearance regularly on cylinder mowers
- keep the whole machine clean and well oiled
- treat the machine with respect – avoid running over stones or grit which could blunt or damage the blades

CULTIVATORS

Follow the manufacturer's maintenance instructions.

HOW TO SHARPEN YOUR TOOLS

Blunt blades mean hard work. They simply won't cut efficiently. Sharpening saw blades is a job for the professional (or possibly the keen handyman), but you should be able to tackle tools such as shears, knives, secateurs, and spades yourself.

You will need either an oil stone or a wet stone (one uses oil, the other water, as a lubricant), which you can buy from a hardware shop. You will need a fine and a coarse finish (sometimes they are on opposite sides of the same stone, otherwise you'll need to buy two stones to cover all sharpening jobs). For hoes and spades you'll need a medium grade, flat metal file.

The exact technique to use will depend on the tool. The general rules are:

- sharpen the blade at the same angle as set by the manufacturer. Some will have to be angled on both sides, some on only one side. Inspect the blade carefully to see how it was when new
- first clean the blade with a plastic scouring pad and white spirit or paraffin
- hold the blade or stone firmly at a constant angle (keep your fingers out of the way of the blade). For most tools use the coarser side of the stone, but for tools with a fine cutting edge such as a knife use the fine side
- keep the stone lubricated (with an oil stone wipe surplus oil from the surface) and then move the blade (or stone) in a circular motion
- when the blade becomes sharper you should detect a different sound and feel as it begins to 'bite' into the stone. Wipe the blade frequently with a rag
- check sharpness at intervals. When sharp you may find a slight burr on the cutting edge. For fine edges you need to remove this by using light strokes on either side of the cutting edge (for blades only sharpened on one side, you'll have to keep the blade absolutely flat when stroking the other side against the stone). This breaks off the burr leaving a clean, sharp edge
- finish off with one or two **light** strokes

How to sharpen tools was dealt with in **Gardening from Which?** *December 1983, servicing mowers in February 1983, and DIY sharpening devices for lawnmowers in December 1984.*

Getting it done for you

Some manufacturers will sharpen tools such as secateurs and loppers for you – if you don't want to do the job yourself it could be worth checking.

Machinery dealers, tool shops, and specialist grinders may also do the job for you.

'Own brand' tools made for supermarkets and chain stores may be well worth considering. **Gardening from Which?** *tests have often shown these to be good value for money.*

Hiring tools

Several times we have suggested hiring tools, either because it is more sensible than buying an expensive tool that you might only use once a year, or because it will give you the opportunity to try out a piece of equipment that you are thinking about buying.

Hire tools take a lot of punishment and you will need to make sure the equipment is in good condition – for your own safety and to be able to judge how much help the tool might be to you.

Most problems are likely to come with mechanical tools – cultivators and lawnmowers for instance. **Gardening from Which?** experience has shown that these can be so poor that they won't work properly, and may even be potentially dangerous. Below we suggest some things to check for if you hire tools of this type. There are other tools that should be more trouble-free, and it's easier to judge their condition at a glance – post-hole borers and wheelbarrows for example.

TOOLS WORTH HIRING

Expensive tools that it is worth considering hiring if you will not use them often include: brushcutter, chainsaw, cultivator, powered lawn aerator, powerful hedgetrimmer, large rotary lawnmower (which you may need to deal with long spring grass).

Other tools may be worth hiring for one-off jobs (such as garden construction). These include: angle grinder, cement mixer, pickaxe, post driver, post-hole borer, rammer, wheelbarrow.

WHERE TO HIRE

There are some large hire shop chains and lots of regional or local hire companies. You should find several to choose from in the Yellow Pages (look under *Hire services – tools and equipment*). Hiring from a large group is no guarantee of better service or condition of tools. It's worth phoning around for prices, but bear in mind that if you go to a shop some distance away, you will have additional travel or delivery costs.

THE CONTRACT

You will almost certainly have to sign a contract when you hire a tool. You will have to sign a declaration on the lines of: *the above items were received by me in good order and I agree to the conditions of hire as stated on the copy of this agreement, a copy of which is in my possession*. Don't sign it until you have made sure the equipment is in good order. If there are any obvious faults and you are still prepared to accept it, write the faults down and get the person in the shop to sign it. Have the person in the shop start and operate the equipment if possible – this will ensure you know how to operate it, and give you a chance to see that it works.

The hire contract is likely to be lengthy and full of legal jargon, but you are protected from any unfair clause by the Unfair Contract Terms Act, and the hire company is required to provide you with a tool or piece of equipment that is suitable for your purpose, so they can't make you pay for equipment that doesn't work at all, or doesn't do its job properly.

CHARGES

Compare charges carefully, and ask for prices by the day, week, and weekend. Sometimes it's as cheap to hire a tool for a week as half a week, and hiring for a weekend may be no more expensive than hiring for 24 hours. It pays to book the equipment you need in advance, especially if demand for it is seasonal. Allow yourself plenty of time for cleaning the equipment before you return it. If you want the equipment delivered check the charges.

FINALLY A CHECKLIST

Before you accept the equipment, it's worth running through this checklist, where it is relevant:

- look for wear, and damage. Look particularly for loose, worn or missing parts. Don't accept anything that's doubtful
- make sure that adjustable things can actually be adjusted properly
- make sure that you know how it works. Get a demonstration if possible. For powered equipment, check for excessive noise or vibration. Ask for written instructions – if these can't be supplied, write down everything you are told
- check that electrical tools are for the right voltage. Once you have got the equipment home, check the wiring in the plugs
- for 4-stroke engines, check the oil levels in engine and transmission
- make sure you have appropriate accessories, such as goggles or protective gloves (you may have to buy or hire them separately)

Hiring tools and equipment was reviewed in **Gardening from Which?** *August 1984.*

Cloches and frames

If you want to extend the growing season, particularly in the vegetable garden, cloches and frames will be invaluable. They are sometimes useful for protecting vulnerable plants during the winter too.

CLOCHES

You need to use the more expensive cloches intensively to justify them on purely economic grounds – they can cost over £10 per square metre of

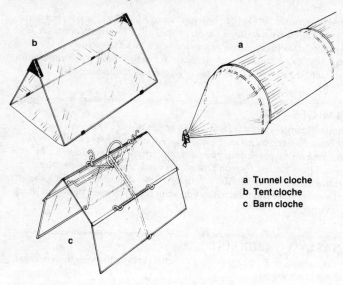

a Tunnel cloche
b Tent cloche
c Barn cloche

cover, and a few can be more than double this price. At the other extreme you may be able to provide cover for the same area with a polythene cloche for less than £1, although the polythene covers will need replacing every few years.

Size and shape

Although individual designs vary a lot, most cloches fall into one of the following groups. Decide what you want to use your cloches for and this will tell you the type of cloche that you need.

Tent cloches have a triangular profile, with the ground forming the base. They are usually no more than 30cm (1ft) high in the centre, with little useable headroom at the sides. This restricts the sort of crop you can grow. They can be used for things like lettuces and radishes, but are ideally suited to germinating seeds, when the lack of height is no disadvantage.

Barn cloches have more or less upright sides, with an inverted V top. 'Low barn' cloches have sides no more than 30cm (1ft) high, 'high barn' cloches have perhaps another 15cm (6in) of height at the sides. The larger ones are useful for tall crops such as peppers, but even the low barn type have much more useable space than tent cloches.

Dome-shaped cloches have roughly vertical sides and a slightly dome-shaped top. Although they can be roomier than tunnel cloches for bushy and sprawling plants, they lack the height for tall plants.

Tunnel cloches are usually formed from a long, continuous sheet of plastic, secured over wire hoops. There are, however, some tunnel-shaped cloches made in individual sections about 1 to 1.2m (3 to 4ft) long. Generally they are best for germinating seeds and getting seedlings off to a good start, but some are quite roomy and can be used for advancing low-growing crops such as strawberries or even bushier plants such as tomatoes, until they get too big.

Materials

Glass is the traditional material, but it's expensive and over the years has come under increasing competition from plastics. However, glass does not deteriorate like some plastics, and will have the longest life barring breakages (the risk of which may rule it out if you have small children). More heat is retained at night by glass than by any other cloche material, and light transmission is very good.

Polythene is widely used for tunnel cloches. Sometimes the fairly lightweight 150 gauge is used, but the more substantial 300 and 600 gauge may also be used. It transmits light well, but condensation tends to cling and can reduce light by about 10 per cent, though in practice this probably won't affect the plants noticeably. It does not retain heat well at night.

Polythene is the least durable of the options, but the cheapest to replace. Untreated 150 gauge is only likely to last a season, but if treated with an ultra-violet inhibitor should last two or three seasons. The thicker the polythene, the longer it should last.

Polypropylene is widely used for semi-flat or corrugated sheets (it is available as a corrugated double layer as Norplex, and Stewart cloches are rigid, injection-moulded polypropylene). The double-layered polypropylene is opaque and does not transmit light as well as most other materials, but the plants still seem to do well (it is possible that the extra heat retained goes some way to offsetting the poorer light).

Heat loss from ordinary polypropylene is substantial at night, but is less from the double-walled material.

Polypropylene treated with ultra-violet inhibitors should last for at least five years. The less rigid, double-layered type should last three to five years with an inhibitor.

PVC domes are closest to glass in light transmission and heat retention at night, and should last for five years.

Points to look for

Robustness Wind can lift a flimsy cloche once it gets under it. Glass should not be a problem because of its weight. Plastic cloches need strong anchorage pins that can penetrate at least 7.5 to 10cm (3 to 4in), or have some alternative strong method of anchorage.

Easy ventilation is especially important in summer, but also necessary earlier for crops such as strawberries which need to be pollinated by insects.

Some cloches have a built-in ventilating system, such as roof panels or small panes in the roof that can be raised or removed, or sides that roll up. If there isn't some means of ventilation you might have to move the cloches apart to leave gaps, or remove them altogether.

Polythene tunnels don't have any means of ventilation other than pulling the sheet up at one or both sides, but this should be perfectly adequate.

> ## Cloche clips
>
> *You can buy cloche clips to hold pieces of glass, usually to form a tent cloche. These are worth considering especially if you already have a supply of suitable glass. If you buy glass, make sure that you ask for horticultural glass – it's cheaper and perfectly adequate.*

Ease of handling To get the most use out of your cloches you'll need to move them from one crop to another. With most you can do this without dismantling them, but polythene tunnels, for example, will probably need to be taken apart to move them.

Ease of watering Although some moisture will seep sideways beneath the cloche after heavy rain, generally you will have to be prepared to water occasionally. Ask yourself how difficult this will be – how easy is it to remove enough of the cloche to allow you to water?

Some cloches have a self-watering system built into the design, and these can be useful. Some have a built-in piped watering system (utilising the tubular ridge pieces) that you connect to a hose-pipe – a good system if you are organised with a water supply from a hose. Some made from moulded plastic have a trough in the top to collect water, which then drips through holes, and one model allows water to come through the self-ventilating flap when it rains. There can be a problem with those that let through rainwater – in winter the ground may become too wet and the continual dripping may be damaging to plants.

Bird protection is a very useful feature. Often birds will make a feast of the succulent young plants while you are ventilating the cloches. Cloches that incorporate netting, or facilities for it, can be very useful – with some the panels can be replaced by netting. You may want to use the cloches just for this feature at times, to keep the birds off strawberries, for instance.

Easy access for harvesting and weeding can be important. If you have to lift the whole cloche off, make sure the design allows you to replace it over the growing crop easily (if the bottom curves inwards, for instance, this could be difficult).

Cloches were reviewed in **Gardening from Which?** *February 1983.*

COLD FRAMES

A cold frame can be useful in any garden, for an early start or for overwintering, but it will be most useful if you have a greenhouse: it will be invaluable for hardening off seedlings, and for relieving pressure within the greenhouse at peak times.

The traditional cold frame had a glazed frame supported on brickwork. Nowadays aluminium frames are popular (though wood is still used) and glass no longer has a monopoly – many frames use plastics instead. Many of them are glazed to the ground, which provides much more light for the plants but makes them less cosy in cold weather unless you insulate them in some way.

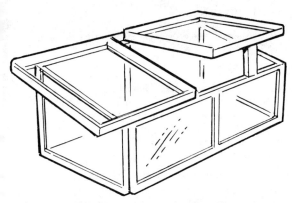

Aluminium and glass cold frame, one of the most popular types. The panels (lights) can be lifted up or slid sideways for ventilation, and removed altogether for easy access.

Size

If you want to grow vegetables in your frame, perhaps to get them that bit earlier, you will need one at least 1.2m x 60cm (4ft x 2ft) to make it worthwhile.

Height is not important for crops such as lettuces and radishes, but for plants such as dwarf beans and pot plants, you will need more height – say 60cm (2ft). You could, of course, increase the useful height by raising the frame up on timber or bricks.

Insulation

Wood and brick sides will retain heat much better than glass or metal – but you could insulate these with expanded polystyrene sheets during cold weather.

Light

Plants need as much light as possible in spring. Glass is best in this respect. Plastics vary a lot but don't generally let through as much light, and can discolour with age and become scratched.

Ventilation

It's important to be able to ventilate the frame adequately. The ventilation should be easy to adjust and ideally should leave the plants protected so they are not exposed if there is a sudden downpour of rain. It's also worth thinking about how easy it is to work with the frame. Many frames have panels which can be raised at one end for ventilation, leaving the plants protected, but which can also be slid open or taken off altogether for easy access to the plants. This may restrict where you can site the frame – you will need room to slide the top beyond the limits of the frame.

Durability

Aluminium and galvanised steel frames are generally strong and, if well-constructed, should last a long time. The life-expectancy of timber will depend on the type of wood and its treatment. Cedar is usually the most expensive, but is the most resistant to decay. Whatever wood is used it should have been well seasoned, and ordinary softwoods treated with a preservative.

Glass or plastic?

Glass is the most satisfactory glazing material generally, but if you have children one of the plastics may be a safer bet. If using glass, bear in mind that smaller panes will be cheaper to replace than large ones.

Rigid and semi-rigid plastics are generally quite strong (some are wire-reinforced), but because they are light you may have to be careful to ensure the frame is adequately anchored.

Cold frames were reviewed in **Gardening from Which?** *April 1983.*

Buying a shed

Although most garden sheds look similar, the quality varies enormously. For that reason it always pays to inspect the shed first, if possible, before you buy it. This may mean visiting a number of garden centres and display grounds before you make up your mind. If you can't find the exact shed that you want on display, try looking at a different model in the same range to get an idea of quality.

Some sheds are available nationally, but many are sold locally or in one region only. They are often advertised in local papers; it's worth checking.

Don't be tempted by price alone, however, for quality is important in a shed. If it isn't reasonably weatherproof it won't last long, the tools inside will rust and fertilisers become damp and hard.

CHOOSING THE RIGHT SIZE

It makes sense to buy the largest shed you can afford and have space for. A shed that's too small will quickly be filled to overflowing, making it difficult to organise the storage space and to find things when you need them.

If you only want to store a few garden tools, a small shed about 1.2m x 0.9m (4ft x 3ft) might be adequate, but the most popular sizes are around 2.1m x 1.5m (7ft x 5ft) or 2.4m x 1.8m (8ft x 6ft), big enough to accommodate a small workbench. If you want to use your shed as a workshop, however, then 3m x 2.4m (10ft x 8ft) is a better size.

SHAPE

The choice will be between an apex roof (like an inverted V) or a pent roof (slopes from front to back or vice-versa). The latter is likely to cost slightly less for a shed of similar size and quality. One drawback of a pent roof is that if you place a workbench under the window you may find the headroom too restrictive to work comfortably. However, you may find the possibility of having the door at the front instead of at the end a useful attribute in some situations.

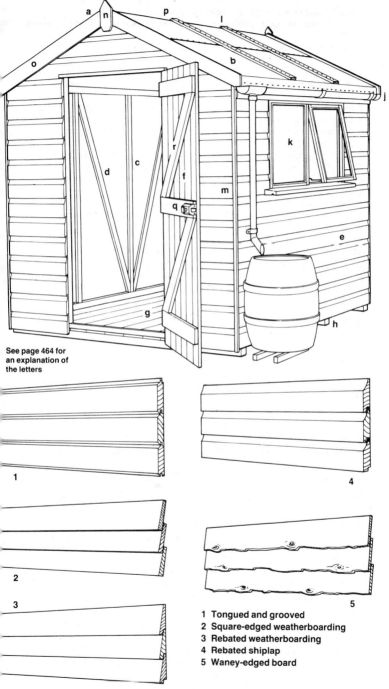

See page 464 for
an explanation of
the letters

1 Tongued and grooved
2 Square-edged weatherboarding
3 Rebated weatherboarding
4 Rebated shiplap
5 Waney-edged board

a Roof should allow enough headroom, especially if you plan to use it as a workshop.

b Felt, the thicker the better. A mineral felt with a chip finish on the upper surface is an advantage. A double layer is a good idea. Joints should overlap.

c Frame should have a strong, rigid construction, and firm joints.

d Cross-braces provide extra strength.

e Cladding should be weatherproof.

f Door: should fit well and be solidly constructed (with ledges and braces). Check whether it can be hung on either side if this is important to you. A fitted lock is desirable.

g Floor should be firm (try bouncing up and down on it) and treated with a preservative. Check whether the floor is included when comparing prices. Sometimes it's an extra. As an alternative you could make a concrete base, but this is also costly, and can be hard work to lay; a concrete floor can be cold and damp in winter.

h Bearers keep the floor off the ground and therefore prolong its life. Make sure the bearers are pressure-impregnated with a preservative.

i Eaves should be generous as they help to throw water clear of the walls, but guttering is better.

j Guttering helps to keep the sides of the shed dry, so can prolong the life of the shed.

k Window should be hinged at the top and open outwards for the best weatherproofing. It will not matter then if you leave it open and it rains. At least one window should open. The sill should slope and have a drip groove cut in the bottom.

l Roof battens help to hold down the felt.

m Cover fillets protect the sawn ends of boards at the corners.

n Finial

o Barge board

p Ridge purlin (not visible)

q Ledge

r Brace

MATERIALS

Timber is the most popular choice for a shed, but metal and concrete are among the alternatives.

Metal can be more attractive than it sounds. In the right setting a metal shed can look quite neat. Most have a low-pitched apex roof and a sliding door.

Steel may tend to have a 'tinny' feel that can be offputting to some people, and they are generally best regarded strictly as tool sheds rather than workshops. Some are inexpensive compared with similar timber sheds. Look for a rust-resisting finish and perhaps a galvanised floor frame.

Concrete sounds very unattractive, but positioned near existing brick or concrete structures may not look out of place. The roof is normally flat, but the walls need not look like concrete; some have an imitation brick finish that can be difficult to tell from the real thing without close inspection. They are strong and have good weather-resistance. You will need to lay a proper concrete foundation, so allow for this when costing the alternatives.

Timber is the most popular choice: it combines a pleasing appearance with reasonable cost, and generally blends in well in a garden setting.

The cheaper kinds of shed are made from softwood timbers, usually deal (some manufacturers use the term whitewood or softwood; European redwood may also come under this heading). They are not naturally durable timbers and must be treated with a preservative. It is best to buy one made from pressure-impregnated timber, but you may have to place a special order for this and pay extra. Painting it with a preservative yourself will not have the same effect – the preservative will not penetrate as well.

Sometimes the timber is described as vacuum treated or dipped, but how good these methods are depends on how well the treatment has been carried out. Bear in mind whether the timber has been treated when comparing costs – treatment might add perhaps 7.5 to 10 per cent to the cost.

Western red cedar is a more expensive timber, but it has a natural rot resistance. It will weather to a silver-grey colour if not painted with a cedar preparation periodically.

CLADDING

The type of cladding is no guarantee of quality, but some types are generally more robust and weatherproof than others. The thickness of the boards should be at least 25mm (1in) nominal or 19mm (¾in) nominal if lined (bear in mind that the actual thickness after preparation will be less than the nominal size).

Tongued and grooved boards look good and usually offer good weatherproofing – but check that there are no splits or knot holes in the timber.

Square and feather-edged weatherboarding can be very weatherproof, but can also be variable in quality. Check that the overlap is adequate and even, and that you can't see gaps. The boards should not be thin or bowed.

Waney-edged boards have a rustic look, but make sure the boards overlap properly and that there are no gaps or knot holes showing.

Rebated weatherboarding has a neat finish and should be weatherproof, but again look for obvious faults.

Rebated shiplap gives a distinctive appearance (see illustration) that you may like. Sometimes tongued and grooved shiplap is used, but the outward appearance is the same.

INSULATION

Even a lining of building paper will improve insulation and help to keep tools drier. This is sometimes included in the price, or may be offered as an extra. Failing that, you can line the shed yourself (a builders' merchant will advise you).

GETTING IT ERECTED

A shed is not difficult to erect yourself if you have a helper – the sections are simply bolted together (some nailed, but this is not usually as satisfactory). But if you do not fancy doing this, you should be able to get it erected for about ten per cent of the cost for, say, a 2.4m x 1.8m (8ft x 6ft) model.

Garden sheds were reviewed in **Gardening from Which?** *October 1982 and September 1984.*

Buying a greenhouse

A greenhouse can be a major financial investment and a visually dominating feature in your garden, so you need to think carefully about the alternatives available.

It's worth breaking the decision-making down into two areas: the **shape** of greenhouse you want (conventional, dome-shaped, polygonal, for instance), and then the **materials and features** that will best meet your needs.

WHAT SHAPE?

You may find a few greenhouses that don't fall conveniently into the categories below, but these are very uncommon.

Curvilinear greenhouses have roof panels that slope at different angles to give a curved effect. This is claimed to improve light transmission, but the benefit of this will depend to some extent on where you site the greenhouse, and the time of year. The shape is more interesting than a traditional greenhouse, but it is not so easy to grow tall plants near to the glass.

Domes make more of a feature of the greenhouse, and are especially useful in windy or exposed sites, where the shape has the benefit of offering low wind resistance. The shape itself has considerable strength and means that individual glazing bars can be slim, and light transmission should be good. The frames are usually aluminium or galvanised steel. The shape, though interesting, is not an easy one to fit into a small garden.

It can be difficult to utilise for growing a range of plants, and you will have to buy specialised fittings (shelves, benches, etc).

Lean-to greenhouses are intended to fit against a wall (though you can buy some with a potting shed for the other half). Not so expensive to heat in winter if placed against the house, because heat loss is less through the house wall, and they can be useful where space is limited. Some of the more elegantly designed types can double as a conservatory if placed against French windows or a patio door. Useful if you want to grow climbers (the back wall is ideal). They need careful siting – facing south they will probably become too hot in summer, facing north there will be too much shade for most plants. South-easterly and south-westerly aspects are usually the best compromise.

Mini plant-houses are usually only large enough to take plants but not the gardener. You have to do the work from the outside. Generally they are lean-tos, and worth considering where space is at a premium. The small size makes winter heating relatively cheap, but they can easily overheat in summer. No substitute for a proper greenhouse, but useful if you haven't space for anything else.

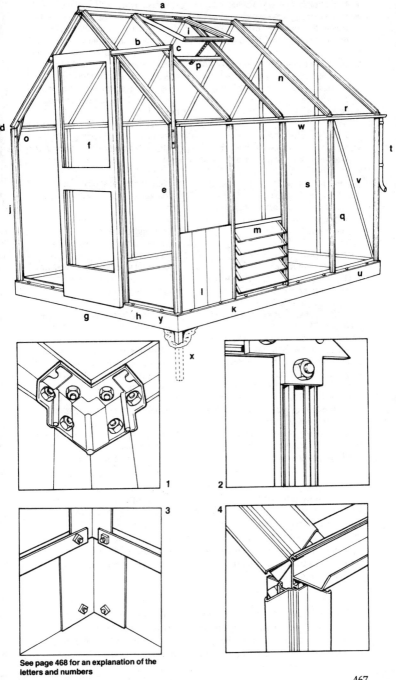

See page 468 for an explanation of the letters and numbers

a Ridge height needs to provide sufficient roof angle to shed condensation and snow; this means an extra 2ft over eaves height for a 6ft-wide house, 2ft 6in for 8ft-wide.

b Locking device to hold door open and lock it shut is useful.

c Runners on top rail should be large, at least 1in diameter, for smooth running.

d Eaves height needs to be 5ft 6in for tall crops.

e Draughts: check that door and ventilators fit well to reduce draughts.

f Doorway should be at least 6ft high and 2ft wide.

g Threshold: choose as low a one as possible to avoid tripping.

h Kick panel helps to reduce breakages.

i Hinged ventilator

j Main frame

k Base

l Infilling

m Louvre ventilator

n Glazing strip which fits between the frame and glass. It should be draughtproof, flexible and resilient.

Ventilation area needed is a sixth of floor area, or two 2 x 2ft vents in a 6 x 8ft house – this is rarely provided as standard, so check that extras are available. For good air flow, some vents should be low down on sides, others at top of roof.

o Support for upper rail must be adequately secured.

p Plastic fittings are sometimes used for vent openers but there are disadvantages – they deteriorate in sunlight and can snap in cold weather.

q Glazing bars should be strong enough to support crops like tomatoes.

r Glass must overlap gutter so water runs off roof, not back into house.

s Standard sized glass, either 24 x 24in or 24 x 18in, is least expensive to replace. Larger panes admit more light and are easier to clean but can be expensive.

t Downpipe provision is essential if you want to collect rainwater – downpipes are rarely standard.

u Bolts to secure base to frame should be no more than 2ft apart.

v Cross bracing must be adequate to give a rigid structure even without glass in position.

w Gutter size must be enough to catch all rainwater – about 1 x 2in for small greenhouses.

x Anchorage to ground – are legs, ground anchors etc provided, for setting in concrete, or must a brick base be constructed?

y Channel for base of door best avoided as it collects dirt; an overhanging arrangement is preferable.

1 Diecast corner pieces greatly add to strength and rigidity and make erection easier.

2 Channels for captive bolts or plastic plugs should be provided in main members as well as in glazing bars to allow maximum use of fittings.

3 Corner pieces which secure base together should overlap sides by at least 2in.

4 Sharp edges can be dangerous – check particularly around the doorway, corners of base and gutter ends.

Polygonal greenhouses, with say six, seven, or nine sides, are made by several manufacturers. They have the merit of looking much more attractive than the traditional greenhouse, and for this reason may be a good choice where they have to be sited in a conspicuous place, such as on a patio or in a very small garden. The drawbacks are the relatively high cost for the growing area provided and the fact that you need specialised fittings (benches and so on).

Traditional greenhouses have upright sides and an even-span roof. They are practical, and fit easily into most gardens. There is a vast range from which to choose, in many different sizes. This type gives the largest possible bench area for the area of ground covered, and most standard fittings can be used. Glass-to-ground models are useful for growing crops

---

Curved eaves

Some modern designs have curved eaves. The curved panels are usually made from polycarbonate or acrylic, which transmits light well but does not shed condensation so well and will deteriorate more quickly than glass. This is something you may be happy to accept for the enhanced appearance.

---

in the borders, but if you will be growing mainly pot-plants on staging, one with a brick, wood, concrete, or even metal, lower part will reduce heat loss in winter.

Some have **sloping sides** which can admit more light in winter when the sun is low in the sky. An angle of 18° is the optimum slope. However, if you do not use your greenhouse much in winter, the benefit to you may be marginal. Tall plants can only be grown close to the sides if they are trained on wires.

Polythene tunnels are used a lot commercially where they provide protection at low cost. In the garden they have less appeal, apart from perhaps in the kitchen garden. You will have to re-cover the structure every year or two, but the cost is low. Tall plants can not be grown at the sides, and the limited amount of framework makes it difficult to put up fixtures such as shelves. Ventilation can be a problem, and heat loss is likely to be high if you attempt to use a heater. Visually they are not attractive.

Uneven span greenhouses are not common. They have a larger roof span on one side, which is supposed to be arranged to face south so that it admits more light. The benefits are not that clear-cut: you may not find it convenient to give it that aspect, and the benefit is most likely to be noticed in winter, which is not relevant if you do not use it then or just keep it ticking over during the winter.

HOW BIG?

In short, buy the largest you can afford and have space for. If you make good use of your greenhouse, you'll almost certainly find a small one too restrictive after a while. If you can't afford a large one initially, but realise that you may want something larger later, think about choosing one that can be extended.

Also bear in mind the height – at the ridge (for your own comfort) and at the eaves. A ridge of 2.1m (7ft) is usually necessary to provide a door of reasonable proportions, and an eaves height of 1.7m (5ft 6in) is needed for plants such as tomatoes and late-flowering chrysanthemums.

WOOD OR METAL?

Metal greenhouses are most likely to be made from aluminium alloy extrusions. Galvanised steel is now rare: no matter how good the galvanising it is likely to be damaged at some time and will then need painting to avoid rust.

Aluminium is less expensive than wood and virtually maintenance-free (though salt spray will cause problems). There is a wide choice from which to select, and the narrow glazing bars mean good light penetration. Glazing will probably be quicker and easier than with a timber greenhouse (though other aspects of erection can be fiddly).

The appearance can be rather stark, though plastic-coated and enamelled versions are available for some designs. The metal is a good heat conductor and will lose heat more rapidly than timber at night, though this is still only a fraction of what's lost through the glass. It is not so easy to fix glass into the framework as in timber models, but you can buy special hooks, supports, and so on.

Timber is generally more attractive in appearance, it's easy to attach fittings to, and is generally warmer than metal (though wooden glazing bars may be thicker and reduce the amount of light the plants receive). A timber greenhouse is likely to be easier to erect: they usually come in large sections to bolt together whereas aluminium ones usually have to be bolted together from lots of bits and pieces, like a construction set.

Unfortunately, a timber greenhouse will probably be more expensive, size for size, not so strong, and need much more maintenance. Because prefabricated bases are rarely available, you will also need to build foundations.

Western red cedar is a popular choice – it has a natural rot resistance. But you will find other woods used, such as Scots pine and Norway spruce. These timbers are usually stronger than Western red cedar so the glazing bars may be thinner, but they will rot more easily and need treating with a preservative and painting regularly.

GLASS OR PLASTIC?
Glass is still the most popular choice, despite the advances in plastics.

Glass has excellent light transmission, traps long-wave radiation well (this creates the 'greenhouse effect'), can last as long as the frame, and condensation does not cling.

Unfortunately, it's heavy, difficult to handle, expensive (and because of its weight needs an expensive framework to support it too), and is dangerous when broken.

Polythene is cheap, light, and safe. It suffers from a short life (even when treated with ultra-violet inhibitors), does not transmit light as well as glass, is more difficult to clean, lets heat escape more quickly than glass, and condensation drips are likely to cling to the surface rather than run down.

Other plastics have severe limitations. PVC weathers quite well but still has a limited life (say four or five years), and is more expensive than polythene.

Rigid polycarbonate sheets have properties similar to glass, with the advantages of light weight and being unbreakable. Unfortunately they are easily scratched and likely to be two to four times the cost of glass.

If you have trouble buying more unusual gardening equipment, contact the British Agricultural and Garden Machinery Association (see SOCIETIES AND ORGANISATIONS) – they will be able to refer you to appropriate manufacturers.

DON'T FORGET THE EXTRAS

You may need to provide a base; sometimes this is offered as an optional extra, occasionally it is included in the price – check when comparing prices.

There will be other 'extras' that you will need to consider. Some of them could be essentials.

Staging and shelves The manufacturer will almost certainly be able to offer suitable staging, but unless you have a greenhouse of unusual shape (such as a polygonal), it may pay to look at those produced by other manufacturers too. You might find a style or cost that is more acceptable.

Additional ventilators are well worth considering. The number in most greenhouses as sold is inadequate. If there isn't a side ventilator, consider putting in a louvre ventilator low down in one side or at the end. It is easier to install these while you are erecting the greenhouse than afterwards.

Automatic ventilator openers are always useful, especially if you are away from home much, but if you don't want to incur this cost now, you can wait and add them later. They can be bought for conventional and louvre ventilators.

Watering systems will probably help you to grow better plants if you can't be on hand regularly. There are several systems, most based on either the drip feed principle (the water is supplied through a network of pipes to individual containers) or on capillary action (mats or sand beds from which the water seeps up into the pot). These are fed direct from a mains supply, or from a reservoir that you top up by hand. The pros and cons of the various systems were discussed in **Gardening from Which?** April 1983 and May 1983.

A power supply may be necessary for propagators (see page 452) or for supplementary or working lighting, and possibly a heater. This can be an expensive item – especially if the greenhouse is some distance from the present mains supply.

Heaters Heating your greenhouse will add considerably to the cost of your hobby, especially if you want to maintain it at a growing temperature rather than just frostproof. It's worth considering the pros and cons of the various systems, the initial outlay, and the likely running costs. You will need to do this carefully: **Gardening from Which?** compared the various forms of heating in September 1982, with prices updated in September 1984. Paraffin heaters were also reviewed in September 1984, and electric fan heaters in September 1983.

Buying a greenhouse was reviewed in **Gardening from Which?** *April 1984 and August 1984.*

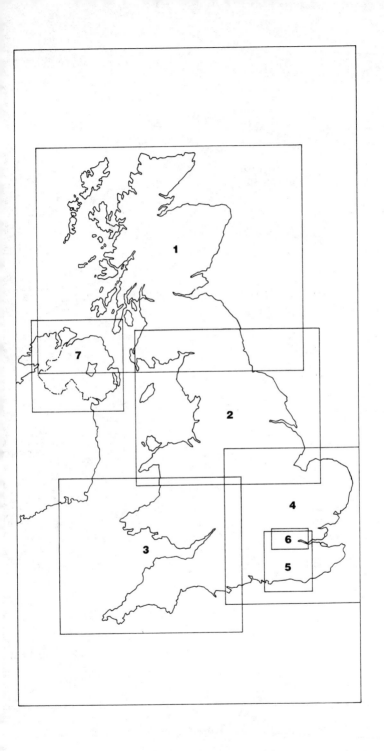

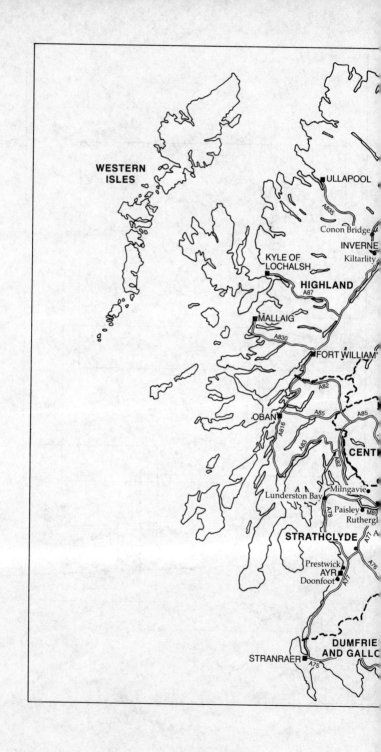

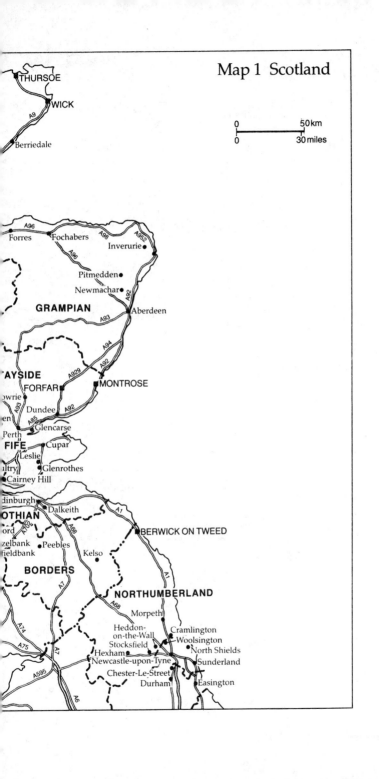

Map 1 Scotland

THURSOE

WICK

Berriedale

0   50 km
0   30 miles

Forres   Fochabers

Inverurie

Pitmedden

Newmachar

GRAMPIAN   Aberdeen

AYSIDE

FORFAR   **MONTROSE**

owrie

Dundee

en

Perth   Glencarse

FIFE   Cupar

Leslie

iltry   Glenrothes

Cairney Hill

dinburgh   Dalkeith

OTHIAN

ord

zelbank   Peebles

ieldbank   Kelso

BORDERS

NORTHUMBERLAND

Morpeth

Heddon-on-the-Wall   Cramlington

Stocksfield   Woolsington

Hexham   North Shields

Newcastle-upon-Tyne

Sunderland

Chester-Le-Street

Durham   Easington

BERWICK ON TWEED

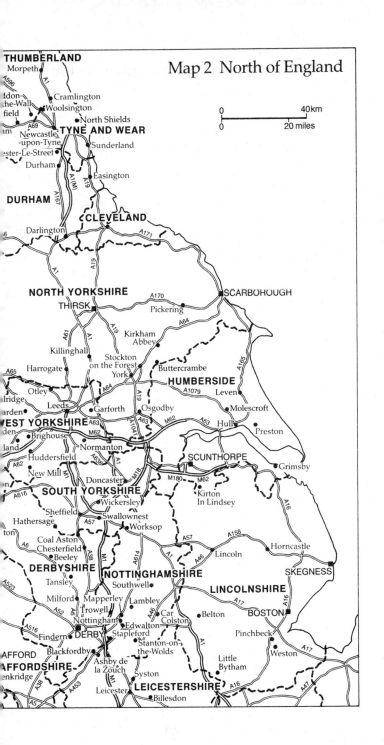

Map 2 North of England

THUMBERLAND
Morpeth
A596
A1
ldon-
he-Wall
field
Cramlington
Woolsington
A69
North Shields
Newcastle
-upon-Tyne
TYNE AND WEAR
am
ester-Le-Street
Durham
Sunderland
A1(M)
A19
Easington
DURHAM
A167
CLEVELAND
Darlington
A171
6
A1
A19
NORTH YORKSHIRE
A170
SCARBOROUGH
THIRSK
Pickering
A61
A1
A19
Kirkham
Abbey
A64
Killinghall
Stockton
on the Forest
York
Buttercrambe
A65
Harrogate
A64
HUMBERSIDE
A165
Otley
A1079
Leven
lridge
Leeds
Garforth
A19
Osgodby
Molescroft
arden
EST YORKSHIRE
A63
A1041
A63
A62
M62
Hull
Preston
den
M62
Brighouse
A1
land
Normanton
SCUNTHORPE
Huddersfield
A628
Grimsby
New Mill
M18
M180
M62
Doncaster
Kirton
In Lindsey
A616
SOUTH YORKSHIRE
A16
n
Wickersley
Sheffield
Swallownest
A57
A158
Hathersage
A57
Worksop
Horncastle
ton
A6
Coal Aston
A614
A1
A46
Lincoln
Chesterfield
Beeley
A38
M1
SKEGNESS
DERBYSHIRE
NOTTINGHAMSHIRE
LINCOLNSHIRE
A523
Tansley
Southwell
Milford
Mapperley
Lambley
A17
A16
Trowell
A52
A6
Nottingham
Car
Colston
Belton
BOSTON
A516
Edwalton
Findern
DERBY
Stapleford
Pinchbeck
AFFORD
Blackfordby
Stanton-on-
the-Wolds
Weston
A17
AFFORDSHIRE
Ashby de
la Zouch
Little
Bytham
A1
enkridge
A38
A453
Syston
A16
A47
A5
LEICESTERSHIRE
Leicester
Billesdon

0   40km
0   20 miles

Map 3 South Wales and South-west England

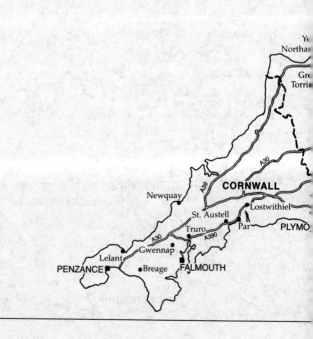

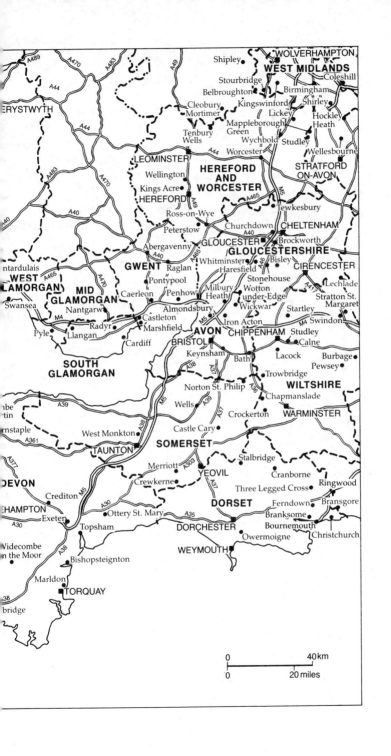

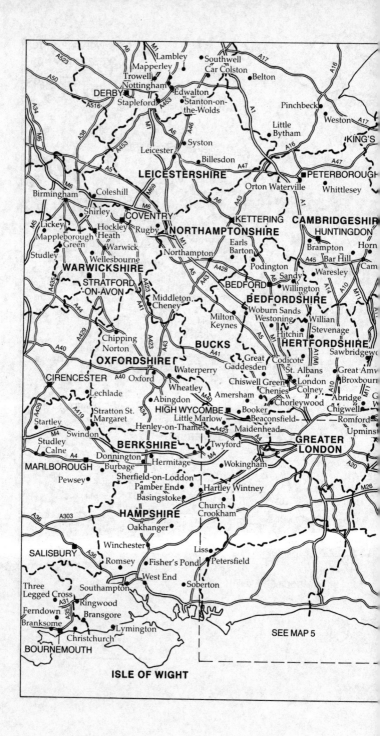

SEE MAP 5

ISLE OF WIGHT

Map 4 Central and
Southern England

Holkham
CROMER
North Walsham
A148
A140
Taverham
Costessey
Sprowston
Norwich
Acle
A47
NORFOLK
A11
Lowestoft
A140
A12
Thetford
Bury St Edmunds
Stonham Aspal
Stowmarket
SUFFOLK
Woodbridge
Flowton
A45
Sudbury
A12
IPSWICH
rook
Capel St. Mary
Colchester
Ardleigh
HARWICH
Elmstead
Market
Kirby Cross
SEX
msford
ford
Rayleigh
27
CHESTER
MARGATE
M2
A299
ngton
Canterbury
dstone
Sheldwich
A2
KENT
Ashford
DOVER
A259
RYE
Bulverhythe

0   40 km
0   20 miles

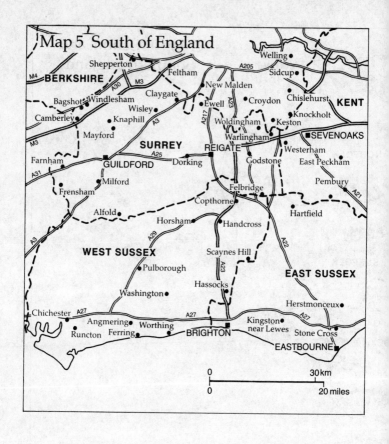

Map 5 South of England

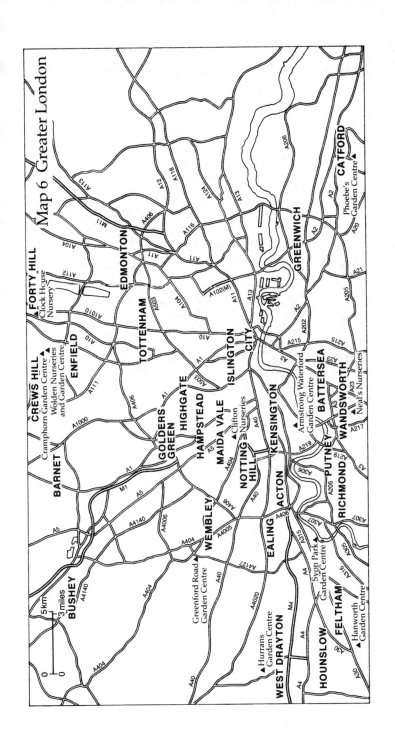

Map 6 Greater London

FORTY HILL
Clock House
Nursery

CREWS HILL
Cramphorn Garden Centre ▲
Wolden Nurseries
and Garden Centre ▲

ENFIELD

EDMONTON

BARNET

TOTTENHAM

GOLDERS
GREEN

HIGHGATE

HAMPSTEAD

MAIDA VALE

Clifton
Nurseries ▲

ISLINGTON

CITY

GREENWICH

CATFORD

Phoebe's
Garden Centre ▲

Armstrong Waterford
Garden Centre ▲

BATTERSEA

Neal's Nurseries ▲

WANDSWORTH

KENSINGTON

NOTTING
HILL

ACTON

PUTNEY

RICHMOND

WEMBLEY

EALING

Greenford Road
Garden Centre ▲

BUSHEY

Hurrans
Garden Centre ▲

WEST DRAYTON

HOUNSLOW

FELTHAM

Hanworth
Garden Centre ▲

Syon Park
Garden Centre ▲

5km

3 miles

0

0

Map 7 Northern Ireland

Report forms

Garden centres and nurseries are changing all the time and we need your help to keep up-to-date. We would like to hear about garden centres and nurseries that are already in the *Guide* as well as those that have yet to make an appearance.

Please use a separate report form (or sheet of paper if you prefer) for each garden centre or nursery, so that we can file each report separately in its own garden centre or nursery file.

Try to give us the following information when writing your report: the range and quality of plants, the selection of tools and equipment, the space for indoor and outdoor displays and how well they were set out, and any exceptional facilities. Let us know what sort of place it was – a small, family-run nursery, a big, modern garden centre, for example. What was your overall impression? Would you go back there again?

Ask for more forms if you need them; write to *The Good Gardener's Guide*, FREEPOST, 14 Buckingham Street, London WC2N 4BR. No stamp needed if you live in the United Kingdom.

REPORT FORM *The Good Gardener's Guide*

Send your completed form (or any other report) to
The Good Gardener's Guide
FREEPOST, 14 Buckingham Street, London WC2N 4BR

Name of place you visited _____

_____

Address _____

_____

Date of your visit _____

What did you buy? _____

_____

Your report

Signed _____
*continue overleaf if necessary
or use separate piece of paper*

Name and address _____

_____

_____

REPORT FORM *The Good Gardener's Guide*

Send your completed form (or any other report) to
The Good Gardener's Guide
FREEPOST, 14 Buckingham Street, London WC2N 4BR

Name of place you visited _____

_____

Address _____

_____

Date of your visit _____

What did you buy? _____

_____

Your report

*continue overleaf if necessary
or use separate piece of paper*

Signed _____

Name and address _____

_____

_____

REPORT FORM *The Good Gardener's Guide*

Send your completed form (or any other report) to
The Good Gardener's Guide
FREEPOST, 14 Buckingham Street, London WC2N 4BR

Name of place you visited _____

_____

Address _____

_____

Date of your visit _____

What did you buy? _____

_____

Your report

continue overleaf if necessary
Signed _____ *or use separate piece of paper*

Name and address _____

_____

_____

REPORT FORM *The Good Gardener's Guide*

Send your completed form (or any other report) to
The Good Gardener's Guide
FREEPOST, 14 Buckingham Street, London WC2N 4BR

Name of place you visited _____

_____

Address _____

_____

Date of your visit _____

What did you buy? _____

_____

Your report

*continue overleaf if necessary
or use separate piece of paper*

Signed _____

Name and address _____

_____

_____

REPORT FORM *The Good Gardener's Guide*

Send your completed form (or any other report) to
The Good Gardener's Guide
FREEPOST, 14 Buckingham Street, London WC2N 4BR

Name of place you visited _____

_____

Address _____

_____

Date of your visit _____

What did you buy? _____

_____

Your report

continue overleaf if necessary
or use separate piece of paper

Signed _____

Name and address _____

_____

_____